Visit classzone.com and get connected

Online resources for students and parents

ClassZone resources provide instruction, practice, and learning support.

eEdition Plus ONLINE

This interactive version of the text encourages students to explore science.

Content Review Online

Interactive review reinforces the big idea and key concepts of each chapter.

SciLinks

NSTA-selected links provide relevant Web resources correlated to the text.

Chapter-Based Support

Math tutorials, news, resources, test practice, and a misconceptions database help students succeed.

Now it all clicks!™

CLASSZONE.COM

McDougal Littell

McDougal Littell

Life SCIENCE

Human
Biology

Ecology

Life Over
Time

Diversity of
Living Things

Cells and
Heredity

LIFE SCIENCE

ISBN: 0-618-30367-7   1 2 3 4 5 6 7 8 VJM 08 07 06 05 04

Internet Web Site: http://www.mcdougallittell.com

Science Consultants

Chief Science Consultant

James Trefil, Ph.D. is the Clarence J. Robinson Professor of Physics at George Mason University. He is the author or co-author of more than 25 books, including *Science Matters* and *The Nature of Science*. Dr. Trefil is a member of the American Association for the Advancement of Science's Committee on the Public Understanding of Science and Technology. He is also a fellow of the World Economic Forum and a frequent contributor to *Smithsonian* magazine.

Rita Ann Calvo, Ph.D. is Senior Lecturer in Molecular Biology and Genetics at Cornell University, where for 12 years she also directed the Cornell Institute for Biology Teachers. Dr. Calvo is the 1999 recipient of the College and University Teaching Award from the National Association of Biology Teachers.

Kenneth Cutler, M.S. is the Education Coordinator for the Julius L. Chambers Biomedical Biotechnology Research Institute at North Carolina Central University. A former middle school and high school science teacher, he received a 1999 Presidential Award for Excellence in Science Teaching.

Instructional Design Consultants

Douglas Carnine, Ph.D. is Professor of Education and Director of the National Center for Improving the Tools of Educators at the University of Oregon. He is the author of seven books and over 100 other scholarly publications, primarily in the areas of instructional design and effective instructional strategies and tools for diverse learners. Dr. Carnine also serves as a member of the National Institute for Literacy Advisory Board.

Linda Carnine, Ph.D. consults with school districts on curriculum development and effective instruction for students struggling academically. A former teacher and school administrator, Dr. Carnine also co-authored a popular remedial reading program.

Donald Steely, Ph.D. serves as principal investigator at the Oregon Center for Applied Science (ORCAS) on federal grants for science and language arts programs. His background also includes teaching and authoring of print and multimedia programs in science, mathematics, history, and spelling.

Sam Miller, Ph.D. is a middle school science teacher and the Teacher Development Liaison for the Eugene, Oregon, Public Schools. He is the author of curricula for teaching science, mathematics, computer skills, and language arts.

Vicky Vachon, Ph.D. consults with school districts throughout the United States and Canada on improving overall academic achievement with a focus on literacy. She is also co-author of a widely used program for remedial readers.

Content Reviewers

John Beaver, Ph.D.
Ecology
Professor, Director of Science Education Center
College of Education and Human Services
Western Illinois University
Macomb, IL

Donald J. DeCoste, Ph.D.
Matter and Energy, Chemical Interactions
Chemistry Instructor
University of Illinois
Urbana-Champaign, IL

Dorothy Ann Fallows, Ph.D., MSc
Diversity of Living Things, Microbiology
Partners in Health
Boston, MA

Michael Foote, Ph.D.
The Changing Earth, Life Over Time
Associate Professor
Department of the Geophysical Sciences
The University of Chicago
Chicago, IL

Lucy Fortson, Ph.D.
Space Science
Director of Astronomy
Adler Planetarium and Astronomy Museum
Chicago, IL

Elizabeth Godrick, Ph.D.
Human Biology
Professor, CAS Biology
Boston University
Boston, MA

Isabelle Sacramento Grilo, M.S.
The Changing Earth
Lecturer, Department of the Geological Sciences
Montana State University
Bozeman, MT

David Harbster, MSc
Diversity of Living Things
Professor of Biology
Paradise Valley Community College
Phoenix, AZ

Richard D. Norris, Ph.D.
Earth's Waters
Professor of Paleobiology
Scripps Institution of Oceanography
University of California, San Diego
La Jolla, CA

Donald B. Peck, M.S.
*Motion and Forces; Waves, Sound, and Light;
 Electricity and Magnetism*
Director of the Center for Science Education (retired)
Fairleigh Dickinson University
Madison, NJ

Javier Penalosa, Ph.D.
Diversity of Living Things, Plants
Associate Professor, Biology Department
Buffalo State College
Buffalo, NY

Raymond T. Pierrehumbert, Ph.D.
Earth's Atmosphere
Professor in Geophysical Sciences (Atmospheric Science)
The University of Chicago
Chicago, IL

Brian J. Skinner, Ph.D.
Earth's Surface
Eugene Higgins Professor of Geology and Geophysics
Yale University
New Haven, CT

Nancy E. Spaulding, M.S.
Earth's Surface, The Changing Earth, Earth's Waters
Earth Science Teacher (retired)
Elmira Free Academy
Elmira, NY

Steven S. Zumdahl, Ph.D.
Matter and Energy, Chemical Interactions
Professor Emeritus of Chemistry
University of Illinois
Urbana-Champaign, IL

Susan L. Zumdahl, M.S.
Matter and Energy, Chemical Interactions
Chemistry Education Specialist
University of Illinois
Urbana-Champaign, IL

Safety Consultant

Juliana Texley, Ph.D.
Former K–12 Science Teacher and School Superintendent
Boca Raton, FL

English Language Advisor

Judy Lewis, M.A.
Director, State and Federal Programs for reading proficiency
and high risk populations
Rancho Cordova, CA

Teacher Panel Members

Carol Arbour
Tallmadge Middle School,
Tallmadge, OH

Patty Belcher
Goodrich Middle School,
Akron, OH

Gwen Broestl
Luis Munoz Marin Middle School,
Cleveland, OH

Al Brofman
Tehipite Middle School,
Fresno, CA

John Cockrell
Clinton Middle School,
Columbus, OH

Jenifer Cox
Sylvan Middle School,
Citrus Heights, CA

Linda Culpepper
Martin Middle School,
Charlotte, NC

Kathleen Ann DeMatteo
Margate Middle School,
Margate, FL

Melvin Figueroa
New River Middle School,
Ft. Lauderdale, FL

Doretha Grier
Kannapolis Middle School,
Kannapolis, NC

Robert Hood
Alexander Hamilton Middle School,
Cleveland, OH

Scott Hudson
Coverdale Elementary School,
Cincinnati, OH

Loretta Langdon
Princeton Middle School,
Princeton, NC

Carlyn Little
Glades Middle School,
Miami, FL

Ann Marie Lynn
Amelia Earhart Middle School,
Riverside, CA

James Minogue
Lowe's Grove Middle School,
Durham, NC

Joann Myers
Buchanan Middle School,
Tampa, FL

Barbara Newell
Charles Evans Hughes Middle School,
Long Beach, CA

Anita Parker
Kannapolis Middle School,
Kannapolis, NC

Greg Pirolo
Golden Valley Middle School,
San Bernardino, CA

Laura Pottmyer
Apex Middle School,
Apex, NC

Lynn Prichard
Booker T. Washington Middle Magnet
School, Tampa, FL

Jacque Quick
Walter Williams High School,
Burlington, NC

Robert Glenn Reynolds
Hillman Middle School,
Youngstown, OH

Theresa Short
Abbott Middle School,
Fayetteville, NC

Rita Slivka
Alexander Hamilton Middle School,
Cleveland, OH

Marie Sofsak
B F Stanton Middle School,
Alliance, OH

Nancy Stubbs
Sweetwater Union Unified School District,
Chula Vista, CA

Sharon Stull
Quail Hollow Middle School,
Charlotte, NC

Donna Taylor
Okeeheelee Middle School,
West Palm Beach, FL

Sandi Thompson
Harding Middle School,
Lakewood, OH

Lori Walker
Audubon Middle School & Magnet Center,
Los Angeles, CA

Teacher Lab Evaluators

Jill Brimm-Byrne
Albany Park Academy,
Chicago, IL

Gwen Broestl
Luis Munoz Marin Middle School,
Cleveland, OH

Al Brofman
Tehipite Middle School,
Fresno, CA

Michael A. Burstein
The Rashi School,
Newton, MA

Trudi Coutts
Madison Middle School,
Naperville, IL

Jenifer Cox
Sylvan Middle School,
Citrus Heights, CA

Larry Cwik
Madison Middle School,
Naperville, IL

Jennifer Donatelli
Kennedy Junior High School,
Lisle, IL

Paige Fullhart
Highland Middle School,
Libertyville, IL

Sue Hood
Glen Crest Middle School,
Glen Ellyn, IL

Ann Min
Beardsley Middle School,
Crystal Lake, IL

Aileen Mueller
Kennedy Junior High School,
Lisle, IL

Nancy Nega
Churchville Middle School,
Elmhurst, IL

Oscar Newman
Sumner Math and Science Academy,
Chicago, IL

Marina Penalver
Moore Middle School,
Portland, ME

Lynn Prichard
Booker T. Washington Middle Magnet
School, Tampa, FL

Jacque Quick
Walter Williams High School,
Burlington, NC

Seth Robey
Gwendolyn Brooks Middle School,
Oak Park, IL

Kevin Steele
Grissom Middle School,
Tinley Park, IL

UNIT A
Cells and Heredity

McDougal Littell Science
Cells and Heredity
mitochondria
membrane
NUCLEUS
heredity

eEdition

Unit Features

1 The Cell
A6

the **BIG** idea

All living things are made up of cells.

2 How Cells Function
A38

the **BIG** idea

All cells need energy and materials for life processes.

How do plants like these sunflowers change energy from the Sun? page A38

McDougal Littell Science
Life Over Time

eEdition

UNIT B
Life Over Time

Unit Features

1 The History of Life on Earth   B6

the **BIG** idea

Living things, like Earth itself, change over time.

How do scientists learn about the history of life on Earth? page B6

How many different types of organisms do you see and how would you group them? page B40

Visual Highlights

UNIT C
Diversity of Living Things

eEdition

Unit Features

1 Single-Celled Organisms and Viruses C6

the BIG idea

Bacteria and protists have the characteristics of living things, while viruses are not alive.

2 Introduction to Multicellular Organisms C40

the BIG idea

Multicellular organisms live in and get energy from a variety of environments.

How does an organism get energy and materials from its environment? page C40

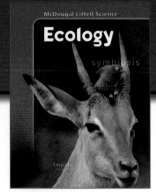

eEdition

UNIT D
Ecology

Unit Features

the BIG idea

Matter and energy together
support life within
an environment.

*How many living and nonliving things can
you identify in this photograph? page D6*

How do living things interact? page D42

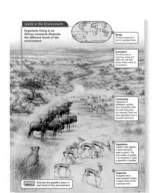

Visual Highlights

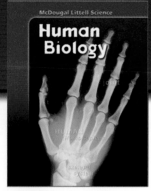

McDougal Littell Science

Human Biology

eEdition

UNIT E
Human Biology

Unit Features

1 Systems, Support, and Movement   E6

the BIG idea

The human body is made up of systems that work together to perform necessary functions.

2 Absorption, Digestion, and Exchange   E34

the BIG idea

Systems in the body obtain and process materials and remove waste.

What materials does your body need to function properly? page E34

Red blood cells travel through a blood vessel. How do you think blood carries materials around your body? page E62

3 Transport and Protection E62

4 Control and Reproduction E98

5 Growth, Development, and Health E130

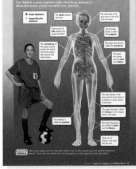

Visual Highlights

Features

Think Science

Math in Science

Connecting Sciences

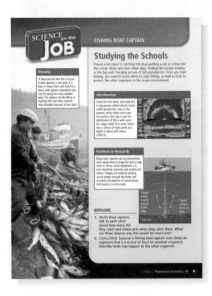

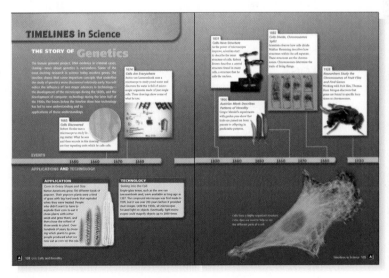

Internet Resources @ ClassZone.com

Simulations

Visualizations

Career Centers

Resource Centers

CELLS AND HEREDITY

Resources for the following topics may be found at ClassZone.com: *Cell Structures, Unicellular Organisms, Macromolecules, Diffusion, Nerve Regeneration, Cell Cycle, Asexual Reproduction, Sexual Reproduction, Meiosis, Genetics Research, Human Genome Project, DNA, Mutations, DNA Technology*

LIFE OVER TIME

Resources for the following topics may be found at ClassZone.com: *Mass Extinctions, Natural Selection, Evidence Supporting Evolution, Linnaeus, Taxonomy, New Insect Species, Modern Classification, Current Fossil and Living Fossil Finds, Population Dynamics, Human Population Growth, Introduced Species in the United States*

DIVERSITY OF LIVING THINGS

Resources for the following topics may be found at ClassZone.com: *Single-Celled Organisms and the Human Body, Bacteria, Viruses, Bee Dance, Plant Adaptations, Animal Adaptations, Fungi, Biodiversity Discoveries and Research, Plant Systems, Plant Evolution, Seeds, Extreme Seeds, Invertebrate Diversity, Worms, Mollusks, Arthropods, Fish, Amphibians, Reptiles, Mammals*

ECOLOGY

Resources for the following topics may be found at ClassZone.com: *Ecosystems, Cycles in Nature, Land and Aquatic Biomes, Symbiotic Relationships, Succession, Conservation Efforts, The Environment, Urban Expansion, Natural Resources, Ecosystem Recovery*

HUMAN BIOLOGY

Resources for the following topics may be found at ClassZone.com: *Skeletal System, Muscles, Respiratory System, Urinary System, Circulatory System, Blood Types, Lymphatic System, Skin, Current Medical Imaging Techniques, Senses, Nervous System, Endocrine System, Human Health, Nutrition, Fighting Disease*

Math Tutorials

NSTA SciLinks

Codes for use with the NSTA SciLinks site may be found on every chapter opener.

Content Review

There is a content review for every chapter at ClassZone.com

Test Practice

There is a standardized test practice for every chapter at ClassZone.com

Explore the Big idea

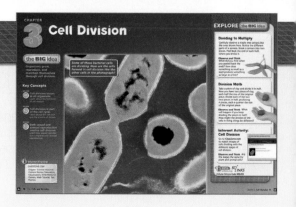

Chapter Opening Inquiry

Each chapter opens with hands-on explorations that introduce the chapter's Big Idea.

Chapter Investigations

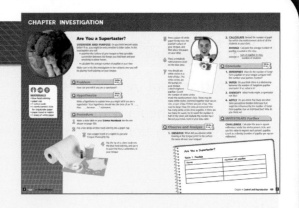

Full-Period Labs

The Chapter Investigations are in-depth labs that let you form and test a hypothesis, build a model, or sometimes design your own investigation.

Explore

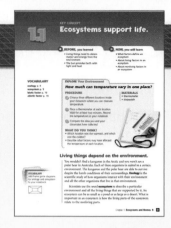

Introductory Inquiry Activities

Most sections begin with a simple activity that lets you explore the Key Concept before you read the section.

Investigate

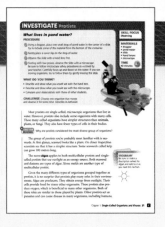

Skill Labs

Each Investigate activity gives you a chance to practice a specific science skill related to the content that you're studying.

Standards and Benchmarks

Each unit in **Life Science** addresses some of the learning goals described in the *National Science Education Standards* (NSES) and the Project 2061 *Benchmarks for Science Literacy*. The following National Science Education Standards are also addressed in the book introduction, unit and chapter features, and lab investigations in all the units: A.9 Understandings About Scientific Inquiry, E.6 Understandings About Science and Technology, F.5 Science and Technology in Society, G.1 Science as a Human Endeavor, G.2 Nature of Science, G.3 History of Science.

National Science Education Standards

Content Standards

UNIT A Cells and Heredity

B.1.c	There are more than 100 known elements that combine in many ways to produce living and nonliving substances.	C.2.b	In many species, females produce eggs and males produce sperm. The egg and sperm come together to produce offspring with genetic material from both parents.
B.3.a	Energy is a property of many substances. Energy is transferred many ways.	C.2.c	Every organism requires a set of instructions for specifying its traits.
C.1.a	Levels of organization for living systems include cells, tissues, organs, organ systems, whole organisms, and ecosystems.	C.2.d	Heredity information is contained in genes in the chromosomes of each cell.
C.1.b	All organisms are composed of cells—the basic unit of life. Most are single cells; others, including humans, are multicellular.	C.2.e	The characteristics of an organism are a combination of traits. Some traits are inherited and others result from interactions with the environment.
C.1.c	Cells perform the functions of life.	F.5.c	Needs, attitudes, and values influence decisions about technology.
C.1.d	Specialized cells perform specialized functions in multicellular organisms.		
C.2.a	Reproduction is a characteristic of all living systems. Some organisms reproduce asexually. Others reproduce sexually.		

UNIT B Life Over Time

C.2.e	The characteristics of an organism are a combination of traits. Some traits are inherited and others result from interactions with the environment.	C.5.b	Biological evolution has led to greater species diversity over time. Biological adaptations include changes in structures, behaviors, or physiology that enhance survival in a particular environment.
C.4.a	A population consists of all individuals of a species that occur together at a given place and time.	C.5.c	Species may become extinct if they cannot survive changes in the environment.
C.4.d	Resources and other factors can limit population growth.	D.2.b	Fossils provide evidence of how life and the environment have changed.
C.5.a	Millions of species of animals, plants, and microorganisms are alive today. Relationships among organisms can be found by looking at internal structures, chemical processes, and the evidence of common ancestry.	F.2.a	When an area becomes overpopulated, increased use of resources degrades the environment.
		G.2.a	Scientists change their ideas about nature when they find new evidence that does not match their existing explanations.

UNIT C Diversity of Living Things

C.1.b | All organisms are composed of cells—the basic unit of life. Most are single cells; others, including humans, are multicellular.

C.1.c | Cells perform the functions of life. They grow and divide. They take in nutrients for energy and materials.

C.1.d | Specialized cells perform specialized functions in multicellular organisms.

C.1.f | Some diseases are the result of breakdown of structures or by infection by other organisms.

C.2.a | Reproduction is a characteristic of all living systems. Some organisms reproduce asexually. Others reproduce sexually.

C.2.b | In many species, females produce eggs and males produce sperm. The egg and sperm come together to produce offspring with genetic material from both parents.

C.3.a | All organisms must be able to obtain and use resources, grow, reproduce, and maintain stable internal conditions.

C.3.b | Regulation of an organism's internal environment keeps conditions within the range required to survive.

C.3.c | Behavior is one kind of response an organism makes.

C.4.c | Most energy in ecosystems enters as sunlight, gets transferred by producers into chemical energy, and passes from organism to organism as food.

C.5.a | Millions of species of animals, plants, and microorganisms are alive today.

F.1.e | Food provides energy and nutrients for growth and development.

UNIT D Ecology

C.4.a | A population consists of all individuals of a species that occur together at a given place and time. An ecosystem includes both living and nonliving things.

C.4.b | Different populations have different roles in an ecosystem. Food webs show the relationship between producers and consumers.

C.4.c | Most energy in ecosystems enters as sunlight, gets transferred by producers into chemical energy through photosynthesis, and passes from organism to organism as food.

C.4.d | Factors can limit population growth.

D.1.f | Water circulates through Earth's crust, oceans, and atmosphere.

D.3.d | The Sun is the major source of energy affecting plant growth, winds, ocean currents, the water cycle, and seasonal variations.

E.6.e | All designs have limits, including availability, safety, and environmental impact.

F.2.a | Human overpopulation can cause increased use of resources, decline in resources, and decline in other populations.

F.2.b | Causes of pollution and resource loss vary from place to place.

UNIT E Human Biology

C.1.a | Levels of organization for living systems include: cells, tissues, organs, organ systems, whole organisms, and ecosystems.

C.1.e | The human organism has systems that perform specific functions.

C.1.f | Some diseases are the result of infection by other organisms.

C.2.a | Reproduction is a characteristic of all living systems.

C.2.b | In many species, females produce eggs and males produce sperm. The egg and sperm come together to produce offspring with genetic material from both parents.

C.3.a | All organisms must be able to obtain and use resources, grow, reproduce, and maintain stable internal conditions.

C.3.b | Regulation of an organism's internal environment keeps conditions within the range required to survive.

F.1.c | Tobacco use increases the risk of illness.

F.1.d | Alcohol and other drugs can increase the risk of illness.

F.1.e | Food provides energy and nutrients for growth and development.

Process and Skill Standards

A.1	Identify questions that can be answered through scientific methods.	A.8	Use mathematics in scientific inquiry.
A.2	Design and conduct a scientific investigation.	A.9.a	Different types of questions suggest different types of scientific investigations.
A.3	Use appropriate tools and techniques to gather and analyze data.	A.9.b	Current scientific knowledge guides scientific investigations.
A.4	Use evidence to describe, predict, explain, and model.	E.6.b	Many different people in different cultures have made and continue to make contributions to science and technology.
A.5	Think critically to find relationships between results and interpretations.	G.1.b	The work of science relies on qualities, such as reasoning, insight, energy, skill, and creativity.
A.6	Give alternative explanations and predictions.		
A.7	Communicate procedures and explanations.		

Project 2061 Benchmarks

Content Benchmarks

UNIT A Cells and Heredity

5.B.1	In some organisms, all genes come from a single parent. In organisms that have sexes, typically half of the genes come from each parent.	5.E.1	Food provides fuel and building material for all organisms.
		5.E.3	Energy can change form in living things.
5.B.2	In sexual reproduction, a specialized cell from a female joins one from a male.	5.F.1	Differences between parents and offspring enlarge over generations.
5.C.1	All living things are made of cells.	8.A.2	People control characteristics of plants and animals by selective breeding.
5.C.2	Cells continually divide to make more cells.	10.I.1	Many diseases are caused by microorganisms. This is the germ theory.
5.C.3	Cells carry out the functions of organisms.	10.I.2	Pasteur showed food spoils as germs enter, and heat can destroy germs.
5.C.4	About 2/3 of the weight of cells is water which gives cells certain properties.		

UNIT B Life Over Time

5.A.3	In classifying organisms, biologists consider internal and external structures.	5.F.1	Small differences between parents and offspring accumulate in successive generating.
5.B.3	New species have resulted from selective breeding.	5.F.2	Individual organisms with certain traits are more likely than others to survive.
5.D.1	In all environments, organisms with similar needs may compete.		

UNIT C Diversity of Living Things

5.A.1	One general distinction among organisms is between plants and animals. Many organisms are neither plants or animals.	5.E.1	Food provides organisms with fuel and materials.
		5.E.3	Energy can change form in living things.
5.A.2	Organisms have diverse body plans.	6.B.3	Patterns of human development are similar to those of other vertebrates.
5.A.3	Organisms share similar features.		
5.B.2	In sexual reproduction a specialized cell from a female joins one from a male.	6.C.1	Organs and organ systems are composed of cells and help provide basic needs.
5.C.1	All living things are made of cells.	6.E.3	Viruses, bacteria, fungi, and parasites may infect the human body.

UNIT D Ecology

3.C.6	Rarely are technology issues simple.
4.B.8	Water is, necessary for life, limited, and becoming depleted and polluted.
4.C.7	Human activities affect the environment.
5.A.5	All organisms are part of two connected food webs.
5.D.1	Species with similar needs may compete.
5.D.2	Populations may interact in diverse ways.
5.E.2	Matter is transferred between living things and the environment.
5.E.3	Energy can change form in living things.
6.E.5	The health of individuals requires keeping soil, air, and water safe.
11.A.2	Studying a system involves studying interactions among its parts.

UNIT E Human Biology

6.A.1	Human beings have body systems for diverse body functions
6.C.2	For the body to use food it must be digested and transported to cells.
6.C.3	Cells take in oxygen for combustion of food, and eliminate carbon dioxide.
6.C.4	Specialized cells and molecules identify and/or destroy microbes.
6.B.1	Fertilization occurs when a sperm cell enters an egg cell.
6.B.3	Cells divide and specialize as a fetus develops from the embryo.
6.B.5	Body changes occur as humans age.
6.C.5	Hormones are chemical messengers.
6.C.6	Interactions among senses, nerves, and the brain make learning possible.
6.E.2	Toxic substances, diet, and behavior may harm one's health.
6.E.4	White blood cells engulf invaders or produce antibodies.

Process and Skill Benchmarks

9.A.2	Use a number line and negative numbers.
9.A.3	Write numbers in different forms.
9.A.4	Use addition, subtraction, multiplication, division.
9.B.2	Use mathematics to describe change.
9.B.3	Use graphs to show relationships.
9.C.4	Use a graphic display of numbers to show trends, rates, gaps, or clusters.
9.D.3	The mean, median, and mode tell different things about a data set.
9.D.5	Use a large, well-chosen sample to represent the whole.
11.A.2	Think about things as systems.
11.A.3	See how systems are interconnected.
11.B.1	Use models to think about processes.
11.C.4	Use equations to summarize changes.
11.C.5	Understand how symmetry (or the lack of it) can determine properties.
11.D.	With complex systems, use summaries, averages, ranges, and examples.
12.A.1	Know why it is important in science to keep honest, clear, and accurate records.
12.A.2	Investigate, using hypotheses.
12.A.3	See multiple ways to interpret results.
12.B.3	Calculate volumes of rectangular solids.
12.B.7	Determine, use, and convert units.
12.C.3	Use and read measurement instruments.
12.D.1	Use tables and graphs to organize information and identify relationships.
12.D.2	Read, interpret, and describe tables and graphs.
12.D.3	Locate information in reference books and other resources.
12.D.4	Understand charts and graphs.
12.E.3	Be skeptical of biased samples.
12.E.4	See more than one way to interpret results.
12.E.5	Criticize faulty reasoning.

Introducing Life Science

S cientists are curious. Since ancient times, they have been asking and answering questions about the world around them. Scientists are also very suspicious of the answers they get. They carefully collect evidence and test their answers many times before accepting an idea as correct.

In this book you will see how scientific knowledge keeps growing and changing as scientists ask new questions and rethink what was known before. The following sections will help get you started.

What Is Life Science?

Life science is the study of living things. As you study life science, you will observe and read about a variety of organisms, from huge redwood trees to the tiny bacteria that cause sore throats. Because Earth is home to such a great variety of living things, the study of life science is rich and exciting.

But life science doesn't simply include learning the names of millions of organisms. It includes big ideas that help us to understand how all these livings things interact with their environment. Life science is the study of characteristics and needs that all living things have in common. It's also a study of changes—both daily changes as well as changes that take place over millions of years. Probably most important, in studying life science, you will explore the many ways that all living things—including you—depend upon Earth and its resources.

The text and visuals in this book will invite you into the world of living things and provide you with the key concepts you'll need in your study. Activities offer a chance for you to investigate some aspects of life science on your own. The four unifying principles listed below provide a way for you to connect the information and ideas in this program.

- **All living things share common characteristics.**

- **All living things share common needs.**

- **Living things meet their needs through interactions with the environment.**

- **The types and numbers of living things change over time.**

the **BIG** idea

Each chapter begins with a big idea. Keep in mind that each big idea relates to one or more of the unifying principles.

All living things share common characteristics.

Birds nest in a group of weeds as sunlight shines and a breeze blows. Which of these is alive? Warblers and weeds are living things, but sunlight and breezes are not. All living things share common characteristics that distinguish them from nonliving things.

What It Means

This unifying principle helps you explore one of the biggest questions in science, "What is life?" Let's take a look at four characteristics that distinguish living things from nonliving things: organization, growth, reproduction, and response.

Organization

If you stand a short distance from a reed warbler's nest, you can observe the largest level of organization in a living thing—the **organism** itself. Each bird is an organism. If you look at a leaf under a microscope, you can observe the smallest level of organization capable of performing all the activities of life, a **cell.** All living things are made of cells.

Growth

Most living things grow and develop. Growth often involves not only an increase in size, but also an increase in complexity, such as a tadpole growing into a frog. If all goes well, the small warblers in the picture will grow to the size of their parent.

Reproduction

Most living things produce offspring like themselves. Those offspring are also able to reproduce. That means that reed warblers produce reed warblers which in turn reproduce more reed warblers.

Response

You've probably noticed that your body adjusts to changes in your surroundings. If you are exploring outside on a hot day, you may notice that you sweat. On a cold day, you may shiver. Sweating and shivering are examples of response.

Why It's Important

People of all ages experience the urge to explore and understand the living world. Understanding the characteristics of living things is a good way to start this exploration of life. In addition, knowing about the characteristics of living things helps you identify

- similarities and differences among various organisms
- key questions to ask about any organism you study

All living things share common needs.

What do you need to stay alive?
What does an animal like a fish or a
coral need to stay alive? All living
things have common needs.

What It Means

Inside every living thing, chemical reactions constantly change materials into new materials. For these reactions to occur, an organism needs energy, water and other materials, and living space.

Energy

You use energy all the time. Movement, growth, and sleep all require energy, which you get from food. Plants use the energy of sunlight to make their own food. All animals get their energy by eating either plants or other animals that eat plants.

Water and Other Materials

Water is the main ingredient in the cells of all living things. The chemical reactions inside cells take place in water, and water plays a part in moving materials around within organisms.

Other materials are also essential for life. For example, plants must have carbon dioxide from the air to make their own food. Plants and animals both use oxygen to release the energy stored in their food. You and other animals that live on land get oxygen when you breathe in air. The fish swimming around the coral reef in the picture have gills, which allow them to get oxygen that is dissolved in the water.

Living Space

You can think of living space as a home—a space that protects you from external conditions and a place where you can get materials such as water and air. The ocean provides living space for the coral that makes up this coral reef. The coral itself provides living space for many other organisms.

Why It's Important

Understanding the needs of living things helps people make wise decisions about resources. This knowledge can also help you think carefully about
- the different ways in which various organisms meet their needs for energy and materials
- the effects of adding chemicals to the water and air around us
- the reasons why some types of plants or animals may disappear from an area

Living things meet their needs through interactions with the environment.

A moose chomps on the leaves of a plant. This ordinary event involves many interactions among living and nonliving things within the forest.

What It Means

To understand this unifying principle, take a closer look at the words *environment* and *interactions*.

Environment

The **environment** is everything that surrounds a living thing. An environment is made up of both living and nonliving factors. For example, the environment in this forest includes rainfall, rocks, and soil as well as the moose, the evergreen trees, and the birch trees. In fact, the soil in these forests is called "moose and spruce" soil because it contains materials provided by the animals and evergreens in the area.

Interaction

All living things in an environment meet their needs through interactions. An **interaction** occurs when two or more things act in ways that affect one another. For example, trees and other forest plants can meet their need for energy and materials through interactions with materials in soil and air, and light from the Sun. New plants get living space as birds, wind, and other factors carry seeds from one location to another.

Animals like this moose meet their need for food through interactions with other living things. The moose gets food by eating leaves off trees and other plants. In turn, the moose becomes food for wolves.

Why It's Important

Learning about living things and their environment helps scientists and decision makers address issues such as:

- developing land for human use without damaging the environment
- predicting how a change in the moose population would affect the soil in the forest
- determining the ways in which animals harm or benefit the trees in a forest

The types and numbers of living things change over time.

The story of life on Earth is a story of changes. Some changes take place over millions of years. At one time, animals similar to modern fish swam in the area where this lizard now runs.

What It Means

To understand how living things change over time, let's look closely at the terms *diversity* and *adaptation*.

Diversity

You are surrounded by an astonishing variety of living things. This variety is called **biodiversity.** Today, scientists have described and named 1.4 million species. There are even more species that haven't been named. Scientists use the term *species* to describe a group of closely related living things. Members of a **species** are so similar that they can reproduce offspring that are able to reproduce. Lizards, such as the one you see in the photograph, are so diverse that they make up many different species.

Over the millions of years that life has existed on Earth, new species have originated and others have disappeared. The disappearance of a species is called **extinction.** Fossils, like the one in the photograph, provide evidence that some types of organisms that lived millions of years ago became extinct.

Adaptation

Scientists use the term **adaptation** to mean a characteristic of a species that allows members of that species to survive in a particular environment. Adaptations are related to needs. A salamander's legs are an adaptation that allows it to move on land.

Over time, species either develop adaptations to changing environments or they become extinct. The history of living things on Earth is related to the history of the changing Earth. The presence of a fish-like fossil indicates that the area shown in this photograph was once covered by water.

Why It's Important

By learning how living things change over time, you will gain a better understanding of the life that surrounds you and how it survives. Discovering more about the history of life helps scientists to

- identify patterns of relationships among various species
- predict how changes in the environment may affect species in the future

The Nature of Science

You may think of science as a body of knowledge or a collection of facts. More important, however, science is an active process that involves certain ways of looking at the world.

Scientific Habits of Mind

Scientists are curious. They are always asking questions. A scientist who observes that the number of plants in a forest preserve has decreased might ask questions such as, "Are more animals eating the plants?" or "Has the way the land is used affected the numbers of plants?" Scientists around the world investigate these and other important questions.

Scientists are observant. They are always looking closely at the world around them. A scientist who studies plants often sees details such as the height of a plant, its flowers, and how many plants live in a particular area.

Scientists are creative. They draw on what they know to form a possible explanation for a pattern, an event, or a behavior that they have observed. Then scientists create a plan for testing their ideas.

Scientists are skeptical. Scientists don't accept an explanation or answer unless it is based on evidence and logical reasoning. They continually question their own conclusions as well as conclusions suggested by other scientists. Scientists trust only evidence that is confirmed by other people or methods.

A white-tailed deer feeds on many plants including the trillium shown here.

By measuring the growth of this tree, a scientist can study interactions in the ecosystem.

Science Processes at Work

You can think of science as a continuous cycle of asking and seeking answers to questions about the world. Although there are many processes that scientists use, scientists typically do each of the following:

- Ask a question
- Determine what is known
- Investigate
- Interpret results
- Share results

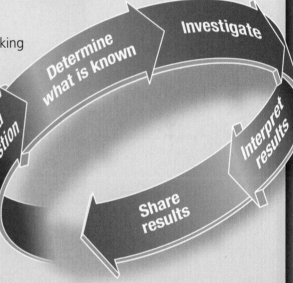

Ask a Question

It may surprise you that asking questions is an important skill. A scientific investigation may start when a scientist asks a question. Perhaps scientists observe an event or a process that they don't understand, or perhaps answering one question leads to another.

Determine What Is Known

When beginning an inquiry, scientists find out what is already known about a question. They study results from other scientific investigations, read journals, and talk with other scientists. A biologist who is trying to understand how the change in the number of deer in an area affects plants will study reports of censuses taken for both plants and animals.

Investigate

Investigating is the process of collecting evidence. Two important ways of collecting evidence are observing and experimenting.

Observing is the act of noting and recording an event, a characteristic, a behavior, or anything else detected with an instrument or with the senses. For example, a scientist notices that plants in one part of the forest are not thriving. She sees broken plants and compares the height of the plants in one area with those in another.

An **experiment** is an organized procedure during which all factors but the one being studied are controlled. For example, the scientist thinks the reason that some plants in the forest are not thriving may be because deer are eating the flowers off the plants. An experiment she might try is to mark two similar parts of an area where the plants grow and then to build a fence around one part so the deer can't get to the plants there. The fence must be constructed so the same amount of light, air, and water reach the plants. The only factor that changes is contact between plants and the deer.

Close observation of the Colorado Potatobeetle led scientists to answers that help farmers control this insect pest.

Forming hypotheses and making predictions are two other skills involved in scientific investigations. A **hypothesis** is a tentative explanation for an observation or a scientific problem that can be tested by further investigation. For example, since at least 1900, Colorado Potatobeetles were able to resist chemical insecticides. It was hypothesized that bacteria living in the beetles' environment were killing many beetles, because otherwise the beetles would be found in larger numbers. A **prediction** is an expectation of what will be observed or what will happen and can be used to test a hypothesis. It was predicted that certain bacteria would kill Colorado Potatobeetles. This prediction was confirmed when bacteria called *Bt* was discovered to kill Colorado Potatobeetles and other insect pests.

Interpret Results

As scientists investigate, they analyze their evidence, or data, and begin to draw conclusions. **Analyzing data** involves looking at the evidence gathered through observations or experiments and trying to identify any patterns that might exist in the data. Often scientists need to make additional observations or perform more experiments before they are sure of their conclusions. Many times scientists make new predictions or revise their hypotheses.

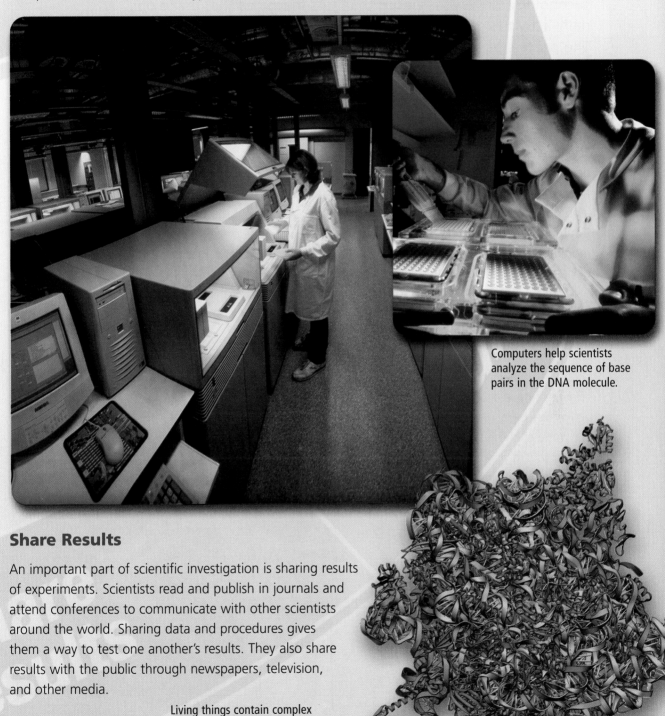

Computers help scientists analyze the sequence of base pairs in the DNA molecule.

Share Results

An important part of scientific investigation is sharing results of experiments. Scientists read and publish in journals and attend conferences to communicate with other scientists around the world. Sharing data and procedures gives them a way to test one another's results. They also share results with the public through newspapers, television, and other media.

Living things contain complex molecules such as RNA and DNA. To study them scientists often use models like the one shown here.

The Nature of Technology

Imagine what life would be like without cars, computers, and cell phones. Imagine having no refrigerator or radio. It's difficult to think of a world without these items we call technology. Technology, however, is more than just machines that make our daily activities easier. Like science, technology is also a process. The process of technology uses scientific knowledge to design solutions to real-world problems.

Science and Technology

Science and technology go hand in hand. Each depends upon the other. Even designing a device as simple as a toaster requires knowledge of how heat flows and which materials are the best conductors of heat. Scientists also use a number of devices to help them collect data. Microscopes, telescopes, spectrographs, and computers are just a few of the tools that help scientists learn more about the world. The more information these tools provide, the more devices can be developed to aid scientific research and to improve modern lives.

The Process of Technological Design

Heart disease is among the leading causes of death today. Doctors have successfully replaced damaged hearts with hearts from donors. Medical engineers have developed pacemakers that improve the ability of a damaged heart to pump blood. But none of these solutions is perfect. Although it is very complex, the heart is really a pump for blood, thus, using technology to build a better replacement pump should be possible. The process of technological design involves many choices. In the case of an artificial heart, choices about how and what to develop involve cost, safety, and patient preference. What kind of technology will result in the best quality of life for the patient?

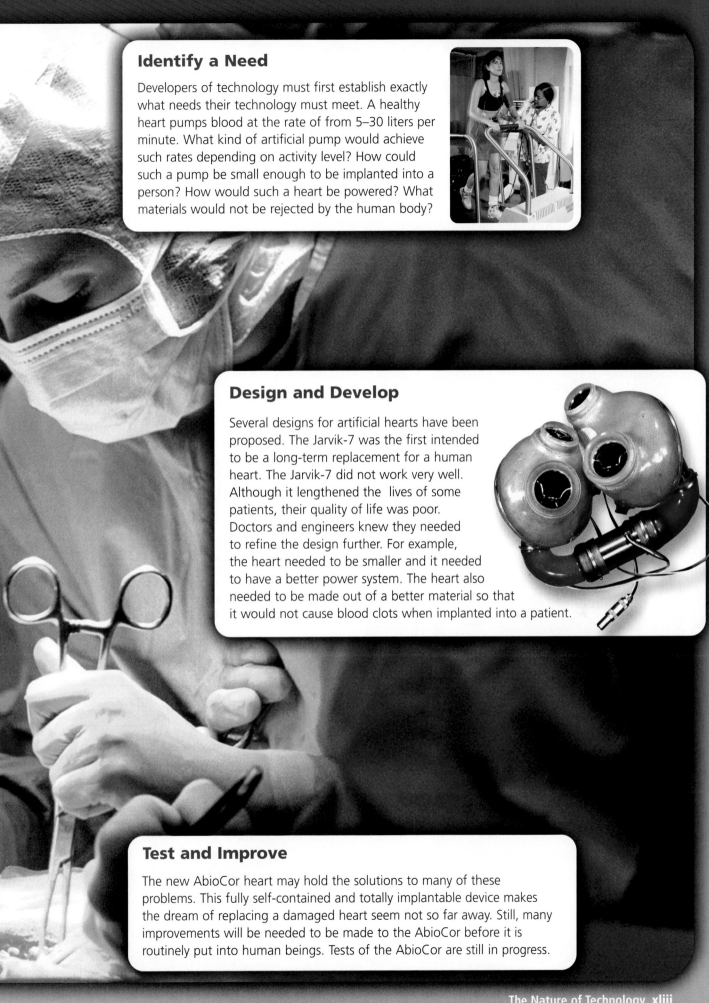

Identify a Need

Developers of technology must first establish exactly what needs their technology must meet. A healthy heart pumps blood at the rate of from 5–30 liters per minute. What kind of artificial pump would achieve such rates depending on activity level? How could such a pump be small enough to be implanted into a person? How would such a heart be powered? What materials would not be rejected by the human body?

Design and Develop

Several designs for artificial hearts have been proposed. The Jarvik-7 was the first intended to be a long-term replacement for a human heart. The Jarvik-7 did not work very well. Although it lengthened the lives of some patients, their quality of life was poor. Doctors and engineers knew they needed to refine the design further. For example, the heart needed to be smaller and it needed to have a better power system. The heart also needed to be made out of a better material so that it would not cause blood clots when implanted into a patient.

Test and Improve

The new AbioCor heart may hold the solutions to many of these problems. This fully self-contained and totally implantable device makes the dream of replacing a damaged heart seem not so far away. Still, many improvements will be needed to be made to the AbioCor before it is routinely put into human beings. Tests of the AbioCor are still in progress.

Using McDougal Littell Science

Reading Text and Visuals

This book is organized to help you learn. Use these boxed pointers as a path to help you learn and remember the **Big Ideas** and **Key Concepts**.

Take notes.

Use the strategies on the **Getting Ready to Learn** page.

Read the Big Idea.

As you read **Key Concepts** for the chapter, relate them to **the Big Idea**.

CHAPTER 3

Transp Protec

the **BIG** idea

Systems function to transport materials and to defend and protect the body.

Key Concepts

SECTION 3.1 The circulatory system transports materials.
Learn how materials move through blood vessels.

SECTION 3.2 The immune system defends the body.
Learn about the body's defenses and responses to foreign materials.

SECTION 3.3 The integumentary system shields the body.
Learn about the structure of skin and how it protects the body.

Internet Preview

CLASSZONE.COM
Chapter 3 online resources: Content Review, two Visualizations, four Resource Centers, Math Tutorial, Test Practice

E 62 Unit: Human Biology

CHAPTER 3
Getting Ready to Learn

 CONCEPT REVIEW

- The body's systems interact.
- The body's systems work to maintain internal conditions.
- The digestive system breaks down food.
- The respiratory system gets oxygen and removes carbon dioxide.

 VOCABULARY REVIEW

organ p. 11
organ system p. 12
homeostasis p. 12
nutrient p. 45

CONTENT REVIEW
CLASSZONE.COM
Review concepts and vocabulary.

 TAKING NOTES

MAIN IDEA AND DETAIL NOTES

Make a two-column chart. Write the main ideas, such as those in the blue headings, in the column on the left. Write details about each of those main heads in the column on the right.

VOCABULARY STRATEGY

Write each new vocabulary term in the center of a **frame game** diagram. Decide what information to frame it with. Use examples, descriptions, parts, sentences that use the term in context, or pictures. You can change the frame to fit each term.

See the Note-Taking Handbook on pages R45–R51.

SCIENCE NOTEBOOK

MAIN IDEAS	DETAIL NOTES
1. The circulatory system works with other body systems.	1. Transports materials from digestive and respiratory systems to cells 2. Blood is fluid that carries materials and wastes 3. Blood is always moving through the body 4. Blood delivers oxygen, takes away carbon dioxide

carries material to cells

moves continuously through body | **BLOOD** | carries waste away from cells

circulatory system

E 64 Unit: Human Biology

---

xliv

Read each heading.

See how it fits in the outline of the chapter.

KEY CONCEPT

3.1 The circulatory system transports materials.

◄ BEFORE, you learned
- The urinary system removes waste
- The kidneys play a role in homeostasis

► NOW, you will learn
- How different structures of the circulatory system work together
- About the structure and function of blood
- What blood pressure is and why it is important

Remember what you know.

Think about concepts you learned earlier and preview what you'll learn now.

VOCABULARY
circulatory system p. 65
blood p. 65
red blood cell p. 67
artery p. 69
vein p. 69
capillary p. 69

EXPLORE The Circulatory System

How fast does your heart beat?

PROCEDURE

1. Hold out your left hand with your palm facing up.

2. Place the first two fingers of your right hand on your left wrist below your thumb. Move your fingertips slightly until you can feel your pulse.

3. Use the stopwatch to determine how many times your heart beats in one minute.

MATERIALS
stopwatch

WHAT DO YOU THINK?
- How many times did your heart beat?
- What do you think you would find if you took your pulse after exercising?

Try the activities.

They will introduce you to science concepts.

The circulatory system works with other body systems.

VOCABULARY
Add a frame game diagram for the term *circulatory system* to your notebook.

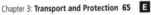

You have read that the systems in your body provide materials and energy. The digestive system breaks down food and nutrients, and the respiratory system provides the oxygen that cells need to release energy. Another system, called the **circulatory system,** transports products from the digestive and the respiratory systems to the cells.

Materials and wastes are carried in a fluid called **blood**. Blood moves continuously through the body, delivering oxygen and other materials to cells and removing carbon dioxide and other wastes from cells.

Learn the vocabulary.

Take notes on each term.

Chapter 3: **Transport and Protection** 65 **E**

Reading Text and Visuals

Read one paragraph at a time.

Look for a topic sentence that explains the main idea of the paragraph. Figure out how the details relate to that idea. One paragraph might have several important ideas; you may have to reread to understand.

Answer the questions.

Check Your Reading questions will help you remember what you read.

Study the visuals.

- Read the title.
- Read all labels and captions.
- Figure out what the picture is showing. Notice the information in the captions.

Exchanging Oxygen and Carbon Dioxide

Like almost all living things, the human body needs oxygen to survive. Without oxygen, cells in the body die quickly. How does the oxygen you need get to your cells? Oxygen, along with other gases, enters the body when you inhale. Oxygen is then transported to cells throughout the body.

The air that you breathe contains only about 20 percent oxygen and less than 1 percent carbon dioxide. Almost 80 percent of air is nitrogen gas. The air that you exhale contains more carbon dioxide and less oxygen than the air that you inhale. It's important that you exhale carbon dioxide because high levels of it will damage, even destroy, cells.

In cells and tissues, proper levels of both oxygen and carbon dioxide are essential. Recall that systems in the body work together to maintain homeostasis. If levels of oxygen or carbon dioxide change, your brain or blood vessels signal the body to breathe faster or slower.

The photograph shows how someone underwater maintains proper levels of carbon dioxide and oxygen. The scuba diver needs to inhale oxygen from a tank. She removes carbon dioxide wastes with other gases when she exhales into the water. The bubbles you see in the water are formed when she exhales.

CHECK YOUR READING What gases are in the air that you breathe?

Gas Exchange

This scuba diver breathes the same mixture of gases present in air.

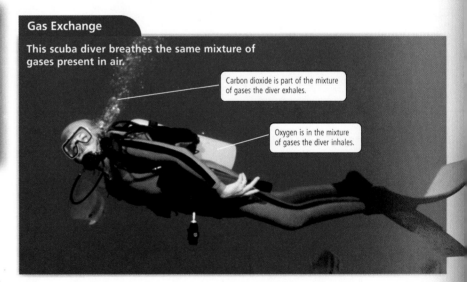

Carbon dioxide is part of the mixture of gases the diver exhales.

Oxygen is in the mixture of gases the diver inhales.

Doing Labs

To understand science, you have to see it in action. Doing labs helps you understand how things really work.

(1) Read the entire lab first.

(2) Form a hypothesis.

(3) Follow the procedure.

(4) Record the data.

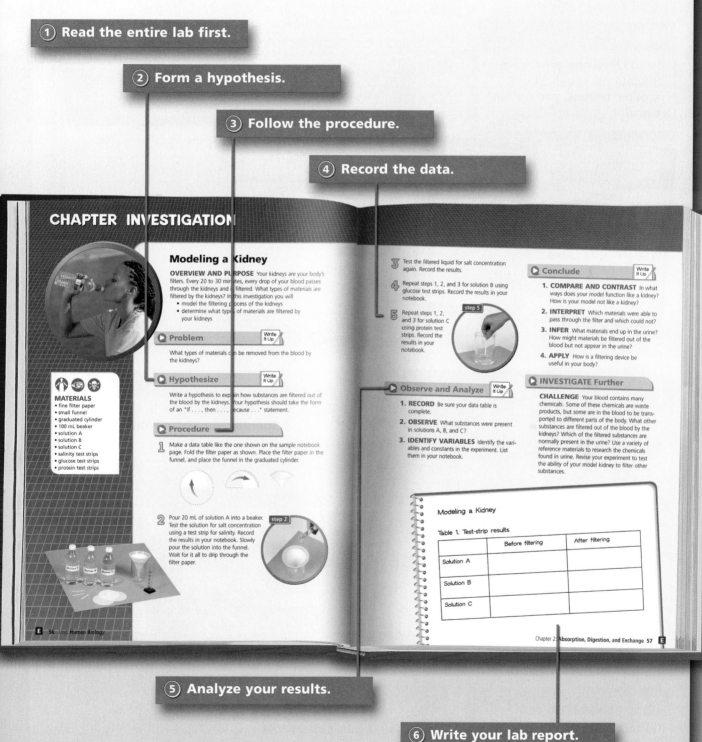

CHAPTER INVESTIGATION

Modeling a Kidney

OVERVIEW AND PURPOSE Your kidneys are your body's filters. Every 20 to 30 minutes, every drop of your blood passes through the kidneys and is filtered. What types of materials are filtered by the kidneys? In this investigation you will
- model the filtering process of the kidneys
- determine what types of materials are filtered by your kidneys

Problem
Write it Up

What types of materials can be removed from the blood by the kidneys?

Hypothesize
Write it Up

Write a hypothesis to explain how substances are filtered out of the blood by the kidneys. Your hypothesis should take the form of an "If . . . , then . . . , because . . ." statement.

Procedure

1. Make a data table like the one shown on the sample notebook page. Fold the filter paper as shown. Place the filter paper in the funnel, and place the funnel in the graduated cylinder.

2. Pour 20 mL of solution A into a beaker. Test the solution for salt concentration using a test strip for salinity. Record the results in your notebook. Slowly pour the solution into the funnel. Wait for it all to drip through the filter paper. **step 2**

MATERIALS
- fine filter paper
- small funnel
- graduated cylinder
- 100 mL beaker
- solution A
- solution B
- solution C
- salinity test strips
- glucose test strips
- protein test strips

3. Test the filtered liquid for salt concentration again. Record the results.

4. Repeat steps 1, 2, and 3 for solution B using glucose test strips. Record the results in your notebook.

5. Repeat steps 1, 2, and 3 for solution C using protein test strips. Record the results in your notebook. **step 5**

Observe and Analyze
Write it Up

1. **RECORD** Be sure your data table is complete.

2. **OBSERVE** What substances were present in solutions A, B, and C?

3. **IDENTIFY VARIABLES** Identify the variables and constants in the experiment. List them in your notebook.

Conclude
Write it Up

1. **COMPARE AND CONTRAST** In what ways does your model function like a kidney? How is your model not like a kidney?

2. **INTERPRET** Which materials were able to pass through the filter and which could not?

3. **INFER** What materials end up in the urine? How might materials be filtered out of the blood but not appear in the urine?

4. **APPLY** How is a filtering device useful in your body?

INVESTIGATE Further

CHALLENGE Your blood contains many chemicals. Some of these chemicals are waste products, but some are in the blood to be transported to different parts of the body. What other substances are filtered out of the blood by the kidneys? Which of the filtered substances are normally present in the urine? Use a variety of reference materials to research the chemicals found in urine. Revise your experiment to test the ability of your model kidney to filter other substances.

Modeling a Kidney

Table 1. Test-strip results

	Before filtering	After filtering
Solution A		
Solution B		
Solution C		

E 56 Unit: Human Biology

Chapter 2: Absorption, Digestion, and Exchange 57 E

(5) Analyze your results.

(6) Write your lab report.

Using Technology

The Internet is a great source of information about up-to-date science.
The ClassZone Web site and NSTA SciLinks have exciting sites for you to
explore. Video clips and simulations can make science come alive.

Look for red banners.

Go to **ClassZone.com** to see
simulations, visualizations,
resource centers, and content
review.

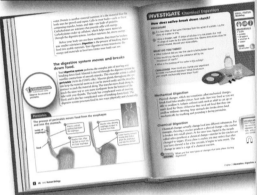

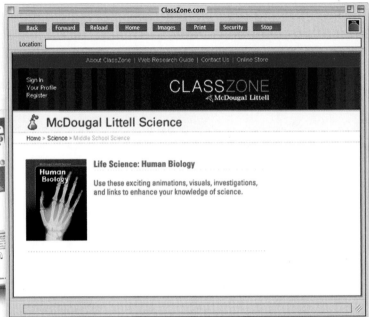

Watch the video.

See science at work in the
**Scientific American Frontiers
video.**

Look up SciLinks.

Go to **scilinks.org** to explore
the topic.

Tissues and Organs **Code: MDL044**

UNIT A

Cells and Heredity

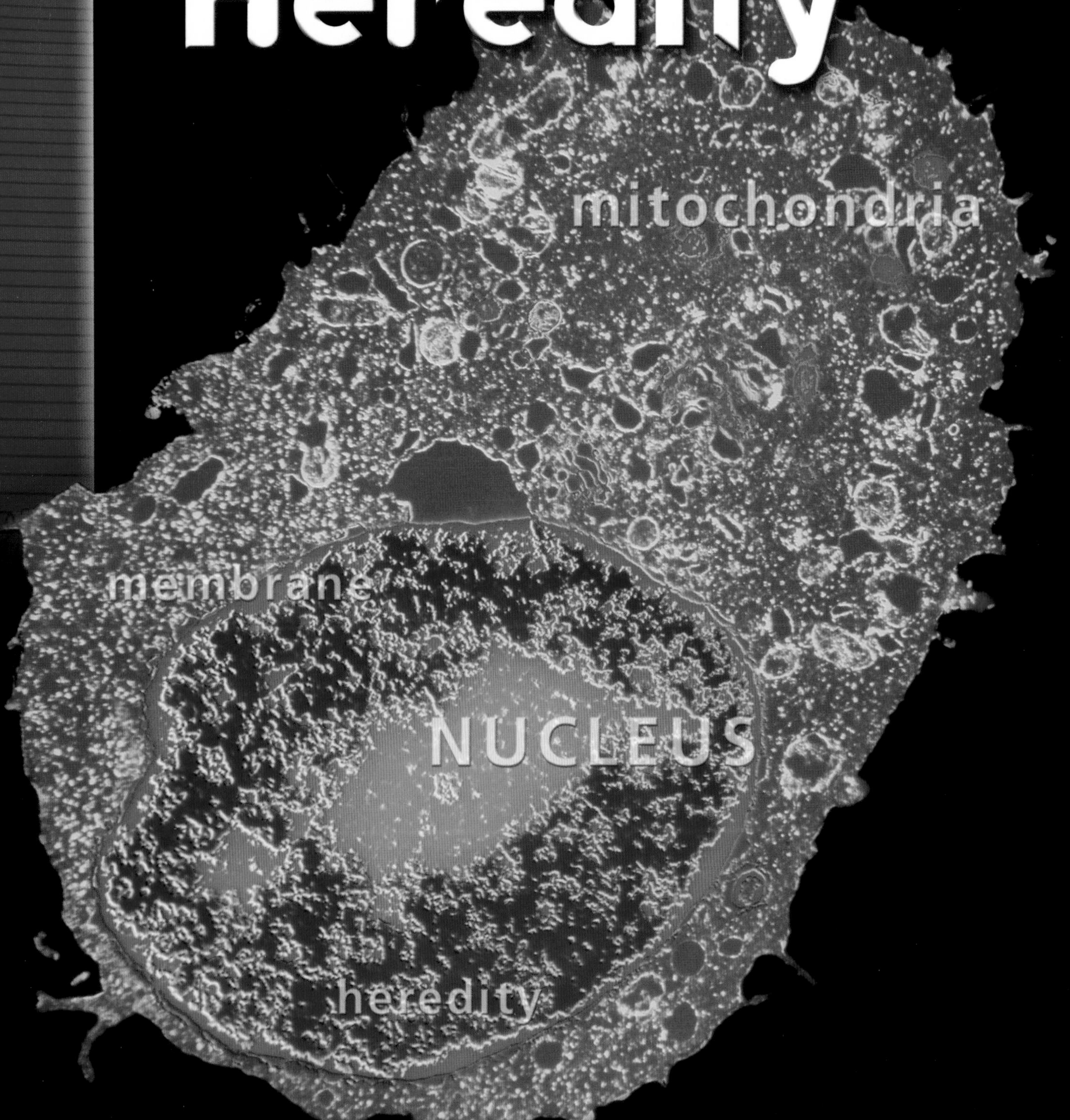
mitochondria
membrane
NUCLEUS
heredity

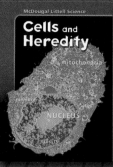

McDougal Littell Science

Cells and Heredity
Contents Overview

Unit Features

1 The Cell

(the **BIG** idea)

All living things are made up
of cells.

2 How Cells Function

(the **BIG** idea)

All cells need energy and materials
for life processes.

3 Cell Division

(the **BIG** idea)

Organisms grow, reproduce, and
maintain themselves through cell
division.

4 Patterns of Heredity

(the **BIG** idea)

In sexual reproduction, genes are
passed from parents to offspring in
predictable patterns.

5 DNA and Modern Genetics

(the **BIG** idea)

DNA is a set of instructions for
making cell parts.

Genes that MAP the Body

What signals a monkey to grow a tail and a fish to grow fins? The answer is in their genes.

SCIENTIFIC AMERICAN FRONTIERS

Learn about genes that affect aging. See the video "Genes for Youth."

What's in a Gene?

Humans and fish are are about as different as one animal can be from another. Yet both organisms have a similar body pattern: front and back, top and bottom, left side and right side. The head is at one end and limbs extend from the body—fins in a fish, arms and legs in a human. Inside are similar structures—brains, hearts, and stomachs—and cells that function in similar ways.

DNA is the genetic material found in all living things. DNA determines how cells grow, develop, and function. Within the DNA are genes, segments of DNA, that determine whether a cell becomes a brain cell or a heart cell. Both a fish and a human start out life as a single cell. As the cell divides again and again, each organism grows into its familiar shape. Scientists are studying what it is that maps out the head-to-tail development that gets every part of a body in the right place.

One group of genes, called *Hox* genes, are critical in the early development of an animal's body. These genes are found in the DNA of every animal—from humans to fruit flies. The position of *Hox* genes, from top to bottom along the DNA, matches up to the particular parts they control of an organism's body.

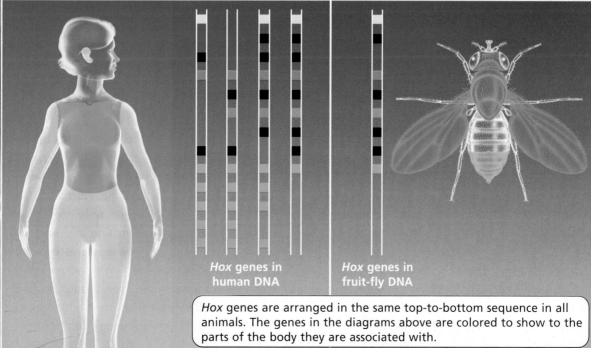

Hox genes in
human DNA

Hox genes in
fruit-fly DNA

Hox genes are arranged in the same top-to-bottom sequence in all animals. The genes in the diagrams above are colored to show to the parts of the body they are associated with.

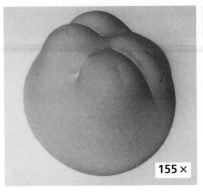

155 ×

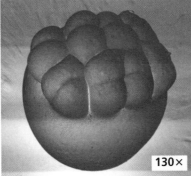

130 ×

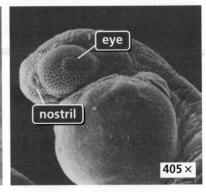

eye

nostril

405 ×

The egg of a zebrafish starts to divide after fertilization.

SOURCE for three images, Dr. Richard Kessel and Dr. Gene Shih/Visuals Unlimited

The egg now has 16 cells, all of which are similar in size and shape.

Many hours later, the cells have started to develop into different parts of the body.

How *Hox* Genes Work

Hox genes act like switches. A particular *Hox* gene turns on the development of a particular structure in an animal's body. One type of *Hox* gene switches on the development of structures in the head—for example, eyes and ears. Another switches on the development of limbs—the arms, legs, fins, or wings of an animal. The position of the genes within an animal's DNA matches to the part of the body it controls. *Hox* genes at the top control development of parts of the head. Those toward the middle control development of the main part of the body and the limbs.

How a Limb Develops

What happens if a *Hox* gene gets out of position? If the *Hox* gene that controls the development of legs in a fruit fly is placed in with the *Hox* genes that control development of the head, the fruit fly will grow legs from its head. The gene functions as it should, it's just that it's not doing its job in the right place.

Another interesting thing about *Hox* genes is that they are active only for a certain period of time. They "switch off" when the part of the body they control has developed. Studies of the zebrafish have provided clues as to how this happens.

SCIENTIFIC AMERICAN FRONTIERS

View the "Genes for Youth" segment of your Scientific American Frontiers video to learn about the role of genes in aging. ▶

IN THIS SCENE FROM THE VIDEO biologist Cynthia Kenyon observes the activity level of some unusual worms that remain active much longer than other worms.

Kenyon is interested in what controls aging in worms. She studies how the genes in long-living worms affect the activity of their cells. She looks for differences between the cells of unusual worms and those of normal worms.

Because cells of animals function in similar ways, she is interested in how

UNDERSTANDING AGING A multicellular organism starts life as a single cell. As an organism grows, it goes through different stages of development. Think of the differences between a baby, a teenager, a young adult, and an older person.

what she learns about aging in worms might apply to other animals. Even though a worm is far less complex an animal than a human, studying these worms may provide clues into how humans age.

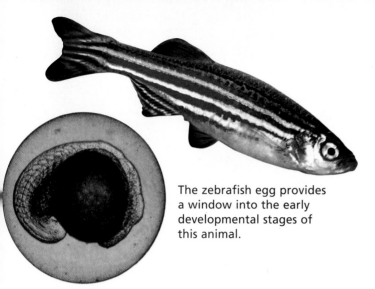

The zebrafish egg provides a window into the early developmental stages of this animal.

A Window on Development

Zebrafish are tiny fish that hatch in about three days. Scientists can actually see through the fish egg to watch its body develop. Working with the *Hox* genes of zebrafish, one researcher studied the amount of time that the *Hox* gene that controls fin development was active. The gene "turned on" for a short period of time, the fin developed, then the gene "turned off."

This research led scientists to think about the length of time the same *Hox* gene is active in other animals. It's possible that limbs are longer in larger animals because their *Hox* genes are active for a longer period of time. Researchers are excited because what they learn about the *Hox* genes of a simple animal can provide clues into the development of larger, more complex animals.

UNANSWERED Questions

There are many unanswered questions about the role *Hox* genes play in the development of body plans:

- Which *Hox* genes control which stages of development and how long are the genes active?

- What is it that signals the genes to "turn on and off"?

- How can research on *Hox* genes be used by medical researchers to help them treat genetic diseases or disorders that affect how a body develops?

UNIT PROJECTS

As you study this unit, work alone or with a group on one of the projects below.

Design an Experiment

Use fast plants to observe differences among plants.

- Follow directions for growing fast plants.

- Observe the plants as they grow and identify different characteristics.

- Use your observations to form a question about genes and plant characteristics.

- Design an experiment to answer your question.

Living Cell

Work cooperatively to present a "living cell" demonstration. Model cell processes, such as photosynthesis and cellular respiration.

- Design a model that shows parts of the cell at work.

- Include structures such as membranes, the nucleus, chloroplasts, and mitochondria. Represent energy and materials that move into and out of a cell.

- Have one student narrate each process.

DNA Detective Work

Prepare an oral presentation about how DNA technology is used to solve crimes.

Explain the science behind police and detective work.

CAREER CENTER
CLASSZONE.COM

Learn more about careers in molecular biology.

The Cell

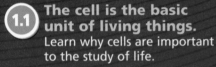

All living things are made up of cells.

Key Concepts

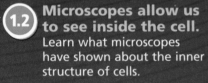

Internet Preview

CLASSZONE.COM

Chapter 1 online resources: Content Review, two Simulations, two Resource Centers, Math Tutorial, Test Practice

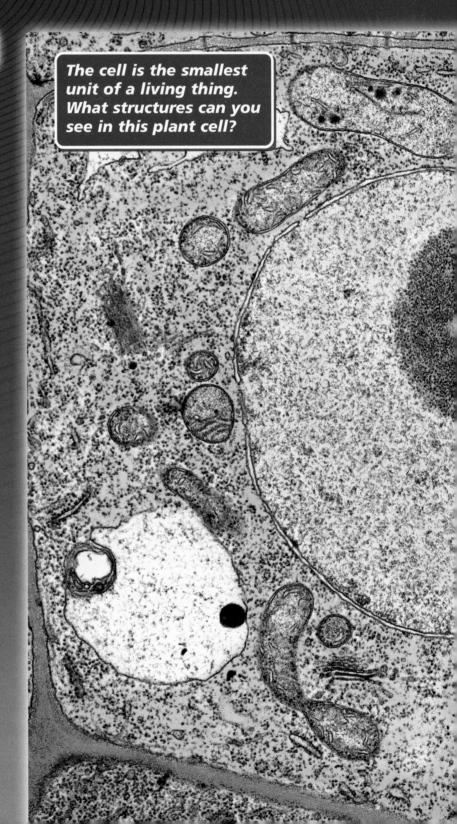

The cell is the smallest unit of a living thing. What structures can you see in this plant cell?

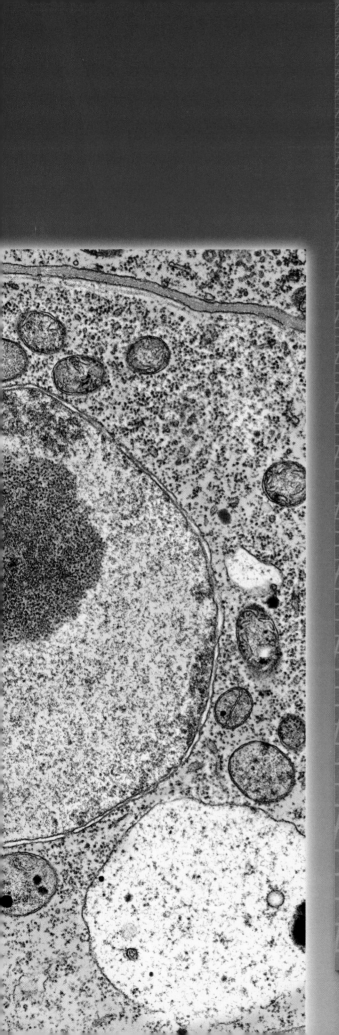

Seeing and Understanding

Cut out a color photograph or drawing from a magazine or newspaper and place it on a flat surface. Use a magnifying glass to look at the image. Start with the magnifying glass right on top of the image and then slowly move the magnifying glass away, studying the photograph as you do.

Observe and Think What happens as you move the magnifying glass away from the image? How can a simple magnifying tool help you understand better how the image was printed?

Bits and Pieces

Find a sentence approximately ten words long in a newspaper or magazine and cut it out. Then cut the sentence into words. Ask a friend to put the words back together into a sentence.

Observe and Think What clues can your friend use to put the sentence back together? How can the parts of something help you understand how the whole works?

Internet Activity: Cells

Go to **ClassZone.com** to take a virtual tour of a cell.

Observe and Think What functions do the different parts of the cell perform?

NSTA
scilinks.org
SCiLINKS

Cell Theory **Code: MDL031**

Getting Ready to Learn

◀ CONCEPT REVIEW

- Living things share certain characteristics that distinguish them from nonliving things.
- Living things have common needs, including energy, matter, and living space.

◀ VOCABULARY REVIEW

See Glossary for definitions.

cell

DNA

genetic material

theory

CONTENT REVIEW
CLASSZONE.COM

Review concepts and vocabulary.

▶ TAKING NOTES

MAIN IDEA WEB

Write each new blue heading, or main idea, in the top box. In the boxes around it, take notes about important terms and details that relate to the main idea.

VOCABULARY STRATEGY

Write each new vocabulary term in the center of a **four square** diagram. Write notes in the squares around each term. Include a definition, some characteristics, and some possible examples of the term. If possible, write some things that are not examples of the term.

See the Note-Taking Handbook on pages R45–R51.

SCIENCE NOTEBOOK

All living things are made of cells.

| The cell is the smallest unit that performs the activities of life. | Multicellular organisms have many different types of cells working together. | In a unicellular organism a single cell carries out all the activities of life. |

Definition	Characteristics
Any living thing	Needs energy, materials from the environment, and living space.
	Grows, develops, responds to environment, reproduces.
	Is made up of one or more cells.

ORGANISM

Examples	Nonexamples
Dogs, cats, birds, insects, moss, trees, bacteria	Rocks, water, dirt

The cell is the basic unit of living things.

◀ BEFORE, you learned

- Living things have common characteristics
- Living things have common needs
- A theory is something that explains what is observed in nature

▶ NOW, you will learn

- How living things are different from nonliving things
- How the microscope led to the discovery of cells
- About the cell theory

VOCABULARY

organism p. 9
unicellular p. 11
multicellular p. 11
microscope p. 12
bacteria p. 14

EXPLORE Activity and Life

Does a candle show signs of life?

PROCEDURE

① Carefully light one candle.

② Sit quietly and observe the candle. Note its behavior. What does the flame do? What happens to the wax?

WHAT DO YOU THINK?

- How does a lit candle seem alive?
- How do you know for sure that it is not?

MATERIALS

- small candle
- candleholder
- matches

Living things are different from nonliving things.

MAIN IDEA WEB
Make a main idea web about living things, including how they differ from nonliving things.

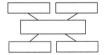

You know life when you see it. Perhaps your class takes a field trip to a local state park to collect water samples. You are surrounded by trees. There is a stream, with rocks covered with moss and green algae. There are fish and frogs; there are birds and insects. You are surrounded by life. But how would you define it?

One way to answer the question is to think about what makes a living thing different from a nonliving thing. You might ask if a thing uses energy. Or maybe you would observe it to see if it moves. You could investigate whether it consumes food and water. These are characteristics of living things, or organisms. Any individual form of life that uses energy to carry out its activities is an **organism.** Most organisms move. All organisms get water and other materials from the environment.

Characteristics of Life

Living things have these characteristics:

- organization
- the ability to develop and grow
- the ability to respond to the environment
- the ability to reproduce

An organism's body must be organized in a way that enables it to meet its needs. Some organisms, like bacteria, are very simple. A more complex organism, such as the kingfisher shown in the photograph below, is organized so that different parts of its body perform different jobs, called functions. For example, a kingfisher has wings for flying, a heart for pumping blood, and eyes for seeing.

Another characteristic of organisms is that they grow and, in most cases, develop into adult forms. Some organisms change a great deal in size and appearance throughout their lifetimes, whereas others grow and change very little. Organisms also respond to the world outside them. Think of how the pupils of your eyes get smaller in bright light. Finally, organisms can reproduce, producing new organisms that are similar to themselves.

CHECK YOUR READING What four characteristics are common to all living things?

Needs of Life

Organisms cannot carry out the activities that characterize life without a few necessities: energy, materials, and living space. What does it mean to need energy? You know that if you want to run a race, you need energy. But did you know that your body also needs energy to sleep or to breathe or even to think? All organisms require a steady supply of energy to stay alive. Where does this energy come from, and how does an organism get it?

APPLY Identify three living things in this photograph. How do they meet their needs?

Food is a source of **energy** and **materials**.

Water provides **materials** and **living space**.

The energy used by almost all forms of life on Earth comes from the Sun. Some organisms, like plants and some bacteria, are able to capture this energy directly. Your body, like the bodies of other animals, uses food as a source of energy. The food animals eat comes from plants or from organisms that eat plants. Food also provides the materials necessary for growth and reproduction. These materials include substances such as carbon dioxide, nitrogen, oxygen, and water. Finally, all organisms need space to live and grow. If any one of these requirements is missing, an organism will die.

All living things are made of cells.

The cell is the smallest unit of a living thing. Some organisms are made of a single cell. These organisms are **unicellular** and usually too small for you to see directly. Pond water is full of tiny unicellular organisms. Most of the organisms you can see, such as a frog or a water lily, are made up of many cells. Organisms made up of many cells are called **multicellular** organisms.

The needs and characteristics of a single cell in a unicellular organism are the same as those for any organism. Each of the tiny single-celled organisms found in a drop of pond water performs all the activities that characterize life. Multicellular organisms, like a frog or a water lily, have bodies that are more complex. Different parts of the body of a multicellular organism perform different functions. A water lily's roots hold it in the soil and its leaves capture energy from the Sun. A frog moves with its arms and legs and eats with its mouth.

Multicellular organisms have different types of cells that make up their body parts and help the organisms meet their needs. Roots are made of root cells, which are different from leaf cells. Muscle cells have special parts that allow them to move. In a multicellular organism, many cells work together to carry out the basic activities of life.

VOCABULARY
Add four squares for *unicellular* and *multicellular* to your notebook. You may want to add to your lists of characteristics and examples as you read through the chapter.

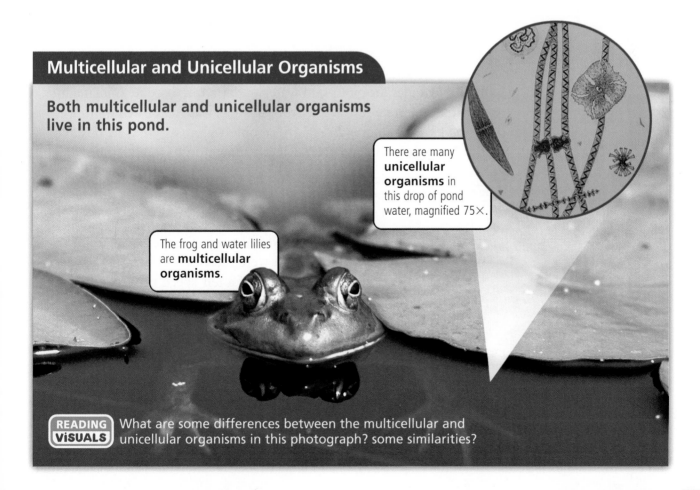

Multicellular and Unicellular Organisms

Both multicellular and unicellular organisms live in this pond.

There are many **unicellular organisms** in this drop of pond water, magnified 75×.

The frog and water lilies are **multicellular organisms**.

READING VISUALS What are some differences between the multicellular and unicellular organisms in this photograph? some similarities?

The microscope led to the discovery of cells.

Most cells are microscopic, too small to see without the aid of a microscope. A **microscope** is an instrument which makes an object appear bigger than it is. It took the invention of this relatively simple tool to lead to the discovery of cells. In the 1660s, Robert Hooke began using microscopes to look at all sorts of materials. Anton van Leeuwenhoek took up similar work in the 1670s. They were among the first people to describe cells.

READING TiP

The word *microscopic* is an adjective made from the noun *microscope.* Things that are microscopic are too small to see without the use of a microscope.

Robert Hooke gave the cell its name. While looking at a sample of cork, a layer of bark taken from an oak tree, he saw a group of similarly shaped compartments that looked to him like tiny empty rooms, or cells. You can see from his drawing, shown at right, how well these cells fit Hooke's description. Hooke used a microscope that magnified objects 30 times (30×). In other words, objects appeared thirty times larger than their actual size.

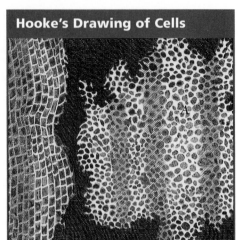

Hooke's Drawing of Cells

Robert Hooke published this drawing of dead cork cells in 1665. The microscope he used, shown at left, has two lenses.

The bark cells Hooke saw were actually dead cells, which is why they appeared empty. Anton van Leeuwenhoek was one of the first people to describe living cells. He looked at a drop of pond water under a microscope. Imagine his surprise when he saw that a drop of water was full of living things! Using lenses that could magnify an object almost 300×, he observed tiny unicellular organisms like those shown on page 11.

CHECK YOUR READING How did the invention of the microscope change the study of biology?

You can understand how powerful a microscope is if you think of how big a penny would be if it were increased in size 30 ×. It would be a little bigger than the tire of a ten-speed bicycle. Enlarged 300 ×, that penny would be so big that you would need a tractor-trailer to move it. Magnify your best friend 30× (supposing a height of 1.5 meters, or almost 5 ft), and your friend would appear to be 45 meters (147 ft) tall. That's almost the height of Niagara Falls. Change the magnification to 300 ×, and your friend would appear to be 450 meters (1470 ft) tall—taller than the Empire State Building.

Cells come from other cells.

The studies of Hooke and Leeuwenhoek made people ask if all living things have cells. People continued to observe samples taken from all sorts of living matter. They continued to find cells, although often these cells looked very different from one another. Still, it was clear that all living matter was made of cells.

There was another important question scientists were trying to answer: Where do cells come from? The answer to this question was settled by the 1850s. People studying all types of living cells observed the same thing—that cells divide. One living cell divides into two living cells. Here, under the microscope, was evidence of where cells come from. Life comes from life—that is, one cell comes from another cell.

 CHECK YOUR READING What do scientists mean when they say that life comes from life? Your answer should include the word *cells*.

The observations and evidence gathered over a long time by many scientists are summarized in the three concepts of the cell theory:

1. Every living thing is made of one or more cells.

2. Cells carry out the functions needed to support life.

3. Cells come only from other living cells.

The Cell Theory

The importance of the cell to life is summarized in the cell theory.

1 **Every living thing is made up of one or more cells.** A polar bear is a multicellular organism.

2 **Cells carry out the functions needed to support life.** Fat cells are animal cells that provide energy as well as insulation.

400×

3 **Cells come only from other living cells.** Each polar bear cub began as a single cell.

The cell theory is important to the study of biology.

The importance of the cell theory is indicated by the word *theory*. A scientific theory is a widely accepted explanation of things observed in nature. A theory must be supported by evidence, including experimental evidence and observations. A theory proves its value when it explains new discoveries and observations.

 CHECK YOUR READING What are two characteristics of scientific theory?

Theories are important for a number of reasons. Certainly they satisfy scientists' desire to understand the natural world, and they serve as foundations for further research and study. Theories can also lead to research that has some practical benefit for society.

Louis Pasteur

The work of the French scientist Louis Pasteur shows how an understanding of cell theory can have practical uses. Pasteur lived in the 1800s, when there was no mechanical refrigeration in homes. People were used to having foods spoil and milk go sour. During this time, many people died from diseases such as typhoid fever, tuberculosis, and diphtheria. Pasteur's work showed that microscopic organisms were involved both in the spoilage of food and in disease.

The milk that you get from the school cafeteria has been pasteurized so that it will stay fresh longer.

Pasteur observed that milk that turned sour contained large numbers of tiny single-celled organisms called **bacteria** (bak-TEER-ee-uh). He developed a process, now known as pasteurization, in which heat is used to kill the bacteria. Killing the bacteria keeps milk fresh longer. The fact that bacteria cause milk to sour or "sicken" made Pasteur wonder whether microscopic organisms could also be the cause of sickness in humans and animals.

Bacteria and Spontaneous Generation

Using a microscope to study air, water, and soil, Pasteur found microorganisms everywhere. He found bacteria in the blood of animals, including people who were sick. Pasteur referred to the microorganisms he observed as "germs." He realized that an understanding of germs might help prevent disease. Pasteur's work led to the first animal vaccinations for cholera and anthrax and to a treatment for rabies in humans.

At the time that Pasteur was doing his research, there were scientists who thought that bacteria grew from nonliving materials, in a process known as spontaneous generation. Pasteur conducted

Pasteur's Experiments

Pasteur's experiments showed that bacteria are present in the air. They do not grow spontaneously.

— End of flask is sealed.

1 Broth is boiled to destroy any living bacteria, and the flask is sealed.

2 A few days pass, and the broth is still clear. No bacteria have grown.

3 Two to three days pass, and the broth is still clear. No bacteria have grown.

— End of flask is broken.

1 Broth is boiled to destroy any living bacteria, and the flask is sealed.

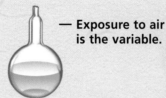
— Exposure to air is the variable.

2 The end of the flask is broken to expose the broth to the air. The broth is clear.

3 Two to three days pass, and the broth is cloudy because of the growth of bacteria.

a now-famous series of experiments that disproved spontaneous generation and confirmed the cell theory. He showed that cells come only from other cells. Two of those experiments are shown above. Both began with a sealed flask containing boiled broth. In the first experiment, the flask remained sealed, while in the second experiment, the top of the flask was broken to expose the contents to air. Bacteria grew only in the second flask.

1.1 Review

KEY CONCEPTS

1. Name four characteristics of living things.

2. How did the microscope change human understanding of life?

3. Explain the three concepts that make up the cell theory.

CRITICAL THINKING

4. **Analyze** Relate the characteristics of a scientific theory to the cell theory.

5. **Compare and Contrast** Draw a Venn diagram to compare and contrast multicellular and unicellular organisms.

⚠ CHALLENGE

6. **Synthesize** Explain how Pasteur's experiment supported the cell theory and disproved the theory of spontaneous generation.

CHAPTER INVESTIGATION

Using a Microscope

OVERVIEW AND PURPOSE The smallest forms of life are not visible to the human eye. You will use a light microscope as a tool to observe unicellular and multicellular organisms. Then you will compare the organisms you see under the microscope to the Identification Key. Refer to pages R14 and R15 of the Lab Handbook for more information about using a microscope and preparing a slide.

▶ Procedure

1. Make a data table like the one shown on page 17. To observe the microscopic organisms, you need to make a wet-mount slide. Obtain a slide and use the eyedropper to place 2–3 drops of pond water in the center of the slide.

2. Obtain a cover slip for your slide. Place one edge of the cover slip on the slide, at the left edge of the pond water. Slowly lower the cover slip as if you were closing the cover of a book. The cover slip should lie flat on the slide. If you see air bubbles, pick up the cover slip and lower it again.

   step 2

3. Clean the lenses of the microscope with lens paper. Choose the lowest magnification, then place the slide on the stage. Start with the objective at its lowest point and raise the objective to focus. First focus with the coarse adjustment, which is usually the larger knob. Begin your search for living organisms. Use the fine adjustment to make the image clearer. Be patient when looking for life on your slide. It may take some time.

4. When you find something interesting, carefully switch to a higher magnification. Turn the nose of the microscope until another objective snaps into place. Use only the fine adjustment when viewing at high power, to avoid scratching the microscope or the slide. Move the slide gently from side to side as you look through the microscope. Search different parts of the sample for different organisms.

   step 4

MATERIALS
- slides
- eyedropper
- pond water
- cover slip
- light microscope
- lens paper
- Identification Key

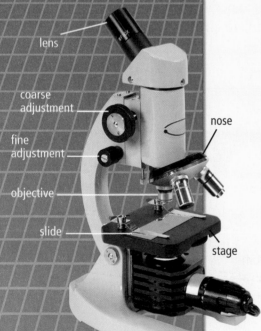

lens

coarse adjustment

fine adjustment

objective

slide

nose

stage

Euglena
(unicellular)

Paramecium
(unicellular)

Stentor
(unicellular)

Desmid
(unicellular)

Water flea
(multicellular)

Hydra
(multicellular)

Copepod
(multicellular)

Volvox
(multicellular)

5 Make a sketch of each of the different organisms that you see. Record any movement or behavior you observe. Include the magnification of the objective lens that you used.

▶ Observe and Analyze   [Write It Up]

1. **CLASSIFY** Use the Identification Key above to identify the organism. If you cannot make an identification, write *unknown*.

▶ Conclude   [Write It Up]

1. **COLLECT DATA** Compare your sketches with those of your classmates. How many different organisms in total did your class find? How many were identified as unicellular? How many were identified as multicellular?

2. **COMMUNICATE** Why is the microscope an important tool for studying cells and entire organisms?

3. **INTERPRET** Using what you learned in this chapter and in this investigation, explain the ways in which you would use the different objectives on a microscope.

4. **APPLY** Many diseases, such as strep throat, are caused by microscopic organisms. Why might a microscope be an important tool for a doctor?

5. **APPLY** How might the way a biologist uses a microscope be different from the way a doctor uses a microscope?

▶ INVESTIGATE Further

Collect a small sample of soil from outside the school or your home. Mix the soil with enough tap water to make it liquid. Then take a sample of the soil mixture and examine it under the microscope. Sketch some of the organisms you see. Are they similar to those in the pond-water sample? Why do you think different types of organisms live in different environments?

Using a Microscope

Table 1. Identifying Microorganisms

Organism 1
  Magnification used:
  Movement/behavior:
  Sketch:

  Name:

Organism 2
  Magnification used:
  Movement/behavior:
  Sketch:

  Name:

Microscopes allow us to see inside the cell.

◀ BEFORE, you learned

- Some organisms are unicellular and some are multicellular
- A microscope is necessary to study most cells
- The cell theory describes the cell as the fundamental unit of life

▶ NOW, you will learn

- About different types of microscopes
- About prokaryotic and eukaryotic cells
- How plant and animal cells are similar and different

VOCABULARY

cell membrane p. 20
cytoplasm p. 20
nucleus p. 20
eukaryotic cell p. 20
prokaryotic cell p. 20
organelle p. 20
cell wall p. 21
chloroplast p. 23
mitochondria p. 23

THINK ABOUT

How small are cells?

Because cells are so small, describing them requires a very small unit of measure: the micrometer (μm). A micrometer is one millionth of a meter. Cells vary in size from about 1 micrometer (some bacteria) to 1000 micrometers (some plant and animal cells). To get a sense of the sizes of cells, consider that it would take about 17,000 tiny bacterial cells lined up to reach across a dime. How many of these cells might fit on your fingertip?

The microscope is an important tool.

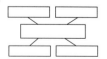

MAIN IDEA WEB
Make a main idea web that explains the importance of the microscope.

The invention of the light microscope led to the discovery of cells and to the development of cell theory. In light microscopes, lenses are used to bend light and make objects appear bigger than they are. Modern light microscopes can magnify objects up to 1000 times.

The light microscope is still used today to study cells. Over many years scientists have found ways to make light microscopes more useful. Cell samples are treated with dyes to make structures in the cells easier to see. Scientists use video cameras and computer processing to observe the movement of cell parts and materials within cells. One important advantage of light microscopes is that scientists can observe living cells with them.

Two other types of microscopes are important in the study of cells. The scanning electron microscope (SEM) and the transmission electron microscope (TEM) can produce images of objects as small as 0.002 micrometers. The light microscope can be used only for objects that are larger than 0.2 micrometers. Therefore, although a light microscope can be used to see many of the parts of a cell, only the SEM and TEM can be used for looking at the details of those parts.

In both the SEM and the TEM, tiny particles called electrons, not light, are used to produce images. The advantage of these microscopes is that they can magnify objects up to a million times. The disadvantage is that they cannot be used to study live specimens.

SIMULATION
CLASSZONE.COM

View cells through different types of microscopes.

CHECK YOUR READING Compare light microscopes with electron microscopes. What are the advantages and disadvantages of each?

To be viewed with an SEM, a cell sample is coated in a heavy metal, such as gold. Then a beam of electrons is run back and forth over the surface of the cell. The electrons bounce off the coating and are read by a detector that produces a three-dimensional image of the surface.

A cell viewed with a TEM, is sliced extremely thin. Electrons pass through a section. Images produced by a TEM appear two-dimensional.

Electron Microscopes

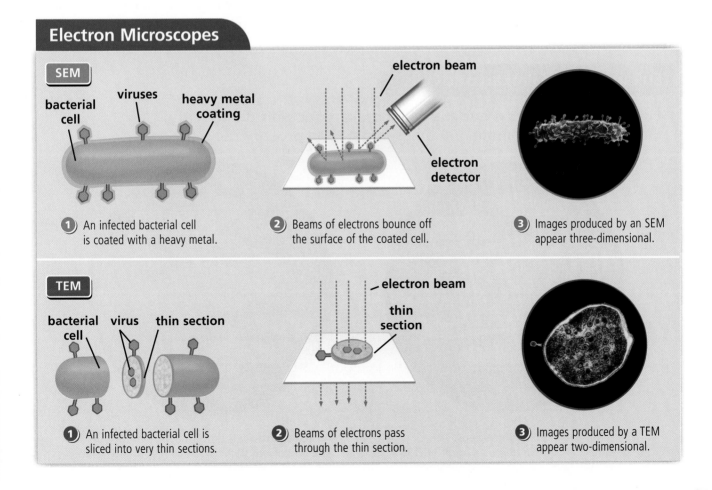

SEM

1. An infected bacterial cell is coated with a heavy metal.
2. Beams of electrons bounce off the surface of the coated cell.
3. Images produced by an SEM appear three-dimensional.

TEM

1. An infected bacterial cell is sliced into very thin sections.
2. Beams of electrons pass through the thin section.
3. Images produced by a TEM appear two-dimensional.

Cells are diverse.

Very early on, the people studying cells knew that cells have a great diversity of sizes and shapes. As microscopes were improved, scientists could see more and more details of cells. What they saw was that the inside of one cell can be very different from that of another cell.

Every cell has a boundary that separates the inside from the outside. That boundary is the **cell membrane,** a protective covering that encloses the entire cell. Any material coming into or out of the cell must pass through the cell membrane. Contained inside the cell membrane is a gelatin-like fluid called **cytoplasm** (SY-tuh-PLAZ-uhm). Most of the work of the cell is carried out in the cytoplasm.

Scientists separate cells into two broad categories based on one key difference: the location of the genetic material cells need to reproduce and function. In a **eukaryotic cell** (yoo-KAR-ee-AHT-ihk) the genetic material is in a structure called the **nucleus** (NOO-klee-uhs), a structure enclosed by its own membrane. Scientists use the word **organelle** (AWR-guh-NEHL) to describe any part of a cell that is enclosed by membrane.

In a **prokaryotic cell** (proh-KAR-ee-AWT-ihk) there is no separate compartment for the genetic material. Instead, it is in the cytoplasm. There are no organelles. Most unicellular organisms are prokaryotic cells. Almost all multicellular organisms are eukaryotic.

VOCABULARY
Add a four square for *cell membrane* to your notebook. Try to include the word *cytoplasm* in your diagram.

Eukaryotic and Prokaryotic Cells

Eukaryotic cells have a nucleus while prokaryotic cells do not. Eukaryotic cells are about 100 times larger than prokaryotic cells.

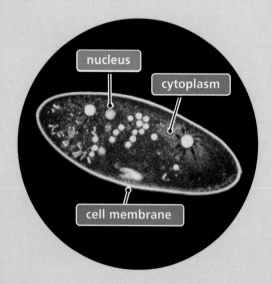

nucleus

cytoplasm

cell membrane

A **eukaryotic cell** has a nucleus. The paramecium shown here is magnified 133×.

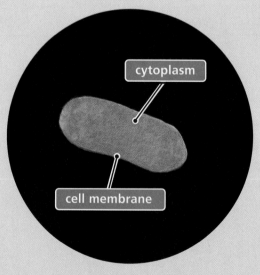

cytoplasm

cell membrane

A **prokaryotic cell** does not have a nucleus. The bacterium shown here is magnified 12,000×.

INVESTIGATE Plant and Animal Cells

How do plant and animal cells compare?

PROCEDURE

1. Choose the objective lens with the lowest magnification. Place the plant-cell slide on the stage and turn on the light source. Handle the slide carefully.

2. Observe the cells at low magnification. Make a drawing of one of the cells.

3. Observe the cells at high magnification. Fill in details. Return to the low-magnification lens before removing the slide.

4. Repeat steps 1–3 with the animal-cell slide.

WHAT DO YOU THINK?

- Compare the drawings you made. How are the plant and animal cells alike, and how are they different?

- Compare the thickness of plant cell's cell membrane and cell wall with the thickness of the animal cell's cell membrane?

CHALLENGE Placing a ruler on top of the slides, view each slide at low power. Estimate and compare the sizes of the two cells.

SKILL FOCUS
Observing

MATERIALS
- prepared slides
- microscope
- *for Challenge:* millimeter ruler

TIME
30 minutes

Plants and animals have eukaryotic cells.

Plant and animal cells, like all eukaryotic cells, are divided into two main compartments. The nucleus, the largest organelle, is the compartment that stores all the instructions a cell needs to function. You will learn more about how cells use this information in Chapter 5.

Surrounding the nucleus is the cytoplasm. The cell membrane is the boundary between the cytoplasm and the outside of the cell. Plant cells also have cell walls. A **cell wall** is a tough outer covering that lies just outside the cell membrane. The cell wall supports and protects the cell. Having a cell wall is one important way in which plant cells differ from animal cells.

RESOURCE CENTER
CLASSZONE.COM

Find out more about cell structures.

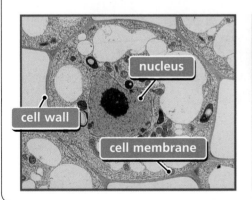

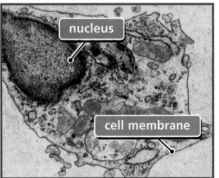

Both a plant cell (shown at left magnified 1750×) and an animal cell (shown at right magnified 12,000×) have a nucleus and a cell membrane. Only plant cells have a cell wall.

Plant Cell

Found in plant cells, not animal cells:

chloroplast

central vacuole

cell wall

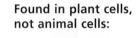

nucleus

endoplasmic reticulum

ribosomes

Golgi apparatus

vesicles

mitochondrion

cell membrane

Animal Cell

Found in animal cells, not plant cells:

lysosome

nucleus

endoplasmic reticulum

ribosomes

Golgi apparatus

vesicles

mitochondrion

cell membrane

Structures That Process Information

The nucleus is often the largest organelle in a cell. It contains all the information a cell needs to function. The information is translated by ribosomes, tiny structures located just outside the nucleus. Ribosomes use the information to gather the materials a cell needs to build important molecules called proteins.

Organelles That Provide Energy

No cell can stay alive without energy. Cells need energy to perform all the activities of life. Plants get their energy directly from the Sun. Within plant cells are **chloroplasts** (KLAWR-uh-PLASTS), organelles in which the energy from sunlight is used to make sugar. Plants use some of the sugar immediately, to keep their cells functioning. The rest of the sugar is stored in the cells.

Animal cells do not contain chloroplasts. As a result, animals are not able to use the energy of the Sun directly. Instead, animals get their energy from food. Much of the food an animal uses for energy comes from the sugar that plant cells have stored. Animals can get this energy by eating plants or by eating animals that have eaten plants.

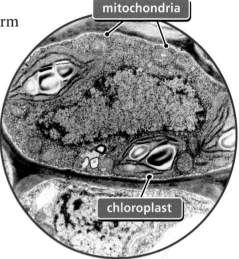

This plant cell is magnified 6000×.

⬛ **CHECK YOUR READING** How can a chloroplast, a structure found in plant cells but not in animal cells, provide energy for both plants and animals?

Both plant cells and animal cells must be able to use energy to do work. The energy is made available by organelles found in all eukaryotic cells. **Mitochondria** (MY-tuh-KAHN-dree-uh) are the organelles that use oxygen to process food in order to manufacture energy in both plant and animal cells.

READING TiP

Mitochondria is plural. The singular form is mitochondrion.

Organelles That Process and Transport

You know that plant and animal cells get their energy from the sugars that the organisms make or consume. Sugars are also an important part of the starting materials that cells use to maintain themselves and grow. The job of making cell parts from the starting materials that enter a cell is divided among a number of structures in the cytoplasm.

Just outside the nucleus, the endoplasmic reticulum begins. In the illustrations on page 22, you can see that the endoplasmic reticulum is a system of twisting and winding membranes. The endoplasmic reticulum processes materials it gets from ribosomes and uses them to manufacture proteins and parts of cell membrane.

The endoplasmic reticulum is also part of the cellular transport system. Portions of endoplasmic reticulum break off to form small packages called vesicles. The vesicles transport processed materials to an organelle called the Golgi apparatus. The folded membranes of the Golgi apparatus make it look something like a stack of pancakes. The Golgi apparatus takes the materials manufactured by the endoplasmic reticulum and finishes processing them.

Organelles for Storage, Recycling, and Waste

Cells store water, sugar, and other materials, which they use to function continuously. Cells must also store waste materials until they can be removed. Inside cells are sacs called vacuoles. Vacuoles are made of membrane and can hold water, waste, and other materials. Vacuoles function with the cell membrane to move materials either into or out of the cell. A plant cell has a large central vacuole in which water and other materials can be stored. Water in the vacuole provides support for smaller plants.

Animal cells do not have central vacuoles. What animal cells do have are structures called lysosomes. Lysosomes are vacuoles that contain chemicals that break down materials taken into the cell, as well as old cell parts. Remember that animals, unlike plants, take in food. Nutrients brought into the cell need to be broken down, as well as wastes contained.

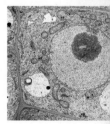
central vacuole

 Compare and contrast lysosomes and central vacuoles.

1.2 Review

KEY CONCEPTS

1. What advantages and disadvantages does a light microscope have in comparison with an electron microscope?

2. What is the difference between a eukaryotic cell and a prokaryotic cell?

3. List three structures found in plant cells that are not in animal cells.

CRITICAL THINKING

5. **Synthesize** What organelles can be said to act like an assembly line within a cell? Explain.

4. **Compare and Contrast** Make a Venn diagram comparing and contrasting plant and animal cells.

CHALLENGE

6. **Synthesize** Identify the type of microscope used to capture the image at the right, and indicate whether the cell is a plant cell or an animal cell. How do you know?

(magnified 27,900

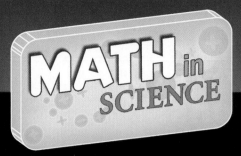

MATH TUTORIAL
CLASSZONE.COM

Click on Math Tutorial
for more help with
scientific notation.

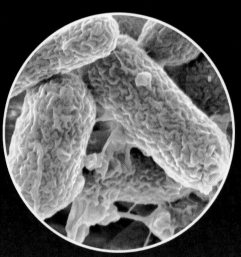

How many bacteria can fit on
the head of a pin? The bacteria
are magnified 50,000× in this
photograph. The head of the
pin below is
magnified 7×.

SKILL: USING SCIENTIFIC NOTATION

Comparing Sizes

Measuring the sizes of very small things like atoms or very large things like planets requires numbers with many places. For example, the diameter of the nucleus of a cell is around 1/100,000 of a meter, while the diameter of Earth is 12,756,000 meters. How can you compare these sizes?

Example

(1) Express a large number as a number between 1 and 10 multiplied by a power of 10.

$$12,756,000 = 1.2756 \times 10^7$$

The exponent is the number of places following the first place.

(2) Express any number smaller than 1 as a negative power of 10.

$$\frac{1}{1000,000} = 0.00001 = 1 \times 10^{-5}$$

The exponent is the number of places following the decimal point.

(3) Compare -5 and 7 to see that 7 is 12 more than -5.

ANSWER Earth's diameter is roughly 10^{12} times bigger than the diameter of a cell's nucleus.

Answer the following questions.

1. An oxygen atom measures 14/100,000,000,000 of a meter across. Write the width of the oxygen atom in standard form as a decimal number.

2. Write the width of the oxygen atom in scientific notation.

3. A chloroplast measures 5 millionths of a meter across. Write its width in standard form and in scientific notation.

4. A redwood tree stands 100 meters tall. There are 1000 millimeters in a meter. Express the height of the redwood tree in millimeters. Write the number in scientific notation.

5. A typical plant cell measures 1 millionth of a meter in width. Express the width in standard form and in scientific notation.

CHALLENGE The yolk of an ostrich egg is about 8 centimeters in diameter. The ostrich itself is about 2.4 meters tall. Write each of these lengths in the same unit, and express them in scientific notation. Then tell how many times taller the ostrich is than the yolk.

KEY CONCEPT

Different cells perform various functions.

◀ BEFORE, you learned	▶ NOW, you will learn
• Modern microscopes reveal details of cell structures	• How organisms are classified into three domains
• Some cells are prokaryotic and some are eukaryotic	• About specialization in multi-cellular organisms
• Plant and animal cells have similarities and differences	• How cells, tissues, and organs are organized

VOCABULARY

specialization p. 28
tissue p. 29
organ p. 30

EXPLORE Specialization

How do roots differ from leaves?

PROCEDURE

1. Soak the grass plant in a cup of water to clean away any dirt.

2. Compare the color of the roots with the color of the blades or leaves. Record your observations.

3. Wash your hands when you have finished.

WHAT DO YOU THINK?

• How does the color of the grass roots compare with that of the grass blades?

• Chloroplasts contain a chemical that gives leaves their green color. What does this suggest to you about the functions of the grass blades and roots?

MATERIALS
• grass plants
• cup
• water

Organisms can be classified by their cell type.

MAIN IDEA WEB
Make a web of the important terms and details about the main idea: *Organisms can be classified by their cell type.*

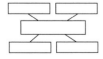

Look around you at this moment. The living organisms you see may number 10, 20, 100, or 1000, depending on where you are. What you are not seeing, but what is also there, is a huge number of unicellular organisms. For example, there are at least 2–3 million bacteria living on each square centimeter of your skin.

Most of the organisms alive on Earth today are made of a single cell. One of the most interesting scientific discoveries made recently had to do with a group of unicellular organisms. These organisms were found living where no one expected to find any life at all.

Archaea and Bacteria

In the early 1980s, scientists discovered unicellular organisms living in rather extreme environments. Some were living deep in the ocean, at thermal vents where there is extreme heat and no oxygen. Others were found in the salty waters of the Great Salt Lake and in the hot sulfur springs of Yellowstone Park.

At first, these organisms were referred to as archaebacteria. The organisms were similar in appearance to bacteria. The prefix *archae* comes from a Greek word that means "ancient." Many of these organisms live in environments that are like the environments of ancient Earth.

▼ REMINDER

The genetic material in a prokaryotic cell is not enclosed in a nucleus. In eukaryotic cells genetic material is stored in a nucleus.

thermal vent

archaea

Archaea are prokaryotic organisms that can live in extreme environments like these thermal vents. In a thermal vent, temperatures can reach 600 degrees Celsius.

It took a while for scientists to realize that these organisms that looked like bacteria were genetically very different from bacteria. Scientists decided to establish a separate category for them, a domain called Archaea (AHR-kee-uh). A domain is a broad category of living things that is based on characteristics of their cells. Scientists have identified three domains. Bacteria are classified in the domain Bacteria. A third domain includes organisms with eukaryotic cells.

Organisms that belong to the domains Bacteria and Archaea are similar in some important ways. They are prokaryotes, which are unicelluar organisms made of prokarytic cells. Their cytoplasm contains ribosomes but no organelles, so the structure of a prokaryote is simple. Another feature of a prokaryote is a tough cell wall that protects the organism.

RESOURCE CENTER
CLASSZONE.COM

Learn more about unicellular organisms.

CHECK YOUR READING Why did scientists decide to establish separate domains for archaea and bacteria?

Eukarya

The third domain is the domain Eukarya. Organisms in this domain have cells with a nucleus. This domain includes almost all the multi-cellular organisms on Earth: plants, animals, and fungi. It also includes many unicellular organisms called protists. The cells of uni-cellular eukaryotes are more complex in structure and larger than the cells of prokaryotes.

 CHECK YOUR READING How are eukaryotes different from prokaryotes?

The paramecium is one of the most complex of all unicellular eukaryotes. Its body is lined with hairlike strands, called cilia (SIHL-ee-uh), that allow it to move. It has dartlike structures that carry a substance used in healing and, perhaps, defense. Along the outside of the cell is a long oral groove lined with cilia that leads to a mouth pore. In addition to a nucleus, the cell of a paramecium has organelles that enable it to digest food and remove water and wastes. The paramecium has all it needs to live as a single cell. By compari-son, in most multicellular eukaryotes, no individual cell can survive on its own.

paramecium 1000×

mouth pore

oral groove

cilia

Cells in multicellular organisms specialize.

VOCABULARY
Remember to add a four square for *specialization* to your notebook.

Most multicellular organisms consist of many different types of cells that do different jobs. For example, most animals have blood cells, nerve cells, and muscle cells. The cells are specialized. **Specialization** of cells means that specific cells perform specific functions. This spe-cialization is why a single cell from a multicellular organism cannot survive on its own. A blood cell can help you fight infection or deliver oxygen to your muscles, but it cannot cause your body to move as a muscle cell can. Plants have cells that function in photosynthesis, and other cells that draw water from the soil, and still others that function mainly to support the plant's weight.

 CHECK YOUR READING What does it mean for a cell to be specialized?

A fully grown salamander has many specialized cells.

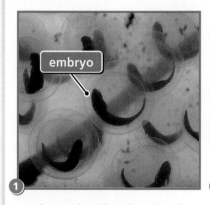

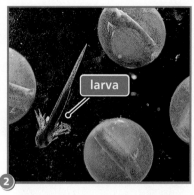

① A salamander, like all multicellular organisms, begins life as an egg. After fertilization, the egg develops into an embryo.

② As the cells divide, they begin to specialize. The amount of specialization depends on the complexity of the organism.

③ A salamander's body has many specialized cells. These include skin cells, blood cells, bone cells, muscle cells, and nerve cells.

A multicellular organism is a community of cells.

Cells in a multicellular organism are specialized. The ways in which the cells work together and interact depend on the organism. You can think of the cells of an organism as members of a community. The size and complexity of the community differ from organism to organism.

A sponge is an animal that is fairly simple in its organization. It spends its life attached to the ocean floor, filtering food and other nutrients from the water. Like all animals, the sponge is organized at a cellular level. Different types of cells in its body perform different functions. For example, certain cells take in food, and other cells digest it. However, cells in a sponge are not very highly specialized. A piece broken from a living sponge will actually regenerate itself as new cells replace the lost ones.

In more complex organisms, such as plants and animals, cells are not only specialized but grouped together in tissues. A **tissue** is a group of similar cells that are organized to do a specific job. If you look at your hand, you will see the top layer of tissue in your skin. Humans have two layers of skin tissue, layered one on top of the other. Together these skin tissues provide protection and support.

 CHECK YOUR READING In what way is a tissue an organization of cells?

Levels of Organization

Levels of organization in multicellular organisms include cells, tissues, organs, organ systems, and the organism itself.

Plant cell

Tissue

Organ: leaf

Organ system: leaves, stems, roots

Organism: lilac tree

Animal cell

Tissue

Organ: eye

Organ system: eyes, brain, nerves

Organism: tarsier

Different tissues working together to perform a particular function represent another level of organization, the **organ.** The eye is an organ that functions with the tarsier's brain to allow sight. A leaf is an organ that provides a plant with energy and materials. It has tissue that brings in water and nutrients, tissue that uses the Sun's energy to make sugar, and tissue that moves sugar to other parts of the plant.

CHECK YOUR READING   What is the relationship between tissues and organs?

Different organs and tissues working together form an organ system. An organism may have only a few organ systems. The organ systems of plants include roots, stems, and leaves. Other organisms have many organ systems. Humans have 11 major organ systems, made up of about 40 organs and over 200 types of tissue. The human nervous system, for example, includes the brain, the spinal cord, nerves, and sensory organs, such as the ears and eyes.

An organism itself represents the highest level of organization. It is at this level that we see all the characteristics we associate with life. If an organism is a complex organism—a human—for example, it will consist of trillions of cells grouped into tissues, organs, and organ systems. However, a simple organism, like a sponge, meets its needs with a body made up of only a few types of specialized cells.

 CHECK YOUR READING What level of organization is an organism? What do we see at this level of organization?

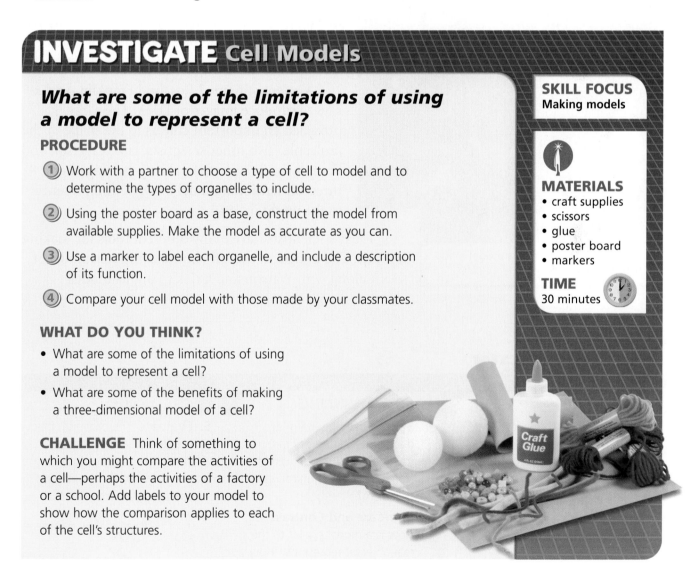

INVESTIGATE Cell Models

What are some of the limitations of using a model to represent a cell?

PROCEDURE

1. Work with a partner to choose a type of cell to model and to determine the types of organelles to include.

2. Using the poster board as a base, construct the model from available supplies. Make the model as accurate as you can.

3. Use a marker to label each organelle, and include a description of its function.

4. Compare your cell model with those made by your classmates.

WHAT DO YOU THINK?

• What are some of the limitations of using a model to represent a cell?

• What are some of the benefits of making a three-dimensional model of a cell?

CHALLENGE Think of something to which you might compare the activities of a cell—perhaps the activities of a factory or a school. Add labels to your model to show how the comparison applies to each of the cell's structures.

SKILL FOCUS
Making models

MATERIALS
• craft supplies
• scissors
• glue
• poster board
• markers

TIME
30 minutes

Scientists use models to study cells.

Watson and Crick used a model made from wire and tin.

Any drawing or photograph on a flat page is two-dimensional. In addition, diagrams of cells are often simplified to make them easier to understand. If you look at plant or animal cells under a microscope, you will notice some differences between real cells and the diagrams on page 22. In order to study cell structures and their functions, scientists use many types of models, including three-dimensional models. One of the most important discoveries in science involved the use of models.

DNA is the genetic material common to all cells. (You will read more about the structure and function of DNA later in this unit.) In the early 1950s, scientists had a good idea what DNA was made up of. The problem was that they could not figure out how all the pieces of the molecule fit together.

A scientist named Rosalind Franklin used x-rays to produce images of DNA. The x-ray provided an important clue as to the shape of the molecule. Two other scientists, James Watson and Francis Crick, were then able to put together a three-dimensional model of DNA and present it to the world in 1953.

Today's scientists have many different tools for making models. The images at the left show a computer model of DNA along with Watson and Crick's famous model.

1.3 Review

KEY CONCEPTS

1. What are the three domains, and what type of cells do the organisms in each domain have?

2. Define specialization in your own words.

3. Describe the levels of organization in a tree.

CRITICAL THINKING

4. **Synthesize** In what way does a specialized cell in a multicellular organism differ from the cell of a unicellular organism?

5. **Compare and Contrast** How is a model similar to the real object it represents? How is it different?

◯ CHALLENGE

6. **Evaluate** The organism below is called *Chlamydomonas*. What domain does it belong to, and what do the internal structures tell you about it?

flagella (allow movement)

cell wall — — cell membrane

chloroplast — — nucleus

— mitochondrion

Cells and Spacesuits

What do a space suit and a unicellular organism have in common? Both have to support life. And both can support life in difficult environments. What are some of the similarities—and differences—between the cell body of a unicellular organism and a space suit that supports an astronaut in outer space?

▶ Some Features of Spacesuits

FEATURE	FUNCTION
Strong outer material...	...protects the astronaut from space particles.
A special jet-propelled backpack...	...helps the astronaut move in the weightlessness of space.
Tanks of compressed air...	...provide oxygen for the astronaut to breathe.

▶ Some Features of Cells

FEATURE	FUNCTION
Tail-like flagella on the outside of some cells...	...help cells move.
An outer membrane...	...keeps harmful particles out.
Tiny openings in a cell's membrane...	...let oxygen move into the cell.

▶ Make Comparisons

On Your Own Match each cell feature with a similar spacesuit feature. What characteristics do the cell and spacesuit have in common? What is one key difference?

As a Group Use your comparisons to make a Venn diagram.

CHALLENGE An analogy uses a familiar thing to help explain or describe something new. Come up with your own analogies to describe the cell or some of its organelles.

flagella

This cell has flagella, which help it move.

Chapter Review

the BIG idea

All living things are made up of cells.

CONTENT REVIEW
CLASSZONE.COM

◄ **KEY CONCEPTS SUMMARY**

1.1 The cell is the basic unit of living things.

All living things are made up of one or more cells. **Organisms** share the following characteristics:

- organization
- ability to grow and develop
- ability to respond
- ability to reproduce

Multicellular organisms include this frog and these water-lily plants.

Many unicellular organisms live in pond water.

VOCABULARY
organism p. 9
unicellular p. 11
multicellular p. 11
microscope p. 12
bacteria p. 14

1.2 Microscopes allow us to see inside the cell.

A **prokaryotic cell** is relatively simple in structure, with no nucleus or other organelles. A **eukaryotic cell** is more complex, with many different organelles inside it.

bacterium

A bacterium consists of a single prokaryotic cell.

plant cell   animal cell

Plants and animals are made up of many eukaryotic cells.

VOCABULARY
cell membrane p. 20
cytoplasm p. 20
nucleus p. 20
eukaryotic cell p. 20
prokaryotic cell p. 20
organelle p. 20
cell wall p. 21
chloroplast p. 23
mitochondria p. 23

1.3 Different cells perform various functions.

- The single cell of a unicellular organism does all that
  is necessary for the organism to survive.
- A multicellular organism is a community of **specialized** cells.
- Scientific models make it easier to understand cells.

The tarsier has many levels of organization in its body.

tarsier

VOCABULARY
specialization p. 28
tissue p. 29
organ p. 30

Reviewing Vocabulary

1–5. *Use a vocabulary term to identify each numbered part of this plant cell.*

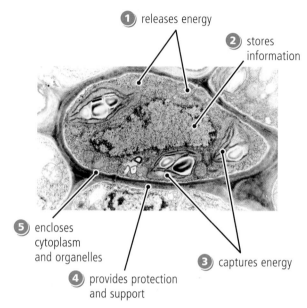

1 releases energy

2 stores information

5 encloses cytoplasm and organelles

4 provides protection and support

3 captures energy

In one or two sentences, describe how the terms in each of the following pairs are related. Underline each term in your answer.

6. unicellular, multicellular

7. cell, organelle

8. prokaryotic cell, eukaryotic cell

9. tissue, organ

Reviewing Key Concepts

Multiple Choice *Choose the letter of the best answer.*

10. Which statement about cells is part of the cell theory?
   a. Cells are found in most living things.
   b. Cells with cell walls do not have cell membranes.
   c. All cells capture energy from sunlight.
   d. Cells come only from other living cells.

11. What structure does a plant cell have that is not found in an animal cell and that allows a plant cell to capture energy from the Sun?
   a. cell wall
   b. chloroplast
   c. mitochondrion
   d. central vacuole

12. Which technology was important to the development of the cell theory?
   a. computer
   b. scientific model
   c. microscope
   d. refrigeration

13. Organisms can be divided into domains on the basis of the characteristics of their cells. What are these domains?
   a. Archaea, Bacteria, and Eukarya
   b. prokaryotes and eukaryotes
   c. plants, animals, and bacteria
   d. unicellular and multicellular

14. Cells in a complex multicellular organism have different levels of organization. What is the order of these levels?
   a. cell membrane, cytoplasm, nucleus
   b. tissues, organs, organ systems
   c. tissues, organs, specialized cells
   d. cell membrane, organelles, nucleus

15. What is the function of the genetic material in a cell?
   a. provides transport of materials from the nucleus to the cell membrane
   b. breaks down materials brought into the cell
   c. provides information a cell needs to function and grow
   d. controls what comes into a cell and what goes out

Short Answer *Write a short answer to each question.*

16. What are four characteristics common to all living things?

17. What are three needs common to all living things?

Thinking Critically

Questions 18–20 refer to polar bears and their cells as examples of animals and animal cells.

18. PREDICT Some polar bears go through long periods of sleep during the cold winter months. In what two ways might their fat cells help the bears survive during these periods?

19. PROVIDE EXAMPLES Animals do not get energy directly from the Sun as plants do. Give one or two examples of body systems in a polar bear that help it obtain and process food.

20. COMPARE AND CONTRAST Consider the fat cells in a polar bear and compare them with the single body cell of a bacterium. How are the cells alike, and how are they different?

21. CONNECT The cell theory applies to all organisms, including you. State the three parts of the cell theory and describe briefly how they relate to you.

22. ANALYZE Louis Pasteur designed the swan-necked flask to use in his experiments. In one experiment, he used two flasks of nutrient broth. One flask he heated; the other he left untouched. Bacteria grew in the untouched flask. Nothing grew in the flask that had been heated, or sterilized. How did this experiment help disprove the theory of spontaneous generation?

Both ends of flasks are open.

23. PREDICT What would happen if the neck of the sterilized swan-necked flask were broken?

24. IDENTIFY CAUSE Why does pasteurized milk eventually spoil?

25. COMPARE AND CONTRAST A plant cell has a number of structures and organelles that an animal cell does not. Copy the table below and place a check in the appropriate box of each row. The first two are done for you.

	Animal Cell	Plant Cell
Cell wall		✓
Cell membrane	✓	✓
Cytoplasm		
Nucleus		
Central vacuole		
Chloroplast		
Mitochondrion		

the BIG idea

26. CLASSIFY Look again at the photograph on pages 6–7. Can you identify any of the structures shown? Can you identify the type of microscope used to make the photograph? How do you know?

27. CONNECT What are three ways that an understanding of cells has changed the way people live? **Hint:** Think about Pasteur and his work.

UNIT PROJECTS

If you are doing a unit project, make a folder for your project. Include in your folder a list of the resources you will need, the date on which the project is due, and a schedule to track your progress. Begin gathering data.

Standardized Test Practice

For practice on your
state test, go to . . .
TEST PRACTICE
CLASSZONE.COM

The Euglena Puzzle

Read the following description of euglenas and how scientists classify them. Then answer the questions below.

Plants and animals are typically multicellular organisms. For a long time, scientists tried to classify any unicellular organism that had a nucleus as either a single-celled plant or a single-celled animal. One group of unicellular organisms, *Euglenas,* was particularly difficult to classify. These tiny organisms can be found living in most ponds. What is puzzling about *Euglenas* is that they have characteristics of both plants and animals.

Some scientists argued that *Euglenas* are more like plants because many of them have chloroplasts. Chloroplasts are cellular structures that enable both plants and *Euglenas* to capture energy from the Sun. Other scientists argued that *Euglenas* are more like animals because they can take in food particles from the water. *Euglenas* also have flagella, tail-like structures that enable them to swim. The *Euglena* even has an eyespot for sensing light.

1. What cellular structures enable plants and *Euglenas* to capture energy from the Sun?
  a. flagella   **c.** nuclei
  b. chloroplasts   **d.** eyespots

2. What cellular structures are common to plants, animals, and *Euglenas*?
  a. flagella   **c.** nuclei
  b. chloroplasts   **d.** eyespots

3. In what way are *Euglenas* different from both plants and animals?
  a. They have no nuclei.   **c.** They live in ponds.
  b. They are unicellular.   **d.** They get energy from food.

4. What does an eyespot do?
  a. senses light   **c.** provides energy
  b. captures food   **d.** senses movement

5. Having flagella makes *Euglenas* similar to animals because it allows *Euglenas* to do what?
  a. eat food   **c.** sense light
  b. get energy   **d.** move about

Extended Response

Answer the following questions in detail. Include some of the terms in the word box. In your answers, underline each term you use.

| organelle | unicellular | microscope |
| chloroplast | response | organism |

6. A jar of water containing *Euglenas* is placed in a sunny window. After a while, a noticeable cloud forms in the water, near where the light shines into the water. Over the course of the day, the position of the Sun changes. As it does, the cloud keeps moving toward the light. On the basis of your reading, what do you think is happening and why?

7. Suppose there is a small pond near your school. The pond is surrounded by many tall trees that tend to block sunlight around the edges of the pond. In this situation, explain why it is an advantage for *Euglenas* to have the characteristics they do. Which of these characteristics do you associate with plants? with animals?

How Cells Function

the **BIG** idea

All cells need energy and materials for life processes.

How do plants like these sunflowers change energy from the Sun?

Key Concepts

SECTION

 2.1 Chemical reactions take place inside cells.
Learn why water and four types of large molecules are important for cell functions.

SECTION

 2.2 Cells capture and release energy.
Learn about the process of photosynthesis and the two ways cells release energy.

SECTION

 2.3 Materials move across the cell's membranes.
Learn about the different ways materials move through cells.

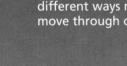 **Internet Preview**

CLASSZONE.COM

Chapter 2 online resources: Content Review, two Visualizations, two Resource Centers, Math Tutorial, and Test Practice.

EXPLORE (the BIG idea)

Leaves Underwater

Put a dish, two plant leaves, and two baby food jars in a sink full of water. Fill one jar with water and both leaves, then turn the jar upside down on the dish. Fill the other jar with just water and do the same. Remove your set-up from the sink and place it in sunlight for two hours.

Observe and Think
What happened in the jars? Why do you think these things happened?

Just a Spoonful of Sugar

Pour a little warm water into each of two cups. Stir a spoonful of sugar into one of the cups. Drop several raisins into each cup and wait for four hours. After four hours, compare the raisins in each cup.

Observe and Think How are the raisins different? How would you explain your observation?

Internet Activity: Photosynthesis

Go to **ClassZone.com** to examine how plants use sunlight to make sugar molecules.

Observe and Think
What are the starting materials of photo-synthesis? What are the products?

NSTA
scilinks.org

SCiLINKS

Photosynthesis **Code: MDL032**

Getting Ready to Learn

◀ CONCEPT REVIEW

- Cells are the basic units of living things.
- Some cells have organelles that perform special functions for the cell.
- Animal cells and plant cells have similar structures, but only plant cells have cell walls and chloroplasts.

◀ VOCABULARY REVIEW

cell membrane, p. 20

organelle, p. 21

chloroplast, p. 23

mitochondria, p. 23

ⓘ CONTENT REVIEW
CLASSZONE.COM

Review concepts and vocabulary.

▶ TAKING NOTES

OUTLINE

As you read, copy the headings on your paper in the form of an outline. Then add notes in your own words that summarize what you read.

VOCABULARY STRATEGY

Draw a **word triangle** diagram for each new vocabulary term. On the bottom line, write and define the term. Above that, write a sentence that uses the term correctly. At the top, draw a small picture to show what the term looks like.

See the Note-Taking Handbook on pages R45–R51.

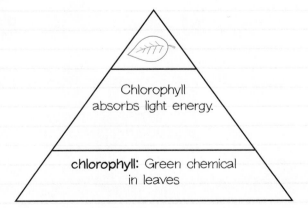

SCIENCE NOTEBOOK

OUTLINE

I. ALL CELLS ARE MADE OF THE SAME ELEMENTS.

  A. ALL MATTER MADE OF ELEMENTS.

      1. 6 make up most of human body

      2. elements interact to produce new materials
         a. smallest unit of element is atom

Chlorophyll absorbs light energy.

chlorophyll: Green chemical in leaves

Chemical reactions take place inside cells.

BEFORE, you learned

- All living things are made of cells
- Cells need energy to sustain life
- Plant and animal cells have similarities and differences

NOW, you will learn

- About the types of elements found in all cells
- About the functions of large molecules in the cell
- Why water is important to the activities of the cell

VOCABULARY

chemical reaction p. 42
carbohydrate p. 42
lipid p. 43
protein p. 43
nucleic acid p. 43

EXPLORE Food Molecules

How are different types of molecules important in your everyday life?

PROCEDURE

① Examine the foods shown in the photograph. Protein, carbohydrates, and lipids (fats) are important substances in the food you eat. Locate at least one source of protein, carbohydrates, and lipids in the food.

② Use your textbook and additional resource materials to find out a little more about these molecules in our food supply.

WHAT DO YOU THINK?
What foods do you eat that supply protein, carbohydrates, and lipids?

MATERIALS
- notebook
- reference materials

OUTLINE
Continue the outline begun on page 40.

I. Main idea
  A. Supporting idea
    1. Detail
    2. Detail
  B. Supporting idea

All cells are made of the same elements.

The microscope allowed people to observe the tiny cells that make up all living things. Even smaller, too small for a light microscope to show, is the matter that makes up the cell itself.

All matter in the universe—living and nonliving—can be broken down into basic substances called elements. About a hundred different elements are found on Earth. Each element has its own set of properties and characteristics. For example, the characteristics of oxygen include that it is colorless, odorless, and on Earth, it exists in the form of a gas.

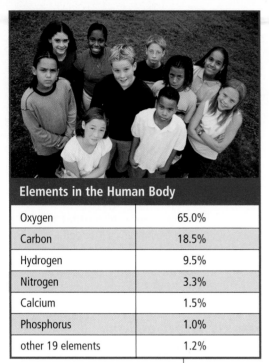

Elements in the Human Body

Oxygen	65.0%
Carbon	18.5%
Hydrogen	9.5%
Nitrogen	3.3%
Calcium	1.5%
Phosphorus	1.0%
other 19 elements	1.2%

Source: CRC Handbook of Chemistry and Physics

Of all the elements found on Earth, about 25 are essential for life. As you can see from the table, just 6 elements account for about 99 percent of the mass of the human body. But very little of this matter exists as pure elements. Instead, most is in the form of compounds, which are substances made up of two or more different elements. For example, water is a compound made of hydrogen and oxygen.

The smallest unit of any element is called an atom. In a compound, atoms of two or more elements are joined together by chemical bonds. Most compounds in cells are made up of atoms bonded together in molecules. For example, a molecule of water is made of one atom of oxygen bonded to two atoms of hydrogen.

Most activities that take place within cells involve atoms and molecules interacting. In this process, called a **chemical reaction,** bonds between atoms are broken and new bonds form to make different molecules. Energy is needed to form bonds between atoms, and energy is released when bonds break. Thus the energy that cells use for life activities is chemical energy.

Large molecules support cell function.

RESOURCE CENTER
CLASSZONE.COM

Explore molecules in living things.

In living things, there are four main types of large molecules: (1) carbohydrates, (2) lipids, (3) proteins, and (4) nucleic acids. Thousands of these molecules work together in a cell. The four types of molecules in all living things share one important characteristic. They all contain carbon atoms. These large molecules are made up of smaller parts called subunits.

Carbohydrates

sugars

Carbohydrates are used for structure and energy storage. Carbohydrates, such as cellulose, are made of **sugars.**

Carbohydrates (KAHR-boh-HY-DRAYTS) provide the cell with energy. Simple carbohydrates are sugars made from atoms of carbon, oxygen, and hydrogen. Inside cells, the bonds in sugar molecules are broken. Breaking those bonds releases energy. Simple sugar molecules can also be linked into long chains to form more complex carbohydrates, such as starch, cellulose, and glycogen.

Starch and cellulose are complex carbohydrates made by plant cells. When a plant cell makes more sugar than it can use, extra sugar molecules are stored in long chains called starch. Plants also make cellulose, which is the material that makes up the cell wall. Animals get their energy by eating plants or other animals that eat plants.

Lipids

Lipids are the fats, oils, and waxes found in living things. Like carbohydrates, simple lipids are made of atoms of carbon, oxygen, and hydrogen and can be used by cells for energy and for structural support. However, the atoms in all lipids are arranged differently from the atoms in carbohydrates. Many common lipids consist of a molecule called glycerol bonded to long chains of carbon and hydrogen atoms called fatty acids. This structure gives lipids unique properties. One extremely important property of lipids is that they cannot mix with water.

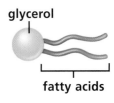

glycerol

fatty acids

Lipids make up the membranes surrounding the cell and organelles. Lipids are made of **fatty acids** and **glycerol**.

CHECK YOUR READING How do cells use carbohydrates?

Proteins

Proteins are made of smaller molecules called amino acids. Amino acids contain the elements carbon, oxygen, hydrogen, nitrogen, and sometimes phosphorus and sulfur. In proteins, amino acids are linked together into long chains that fold into three-dimensional shapes. The structure and function of a protein is determined by the type, number, and order of the amino acids in it.

Your body gets amino acids from protein in food, such as meat, eggs, cheese, and some beans. After taking in amino acids, your cells use them to build proteins needed for proper cell functioning. Some amino acids can be made by the body, but others must be taken in from an outside food source.

There are many types of proteins. Enzymes are proteins that control chemical reactions in the cells. Other proteins support the growth and repair of living matter. The action of proteins in your muscles allows you to move. Some of the proteins in your blood fight infections. Another protein in your blood delivers oxygen to all the cells in your body. Proteins are also important parts of cell membranes. Some proteins in the cell membrane transport materials into and out of the cell.

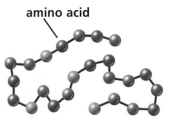

amino acid

Proteins are made up of **amino acids**. Proteins carry out most of the chemical activity in cells.

Nucleic Acids

Nucleic acids (noo-KLEE-ihk) are the molecules that hold the instructions for the maintenance, growth, and reproduction of a cell. There are two types of nucleic acids: DNA and RNA. Both DNA and RNA are made from carbon, oxygen, hydrogen, nitrogen, and phosphorus. The subunits of nucleic acids are called nucleotides.

DNA provides the information used by the cell for making all of the protein the cell needs. Within the DNA, this information is code formed by the specific order of different nucleotides. The pattern

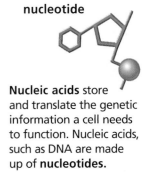

nucleotide

Nucleic acids store and translate the genetic information a cell needs to function. Nucleic acids, such as DNA are made up of **nucleotides**.

of nucleotides in the DNA is copied as RNA, which delivers the information into the cytoplasm. Other RNA molecules in the cytoplasm control chemical reactions and form structures.

 What is the function of DNA and RNA?

About two thirds of every cell is water.

hydrogen

oxygen

Each **water** molecule is made of two **hydrogen** atoms bonded to one **oxygen** atom.

All of the chemical reactions inside the cell take place in water. Water is also in the environment outside the cell. For example, water inside cells makes up about 46 percent of your body's mass, and water outside the cells in body fluids accounts for another 23 percent.

A water molecule consists of two atoms of hydrogen bonded to one atom of oxygen. Because of its structure, a water molecule has a slight positive charge near the hydrogen atoms and a slight negative charge near the oxygen atom. Molecules that have slightly charged ends are said to be polar. Like a magnet, the ends of a polar molecule attract opposite charges and repel charges that are the same. Because water is a polar molecule, many substances dissolve in water. However, not all materials dissolve in water. If you have ever shaken a bottle of salad dressing, you've probably observed that oil and water don't mix.

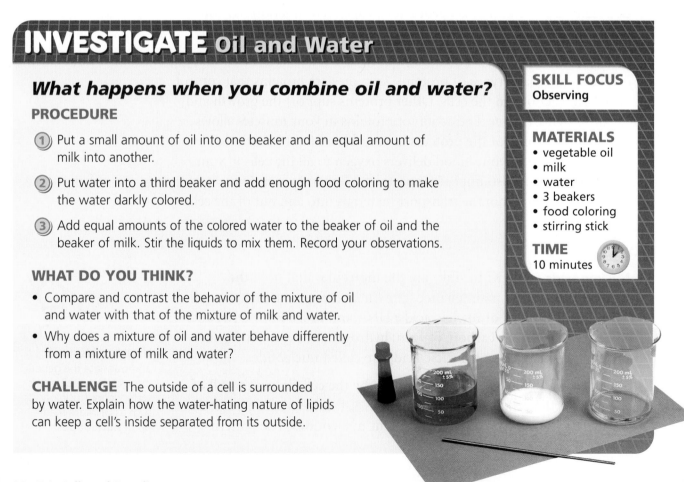

INVESTIGATE Oil and Water

What happens when you combine oil and water?

PROCEDURE

(1) Put a small amount of oil into one beaker and an equal amount of milk into another.

(2) Put water into a third beaker and add enough food coloring to make the water darkly colored.

(3) Add equal amounts of the colored water to the beaker of oil and the beaker of milk. Stir the liquids to mix them. Record your observations.

WHAT DO YOU THINK?

• Compare and contrast the behavior of the mixture of oil and water with that of the mixture of milk and water.

• Why does a mixture of oil and water behave differently from a mixture of milk and water?

CHALLENGE The outside of a cell is surrounded by water. Explain how the water-hating nature of lipids can keep a cell's inside separated from its outside.

SKILL FOCUS
Observing

MATERIALS
• vegetable oil
• milk
• water
• 3 beakers
• food coloring
• stirring stick

TIME
10 minutes

Cell Membrane

The cell membrane is made of a double layer of lipids.

Lipids have a water-loving head and a water-hating tail.

head

tail

cell membrane

inside of cell

outside of cell

Most lipids do not dissolve in water. A special type of lipid is the major molecule that makes up cell membranes. These special lipid molecules have two parts: a water-loving head and two water-hating tails. In other words, the head of the lipid molecule is polar, while the tails are nonpolar.

Why is it important that cell membranes contain lipids? Remember that cell membranes function as boundaries. That is, they separate the inside of a cell from the outside. Most of the material inside and outside the cell is water. As you can see in the diagram above, the water-hating tails in the lipids repels the water while the head clings to water.

READING TiP

As you read about the properties of cell, notice the arrangements of lipids in the diagram of the cell.

2.1 Review

KEY CONCEPTS

1. Explain how just a few elements can make up all living things.

2. What functions do proteins, carbohydrates, lipids, and nucleic acids perform?

3. What does it mean to describe water molecules as being polar?

CRITICAL THINKING

4. **Compare and Contrast** How are carbohydrates and lipids similar? How are they different?

5. **Draw Conclusions** What unusual property of carbon makes it so important to living things?

● CHALLENGE

6. **Model** Some people have compared the nucleic acids DNA and RNA to a blueprint for life. How are DNA and RNA like blueprints? How are they different?

Natural Dyes and Cells

Where does the blue in your blue jeans come from? How about the red, yellow, green, or pink in your favorite wool or cotton sweater? Most fabrics are colored with dyes made up in labs, but some designers prefer to use natural dyes and natural cloth. All textile designers must understand the science of dyes and fibers to produce the colors they want.

Fibers

Natural fibers come either from plants or animals. Wool is an animal fiber. Silk, too, is made up of animal cells. Cotton, linen, and rayon are fibers made from plants. Plant fibers have thick cell walls, made mostly of cellulose. Animal fibers, on the other hand, contain mainly proteins.

silk

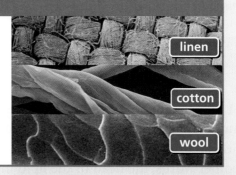

linen

cotton

wool

Dyes

Most natural dyes come from plants, but sometimes insects are used too. The indigo plant is used for most blue, including the original blue jeans. Insects are most often used to make reds. All dyes are made of molecules—carbon, oxygen, hydrogen, and other atoms. The molecules of the dye bind to the molecules of the fibers, adding the dye's color to the fiber.

Color Fixers

A mordant is a chemical compound that combines with dye as a color fixer, or color keeper. The mordant must strengthen the bonds between natural dye molecules and fibers. A stronger bond means the color is less likely to fade or wash out of the fibers. Most mordants are liquid solutions containing metals, such as chromium.

EXPLORE

1. **EXPERIMENT** Design an experiment using onion skins, beets, or blackberries to color white wool and white cotton. The procedure should include chopping the plant and heating it with water to make the dye. Be sure that your experiment procedure includes only one variable. Your experiment should start with a question, such as How do the dyes differ? Or Which dye works best?

2. **CHALLENGE** Using different mordants with the same dye can give different colors. For example, dandelion leaf dye gives yellow-green, gray-green, tan, or gold with different mordants. Explain why this happens.

2.2 Cells capture and release energy.

◀ BEFORE, you learned

- The cell is the basic unit of all living things
- Plant cells and animal cells have similarities and differences
- Plants and animals need energy and materials

▶ NOW, you will learn

- Why cells need energy
- How energy is captured and stored
- How plants and animals get energy

VOCABULARY

chemical energy p. 47
glucose p. 47
photosynthesis p. 48
chlorophyll p. 48
cellular respiration p. 50
fermentation p. 52

THINK ABOUT

What do these cells have in common?

Both muscle cells and plant cells need energy to live. Your muscle cells need energy to help you move and perform other functions. Even though plant cells don't move in the same way that muscles move, they still need energy. How do human muscle cells and plant cells get energy?

leaf cells

muscle cells

OUTLINE

Remember to include this heading in your outline of this section.

I. Main idea
  A. Supporting idea
    1. Detail
    2. Detail
  B. Supporting idea

All cells need energy.

To stay alive, cells need a constant supply of energy. Animal cells get energy from food, while plant cells get energy from sunlight. All cells use chemical energy. **Chemical energy** is the energy stored in the bonds between atoms of every molecule. To stay alive, cells must be able to release the chemical energy in the bonds.

A major energy source for most cells is stored in a sugar molecule called **glucose.** When you need energy, cells release chemical energy from glucose. You need food energy to run, walk, and even during sleep. Your cells use energy from food to carry out all of their activities.

Think about muscle cells. When you run, muscle cells release chemical energy from glucose to move your legs. The more you run, the more glucose your muscle cells need. You eat food to restore the glucose supply in muscles. But how do plant cells get more glucose? Plants transform the energy in sunlight into the chemical energy in glucose.

Some cells capture light energy.

The source of energy for all organisms ultimately comes from the Sun. Plants change the energy in sunlight into a form of energy their cells can use—the chemical energy in glucose. All animals benefit from the ability of plants to convert sunlight to food energy. Animals either eat plants, or they eat other animals that have eaten plants.

Photosynthesis (FOH-toh-SIHN-thih-sihs) is the process that plant cells use to change the energy from sunlight into chemical energy. Photosynthesis takes place in plant cells that have chloroplasts. Chloroplasts contain **chlorophyll** (KLAWR-uh-fhil), a light-absorbing pigment, or colored substance, that traps the energy in sunlight.

The process of photosynthesis involves a series of chemical steps, or reactions. The illustration on the next page shows an overview of how photosynthesis changes starting materials into new products.

READING TiP

As you read each numbered item here, find the number on the diagram on page 49.

① **The starting materials** of photosynthesis are carbon dioxide and water. The plant takes in carbon dioxide from the air and water from the soil.

② **The process** takes place when carbon dioxide and water enter the plant's chloroplasts. Chlorophyll captures energy from sunlight, which is used to change carbon dioxide and water into new products.

③ **The products** of photosynthesis are glucose and oxygen. The plant releases most of the oxygen to the air as a waste product and keeps the glucose for its energy needs.

CHECK YOUR READING Summarize photosynthesis. Remember that a summary includes only the most important information.

Plants do not immediately use all of the glucose they make. Some of the glucose molecules are linked together to build large carbohydrates called starch. Plants can store starch and later break it back down into glucose or other sugars when they need energy. Sugars and starches supply food for animals that eat plants.

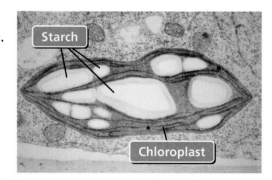

Starch

Chloroplast

The starch in this plant cell stores energy.

Photosynthesis

Chloroplast

Leaf cell (magnified 2200×)

1. **The starting materials** Carbon dioxide from the air and water from the soil enter the chloroplasts.

2. **The process** Inside the chloroplasts, chlorophyll captures energy from sunlight. This energy is used to change starting materials into new products.

3. **The products** Glucose supplies energy and is a source of materials for the plant; most oxygen is released into the air.

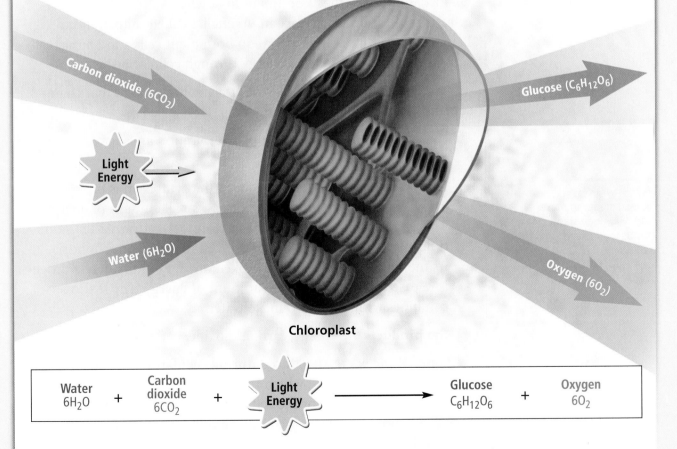

Carbon dioxide ($6CO_2$)

Light Energy

Water ($6H_2O$)

Glucose ($C_6H_{12}O_6$)

Oxygen ($6O_2$)

Chloroplast

| Water $6H_2O$ | + | Carbon dioxide $6CO_2$ | + | Light Energy | → | Glucose $C_6H_{12}O_6$ | + | Oxygen $6O_2$ |

READING VISUALS What part of the diagram shows starting materials being changed?

All cells release energy.

All cells must have energy to function. Glucose and other sugars are cell food—they are the power source for cell activities in almost all living things. When glucose is stored as glycogen or taken in as starch, it must be broken down into individual molecules before cells are able to use it. Chemical energy is stored in the bonds of sugars. When the bonds of a sugar molecule are broken, a burst of energy is released that the cell can use.

Cells can release energy in two basic processes: cellular respiration and fermentation. Cellular respiration requires oxygen, but fermentation does not. In addition, cellular respiration releases much more usable energy than does fermentation.

 What is released when a sugar molecule is broken down?

Cellular Respiration

In **cellular respiration,** cells use oxygen to release energy stored in sugars such as glucose. In fact, most of the energy used by the cells in your body is provided by cellular respiration.

Just as photosynthesis occurs in organelles called chloroplasts, cellular respiration takes place in organelles called mitochondria. Remember that mitochondria are in both plant cells and animal cells, so both kinds of cells release energy through cellular respiration.

Like photosynthesis, cellular respiration is a process that changes starting materials into new products.

① The starting materials of cellular respiration are sugars—such as glucose—and oxygen.

② The process begins when glucose in the cytoplasm is broken down into smaller molecules. This releases a small amount of energy. These molecules then move into the mitochondria. At the same time, oxygen enters the cell and travels into the mitochondria. As the smaller molecules are broken down even further, hydrogen is released along with a large amount of energy. The hydrogen combines with oxygen to make water.

③ The products are energy, carbon dioxide, and water.

Some of the energy produced during cellular respiration is transferred to other molecules, which then carry the energy where it is needed for the activities of the cell. The rest of the energy is released as heat. Carbon dioxide formed during cellular respiration is released by the cell.

 What are the three products of cellular respiration?

> **READING TiP**
> Reread step 2 to make sure you understand what happens to oxygen and glucose.

Cellular Respiration

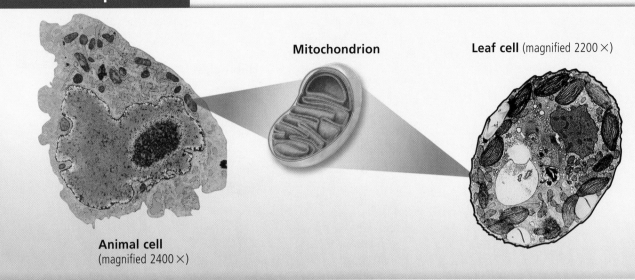

Mitochondrion

Leaf cell (magnified 2200 ×)

Animal cell
(magnified 2400 ×)

1 **The starting materials** Glucose and oxygen enter the cell. Glucose is split into smaller molecules.

2 **The process** Inside the mitochondria more chemical bonds are broken in the smaller molecules. Oxygen is needed for this process.

3 **The products** Energy is released, and water and carbon dioxide are produced.

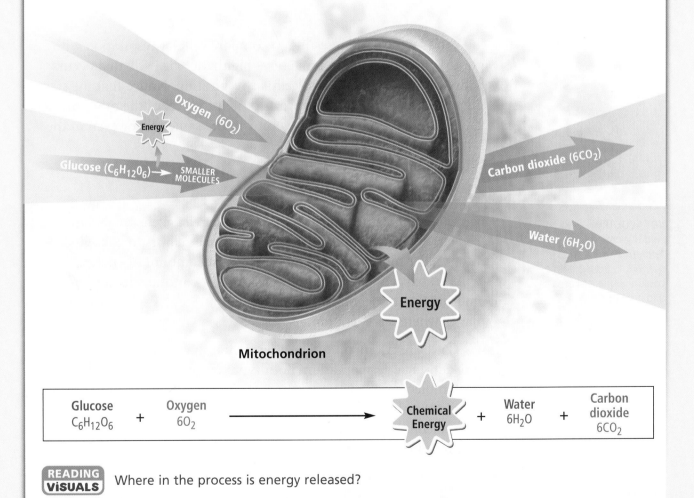

Energy

Oxygen ($6O_2$)

Glucose ($C_6H_{12}O_6$) → SMALLER MOLECULES

Carbon dioxide ($6CO_2$)

Water ($6H_2O$)

Energy

Mitochondrion

Glucose $C_6H_{12}O_6$	+	Oxygen $6O_2$	→	Chemical Energy	+	Water $6H_2O$	+	Carbon dioxide $6CO_2$

READING VISUALS Where in the process is energy released?

Photosynthesis and Respiration Cycle

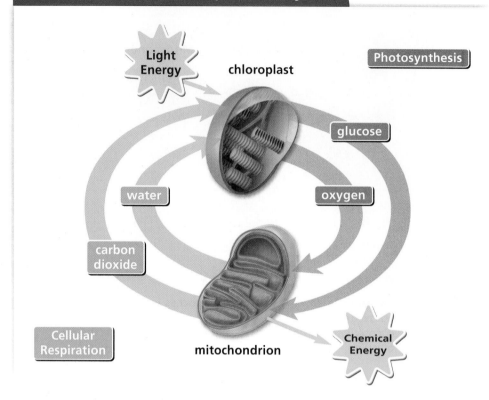

Light Energy · chloroplast · Photosynthesis · glucose · water · oxygen · carbon dioxide · Cellular Respiration · mitochondrion · Chemical Energy

You may find it interesting to compare cellular respiration with photosynthesis. The diagram above highlights the cycle that occurs between photosynthesis and cellular respiration. Notice that the starting materials of one process are also the products of the other process. This cycle does not necessarily occur in the same cell, or even in the same organism.

Fermentation

VOCABULARY
Add a word triangle for *fermentation* to your notebook. Your triangle could include a sketch of a loaf of bread.

Fermentation is the process by which cells release energy without oxygen. Recall that in cellular respiration the cell first breaks glucose into smaller molecules. This releases a small amount of energy. Without oxygen, cellular respiration cannot continue. Instead of entering the mitochondria, these smaller molecules stay in the cytoplasm, where fermentation occurs.

There are two main types of fermentation: alcoholic fermentation and lactic acid fermentation. Both types of fermentation start with the small molecules made from sugars at the beginning of cellular respiration. In the absence of oxygen, different reactions occur that produce either alcohol and carbon dioxide or lactic acid. In both cases, a small amount of energy is released.

CHECK YOUR READING Use a Venn diagram to compare and contrast fermentation and cellular respiration.

The production of many foods that people eat every day involve either alcoholic fermentation or lactic acid fermentation. Three important foods are bread, yogurt, and cheese.

Bread is often made by mixing flour, milk, and sugar with a microorganism you know as yeast. If the mixture is kept in a warm place, yeast runs out of oxygen and uses fermentation to convert the sugar into alcohol and carbon dioxide. Bubbles of carbon dioxide gas forming inside the dough cause it to rise. When the dough is baked, the small amount of alcohol evaporates, the yeast is killed, and the carbon dioxide bubbles give the bread a light, spongy structure.

Some bacteria release energy through lactic acid fermentation. These bacteria convert the sugar found in milk into lactic acid and are used to make yogurt, cheese, and sourdough bread. Lactic acid changes the acidity of a bread mixture to give it a slightly sour flavor. In yogurt and cheese, the buildup of lactic acid causes the milk to partially solidify, producing the creamy texture of yogurt. If fermentation continues for a long time, the milk eventually turns into cheese.

INVESTIGATE Fermentation

How can you tell if fermentation releases material?

PROCEDURE

1. Add 1/2 teaspoon of yeast to the empty water bottle.
2. Fill the bottle about three-quarters full with the sugar solution.
3. Place the balloon tightly around the mouth of the bottle.
4. Gently swirl the bottle to mix the yeast and sugar solution.
5. After 20 minutes, observe the balloon and record your observations.

WHAT DO YOU THINK?

- What changes did you observe? What do you think is the source of energy that caused these changes?
- What accounts for the change in the amount of gas inside the balloon?

CHALLENGE Design an experiment to answer the following questions. How might the temperature of the sugar solution affect the process?

SKILL FOCUS
Observing

MATERIALS
- dry yeast
- spoon
- small water bottle
- warm sugar solution
- balloon

TIME
30 minutes

Energy and Exercise

Your muscle cells, like some organisms, are able to release energy by both cellular respiration and fermentation. While you are at rest, your muscle cells use specialized molecules to store both energy and oxygen.

During hard or prolonged exercise, your muscle cells may use up all their stores of energy and oxygen. Then your muscle cells rely on fermentation to break down sugars. There is much less energy available to cells that use fermentation, which is why you cannot continue to run rapidly for long distances. When your cells use fermentation to release energy, one of the waste products is lactic acid, which can cause a burning sensation in your muscles.

APPLY Why might these students feel a burning sensation in their arms muscles while doing pull-ups?

When you stop after this type of exercise, your muscles continue to hurt and you continue to breathe hard for many minutes. During this time, your muscles are playing catch-up. They use the oxygen brought into your blood by your heavy breathing to finish breaking down the byproducts of fermentation. As the lactic acid is converted into carbon dioxide and water, the burning sensation in your muscles goes away. Your muscles build back up their stores of energy and oxygen until the next time they are needed.

2.2 Review

KEY CONCEPTS

1. Which form of energy is especially important for living things? Why?

2. How is photosynthesis important to life on Earth?

3. What starting materials do cells need for cellular respiration?

CRITICAL THINKING

4. **Compare and Contrast** How are photosynthesis and cellular respiration similar? How are they different?

5. **Predict** Suppose that in a lab you could remove all the oxygen from a terrarium. What would happen to the plants? Why?

○ CHALLENGE

6. **Synthesize** In everyday language, the word *respiration* refers to breathing. How is breathing related to *cellular respiration*? Hint: The air we breathe out contains more carbon dioxide than the air we breathe in.

MATH in SCIENCE

MATH TUTORIAL
CLASSZONE.COM

Click on Math Tutorial
for more help with
interpreting line graphs.

Carbon Dioxide Levels in Biosphere 2

Biosphere 2 is a research and education center in Arizona that can house people, plants, and animals. It was built to find out whether people could get the food and breathable air needed to survive in a small sealed environment over a two-year period.

Example

Data on carbon dioxide levels in the air of Biosphere 2 were collected at 15-minute intervals for several weeks. The graph below shows the amounts of carbon dioxide (CO_2) in the air on January 20, 1996.

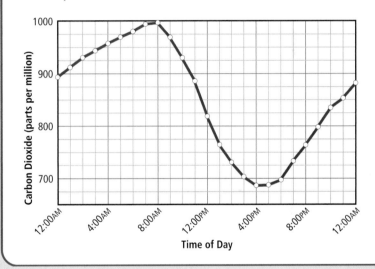

Answer the following questions.

1. What intervals are shown on the *x*-axis? What is shown on the *y*-axis?

2. At what time of day does the carbon dioxide concentration reach its highest point? About how many parts per million of CO_2 are in the air at that time?

3. Between what hours is the CO_2 level decreasing?

CHALLENGE The data in the graph were collected on a sunny day. How might the graph look different if the day had been overcast?

2.3 Materials move across the cell's membranes.

 BEFORE, you learned

- All cells have an outer covering called the cell membrane
- Cells need starting materials for life-sustaining processes
- Cells need to get rid of waste products

 NOW, you will learn

- How materials move into and out of the cell through the cell membrane
- How energy is involved in transporting some materials into and out of cells
- How surface area affects transport in cells

VOCABULARY

diffusion p. 56
passive transport
 p. 58
osmosis p. 59
active transport p. 60

EXPLORE Diffusion

How do particles move?

PROCEDURE

MATERIALS
- beaker
- water
- food coloring

① Fill the beaker with tap water.

② Add 3 drops of food coloring to the water.

③ For 10 minutes, observe what happens. Write down your observations.

WHAT DO YOU THINK?
- What changes did you observe?
- What might have caused the changes?

VOCABULARY
Add a word triangle for *diffusion* to your notebook. Your triangle could include a sketch of the sun.

Some materials move by diffusion.

When you walk toward the shampoo section in a store, you can probably smell a fragrance even before you get close. The process by which the scent spreads through the air is an example of diffusion. **Diffusion** (dih-FYOO-zhuhn) is the process by which molecules spread out, or move from areas where there are many of them to areas where there are fewer of them.

Diffusion occurs because the molecules in gases, liquids, and even solids are in constant motion in all directions. This random movement of molecules tends to spread molecules out until they are evenly distributed. But diffusion does more than just spread a scent around a room. Cells use diffusion to carry out important life functions. Diffusion helps cells maintain conditions necessary for life. For example, the oxygen needed for respiration enters cells by diffusion. Similarly, the carbon dioxide produced by respiration leaves cells by diffusion.

Concentration

Diffusion occurs naturally as particles move from an area of higher concentration to an area of lower concentration. The concentration of a substance is the number of particles of that substance in a specific volume. For example, if you dissolved 9 grams of sugar in 1 liter of water, the concentration of the sugar solution would be 9 g/L. When there is a difference of concentration of a substance between two areas, diffusion occurs.

Generally, the greater the difference in concentration between two areas, the more rapidly diffusion occurs. As the difference of concentration decreases, diffusion slows down, the number of particles moving to one area is balanced by the number moving in the other direction. Particles are still moving in all directions, but these movements do not change the concentrations.

 CHECK YOUR READING Summarize what happens during diffusion. (Remember, a summary includes only the most important information.)

Concentration and Diffusion

A sugar cube dissolving in water provides an example of diffusion.

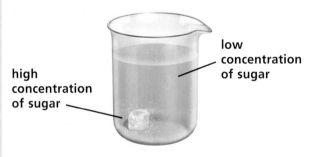

high concentration of sugar

low concentration of sugar

1 Shortly after a sugar cube is placed in a beaker of water, the concentration of sugar is high near the sugar cube and very low elsewhere in the beaker.

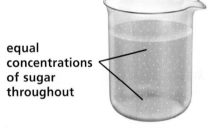

equal concentrations of sugar throughout

2 Over time, diffusion causes the concentration of sugar to become the same throughout the beaker. Particles are still moving.

Diffusion in Cells

Diffusion is one way by which materials move in and out of cells. Small molecules such as oxygen can pass through tiny gaps in the cell membrane by diffusion. For example, consider the conditions that result from photosynthesis in a leaf cell.

RESOURCE CENTER
CLASSZONE.COM

Learn more about diffusion.

- Photosynthesis produces oxygen inside the cell.
- The concentration of oxygen molecules becomes higher inside the cell than outside.
- Oxygen molecules move out of the cell by diffusion.

In a plant cell, some of the oxygen produced by photosynthesis is used in cellular respiration. The remaining oxygen diffuses out of the cell. Much of it escapes to the air. Some of it diffuses to other cells where there is a lower concentration of oxygen. This process of diffusion continues from one cell to the next.

Diffusion is a form of passive transport. In **passive transport,** materials move without using the cell's energy. Cells benefit from passive transport because some materials can move through various cell membranes without any input of energy. Whether or not a substance can diffuse across a cell membrane depends on how well the substance dissolves in the lipids that make up the cell membrane. A special form of passive transport allows polar substances, such as glucose, salts, and amino acids, to pass through cell membranes.

All cells need the food energy supplied by glucose. Yet glucose is produced in just some plant cells. Polar substances move into the cell through protein channels—or openings—in their membranes that are specific for each substance. This type of diffusion is still passive transport because it uses no energy.

CHECK YOUR READING What is passive transport? Your answer should mention energy.

VOCABULARY
Add a word diagram for *passive transport* to your notebook. You may want to use words instead of a sketch in part of your triangle.

Passive Transport

Materials move across a cell membrane continuously.

= oxygen
= glucose

Different concentrations

More **oxygen** moves out of the cell than into the cell.

outside of cell

Special **proteins** allow passive transport of some molecules, such as glucose.

inside of cell

The concentration of oxygen is greater inside the cell than outside.

Equal concentrations

Equal amounts of **oxygen** move into and out of the cell.

The concentration of oxygen is the same inside and outside the cell.

Osmosis

You have read about the importance of water. Water molecules move through cell membranes by diffusion. The diffusion of water through a membrane is given a special name, **osmosis** (ahz-MOH-sihs). If the concentration of water is higher outside a cell than inside, water moves into the cell. If the concentration of water is lower outside a cell, water moves out of the cell.

You can easily observe the effect of osmosis on plants. If you forget to water a plant, it wilts. Why? The soil dries out, and the plant's roots have no water to absorb. As a result, water leaves the plant cells by osmosis and they shrink. If you water the plant, water becomes available to enter the shrunken cells by osmosis. The leaves will return to normal as water moves into the cells.

Without water, a plant droops. The cells have little water in their vacuoles, shown in blue. (magnified 1200×)

Water moves into leaf cells by osmosis and fills the vacuoles, shown in blue. (magnified 1200×)

Some transport requires energy.

Not all materials that move in and out of a cell can do so by diffusion. For cells to carry out life functions, materials must often move from areas of low concentration into areas of high concentration. This process of moving materials against a concentration requires energy.

Active Transport

Active transport is the process of using energy to move materials through a membrane. This process is different from diffusion and other types of passive transport, which do not require energy.

 CHECK YOUR READING How is active transport different from passive transport?

VISUALIZATION
CLASSZONE.COM

Observe active transport at work.

Cells use active transport to perform important life functions, including the removal of excess salt from the body. Consider the example of active transport in marine iguanas, shown below. These lizards swim and feed in the salty ocean. As a result they soak up a lot of salt. Too much salt would seriously damage the iguanas' cells, so the cells must get rid of the excess.

The solution to the marine iguana's salt problem is found in two small glands above its eyes. Cells in these glands remove excess salt from the blood by active transport. Even when cells in these glands have a higher concentration of salt than that of the blood, the cells use chemical energy to continue taking salt out of the blood. The gland forms a droplet of salt, which the iguana easily blows out through its nostrils.

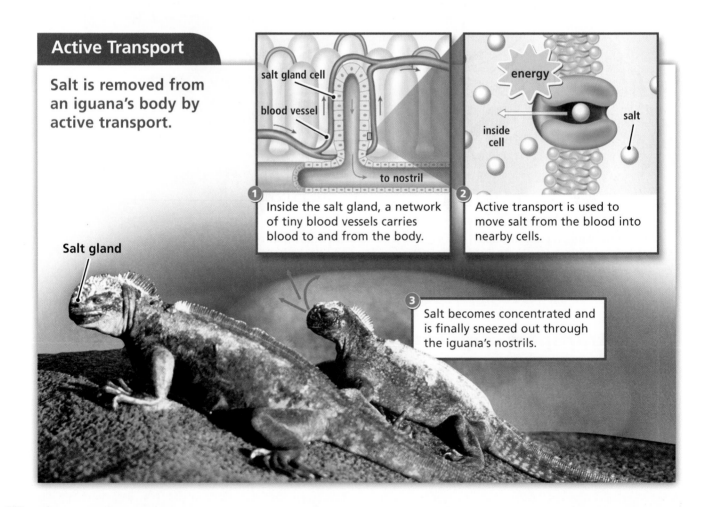

Active Transport

Salt is removed from an iguana's body by active transport.

salt gland cell

blood vessel

to nostril

1 Inside the salt gland, a network of tiny blood vessels carries blood to and from the body.

energy

inside cell

salt

2 Active transport is used to move salt from the blood into nearby cells.

Salt gland

3 Salt becomes concentrated and is finally sneezed out through the iguana's nostrils.

You may not be able to blow salt out of your nostrils, but your kidneys help to keep healthy salt levels in your body. Kidneys filter wastes from your blood by active transport. Cells in the kidneys remove excess salt from the blood.

Endocytosis

Cells also need to move materials that are too large to go through the cell membrane or a protein channel. As the diagram below illustrates, endocytosis (EHN-doh-sy-TOH-sihs) occurs when a large bit of material is captured within a pocket of the membrane. This pocket breaks off and forms a package that moves into the cell. Cells in your body can use endocytosis to fight bacteria and viruses by absorbing them.

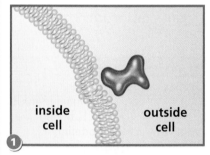
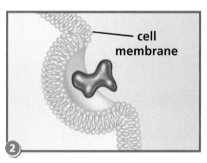
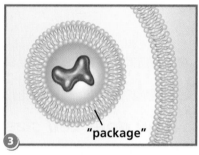

As a particle approaches, the cell membrane folds inward, creating a pocket.

The particle moves into the pocket, and the membrane closes around it, forming a "package."

The "package" breaks away from the cell membrane, bringing the particle into the cell.

Exocytosis

When a cell needs to get rid of large materials, the process of endocytosis is reversed. In exocytosis (EHK-soh-sy-TOH-sihs), a membrane within the cell encloses the material that needs to be removed. This package moves to the cell membrane, joins with it, and the material is expelled. Cells often use exocytosis to flush out waste materials or to expel proteins or hormones made by the cell.

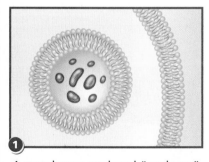
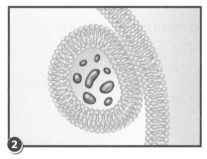
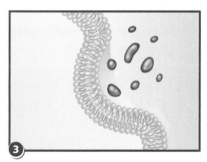

A membrane-enclosed "package" carries materials from inside the cell to the cell membrane.

The membrane of the "package" attaches to the cell membrane, and the two membranes merge.

The materials are pushed out of the cell as the membrane of the "package" becomes part of the cell membrane.

Cell size affects transport.

Most cells are very small. In fact, most cells are too small to be seen without a microscope. The average cell in your body is about 50 micrometers (0.05 mm) in diameter. Most of the cells on this planet are bacteria, which are only 3 to 5 micrometers in diameter. How can something as important as a cell be so tiny? Actually, if cells were not so small, they could never do their jobs.

Everything the cell needs or has to get rid of has to go through the cell membrane. The amount of cell membrane limits the ability of cells to either get substances from the outside or transport waste and other materials to the outside. This ability is related to surface area. The relationship between surface area and volume controls cell size. As a cell gets larger, its volume increases faster than its surface area if the cell maintains the same shape. Why does this matter?

INVESTIGATE Cells

How does cell size affect transport?

Demonstrate how small size helps make it possible for cells to get resources.

SKILL FOCUS
Modeling

PROCEDURE

1. Cut a 1-cm-thick slice of egg white off the top of one of the eggs.

2. Use a ruler and a knife to trim the piece of egg white into a cube approximately 1-cm on each side.

3. Pour 100 mL of water into the beaker. Add 10 drops of blue food coloring and stir. Place the whole egg and the cube of egg white into the solution. Let both stand in the colored water overnight.

4. Remove each gently from the water with a spoon. Place both on a paper towel. With the knife, cut each in half. Use the ruler to measure how far the blue water penetrated into the surface of each one.

MATERIALS
- 2 hard-boiled, peeled eggs
- knife
- ruler
- 100 mL water
- glass beaker
- dark blue food coloring
- spoon
- paper towel

TIME
30 minutes

WHAT DO YOU THINK?

- Record your observations. Which piece of egg was penetrated more, compared to its total diameter, by the blue water?
- Why was there a difference in water penetration?

CHALLENGE What do you predict would happen to an egg left in its shell?

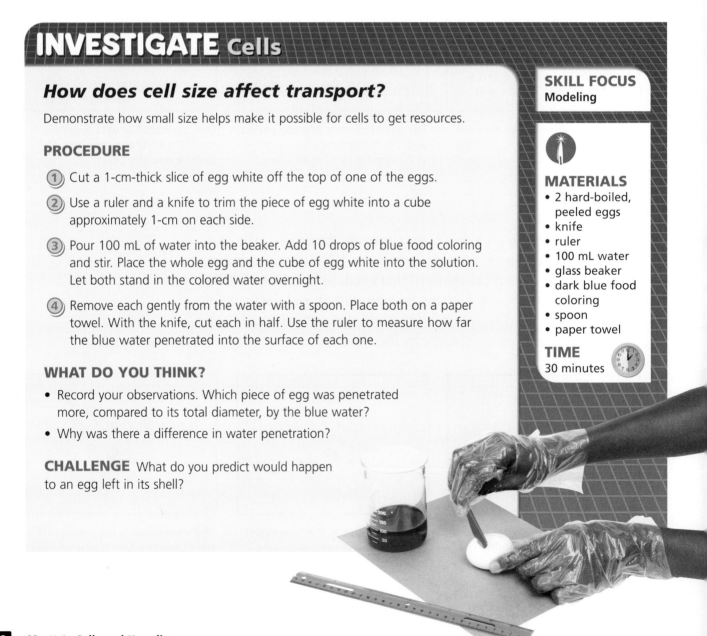

Surface Area and Volumes of Cubes

	Number of Cubes	Side Length	Surface Area	Volume
4 cm	1	4 cm	96 cm²	64 cm³
2 cm	8	2 cm	192 cm²	64 cm³
1 cm	64	1 cm	384 cm²	64 cm³

As the cell gets bigger, there comes a time when its surface area is not large enough to allow resources to travel to all parts of the cell. So the cell stops growing. Bird eggs and frog eggs are much larger than typical cells, but they have a storehouse of food and also rapidly divide to give rise to multicellular embryos. In fact, this multicellular embryo is a good illustration of another way cells get around the surface-area-to-volume problem: they divide. The ratio of surface area to volume in newly divided cells is much higher, giving more surface area for exchanging materials with the outside of cells.

A cell's shape also affects its surface area. For example, some single-celled organisms are thin and flat, providing increased surface area. Other cells, such as nerve cells and muscle cells, are long and skinny, which also gives them a higher ratio of surface area to volume.

READING TiP

Look at the chart above. Notice that the volumes are all the same, but the surface area changes.

2.3 Review

KEY CONCEPTS

1. How are the processes of diffusion and osmosis alike?

2. What is the difference between active and passive transport? Use the term *energy* in your answer.

3. How does the surface area of a cell limit the growth of the cell?

CRITICAL THINKING

4. **Apply** If you put a bouquet of carnations in water, through what process does the water enter the stems?

5. **Predict** If a marine iguana were to spend a few days in a freshwater tank, would it continue to blow salt droplets from its nostrils? Why or why not?

◇ CHALLENGE

6. **Predict** Freshwater protozoa, which are unicellular organisms, have a greater concentration of salt inside them than does the surrounding water. Does water diffuse into or out of the protozoa?

CHAPTER INVESTIGATION

Diffusion

OVERVIEW AND PURPOSE The cell membrane controls what diffuses into and out of a cell. What factors affect the diffusion of substances across the cell membrane? In this investigation, you will

- observe the affect of concentration on rate of diffusion
- determine the relative concentrations of the iodine solutions used

▶ Problem

How does the concentration of a substance affect its diffusion through a membrane?

▶ Hypothesize

Write a hypothesis to explain how concentration will affect diffusion of material through a membrane. Your hypothesis should take the form of an "If . . ., then . . ., because. . ." statement.

▶ Procedure

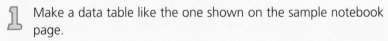

1. Make a data table like the one shown on the sample notebook page.

2. To test for the presence of starch, use one eyedropper to put several drops of cornstarch solution on the lid of the baby food jar. With another eyedropper, add a few drops of iodine to the solution on the jar lid. Observe and record what happens.

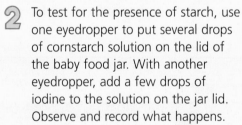

step 2

3. Fill the baby food jar about three-fourths full with the cornstarch solution.

   Place the plastic wrap inside the jar so that the plastic extends a little below the surface of the cornstarch solution.

4. Pour 10 mL of the iodine solution that you are given (A, B, or C) on the plastic wrap membrane, enough to cover the top of the plastic wrap. Record your observations.

step 4

MATERIALS
- eyedroppers
- cornstarch solution
- baby food jar with lid
- plastic wrap
- iodine solution
- graduated cylinder (if available)

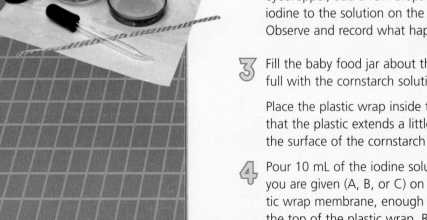

5 Examine the solutions above and below the membrane after 20 minutes. Record any color changes, as well as the intensity of any changes, that you observe.

▶ Observe and Analyze *Write It Up*

1. **IDENTIFY VARIABLES** Identify the constants. What will stay the same in the experiment for all groups?

   Identify the independent variable. What is being changed?

   Identify the dependent variable. What is being observed and measured?

2. **RECORD OBSERVATIONS** Draw before and after pictures of your setup and label each drawing. Be sure to show the colors of the solutions on both sides of the membrane in each drawing.

   Make a drawing to show the direction in which molecules diffused through the membrane in your experiment.

   Compare the observations you made from your iodine solution with the observations made by your classmates. Be sure to record which iodine solution (A, B, or C) produced which changes.

▶ Conclude *Write It Up*

1. **INTERPRET** Did starch diffuse through the membrane into the iodine solution? How do you know? Did iodine diffuse through the membrane into the cornstarch solution? How do you know?

2. **INTERPRET** What factors affect the diffusion of different substances through a membrane?

3. **INFER** From what you've observed, which solution contains larger molecules, cornstarch or iodine? Why weren't the larger molecules able to diffuse through the membrane?

4. **INTERPRET** Which iodine solution (A, B, or C) produced the largest color change?

5. **INTERPRET** Which solution had the highest concentration of iodine, and how do you know?

6. **IDENTIFY LIMITS** Describe any errors that you made in your procedure, or places where errors might have occurred.

7. **APPLY** Identify two real-life situations in which diffusion occurs.

▶ INVESTIGATE Further

CHALLENGE Investigate the role of temperature in diffusion. Predict how changes in the temperature of the iodine solution will affect the speed of diffusion through the plastic membrane. Why do you think temperature would affect the diffusion process?

Diffusion

Table 1. Color Changes

Solution	Color at 0 min		Color at 20 min	
	cornstarch solution	iodine solution	cornstarch solution	iodine solution
A				
B				
C				

Chapter Review

the BIG idea

All cells need energy and materials for life processes.

CONTENT REVIEW
CLASSZONE.COM

◀ KEY CONCEPTS SUMMARY

2.1 Chemical reactions take place inside cells.

All cells are made of the same elements. Cells contain four types of large molecules—**carbohydrates, lipids, proteins,** and **nucleic acids**—that support cell function.

About two thirds of every cell is water. The properties of water are important to cell function.

carbohydrates

lipids

proteins

nucleic acids

VOCABULARY
chemical reaction p. 42
carbohydrate p. 42
lipid p. 43
protein p. 43
nucleic acid p. 43

2.2 Cells capture and release energy.

All cells need energy. Some cells capture light energy through **photosynthesis.** All cells release chemical energy from glucose.

Cellular respiration and **fermentation** are two ways that cells release energy from glucose.

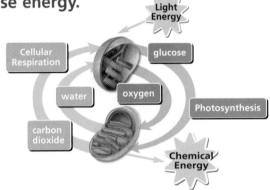

Light Energy

Cellular Respiration

glucose

water

oxygen

Photosynthesis

carbon dioxide

Chemical Energy

VOCABULARY
chemical energy p. 47
glucose p. 47
photosynthesis p. 48
chlorophyll p. 48
cellular respiration
   p. 50
fermentation p. 52

2.3 Materials move across the cell's membranes.

Passive transport is the movement of materials from an area of higher concentration to an area of lower concentration. **Diffusion** and **osmosis** are examples of passive transport.

Active transport is the movement of materials from an area of lower concentration to an area of higher concentration. Cells need energy to perform active transport.

passive transport

active transport

VOCABULARY
diffusion p. 56
passive transport p. 58
osmosis p. 59
active transport p. 60

Reviewing Vocabulary

Use words from the vocabulary lists on page 66 to answer these questions.

1. Which molecule carries information?

2. Which word describes the process when two or more atoms bond together?

3. What kind of energy do cells use?

4. Which term describes the process in which cells release energy without using oxygen?

5. Which word means "putting together with light"?

6. From what sugar molecule do many living things release energy?

7. Which chemical that aids in photosynthesis do you find in a chloroplast?

8. Which word means "diffusion of water across cell membranes"?

9. Choose two pairs of opposite processes.

10. Use a Venn diagram to compare and contrast passive transport and active transport.

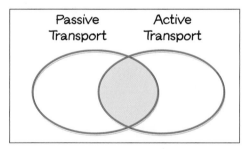

Reviewing Key Concepts

Multiple Choice *Choose the letter of the best answer.*

11. The fats, oils, and waxes found in living things are known as
  a. lipids   **c.** carbohydrates
  b. proteins   **d.** glucose

12. What do cells use as a source of energy and for energy storage?
  a. proteins   **c.** cytoplasm
  b. water   **d.** carbohydrates

13. Leaf cells use chlorophyll to absorb
  a. oxygen   **c.** carbon dioxide
  b. light energy   **d.** glucose

14. The cells of a redwood tree require oxygen for the process of
  a. photosynthesis   **c.** fermentation
  b. cellular respiration   **d.** endocytosis

15. In fermentation, cells release energy without
  a. alcohol   **c.** glucose
  b. water   **d.** oxygen

16. Both a whale and a seaweed plant use which of the following to change glucose into energy?
  a. water   **c.** cellular respiration
  b. photosynthesis   **d.** bonding

17. The movement of materials across a cell membrane, requiring energy, is called
  a. diffusion   **c.** homeostasis
  b. osmosis   **d.** active transport

Short Answer *Write a short answer to each question.*

18. Why is water needed by cells?

19. Explain how the nucleic acids DNA and RNA are related to the process by which two cells come from one cell.

20. What is the role of chlorophyll in a plant's leaves?

21. Explain why a carrot feels spongy after being soaked in salt water.

22. Explain how the ways in which plants and animals get their energy differ.

23. RECOGNIZE CAUSE AND EFFECT Explain why chemical reactions are essential to living creatures.

24. MODEL How does a glass filled with oil and water illustrate the properties of a cell membrane? What properties does it not illustrate?

The illustration below summarizes the relationship between photosynthesis and cellular respiration. Use it to answer the next three questions.

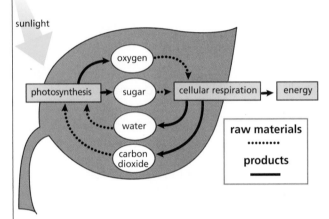

25. OBSERVE What are the starting materials of photosynthesis? What are the starting materials of cellular respiration?

26. OBSERVE What are the products of photosynthesis? What are the products of cellular respiration?

27. DRAW CONCLUSIONS What does this diagram reveal about the connections between photosynthesis and cellular respiration?

Process	Requires Energy?	Moves from Higher to Lower Concentration?
Diffusion	no	yes
Osmosis		
Active transport		
Passive transport		

28. CHART INFORMATION Copy and complete this chart. The first line is done for you.

29. INFER The French scientist Louis Pasteur mixed yeast and grape juice in a sealed container. When he opened the container, the grape juice contained alcohol. Explain what happened.

30. DRAW CONCLUSIONS Why would it be harmful to your health to drink seawater?

31. PREDICT Look at the diagram at the right. The bag has pores that are bigger than the sugar molecules. What will be true of the concentration of the sugar water after a few hours?

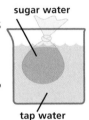

sugar water

tap water

the BIG idea

32. COMPARE AND CONTRAST Look again at the picture on pages 40–41. Why do you think the sunflowers are facing the Sun?

33. INFER Does your body get all its energy from the Sun? Explain.

34. WRITE Imagine that your community has a high level of carbon dioxide emission from cars and factories. A developer wants to build a shopping center on the remaining forest land. Would this action increase or decrease carbon dioxide levels? Why? Write a paragraph explaining your answer.

UNIT PROJECTS

Check your schedule for your unit project. How are you doing? Be sure that you have placed data or notes from your research in your project folder.

Analyzing Data

Elodea plants in beakers of water were placed at different distances from a light source. The number of bubbles that formed on the plants was counted and recorded. The data table shows the results.

Beaker	Distance from light	Bubbles per minute
1	200 cm	2
2	100 cm	10
3	50 cm	45
4	20 cm	83

Study the data and answer the questions below.

1. What gas do the bubbles consist of?

  a. carbon dioxide   **c.** water vapor

  b. hydrogen   **d.** oxygen

2. What is the relationship between the distance from the light source and the rate of bubble formation?

  a. The rate increases as the distance increases.

  b. The rate decreases as the distance increases.

  c. The rate stays the same as the distance increases.

  d. The rate changes in a way unrelated to distance.

3. If another beaker with elodea were placed 150 cm from the light, about how many bubbles would form each minute?

  a. 1   **c.** 11

  b. 7   **d.** 24

4. What is the independent variable in this experiment?

  a. type of plant   **c.** distance from light

  b. number of bubbles   **d.** amount of time

5. Which graph best represents the data shown in the table?

a.

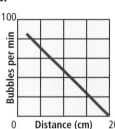

c.

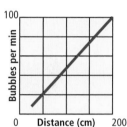

b.

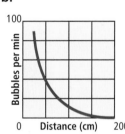

d.

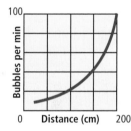

Extended Response

Answer each question. Include some of the terms shown in the word box. In your answers underline each term you use.

chemical energy	cellular respiration
osmosis	chloroplasts
fermentation	glucose
photosynthesis	diffusion

6. A person rides his bicycle several miles. What process is used by the cells in his legs to release energy at the beginning of the ride? At the end of the ride? Explain.

7. A student places a plant in a sealed container and puts the container on a window sill. She leaves the plant there for a week. Will the plant have the starting materials it needs to carry out photosynthesis during the entire week? Explain.

3 Cell Division

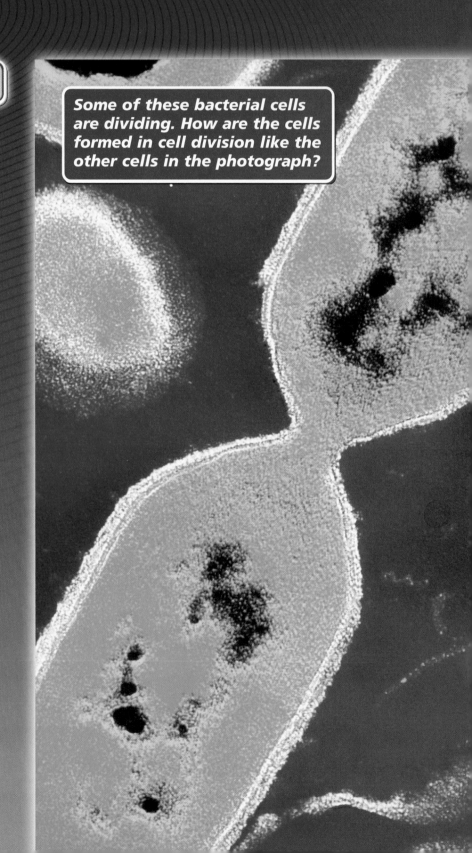

> *Some of these bacterial cells are dividing. How are the cells formed in cell division like the other cells in the photograph?*

the **BIG** idea

Organisms grow, reproduce, and maintain themselves through cell division.

Key Concepts

SECTION

3.1 Cell division occurs in all organisms.
Learn about the functions of cell division.

SECTION

3.2 Cell division is part of the cell cycle.
Learn about the cell cycle and the process of mitosis.

SECTION

3.3 Both sexual and asexual reproduction involve cell division.
Learn how sexual reproduction compares with asexual reproduction.

Internet Preview

CLASSZONE.COM

Chapter 3 online resources: Content Review, Simulation, Visualization, three Resource Centers, Math Tutorial, Test Practice

EXPLORE (the BIG idea)

Dividing to Multiply

Carefully observe a maple tree samara like the ones shown here. Notice the different parts of a samara. Break a samara into two pieces. Peel back the end of each half, where you broke it.

Observe and Think
What did you find when you peeled back the ends? How does something as small as a seed produce something as large as a tree?

Division Math

Take a piece of clay and divide it in half. Now you have two pieces of clay, each half the size of the original piece. Divide each of the two new pieces in half, producing 4 pieces, each a quarter the size of the original piece.

Observe and Think What will happen if you keep dividing the pieces in half? How might the division of the cells in living things be different?

Internet Activity: Cell Division

Go to **ClassZone.com** to match images of cells dividing with the different stages of cell division.

Observe and Think Are the stages the same for plant and animal cells?

NSTA
scilinks.org
SCiLINKS

Cellular Mitosis **Code: MDL033**

Getting Ready to Learn

◀ CONCEPT REVIEW

- The cell is the basic unit of structure and function in living things.
- All cells come from other cells.
- DNA provides the instructions a cell needs to function and reproduce.

◀ VOCABULARY REVIEW

cell membrane p. 20

nucleus p. 20

cycle *See Glossary.*

CONTENT REVIEW
CLASSZONE.COM
Review concepts and vocabulary.

▶ TAKING NOTES

COMBINATION NOTES

To take notes about a new concept, first make an informal outline of the information. Then make a sketch of the concept and label it so you can study it later.

VOCABULARY STRATEGY

Write each new vocabulary term in the center of a **frame game** diagram. Decide what information to frame it with. Use examples, description, parts, sentences that use the term in context, or pictures. You can change the frame to fit each term.

See the Note-Taking Handbook on pages R45–R51.

SCIENCE NOTEBOOK

NOTES

Mitosis has four phases

- prophase: chromosomes form

- metaphase: chromosomes line up in middle

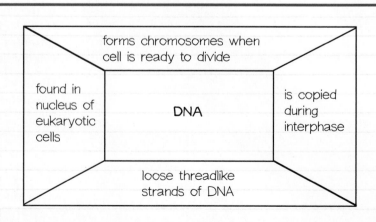

	forms chromosomes when cell is ready to divide	
found in nucleus of eukaryotic cells	**DNA**	is copied during interphase
	loose threadlike strands of DNA	

3.1

Cell division occurs in all organisms.

◀ **BEFORE,** you learned

- Cells come from other cells
- Cells take in and release energy and materials
- In a multicellular organism, some cells specialize

▶ **NOW,** you will learn

- How genetic material is organized in cells
- About the functions of cell division in multicellular organisms

VOCABULARY

DNA p. 74
chromosome p. 75

EXPLORE Cell Division

How is organization helpful?

PROCEDURE

1. Work with two other students. Obtain paired and unpaired groups of socks.

2. Two of the students put on blindfolds. One takes the paired group of socks and the other takes the unpaired group.

3. Each blindfolded student tries to separate his or her group of socks into two piles of single socks, one from each pair. The third student keeps track of time and stops the activity after 2 min.

MATERIALS
- 2 blindfolds
- socks
- stopwatch

WHAT DO YOU THINK?
Which group of socks was more accurately separated into two identical sets? Why?

Cell division is involved in many functions.

REMINDER

Multicellular organisms are made up of eukaryotic cells. Most genetic material in eukaryotic cells is contained in the nucleus.

Cell division occurs in all organisms, but performs different functions. Unicellular organisms reproduce through cell division. In multicellular organisms, all division is involved in growth, development, and repair.

You are probably bigger this year than you were last year. One characteristic of all living things is that they grow. Your body is made up of cells. Although cells themselves grow, most growth in multicellular organisms occurs when cells dividing produce new cells. In this chapter you will read about cell division in eukaryotic cells.

The genetic material of eukaryotic cells is organized in chromosomes.

The genetic material of a cell contains information needed for the cell's growth and other activities. When a cell divides into two new cells, each new cell receives a full set of genetic material. Most of the genetic material in cells is contained in a molecule called DNA.

DNA

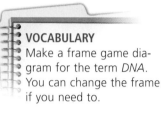

VOCABULARY
Make a frame game diagram for the term *DNA*. You can change the frame if you need to.

The genetic material in cells is DNA—deoxyribonucleic acid (dee-AHK-see-RY-boh-noo-KLEE-ihk). **DNA** is a chemical that contains information for an organism's growth, and functions. You read in chapter 1 that James Watson and Francis Crick worked with other scientists to build a model of DNA in 1953. They showed that DNA is made of two strands of molecules joined in a structure that resembles a twisted ladder or a double helix. You will learn more about DNA later in the unit.

 What is DNA?

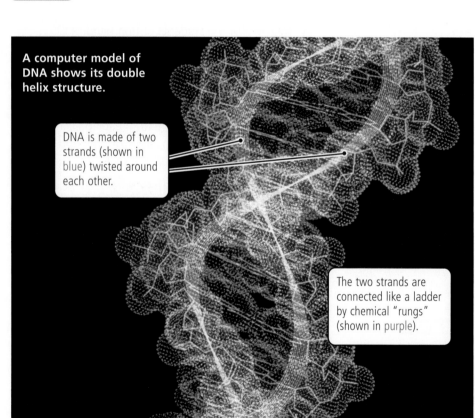

A computer model of DNA shows its double helix structure.

DNA is made of two strands (shown in blue) twisted around each other.

The two strands are connected like a ladder by chemical "rungs" (shown in purple).

Chromosomes

In a eukaryotic cell, most of the cell's DNA is in the nucleus. During most of a cell's life cycle, DNA exists as a mass of loose strands. While the DNA is spread throughout the nucleus, the cell performs the functions needed for survival. During this time, the DNA is duplicated, or copied.

Before a cell divides, the DNA becomes wrapped around proteins like thread around a spool. The DNA is then further compacted into structures called **chromosomes** (KROH-muh-SOHMZ). As shown, a duplicated chromosome consists of two identical structures called chromatids that are held together near the center by a structure called a centromere.

Within each species of organism, the pattern and number of chromosomes formed is the same every time a cell divides. For example, humans have 46 chromosomes. Fruit flies, however, have 8 chromosomes, and corn plants have 20.

READING TiP

Compare the diagram of DNA with the computer model on page 74.

  Describe the relationship between DNA and chromosomes.

Organization of Genetic Material

The DNA in chromosomes is wrapped around a protein core until it is very condensed.

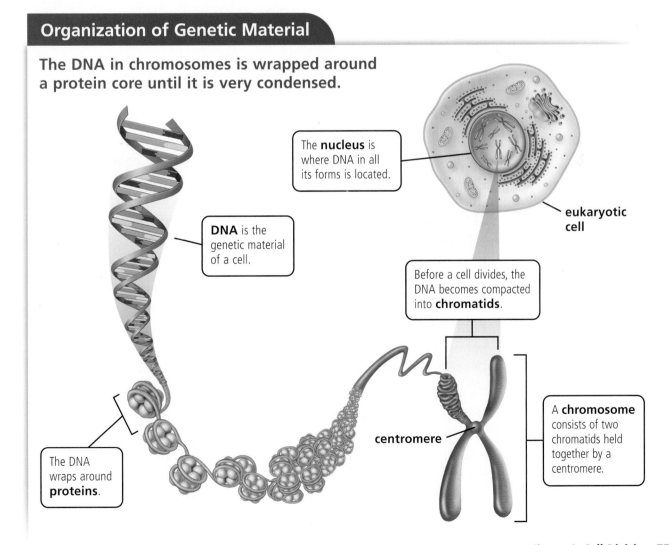

The **nucleus** is where DNA in all its forms is located.

eukaryotic cell

DNA is the genetic material of a cell.

Before a cell divides, the DNA becomes compacted into **chromatids**.

The DNA wraps around **proteins**.

centromere

A **chromosome** consists of two chromatids held together by a centromere.

How does DNA form chromosomes?

PROCEDURE

1. Select four pieces of yarn of different colors and four craft sticks. Push the yarn together into a loose ball. Observe how much space it takes up and how the individual pieces are organized.

2. Wrap each piece of yarn around a craft stick. Wrap the yarn so that the coils are tightly packed but do not overlap.

WHAT DO YOU THINK?

- What did you observe about the loosely balled yarn?
- What does the loosely balled yarn represent?
- What does the yarn on the craft sticks represent?
- Why does the yarn on the craft sticks take up less space than the ball of yarn?

CHALLENGE How does the yarn's being wrapped on the craft sticks make it easier to separate the different colors?

SKILL FOCUS
Modeling

MATERIALS
- yarn
- craft sticks

TIME
20 minutes

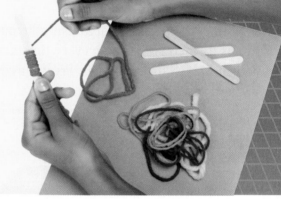

Cell division is involved in growth, development, and repair.

COMBINATION NOTES
Remember to take notes and draw sketches to help you understand the main idea: *Cell division is involved in growth, development, and repair.* Be sure to include the red heads in your notes.

Multicellular organisms vary greatly in size and complexity. You may not think that you have much in common with an ant or an oak tree. Actually, you share many characteristics with these organisms. One of the most important characteristic is that both you and they are made of trillions of cells. But, like most organisms, you and they started out as single cells. In multicellular organisms, cell division is essential for three major functions: growth, development, and repair.

Through cell division, a single cell becomes two cells. Those two cells divide into four, and the four cells divide into eight, and so on. A multicellular organism grows because cell division increases the number of cells in it. As the organism develops and its cells divide, many of the cells become specialized, and most of them continue to divide.

Even when growth and development appear to stop, cell division is still occurring. When an organism ages or is injured, the worn-out or damaged cells need to be replaced by new cells formed when healthy cells divide. For example, the cells that make up the lining of your throat have a short life span—two to three days. Living throat cells are constantly dividing and replacing the cells that have died.

Growth

In general, a large organism does not have larger cells than a small organism; it simply has many more cells than the small organism. When you were small, your body contained fewer cells than it has now. By the time you reach adulthood, your body will be made up of about 100 trillion cells.

Individual cells grow in size, but there are limits to the size that cells can reach. As you learned in Chapter 2, cells need a high ratio of surface area to volume in order to function. As a cell grows, that ratio decreases. When the cell divides into two smaller cells, the ratio of surface area to volume for each cell increases.

Another limit on cell growth is related to the amount of information a cell needs from its DNA. As the cell grows, more processes are needed for it to function, so its demand for instructions from DNA increases. However, the amount of DNA in the cell remains constant.

 CHECK YOUR READING — Describe how the number of cells in a multicellular organism changes as the organism grows?

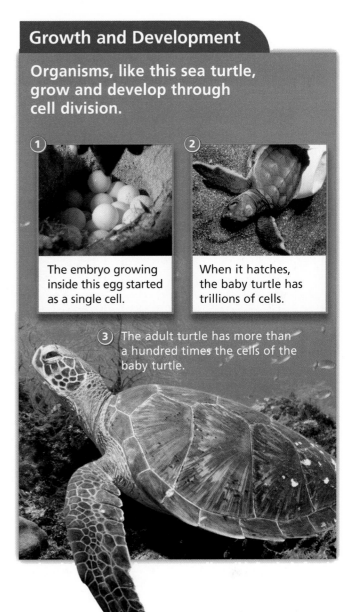

Growth and Development

Organisms, like this sea turtle, grow and develop through cell division.

① The embryo growing inside this egg started as a single cell.

② When it hatches, the baby turtle has trillions of cells.

③ The adult turtle has more than a hundred times the cells of the baby turtle.

Development

Although multicellular organisms begin as single cells, they grow into larger organisms through cell division. However, cell division alone does not allow organisms to develop. If cell division were the only process occurring in cells, all multicellular organisms would end up as spheres of identical cells. But during development, cells become specialized to perform particular functions.

These cells may take on shapes or structures that help them to perform their functions. Some cells might become layered skin cells, while others might become long, thin nerve cells. These cells still have the same set of genetic material as all the other cells in an organism's body, but as the organism develops they specialize.

 CHECK YOUR READING — Give two examples of specialized cells from the paragraph above.

READING TiP

Connect what you have read about growth and development with the series of sea turtle photographs above.

Repair

You may have cut yourself at one time or another. Perhaps you have even broken a bone in your arm or leg. The body repairs injuries like these by means of cell division. For example, when your skin is cut, skin cells on either side of the cut make new cells to heal the wound. You can see the process of healing in the diagram below.

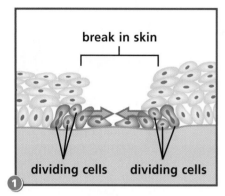

break in skin

dividing cells   dividing cells

① Cells in the lower layer begin to divide quickly and move into the break.

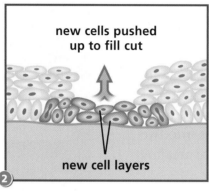

new cells pushed up to fill cut

new cell layers

② New cells begin to fill the area as cells continue to divide.

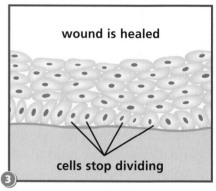

wound is healed

cells stop dividing

③ Cells stop their rapid dividing once the break is filled.

As cells age and die, they need to be replaced. In the human body—which is made up of about 200 different types of cells—cells are replaced at different rates. Your skin cells wear out quickly, so they need to be replaced often. Every minute or so, your skin loses about 40,000 cells, which are replaced with new ones. In contrast, most of the cells in your brain live a long time and do not divide very often.

 CHECK YOUR READING   What role does cell division play in healing the body?

3.1 Review

KEY CONCEPTS

1. Why is cell division important?
2. How is genetic material organized in eukaryotic cells?
3. Explain how cell division is involved in the growth, development, and repair of an organism.

CRITICAL THINKING

4. **Summarize** Explain how DNA changes form before a eukaryotic cell divides.
5. **Infer** Why do you think that injuries to the skin generally heal faster than injuries to the brain?

⬥ CHALLENGE

6. **Apply** Describe the stages of development in a multicellular organism that is familiar to you.

Chemical Dyes Show Nerve Growth

For years, the medical community has agreed that nerve tissue, once damaged, does not repair itself. In fact, the opinion was that new nerve cells didn't grow in adults at all. However, a surprising discovery has shown that new nerve cells do grow in the mature brains of both monkeys and people!

Elizabeth Gould noticed that new nerve cells can grow in adult brains

The Discovery

The discovery involves a chemical known as bromodeoxyuridine (BrdU), which can be used to detect new cancer cells.

1. BrdU highlights the DNA of cells that are reproducing, such as cancer cells.

2. BrdU also makes it possible to count the new cells that are being created, because they stand out as well.

3. The cells that have been highlighted with BrdU can be seen under a microscope when they are illuminated with a special light.

When scientists used this technique to examine certain areas in the brains of monkeys and of adult humans who had died of cancer, they found that new nerve cells had grown in the brains of each. Thus, the chemical properties of BrdU allowed scientists to discover new nerve cells growing in places where scientists had previously never expected to see them.

Hope for the Future

If new nerve cells grow in these tissues, it may be possible to stimulate growth in damaged nerve tissue such as that in the spinal cord. If researchers discover how new growth in nerve cells is stimulated, there may be new hope for people who have nervous systems damaged by accidents or by diseases such as Parkinson's disease.

ON YOUR ON

1. **SYNTHESIZE** How could you use chemicals, such as small dots with a pen, in an experiment to show how your fingernails grow?

2. **CHALLENGE** What are some possible effects of being able to grow new nerve cells?

RESOURCE CENTER
CLASSZONE.COM

Find out more about new nerve cell growth.

3.2 Cell division is part of the cell cycle.

BEFORE, you learned

- Cells come from other cells through cell division
- A cell must have a full set of genetic material to function
- Cell division enables multicellular organisms to develop, grow, and repair themselves

NOW, you will learn

- About two main stages in the cell cycle
- About the changes that occur in cells before mitosis
- About the events that take place during mitosis

VOCABULARY

cell cycle p. 80
interphase p. 81
mitosis p. 81
cytokinesis p. 81

THINK ABOUT

What is a cycle?

Many things in your everyday life are cycles. A cycle is any activity or set of events that regularly repeats. Cycles can be short, like the sequence of events that make your heart beat, or they can be very long, like the turning of our galaxy. One example of a cycle is shown at the right. The photographs show a tree during four seasons in a northern climate. How are these seasons a cycle?

The cell cycle includes interphase and cell division.

All living things live, grow, reproduce, and die in a process called a life cycle. The life cycle of a tree, for example, begins with a seed. Under the right conditions, the seed begins to grow. It produces a very small plant, which may grow over many years into a towering tree. When it is mature, the tree makes its own seeds, and the cycle begins again.

Cells have a life cycle too, called the cell cycle. The **cell cycle** is the normal sequence of development and division of a cell. The cell cycle consists of two main phases: one in which the cell carries out its functions, called interphase, and one in which the cell divides, which can include mitosis and cytokinesis. All cells divide, but only eukaryotes undergo mitosis. Each phase in the cell cycle requires a certain period of time—from hours to days or years, depending on the type of cell.

RESOURCE CENTER
CLASSZONE.COM

Learn about the cell cycle.

Interphase

Interphase is the part of the cell cycle during which a cell is not dividing. Much activity takes place in this phase of the cell's life. During interphase, the cell grows to about twice the size it was when it was first produced. The cell also engages in normal life activities, such as transporting materials in and transporting wastes out. Also, cellular respiration occurs, which provides the energy the cell needs.

Changes that occur during interphase prepare a cell for division. Before a cell can divide, it duplicates its DNA exactly. Correct copying of the DNA is very important. It ensures that, after cell division, each new cell gets a complete set of DNA. During most of interphase, the DNA is in chromatin form.

CHECK YOUR READING What cell processes occur during interphase?

VOCABULARY
Make a frame game diagram for *interphase*.

Cell Division Phase

Mitosis is the part of the cell cycle during which the nucleus divides. Prokaryotes do not undergo mitosis because they have only one chromosome and no nucleus. In most cells, mitosis is the shortest period in the life cycle. The function of mitosis is to move the DNA and other material in the parent cell into position for cell division. When the cell divides, each new cell gets a full set of DNA and other cell structures. **Cytokinesis** (sy-toh-kuh-NEE-sihs) is the division of the parent cell's cytoplasm. Cytokinesis occurs immediately after mitosis.

Cell Cycle

The events that happen during the life of a cell are called the cell cycle.

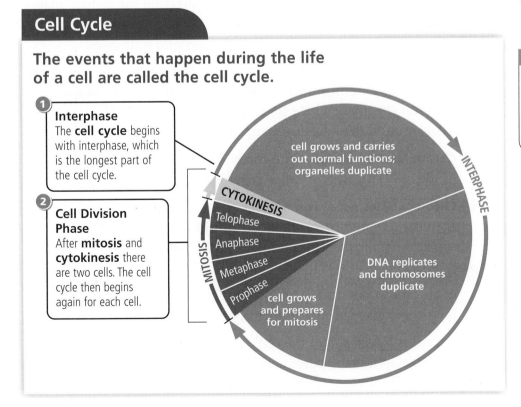

1 Interphase
The **cell cycle** begins with interphase, which is the longest part of the cell cycle.

2 Cell Division Phase
After **mitosis** and **cytokinesis** there are two cells. The cell cycle then begins again for each cell.

cell grows and carries out normal functions; organelles duplicate

CYTOKINESIS
Telophase
Anaphase
Metaphase
Prophase

INTERPHASE

MITOSIS

DNA replicates and chromosomes duplicate

cell grows and prepares for mitosis

READING TiP
The arrows in the Cell Cycle diagram represent the passage of time. Interphase is in red, mitosis is in purple, and cytokinesis is in yellow.

As a result of mitosis and cytokinesis, the original—or parent—cell splits into two genetically identical daughter cells. In this case, the term *daughter cell* does not imply gender. It is a term scientists use to refer to these new cells. Each daughter cell comes from half of the parent cell. Each daughter cell also receives a complete set of DNA from the parent cell.

Cell division produces two genetically identical cells.

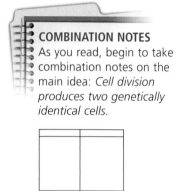
Recall that many cells in your body are continually dividing into new cells. The new cells help your body grow, develop, repair itself, and replace worn-out parts. Though your body cells divide at different rates, the same process—mitosis—divides their genetic material.

Cell division produces daughter cells that are genetically identical to each other, as well as to their parent cell, which no longer exists. Being genetically identical to their parent cell helps the new cells function properly. A skin cell, for example, divides and produces skin cells genetically identical to it. The new skin cells will function in exactly the same way as the parent.

 CHECK YOUR READING   How are daughter cells like the parent cell?

Steps of Mitosis

The process of mitosis is essential in evenly dividing the genetic material between the daughter cells. Although mitosis is a continuous process, scientists divide the events of mitosis into four phases.

1 **Chromosomes form.** During prophase, the DNA in the nucleus of a cell forms chromosomes. Each chromosome consists of two identical chromatids held together by a centromere. The membrane around the nucleus disappears.

2 **Chromosomes line up.** The chromosomes line up in the middle of the cell. This stage is called metaphase.

3 **Chromosomes separate.** During the stage called anaphase, the chromatids split up, forming two chromosomes. The chromosomes are pulled to opposite sides of the cell.

4 **Nuclei form.** A new nuclear membrane forms around each group of chromosomes during telophase. The chromosomes return to their threadlike chromatin form.

Mitosis is finished, and the cell's genetic material has been divided. Following telophase the parent cell's cytoplasm is divided to complete the parent cell's division into two entirely separate daughter cells.

Cell Division

Before mitosis, the cell's DNA is copied during interphase.

Interphase

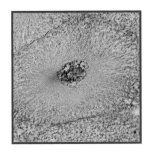

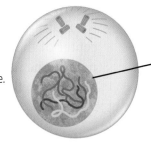

The cell has grown and is ready to divide.

The nucleus contains two complete copies of DNA.

Mitosis produces two new cells with identical copies of DNA.

1 Chromosomes form.
Prophase

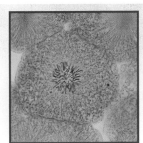

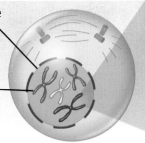

The nuclear membrane disappears.

Long strands of DNA condense to distinct chromosomes, each with two chromatids that are exact copies of each other.

Chromosome

chromatids

centromere

2 Chromosomes line up.
Metaphase

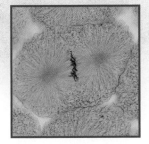

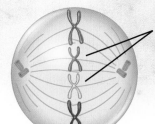

Chromosomes line up in the middle of the cell.

3 Chromosomes separate.
Anaphase

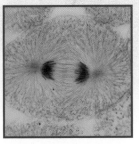

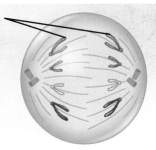

Each chromosome splits into two chromatids.

Chromatids pull to the opposite ends of the cell.

4 Nuclei form.
Telophase, Cytokinesis

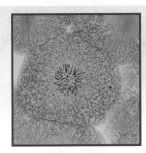

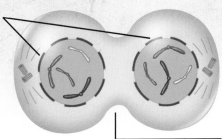

New nuclear membranes form.

Cell pinches and divides

Division of the Cytoplasm

READING TiP

As you read about cytokinesis refer to the images of plant and animal cells on page 85.

Cytokinesis, or the division of the parent cell's cytoplasm, immediately follows mitosis in eukaryotic cells. Cytokinesis differs slightly in animal cells and plant cells.

During cytokinesis in an animal cell, a fiber ring forms in the center of the dividing cell. The fiber ring contracts, pulling the cell membrane inward. Eventually, the cell is pinched into two daughter cells.

In a plant cell, the cell wall prevents the cell membrane from being pulled inward. A structure called a cell plate grows between the two new nuclei. The cell plate develops into a membrane and eventually becomes part of the cell wall of each of the new cells.

CHECK YOUR READING How does cytokinesis differ in plant cells and animal cells?

INVESTIGATE Cell Division

How can you model mitosis?

PROCEDURE

1. Divide the poster board into six spaces, and draw arrows from one space to the next to indicate a cycle. Label the spaces, in order, "Interphase," "Prophase," "Metaphase," "Anaphase," "Telophase," and "Cytokinesis."

2. In each space, make a model of a cell and its DNA in the indicated phase. Make sure you represent the cell membrane, the nuclear membrane—when it is present—and the DNA.

WHAT DO YOU THINK?

- In which phases is the nuclear membrane present?
- In which phases is the DNA present as chromosomes?
- What do the arrows in your model show?

CHALLENGE How do you think cell division would differ in prokaryotic cells? Do you think cell division in prokaryotic cells would be more or less complex than in eukaryotic cells? Make drawings to show how you think a prokaryotic cell might divide.

SKILL FOCUS
Making models

MATERIALS
- poster board
- markers
- pipe cleaners
- packing peanuts
- glue
- scissors
- yarn

TIME
30 minutes

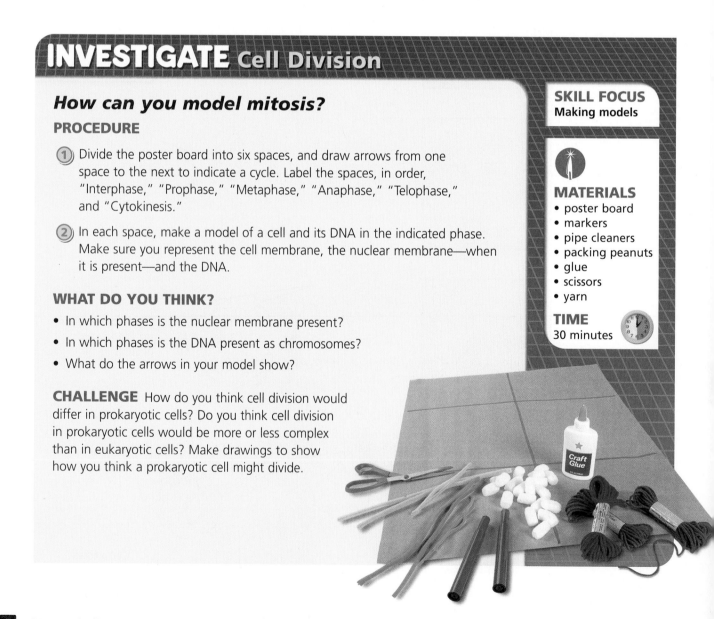

Cytokinesis happens in both plant and animal cells.

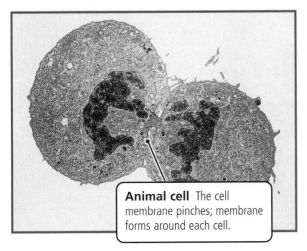

Animal cell The cell membrane pinches; membrane forms around each cell.

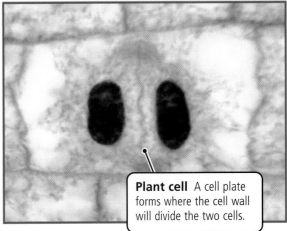

Plant cell A cell plate forms where the cell wall will divide the two cells.

 READING VISUALS COMPARE AND CONTRAST How does the process of cytokinesis in the animal cell on the left differ from that of the plant cell on the right?

The two daughter cells are now completely separated. Each is surrounded by a cell membrane. Each daughter cell has about half of its parent cell's cytoplasm. Though daughter cells are identical to their parent cell, they are smaller. After division, cells enter a period of growth, during which they take in the resources they need to increase the amount of their cytoplasm and to grow to full size. When cells are fully grown, they are about the same size as the parent cell was before division.

CHECK YOUR READING What happens to cells after cytokinesis?

3.2 Review

KEY CONCEPTS

1. What are the two main parts of the cell cycle?

2. Describe the state of a cell about to start mitosis.

3. How is the genetic material in two daughter cells similar to the genetic material in a parent cell?

CRITICAL THINKING

4. **Sequence** Describe in order the steps that occur during mitosis.

5. **Compare and Contrast** How is cytokinesis in plant cells similar to cytokinesis in animal cells? How is it different?

CHALLENGE

6. **Infer** You know that mitosis does not happen in prokaryotes. Do you think cytokinesis happens in prokaryotes? Explain your answer.

CHAPTER INVESTIGATION

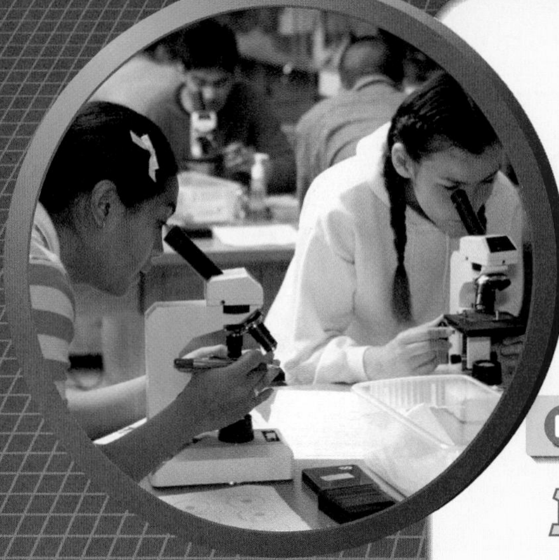

Stages of the Cell Cycle

OVERVIEW AND PURPOSE In this activity you will observe cells from an onion root tip that are undergoing mitosis. You will identify and draw cells in different stages of mitosis and the cell cycle. Then you will count the number of cells in each stage. Remember to record this information in your **Science Notebook.**

▶ Procedure

1. Make a data table like the one shown on the sample notebook page.

2. Obtain a prepared slide of an onion root tip. Place the slide on the microscope stage. Using the low-power objective, adjust the focus until the root tip is clear.

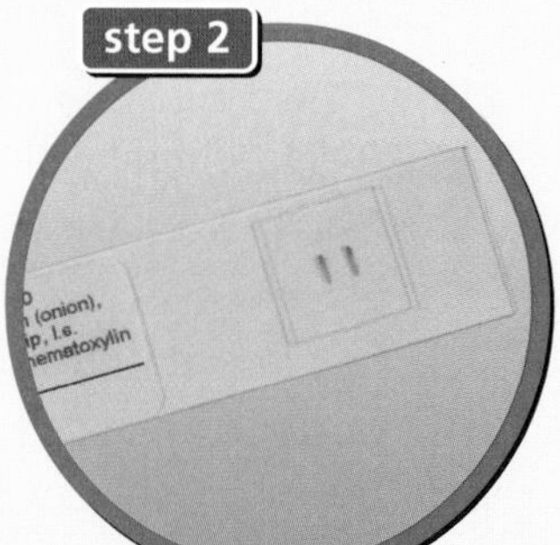

step 2

3. Move the slide until you are looking at the region just above the root tip. The cells in this area were in the process of mitosis when the slide was made.

4. Look at the boxlike cells arranged in rows. The DNA in these cells has been stained to make it more visible. Select a cell in interphase. Switch to high power and sketch this cell in your notebook.

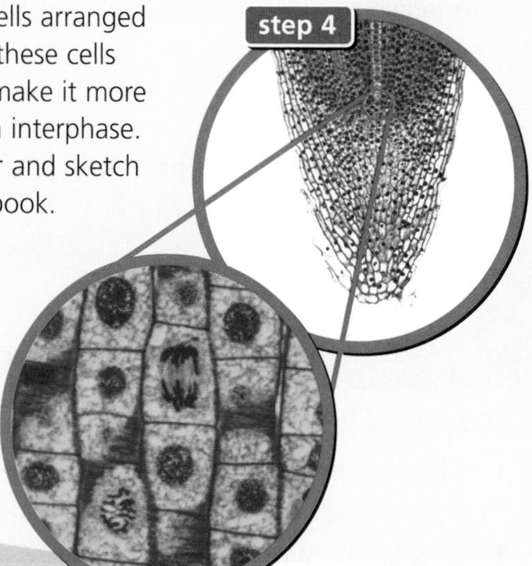

step 4

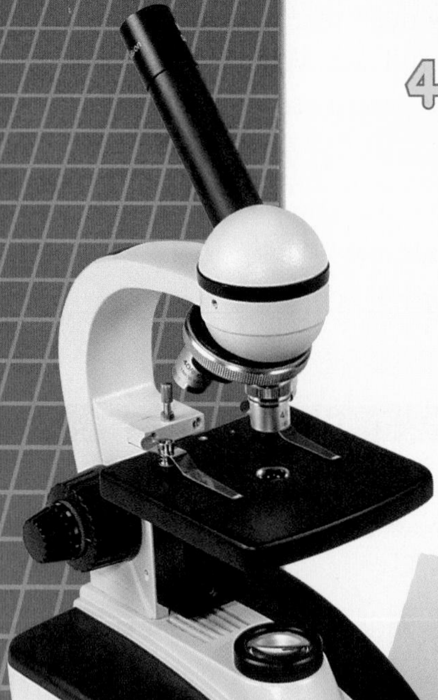

MATERIALS
- prepared slides of onion root tip cells
- light microscope

5 Repeat step 3 for cells in the various stages of mitosis: prophase, metaphase, anaphase, and telophase. Refer to the diagram on page 83 to identify cells in each stage.

6 Arrange your sketches to represent the order of the process of mitosis.

7 Under low-power magnification, choose 25 cells at random. Decide which stage of the cell cycle each cell is in. Record the number of cells in each stage in your data table.

▶ Observe and Analyze

Write It Up

1. OBSERVE Look at your sketches of the stages of mitosis. Describe the events in each stage.

2. ANALYZING DATA Was there any one stage of the cell cycle that was occurring in the majority of cells you observed? If so, which was it?

▶ Conclude

Write It Up

1. INFER What might the differences in the number of cells in each stage of the cell cycle mean?

2. IDENTIFY LIMITS Were there any cells that were difficult to classify as being in one particular phase of the cell cycle? What do these cells suggest to you about the process of mitosis?

3. APPLY Where does new root growth take place? Explain your answer.

▶ INVESTIGATE Further

CHALLENGE From your data table, calculate the percent of cells in each stage of the cell cycle. Use those numbers to predict how much time a cell spends in each stage. You can base your calculation on a total cell cycle of 24 hours.

Stages of the Cell Cycle

Table 1. Number of Cells in Each Stage of the Cell Cycle

Stage	Number of Cells Observed
Interphase	
Prophase	
Metaphase	
Anaphase	
Telophase	

KEY CONCEPT

Both sexual and asexual reproduction involve cell division.

 BEFORE, you learned

- Cells go through a cycle of growth and division
- Mitosis produces two genetically identical cells

NOW, you will learn

- About cell division and asexual reproduction
- How sexual reproduction and asexual reproduction compare

VOCABULARY

asexual reproduction
p. 88
binary fission p. 89
regeneration p. 90

THINK ABOUT

How does cell division affect single-celled organisms?

In multicellular organisms, cell division functions in growth, repair, and development. But in unicellular organisms, each cell is itself an organism. Unicellular organisms, like this paramecium, also undergo cell division. What are some possible results of cell division in unicellular organisms? How might they compare with the results of cell division in multicellular organisms?

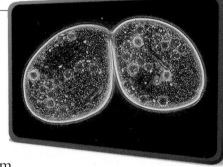

Asexual reproduction involves one parent.

COMBINATION NOTES
Begin taking notes on the main idea: *Asexual reproduction involves one parent.* Be sure to include sketches of each method of reproducing.

Mitosis and cytokinesis are the processes by which cells divide. In multicellular organisms, the daughter cells that arise from these processes are separate cells but do not live independent lives. For example, new skin cells are part of skin tissue and cannot live independently. In multicellular organisms, mitosis and cytokinesis are not considered methods by which an organism reproduces.

Most unicellular organisms, and a few multicellular organisms, use cell division to reproduce, in a process called asexual reproduction. In **asexual reproduction,** one organism produces one or more new organisms that are identical to itself and that live independently of it. The organism that produces the new organism or organisms is the parent. Each new organism is an offspring. The offspring produced by asexual reproduction are genetically identical to their parents.

Cell Division in Unicellular Organisms

Cell division and reproduction are the same thing in all single-celled organisms. However, the process of cell division in prokaryotes and in single-celled eukaryotes differs.

Binary fission is the form of asexual reproduction occurring in prokaryotes. Binary fission occurs when the parent organism splits in two, producing two completely independent daughter cells. Genetically, the daughter cells are exactly like the parent cell. Since all prokaryotic organisms are single-celled, cell division and reproduction by binary fission are the same process for them.

In single-celled eukaryotic organisms, however, reproduction by cell division involves mitosis and cytokinesis. The unicellular organism undergoes mitosis, duplicating and separating its chromosomes. Then its cytoplasm is divided through cytokinesis. The result is two separate, independent, and genetically identical offspring. Examples of single-celled eukaryotic organisms that reproduce by cell division include algae, some yeasts, and protozoans, such as paramecium.

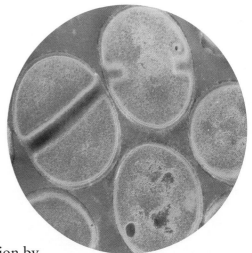

Binary fission results in two nearly equal, independent cells, as shown in these bacteria.

Budding

Both unicellular and multicellular organisms can reproduce by budding. Budding is a process in which an organism develops tiny buds on its body. Each bud forms from the parents' cells, so the bud's genetic material is the same as the parents'. The bud grows until it forms a complete or nearly complete new organism that is genetically identical to the parent.

In some budding organisms, buds can form from any part of the body. In other organisms, buds can be produced only by specialized cells in particular parts of the body. A new organism produced by budding may remain attached to its parent. Most often, when a bud reaches a certain size, it breaks free of the parent and becomes a separate, independent organism.

Some yeast and single-celled organisms reproduce asexually by budding. But budding is most notable in multicellular organisms. Hydras are freshwater animals that are famous for reproducing by budding. Among plants, the kalanchoe (KAL-uhn-KOH-ee) produces tiny buds from the tips of its leaves. Each kalanchoe bud that lands on a suitable growing surface will develop into a mature kalanchoe plant that is genetically identical to the parent plant.

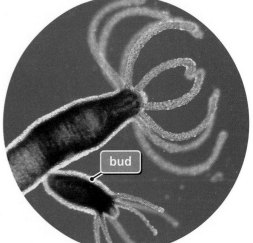

Budding Hydras reproduce by pinching off small buds.

CHECK YOUR READING How is budding different in unicellular and multicellular organisms?

Regeneration

In certain multicellular organisms, specialized cells at the site of a wound or lost limb are able to become different types of tissues. The process of new tissue growth at these sites is called **regeneration.**

Regeneration
This starfish is regenerating its legs that were lost.

Although one function of regeneration is the regrowth of damaged or missing body parts, in some organisms asexual reproduction is another function of regeneration.

Regeneration can be observed in many animals called starfish. If a starfish is cut in half, each half can regenerate its missing body parts from its own cells. The result is two complete, independent, and genetically identical starfish. Sometimes a starfish will drop off one of its limbs. The animal will eventually form a new limb. In these cases, regeneration is considered a form of asexual reproduction.

The growth of plants from cuttings is also a kind of asexual reproduction through regeneration. Cells near a cut made in a plant's stem begin to produce the missing part of the plant. Once the missing part is grown, the cutting can be planted in soil. The cutting will grow into a new, independent plant that is genetically identical to the plant from which the cutting was taken.

 CHECK YOUR READING Describe the process of regeneration in starfish.

Asexual Reproduction and Health.

RESOURCE CENTER
CLASSZONE.COM

Learn more about asexual reproduction.

You have probably had the following experience. In the morning you feel fine. By afternoon, you have a strange feeling that something is not quite right, but you are well enough to function normally. You may even continue to feel well at dinner, and you eat heartily. Then, later that evening, it hits you. You're sick. That tickle in your throat has become a sore throat requiring a visit to the doctor and antibiotics. How did you get so sick so fast?

You could have picked up bacteria in school that morning. Perhaps another student coughed, spreading the bacteria that causes strep throat. A population of bacteria, like populations of other organisms that reproduce asexually through binary fission, increases in number geometrically. Two cells become 4, which become 8, which become 16, and so on.

The reason you get sick so fast is that for many bacteria the generation time is very short. Generation time is the time it takes for one generation to produce offspring—the next generation. In fact, some types of bacteria can produce a new generation of cells in less than 30 minutes. In about an hour the number of bacteria can increase to four times the starting number.

Asexual reproduction
These bacteria are quickly multiplying through asexual reproduction.

Although all offspring are genetically identical, the rare genetic random change does occasionally occur during cell division. The rapid reproduction rate makes it more likely that some offspring will have a random genetic change that may be beneficial.

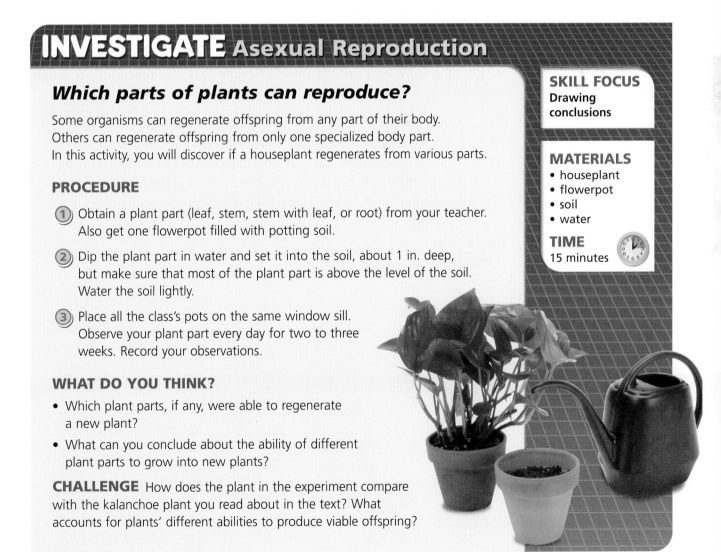

INVESTIGATE Asexual Reproduction

Which parts of plants can reproduce?

Some organisms can regenerate offspring from any part of their body. Others can regenerate offspring from only one specialized body part. In this activity, you will discover if a houseplant regenerates from various parts.

PROCEDURE

1. Obtain a plant part (leaf, stem, stem with leaf, or root) from your teacher. Also get one flowerpot filled with potting soil.

2. Dip the plant part in water and set it into the soil, about 1 in. deep, but make sure that most of the plant part is above the level of the soil. Water the soil lightly.

3. Place all the class's pots on the same window sill. Observe your plant part every day for two to three weeks. Record your observations.

WHAT DO YOU THINK?

- Which plant parts, if any, were able to regenerate a new plant?
- What can you conclude about the ability of different plant parts to grow into new plants?

CHALLENGE How does the plant in the experiment compare with the kalanchoe plant you read about in the text? What accounts for plants' different abilities to produce viable offspring?

SKILL FOCUS
Drawing conclusions

MATERIALS
- houseplant
- flowerpot
- soil
- water

TIME
15 minutes

Sexual reproduction involves two parent organisms.

Reproduction of multicellular organisms often involves sexual reproduction as well as asexual cell division. The table shows some differences between asexual and sexual reproduction.

Comparing Asexual and Sexual Reproduction	
Asexual Reproduction	**Sexual Reproduction**
Cell Division	Cell division and other processes
One parent organism	Two parent organisms
Rate of reproduction is rapid	Rate of reproduction is slower than rate for asexual reproduction
Offspring identical to parents	Offspring have genetic information from two parents

If you grow a plant from a cutting, the new plant will be identical to the parent. However, plants that grow from seeds contain genetic material from two parents. Plants growing from seeds and animals growing from eggs are examples of organisms that reproduce through sexual reproduction.

Cell division is part of both sexual and asexual reproduction. The process of mitosis produces cells identical to the parent cells. The diversity of life on Earth is possible because of the combining of genetic materials from two parents in sexual reproduction. In the next chapter, you will read about cell processes involved in sexual reproduction.

 CHECK YOUR READING List two major differences between asexual and sexual reproduction.

3.3 Review

KEY CONCEPTS

1. How does binary fission relate to cell division?

2. What is a bud, and where does it form on an organism that reproduces asexually?

3. Compare sexual and asexual reproduction.

CRITICAL THINKING

4. **Predict** Do you think prokaryotes undergo regeneration? Why or why not?

5. **Compare and Contrast** How is the process of binary fission similar and different in prokaryotic and eukaryotic organisms?

⚠ CHALLENGE

6. **Synthesize** Some bacteria can exchange genetic material with one another through a process called conjugation. How do you think offspring produced during conjugation would compare with offspring produced in cell division?

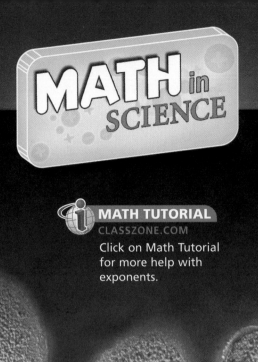

MATH in SCIENCE

MATH TUTORIAL
CLASSZONE.COM
Click on Math Tutorial for more help with exponents.

Divide and Multiply

Each time a parent cell divides, the result is two new cells. The new cells are a new generation that in turn divides again. The increase in the number of cells can be shown using exponents. Each cell of each new generation produces two cells. This type of increase in the number of objects is often called exponential growth.

Example

What is the numerical sequence when cells divide to form new cells? You can model this type of progression by using a plain piece of paper.

(1) To represent the first division, fold the piece of paper in half.

(2) Fold it in half again, and it will show the second division. Fold it again and again to represent succeeding divisions.

(3) Write the sequence that shows the number of boxes on the paper after each fold.

2, 4, 8, 16, . . .

(4) Notice that after one division (fold), there are 2 cells (boxes), or 2^1. Two divisions yield 2 • 2 cells, or 2^2. And after three divisions, there are 2 • 2 • 2 cells, or 2^3.

ANSWER The sequence can be written with exponents:
$2^1, 2^2, 2^3, 2^4, . . .$

Answer the following questions.

1. Suppose the cells divide for one more generation after the 4 described above. How can this be written as an exponent of 2? How many cells will there be?

2. How many cells would exist in the tenth generation? Write the number using an exponent.

3. Suppose you took the paper in the example and folded it in thirds each time, rather than in half. Make a table showing the number of boxes after each folding. Use numbers with exponents to write the sequence.

4. Write the following number sequence as a sequence of numbers with exponents: 5, 25, 125, 625, . . .

5. Write the following number sequence as a sequence of numbers with NO exponents: $10^1, 10^2, 10^3, 10^4, . . .$

CHALLENGE Before you begin folding, you have a single sheet of paper, or 1 box. The parent cell is also a single unit. Use this information to explain why $2^0 = 3^0$.

Chapter Review

the **BIG** idea

Organisms grow, reproduce, and maintain themselves through cell division.

CONTENT REVIEW
CLASSZONE.COM

KEY CONCEPTS SUMMARY

3.1 **Cell division occurs in all organisms.**

- In unicellular organisms functions of cell division include reproduction
- In multicellular organisms functions of cell division include growth, development, and repair.

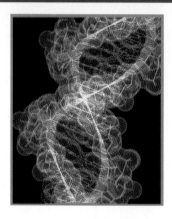

VOCABULARY
DNA p. 74
chromosome p. 75

3.2 **Cell division is part of a cell cycle.**

The **cell cycle** has two main phases, **interphase** and **mitosis.** Most of the life cycle of a cell is spent in interphase. During mitosis, cells divide.

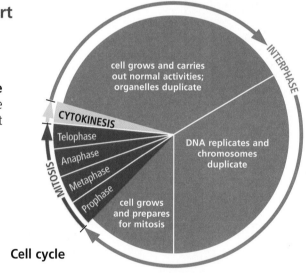

cell grows and carries out normal activities; organelles duplicate

INTERPHASE

CYTOKINESIS
Telophase
Anaphase
Metaphase
Prophase
MITOSIS

DNA replicates and chromosomes duplicate

cell grows and prepares for mitosis

Cell cycle

VOCABULARY
cell cycle p. 80
interphase p. 81
mitosis p. 81
cytokinesis p. 81

3.3 **Both sexual and asexual reproduction involve cell division.**

Some organisms reproduce asexually. Both asexual and sexual reproduction involve cell division.

Comparing Asexual and Sexual Reproduction	
Asexual Reproduction	**Sexual Reproduction**
Cell Division	Cell division and other processes
One parent organism	Two parent organisms
Rate of reproduction is rapid	Rate of reproduction is slower than rate for asexual reproduction
Offspring identical to parents	Offspring have genetic information from two parents

VOCABULARY
asexual reproduction p. 88
binary fission p. 89
regeneration p. 90

On a separate sheet of paper, write a sentence describing the relationship between the two vocabulary words in each pair.

1. cell cycle, interphase

2. mitosis, cytokinesis

3. chromosome, DNA

4. parent, offspring

Reviewing Key Concepts

Multiple Choice *Choose the letter of the best answer.*

5. Most of the growth in your body occurs because your cells

   a. grow larger   **c.** make proteins

   b. take in oxygen   **d.** divide

6. The stage in a cell's life when it is not in the process of dividing is called

   a. interphase   **c.** mitosis

   b. the cell cycle   **d.** cell division

7. What material in the cell makes up DNA?

   a. carbohydrates   **c.** the nucleus

   b. chromatids   **d.** nucleic acid

8. What increases when a cell divides into two smaller cells?

   a. volume   **c.** surface area

   b. length   **d.** width

9. The process of mitosis results in

   a. two daughter cells that are different from one another

   b. two genetically identical daughter cells

   c. identical pairs of chromosomes

   d. identical pairs of chromatids

10. What is the step that follows mitosis, in which the cytoplasm divides?

   a. prophase   **c.** anaphase

   b. synthesis   **d.** cytokinesis

11. A cell's chromosomes must be duplicated before mitosis occurs so that

   a. they can form chromatids

   b. they can attach to the spindle

   c. each daughter cell gets a full number of chromosomes

   d. each daughter cell does not have to duplicate its own chromosomes

12. Binary fission differs from mitosis because the new cells

   a. cannot function without the parent

   b. grow from missing limbs

   c. have half the normal number of chromosomes

   d. live independently of the parent cell

13. If a starfish is cut in half, it can regenerate its missing body through

   a. binary fission   **c.** healing

   b. budding   **d.** regeneration

14. Which is an example of reproduction?

   a. binary fission in unicellular organisms

   b. cell division in a multicellular organism

   c. cell division around a broken bone

   d. division of cytoplasm

15. Which sequence is correct for mitosis?

   a. chromosomes form, chromosomes separate, chromosomes line up, nuclei form

   b. chromosomes form, chromosomes line up, chromosomes separate, nuclei form

   c. chromosomes line up, nuclei form, chromosomes separate, chromosomes form

   d. chromosomes separate, chromosomes form, nuclei form, chromosomes line up

Short Answer *Write a short answer to each question.*

16. What is the difference between mitosis in plant and animal cells?

17. Describe what happens in a cell during interphase. Your answer should mention DNA.

18. Describe the functions of cell division in both unicellular and multicellular organisms.

Thinking Critically

19. IDENTIFY CAUSE Describe some of the reasons that cells reproduce.

This illustration shows a plant and the cutting that was taken from it, which is growing in a container of water. Use the illustration to answer the next six questions.

20. OBSERVE From which part of the plant was the cutting taken?

21. INFER Where did the cutting get the genetic information that controls its development?

22. INFER What is the genetic relationship between the original plant and the cutting?

23. SYNTHESIZE What process causes both the cutting and the original plant to grow?

24. SUMMARIZE Write a brief summary of the process that causes growth in both plants.

25. PREDICT These plants also reproduce when seeds form when a different plant fertilizes them. How is the cutting the same as the plant that would grow from a seed? How is the cutting different?

26. CALCULATE A single bacterium enters your body at 10:00 A.M. These type of bacteria reproduce at a rate of one generation every 30 minutes. How many bacteria will be in your body by 8:00 P.M. that evening?

The diagrams below show 4 parts of a process. Use them to answer the following two questions.

a.

c.

b.

d.

27. SEQUENCE What is the correct order of the four diagrams above?

28. SYNTHESIZE Draw two diagrams, one showing what you would see before the process shown above begins, and one showing what you would see after the conclusion of the process.

29. MODEL On a separate sheet of paper, draw your own simple model of the process of mitosis.

the BIG idea

30. SUMMARIZE Look again at the question on the photograph on pages 132–133. Now that you have studied this chapter, how would you change your answer to the question?

31. SYNTHESIZE How do the concepts in this chapter relate to the concepts in the cell theory?

UNIT PROJECTS

If you need to do an experiment for your unit project, gather the materials. Be sure to allow enough time to observe results before the project is due.

Analyzing Data

This diagram shows the length of the cell cycle for a typical skin cell
in the human body.

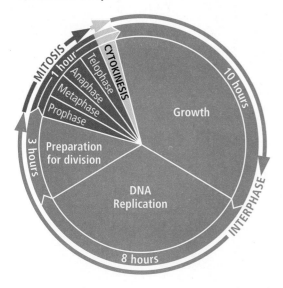

Use the diagram to answer the questions below.

1. How long does the growth phase of the cell cycle take?

a. 1 hour   c. 8 hours

b. 3 hours   d. 10 hours

2. How much time does the cell cycle spend in interphase?

a. 1 hour   c. 21 hours

b. 10 hours   d. 22 hours

3. What is the total length of time it takes for the skin cell to complete one full cell cycle?

a. 10 hours   c. 21 hours

b. 18 hours   d. 22 hours

4. What phase of the cell cycle takes about 8 hours?

a. DNA replication

b. mitosis

c. growth

d. preparation for cell division

5. Suppose another type of skin cell takes 44 hours to complete one cell cycle. If all of the phases are proportional to the length of time shown in the diagram, how long will the preparation for cell division phase last?

a. 3 hours   c. 10 hours

b. 6 hours   d. 20 hours

6. According to the diagram, what is the second stage in mitosis?

a. prophase   c. telophase

b. metaphase   d. cytokinesis

Extended Response

Answer the two questions. Include some of the terms shown in the word box. Underline each term you use in your answers.

cell cycle	metaphase	mitosis
anaphase	prophase	telophase

7. A scientist is studying the stages of cell division in the cells of an onion root. The scientist counts 100 cells and identifies which stage of cell division each cell is in at a given moment. He counts a total of 85 cells in interphase, 8 cells in prophase, 3 cells in metaphase, and 2 cells each in anaphase and telophase. A typical onion cell takes about 12 hours to complete the cell cycle. Using the information in the diagram and the data given here, how can you account for these numbers?

8. Your science class is investigating the effect of temperature on the rate of mitosis in onion plants. You hypothesize that the higher the temperature, the faster cells undergo mitosis. How could you set up an experiment to support your hypothesis? Describe the materials you would use and the steps you would take in your procedure.

Patterns of Heredity

the **BIG** idea

In sexual reproduction, genes are passed from parents to offspring in predictable patterns.

Key Concepts

SECTION
4.1 **Living things inherit traits in patterns.**
Learn about traits and how living things inherit traits from their parents.

SECTION
4.2 **Patterns of heredity can be predicted.**
Learn how math can be used to predict patterns of heredity.

SECTION
4.3 **Meiosis is a special form of cell division.**
Learn about the process of meiosis.

 Internet Preview

CLASSZONE.COM

Chapter 4 online resources: Content Review, two Simulations, two Resource Centers, Math Tutorial, Test Practice

> **What similarities can you see between this mother wolf and her two offspring?**

EXPLORE (the BIG idea)

How Are Traits Distributed?

Ask 10 people you know if they are left-handed or right-handed, if they have dimples, and if they can roll their tongue. For each trait, write down how many people have that trait.

Observe and Think Were any of the traits evenly distributed? Why do you think that is?

Combinations

Take one bag with 4 blue slips of paper and one bag with 4 red slips of paper. Consider different ways to mix or combine the materials in the bags.

Observe and Think How many ways could you think of mixing the materials? How were the combinations similar and different?

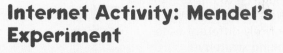

Internet Activity: Mendel's Experiment

Go to **ClassZone.com** to try a virtual version of Mendel's experiments with peas. Learn about heredity as you breed plants with different traits.

Observe and Think What does Mendel's experiment teach us about heredity?

NSTA scilinks.org *SCiLINKS*

Heredity **Code: MDL034**

Getting Ready to Learn

CONCEPT REVIEW

- Life comes from life.
- Mitosis produces identical cells.
- Some organisms reproduce with asexual reproduction.

VOCABULARY REVIEW

cell p. 11

chromosome p. 79

mitosis p. 86

asexual reproduction p. 92

parent, offspring p. 93

CONTENT REVIEW
CLASSZONE.COM
Review concepts and vocabulary.

TAKING NOTES

CHOOSE YOUR OWN STRATEGY

Take notes using one or more of the strategies from earlier chapters—**main idea webs, combination notes,** or **mind maps.** Feel free to mix and match the strategies, or use an entirely different note-taking strategy.

VOCABULARY STRATEGY

Think about a vocabulary term as a **magnet word** diagram. Write the other terms or ideas related to that term around it.

See the Note-Taking Handbook on pages R45–R51.

SCIENCE NOTEBOOK

Main Idea Web

Combination Notes

Mind Map

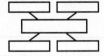

ALLELE

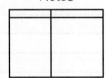

pairs of chromosomes

genes

traits

alternate forms of one gene

on a homolog

have 2 alleles of each gene

KEY CONCEPT

Living things inherit traits in patterns.

BEFORE, you learned

- Life comes from life
- Cells contain chromosomes
- Some organisms reproduce with asexual reproduction

NOW, you will learn

- How traits are passed from parent to offspring
- About discoveries made by Gregor Mendel
- About dominant and recessive traits

VOCABULARY

sexual reproduction
  p. 102
gene p. 102
heredity p. 102
allele p. 103
phenotype p. 106
genotype p. 106
dominant p. 107
recessive p. 107

THINK ABOUT

What characteristics might be inherited?

Make a list of characteristics you can observe about the girl in the photograph to the right. Perhaps your list includes the fact that she has pale skin, or that she can read. Some of these characteristics are qualities or abilities learned or acquired from the environment around her. However, some of the characteristics were probably inherited from her parents. Of the characteristics on your list, which do you think were inherited and which do you think were acquired?

NOTETAKING STRATEGY
Take notes on the idea that parents and offspring are similar by using a strategy from an earlier chapter or one of your own.

Parents and offspring are similar.

You are an individual who has a unique combination of characteristics. These characteristics are also known as traits. Many of your traits may resemble those your parents have, including your hair color, eye color, and blood type. These characteristics are called inherited traits.

Some traits are acquired, not inherited. An acquired trait is developed during your life. Learned behaviors are one type of acquired trait. For example, your ability to read and write is an acquired trait—a skill you learned. You were not born knowing how to ride a bike, and if you have children, they will not be born knowing how to do it either. They will have to learn the skill just as you did.

Some acquired traits are not learned but result from interaction with the environment. Skin color, for example, has both an inherited component and an environmental one. The skin color of many light-skinned people darkens when they are exposed to the Sun.

CHECK YOUR READING   How are inherited traits and acquired traits different? Give one example of each.

Find out more about sexual reproduction.

In this chapter, you will learn about inheritance that happens through sexual reproduction. During **sexual reproduction** a cell containing genetic information from the mother and a cell containing genetic information from the father combine into a completely new cell, which becomes the offspring. You will learn more about the mechanics of sexual reproduction in Section 4.3.

Genes are on chromosome pairs.

Inherited traits are controlled by the structures, materials, and processes you learned about in Chapters 1 and 2. In turn, these structures, materials, and processes are coded for by genes. A **gene** is a unit of heredity that occupies a specific location on a chromosome and codes for a particular product. **Heredity** is the passing of genes from parents to offspring.

Individuals inherit their genes from their parents. The genes code for the expression of traits. It is important to understand that an organism does not inherit the traits themselves from its parents. It inherits the genes that code for the traits it has. Most traits are not coded for by just one gene. Some characteristics are affected by many genes in complicated ways. We have much to learn about which genes might affect which characteristics.

Cells contain pairs of chromosomes, with one chromosome of each pair coming from each of two parents. The chromosomes in a pair are called homologs. They resemble each other, having the same size and shape, and carrying genetic information for particular traits.

On each homolog are sites where specific genes are located. Let us say, for example, that the gene that determines

Chromosomes and Genes

The letters on the pair of chromosomes below represent alleles.

Chromosomes come in pairs called homologs.

A **gene** occupies a specific location on both chromosomes in a pair.

Alleles, which come in pairs, are alternate forms of the same gene.

A | a
B | B
c | C
d | d
E | e
F | F
g | G
h | H

whether or not a plant is tall is located at place A on a pair of homologs. Though both homologs have the gene for height at site A, the genes may not be identical. They may be variations instead. The various forms of the same gene are called **alleles** (uh-LEELZ).

Thus, the homolog from one parent might have an allele for regular height at site A, while the gene from the other parent might have an allele for short height at site A. The alleles on a pair of homologs may or may not be different. Though any one plant can have only two alleles of a gene, there can be many alleles for a particular gene within a population.

CHECK YOUR READING
What are alleles?

READING **TiP**
The word *homolog* comes from the Greek words *homos,* which means "same," and *logos,* which means "proportion."

Each species has a characteristic number of chromosomes. Chimpanzees have 24 pairs of chromosomes, for a total of 48 chromosomes. Fruit flies have 4 pairs of chromosomes, or 8 in all. Humans have 23 pairs, for a total of 46 chromosomes. Scientists refer to chromosomes by their number. Human chromosomes are numbered 1 through 22; the 23rd pair are the sex chromosomes.

In humans, the sex chromosomes are called the X-chromosome and the Y-chromosome. A human female has two X-chromosomes, while a human male has one X-chromosome and one Y-chromosome. In addition to determining the sex of an offspring, the X- and Y-chromosomes contain important genes, just as the other, numbered chromosomes do.

Human Chromosomes

Humans have 23 pairs of chromosomes, for a total of 46. One of these pairs, shown below, determines the sex of a human offspring.

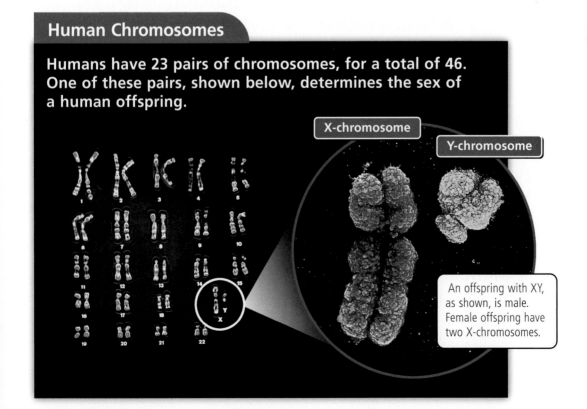

X-chromosome

Y-chromosome

An offspring with XY, as shown, is male. Female offspring have two X-chromosomes.

Gregor Mendel made some important discoveries about heredity.

The first major experiments investigating heredity were performed by a monk named Gregor Mendel, who lived in Austria during the mid-1800s. Before Mendel became a monk, he attended university and received training in science and mathematics. This training served him well when he began investigating the inheritance of traits among the pea plants in the monastery's garden.

Mendel took very detailed notes, carefully recording all the data from his many experiments. He worked with seven different traits: plant height, flower and pod position, seed shape, seed color, pod shape, pod color, and flower color. He studied each trait separately, always starting with plants that were true-breeding for that one particular trait. A true-breeding plant is one that will always produce offspring with a particular trait when allowed to self-pollinate.

READING TiP

The root of the word *trait* means to "draw out." It was originally used in the sense of drawing out a line. This same idea works in heredity if you link of drawing a connection between parents and offspring.

One Example

In his experiments with plant height, Mendel took two sets of plants, one true-breeding for plants of regular height and the other true-breeding for plants of short or dwarf height.

1. Instead of letting the plants self-pollinate as they do naturally, he deliberately paired as parents one plant from each set. Mendel called the plants that resulted from this cross the first generation. All of the plants from this first generation were of regular height. The dwarf-height trait seemed to have disappeared entirely.

2. Mendel then let the first-generation plants self-pollinate. He called the offspring that resulted from this self-pollination the second generation. About three fourths of the second-generation plants were of regular height, but about one fourth were of dwarf height. So the trait that seemed to disappear in the first generation reappeared in the second generation.

Mendel's experiments with other traits showed similar patterns.

 CHECK YOUR READING Summarize the pattern shown in Mendel's experiments with plant height.

Mendel's Conclusions

Mendel drew upon his knowledge of mathematics while analyzing his data in order to suggest a hypothesis that would explain the patterns he observed. Mendel realized that each plant must have two "factors" for each possible trait, one factor from each parent. Some traits, such as dwarf height, could be masked—dwarf height could be seen in the

Mendel's Pea Plants

Mendel observed variation in the height of pea plants (regular or dwarf height). By crossing plants with specific traits, he deduced that offspring get factors for each trait from both parents.

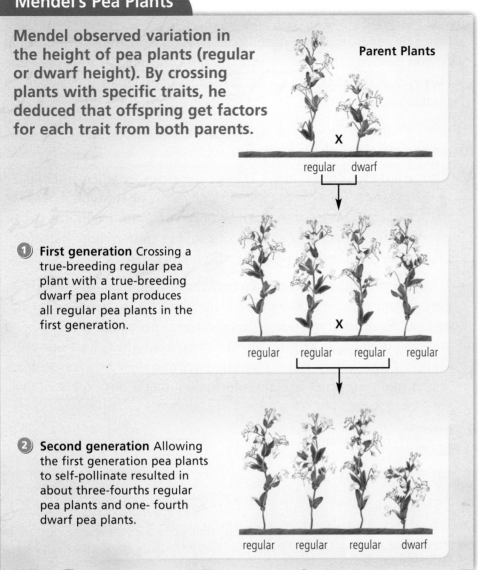

Parent Plants

regular   dwarf

1. **First generation** Crossing a true-breeding regular pea plant with a true-breeding dwarf pea plant produces all regular pea plants in the first generation.

regular   regular   regular   regular

2. **Second generation** Allowing the first generation pea plants to self-pollinate resulted in about three-fourths regular pea plants and one- fourth dwarf pea plants.

regular   regular   regular   dwarf

plant only if both of the plant's factors were for dwarf height. All of the plants in the first generation had one dwarf factor and one regular factor. A plant with one dwarf-height factor and one regular-height factor would be of regular height, because the regular-height factor masks the dwarf-height factor.

Later experiments allowed Mendel to draw a number of other conclusions about how these factors are distributed. Since the mid-1800s, Mendel's experiments and conclusions have been the basis for most of the scientific thought about heredity. Those things he called "factors" are what we now call genes and alleles.

CHECK YOUR READING How many factors or genes does each plant have for each possible trait?

Alleles interact to produce traits.

The pea-plant traits Gregor Mendel chose to study were all controlled by single genes, and each of the genes was on a different chromosome. As you learned earlier, most traits are not controlled by only one gene. However, simple examples such as Mendel's peas do help us better understand heredity.

Phenotype and Genotype

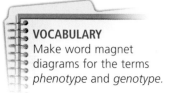

What color eyes do you have? The eye color you see when you look in the mirror is your phenotype. An organism's **phenotype** describes the actual characteristics that can be observed. Your height, the size of your feet, the presence or absence of a fold in your eyelids—all are observable traits and are part of your phenotype.

By contrast, the genes that control the development of eyefolds are part of your genotype. **Genotype** is the name for the genes an organism has. Your genotype is not always obvious from your phenotype. If you have eyefolds, your genotype definitely contains at least one eyefold-producing allele. But it may also have one allele for no eyefolds. Sometimes your genes contain information that is not expressed in your phenotype.

CHECK YOUR READING Is eye color a phenotype or a genotype? How do you know?

eye with folds at the corner of the eyelids

eye without folds at the corner of the eyelids

COMPARE The photograph above shows **phenotypes** of the eyefold gene. A person with eyefolds is shown to the left, a person without eyefolds to the right.

Dominant and Recessive Alleles

The eyefold gene, which controls development folds in the eyelids, comes in two alleles: eyefolds and no-eyefolds. If you have even one copy of the allele for eyefolds, you will have eyefolds. This happens because the allele for producing eyefolds is dominant. A **dominant** allele is one that is expressed in the phenotype even if only one copy is present in the genotype—that is, even if the other allele is an alternative form.

Suppose your genotype contains a no-eyefolds allele. The no-eyefolds allele is recessive. A **recessive** allele is one that is expressed in the phenotype only when two copies of it are present on the homologs. If one chromosome in the pair contains a dominant allele and the other contains a recessive allele, the dominant phenotype will appear. If you do not have eyefolds, it is because you got two no-eyefolds genes—one from each parent.

The interaction of dominant and recessive alleles means that it is possible for two brown-haired parents to have a blond child.

 CHECK YOUR READING — Under what conditions is a recessive allele expressed in an offspring's phenotype?

Hair color is determined by multiple genes, can be affected by the environment, and sometimes changes over time. However, in some cases it has a dominant-recessive pattern similar to that of the eyefold gene. As in the family shown at right, parents who both have brown hair can have a blond child. Brown hair is dominant, so if both parents have alleles for both brown hair and blond hair, the brown-hair allele is more likely to be expressed. Their child, however, could have two blond-hair alleles (one from each parent) and therefore have blond hair instead of brown.

4.1 Review

KEY CONCEPTS

1. Explain the difference between acquired and inherited traits.

2. Describe the conclusions that Mendel drew from his experiments with pea plants.

3. What type of alleles a.e expressed only if an identical pair exist on the chromosome of the offspring?

CRITICAL THINKING

4. **Compare and Contrast** What is the difference between a genotype and a phenotype?

5. **Analyze** Explain why a person with an allele for a particular trait may not have a phenotype that shows the trait.

CHALLENGE

6. **Apply** In guinea pigs, the allele for black fur is dominant over the allele for brown fur. If you had two parent guinea pigs, each with brown fur, what color fur might the offspring have, and why?

CHAPTER INVESTIGATION

Offspring Models

OVERVIEW AND PURPOSE Sexual reproduction combines genes from two parent organisms and results in diversity among offspring. In this activity, you will
- design a model of an offspring
- determine how the offspring exhibits portions of both genotype and phenotype from its parents

▶ Problem

How are traits passed from parent to offspring?

▶ Procedure

1. Make data tables like those shown on the sample notebook page.

2. Your teacher will supply bags containing alleles written on slips. Capital letters represent dominant alleles, and lower-case letters represent recessive alleles. Each bag will have two alleles for one trait. Six of the bags, one for each of 6 traits, will represent the female parent's alleles. Another set of 6 bags will represent the male parent's alleles. From each bag, choose one allele.

3. In Table 1, record the alleles for both parents, and the allele pairs for the offspring. Then place the slips back into the bags. You will use the alleles to build a model offspring.

4. Use the information in the table below to determine the phenotype of the offspring. Write the phenotype in the fourth column in Table 1.

MATERIALS
- foam balls (body segments)
- colored toothpicks (antennae)
- small paperclips (wings)
- colored pipe cleaners (legs)
- colored pushpins (eyes)

Genotypes and Phenotypes	
BB or Bb = 3 body segments	bb = 2 body segments
WW or Ww = 2 pairs of wings	ww = 1 pair of wings
AA or Aa = purple antennae	aa = red antennae
PP or Pp = 3 pairs of legs	pp = 2 pairs of legs
CC or Cc = yellow legs	cc = orange legs
EE or Ee = blue eyes	ee = green eyes

5 Choose the materials you need to assemble the offspring. You can use toothpicks to attach the body segments. Push the pipe cleaners, toothpicks, and wings into the foam balls. **CAUTION: Take care when handling the pushpins.**

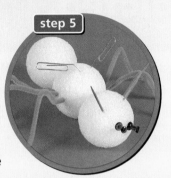

step 5

▶ Observe and Analyze

Write It Up

1. **OBSERVE** Does your offspring look the way you would expect either parent to look? Explain.

2. **ANALYZE** How many different genotypes are possible for each trait? Explain.

▶ Conclude

Write It Up

1. **INFER** What are the possible genotypes of the parents? Fill in Table 2.

2. **INTERPRET** Can you tell how the genotypes of the parents differ from that of the offspring? Explain.

3. **INTERPRET** How does your offspring model illustrate what you have learned about heredity?

4. **IDENTIFY LIMITS** What sources of error might you have experienced?

5. **APPLY** Blue eyes are the phenotype for two recessive alleles. Can parents with blue eyes have a brown-eyed offspring? Explain.

▶ INVESTIGATE Further

CHALLENGE Predict the genotypes and phenotypes of the offspring of a cross between your model offspring and the model made by one of your classmates.

Offspring Models

Table 1. Parent and Offspring Family Traits

	Female Parent	Male Parent	Offspring Genotype	Offspring Phenotype
Body segments				
Pairs of wings				
Antennae color				
Pairs of legs				
Color of legs				
Color of eyes				

Table 2. Possible Parent Genotypes

Trait	Female Parent	Male Parent
Body segments		
Pairs of wings		
Antennae color		
Pairs of legs		
Color of legs		
Color of eyes		

4.2 Patterns of heredity can be predicted.

BEFORE, you learned	NOW, you will learn
• Genes are passed from parents to offspring • Offspring inherit genes in predictable patterns	• How Punnett squares can be used to predict patterns of heredity • How ratios and probability can be used to predict patterns of heredity

VOCABULARY

Punnett square p. 110
ratio p. 112
probability p. 112
percentage p. 112

EXPLORE Probability

How can probability help predict results?

PROCEDURE

1. Toss both coins 10 times. For each toss, record the combination of heads and/or tails.

2. For each combination (two heads, two tails, or a head and a tail), add up the number of tosses.

WHAT DO YOU THINK?

• Which combination happened most often?
• If you tossed both coins one more time, which combination would be the most likely result? Can you know for sure? Why or why not?

MATERIALS
• two coins
• pencil and paper

Punnett squares show possible outcomes for inheritance.

NOTETAKING STRATEGY
Use a strategy from an earlier chapter or design one of your own to take notes on how Punnett squares show possible patterns of heredity.

Mendel noticed that traits are inherited in patterns. One tool for understanding the patterns of heredity is a graphic called a Punnett square. A **Punnett square** illustrates how the parents' alleles might combine in offspring.

Each parent has two alleles for a particular gene. An offspring receives one allele from each parent. A Punnett square shows how the parents' alleles may be passed on to potential offspring.

The Punnett square on page 111 shows how alleles for pea-plant height would be distributed among offspring in Mendel's first-generation cross. The dominant allele (D) is regular height, and the recessive allele (d) is dwarf height.

The top of the Punnett square shows one parent's alleles for this trait—two dominant regular alleles (DD). The side of the Punnett square shows the other parent's alleles for this trait—two recessive dwarf alleles (dd).

Each box in the Punnett square shows a way the alleles from each parent would combine in potential offspring. You can see that each potential offspring would have the same genotype: one dominant and one recessive allele (Dd). The phenotype of each offspring would show the dominant allele, in this case regular height.

 CHECK YOUR READING What is a Punnett square?

READING TiP

As you read about Punnett squares, connect each sentence with the diagram below.

Using Punnett Squares

The Punnett square below shows the possible allele combinations for an offspring of one parent with two dominant (D) regular-height alleles and one parent with two recessive (d) dwarf-height alleles.

 **SIMULATION** CLASSZONE.COM

Predict offspring traits with virtual Punnett squares.

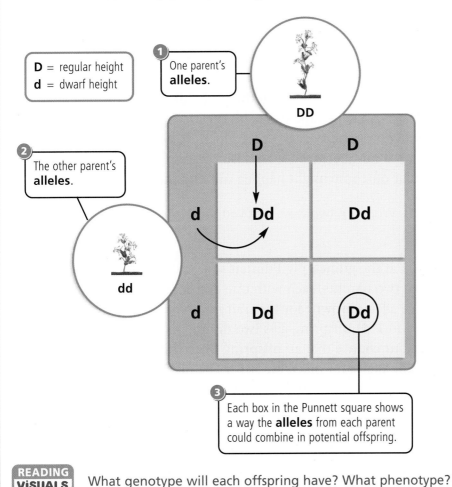

D = regular height
d = dwarf height

1 One parent's **alleles**.

DD

2 The other parent's **alleles**.

dd

	D	D
d	Dd	Dd
d	Dd	(Dd)

3 Each box in the Punnett square shows a way the **alleles** from each parent could combine in potential offspring.

READING VISUALS What genotype will each offspring have? What phenotype?

Ratios and percentages can express the probability of outcomes.

The Punnett square on page 111 for the first generation of pea plants shows that all potential offspring will be of regular height, because they all have one dominant allele. You can say that 100 percent of the offspring will be of regular height. Or you could say that the ratio of regular-height offspring to total offspring is four to four. A **ratio** compares, or shows the relationship between, two quantities. A ratio is usually written 4:4 and read as "four to four." This can be interpreted as "four out of four." The Punnett square shows that four out of four offspring will express the dominant gene for regular height.

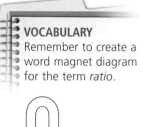

VOCABULARY
Remember to create a word magnet diagram for the term *ratio*.

4:4
ratio of blue squares to total squares

1:4 red
3:4 blue

Punnett squares and the ratios they show express probability. **Probability** is the likelihood, or chance, of a specific outcome in relation to the total number of possible outcomes. The ratios derived from a Punnett square tell you the probability that any one offspring will get certain genes and express a certain trait. Another way of expressing probability is as a percentage. A **percentage** is a ratio that compares a number to 100. That is, it states the number of times a particular outcome might happen out of a hundred chances.

CHECK YOUR READING What are two ways that you can express a probability?

Look at the guinea-pig Punnett square on page 113. This cross is between two parents, each with one dominant allele (black) and one recessive allele (brown) for the trait fur color. In this cross, only one in four (ratio 1:4) offspring gets two dominant alleles. That is, there is a one in four chance that an offspring from this cross will have two dominant alleles for black fur (BB). The likelihood that the offspring will get one dominant and one recessive allele (Bb) is 2:4—two out of every four offspring would have this genotype. Like the one offspring with two dominant alleles (BB), the two offspring with the genotype Bb will have black fur. This makes a total of three offspring (3:4) with the phenotype black fur. Only 1:4 offspring of this cross will have the genotype and phenotype brown fur (bb).

Punnett Square and Probability

The Punnett square below shows the possible ways alleles could combine in the offspring of two parent guinea pigs. Each parent has one dominant allele for black fur (B) and one recessive allele for brown fur (b).

B = black fur
b = brown fur

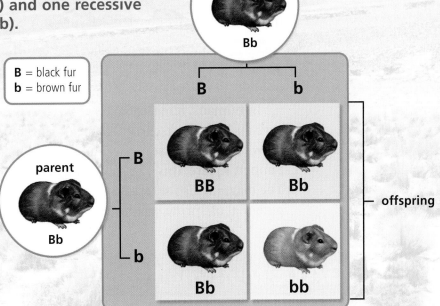

parent
Bb

parent
Bb

B   b

B

BB   Bb

b

Bb   bb

offspring

The table below shows the probability of the various genotypes and phenotypes from the Punnett square above. Each probability is shown as both a ratio and a percentage.

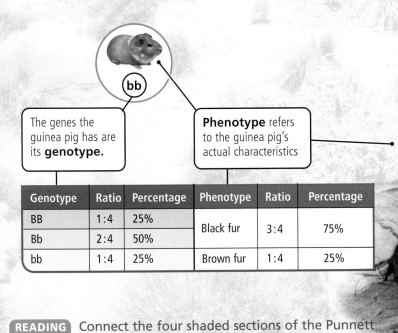

bb

The genes the guinea pig has are its **genotype.**

Phenotype refers to the guinea pig's actual characteristics

Genotype	Ratio	Percentage	Phenotype	Ratio	Percentage
BB	1:4	25%	Black fur	3:4	75%
Bb	2:4	50%			
bb	1:4	25%	Brown fur	1:4	25%

READING VISUALS Connect the four shaded sections of the Punnett square to the matching genotypes in the chart.

When one parent has two dominant alleles and the other has two recessive alleles, there is a 100 percent chance that an offspring will have the dominant phenotype. The pea-plant example on page 111 shows this pattern. All the offspring are of regular height. When both parents have one dominant and one recessive allele, there is a 75 percent chance that an offspring will have the dominant phenotype. The guinea-pig example on page 113 shows this pattern. Chances are that more offspring will have black fur than brown fur.

CHECK YOUR READING What is the probability that an offspring from the pea plant cross on page 111 will be of dwarf height?

In humans, females have two X-chromosomes (XX), and males have an X- and a Y-chromosome (XY). The Punnett square on page 115 shows the possible sexes of human offspring. Unlike the guinea-pig Punnett square, this one shows only two possible outcomes, XX and XY. The diagram also shows how to find the percentage chance that a potential offspring will be female.

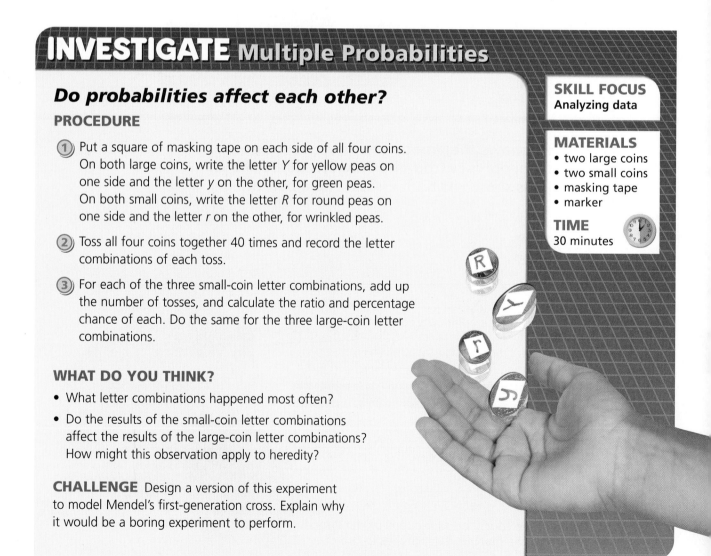

INVESTIGATE Multiple Probabilities

Do probabilities affect each other?

PROCEDURE

1. Put a square of masking tape on each side of all four coins. On both large coins, write the letter Y for yellow peas on one side and the letter y on the other, for green peas. On both small coins, write the letter R for round peas on one side and the letter r on the other, for wrinkled peas.

2. Toss all four coins together 40 times and record the letter combinations of each toss.

3. For each of the three small-coin letter combinations, add up the number of tosses, and calculate the ratio and percentage chance of each. Do the same for the three large-coin letter combinations.

WHAT DO YOU THINK?

- What letter combinations happened most often?

- Do the results of the small-coin letter combinations affect the results of the large-coin letter combinations? How might this observation apply to heredity?

CHALLENGE Design a version of this experiment to model Mendel's first-generation cross. Explain why it would be a boring experiment to perform.

SKILL FOCUS
Analyzing data

MATERIALS
- two large coins
- two small coins
- masking tape
- marker

TIME
30 minutes

Calculating Probability

Two humans, a female (XX) and a male (XY), have an offspring. The Punnett square below can be used to calculate the probability that an offspring will be female or male.

① To find the percentage chance of a female offspring, first find the ratio by counting the number of XX offspring out of the four possible outcomes.

② Two out of 4 (ratio 2:4, or 2/4) offspring will be female.

③ Multiply this ratio by 100 to find the probability as a percentage.

④ Two fourths equal 1/2, and 1/2 of 100 is 50. So there is a 50 percent chance that an offspring will be female.

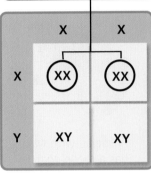

	X	X
X	(XX)	(XX)
Y	XY	XY

READING VISUALS Compare this Punnett square with the pea-plant Punnett square on page 111 and the guinea-pig Punnett square on page 113. How is it similar? How is it different?

It is important to realize that Punnett squares and probability do not guarantee the outcome of a genetic cross. They indicate the probability of different outcomes. While there is a 75 percent chance that an offspring will have black fur according to the Punnett square on page 113, you cannot know with any certainty what color fur a particular offspring will actually have. Actual experimental results may not match predicted outcomes.

CHECK YOUR READING Can a Punnett square tell you the specific outcome of a genetic cross? Why or why not?

4.2 Review

KEY CONCEPTS

1. Explain how Punnett squares predict the outcomes of heredity.

2. How are ratio and percentages related?

3. How can you find a percentage chance from a Punnett square?

CRITICAL THINKING

4. **Predict** Mendel studied the colors of seeds in his experiments with pea plants. Let G stand for green and g stand for yellow. Green is dominant. Make a Punnett square for seed color. Find the percentage chance for each outcome.

⬤ CHALLENGE

5. **Apply** In pea plants, the allele for smooth peas is dominant over the allele for wrinkled peas. Create a Punnett square and calculate the probability that two smooth-pea plants will have an offspring with wrinkled peas if each parent has one smooth and one wrinkled allele.

MATH TUTORIAL
CLASSZONE.COM
Click on Math Tutorial for
more help with probability.

Coat Coloring

The Shetland sheepdog, or Sheltie, has patches of color on its silky coat. A gene controls marbling of the colors, or merling. The merle gene comes in two forms: M for merle, or m for no merle.

A Sheltie with Mm has a merle coat.

A Sheltie with MM is mostly white.

A Sheltie with mm has solid patches, no merling

Example

One Sheltie parent has a merle coat (Mm), and one has no merling (mm). With these two parents, what is the probability of a puppy with a merle coat?

(1) Make a Punnett square. Put the alleles from one parent on top. Put those of the other on the side.

(2) Fill in the blocks by combining the alleles.

(3) The total number of blocks is the second part of a ratio.
___ : 4

(4) To find the probability of an outcome, count the blocks of that outcome.

ANSWER: There is a 2 : 4, or 2 out of 4 probability.

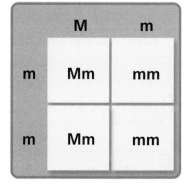

	M	m
m	Mm	mm
m	Mm	mm

Now, make your own Punnett square for Shelties.

1. Make a Punnett square to show two Sheltie parents, both with merle coats (Mm).

2. What is the probability of a merle puppy?

3. What are the chances of a puppy with no merling?

CHALLENGE Write each of the probabilities in questions 2 and 3 and the example as a percentage.

Meiosis is a special form of cell division.

A

◀ **BEFORE,** you learned	▶ **NOW,** you will learn
• Mitosis produces two genetically identical cells	• Why meiosis is necessary for sexual reproduction
• In sexual reproduction, offspring inherit traits from both parents	• How cells and chromosomes divide during meiosis
• Genetic traits are inherited in predictable patterns	• How meiosis differs from mitosis

VOCABULARY

gamete p. 118
egg p. 118
sperm p. 118
fertilization p. 118
meiosis p. 119

EXPLORE Meiosis

Why does sexual reproduction need a special form of cell division?

PROCEDURE

MATERIALS
• 2 blue pipe cleaners
• 2 red pipe cleaners

① Suppose the cells that combine during sexual reproduction are produced by mitosis, with the same pairs of chromosomes as most cells. Model this combination with the pipe cleaners; both red pipe cleaners and both blue pipe cleaners end up in the new cell.

② Now model a way for the new cell to end up with the same number of chromosomes as most other cells.

WHAT DO YOU THINK?
• What was wrong with the new cell produced at the end of step 1?
• Describe your model of the way a new cell could end up with the correct number of chromosomes.

Meiosis is necessary for sexual reproduction.

In Section 4.1 you learned that two cells combine during the process of sexual reproduction. One of the cells contains genetic information from the mother. The other contains genetic information from the father. The two cells combine into a completely new cell, which becomes the offspring.

 How does the genetic material of offspring produced by sexual reproduction compare with the genetic material of the parents?

Most human cells, which can be referred to as body cells, contain 46 chromosomes—the full number of chromosomes that is normal for a human being. Any cell that contains the full number of chromosomes (two sets) for a species is a 2*n* cell, also called a diploid cell. The 2*n* cells for a fruit fly, for example, contain 8 chromosomes.

Think about what would happen if two body cells were to combine. The resulting cell would have twice the normal number of chromosomes. A special type of cell, called a gamete, is needed.

Gametes are cells that contain half the usual number of chromosomes—one chromosome from each pair. Gametes are 1*n* cells, also called haploid cells. Human gametes contain 23 unpaired chromosomes. The gametes of a fruit fly contain 4 unpaired chromosomes. Gametes are found only in the reproductive organs of plants and animals. An **egg** is a gamete that forms in the reproductive organs of a female. A gamete that forms in the reproductive organs of a male is a **sperm**.

 CHECK YOUR READING What is a gamete?

During sexual reproduction two gametes combine to become a 2*n* cell that can grow into a new offspring. **Fertilization** is the process that takes place when a sperm and an egg combine to form one new cell. The diagram below shows what happens to the chromosomes in gametes during fertilization. In humans, an egg cell with 23 chromosomes joins a sperm cell with 23 chromosomes to form a new 2*n* cell with 46 chromosomes.

Fertilization

During fertilization, a 1*n* egg cell from a female combines with a 1*n* sperm cell from a male, producing a 2*n* fertilized egg cell, which develops into an offspring.

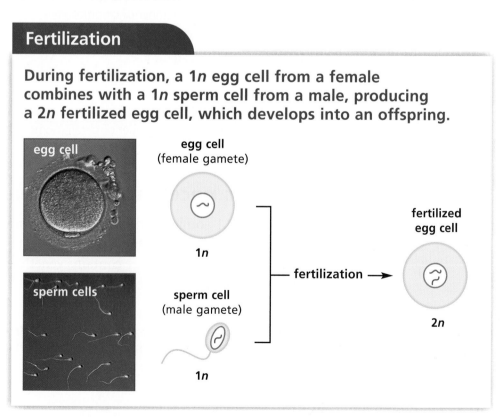

egg cell

egg cell
(female gamete)

1*n*

sperm cells

sperm cell
(male gamete)

1*n*

— fertilization →

fertilized
egg cell

2*n*

How can you model fertilization?

In fertilization, a sperm and an egg combine to form a new cell. Design a model of fertilization.

DESIGN — YOUR OWN — EXPERIMENT

PROCEDURE

1. Use the materials provided to make simple models of an egg and a sperm.
2. Use the sperm and egg models to show the fertilization process.

WHAT DO YOU THINK?

- Describe your model of the cell that exists at the end of the fertilization process.
- How is it different from the sperm cell and egg cell?

CHALLENGE Design a model for fertilization in fruit flies.

SKILL FOCUS
Modeling

MATERIALS
- pipe cleaners
- gallon milk jug
- film canister
- yarn

TIME
25 minutes

You know that body cells divide by the process called mitosis. Mitosis produces two daughter cells, each containing exact copies of the chromosomes in the parent cell. Each daughter cell formed by mitosis is a standard diploid ($2n$) cell.

But to produce gametes, which are haploid, a different kind of cell division is necessary. **Meiosis** is a special kind of cell division that produces haploid ($1n$) cells. During meiosis, a single cell goes through two cell divisions—meiosis I and meiosis II. Meiosis takes place only in the reproductive tissues of an organism.

Cells divide twice during meiosis.

Before meiosis begins, the chromosomes of the parent cell are copied. A cell that is ready to divide contains two copies of each chromosome pair—twice as many chromosomes as usual. So to end up with cells that have half the usual number of chromosomes, there must be two divisions.

Remember that the two chromosomes in a pair are called homologs. At the beginning of meiosis I, the cell has two copies of each homolog. During meiosis I the homologs divide. The starting cell divides into two cells. One cell contains the two copies of one homolog of each pair, while the other cell contains the two copies of the other homolog of each pair. Then, during meiosis II, each of the two cells is divided, producing four haploid cells. Each haploid cell has one unpaired set of chromosomes.

NOTETAKING STRATEGY
Use an earlier strategy or one that you think works well to take notes on the division of cells during meiosis.

Meiosis I

As you can see in the diagram on page 121, there are four steps in meiosis I: prophase I, metaphase I, anaphase I, and telophase I. Included in telophase I is a cytokinesis, the division of the cytoplasm. The diagram shows what would happen during meiosis I in a species that has four chromosomes in its 2n body cells.

READING TiP

As you read about meiosis I and meiosis II, match the numbers in the text to the numbers in the diagram on page 121.

1 Prophase I Chromosomes pair up with their partners. There are two sets of each of the chromosome pairs in the parent cell. The members of each chromosome pair are attached together in sets of doubled homologs.

2 Metaphase I Each set of chromosome pairs lines up along the center of the cell.

3 Anaphase I The two copies of one homolog are pulled apart from the two copies of the other homolog. This dividing of the homologs is the most significant step of meiosis I.

4 Telophase I and Cytokinesis A new cell membrane forms at the center of the cell, dividing the parent cell into two daughter cells.

CHECK YOUR READING What happens to the parent cell during telophase I?

Meiosis II

RESOURCE CENTER
CLASSZONE.COM

Learn more about meiosis.

During meiosis I, two daughter cells are formed. The chromosomes of these two cells are not copied before meiosis II begins. Both of these cells divide during meiosis II, to produce a total of four daughter cells. The four steps in meiosis II, shown on page 121, are prophase II, metaphase II, anaphase II, and telophase II (with cytokinesis).

5 Prophase II In each daughter cell, there are two copies of each of n chromosomes. The copies are attached together.

6 Metaphase II The chromosomes line up along each cell's center.

7 Anaphase II The two attached copies of each chromosome separate and are pulled to opposite poles in each cell.

8 Telophase II and Cytokinesis A new cell membrane forms in the center of each cell, as each cell divides into two 1n daughter cells, producing a total of four 1n cells.

During meiosis, one cell in an organism's reproductive system divides twice to form four 1n cells. In male organisms, these gametes become sperm. In female organisms, at least one of these cells becomes an egg. In some species, including humans, only one of the four daughter cells produced by a female during meiosis becomes an egg. The rest dissolve back into the organism or, in some cases, are never produced.

Meiosis

Meiosis reduces the number of chromosomes by half, producing four 1*n* cells.

Meiosis I: Paired chromosomes separate

① Prophase I

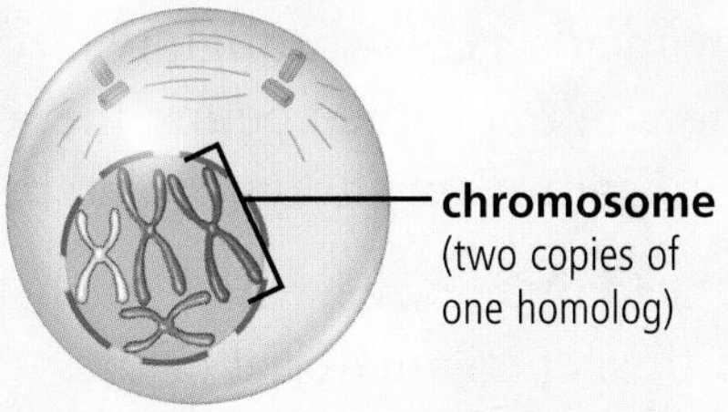

chromosome
(two copies of one homolog)

DNA condenses into chromosomes. The nuclear membrane disappears.

② Metaphase I

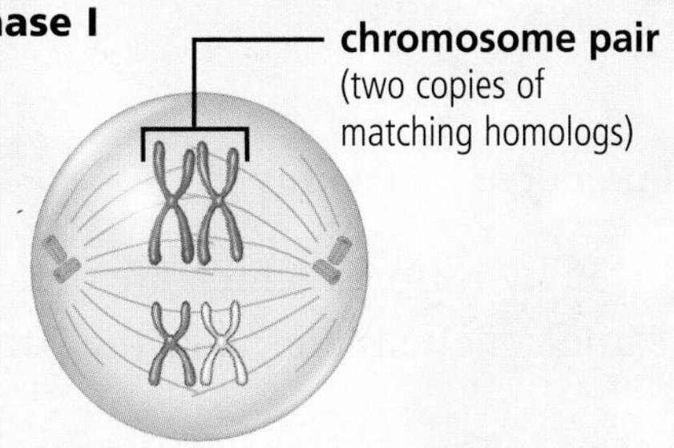

chromosome pair
(two copies of matching homologs)

Chromosomes arrange as pairs in the middle of the cell.

③ Anaphase I

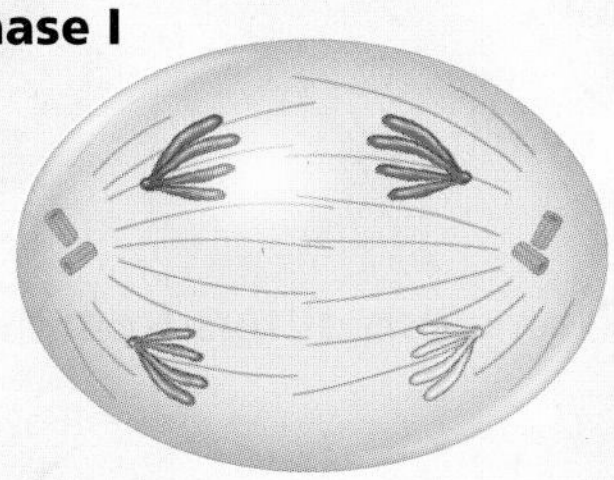

The homologs of each chromosome pair separate and are pulled to opposite ends of the cell.

④ Telophase I and Cytokinesis

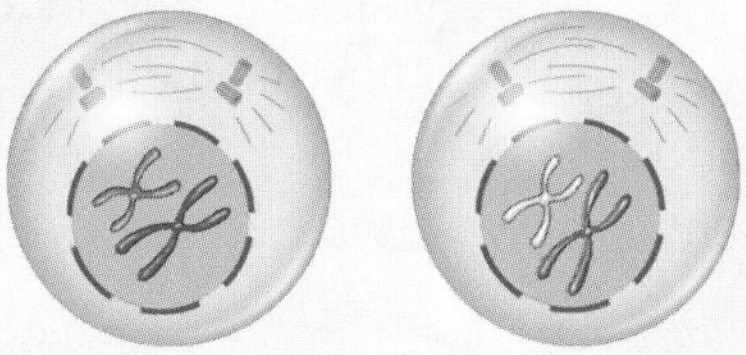

The cell divides into two daughter cells.

Meiosis II: Chromosomes separate

⑤ Prophase II

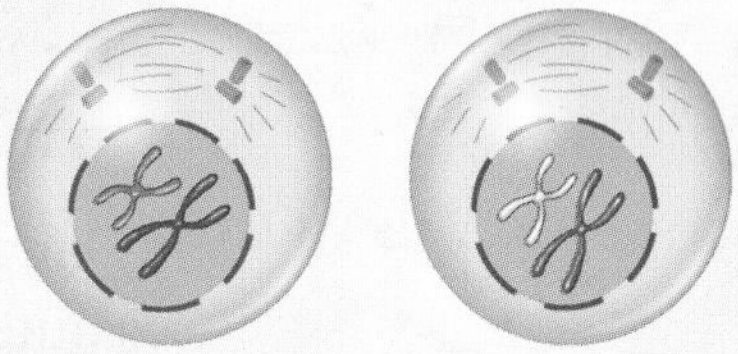

The two copies of each homolog remain attached as chromosomes.

⑥ Metaphase II

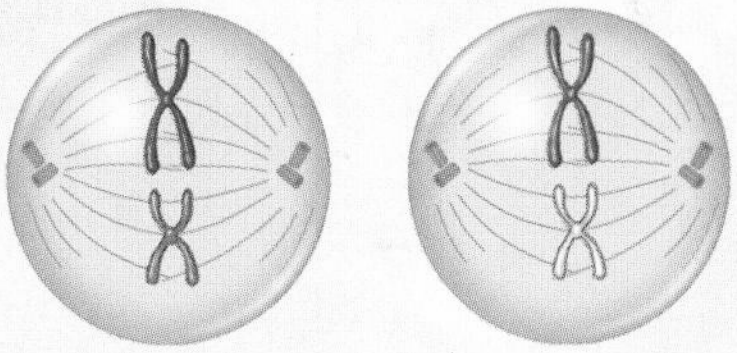

Chromosomes line up in the middle of the cell.

⑦ Anaphase II

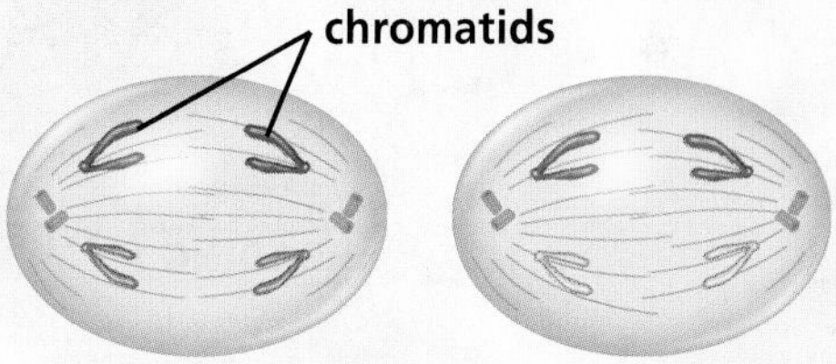

chromatids

Each chromosome splits into chromatids, so that one copy of each homolog is pulled to the opposite ends of the cells.

⑧ Telophase II and Cytokinesis

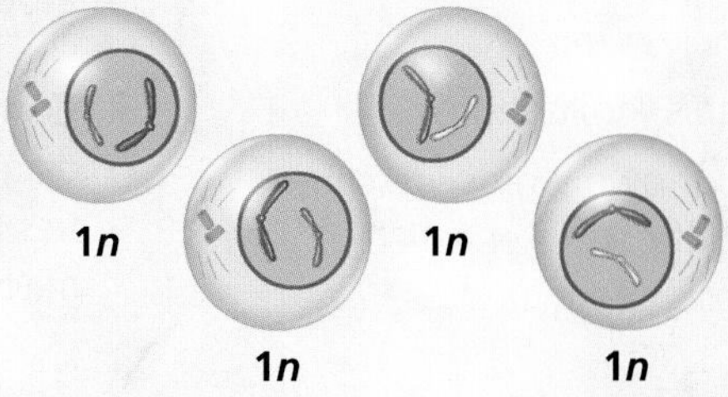

1*n* 1*n* 1*n* 1*n*

Both cells divide, producing four 1*n* cells.

Meiosis and mitosis differ in some important ways.

You can see that the processes of meiosis and mitosis are similar in many ways. However, they also have several very important differences.

READING TiP

As you read about how meiosis and mitosis are different, refer to the diagrams on pages 83 and 121.

- Only cells that are to become gametes go through meiosis. All other cells divide by mitosis.

- A cell that divides by meiosis goes through two cell divisions, but the chromosomes are not copied before the second division. In mitosis, the chromosomes are always copied before division.

- Daughter cells produced by meiosis, which are haploid ($1n$), contain only half of the genetic material of the parent cell (one of each chromosome).

Cell produced by meiosis

- Daughter cells produced by mitosis, which are diploid ($2n$), contain exactly the same genetic material as the parent (pairs of chromosomes).

Cell produced by mitosis

 CHECK YOUR READING What are four ways in which meiosis differs from mitosis?

4.3 Review

KEY CONCEPTS

1. What kind of cell is produced by meiosis?
2. What is fertilization?
3. In your own words, describe the differences between meiosis and mitosis.

CRITICAL THINKING

4. **Compare** How do prophase I and prophase II differ?
5. **Communicate** Make a Venn diagram to show the similarities and differences between mitosis and meiosis.

⚫ CHALLENGE

6. **Synthesize** Why does meiosis II result in four $1n$ cells rather than four $2n$ cells?

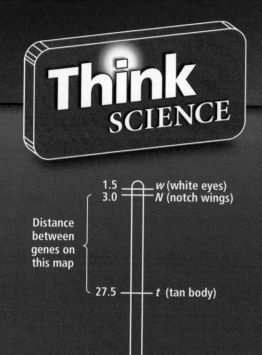

1.5 — w (white eyes)
3.0 — N (notch wings)

Distance between genes on this map

27.5 — t (tan body)

56.7 — f (forked bristles)

Genes have a particular location on a chromosome. A gene map shows the location.

Are Traits Linked?

Fruit flies are easy to breed in a laboratory and have an assortment of easily recognized genetic traits—different eye colors, body patterns, limb characteristics, and wing shapes. For these reasons, early geneticists studied fruit flies to learn how certain traits were inherited. Sometimes the experiments produced puzzling results. Here is an example from the laboratory of Thomas Hunt Morgan.

▶ Observations

- In a batch of fruit flies, most red-eyed individuals were born with short wings.
- In the same batch, at least one fruit fly was born with red eyes and normal-sized wings.

▶ Hypotheses

Morgan and his coworkers made these hypotheses about the inherited traits:

- The genes for red eyes and the gene for short wings are linked together on a fruit fly's chromosomes. These linked genes are usually inherited together.
- Sometimes during meiosis, one of the linked genes will "cross over" from one chromosome to a homologous one. When this happens, a fruit fly will be born with one but not both of the linked genes—red eyes without short wings.
- Genes that are farthest from each other on a chromosome are most likely to become separated and cross over during meiosis. Genes that are closest (linked) to each other are least likely to.

▶ Further Discoveries

By studying the results of many breeding experiments, Morgan and his student, Alfred Sturtevant, could determine which genes were closest and farthest from each other. From this information, they drew a simple map showing the location of each of the fruit fly's linked genes.

▶ Determine Relevance

On Your Own Look at the map of a chromosome on this page. Which of the traits are most likely to be inherited together? Which might be most easily separated and cross over during meiosis?

As a Group Is it reasonable to think that information about a fruit fly's genes could apply to the genes of a human being? Discuss this topic in a small group and see if the group can agree.

the **BIG** idea

In sexual reproduction, genes are passed from parents to offspring in predictable patterns.

KEY CONCEPTS SUMMARY

4.1 Living things inherit traits in patterns.

Offspring inherit **alleles**, which are forms of **genes**, from their parents. Alleles come on chromosome pairs and can be **dominant** or **recessive**. The alleles you have are your **genotype**; the observable characteristics that come from your genotype are your **phenotype**.

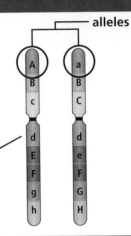

alleles

a gene

VOCABULARY
sexual reproduction p. 102
gene p. 102
heredity p. 102
allele p. 103
phenotype p. 106
genotype p. 106
dominant p. 107
recessive p. 107

4.2 Patterns of heredity can be predicted.

Punnett squares show possible outcomes of heredity. **Ratios** and **percentages** can be used with Punnett squares to express the **probability** of particular outcomes.

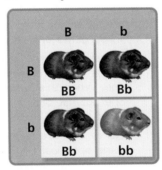

B = black fur
b = brown fur

VOCABULARY
Punnett square p. 110
ratio p. 112
probability p. 112
percentage p. 112

4.3 Meiosis is a special form of cell division.

- At the beginning of meiosis I, the parent cell has two copies of each chromosome pair.
- During meiosis I, the homologs of the chromosome pair separate; there are two cells, each with two copies of one homolog from each pair.
- During meiosis II, the two copies of each homolog separate; each daughter cell has one homolog.

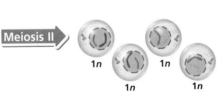

Meiosis I

Meiosis II

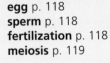

1n 1n 1n 1n

VOCABULARY
gamete p. 118
egg p. 118
sperm p. 118
fertilization p. 118
meiosis p. 119

Reviewing Vocabulary

Make a frame for each of the vocabulary terms listed below. Write the term in the center. Think about how each term is related to the Big Idea of the chapter. Decide what information to frame it with. Use definitions, examples, descriptions, parts, or pictures.

1. allele

3. ratio

2. heredity

4. probability

Describe how the vocabulary terms in the following pairs of words are related to each other. Explain the relationship in a one- or two-sentence answer. Underline each vocabulary word or term in your answers.

5. phenotype, genotype

6. dominant, recessive

Reviewing Key Concepts

Multiple Choice *Choose the letter of the best answer.*

7. Which is an example of an acquired trait?
   a. eye color
   b. hair color
   c. blood type
   d. ability to read

8. The unit of heredity that determines a particular trait is known as
   a. a chromosome
   b. a gamete
   c. a gene
   d. a phenotype

9. A human female would have which set of sex chromosomes?
   a. XX
   b. YY
   c. XY
   d. XXXX

10. If one copy of a dominant allele is present in a genotype, then the trait is
   a. expressed in the phenotype
   b. not expressed in the phenotype
   c. partially expressed in the phenotype
   d. not expressed in an offspring's phenotype

11. In guinea pigs, the allele for black fur (B) is dominant, and the allele for brown fur (b) is recessive. If a BB male mates with a Bb female, what percentage of offspring are likely to have black fur?
   a. 100 percent
   c. 50 percent
   b. 75 percent
   d. 25 percent

12. If one parent has two dominant alleles and another parent has two recessive alleles, the offspring will have
   a. the recessive phenotype
   b. the dominant phenotype
   c. two dominant alleles
   d. two recessive alleles

13. Cells that contain half the usual number of chromosomes are
   a. fertilized egg cells
   c. alleles
   b. gametes
   d. diploid cells

14. The process that produces haploid (1*n*) cells is known as
   a. mitosis
   c. meiosis
   b. reproduction
   d. fertilization

15. What happens when fertilization occurs?
   a. Two 2*n* cells combine in a new cell.
   b. Two 1*n* cells combine into a new cell.
   c. Two 2*n* daughter cells are produced.
   d. Two 1*n* daughter cells are produced.

16. Which does not occur during meiosis?
   a. Two haploid daughter cells are produced.
   b. Two diploid daughter cells are produced.
   c. Only cells that are gametes are produced.
   d. Daughter cells are produced that contain half the chromosomes of the parent cell.

Short Answer *Write a short answer to each question.*

17. In what case would a recessive allele be expressed in the phenotype of an offspring?

18. Describe the purpose of a Punnett square.

19. How does the number of chromosomes in a person's sex cells compare with the number of chromosomes in the body cells?

Thinking Critically

20. INFER How was Mendel able to infer that each offspring of two parent pea plants had a pair of "factors" for a particular trait?

21. COMMUNICATE Briefly describe how heredity works. Use the terms *gene* and *chromosome* in your explanation.

22. APPLY Can a dwarf pea plant ever have a dominant allele? Explain.

23. ANALYZE How is a Punnett Square used to show both the genotype and phenotype of both parents and offspring?

24. APPLY In rabbits, the allele for black fur is dominant over the allele for white fur. Two white rabbits have a litter of eight offspring. Six of the offspring have white hair and two have black hair. What are the genotypes of the parents? Explain.

Use the Punnett square below to answer the next two questions.

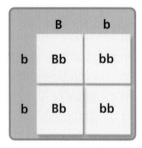

	B	b
b	Bb	bb
b	Bb	bb

25. CALCULATE A parent has one dominant allele for black fur (B) and one recessive allele for white fur (b). The other parent has two recessive alleles for white fur. In this cross what is the ratio of black to white fur in the offspring?

26. CALCULATE What is the percentage chance that an offspring will have the recessive phenotype?

27. ANALYZE This diagram shows the process of fertilization. Which of the cells shown are haploid? Explain.

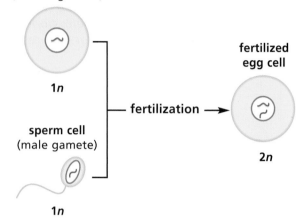

egg cell
(female gamete)

1*n*

sperm cell
(male gamete)

1*n*

fertilization →

fertilized
egg cell

2*n*

28. SUMMARIZE Briefly describe what happens during meiosis I and meiosis II. What is the function of meiosis?

the BIG idea

29. INFER Look again at the picture on pages 98–99. Now that you have finished the chapter, how would you change or add details to your answer to the question on the photograph?

30. SYNTHESIZE Write one or more paragraphs explaining how Mendel's observations of pea plants contributed to the study of modern genetics. Use these terms in your explanation.

gene	phenotype
allele	dominant
trait	recessive
genotype	

UNIT PROJECTS

If you need to create graphs or other visuals for your project, be sure you have grid paper, poster board, markers, or other supplies.

Analyzing data

The chart below shows the phenotypes of pea-plant offspring.

Phenotypes of Pea Plants	
Phenotype	Number of Offspring
Regular (D)	12
Dwarf (d)	4

Use the chart to answer the questions below.

1. What percentage of pea plants showed the dominant phenotype?

a. 100 percent

b. 75 percent

c. 50 percent

d. 25 percent

2. What percentage of pea plants showed the recessive phenotype?

a. 100 percent

b. 75 percent

c. 50 percent

d. 25 percent

3. What is the genotype of the dwarf pea plants?

a. DD

b. Dd

c. dd

d. cannot tell

4. What are the possible genotypes of the regular pea plants?

a. DD and dd

b. DD and Dd

c. Dd and dd

d. cannot tell

5. What are the genotypes of the parents?

a. Dd and DD

b. DD and Dd

c. Dd and dd

d. dd and dd

6. Which statement is true, based on the data in the chart?

a. If both parents were Dd, then none of the offspring would be dwarf.

b. If both parents were DD, then none of the offspring would be dwarf.

c. If one parent were Dd and the other were dd, then none of the offspring would be regular.

d. If one parent were DD and the other parent were dd, then none of the offspring would be regular.

Extended Response

7. Traits for a widow's peak hairline (W) and curly hair (C) are controlled by dominant alleles. A family of eight has three children with widow's peaks. All six children have curly hair. Use your knowledge of heredity to write one or two paragraphs explaining the possible genotypes of the parents.

8. A student proposes a hypothesis that traits that are dominant are more common in the general population than traits with recessive alleles. Describe a procedure you might use to test this hypothesis.

THE STORY OF Genetics

The human genome project, DNA evidence in criminal cases, cloning—news about genetics is everywhere. Some of the most exciting research in science today involves genes. The timeline shows that some important concepts that underline the study of genetics were discovered relatively early. You will notice the influence of two major advances in technology—the development of the microscope during the 1600s, and the development of computer technology during the later half of the 1900s. The boxes below the timeline show how technology has led to new understanding and to applications of those understandings.

1674
Cells Are Everywhere
Anton van Leeuwenhoek uses a microscope to study pond water and discovers the water is full of microscopic organisms made of just single cells. These drawings show some of what he saw.

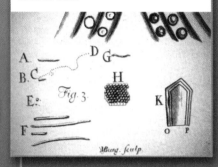

1665
Cells Discovered
Robert Hooke uses a microscope to study living matter. What he sees and then records in this drawing are tiny repeating units which he calls cells.

EVENTS

1650   1660   1670   1680

APPLICATIONS AND TECHNOLOGY

APPLICATION
Corn in Every Shape and Size
Native Americans grew 700 different kinds of popcorn. Their popcorn plants were a kind of grass with big hard seeds that exploded when they were heated. People who didn't want to have to explode their corn to eat it chose plants with softer seeds and grew them, and then chose the softest of those seeds to plant. Over hundreds of years, by choosing which plants to grow, people produced what we now eat as corn on the cob.

TECHNOLOGY
Seeing into the Cell
Single-glass lenses, such as the one van Leeuwenhoek used, were available as long ago as 1267. The compound microscope was first made in 1595, but it was over 200 years before it provided clear images. Until the 1930s, all microscopes focused light on objects. Eventually, light microscopes could magnify objects up to 2000 times.

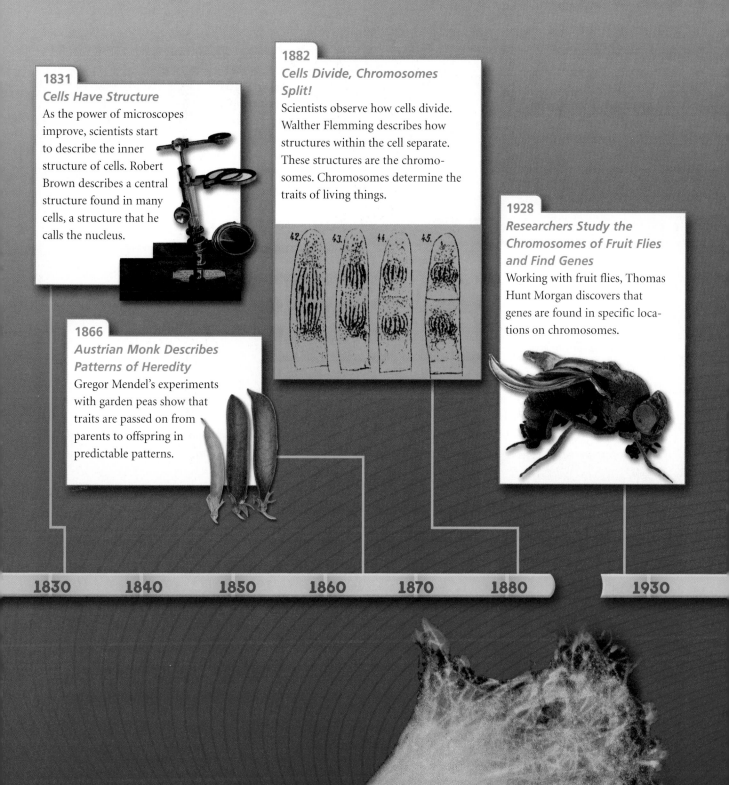

1831
Cells Have Structure
As the power of microscopes improve, scientists start to describe the inner structure of cells. Robert Brown describes a central structure found in many cells, a structure that he calls the nucleus.

1882
Cells Divide, Chromosomes Split!
Scientists observe how cells divide. Walther Flemming describes how structures within the cell separate. These structures are the chromosomes. Chromosomes determine the traits of living things.

1928
Researchers Study the Chromosomes of Fruit Flies and Find Genes
Working with fruit flies, Thomas Hunt Morgan discovers that genes are found in specific locations on chromosomes.

1866
Austrian Monk Describes Patterns of Heredity
Gregor Mendel's experiments with garden peas show that traits are passed on from parents to offspring in predictable patterns.

1830 1840 1850 1860 1870 1880 1930

Cells have a highly organized structure. Color dyes are used to help us see the different parts of a cell.

1944
DNA—Genetic Material
Researchers studying *Streptococcus* transformation find that bacterial cells get their characteristics from DNA.

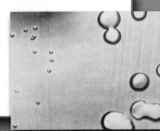

1973
DNA Recombined
In an amazing break-through, scientists have cut DNA from two different sources and recombined the DNA. The new DNA molecule reproduces when placed inside a bacterium. Such bacteria can be used to make proteins useful to humans.

1951
Scientists Capture Image of DNA
Scientists searching for the secret of DNA structure get an enormous clue when Rosalind Franklin uses x-ray crystallography to create an image of DNA. Maurice Wilkin, James Watson, and Francis Crick are awarded the Nobel Prize in 1962 for building a model of the DNA double helix molecule.

1984
Chinese Scientists Clone Fish!
In an effort to produce fast-growing fish for food, a team working with Zuoyan Zhu have made the first genetically modified (GM) fish.

1950   1960   1970   1980

TECHNOLOGY

Seeing Molecules

In the 1930s, a microscope came into use that focuses a beam of electrons, instead of a beam of light, on an object. Now we can see things as small as the molecules inside cells.

The image of the chromosome at left was made using an electron microscope.

APPLICATION

DNA Frees Innocent Prisoner

Kevin Green was convicted of murder and spent 16 years in prison. While he was in jail, the California Department of Justice created a DNA database that contained the DNA fingerprints of many other convicted felons. When Kevin's defenders compared the DNA found at the murder scene with DNA fingerprints in the database, they found that it matched someone else's fingerprint. The real murderer confessed, and Kevin is now a free man, thanks to genetics.

1984
Living Things Have Genetic Fingerprints

Human fingers have their own unique fingerprints. In a similar way, the DNA of different people has its own unique patterns. These DNA fingerprints are compared here.

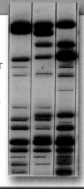

2000
Scientists Sequence Human Genome

Two groups of researchers, Celera and the Human Genome Project, succeed in publishing the first draft of the sequence of DNA for all the chromosomes in the human body.

RESOURCE CENTER
CLASSZONE.COM
Find recent genetics updates.

1990   2000   Today

APPLICATION

Saved by a New Gene

In 1986 a baby girl named Ashanti DeSilva was born. One single mistake in her DNA meant that Ashanti's body could not make an important disease-fighting protein.

In 1981, researchers had figured out how to move a working gene from one mammal to another. Ashanti became the first person ever to receive a gene from someone else. Ashanti's doctors injected some of her white blood cells with healthy copies of the sick gene. Now her white blood cells worked. Researchers and doctors are trying to apply the same techniques to other genetic disorders. There is still much work to be done.

INTO THE FUTURE

Genetics is a young science. The timeline spans 350 years, but the real study of genetics began in 1900 with another look at the work of Gregor Mendel. Since then, scientists have determined the structure and function of DNA—and ways to use this knowledge.

In medicine, genetics is used to identify genes that play a role in inherited diseases. Questions remain about how this knowledge can be used to treat or even prevent disease.

In agriculture, genetics is used to modify the genes of plant and animal stocks to give them desirable traits, such as resistance to disease. Questions remain about what effect modified genes might have once they enter a population of plants or animals.

In biology, genetics is used to determine how different types of organisms have changed over time and how one species relates to another. Questions remain about whether similar genes found in different organisms behave in the same way.

In society, genetic profiles are used to help solve crimes or make identifications. Questions remain about how to protect individuals and their personal information.

ACTIVITIES

Reliving History

Use a hand lens or microscope to study a sample of water from a pond or puddle, see if your sample contains structures similar to those drawn by Leeuwenhoek in 1674.

Writing About Science: Biography

Sharing information is important to scientific discovery. Learn more about individuals or groups involved in the discovery of DNA structure or sequencing the human genome. How important was cooperation in their work?

CHAPTER 5

DNA and Modern Genetics

the **BIG** idea

DNA is a set of instructions for making cell parts.

Key Concepts

SECTION
5.1 **DNA and RNA are required to make proteins.**
Learn about DNA, RNA, and protein synthesis.

SECTION
5.2 **Changes in DNA can produce variation.**
Learn about the effects of changes in DNA and how some changes can cause genetic disorders.

SECTION
5.3 **Modern genetics uses DNA technology.**
Learn about some applications of DNA technology and the Human Genome Project.

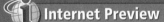

Internet Preview

CLASSZONE.COM

Chapter 5 online resources: Content Review, Visualization, four Resource Centers, Math Tutorial, Test Practice

What can a model of DNA show you about its structure?

EXPLORE (the BIG idea)

What Is the Pattern?

Sometimes by looking at the parts of a whole you can guess how the pieces fit together. Some evidence for the structure of DNA came when people noticed that certain types of chemical subunits came in pairs. Try this activity with a friend. Take 8 index cards and write 2 letters, A T or C G, on each card. Now cut the pairs in half and give your friend the individual pieces. See if he or she can find the pattern.

Observe and Think How long did it take your friend to see the pattern? Were there any other clues that he or she used?

What Vegetable Is That?

Buy a broccoflower from your local supermarket. Describe what it looks like, what it tastes like, and how it smells.

Observe and Think What properties of each vegetable does the broccoflower have? What gives an organism its traits?

Internet Activity: Human Genome

Go to **ClassZone.com** to find out how scientists put together a sequence of the DNA in the human genome.

Observe and Think What are the benefits of having a map of the human genome?

NSTA scilinks.org **SCiLINKS**

Genetics **Code: MDL035**

Getting Ready to Learn

CONCEPT REVIEW

- Traits are controlled by genes on chromosomes.
- Genes can be dominant or recessive.
- Cells have DNA, RNA, and proteins.

VOCABULARY REVIEW

organelle p. 21

protein p. 46

gene p. 102

technology *See Glossary.*

CONTENT REVIEW
CLASSZONE.COM
Review concepts and vocabulary.

TAKING NOTES

SUPPORTING MAIN IDEAS

Make a chart to show main ideas and the information that supports them. Copy each blue heading; then add supporting information, such as reasons, explanations, and examples.

CHOOSE YOUR OWN STRATEGY

Take notes about new vocabulary terms using one or more of the strategies from earlier chapters —**four square, word triangle, frame game,** or **magnet word.** Feel free to mix and match the strategies, or use an entirely different vocabulary strategy.

See the Note-Taking Handbook on pages R45–R51.

SCIENCE NOTEBOOK

DNA sequences can change.

Variations in DNA make one organism different from another.

Human DNA has 6 billion base pairs; yeast DNA has 12 million base pairs.

Definition	Characteristics
TERM	
Examples	Nonexamples

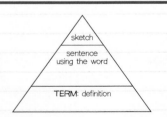

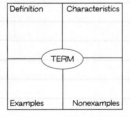

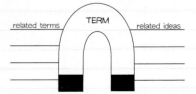

DNA and RNA are required to make proteins.

◀ **BEFORE**, you learned

- Traits pass from parents to off-spring in predictable patterns
- Traits are passed on through genes
- In sexual reproduction, off-spring get half their genes from each parent

▶ **NOW**, you will learn

- How the structure of DNA stores information the cell needs
- How DNA is copied
- How RNA uses the information from DNA to make proteins

VOCABULARY

replication p. 137
RNA p. 138

EXPLORE Templates

How does a template work?

PROCEDURE

MATERIALS
- paper
- pencil

① Write a set of rules to describe how the characters in line A relate to the characters in line B.

② Place a piece of paper just under line C below. Use the rules from step 1 to produce a template—the corresponding pattern that goes with line C.

C ⊙ △ △ □ ○ ○

③ Give the rules and the template to a classmate to produce a copy of line C.

WHAT DO YOU THINK?
What is a template and how does it differ from a copy?

DNA is the information molecule.

SUPPORTING MAIN IDEAS
Make a chart of information supporting the main idea: *DNA is the information molecule.*

DNA is a molecule that stores information—that's all it does. You could compare the information in DNA to the books in your local library. You might find a book describing how to bake a cake, make a model sailboat, or beat your favorite computer game. The books, however, don't actually do any of those things—you do. The "books" in the DNA "library" carry all the information that a cell needs to function, to grow, and to divide. However, DNA doesn't do any of those things. Proteins do most of the work of a cell and also make up much of the structure of a cell.

Proteins and Amino Acids

RESOURCE CENTER
CLASSZONE.COM

Learn more about DNA.

Proteins are large molecules that are made up of chains of amino acids. Twenty different amino acids come together in enough combinations to make up the thousands of different proteins found in the human body. Some proteins are small. For example, lysozyme is a digestive protein that is made up of a sequence of 129 amino acids. Some proteins are large. For example, dystrophin is a huge structural protein that is made up of 3685 amino acids.

CHECK YOUR READING What is the relationship between proteins and amino acids?

DNA stores the information that enables a cell to put together the right sequences of amino acids needed to produce specific proteins. Scientists describe DNA as containing a code. A code is a set of rules and symbols used to carry information. For example, your computer uses a code of ones and zeroes to store data and then translates the code into the numbers, letters, and graphics you see on a computer screen. To understand how DNA functions as a code, you first need to learn about the structure of the DNA molecule.

DNA and the Genetic Code

The DNA molecule takes the shape of a double-stranded spiral, which, as you can see from the diagram, looks something like a twisted ladder. In Chapter 2, you read about different subunits that make up the molecules found in cells. Nucleotide subunits make up each of the two strands of the DNA molecule. One part of the nucleotide forms the side rail of the DNA "ladder." The other part, the nucleotide base, forms the rung. Actually, two bases come together to form the rung, as one nucleotide base attaches to another from the opposite strand. You can see how the parts fit together in the diagram to the left.

There are four different nucleotides in DNA, identified by their bases: adenine (A), thymine (T), cytosine (C), and guanine (G). Because of differences in size and shape, adenine always pairs with thymine (A-T) and cytosine always pairs with guanine (C-G). The bases fit together like two pieces of a jigsaw puzzle. These bases are often referred to simply by their initials—A, T, C, and G. The phrase "all tigers can growl" may help you remember them.

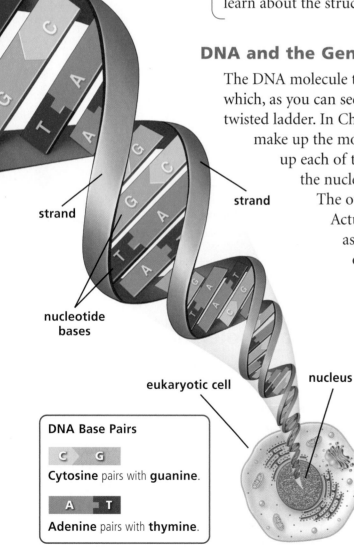

DNA molecule

strand

strand

nucleotide bases

eukaryotic cell

nucleus

DNA Base Pairs

| C | G |

Cytosine pairs with **guanine**.

| A | T |

Adenine pairs with **thymine**.

It is the sequence—the order—of bases in a strand of DNA that forms the code for making proteins. Like a list of ingredients in a recipe book, a set of bases specifies the amino acids needed to form a particular protein. The cookbook uses just 4 bases—A, T, G, and C—to code for 20 amino acids. A code of 2 bases to 1 amino acid gives only 16 possible combinations. However, a code of 3 bases to 1 amino acid gives 64 possible combinations.

The genetic code is, in fact, a triplet code. A specific sequence of 3 nucleotide bases codes for 1 amino acid. For example, the triplet T-C-T on a strand of DNA codes for the amino acid arginine. Some amino acids have two different codes. Others have three, and some have four. A gene is the entire sequence of the bases that codes for all the amino acids in a protein. Each gene is made up of a sequence of bases at a particular location on the DNA.

T – C – T
(DNA triplet)

codes for

arginine
(amino acid)

Replication

When a cell divides into two cells, each daughter cell receives an identical copy of the DNA. Before a cell divides, all of its DNA is copied, a process referred to as **replication.** Let's follow the process through for one DNA molecule. First, the two strands of DNA separate, almost like two threads in a string being unwound. Nucleotides in the area around the DNA match up, base by base, with the nucleotides on each DNA strand. C matches up with G and A matches up with T. When replication is complete, there are two identical DNA molecules. Each molecule has one strand of old DNA and one strand of new DNA.

READING TiP

Replicate includes the root word meaning "to repeat."

Replication

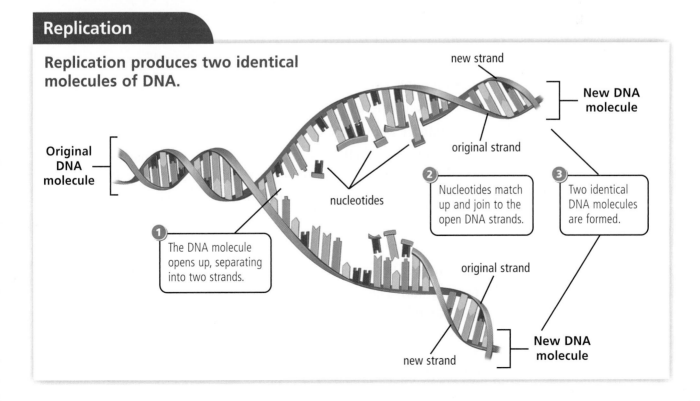

Replication produces two identical molecules of DNA.

Original DNA molecule

nucleotides

new strand

New DNA molecule

original strand

1 The DNA molecule opens up, separating into two strands.

2 Nucleotides match up and join to the open DNA strands.

3 Two identical DNA molecules are formed.

original strand

New DNA molecule

new strand

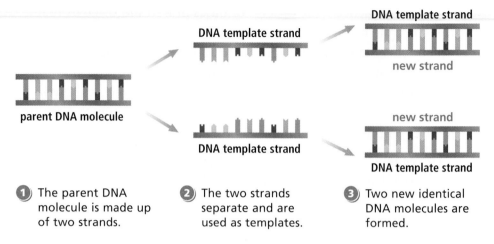

① The parent DNA molecule is made up of two strands.

② The two strands separate and are used as templates.

③ Two new identical DNA molecules are formed.

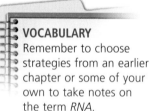

READING TiP

Complementary has a root that means "to complete."

During replication, each strand of DNA is used as a template to produce a copy of the other strand. A template is a pattern or shape that produces a matching, or complementary, product. If you've ever made a plaster model of your hand, you've worked with a template. You press your hand into a soft material that leaves a mold of your hand. You then pour liquid plaster into the mold to produce a copy of your hand. The mold is a template. Its shape allows you to make a complementary shape that matches your hand.

RNA is needed to make proteins.

DNA is not used to make proteins directly. Translating the genetic code of DNA involves another type of molecule, RNA. **RNA,** or ribonucleic acid, carries the information from DNA to a ribosome, where the amino acids are brought together to form a protein. DNA actually codes for RNA. Three different types of RNA are involved in making proteins. They are named for their functions:

- messenger RNA (mRNA)
- ribosomal RNA (rRNA)
- transfer RNA (tRNA)

In prokaryotic cells, RNA and proteins are both made in the cytoplasm. In eukaryotic cells, DNA is copied in the nucleus, then RNA moves to the cytoplasm, where the proteins are made.

VOCABULARY
Remember to choose strategies from an earlier chapter or some of your own to take notes on the term *RNA*.

Transcription

The process of transferring information from DNA to RNA is called transcription. The chemical structure of RNA is quite similar to the structure of DNA. Both are made up of four types of nucleotide subunits. Three of the bases that make up RNA are the same as in DNA: guanine (G), cytosine (C), and adenine (A). However, the fourth base is uracil (U), not thymine.

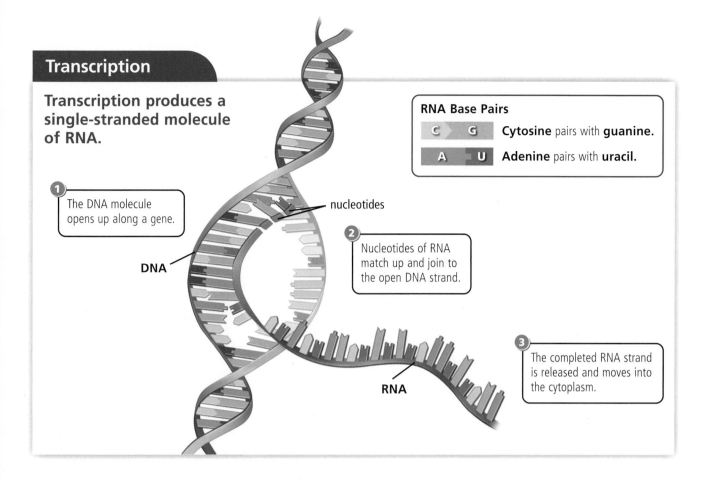

Transcription

Transcription produces a single-stranded molecule of RNA.

RNA Base Pairs

C ▷ G **Cytosine** pairs with **guanine**.

A ▷ U **Adenine** pairs with **uracil**.

1 The DNA molecule opens up along a gene.

nucleotides

DNA

2 Nucleotides of RNA match up and join to the open DNA strand.

3 The completed RNA strand is released and moves into the cytoplasm.

RNA

During transcription, DNA is again used as a template, this time to make a complementary strand of RNA. Only individual genes are transcribed, not a whole DNA molecule. The DNA again opens up, just where the gene is located. As shown in the diagram above, RNA bases match up to complementary bases on the DNA template. Adenine pairs with uracil (A-U) and cytosine pairs with guanine (C-G).

Transcription is different from replication in some important ways. Only one strand of DNA is transcribed, which means just a single strand of RNA is produced. When transcription is complete, the RNA is released, it does not stay attached to DNA. This means that many copies of RNA can be made from the same gene in a short period of time. At the end of transcription, the DNA molecule closes.

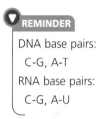

REMINDER

DNA base pairs:
C-G, A-T
RNA base pairs:
C-G, A-U

Translation

Replication and transcription involve passing along information that is coded in the language of nucleotide bases. To make proteins, cells have to translate this language of nucleotide bases into the language of amino acids. Three specific bases equal one amino acid. The actual assembly of the amino acids in their proper sequence is the translation. Translation takes place in the cytoplasm of a cell. It involves all three types of RNA.

DNA

Transcription

RNA

Translation

Protein

The assembling of amino acids to form a protein occurs in the cytoplasm.

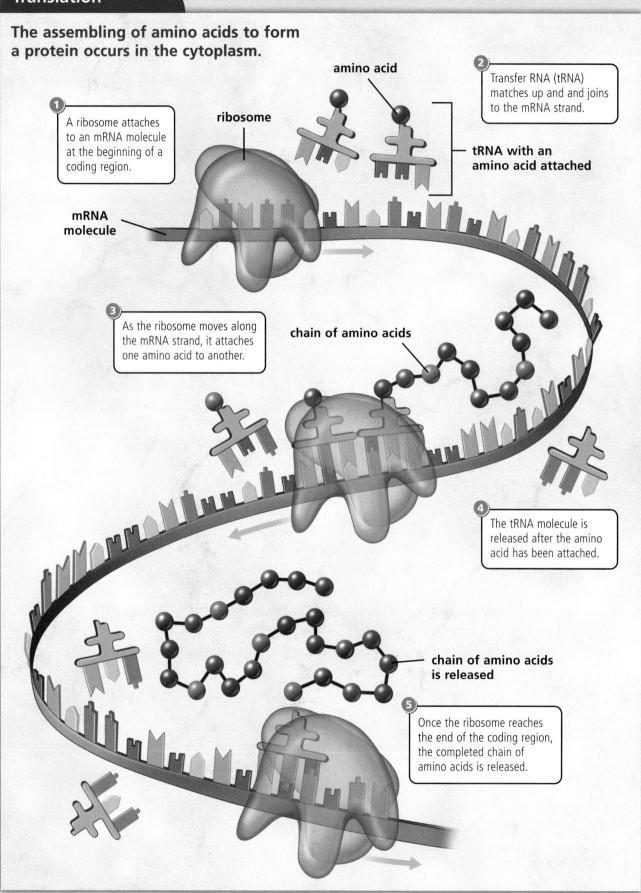

1 A ribosome attaches to an mRNA molecule at the beginning of a coding region.

2 Transfer RNA (tRNA) matches up and and joins to the mRNA strand.

amino acid

ribosome

tRNA with an amino acid attached

mRNA molecule

3 As the ribosome moves along the mRNA strand, it attaches one amino acid to another.

chain of amino acids

4 The tRNA molecule is released after the amino acid has been attached.

chain of amino acids is released

5 Once the ribosome reaches the end of the coding region, the completed chain of amino acids is released.

Proteins are made on ribosomes, structures that are made up of ribosomal RNA and proteins. If you think of DNA as a cookbook for making different proteins, and mRNA as a recipe for making a protein, then the ribosome is the place where the cooking gets done. In this analogy, tRNA gathers the ingredients, which are amino acids.

A tRNA molecule is shaped in such a way that one end of it can attach to a specific amino acid. The other end of tRNA has a triplet of bases that is complementary to a triplet of bases on mRNA. Transfer RNA does the actual translation of bases to amino acid when it matches up with mRNA. The diagram on page 140 shows the whole process.

READING TiP

Refer to the diagram on page 140 as you read the text. The numbers in the text match the numbers in the diagram.

1. Translation begins when a ribosome attaches to the beginning end of an mRNA molecule.

2. A tRNA molecule carrying an amino acid matches up to a complementary mRNA at the ribosome.

3. The ribosome attaches one amino acid to another as it moves along the mRNA molecule.

4. The tRNA molecules are released after the amino acids they carry are attached to the chain of amino acids.

5. The ribosome completes the translation when it reaches the end of the mRNA strand. The newly made protein molecule, in the form of a chain of amino acids, is released.

 CHECK YOUR READING Describe how the three different types of RNA work together in protein synthesis.

The process of making proteins is basically the same in all cells. The flow of information in a cell goes from DNA to RNA to protein.

 **VISUALIZATION** CLASSZONE.COM

Watch an animation of how proteins are made.

5.1 Review

KEY CONCEPTS

1. Describe the shape of the DNA molecule and how nucleotide bases fit into that structure.

2. What is a protein and what is it made up of?

3. Identify three types of RNA involved in protein synthesis and briefly describe what they do.

CRITICAL THINKING

4. **Infer** What might happen if the wrong amino acid is put on a tRNA molecule?

5. **Apply** Copy the following sequence of DNA bases: A-T-C-A-G-G. Write the complementary mRNA and tRNA sequences for this.

CHALLENGE

6. **Synthesize** Study the sequences you wrote for question 5. How does the tRNA sequence compare to the original DNA sequence?

CHAPTER INVESTIGATION

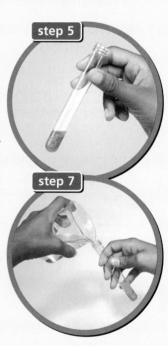

Extract and Observe DNA

OVERVIEW AND PURPOSE In this activity, you will work with several simple chemicals that can break down the membranes of a cell. You will extract DNA from raw wheat germ. Then you will examine the properties of the extracted DNA.

▶ Procedure

1. Make a table in your **Science Notebook** like the one shown on page 143.

2. Place a small scoop of wheat germ in a test tube. The wheat germ should be about 1 cm high in the test tube.

3. Add enough distilled water to wet and cover all of the wheat germ in the test tube.

4. Add 25–30 drops of detergent solution to the test tube.

5. For 3 minutes, gently swirl the test tube contents by rotating your wrist while holding the tube. Try not to make bubbles.

   (step 5)

6. Add 25–30 drops of the salt solution to the test tube, and swirl for 1 more minute.

7. Hold the test tube tilted at an angle. Slowly add alcohol so that it runs down the inside of the test tube and forms a separate layer on top of the the material already in the tube. Add enough alcohol to double the total volume you started with. Let the test tube stand for 2 minutes.

   (step 7)

MATERIALS
- raw wheat germ
- scoop
- test tube
- warm distilled water
- detergent solution
- salt solution
- cold ethyl or isopropyl alcohol
- bent paper clip

8 Watch for stringy, cloudy material to rise up from the bottom layer into the alcohol layer. This is the DNA.

9 Use the bent paper clip to remove some DNA. Be careful to probe only the alcohol layer and not disturb the material at the bottom of the test tube.

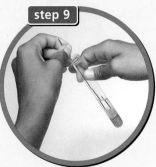

step 9

10 Wash your hands after working with the chemicals.

Observe and Analyze
Write It Up

1. **OBSERVE** How do your observations of the DNA you just extracted compare with what you know about the structure of DNA. Record these comparisons in your notebook in a table similar to the one shown.

2. **INFER** What type of organism is wheat? Where is the DNA located in a wheat germ cell?

3. **INFER** What do you think was the purpose of using detergent in this experiment? Hint: How does soap work on greasy dishes?

4. **IDENTIFY LIMITS** What might happen if the wheat germ were not mixed properly with the detergent solution?

Conclude
Write It Up

1. **INFER** If you had used cooked or toasted wheat germ in this experiment, you would not have gotten good results. Why do you think this is the case?

2. **INFER** Would this experiment work with cells from other organisms, such as bananas, onions, or cells from your own cheek? Why or why not?

3. **INFER** Would DNA from a single cell be visible to the naked eye?

4. **APPLY** The procedure that you performed today is used by many people to obtain DNA for further study. Give some examples of how DNA information is used in the world today.

INVESTIGATE Further

CHALLENGE Repeat the experiment replacing the alcohol with water in step 7. Compare the results with the results you obtained using alcohol.

Extract and Observe DNA

Table 1. Properties and Observations

Properties of DNA	Observations

5.2 Changes in DNA can produce variation.

 BEFORE, you learned

- DNA contains information in the form of a sequence of bases
- Genes code for RNA and proteins
- DNA is transcribed into RNA, which is used to make proteins

 NOW, you will learn

- About mutations, any changes in DNA
- About the possible effects of mutations
- About pedigrees and how they are used

VOCABULARY

mutation p. 145
pedigree p. 147

EXPLORE Codes

What happens to a code if small changes occur?

PROCEDURE

① Language is a type of code. Look at the English sentence below.

One day the cat ate the rat.

② Insert an extra *a* into the word *cat* in the sentence above, but keep the spacing the same. That is, keep a space after every third letter.

WHAT DO YOU THINK?

- Does the sentence still make sense? How were the rest of the words affected?
- How would other small changes affect the meaning of the sentence? Try substituting, removing, and switching letters.

MATERIALS
- pencil
- paper

DNA sequences can change.

SUPPORTING MAIN IDEAS
In your notebook, organize information that supports this main idea: *DNA sequences can change.*

Differences, or variations, in DNA are what make one organism different from another. The number of differences in the DNA sequences between two species is large. Each human cell, with its 46 chromosomes, contains an astounding 6 billion base pairs in its DNA. A yeast cell, by comparison, has 12 million base pairs in its DNA.

The number of differences between any two individuals of the same species is small. For example, about 99.9 percent of the DNA in the cells of two different humans is the same. Just 0.1 percent variation in DNA makes you the unique person you are. That averages out to one base in a thousand.

How can there be such great variety among people if their DNA is so similar? The reason is that of the 6 billion base pairs in human DNA, only 5 percent are in the genes that code for RNA and proteins. As you learned in Chapter 4, genes and their interaction with the environment are what determine the traits of a person.

Differences in genes affect the height of people or the color of their eyes, hair, or skin. Genes produce variation because the type or amount of the proteins they code for can vary from person to person. For example, skin color comes from a protein called melanin. The amount of melanin an individual produces affects the color of their skin.

Many traits, including skin tones, are affected by genes.

Given the huge number of base pairs in the DNA of any organism, it is not surprising that errors occur when DNA is copied. DNA is also affected by the environment. For example, exposure to ultraviolet radiation or x-rays can damage DNA. Both natural and human-made toxins, which are harmful chemicals, can also damage DNA.

Any change in DNA is called a **mutation.** Cells have different ways to repair mistakes in a DNA sequence. Certain enzymes actually proofread DNA, for example correcting mismatched base pairs. Other enzymes enable damaged DNA to be fixed.

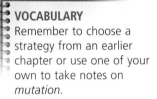

VOCABULARY
Remember to choose a strategy from an earlier chapter or use one of your own to take notes on *mutation.*

 CHECK YOUR READING What is a mutation?

When a mutation occurs in a gene, the coding region of DNA, the wrong amino acid might be placed in the amino-acid chain. If this happens, there are three possible outcomes.

❶ **The mutation causes no effect.** There are two sets of DNA in every cell, which means a pair of genes are coding for the same protein. Even if one gene is not working, the other may still code for enough of the protein to enable a cell to function normally.

❷ **The effect of a mutation is minor.** A change in the genes that control the amount of melanin produced could affect not only how light or dark a person's skin is, it could also affect eye or hair color. The change, in this case, is a change in appearance.

❸ **The effect of a mutation is great.** The effect can be good, such as a plant having an increased resistance to disease. Or the effect can be bad, causing a genetic disorder or disease.

RESOURCE CENTER
CLASSZONE.COM

Find out more about mutations.

Remember, only 5 percent of human DNA is in genes. If a mutation occurs in a noncoding region of DNA, then chances are that the mutation will have no effect. Such a mutation is neutral.

How does a large number of noncoding sequences affect mutations?

SKILL FOCUS
Making models

PROCEDURE

① Circle ten words on the page of a newspaper to represent genes. Place the newspaper on your desk.

② Use a handful of paper-punch circles to represent mutations and scatter them onto the newspaper.

③ Count the number of paper-punch "mutations" that landed on "genes" and those that did not.

WHAT DO YOU THINK?

• What percentage of "mutations" affected gene sequences?

• What does this model suggest about the probability of mutations affecting genes that are only a small part of a DNA sequence?

CHALLENGE Most of the sequences in bacterial DNA are genes. How could you use the same model to evaluate the effect of mutations on bacterial DNA?

MATERIALS
• newspaper
• pen
• paper-punch circles

TIME
15 minutes

Go! Wednesday

Mutations can cause genetic disorders.

A genetic disorder is a disease or condition that results from mutations that affect the normal functioning of a cell. Sometimes these disorders are inherited, passed on from parent to offspring. Examples of inherited disorders include Tay-Sachs disease, cystic fibrosis, sickle cell disease, and albinism. Other genetic disorders result from mutations that occur during a person's lifetime. Most cancers fall into this category.

CHECK YOUR READING What is a genetic disorder?

Sometimes a person carries a tendency for a disease, such as diabetes, glaucoma, Alzheimer's disease, or emphysema. In some cases, a person's behavior can help prevent the disease. Cigarette smoke is a leading cause of lung cancer. Smoke also greatly increases the risk of people with a genetic tendency for emphysema to develop that disease.

Sickle cell disease is an interesting example of how a mutation can have more than one effect. The mutation occurs in one of the genes that code for hemoglobin. Hemoglobin is a protein that carries oxygen in red blood cells. The mutation causes one amino acid to be replaced with another.

normal hemoglobin
(protein)

glutamate
(amino acid)

sickle cell hemoglobin
(protein)

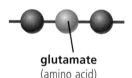

valine
(amino acid)

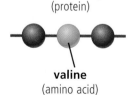

Sickle cell disease is a recessive disorder. Only people who carry two recessive alleles are affected. Recall that an allele is one form of a gene. Because of the amino acid change, some red blood cells can take on a sickle shape. See the photograph at the right. The pedigree below shows the pattern of inheritance of the sickle cell allele through three generations of a family. A **pedigree** is a diagram of family relationships that includes two or more generations.

Sickle cell disease is a severe disease. Sickled red blood cells tend to break more easily than normal red blood cells. People with sickle cell disease do not get enough oxygen delivered to their body tissues, and the tissues become damaged. The disease is common in Africa and parts of India and the Middle East.

What is interesting about the sickle cell allele is that it provides protection against dying of malaria. Malaria is a severe disease, also common in Africa, India, and the Middle East. It is caused by microscopic organisms that reproduce in red blood cells. Scientists do not yet completely understand why people with the sickle cell allele are better able to survive malaria. However the effect of this protection is that the sickle allele remains common in populations that live in regions where malaria is common.

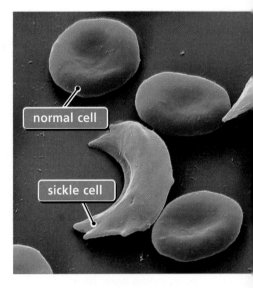

normal cell

sickle cell

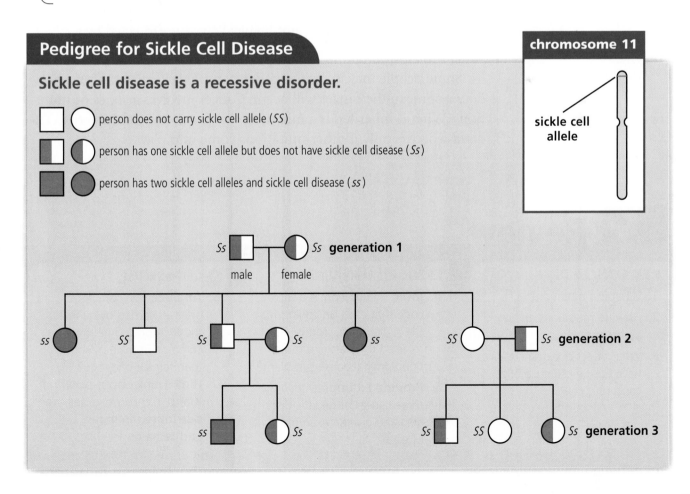

Pedigree for Sickle Cell Disease

chromosome 11

Sickle cell disease is a recessive disorder.

☐ ○ person does not carry sickle cell allele (*SS*)

◨ ◖ person has one sickle cell allele but does not have sickle cell disease (*Ss*)

■ ● person has two sickle cell alleles and sickle cell disease (*ss*)

sickle cell allele

Ss ◨—◖ *Ss* **generation 1**

male | female

ss ● | *SS* ☐ | *Ss* ◨—◖ *Ss* | ● *ss* | *SS* ○—◨ *Ss* **generation 2**

ss ■ | ◖ *Ss* | *Ss* ◨ | *ss* ○ | ◖ *Ss* **generation 3**

Cancer is a genetic disorder that affects the cell cycle.

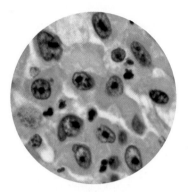

Cancer cells, such as the ones shown here, have abnormal shapes. Cancer cells reproduce uncontrollably and crowd out normal cells.

Cancer is not a single genetic disorder; but rather it is a group of disorders. All cancers are characterized by the uncontrolled division of cells. Normally, cells in a multicellular organism function to maintain the health of an organism. Cell division is controlled so that an organism has the number of cells it needs to function. Cancer cells are, in a way, "selfish" cells. Where normal cells stay within the same tissue, cancer cells spread quickly and can invade other tissues. A normal cell has a definite life span. Cancerous cells become "immortal"—they divide indefinitely.

CHECK YOUR READING What is a characteristic of all cancers?

Most cancers are caused by mutations to DNA that happen during a person's lifetime. Some mutations come from mistakes made during replication. But many are caused by harmful chemicals often referred to as *carcinogens* (kahr-SIHN-uh-juhnz). Many plants naturally produce carcinogens in their tissues. Nicotine is a carcinogen naturally found in tobacco leaves. There are other carcinogens in tobacco.

Ultraviolet and nuclear radiation as well as x-rays can also cause cancer. That is why, if you get an x-ray at the doctor's or dentist's office, the part of your body not being x-rayed is protected by a lead apron.

Some people may inherit a tendency for a particular cancer. That does not mean the cancer will occur. Cancer involves a series of mutations. What is inherited is a mutation that is one step in the series. The disease occurs only if other mutations come into play.

5.2 Review

KEY CONCEPTS

1. What is a mutation?
2. How do mutations affect an organism?
3. What effect does cancer have on the cell cycle of a cancerous cell?

CRITICAL THINKING

4. **Infer** A mutation in a triplet code that ends up coding for the same amino acid is referred to as a silent mutation. In what sense is it silent?
5. **Provide Examples** Identify three causes of genetic disorders and give an example of each.

CHALLENGE

6. **Analyze** Why are genetic diseases carried by genes on the X chromosome more common in male offspring than female offspring?
Hint: Think about how X and Y chromosomes are distributed in males and females.

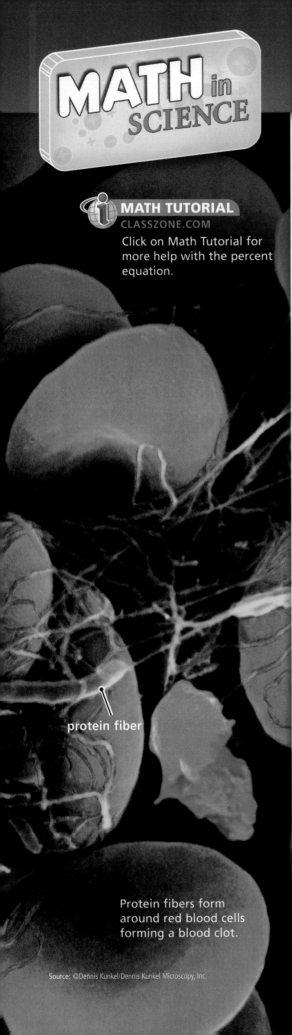

protein fiber

Protein fibers form around red blood cells forming a blood clot.

MATH in SCIENCE

MATH TUTORIAL
CLASSZONE.COM

Click on Math Tutorial for more help with the percent equation.

SKILL: FINDING PERCENT OF A WHOLE

Percents and Populations

Hemophilia is a genetic disorder in which blood does not clot properly. In any group of people who have hemophilia, approximately 80 percent have type A, which is caused by a mutation in one gene. Usually about 12 percent have type B, a different gene mutation.

To express what part of a population carries a gene mutation, scientists can use percentages. Once you know the percentage of a population, you can find out how many individuals that percent represents.

Example

Suppose a doctor is treating a group of people who have the disease hemophilia. The group has 400 people. About how many individuals would you expect to have hemophilia A?

(1) Write the percent as a decimal.

$$80\% = 0.80$$

(2) Multiply the decimal number by the total population.

$$0.80 \cdot 400 = 320.00$$

(3) Be sure the answer has the same number of decimal places as the total number of decimal places in the original factors.

$$0.80 \cdot 400 = 320.00$$
2 decimal places

ANSWER There are probably about 320 people with hemophilia A.

Answer the following questions for a group of 400 hemophilia patients.

1. How many patients are likely to have hemophilia B?

2. Suppose a new doctor begins treatment of 20 percent of the hemophilia A patients. How many individuals is that?

3. In as many as 30 percent of cases of hemophilia, there is no family history of the disorder. In the group of 400, how many individuals probably did not have a family history of hemophilia?

CHALLENGE Write a fraction in simplest terms equal to each percentage: 80 percent, 30 percent, 12 percent, 3 percent. When you multiply these fractions by 400, do you get the same or different results as when you multiply 400 by the percentages? Explain why the results may be different.

5.3 Modern genetics uses DNA technology.

 BEFORE, you learned

- Mutations are changes to DNA
- Not all mutations have an effect on an organism
- Mutations can lead to genetic disorders

 NOW, you will learn

- How scientists can change organisms by changing DNA
- About some applications of DNA technology
- About some issues surrounding the use of DNA technology

VOCABULARY

selective breeding p. 151
genetic engineering p. 151
genome p. 154
cloning p. 154

THiNK ABOUT

What type of animal is this?

Look at the photograph of the animal to the right. The cells in this animal contain DNA from two different species. For a long time humans have been able to mix genes by breeding together animals of different but similar species. Now scientists have the technology to mix together genes from two very different species by inserting genes from one organism into the cells of another. What do the characteristics of this animal suggest about the source of its genes?

Changes in DNA can change an organism.

Organisms change over time. Changes come about because of mutations in DNA. Random changes in DNA may introduce new traits into an organism. Over time, certain traits may become more common in one group of organisms as they interact with the environment and each other.

Are all changes in a group of organisms random? There are dogs, such as bloodhounds, that are particularly well suited to tracking. There are cows that give large quantities of milk and crops that produce large quantities of grain. Changes such as these are not random, but result from careful breeding directed by humans.

Selective Breeding

For thousands of years, humans have been carefully selecting and breeding certain plants and animals that have desirable traits. As the years have passed, horses have gotten faster, pigs have gotten leaner, and corn has become sweeter. **Selective breeding** is the process of selecting and breeding parent organisms to pass on particular traits to the offspring.

Selective breeding can be successful as long as the desirable traits are controlled by genes. In fact, what these early farmers were actually selecting were alleles, particular versions of a gene. The genes were already present in some members of the population. People were not changing DNA, but they were causing certain alleles to become more common in a particular breed. The different dog breeds are a good example of this. All dogs share a common ancestor, the wolf. However, thousands of years of selective breeding have produced dogs with a variety of characteristics.

Bloodhounds, with their strong sense of smell, are used in police work for tracking.

 How does selective breeding affect DNA?

Genetic Engineering

Within the last fifty years it has become possible to directly change the DNA of an organism. **Genetic engineering** is the process in which a sequence of DNA from an organism is first isolated, then changed, and then returned to the organism or to another organism. The DNA that is engineered often codes for some particular trait of interest. Using technology, scientists can take a gene from one species and transfer it into the DNA of an organism from another species. The resulting organisms are referred to as genetically modified (GM), or transgenic.

READING TiP

The root *trans-* means "across." *Transgenic* refers to the movement of genes across species.

 What are three steps involved in genetic engineering?

One application of genetic engineering across species involves making plants more insect-resistant. Genetic engineers have isolated genes in microorganisms that produce natural insect-killing chemicals, or pesticides. They have succeeded in transferring these genes into the DNA of crop plants, such as corn and soybeans. The cells of the genetically modified plants then produce their own pesticide, reducing the amount of chemical pesticide farmers need to use on their fields.

genetically modified tomatoes

These tomatoes have been genetically modified to grow in conditions that would not support naturally occurring tomatoes.

Genetic engineering can address very specific needs. For example, in many parts of the world, soils are poor in nutrients. Or the soil may contain salts. Such soil is not good for growing food crops. Genetic engineers have inserted a gene from a salt-tolerant cabbage into tomatoes. The salt-tolerant tomatoes can grow in soil that natural tomatoes cannot grow in. These tomatoes can also be grown using brackish water, which is water with a higher salt content than fresh water.

There are risks and benefits associated with genetic engineering.

Genetic engineering offers potential benefits to society, but also carries potential risks. Probably most people in the United States have eaten foods made from genetically modified corn or soybeans. The plants have bacterial genes that make them more resistant to plant-eating insects. This increases food production and reduces the amount of chemical pesticides needed. Less chemical pesticide on the ground reduces the risk of environmental pollution.

However, many people worry that the natural pesticides produced by a genetically modified plant might have some effect on humans. What if genetically modified plants cross-breed with other plants, and give protection to plants that are considered weeds? There is also the question of how to let people know if the food they eat is genetically modified. Many people think that such food should be labeled.

CHECK YOUR READING What are some risks and benefits associated with using genetic engineering in food crops?

There is uncertainty about how the DNA of genetically modified organisms might affect natural populations. For example, scientists are working with salmon that are genetically modified to grow more quickly. Fish are an important food source, and natural fish populations are decreasing. However, the salmon are raised in pens set in rivers or the sea. If the fish escape, they may breed with fish from wild populations. Government officials have yet to decide whether the benefit of having these fast-growing fish is worth the risk to wild populations.

salmon pens

ANALYZE How would the genetic material of wild salmon change if they were to breed with genetically modified salmon?

DNA technology has many applications.

DNA technology is used in many different ways. It can be used to add nutrients to foods to make them more nutritious. It can be used to produce new and better drugs for treating disease. DNA technology can also be used to determine whether a particular drug might cause side effects in an individual. And it can be used to screen for and perhaps treat genetic disorders.

DNA Identification

You may have seen news stories about how DNA evidence is used to solve a crime. Law enforcement specialists gather as much DNA evidence as they can from a crime scene—for example, skin, hair, or blood. In a laboratory, they scan about ten regions of the DNA that are known to vary from individual to individual. They use this information to produce a DNA profile—a DNA fingerprint. This fingerprint is unique to a person, unless that person has an identical twin. If DNA analysis of tissue found at the crime scene matches the DNA fingerprint of a suspect, then police know the suspect was at the scene.

The more matches found between crime-scene DNA and the suspect's DNA, the higher the probability that the suspect is guilty. Experts currently recommend that at least four to six DNA regions be matched to establish a person's guilt. The chances are very small that another person would have exactly the same DNA profile for all the DNA regions tested. Of course, the courts also take other forms of evidence into account before an individual is convicted of a crime.

RESOURCE CENTER
CLASSZONE.COM

Learn more about DNA technology.

Studying Genomes

VOCABULARY
Don't forget to choose a strategy to take notes on the term *genome*.

One of the most challenging scientific projects ever undertaken was the Human Genome Project. A **genome** is all the genetic material in an organism. The primary goal of the project was to sequence the 3 billion nucleotide pairs in a single set of human chromosomes. The initial sequence was published in 2001. Scientists are now working to identify the approximately 30,000 genes within the human genome.

Scientists have completed sequencing the genomes of many organisms. These organisms, often referred to as model organisms, enable scientists to compare DNA across species. Many of the genes found in model organisms, such as the fruit fly and mouse, are also found in the human genome.

Scientists are aware that there are many ethical, legal, and social issues that arise from the ability to change DNA. We as a society have to decide when it is acceptable to change DNA and how to use the technology we have. **Cloning** is a technique that uses technology to make copies of DNA. It can be applied to a segment of DNA or to a whole organism. Cloning has been used in bacteria to produce proteins and drugs that help fight disease. Human insulin, which is needed to treat people with a certain form of diabetes, is now produced in large quantities as the result of cloning techniques.

The same technology, which is so helpful in one application, can be a cause of concern when applied in a different way. In 1996, scientists cloned the first mammal, a sheep named Dolly. All of Dolly's DNA came from a single body cell. The ability to clone such a complex animal raised many concerns about future uses of the cloning. This, as well as many other possible applications of technology, makes it important that people understand the science of genetics. Only then can they make informed decisions about how and when the technology should be used.

Dolly was the first successfully cloned mammal.

5.3 Review

KEY CONCEPTS

1. What is a genetically modified organism?
2. What is the Human Genome Project?
3. List three different applications of DNA technology.

CRITICAL THINKING

4. **Compare and Contrast** How is selective breeding different from genetic engineering? How are they the same?
5. **Analyze** Can a genetically modified trait in an organism be undone?

○ CHALLENGE

6. **Analyze** Why might a genetically engineered drug, such as insulin, be better for treatment of disease than a drug that is manufactured chemically?

Modern Genetics Meets the Dodo and the Solitaire

Hunted to Extinction

The dodo bird was first sighted around 1600 by Portuguese sailors arriving on the shores of the island of Mauritius in the Indian Ocean. Portuguese sailors hunted the dodo, which was unable to fly, and used its meat for food. The bird, never having had contact with humans, did not run away. Only a mere 80 years later, the dodo was extinct.

DNA Evidence

Few bone specimens of the dodo bird remain today. Scientists collected and analyzed genetic material from preserved dodo specimens and specimens of another, similar extinct bird called the solitaire bird. The DNA evidence was compared with the genetic material of about 35 species of living pigeons and doves.

The model shows a solitaire bird, a close relative of the dodo.

The DNA had a story to tell. Evidence suggests that the dodo and solitaire bird were close relatives. Their nearest living relative is a species of pigeon found in nearby southeast Asia. From this evidence, scientists hypothesize that the dodo and solitaire birds species became separate almost 25 million years ago. In the geographic location of the island of Mauritius, the dodo developed its distinct characteristics, which eventually led to its extinction.

EXPLORE

1. **MAKE INFERENCES** How can scientists use what they know from analyzing dodo bones to help them form conclusions about the physical characteristics of the bird?

2. **CHALLENGE** Several factors contributed to the extinction of the dodo bird. Look online to find out more about these factors. How can learning about what happened to the dodo help save today's endangered species from extinction?

Chapter Review

the BIG idea

DNA is a set of instructions for making cell parts.

CONTENT REVIEW
CLASSZONE.COM

KEY CONCEPTS SUMMARY

5.1 DNA and RNA are required to make proteins.

DNA contains a code that enables a cell to make RNA and proteins. Replication copies the code before a cell divides.

- DNA's triplet code enables a cell to make RNA
- mRNA, tRNA, and ribosomes translate the code into a sequence of amino acids.
- The amino acids form a protein needed for cell function.

DNA → RNA → Proteins

VOCABULARY
replication p. 137
RNA p. 138

5.2 Changes in DNA can produce variation.

Differences in DNA produce variations. Any change to DNA is a mutation. Many mutations have no or little effect. However, some mutations can change the way a cell works—sometimes helping an organism, sometimes hurting it.

Genetic disorders are caused by mutations in DNA. Some are inherited and can be followed through different generations of a family by using a pedigree. Other genetic disorders, such as cancer, are caused by mutations that occur during a person's lifetime.

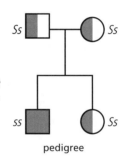

pedigree

VOCABULARY
mutation p. 145
pedigree p. 147

5.3 Modern genetics uses DNA technology.

Changes in DNA can change an organism. Selective breeding changes organisms by choosing for traits already coded for by DNA.

Genetic engineering introduces changes to the DNA of an organism. It can be used to

- introduce new traits into an organism
- produce medicines and other products
- identify individuals
- clone genes as well as organisms
- sequence the genome of an organism

DNA technology raises important issues for society.

Dolly was the first mammal to be cloned.

VOCABULARY
selective breeding
  p. 151
genetic engineering
  p. 151
genome p. 154
cloning p. 154

Reviewing Vocabulary

Copy the chart below and write the definition for each word. Use the meaning of the word's root to help you.

Term	Root Meaning	Definition
1. replication	to repeat	
2. mutation	to change	
3. genome	relating to offspring	
4. cloning	to branch off	

Reviewing Key Concepts

Multiple Choice *Choose the letter of the best answer.*

5. Genes are sequences of DNA, which are made up of
- **a.** nucleotides
- **b.** chromosomes
- **c.** phosphates
- **d.** ribosomes

6. What happens during replication?
- **a.** DNA is copied.
- **b.** RNA is copied.
- **c.** Ribosomes are made.
- **d.** Proteins are made.

7. Which base pair is found only in RNA?
- **a.** thymine-uracil
- **b.** guanine-cytosine
- **c.** thymine-adenine
- **d.** adenine-uracil

8. The main function of mRNA in protein synthesis is to
- **a.** transfer amino acids to a ribosome
- **b.** carry proteins to the ribosome
- **c.** transcribe genes from DNA
- **d.** connect nucleotides together

9. Proteins are made up of a sequence of
- **a.** chromosomes
- **b.** amino acids
- **c.** nucleotides
- **d.** base pairs

10. Mutations are changes in
- **a.** DNA
- **b.** the cell cycle
- **c.** tRNA
- **d.** proteins

11. Which is a known cause of genetic mutations?
- **a.** poor nutrition
- **b.** malaria
- **c.** UV radiation
- **d.** cancer

12. A pedigree shows
- **a.** how proteins are synthesized
- **b.** how members of a family are related
- **c.** where mutations are located in a sequence of DNA
- **d.** which triplet of bases matches up with a particular amino acid

13. The main goal of the Human Genome Project was to
- **a.** find cures for genetic diseases
- **b.** find all mutations in human DNA
- **c.** count the number of genes in human DNA
- **d.** sequence all DNA on human chromosomes

14. Genetic engineering involves
- **a.** inserting changed DNA into an organism
- **b.** cross-breeding plants
- **c.** testing new medicines for genetic diseases
- **d.** using x-rays to change DNA

Short Answer *Write a short answer to each question.*

15. DNA is described as the information molecule. What is the information that DNA carries?

16. What is the difference between selective breeding and genetic engineering?

17. List three applications of DNA technology and how these uses benefit humans.

Thinking Critically

Use the diagram to answer the next three questions.

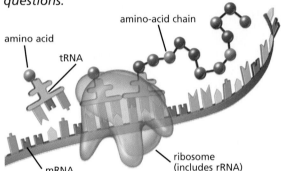

amino-acid chain

amino acid

tRNA

mRNA

ribosome (includes rRNA)

18. ANALYZE How does the mRNA strand above compare with the DNA template that produced it? Use the words *guanine, cytosine, thymine, adenine, and uracil* in your answer.

19. SUMMARIZE Three types of RNA are needed for protein synthesis. What are the three types and what is the function of each?

20. APPLY A protein contains 131 amino acids. How many bases will there be on the mRNA strand corresponding to these amino acids and how do you know?

21. ANALYZE A cell contains two sets of DNA. If the gene on one molecule of DNA has a mutation, how will that affect the gene on the other molecule of DNA?

22. SYNTHESIZE A mutation occurs during DNA replication. The following sequence

A-T-T-A-C-A-G-G-G

is copied as,

A-T-A-C-A-G-G-G

with one base missing. How does that affect the triplet code?

23. SEQUENCE List the steps in making a protein. Start with a gene on a DNA molecule. Include the chemical subunits involved in each step.

24. EVALUATE A person who carries a gene for a genetic disorder may not get the disorder. How can that be?

25. INFER How might a scientist determine if a neutral mutation has occurred in an organism?

26. PREDICT A mutation in an Arctic hare causes brown spots to appear on normally white fur. Explain how the mutation might affect the ability of the hare to survive.

27. EVALUATE Doctors can sometimes cure cancer by removing cancerous cells from a person's body. Why is it important for the doctors to remove all the cells?

28. EVALUATE How might selective breeding of a type of animal limit genetic diversity within the breed?

29. EVALUATE If a scientist compares the genome of a mouse to that of a human and discovers that the two organisms have many of the same genes, what can the scientist infer about how the cells in the two organisms function?

the BIG idea

30. DRAWING CONCLUSIONS Look again at the photograph on pages 132–133. How have models helped scientists understand the function of DNA?

31. CONNECT A local newspaper has written an editorial against the use of genetic engineering. The writer argues that humans should never change the DNA in an organism, even though they have the technology to do so. Write a response to the editorial, stating whether you think the benefits humans get from genetic engineering are worth the risks.

UNIT PROJECTS

Evaluate all the data, results, and information from your project folder. Prepare to present your project. Be ready to answer questions posed by your classmates about your results.

Analyzing Data

Use the following information and the pedigree chart to answer the questions.

Red-green colorblindness is one of the most common genetic conditions in the human population. About 5 percent of males are red-green colorblind. A male receives just one allele for this trait, on the X chromosome he inherits from his mother. If he receives the allele for red-green colorblindness, he will be colorblind. His genotype will be cb/Y.

Females inherit two alleles for the trait. Colorblindness (cb) is recessive and the allele for regular color vision (Cb) is dominant. A female with both the recessive allele and the dominant allele will have normal color vision. Her genotype would be Cb/cb. However, if the female has a male child, her child may be colorblind. The pedigree chart shows colorblindness in three generations.

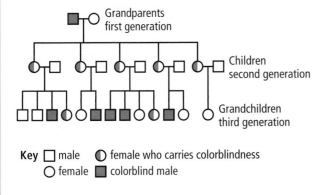

Grandparents
first generation

Children
second generation

Grandchildren
third generation

Key ☐ male   ◖ female who carries colorblindness
   ◯ female   ■ colorblind male

1. How many individuals in the first generation are colorblind?

   a. two
   b. one
   c. none
   d. three

2. How many individuals in the second generation are female?

   a. none
   b. one
   c. two
   d. five

3. Which statement describes the pattern of inheritance for colorblindness?

   a. Grandmother and granddaughter are both colorblind.
   b. Grandmother and son are both colorblind.
   c. Grandfather and granddaughter are both colorblind.
   d. Grandfather and grandson are both colorblind.

4. What are the genotypes of the males in the third generation?

   a. Cb/Y, Cb/Y, Cb/Y, cb/Y, cb/Y, cb/Y, cb/Y
   b. cb/Y, cb/Y, cb/Y, cb/Y,cb/Y, cb/Y, cb/Y
   c. Cb/Y, Cb/Y, Cb/Y, Cb/Y, Cb/Y, Cb/Y, CbY
   d. Cb/Y, Cb/Y, cb/Y, cb/y, cb,y ,cb/Y, cb/Y

Extended Response

5. Write a paragraph explaining why a color-blind man who has three daughters and one son with normal color vision might have two grandsons who are color-blind. Use the terms in the vocabulary box in your answer. Underline each term.

genotype	phenotype	allele
recessive	dominant	generation

6. The same color-blind man has four granddaughters. Would you predict the granddaughters to be colorblind? Explain why or why not. Use the terms in the vocabulary box.

UNIT B

Life Over Time

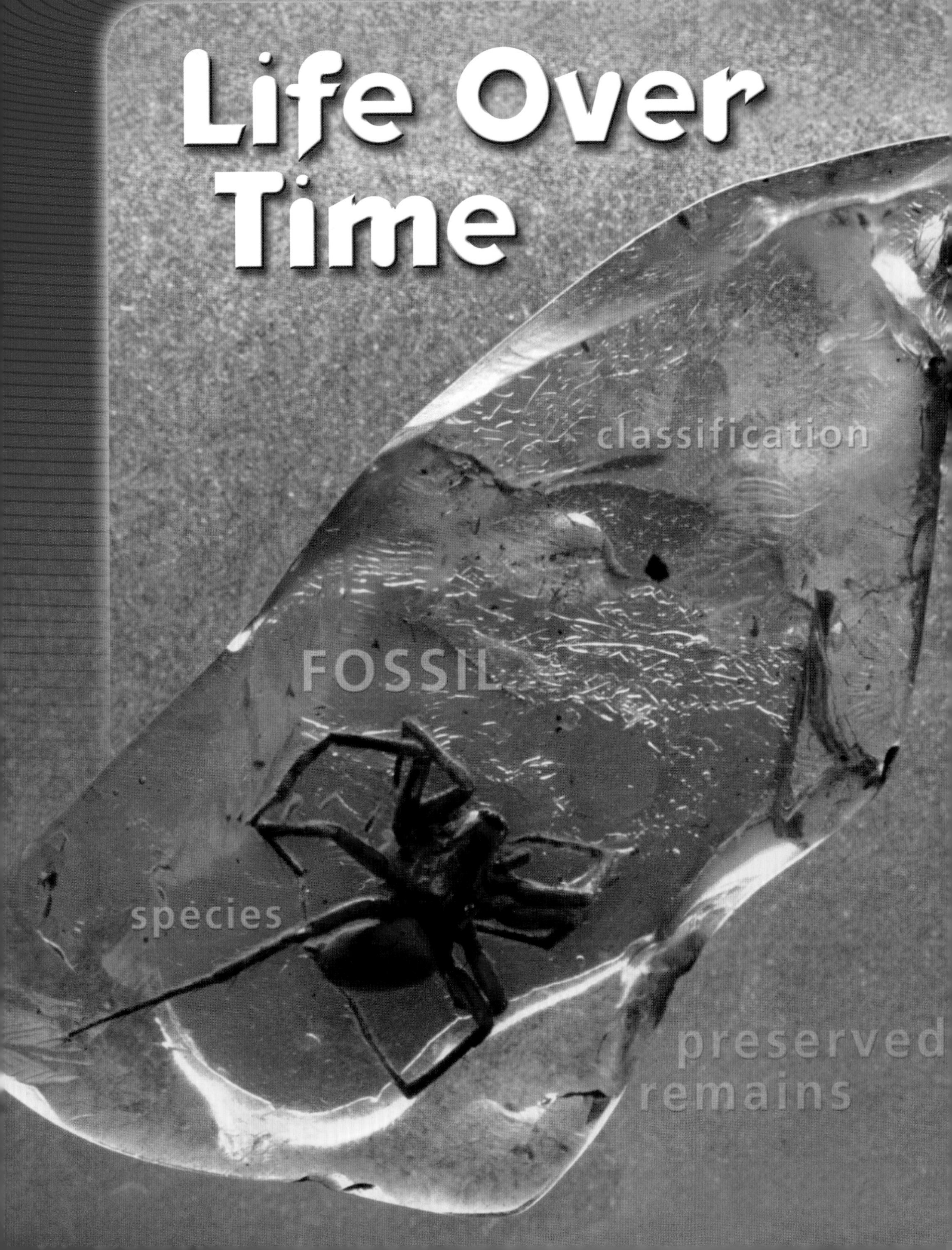
classification
FOSSIL
species
preserved
remains

Life Over Time
Contents Overview

Unit Features

1 The History of Life on Earth   6

the **BIG** idea

Living things, like Earth itself,
change over time.

2 Classification of Living Things   40

the **BIG** idea

Scientists have developed a system
for classifying the great diversity of
living things.

3 Population Dynamics   78

the **BIG** idea

Populations are shaped by
interactions between organisms
and the environment.

Life By Degrees

What happens when Earth's climate changes? Scientists are studying how climate change has influenced the evolution of life on Earth.

SCIENTIFIC AMERICAN FRONTIERS

Learn about how climate change affected life on Earth. See the video "Noah's Snowball."

Climate and Life

Throughout its history, Earth's climate has changed many times. Often the changes are gradual. They may seem small. However, an average global temperature change of just a few degrees can have a large impact on climate. Small changes in climate then cause big changes for plants and animals.

Before there were humans to record events, Earth kept a record of its changes. Parts of the planet stayed intact while other parts changed. Scientists get a sense for Earth's climate at different times in the distant past by looking at fossils, the remains and traces of living things. If scientists find fossils of living things in places where those organisms do not live today, then they may conclude that the climate was different in the past in those places.

Scientists have found that warmer climates lead to a greater diversity of organisms. One researcher examined fossils of tiny organisms called phytoplankton (FY-toh-plank-tuhn). During cooler climate periods, there were fewer types of phytoplankton than during warmer periods. The same is true for other organisms. Peter Wilf and Conrad Labandeira studied fossil plants. They were especially interested in the marks they found on the plants. The marks were left by plant-eating animals who bit the leaves. The warmer the climate was, the more types of plants there were—and the more kinds of animals were eating the plants.

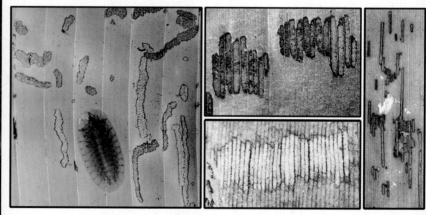

SOURCE: Images © 2000 AAAS

The chew marks of the hispine beatle on living ginger in Panama, beside fossilized chew marks found in Wyoming.

Before and after photographs of the sky show that distinct bands appeared due to dust and ash from the 1991 volcanic eruption of Mt. Pinatubo.

Mass Extinction

Several times in Earth's past, many kinds of animals and plants have disappeared in a relatively short time. These events are called mass extinctions. While we don't know for sure what causes them, most scientists think climate change plays a role in mass extinctions.

The largest mass extinction in Earth's history happened at the end of the Permian (PER-mee-uhn) Period about 248 million years ago. Scientists estimate that 90–95 percent of animal species that lived in the water died out. About three quarters of the vertebrates, or animals with backbones, living on land died out too.

Turn of Events

What caused this extinction? Using fossils, scientists have concluded that Earth's climate became cooler. Material from erupting volcanoes may have blocked sunlight long enough to cool the Earth. The cool temperatures and lack of sunlight may have killed plants and animals.

Scientist Peter Ward has been studying the Permian extinction. He looked at ancient African rivers and found evidence that rivers had became clogged with soil. Plants normally holding soil in place may have been wiped out causing the soil on the riverbanks to loosen. The plant extinction would also have led to animal extinction.

SCIENTIFIC AMERICAN FRONTIERS

View the "Noah's Snowball" segment of your Scientific American Frontiers video to learn about another theory of how climate change affected life on Earth.

IN THIS SCENE FROM THE VIDEO ▶ Fossil hunters examine evidence of early life in China.

DEEP FREEZE Can you imagine what Earth would be like if it were completely covered in ice? Geologists Paul Hoffman and Dan Schrag suggest Earth was frozen solid until about 600 million years ago. They think Earth's climate changed by just a few degrees, but it was enough to make the ice caps cover the planet. The only life that survived was bacteria that were kept warm by volcanoes. And it was the volcanoes that changed the climate again, say Hoffman and Schrag. Suddenly eruptions melted the ice. Ocean levels rose. The scientists think this change might have taken only a hundred years. Not everyone agrees with the snowball hypothesis, but it could explain how life began on Earth.

What Hit Them?

Not all scientists agree about what caused the Permian extinction. Some think an asteroid or comet hit the Earth. But even that event would cause climate change. If an asteroid hit the Earth, it would push massive amounts of dirt and dust into the air. This too could block the sunlight.

The most famous extinction of all took place at the end of the Cretaceous Period. The extended winter that may have followed a meteor impact caused many large land animals—including dinosaurs—to become extinct.

In a new climate some species thrive and survive. They spread out and, over time, evolve to fill empty niches or unique roles in the environment. For example, before the Cretaceous extinction, the only mammals were small. After the dinosaurs became extinct, large mammals could fill the roles of large plant-eaters and meat-eaters.

Even today, climate change continues. Earth's average temperature rose about half a degree Celsius in the twentieth century. Studying how past climate changes shaped life helps scientists predict how it may affect us in the future.

A large plant-eating mammal, *Chalicotherium grande*, roams Asia millions of years ago.

UNANSWERED Questions

Scientists have learned a lot about climate change and mass extinctions by studying fossils. There are many questions still to be answered.

- What caused changes in Earth's climate?
- What else might have caused mass extinctions?
- How might climate change affect life on Earth in the future?

UNIT PROJECTS

As you study this unit, work alone or with a group on one of the projects listed below. Use the bulleted steps to guide your project.

Museum Display

What organisms survived the Permian extinction? What organisms went extinct?

- Create a museum display using art and text.
- Use visuals to show the organisms and the modern relatives that have close connections to them.

Design a Robot

Often, scientists design robots to study dangerous or distant locations.

- Design an artificial robot that would be well-adapted to survive one type of mass extinction.
- Explain why the design would help the robot remain in operation.

Species over Time

Find out more about species that have gone extinct during recorded history.

- Choose one species that is now extinct.
- Present a timeline giving a history of that species.
- Describe what some of its ancestors and surviving related organisms are.
- Describe when it was last seen on record. Include some of the reasons for why it died out.

CAREER CENTER
CLASSZONE.COM

Learn more about careers in paleontology.

The History of Life on Earth

the BIG idea

Living things, like Earth itself, change over time.

Key Concepts

SECTION
1.1 Earth has been home to living things for about 3.8 billion years.
Learn how fossils help explain the development of life on Earth.

SECTION
1.2 Species change over time.
Learn how species develop and change.

SECTION
1.3 Many types of evidence support evolution.
Learn about the evidence scientists use to support evolution.

Internet Preview

CLASSZONE.COM

Chapter 1 online resources: Content Review, Simulation, Visualization, three Resource Centers, Math Tutorial, Test Practice

How do scientists learn about the history of life on Earth?

EXPLORE (the **BIG** idea)

What Can Rocks Show About Earth's History?

Look closely at two rocks from different places or at the two rocks below. What are the characteristics of each rock? Can you see evidence of living things in one of them?

Observe and Think
How could the evidence you gathered from your observations help you describe Earth's history?

Which One of These Things Is Not Like the Other?

Observe a handful of beans. Measure the length of each bean, observe the color, and note how many seeds are in each bean.

Observe and Think
What variety do you observe in the beans?

Investigate Activity: Matching Finch Beaks

Go to **Classzone.com** to match different finch beaks with the foods they eat. Learn how each type of beak functions.

Observe and Think
Can you think of any other beak types birds may have and how they relate to the food they eat?

The Fossil Record **Code: MDL036**

Getting Ready to Learn

◀ CONCEPT REVIEW

- Earth was formed about 4 billion years ago.
- Living things interact with their environment.

◀ VOCABULARY REVIEW

See Glossary for definitions.

cell	organism
DNA	species
genetic material	theory

CONTENT REVIEW
CLASSZONE.COM

Review concepts and vocabulary.

▶ TAKING NOTES

MAIN IDEA AND DETAILS

Make a two-column chart. Write the main ideas, such as those in the blue headings, in the column on the left. Write details about each of those main ideas in the column on the right.

VOCABULARY STRATEGY

Write each new vocabulary term in the center of a **frame game** diagram. Decide what information to frame it with. Use examples, descriptions, and parts of sentences that use the term in context or pictures. You can change the frame to fit each item.

See the Note-Taking Handbook on pages R45–R51.

SCIENCE NOTEBOOK

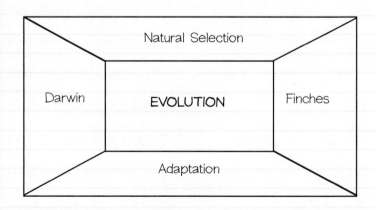

MAIN IDEAS	DETAILS
1. Fossils provide evidence of earlier life	1. Bones, prints, minerals
	1. Relative dating compares fossils
	1. Absolute dating uses the level of radioactivity

Natural Selection

Darwin EVOLUTION Finches

Adaptation

Earth has been home to living things for about 3.8 billion years.

◀ **BEFORE, you learned**

- Living things are diverse
- Living things share common characteristics
- A species is a group of living things that can breed with one another

▶ **NOW, you will learn**

- How scientists use fossils to learn about the history of life
- About patterns in the fossil record
- About mass extinctions

VOCABULARY

fossil p. 9
unicellular organism p. 12
multicellular organism p. 13
mass extinction p. 14

EXPLORE Fossils

What can you infer from the marks an object leaves behind?

PROCEDURE

1. Press a layer of clay into the dish.

2. Choose a small object and press it into the clay to make an imprint of your object.

3. Remove the object carefully and trade your imprint with a classmate.

WHAT DO YOU THINK?

- What object made the imprint?
- What do your observations indicate to you about how the imprint was formed?

MATERIALS
- clay
- petri dish
- small object

Fossils provide evidence of earlier life.

MAIN IDEA AND DETAILS
As you read this section, continue filling in the chart begun on page 8

Imagine watching a movie about the history of life on Earth. The beginning of the movie is set 3.8 billion years ago. At that time, the ocean would have been the setting. All living things lived in the sea. The end of the movie would show Earth today—a planet that is home to millions of species living on land as well as in water.

Of course, learning about the history of life isn't as easy as watching a movie. Modern ideas about life's history involve careful observation of the available evidence. Much of this evidence is provided by fossils. **Fossils** are the remains of organisms preserved in the Earth. Fossils provide a glimpse of a very long story. In some ways, observing a fossil is like hitting the pause button on your video machine or looking at a snapshot of another time.

Fossils

Bones such as this jawbone, are a common type of fossil.

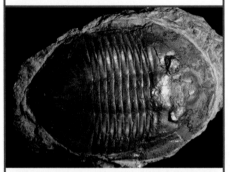

This fossil trilobite formed as minerals replaced the remains of the organism.

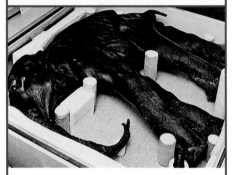

The preserved remains of ancient mammals, like the woolly mammoth, are rare.

VISUALIZATION
CLASSZONE.COM

Explore how a fossil can form.

Types of Fossils

You may have learned that fossils are the imprints or remains of once-living things. Most fossils are hard body parts such as bone. Perhaps you have seen displays of dinosaur skeletons in museums. These displays include fossil bones, such as the jawbone to the left. Other fossils form when minerals replace the remains of organisms or parts of organisms. The trilobite fossil shown in the middle photograph is an example of this type of fossil. Fossils also include prints made by organisms.

Very rarely, people find fossils that are the original remains of entire organisms. Explorers have found the frozen bodies of animals called woolly mammoths that lived about 10,000 years ago. The bodies of insects can be preserved in sap from plants.

Finding the Age of Fossils

How can scientists tell that the first organisms lived in oceans, or that dinosaurs lived on land and that they disappeared 65 million years ago? These questions and others can be addressed by determining the age of fossils. There are two approaches to dating fossils—relative dating and absolute dating. In relative dating, one fossil is compared with another fossil. The relative age tells you whether a fossil formed before or after another fossil.

The places where fossils are discovered provide information about their relative ages. Much of Earth's crust is rock, and rock forms over long periods of time. Understanding when and how rock forms gives scientists information about the sequence of events in Earth's history.

Materials such as sand and mud may settle to the bottom of a body of water. Over many millions of years, layers harden into rock. Shells and other remains of organisms can be trapped in those layers, forming fossils. Newer fossils are usually found in the top layers of rock, while older fossils are in the lower layers.

The absolute age of a fossil tells you when it formed. To find the absolute age of an object, scientists measure its radioactivity. Radioactivity involves changes in some of the atoms that make up materials such as rocks and fossils. Over time, these radioactive particles disappear and the rock material becomes less radioactive. The older a fossil, the less radioactive material it has.

CHECK YOUR READING   What are the two ways scientists can determine the age of fossils?

INVESTIGATE Fossil Records

How do scientists interpret fossil evidence?

PROCEDURE

1. Individually examine each of your group's puzzle pieces. Consider the shape and size of each piece.

2. Arrange the pieces so that they fit together in the best possible way.

3. On the basis of your pieces, try to interpret what the overall puzzle picture may be.

4. Combine your puzzle pieces with another group's. Repeat steps 2 and 3.

WHAT DO YOU THINK?

- How did your interpretation of the puzzle picture change once you had more pieces to work with?

- Explain whether the gaps in the puzzle picture influenced your interpretation.

- Was it easier or more difficult to study the record with more "scientists" in your group?

CHALLENGE Brainstorm other ways scientists could learn about early life on Earth.

SKILL FOCUS
Analyzing

MATERIALS
puzzle pieces

TIME
15 minutes

Assembling the Fossil Record

By combining absolute dating with relative dating, scientists can estimate the age of most fossils. The information about the fossils found in a particular location is called the fossil record. By assembling a fossil record, scientists can identify the periods of time during which different species lived and died. Scientists have used the fossil record to develop an overview of Earth's history. At the back of this book you can find a diagram of Earth's history.

READING TiP

A species is a group of organisms with similar characteristics that can interbreed.

Information from fossils helps scientists and artists describe wooly mammoths.

More complex organisms developed over time.

One of the most striking patterns that scientists find when they study the fossil record involves the development of more complex organisms. Below you will see how scientists have reconstructed the history of a modern city to show how life has developed over time. Recall that the first organisms were made up of single cells. Most organisms living today are single-celled species. However, many species have developed more complex cells and structures.

Unicellular Organisms

READING TIP

Uni- means single and *multi-* means several or many.

Unicellular organisms are organisms made up of a single cell. The organisms in the ocean 3.8 billion years ago were made of simple, single cells. Some of these organisms are responsible for the amount of oxygen that now makes up our atmosphere. The early atmosphere did not contain as much oxygen as it now does. As the atmosphere changed, so did life on Earth.

Different types of single cells developed over time. Over millions of years the cells of organisms became more complex. Today, there are different species of life that include organisms made up of many cells.

Reconstructing the Past

Digging deep into the city of Denver, scientists have been able to reconstruct the ancient past.

55 million years ago The seas have been replaced by a tropical rain forest. The Rocky Mountains have been part of the landscape for over 10 million years.

70 million years ago Colorado is still flat and is now under a shallow sea. Sharks and marine lizards inhabit the water, and large birds fly overhead.

250 million years ago Unicellular organisms cover the land in slimy clumps. The area has no mountains and is covered in shallow, salty water.

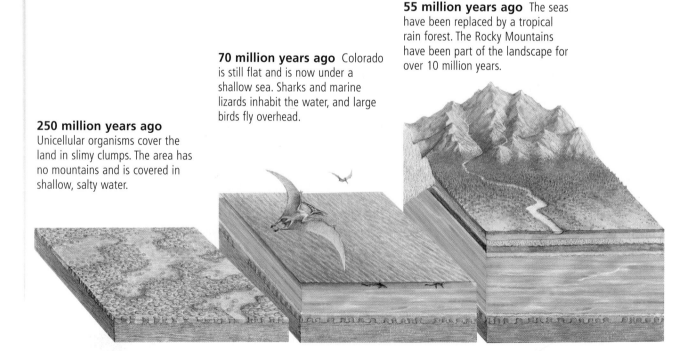

Multicellular Organisms

Around 1.2 billion years ago organisms made up of many cells began to live in Earth's oceans. **Multicellular organisms** are living things made up of many cells. Individual cells within multicellular organisms often perform specific tasks. For example, some cells may capture energy. Other cells might store materials. Still others might carry materials from one part of the organism to another. The most complex species of multicellular organisms have cells that are organized into tissues, organs, and systems.

Recall that all organisms have similar needs for energy, water, materials, and living space. For almost 3 billion years, these needs were met only in oceans. According to fossil records, the earliest multicellular organisms were tiny seaweeds. The earliest animals were similar to today's jellyfish.

Scientists learn about early life by studying different layers of rock

 CHECK YOUR READING Explain how unicellular and multicellular organisms differ.

Life on Land

Consider the importance of water. You use it to meet many different needs. Without it, your life would be very different. This is also true for other living things. About 500 million years ago, the first multicellular organisms moved from water to land.

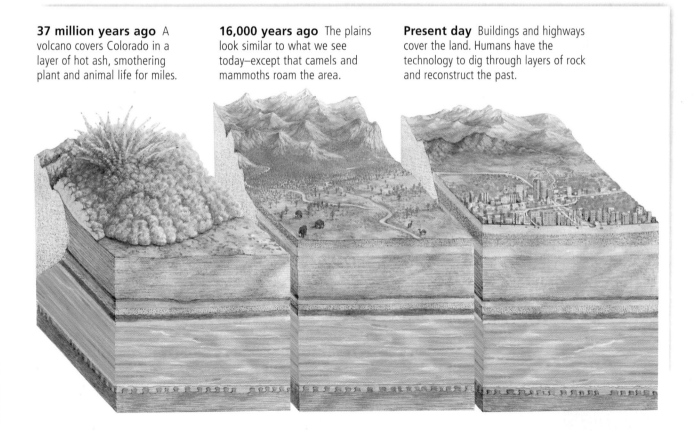

37 million years ago A volcano covers Colorado in a layer of hot ash, smothering plant and animal life for miles.

16,000 years ago The plains look similar to what we see today—except that camels and mammoths roam the area.

Present day Buildings and highways cover the land. Humans have the technology to dig through layers of rock and reconstruct the past.

In order to survive, these living things needed structures to help them get water. The first land-dwelling organisms were simple plants and fungi. Plants were able to obtain water from the soil through structures called roots. Fungi absorbed water from plants as well as from the soil. Insects were also probably among the first living things to inhabit land. Plants provided insects with food and shelter. After insects, animals such as amphibians and reptiles began living on land. They were followed by birds and mammals.

Earth's history includes mass extinctions.

About 10,000 years ago, the last woolly mammoth died without any offspring. At that time, the species became extinct, which means it disappeared. The only way that we know that some species, such as wooly mammoths, ever existed is through the fossil record. During Earth's history, there have been several periods when huge numbers of species have died or become extinct in a very short time. These events are called **mass extinctions.**

Although the fossil record shows a pattern of mass extinctions, two of these extinctions are particularly interesting. These are the Permian Extinction and the Cretaceous Extinction. The causes of these mass extinctions remain unknown.

Permian Extinction

About 250 million years ago, approximately 90 percent of the species living in the ocean became extinct. At the same time, many land-dwelling animals disappeared. Scientists who have studied Earth's history think that Earth's landmasses joined together, forming one enormous continent. This event would have changed the climate on land and the conditions within Earth's waters.

Cretaceous Extinction

Fossils show that around 140 million years ago, animals called dinosaurs lived all over the planet. However, the fossil record for dinosaurs ends about 65 million years ago. At the same time, more than half of the other species living on Earth became extinct.

How do scientists explain the extinction of so many species? One possibility is that a meteorite—a very large object from space—collided with Earth. The collision and its after effects wiped out most of the existing species. The remains of such a collision, the Chicxulub crater, can be found off the coast of Mexico. The computer graphic on page 15 shows the area of impact.

The largest mass extinction, the Permian extinction, affected many different living things but it was the most devastating to organisms that lived in moths.

Chicxulub Crater

Scientists think the impact of a meteorite off the coast of Mexico caused the Cretaceous extinction.

110 mi

The meteorite left a 200 km-wide crater off the Yucatán peninsula in Mexico.

Fragments from the meteorite have been found in the area.

The pattern in the fossil record shows that mass extinctions were followed by periods during which increasing numbers of new species developed. There may be a connection between the extinction of one species and the development of new species. For example, the extinction of dinosaurs may have made it possible for new species of mammals to develop.

 CHECK YOUR READING What do scientists think caused the most recent mass extinction?

1.1 Review

KEY CONCEPTS

1. How do fossils help scientists understand the history of life?

2. How do scientists know that the first organisms were simple, unicellular organisms?

3. What is extinction? Give an example of a mass extinction and its results.

CRITICAL THINKING

4. **Synthesize** How do absolute dating and relative dating help scientists assemble a fossil record for an area?

5. **Sequence** Draw a timeline showing the sequence of three major events in the history of life. Include the following terms on your timeline: *unicellular, multicellular, ocean, land.*

CHALLENGE

6. **Predict** Using the Denver reconstruction as your model, explain how you would reconstruct the history of the environment in your town.

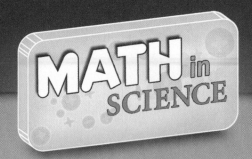

A Span of Time

The history of planet Earth spans from the present to about 5 billion years back. By comparison, the history of life on the planet spans about 4/5 of that time. Such a comparison is called a proportion.

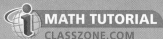
MATH TUTORIAL
CLASSZONE.COM

Click on Math Tutorial for more help writing and solving proportions.

Example

To compare time spans in the history of Earth, you could make a meter-long timeline. Follow these steps:

(1) Measure and cut a piece of paper longer than 1 meter. Draw a straight line that is 1 meter long on your paper.

(2) Mark "0" at the far left to show the present day. Mark "5,000,000,000" at the right to show 5 billion years.

(3) Mark each centimeter along the line with a short stroke.

(4) Make a longer stroke at every 10 pencil marks. Your 5-billion-year span is now divided into 500-million-year sections. Each section is 1/10 in proportion to the total.

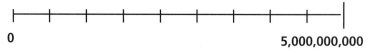

0   5,000,000,000

This fossil is very similar to the modern snail shown above.

Label the timeline by answering the questions below.

1. Each short pencil stroke, or tick, represents 1/100 of the total span. How many years will each centimeter represent?

2. Each of the 10 long pencil marks should have its own label for the amount of time before the present day. The label for the first long pencil mark should be "500 million years." What numbers should label the others?

3. What fractions of the total span do the numbers in Question 2 represent?

CHALLENGE Copy and complete the table.

Event	Years Before Present Time	Number of cm from 0	Fraction of Total Time Span
Life appears on Earth.	3,800,000,000		
Multicellular life appears.	1,500,000,000		
First animals appear on land.	420,000,000		

1.2 Species change over time.

◀ BEFORE, you learned

- Fossils are evidence of earlier life
- More complex organisms have developed over time
- Mass extinctions contributed to the development of Earth's history

▶ NOW, you will learn

- About early ideas and observations on evolution
- How Darwin developed his theory of natural selection
- How new species arise from older species

VOCABULARY

evolution p. 17
natural selection p. 21
adaptation p. 22
speciation p. 24

THINK ABOUT

How have telephones changed over time?

Today people across the world can communicate in many different ways. One of the most common ways is over the telephone. Looking at the two pictures can you describe how this form of communication has changed over time?

Scientists explore the concept of evolution.

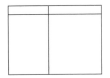

MAIN IDEA AND DETAILS
Make a chart for the main idea *scientists explore the concept of evolution.* Include details about scientists' observations.

In a general sense, evolution involves a gradual change over time. You could say that the way humans communicate has evolved. Certainly telephones have changed over time. The first telephones were the size of a shoebox. Today a telephone can fit in the palm of your hand and can send images as well as sound.

In biology, **evolution** refers to the process though which species change over time. The change results from a change in the genetic material of an organism and is passed from one generation to the next.

CHECK YOUR READING   What is evolution?

Early Ideas

READING TiP

The word *acquire* comes from the root meaning "to add to." Acquired traits are those that are "added" after an organism is born.

In the early 1800s, a French scientist named Jean-Baptiste de Lamarck was the first scientist to propose a model of how life evolves. He became convinced that the fossil record showed that species had changed over time. He proposed an explanation for evolution based on the idea that an individual organism can acquire a new trait during its lifetime and then pass that trait on to its offspring. For example, Lamarck suggested that when giraffes stretched their necks to reach the leaves of tall trees, they passed the result of this stretching—a longer neck—to the next generation. Lamarck was a highly respected scientist, but he was unable to provide any evidence to support his idea.

CHECK YOUR READING How did Lamarck explain the process of evolution?

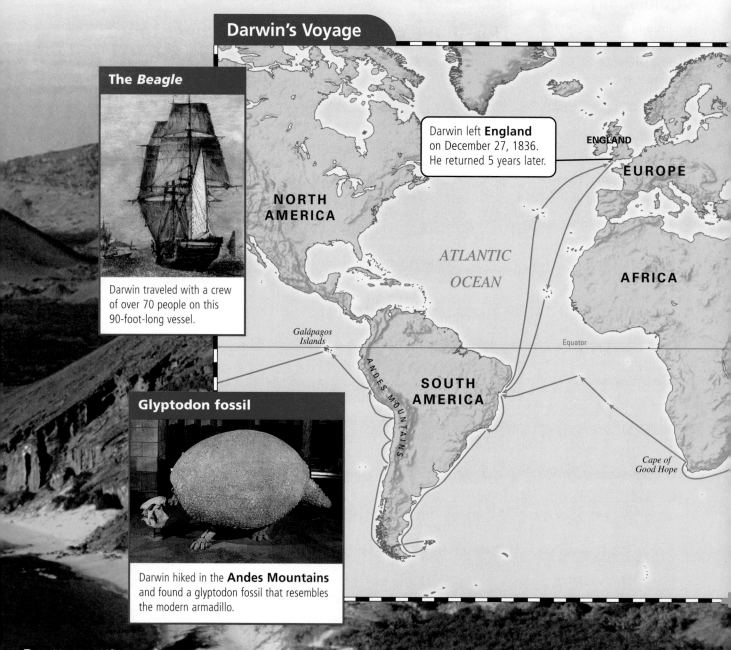

Darwin's Voyage

The Beagle

Darwin traveled with a crew of over 70 people on this 90-foot-long vessel.

Darwin left **England** on December 27, 1836. He returned 5 years later.

ENGLAND

EUROPE

NORTH AMERICA

ATLANTIC OCEAN

AFRICA

Galápagos Islands

Equator

SOUTH AMERICA

ANDES MOUNTAINS

Cape of Good Hope

Glyptodon fossil

Darwin hiked in the **Andes Mountains** and found a glyptodon fossil that resembles the modern armadillo.

Darwin's Observations

About 50 years after Lamarck, the British naturalist Charles Darwin published what would become the basis of the modern theory of evolution. As a young adult, Darwin spent 5 years as a naturalist aboard the *Beagle,* a ship in the British navy. The map below shows the route Darwin traveled. As he sailed along the coast of South America, he studied rock formations and collected fossils. He also began to compare the new animals he was seeing with ones from his own country.

The differences he saw in animals became more obvious when he visited the Galápagos Islands, a chain of volcanic islands about 950 kilometers (600 mi) off the South American coast. On the 18 Galápagos Islands, plants and animals not only differed from those he saw on the mainland, but some differed from island to island.

Darwin was only 20 in 1831 when he joined H.M.S. *Beagle.*

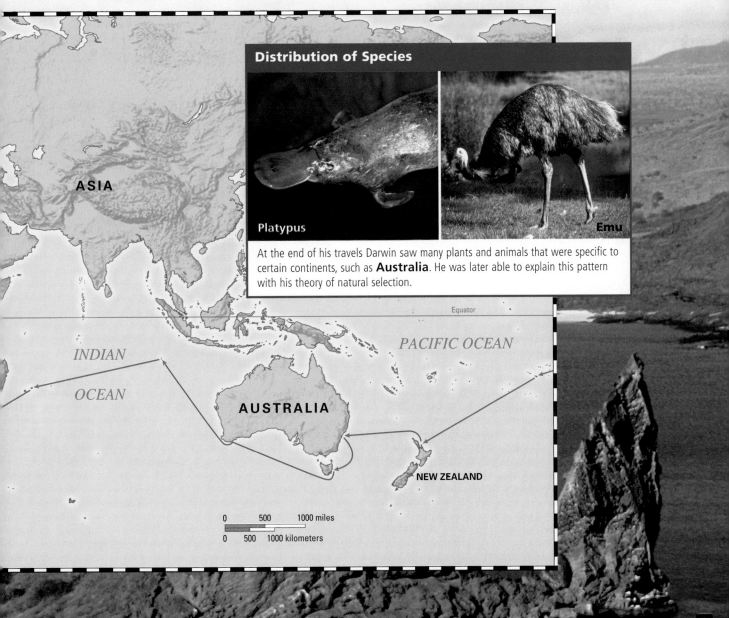

Distribution of Species

Platypus

Emu

At the end of his travels Darwin saw many plants and animals that were specific to certain continents, such as **Australia**. He was later able to explain this pattern with his theory of natural selection.

ASIA

INDIAN
OCEAN

PACIFIC OCEAN

Equator

AUSTRALIA

NEW ZEALAND

| 0 | 500 | 1000 miles |
| 0 | 500 | 1000 kilometers |

Darwin observed several types of tortoises on the islands. Tortoises with short necks were living in damp areas with abundant plant life that grew close to the ground. Longer-necked tortoises were living in dry areas with cacti. He considered whether the length of their necks made it possible for the tortoises to live in different environments.

Darwin also found many different types of birds called finches living on the islands. Some finches were common in the treetops, while others lived in the lower shrubs of a neighboring island. Among the different islands he noticed a variety of beak shapes and sizes. Some finches had heavy, short beaks useful for pecking trees, while others had small, thin beaks that could be used for capturing insects. These observations caused Darwin to question if the birds had evolved differently from one another because they were on different islands.

Darwin's Finches

On the Galápagos Islands, Darwin observed similar-looking birds with very different beaks. These birds are closely related finch species that are suited to different habitats on the island.

Woodpecker Finch

Vegetarian Finch

The woodpecker finch is able to hold a twig in its long pointed beak, which it uses to pull the larvas of insects from a tree. The vegetarian finch has a curved beak, ideal for taking large berries from a branch.

Large Ground Finch

Cactus Finch

The large ground finch has a large beak that it uses to crack open the hard shells of the seeds it feeds on. The cactus finch has a narrow beak that it uses to cut into a cactus and eat the tissue inside.

Natural selection explains how living things evolve.

After Darwin returned home to England in 1836, he spent several years analyzing the observations and specimens he had collected on his voyage. He struggled to develop an explanation that would account for the amazing diversity of species he saw and for the relationships between them. By 1844 he had developed a hypothesis based in part on an insight from one of his hobbies—breeding pigeons.

Darwin knew from personal experience that breeders can produce new varieties of an animal over time. The process breeders use is called artificial selection. For example, breeders produce a new breed of dog by selecting dogs that have certain desired traits and then allowing only those individuals to mate. From the resulting litters, they again selectively breed only the individual dogs with the desired traits. By repeating this process generation after generation, a new breed is produced.

 CHECK YOUR READING What is artificial selection?

Artificial Selection

| Cairne | Airedale | Tibetan |

COMPARE AND CONTRAST These dogs are all terriers, but they have been bred through artificial selection to show very specific traits. How are the dogs similar? How are they different?

Darwin's insight was that a similar process might be going on in nature. He proposed that, through a process he called **natural selection,** members of a species that are best suited to their environment survive and reproduce at a higher rate than other members of the species. Darwin based this idea on a few key principles. These are overproduction, variation, adaptation, and selection.

Overproduction

Take a look at how Darwin's ideas are useful for the study of salmon. When a plant or an animal reproduces, it usually makes more offspring than can possibly survive. As you can see in the diagram on page 23, a female salmon may lay several thousand fertile eggs, but not all of them will hatch. Only a few hundred of the salmon that hatch from the eggs will survive disease and avoid fish-eating predators. Several dozen of these survivors will live to adulthood. An even smaller number will successfully reproduce.

Variation

READING TiP

As you read about the principles of natural selection, refer to the diagrams on page 23.

Within a species there are natural differences, or variations, in traits. For example, if you looked very closely at thousands of salmon, you might see slight differences among individuals. Some might have larger fins. Others might have distinct patterns of spots on their scales. The differences among individuals result from differences in the genetic material of the fish.

Variations are passed on from one generation to the next. Sometimes the genetic material itself changes, causing a new variation to come about. A change in the genetic material is referred to as a mutation. As the fish with the new variation reproduces, the trait gets passed on to its offspring.

Adaptation

Sometimes a mutation occurs that makes an individual better able to survive than other members of the group. An **adaptation** is any inherited trait that gives an organism an advantage in its particular environment. For example, a slight change in the shape of a tail fin may increase a fish's chance of survival by helping it swim faster and avoid predators.

Selection

Darwin reasoned that individual organisms with a particular adaptation are most likely to survive long enough to reproduce. As a result, the adaptation becomes more common in the next generation of offspring. As this process repeats from generation to generation, more members of a species show the adaptation. Consider the shape of the salmon. If a change in the tail fin makes the salmon better able to move upstream and lay eggs, scientists say the environment is selecting this trait. In other words, the species is evolving through natural selection.

Natural Selection

Certain traits become more common in a group of organisms through the process of natural selection.

Overproduction

adult salmon

eggs

A fish may lay hundreds of eggs, but only a small number will survive to reach adulthood.

Variation

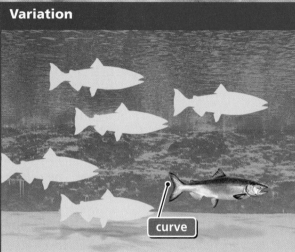

curve

A mutation may cause a slight curve to develop in a fish's tail.

Adaptation

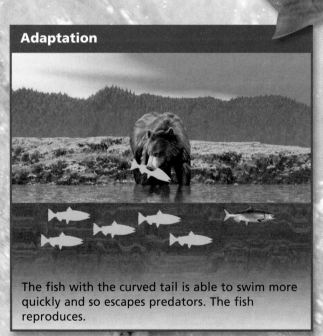

The fish with the curved tail is able to swim more quickly and so escapes predators. The fish reproduces.

Selection

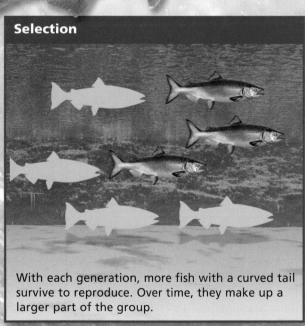

With each generation, more fish with a curved tail survive to reproduce. Over time, they make up a larger part of the group.

READING VISUALS How does natural selection occur for an individual salmon?

New species develop from earlier species.

Darwin's personal observations and the work of another scientist, Alfred Wallace, led Darwin to write about this new concept of evolution. In 1859, after more than twenty years of work, Darwin published his ideas in his book *On the Origin of Species.* This work led the way for our modern understanding of how new species arise.

Speciation

Speciation is the evolution of new species from an existing species. Speciation may occur when the environment changes dramatically. It may also occur when the environment changes gradually. The Galápagos finch populations Darwin studied showed evidence of speciation. The different species of finch had varying characteristics.

Today, scientists continue to find evidence of speciation across the world. In Lake Tanganyika, one of the largest lakes in the world, there are over 150 species of fish called cichlids. One particular species, *tropheus*, originally lived along the rocky shore and couldn't cross the open water. The climate and geology of the area caused the lake's water level to rise and fall many times over thousands of years. As the water level changed, a new, rocky habitat was formed, and some populations of cichlids became isolated from each other.

Speciation

In this African lake, new species of cichlids have evolved.

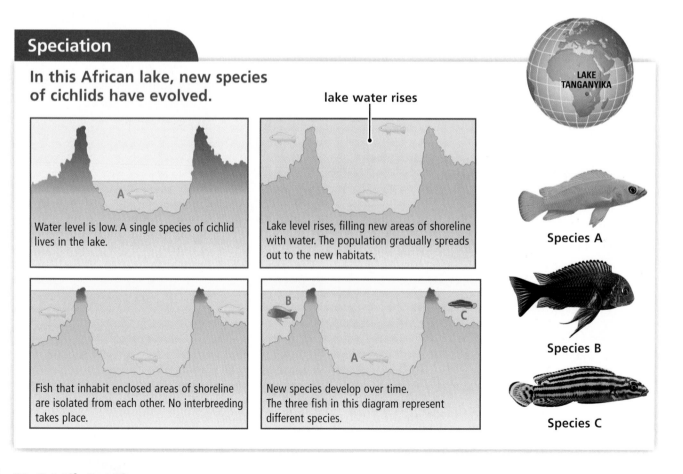

lake water rises

LAKE TANGANYIKA

Water level is low. A single species of cichlid lives in the lake.

Lake level rises, filling new areas of shoreline with water. The population gradually spreads out to the new habitats.

Fish that inhabit enclosed areas of shoreline are isolated from each other. No interbreeding takes place.

New species develop over time. The three fish in this diagram represent different species.

Species A

Species B

Species C

The isolated populations were unable to interact with each other because they couldn't cross open waters. As a result, genetic differences began to add up in these populations. The cichlid populations now represent distinct species. They have developed unique characteristics and cannot breed with each other.

Isolation

Darwin's trip to the Galápagos Islands showed him an important point about speciation. Separated from the mainland by miles of ocean, and unable to breed with their mainland relatives, many new species of living things had evolved. From this, Darwin reasoned that isolation of populations by geographical or other barriers could contribute to the process of speciation.

Today scientists understand that isolation is essential to speciation. For a species to separate, two populations must be prevented from reproducing with each other. A geographic boundary like an ocean or mountain range can result in isolation. Two populations of a species can also be isolated if they feed on different things or reproduce at different times of the year.

As the cichlids in Lake Tanganyika show, the mutations in one isolated group may differ from another. Two or more populations may evolve differently from each other. The result is speciation, which has contributed to the biodiversity on Earth.

The Rocky Mountains are an example of a barrier that can isolate populations.

CHECK YOUR READING What is a key factor that can lead to speciation?

1.2 Review

KEY CONCEPTS

1. How did Lamarck's ideas differ from Darwin's?
2. What did Darwin observe in the finch populations that supported his idea of natural selection?
3. Explain how isolation helps speciation.

CRITICAL THINKING

4. **Hypothesize** Two species of grasses are separated by a tall mountain range. A third species of grass shares some characteristics with each of the other two species. It inhabits a small valley, surrounded on all sides by mountains. Form a hypothesis for the origin of the third species.

⬛ CHALLENGE

5. **Predict** The Arctic hare lives in snow-covered mountains in Canada. The hare is hunted by foxes, wolves, and owls. Which trait is more likely to be inherited by new generations of hares: white fur or black fur?

CHAPTER INVESTIGATION

Modeling Natural Selection

OVERVIEW AND PURPOSE Organisms that are best adapted to their environment tend to survive and reproduce. In this lab you will

- play a game that models the effect of natural selection in an environment
- determine what happens to a group of organisms as a result of natural selection

▶ Question

Write It Up

As you read the steps to the game, think about what makes a population successful in an environment. How will the game model natural selection?

MATERIALS
- pair of number cubes
- 16 red paper clips
- 16 blue paper clips
- 16 yellow paper clips

▶ Procedure

1. Make a game board like the one shown below. In your **Science Notebook** make a table like the one on page 27 to record your data.

	1	2	3	4
1				
2				
3				
4				

2. Count out 10 red paper clips, 4 blue paper clips, and 2 yellow paper clips. Randomly place the paper clips on the board. Keep the rest of the paper clips in a reserve pile.

3 Each color represents a different population of a single species. The board represents the environment. Roll the number cubes to determine which paper clips "live," or remain on the board, and which paper clips "die," or are removed from the board. Predict which color paper clip you think will be the last remaining color. Write down your prediction.

4 Roll the number cubes to determine which square, or part of the environment, will be affected. For example, 2,3 indicates the paper clip in column 2, row 3. If the numbers 5 or 6 come up, roll again until you have a number between 1 and 4 for each cube.

5 Now roll one cube to see what will happen to the paper clip or organism in that square. Use the chart below to determine if the paper clip "lives" or "dies." If the paper clip lives, repeat steps 4 and 5 until one paper clip dies, or is removed from the board. In your table, record which colors live and die.

Red	Remove if you roll a 1, 2, 3, 4, or 5.
Blue	Remove if you roll a 1, 2, or 3.
Yellow	Remove if you roll a 1 or 2.

6 Now that a paper clip has been removed, you need to see what population will reproduce to fill that space. Roll both cubes to choose another square. The color of the paper clip in that square represents the population that will "reproduce." Pick the same color paper clip from your reserve pile and place it on the empty square. All squares on the board should always have a paper clip.

7 Continue playing the game by repeating steps 4–6 until all the paper clips on the board are the same color.

Observe and Analyze

1. **OBSERVE** Which color paper clip filled the board at the end of the game?

2. **PREDICT** Compare the results with your prediction. Do the results support your prediction?

Conclude

1. **INFER** What does the random selection by rolling both number cubes represent? Explain.

2. **INFER** If the individual paper clips represent different members of a single species, then what might the different colors represent?

3. **LIMITATIONS** What problems or sources of error exist in this model? Give examples.

4. **APPLY** How does this game model natural selection?

INVESTIGATE Further

CHALLENGE Occasionally mutations occur in a population that can either help or damage the population's chance of survival. Add another step to the game that would account for mutations.

Modeling Natural Selection

Table 1. Patterns in a Population

Paper Clip Color	Live	Die

Many types of evidence support evolution.

 BEFORE, you learned

- Natural selection explains how living things evolve
- New species develop from earlier species

▶ **NOW, you will learn**

- How scientists develop theories
- About the evidence Darwin used to support evolution
- About additional evidence most scientists use today

VOCABULARY

ancestor p. 29
vestigial organ p. 30
gene p. 33

EXPLORE Evidence

How can observations supply evidence?

PROCEDURE

① Consider the following statement: It rained last night.

② Look at the following observations and determine which pieces of evidence support the statement.
  - There are puddles on the ground.
  - The weather report says there will be scattered showers today.
  - Your sister tells you there was a rain delay during last night's tennis match.

MATERIALS
- paper
- pencil

WHAT DO YOU THINK?
- What other observations can you come up with that would supply evidence for the first statement?
- Could any of the evidence be misleading?

Observations provide evidence for theories.

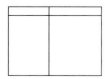

MAIN IDEA AND DETAILS
Don't forget to make a chart of details supporting the main idea that observations provide evidence for theories. Include a definition of *theory* in your chart.

In this chapter, you've learned about important observations that scientists have used to understand the history of living things. These observations provided Darwin with information he used to describe his ideas about evolution.

Darwin, like all good scientists, was skeptical about his observations and conclusions. Although the historic trip on the *Beagle* took place between 1831 and 1836, Darwin didn't publish the book explaining his theory until 1859. In order to understand the importance of Darwin's work, it is also important to understand the meaning of the term *theory*.

Evidence: information from observations and experiments

Evidence for evolution

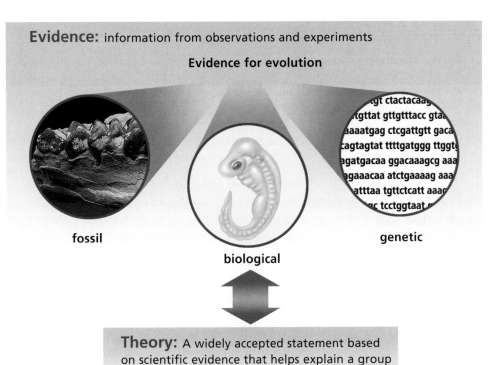

fossil

biological

genetic

Theory: A widely accepted statement based on scientific evidence that helps explain a group of facts

A scientific theory is a statement based on observation and experiment. If continued observation and experiment support the statement, it may become widely accepted. A theory that has been widely accepted is used to explain and predict natural phenomena. The chart above will help give you an idea of how a theory works and what evidence has been used to support evolution and the theory of natural selection.

 CHECK YOUR READING How do scientists support theories?

Fossil evidence supports evolution.

You have read that Darwin collected many specimens of fossils on his trip. These specimens provided evidence that species existing in the past were very similar to species living during Darwin's time. For example, the fossil of an extinct animal called the glyptodon resembles the modern armadillo, an animal found today in South America.

The geographic information about many fossils provides evidence that two species with a common ancestor can develop differently in different locations. An **ancestor** is an early form of an organism from which later forms descend. The idea of common ancestors is important to the theory of natural selection and to the evidence that supports the theory. Scientists comparing modern plants and modern algae to fossil algae can tell that they all share a common ancestor.

 CHECK YOUR READING What is a common ancestor?

Biological evidence supports evolution.

Today scientists continue to study fossil evidence as well as biological evidence to support the concept of evolution. They have even returned to the Galápagos to further investigate Darwin's work. What they have found gives strength to the theory he proposed nearly 150 years ago. Returning year after year, these scientists are able to follow and record evolutionary changes as they are unfolding. The biological evidence they study includes the structure and the development of living things. This work has helped scientists identify relationships between organisms that exist today. In addition, their observations suggest how modern organisms are related to earlier species.

Similarities in Structure

Evidence for evolution can be observed within the physical structures of adult organisms. Scientists who study evolution and development consider two types of structural evidence. They are vestigial (veh-STIHJ-ee-uhl) organs and similar structures with different functions.

 CHECK YOUR READING What are two types of structural evidence?

READING TIP

The root of the word vestigial means "footprint." A vestige refers to visible evidence that is left behind—such as a footprint.

Vestigial organs are physical structures that were fully developed and functional in an earlier group of organisms but are reduced and unused in later species. In the bodies of whales there are small leg bones that are vestigial. The skeletons of snakes also have traces of leglike structures that are not used. These vestigial organs help researchers see how some modern organisms are related to ancestors that had similar structures.

Similar structures with different functions Scientists studying the anatomy of living things have also noticed that many different species share similar structures. But these structures are used differently by each species. For example, lizards, bats, and manatees have forelimbs that have a similar bone structure. As you can see from the diagram on page 31, there is one long bone that goes from a shoulder structure to a wrist structure. But obviously, a lizard, a bat, and a manatee use this structure in different ways.

This similarity in structure indicates that these organisms shared a common ancestor. The process of natural selection caused the variations in form and function that can be observed today. These organisms lived in different environments and so were under different pressures. For lizards the environment was land, for bats it was the air, and for manatees the water. The environment influenced the selection of traits.

Biological Evidence for Evolution

Scientists learn about common ancestors by looking at physical structures.

Vestigial Structures

The small, leglike bones in modern whales indicate that an early ancestor may have had legs.

Ambulocetus, an extinct whalelike animal with four legs

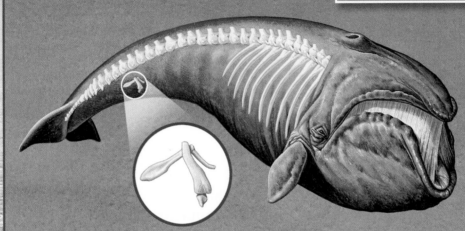

modern whale

Similar Structures, Different Functions

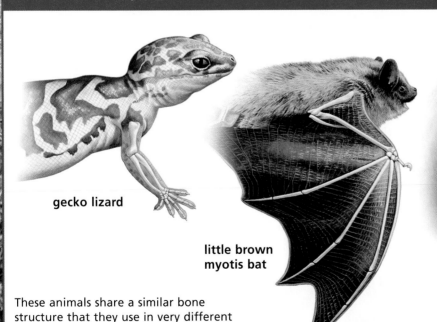

gecko lizard

little brown myotis bat

manatee

These animals share a similar bone structure that they use in very different ways. The presence of this similar structure indicates a common ancestor.

Similarities in Development

READING TiP

As you read about the development of a chicken, rabbit, and salamander, study the diagram below.

Scientists in the 1700s were fascinated by the fact that various animals looked similar in their earliest stages of life. They noted that as the organisms developed, they became less and less alike. Today's scientists continue to compare the developmental stages of different species.

The adult stages of many species do not look similar. For example, a rabbit does not look anything like a chicken. However, studying reveals that the early life stages of a chicken and a rabbit are similar. The early life stage that scientists study is called the embryo.

In the diagram below, notice the development of three different species: a chicken, a rabbit, and a salamander. In the early stages of development, the embryos of all three organisms look similar. As they continue to develop, they begin to take on distinct characteristics. The chicken has a structure that starts to resemble a beak. The salamander begins to look as if it is adapted for life near water. In their adult stages, these three species no longer look similar.

Similarities in Development

The study of embryos shows that animals that appear to be very different as adults are similar during early development.

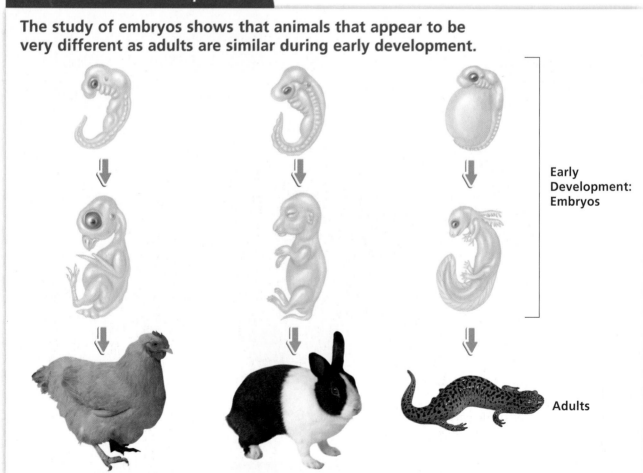

Early Development: Embryos

Adults

How can a sequence communicate information?

PROCEDURE

① From your pile of letters, spell out the word RED.

② Working with a partner, use the letters to spell two more words having three letters.

WHAT DO YOU THINK?

How does rearranging the letters change the meaning of the words?

CHALLENGE Cut out words from a newspaper. Arrange these words to form different phrases. How do these phrases communicate different messages.

SKILL HEAD
Sequencing

MATERIALS
letter cards

TIME
20 minutes

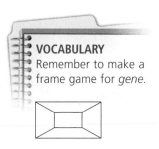

Genetic evidence supports evolution.

The key to understanding how traits are passed from one generation to the next lies in the study of DNA, the genetic material found in all cells. DNA contains the information all organisms need to grow and to maintain themselves. When organisms reproduce, they pass on their genetic material to their offspring.

DNA contains a code that a cell uses to put together all the materials it needs to function properly. The code is made up of four different chemical subunits called bases. The bases are symbolized by the four letters A, T, C, and G. Located within DNA are individual genes. A **gene** is a segment of DNA that relates to a specific trait or function of an organism. Each gene has a particular sequence of bases. The cell takes this sequence and translates it into the chemicals and structures the organism needs.

Scientists studying genes have identified a gene called the clock gene in many mammals. This particular gene relates to the function of sleeping and waking. As scientists learn more they can identify patterns of behavior in different organisms. The chart on page 34 compares the DNA sequence of part of the clock gene in both humans and mice.

VOCABULARY
Remember to make a frame game for *gene*.

 What is a gene?

Comparing Genes

Humans and mice look very different, but the DNA that makes up their genes is surprisingly similar.

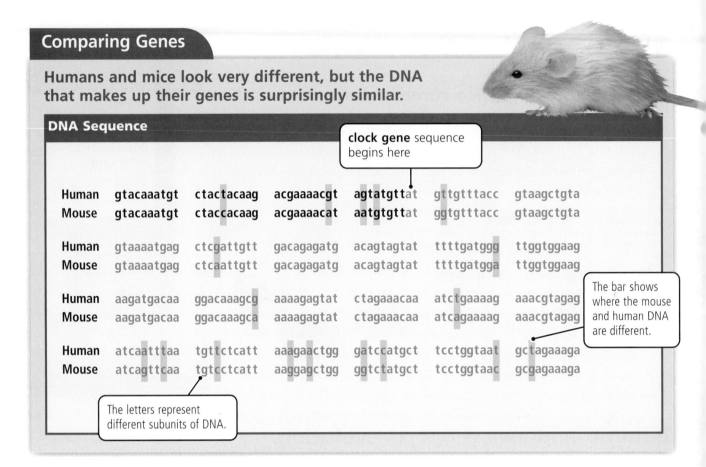

DNA Sequence

clock gene sequence begins here

Human	gtacaaatgt	ctactacaag	acgaaaacgt	agtatgttat	gttgtttacc	gtaagctgta
Mouse	gtacaaatgt	ctaccacaag	acgaaaacat	aatgtgttat	ggtgtttacc	gtaagctgta
Human	gtaaaatgag	ctcgattgtt	gacagagatg	acagtagtat	ttttgatggg	ttggtggaag
Mouse	gtaaaatgag	ctcaattgtt	gacagagatg	acagtagtat	ttttgatgga	ttggtggaag
Human	aagatgacaa	ggacaaagcg	aaaagagtat	ctagaaacaa	atctgaaaag	aaacgtagag
Mouse	aagatgacaa	ggacaaagca	aaaagagtat	ctagaaacaa	atcagaaaag	aaacgtagag
Human	atcaatttaa	tgttctcatt	aaagaactgg	gatccatgct	tcctggtaat	gctagaaaga
Mouse	atcagttcaa	tgtcctcatt	aaggagctgg	ggtctatgct	tcctggtaac	gcgagaaaga

The bar shows where the mouse and human DNA are different.

The letters represent different subunits of DNA.

Scientists can tell how closely organisms are related by comparing their DNA. The more matches there are in the sequence of bases between two organisms, the more closely related they are. For example, almost all the genes found in a mouse are also found in a human. Even though the two organisms appear so different, much of the functioning of their cells is similar.

1.3 Review

KEY CONCEPTS

1. Describe in your own words how scientists use the word *theory*.

2. What type of evidence did Darwin use to support his theory evolution?

3. Identify three different types of evidence that today's scientists use to support evolution.

CRITICAL THINKING

4. **Analyze** Describe three characteristics of a scientific theory. Explain how Darwin's theory of evolution is an example of a scientific theory.

⛰ CHALLENGE

5. **Predict** If you were looking at the sequence within the genes of two species, how would you predict the two species are related?

How Did the Deep-Sea Angler Get Its Glow?

A fish that uses a fishing pole to find food might seem odd. However, anglerfish do just that. The fish have a modified spine that extends from their head, almost like a fishing pole. At the end is a small piece of tissue that is similar in shape to a small worm. The tissue functions like a lure that a fisherman uses to catch fish. The anglerfish wiggles its "lure" to attract prey. If the prey fish moves in close enough, the anglerfish opens its mouth and swallows the prey whole. The "fishing poles" of abyssal anglerfish, anglerfish that live in the deep sea, have an interesting adaptation. The "lure" actually glows in the dark—it is bioluminescent.

▶ Observations

From laboratory research and field studies, scientists made these observations

> There are more than 200 species of anglerfish. Many of these live in deep water.
>
> Shallow-water species do not have glow-in-the-dark "lures."
>
> Only female abyssal anglerfish have a "pole." They do not have pelvic fins and are not strong swimmers.
>
> Other deep-sea organisms, including bacteria, jellyfish, even some squid, are bioluminescent.

▶ Hypotheses

Consider these hypotheses.

> The ancestors of abyssal anglerfish lived in shallow waters. Some of these fish drifted into deep waters. A bioluminescent lure helped some survive.
>
> Light does not reach down to the bottom of the deep sea. Bioluminescence provides an advantage for the anglerfish because it makes its lure noticeable.
>
> A bioluminescent lure is more valuable to a female abyssal anglerfish than the ability to swim.

▶ Evaluate Each Hypothesis

On Your Own For each hypothesis, think about whether all the observations support it. Some facts may rule out some hypotheses. Others may support them.

As a Group Decide which hypothesis is the most reasonable. Discuss your thinking and conclusions in a small group and see if the group can agree.

Chapter Review

the **BIG** idea

Living things, like Earth itself, change over time.

◀ KEY CONCEPTS SUMMARY

1.1 Earth has been home to living things for about 3.8 billion years.

Fossil records inform humans about the development of life on Earth. Information from fossils can help scientists reconstruct Earth's history.

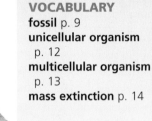

VOCABULARY
fossil p. 9
unicellular organism p. 12
multicellular organism p. 13
mass extinction p. 14

1.2 Species change over time.

Darwin's theory of natural selection explains evolution.

Four principals of natural selection
- overproduction
- variation
- adaptation
- selection

The beak of this cactus finch provides an example of an adaptation.

VOCABULARY
evolution p. 17
natural selection p. 21
adaptation p. 22
speciation p. 24

1.3 Many types of evidence support evolution.

Three different types of evidence provide a bigger picture of evolution

fossil

biological

```
gt ctactacaag
tgttat gttgtttacc gta
aaatgag ctcgattgtt gaca
agtagtat ttttgatggg ttggt
agatgacaa ggacaaagcg aaa
gaaacaa atctgaaaag aaa
atttaa tgttctcatt aaa
gc tcctggtaat
```

genetic

VOCABULARY
ancestor p. 29
vestigial organ p. 30
gene p. 33

Reviewing Vocabulary

Draw a triangle for each of the terms below. On the wide bottom of the triangle, write the term and your own definition of it. Above that, write a sentence in which you use the term correctly. At the top of the triangle, draw a small picture to show what the term looks like.

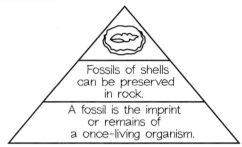

Fossils of shells can be preserved in rock.

A fossil is the imprint or remains of a once-living organism.

1. unicellular organism

2. multicellular organism

3. adaptation

4. vestigial structure

Reviewing Key Concepts

Multiple Choice *Choose the letter of the best answer.*

5. Which is *not* part of the fossil record?
   a. fossil bones
   b. preserved remains
   c. living unicellular organisms
   d. imprints

6. Whether a fossil formed before or after another fossil is described by its
   a. relative age
   b. absolute age
   c. fossil record
   d. radioactive age

7. The earliest multicellular organisms were
   a. jellyfish
   b. simple plants
   c. fungi
   d. tiny seaweeds

8. Which is a possible explanation for mass extinctions?
   a. Earth had no water.
   b. A meteorite collided with Earth.
   c. The continents separated.
   d. Woolly mammoths left no offspring.

9. Darwin's theory that species develop new traits and change over time is known as
   a. natural selection   **c.** speciation
   b. evolution   **d.** adaptation

10. Which describes Lamarck's explanation for changes in the fossil record?
   a. Species best suited to their environments survive better than others.
   b. Variation within a species can be passed on to offspring.
   c. Acquired traits are passed on from one generation to another.
   d. Giraffes adapted to their environment.

11. A slight change in a rabbit's ability to hear its predators better and help it survive is
   a. an adaptation
   b. a vestigial structure
   c. an aquired trait
   d. an isolation

12. Which is necessary for speciation to occur?
   a. adaptation
   b. mass extinction
   c. isolation
   d. acquired traits

13. Which of the following statements explain why the theory of evolution is widely accepted by the scientific community?
   a. It has been proven by experiments.
   b. The fossil record is complete.
   c. It is supported by genetic evidence.
   d. Lamarck's theory was correct.

14. Genetic evidence is based on the study of
   a. embryonic development
   b. mutations
   c. common ancestors
   d. DNA sequences

15. Genetic information that cells use to control the production of new cells is located in

   a. embryos

   b. genes

   c. the environment

   d. vestigial structures

Short Answer *Write a short answer to each question.*

16. Describe how the relative age of a fossil is determined by studying layers of rock.

17. Explain the difference between artificial selection and natural selection.

18. How does common ancestry between two species support evolution?

Thinking Critically

19. **COMMUNICATE** What have scientists learned about past life on Earth from the fossil record?

20. **PROVIDE EXAMPLES** Explain the principle of overproduction. Give an example.

21. **SYNTHESIZE** How might the mass extinction of dinosaurs enable many new species of mammals to develop?

22. **EVALUATE** How would natural selection have led to the development of giraffes with long necks as opposed to giraffes with short necks?

23. **PROVIDE EXAMPLES** How are variation and adaptations related to natural selection? Give an example.

24. **PREDICT** In Africa's Lake Tanganyika different populations of cichlids became isolated from each other. Based on what you already learned, predict how the changing water level helped the cichlid population to change. How do you think the development of new cichlid species affected other living things in the lake?

25. **ANALYZE** How is geographic isolation related to the formation of a new species?

26. **EVALUATE** Pandas were once considered to be closely related to raccoons and red pandas because of their physical similarities. Today, scientists have learned that pandas are more closely related to bears than to raccoons and red pandas. What evidence might scientists have used to draw this conclusion? Explain.

27. **INFER** What does the presence of similar structures in two—organisms such as a dolphin's flipper and a lizard's forelimb—indicate?

the BIG idea

28. **INFER** Look again at the picture on pages 6–7. Now that you have finished the chapter, how would you change or add details to your answer to the question on the photograph?

29. **SYNTHESIZE** The beaks of hummingbirds are adapted to fit into long, thin flowers. Hummingbirds can feed on the nectar inside the flower. Write an explanation for this adaptation that Lamarck might have proposed. Then write an explanation for this adaptation based on Darwin's ideas. Use the terms acquired traits and natural selection in your answer.

UNIT PROJECTS

If you are doing a unit project, make a folder for your project. Include in your folder a list of the resources you will need, the date on which the project is due, and a schedule to track your progress. Begin gathering data.

Standardized Test Practice

Interpreting Diagrams

Choose the letter of the best answer.

This diagram shows how groups of carnivores are related to one another. The Y's in the diagram indicate which groups share a common ancestor.

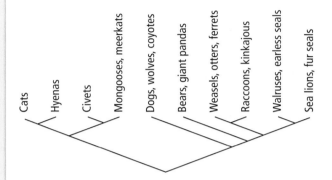

1. Hyenas share a common ancestor with which group?

  a. cats

  b. civets

  c. mongooses and meerkats

  d. raccoons and kinkajous

2. Weasels, otters, and ferrets are most closely related to

  a. bears and giant pandas.

  b. sea lions and fur seals.

  c. raccoons and kinkajous.

  d. mongooses and meerkats.

3. Sea lions and fur seals share a common ancestor with

  a. walruses and earless seals.

  b. raccoons and kinkajous.

  c. mongoose and muskrats.

  d. civets.

4. Which statement is true based on the information in the diagram?

  a. Dogs, wolves, and coyotes do not share a common ancestor with any of the groups.

  b. Raccoons are more closely related to weasels than they are to giant pandas.

  c. None of the groups shown in the diagram share a common ancestor.

  d. Mongooses and meerkats are the same as civets.

5. The branches on the diagram indicate where

  a. mass extinctions might have occurred.

  b. speciation took place.

  c. groups acquired traits and passed them onto their offspring.

  d. there are gaps in the line of evolution.

Extended Response

6. A scientist has discovered a new type of animal in the tundra area near the North Pole. Write a paragraph describing the type of evidence the scientist might use to classify the animal by its evolutionary history in the chart shown. Use these terms in your paragraph. Underline each term in your answer.

embryo	DNA sequences
vestigial structures	common ancestor

7. Write a paragraph in which you describe the traits of one of the animals named in the diagram. Choose several traits and describe how these traits might help the animal survive. Then describe how these might have been the result of adaptations and natural selection.

2 Classification of Living Things

the BIG idea

Scientists have developed a system for classifying the great diversity of living things.

Key Concepts

Internet Preview

CLASSZONE.COM

Chapter 2 online resources: Content Review, Simulation, 4 Resource Centers, Math Tutorial, Test Practice

How many different types of organisms do you see and how would you group them?

EXPLORE (the BIG idea)

How are Fingerprints Different?

Make fingerprints of your thumb and the thumbs of several classmates on separate index cards.

Observe and Think What traits do all fingerprints have in common? What traits of fingerprints allow you to tell them apart?

How Would You Sort Pennies?

Place 20 pennies in a plastic cup. Place your hand over the cup and shake it. Gently pour the pennies onto a table. Without flipping the pennies over, use one trait of the pennies to sort them into groups A and B. Again, without flipping them over, use a second trait to sort the pennies in group A into groups A1 and A2.

Observe and Think What traits do the pennies in each group share? Which group has the largest numbers of pennies?

Internet Activity: Linneaus

Go to Classzone.com to learn more about Carolus Linneaus, who, over 200 years ago, laid the groundwork for how today's scientists classify things.

Observe and Think What evidence did Linneaus use to classify organisms?

NSTA
scilinks.org
SCiLINKS

Classification Systems **Code: MDL037**

Getting Ready to Learn

◀ CONCEPT REVIEW

- Species change over time.
- Fossils and other evidence show that species change.
- New species develop from ancestral species.

◀ VOCABULARY REVIEW

fossil record p. 11
evolution p. 17
ancestor p. 29

See Glossary for definitions.
species, trait, DNA

CONTENT REVIEW
CLASSZONE.COM
Review concepts and vocabulary.

▶ TAKING NOTES

SUPPORTING MAIN IDEAS

Make a chart to show main ideas and the information that supports them. Copy each blue heading. Below each heading, add supporting information, such as reasons, explanations, and examples.

VOCABULARY STRATEGY

Place each vocabulary term at the center of a **description wheel** diagram. Write some words describing it on the spokes.

See the Note-Taking Handbook on pages R45–R51.

SCIENCE NOTEBOOK

Scientists classify millions of species.

Taxonomy is the science of classifying and naming organisms.

Classification is the process of arranging organisms in groups.

To classify organisms, scientists compare their characteristics.

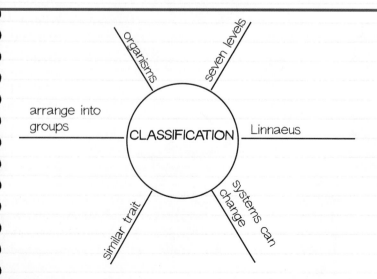

organisms

seven levels

arrange into groups

CLASSIFICATION

Linnaeus

similar trait

systems can change

Scientists develop systems for classifying living things.

- Natural selection helps explain how new species develop
- Evidence indicates that species change over time
- New species develop from ancestral species

- Why scientists classify living things
- That taxonomists study biological relationships
- About evidence used to classify organisms

VOCABULARY

classification p. 44
taxonomy p. 44

THINK ABOUT

How are these organisms similar?

Both a worm and a caterpillar share many characteristics. Both have long, skinny bodies that are divided into segments. But an earthworm moves underground, has no legs or eyes, and can grow back segments that are lost. A caterpillar crawls aboveground and is just one part of a butterfly's life cycle. As you read this chapter, think about whether you would classify these animals together or separately.

Scientists classify millions of species.

About 400 years ago, scientists who studied insects classified them based upon their appearance and behavior. If animals looked alike, researchers concluded that they were related. In the last few centuries scientists have realized that appearances can suggest false connections. Although caterpillars look like worms, they are more like butterflies. In fact, the caterpillar is a stage of a butterfly's life.

For some people, the world seemed to grow larger during the 1600s. Travelers sailed to distant lands and oceans. Scientists went on many of these trips, observing and collecting samples of living things they had never seen before. In addition, the microscope allowed scientists to see tiny organisms that had been invisible before. But how could scientists organize and talk about this wonderful new knowledge?

Classification and Taxonomy

VOCABULARY
Add a description wheel for *classification* to your notebook. Include the word *group* in your diagram.

Two scientific processes deal with classifying and naming living things. **Classification** is the process of arranging organisms into groups based on similarities. **Taxonomy** is the science of naming and classifying organisms. Classification and taxonomy are related studies. A good system of classification allows you to organize a large amount of information so that it is easy to find and to understand. The system should provide a tool for comparing very large groups of organisms as well as smaller groups. Large groups might include all animals. Smaller groups might include birds, reptiles, or mammals.

A good system of taxonomy allows people to communicate about organisms. Before the 1700s, scientists had not agreed on a system of naming and grouping organisms. Take, for example, the common wild briar rose. Some scientists called it *Rosa sylvestris inodora seu canina.* Others used the name *Rosa sylvestris alba cum rubore, folio glabro.* And any scientist studying a species could change the name.

These long Latin names may sound confusing, but even common names can be confusing. In England the bird called a robin—Britain's national bird—is only distantly related to the bird called a robin in the United States, even though they both have red feathers on their chests. And a daddy longlegs could be either a long-legged relative of spiders (in the United States) or a long-legged relative of mosquitoes (in England).

British Daddy Longlegs

American Daddy Longlegs

RESOURCE CENTER
CLASSZONE.COM
Find out more about taxonomy.

Clearly, biologists need both a system for organizing and a system for naming. Each name should refer to one specific type of organism. That way, scientists can use the species name and be sure that everybody knows exactly which organism they are talking about.

CHECK YOUR READING What is the difference between classification and taxonomy?

Using Classification

To classify organisms, scientists use similarities and differences among species. Sometimes these differences are easy to see, such as whether an animal has fur, feathers, or scales. Other times, seeing the differences requires special laboratory equipment, such as equipment to study DNA.

A classification system can help you identify unfamiliar organisms. For example, if you had never heard of a caracal but were told that it was a kind of cat, you already would know many things about it. It has fur, fangs, and sharp claws. It's a meat eater, not a plant eater. You would know these things because the caracal shares those characteristics with all of the members of the cat family.

If you looked up *caracal* in an encyclopedia, you'd find that your guesses were right. The caracal is a small wildcat native to Africa, the Middle East, and India. It weighs about 13 to 19 kilograms (29 to 42 pounds). The name *caracal* comes from a Turkish word meaning "black-eared."

The more characteristics two organisms share, the more similar their names should be in the classification system. The caracal, a pet cat, and all the cats below are different in size, habitat, and other characteristics. But they also have many similarities, and all belong to the cat family, Felidae.

Like other cats, a caracal has fur, sharp fangs, and is a meat eater.

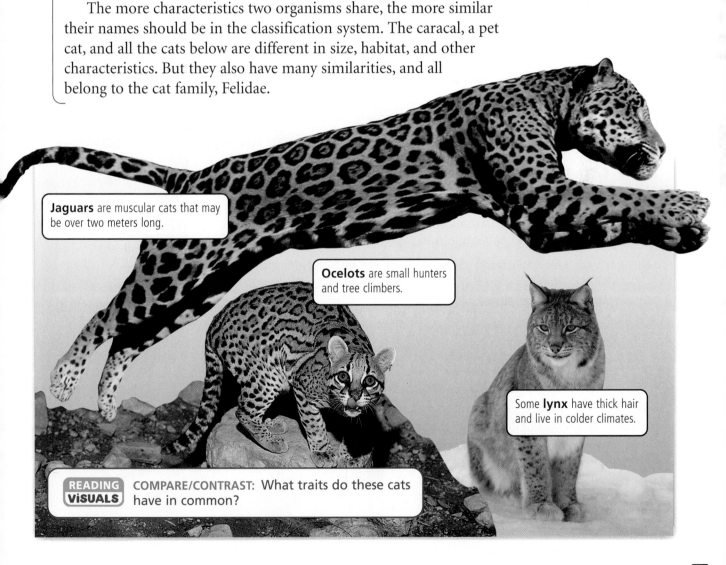

Jaguars are muscular cats that may be over two meters long.

Ocelots are small hunters and tree climbers.

Some **lynx** have thick hair and live in colder climates.

READING VISUALS COMPARE/CONTRAST: What traits do these cats have in common?

Taxonomists study biological relationships.

READING TiP

Taxonomy, taxonomist, and *taxon* all share the same root.

Scientists need a simple, standard way of arranging all of the different species. The science of taxonomy is related to the Greek word *taxis,* which means arrangement. Taxonomists are the scientists who classify and name organisms based on their similarities and differences. A taxon is a group of organisms that share certain traits. Taxons can be broad, like animals and plants, or more specific, like cats and roses.

As you learned in Chapter 1, living things evolve over time. A single species found in a fossil record might be the ancestor of many different species found on Earth today. Taxonomists study the relationships between species, trying to discover how one species evolved as compared to another species. Species that share ancestors are grouped together.

To determine how to classify organisms, scientists compare a variety of characteristics, or traits. A trait is a characteristic or behavior that can be used to tell two species apart, such as size or bone structure. If two organisms share a trait, taxonomists try to determine if they share the trait because they share an ancestor.

CHECK YOUR READING   How do taxonomists use biological relationships to classify organisms?

INVESTIGATE Classifying Leaves

How can you classify leaves?

PROCEDURE

① Decide, as a class, what traits you will use to classify leaves. You may use size, shape, color, vein patterns, texture, or anything else that you observe.

② Work with a few classmates. Sort your leaves into four or five taxons, based on the characteristics chosen in step 1. Give each taxon a name that describes its common traits.

③ Compare your classification scheme with those of other groups.

WHAT DO YOU THINK?

- How did you arrange the leaves into groups?
- Did your methods of classifying leaves match those of other student groups?

CHALLENGE How does the class's classification scheme compare with scientists' schemes for classifying organisms?

SKILL FOCUS
Classifying

MATERIALS
- leaves
- hand lens

TIME
20 minutes

Biological Relationships

Leafy Sea Dragon

The **sargassum fish** and the sea dragon are both fish with wavy fronds.

Both the **sea horse** and sea dragon have the same basic body shape.

This **sargassum seaweed** and the sea dragon both have leafy fronds.

Look at the photographs and try to determine to which organism a leafy sea dragon is more closely related. The leafy sea dragon shares traits with all of the other organisms pictured. For example, the sea dragon and the sargassum seaweed look similar, with greenish wavy fronds. But the sea dragon is an animal that moves, gets food from other organisms, and breathes oxygen. The sargassum seaweed is not an animal, it is a type of algae.

The sargassum fish shares more traits with the sea dragon, but its body is a much different shape and has scales. In fact, the leafy sea dragon is an animal that is closely related to a sea horse. Both have heads and bodies with similar shapes, and neither has scales. The seahorse shares more traits with the leafy sea dragon than with the other two organisms.

Taxonomists take evidence and try to reconstruct the evolution of a species. Then they place the species in the classification system. Scientists use physical evidence, such as fur, bones, and teeth. They also use genetic evidence, which is found within an organism's DNA.

Physical Evidence

Physical Evidence

Steller's Jay
• Lives only west of the Rocky Mountains
• Has a solid black head and neck and almost no white feathers

Blue Jay
• Lives mostly east of the Rocky Mountains
• Has blue, black, and white feathers on its wings and neck

The primary tools early scientists used for taxonomy were their eyes and measuring devices. They collected examples of organisms and noted characteristics, such as color, size, weight, and how groups of organisms obtain energy. Scientists who studied animals observed the internal structure, as well as outward appearances. These physical features are still important today.

Individuals of two species, such as the two jays shown to the left, can have many similarities as well as some differences. One obvious difference is the color pattern. Another is the area of the world in which they live. Blue jays live east of the Rocky Mountains, and steller's jays live west of the Rockies. The common names and the scientific names reflect the differences and the common ancestor: blue jay, *Cyanocitta cristata* and steller's jay, *Cyanocitta stelleri.*

Skeletons, shells, and other hard parts of organisms become fossilized more easily than soft parts do. Scientists can observe and measure fossilized bones or pieces of bones and compare them with each other. They can also compare bones of species that are extinct with bones of modern species. From such studies, scientists can determine many things about how the organism. Physical evidence provides clues about how an organism may have lived, how it moved, or what type of food it ate.

All of this physical evidence helps scientists see that all living organisms are related by evolution. Some are more closely related than others. This means they share a more recent ancestor.

 CHECK YOUR READING How could comparing fossilized bones with a modern animal's bones help you see the modern animal's evolutionary history?

Genetic Evidence

In the early 20th century scientists discovered that organisms inherit their traits through structures called genes. In the mid-1950s they observed that genes are made of DNA and that DNA stores coded information.

Today scientists can use laboratory machines to catalog each component of an organism's DNA. With that information stored on a computer, scientists can compare the components of a gene from one organism with the components of the same gene from another organism.

Genetic evidence usually supports physical evidence, but not always. Consider the example shown on page 49. For years, taxonomists argued about how to classify this small, reddish animal from China. It's scientific name is *Ailurus fulgens*, and the common name is red panda.

Genetic Evidence

Both of these pandas live in the same habitat, have similar faces, and eat bamboo. But genetic evidence shows that red pandas and giant pandas are only distant relatives.

Red Panda

Giant Panda

Red pandas have more DNA in common with **raccoons.**

Giant pandas have more DNA in common with **spectacled bears.**

Racoon

Spectacled Bear

Later, scientists discovered a larger, bearlike animal in China, which they called the giant panda. Both pandas ate only bamboo, shared a common name and their faces looked similar. Scientists concluded they were related to each other and to raccoons. However, molecular evidence has shown that the red panda is more closely related to raccoons and the giant panda is more closely related to bears.

2.1 Review

KEY CONCEPTS

1. Describe the benefits of classifying species.

2. Why do taxonomists study biological relationships?

3. How do scientists use genetic evidence when classifying organisms?

CRITICAL THINKING

4. **Analyze** Why do people need a universal system of naming organisms?

5. **Predict** The animal called a marbled godwit is a bird. What traits would you predict it has?

◯ CHALLENGE

6. **Synthesize** Suppose you found two species of cave-dwelling lizards without eyes living on opposite sides of the world. Explain how you would try to determine if the two species were closely related.

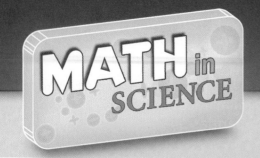

Differences Between Species

MATH TUTORIAL
CLASSZONE.COM

Click on Math Tutorial for more help with percents and fractions.

Does it surprise you to learn that roughly 50 percent of the DNA in your cells is nearly identical to the DNA in the cells of a banana? You probably know from experience that 50 percent is the same as one half. But you can also convert any percent to a fraction by using the number 100 to represent the whole. Fifty parts out of 100 is the same as one half. Another example is shown below.

Example

Comparing the cells of two species, scientists find 40 percent of the DNA is identical. How can you show what fraction that is?

(1) Rewrite the percent as a numerator with a denominator of 100.

$$\frac{40}{100}$$

(2) Reduce the fraction. Use the greatest common factor (GCF) to write the numerator and the denominator as products.

$$\frac{40}{100} = \frac{2 \cdot 20}{5 \cdot 20}$$

(3) Divide the GCF by itself to get $\frac{1}{1}$, or 1.

$$\frac{2}{5} \cdot \frac{20}{20} = \frac{2}{5} \cdot 1 = \frac{2}{5}$$

ANSWER: 40 percent $= \frac{2}{5}$

Rewrite each sentence, changing the percent to a fraction.

1. About 85 percent of the DNA in human cells is similar to the DNA in mouse cells.

2. The tooth of a modern great white shark can be 34 percent of the length of a fossil tooth from a prehistoric shark.

3. There are about 20 percent as many penguin species as there are pine tree species in the world today.

4. There are about 8 percent as many bear species as pine tree species.

CHALLENGE Choose one example or exercise on this page. Tell whether the comparison works better as a fraction or a percent. Explain why.

KEY CONCEPT

Biologists use seven levels of classification.

BEFORE, you learned

- Classification is a system of organization
- Evidence is used to classify organisms

NOW, you will learn

- About scientific names
- About seven levels of classification
- How to use a dichotomous key

VOCABULARY

genus p. 52
binomial nomenclature p. 52
dichotomous key p. 56

EXPLORE Classification

What data do you need to identify objects?

PROCEDURE

① Have one student in your group think of a secret object. The student should then tell the group one characteristic (shape, color, size, type, and so on) of that object.

② The rest of the group guesses the object's identity. Each time someone guesses incorrectly, another characteristic of the object should be given. Record the characteristics and guesses as you go.

③ When the secret object is guessed correctly, begin again with a different student picking a different secret object.

WHAT DO YOU THINK?

- How many characteristics did it usually take to guess an object's identity?
- How does this exercise relate to identifying organisms?

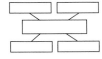

Linnaeus named about 4000 species.

Scientists name species and arrange them into groups. One scientist named Carolus Linnaeus developed systems for both naming species and organizing them into groups. All 4000 species that Linnaeus named were plants or animals. Today, scientists have named over a million species. Linnaeus used appearance to group species. As you have read, modern scientists also use appearance, along with other types of evidence, to arrange species into groups.

Naming Species

Sometimes using only one word to name an organism isn't specific enough. If you are telling a friend about your favorite writer, you might name Mary Oliver or Mary Whitebird or Mary Shelley. Using only "Mary" won't help your friend know of the author you name, so you use two words. In a similar way, scientists use two words to name organisms.

A **genus** (JEE-nuhs) is a group of species that have similar characteristics. For example, the genus *Ursus* groups all of the animals known as bears. Included in this genus are *Ursus arctos* (grizzly bears), and *Ursus maritimus* (polar bears). Members of the same genus are closely related.

The system for naming species developed by Linnaeus is the basis of modern taxonomy. We call this system **binomial nomenclature** (by-NOH-mee-uhl NOH-muhn-KLAY-chuhr). *Binomial* means "two names" and *nomenclature* means "list of names." So binomial nomenclature describes a system of naming something using two names, or words. Most scientific names are Latin terms.

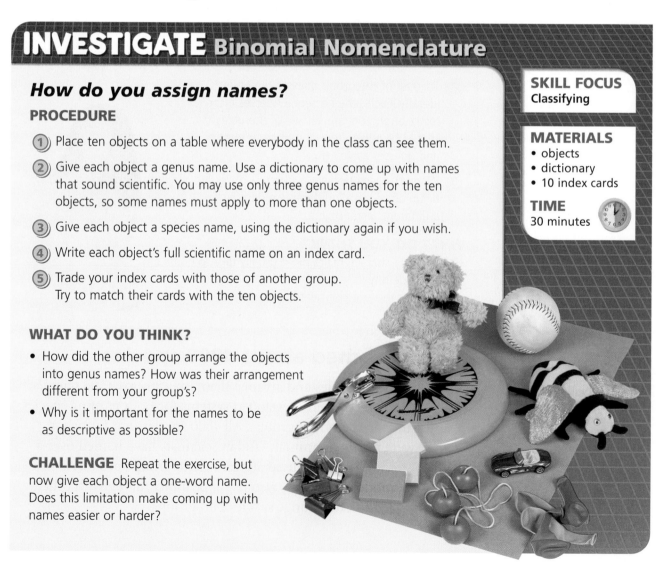

INVESTIGATE Binomial Nomenclature

How do you assign names?

PROCEDURE

1. Place ten objects on a table where everybody in the class can see them.

2. Give each object a genus name. Use a dictionary to come up with names that sound scientific. You may use only three genus names for the ten objects, so some names must apply to more than one objects.

3. Give each object a species name, using the dictionary again if you wish.

4. Write each object's full scientific name on an index card.

5. Trade your index cards with those of another group. Try to match their cards with the ten objects.

SKILL FOCUS
Classifying

MATERIALS
- objects
- dictionary
- 10 index cards

TIME
30 minutes

WHAT DO YOU THINK?

- How did the other group arrange the objects into genus names? How was their arrangement different from your group's?

- Why is it important for the names to be as descriptive as possible?

CHALLENGE Repeat the exercise, but now give each object a one-word name. Does this limitation make coming up with names easier or harder?

Binomial Nomenclature

All organisms are given a unique two-part name. Some organisms have the same species names: *gracilis* means "slender" or "graceful." Without the genus name, the species name is unclear.

Aubrieta gracilis
(false rockcress)

Chameleo gracilis
(gracile chameleon)

Mammillaria gracilis
(thimble cactus)

Using Scientific Names

Linnaeus's system of binomial nomenclature made communication about certain species much easier. When naming an organism, the use of a genus name as well as a species name is necessary.

If the genus name is not included in the scientific name, the identity of a species can be a mystery. For example, the species name of the three different species shown above is *gracilis*. The word *gracilis* means "graceful" or "slender" in Latin.

- *Aubrieta gracilis* is a type of flower found in a rock garden.
- *Chameleo gracilis* is a type of lizard called a chameleon.
- *Mammillaria gracilis* is a type of cactus.

People follow certain rules when they write scientific names. The genus name comes first; the first letter is capitalized and the entire name is in italics. The species name is also written in italics, follows the genus name, and the first letter is in lowercase.

 CHECK YOUR READING What is the difference between a genus and a species?

In addition to species and genus, the classification system includes several larger groups. Each larger group includes one or more smaller groups. Turn to page 54 to read about the larger groups in our modern system of classification.

Organisms can be classified into seven levels.

SUPPORTING MAIN IDEAS
Make a chart to show information that supports the main idea that *organisms can be classified into seven levels.*

You've read about species and genus, the most specific levels of the classification system most scientists use today. There are seven levels that describe a species. The largest level is the kingdom, the group containing the most species. The seven levels of classification for a spotted turtle and a housecat are listed below.

1. Kingdom (Animalia—the animals)
2. Phylum (Chordata—animals with backbones)
3. Class (Mammalia—mammals, or furry animals that nurse their young)
4. Order (Carnivora—carnivores, or animals that kill and eat other animals)
5. Family (Felidae—the cat family)
6. Genus (*Felis*—housecats, cougars, and many others)
7. Species (*catus*—all housecats, no matter what their breed)

Like the cat, the turtle is also classified into seven levels. However, only the two largest levels, Animalia and Chordata, are the same as the classification for a housecat. The more names an organism shares with another organism, the more closely related the two organisms are. Cats and turtles are both animals with backbones, but are otherwise different. Spotted turtles have more traits in common with snakes and lizards than with cats. Lizards, snakes, and turtles all belong in the class Reptilia. Phyla are more specific than kingdoms, classes are more specific than phyla, and so on. The illustration on page 55 shows how kingdom is the broadest grouping of organisms, and species is the most specific.

READING TiP

Phyla is the plural form of *phylum.*

Classification Hierarchy		
	Spotted turtle	Cat
Kingdom	Animalia	Animalia
Phylum	Chordata	Chordata
Class	Reptilia	Mammalia
Order	Testudines	Carnivora
Family	Emydidae	Felidae
Genus	*Clemmys*	*Felis*
Species	*guttata*	*catus*

Clemmys guttata

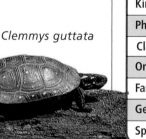

Felis catus

Classifying Organisms

Moving from kingdom to species, each level includes a smaller set of organisms.

① **Kingdom**
Animalia:
Animals

② **Phylum**
Chordata:
With backbone or
similar structure

③ **Class**
Reptilia:
Reptiles

④ **Order**
Testudines:
Turtles

⑤ **Family**
Emydidae:
Water turtles

Spotted turtle
Clemmys guttata

⑥ **Genus**
Clemmys:
North American
pond turtles

⑦ **Species**
guttata:
Spotted turtle

Scientists can compare very broad categories of organisms, such as kingdoms and phyla. Or they can compare very specific categories, such as species. If scientists wish to compare all the different types of turtles to one another, then they will compare the organisms in the order Testudines. But if scientists want to compare turtles that live in or near water, then they will compare only organisms in the family Emydidae.

You can remember the classification levels and their order with this memory aid: Kings Play Chess On Fat Green Stools. The first letter of each word is the same as the first letter in each level of classification: *kingdom, phylum, class, order, family, genus,* and *species.* A complete classification of humans goes like this: kingdom Animalia, phylum Chordata, class Mammalia, order Primates, family Hominidae, genus *Homo,* species *sapiens.*

 CHECK YOUR READING Which level of classification in the seven-level system includes the most species?

Dichotomous keys and field guides help people identify organisms.

With millions of organisms on Earth, how could a specific one be identified? Even if you know some of the larger categories, it can be difficult to find the species, genus, or even family name of many organisms from a long list of possibilities.

Take a beetle, for example. Even if you knew that it is in the kingdom Animalia, phylum Arthropoda (animals with jointed legs), class Insecta (insects), and order Coleoptera (hard-winged insects), you'd still have to choose among 300,000 known species of beetles that have been discovered around the world.

READING TIP

Vocabulary The prefix *di-* means "two".

Taxonomists have come up with a tool to identify organisms such as this beetle. A **dichotomous key** (dy-KAHT-uh-muhs key) asks a series of questions that can be answered in only two ways. Your answer to each question leads you to another question with only two choices. After a number of such questions, you will identify the organism. One example of a dichotomous key for trees is shown on page 57.

The questions in a dichotomous key gradually narrow down the list of possible organisms. The questions can ask about any trait. The idea is simply to make identifying an organism as easy as possible. The dichotomous key for trees, for example, asks a set of questions that only ask about the traits of the leaves. Leaves are usually easy to get from a tree that needs to be identified, and they include many characteristics that can be used to tell different trees apart.

SIMULATION
CLASSZONE.COM

Use an interactive dichotomous key.

Dichotomous Key

Use the dichotomous key below to discover on what tree the circled leaf is found.

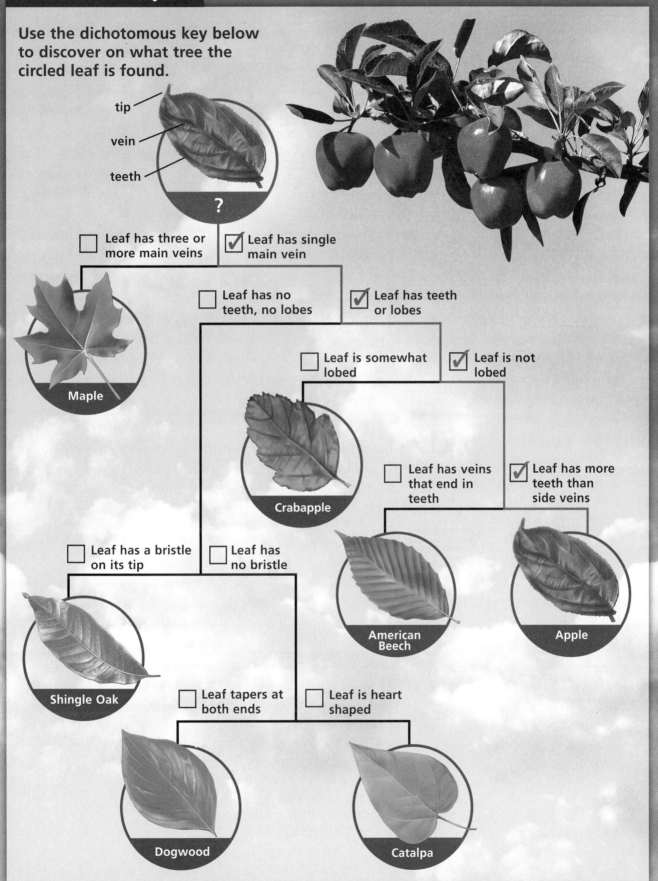

tip

vein

teeth

?

- ☐ Leaf has three or more main veins
- ☑ Leaf has single main vein

Maple

- ☐ Leaf has no teeth, no lobes
- ☑ Leaf has teeth or lobes

- ☐ Leaf is somewhat lobed
- ☑ Leaf is not lobed

Crabapple

- ☐ Leaf has veins that end in teeth
- ☑ Leaf has more teeth than side veins

- ☐ Leaf has a bristle on its tip
- ☐ Leaf has no bristle

American Beech

Apple

Shingle Oak

- ☐ Leaf tapers at both ends
- ☐ Leaf is heart shaped

Dogwood

Catalpa

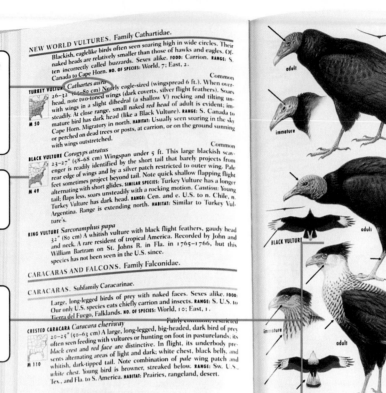

A bird's **scientific name** is shown next to its common name. The first name is the genus, and the second name is the species.

Range maps show where a bird can be found in each season.

Body shape and body size give clues to determining if you have identified the right bird.

Another tool for identifying organisms is a field guide. Field guides include paintings or photographs of familiar species. Flower guides may start with the flower's color. Bird guides are arranged by orders and families. Field guides also include maps showing where organisms live.

 CHECK YOUR READING What two tools have taxonomists developed to identify organisms?

2.2 Review

KEY CONCEPTS

1. What is binomial nomenclature?

2. Write the names of the seven levels of classification. Which level contains the most organisms?

3. What makes a dichotomous key easy to use?

CRITICAL THINKING

4. **Summarize** What were Carolus Linnaeus' main contributions to taxonomy?

5. **Compare and Contrast** Compare a dichotomous key with a typical field guide. What are the strengths and weaknesses of each?

CHALLENGE

6. **Synthesize** Predict what differences you might find among organisms in the same species?.

EXTREME SCIENCE

The Undiscovered

Everyone agrees that insects are the largest group of animals on Earth, but nobody knows exactly how many insect species exist. Some estimates predict that there are as many as 30 million. However, only about 900,000 have been classified. Twenty-nine million insect species may be waiting to be discovered!

Where in the World?

Many of the new insect species are found in tropical forests of South America and Asia. But plenty may be hiding close to your own home.

- The most massive bug in Southern California went undiscovered until April 4, 2002. This wingless relative of the Jerusalem cricket looks something like a puffed-up 3-inch-long ant.

- While studying for her graduate degree, Christina Sandoval captured insects in Santa Barbara, California. She caught an unidentified species of walking stick insect, which she named after herself: *Timema cristinae.*

- The Hanford Nuclear Reservation, in Washington state, was closed to the public for about 50 years. After it opened for cleanup, the Nature Conservancy found 27 new insect species in just 4 years, including a new micromoth less than 1/8 inch long.

Scientists think that over one third of the estimated 164,000 insect species in the United States have yet to be discovered and named. Start looking. Who knows where they'll be!

A Whole New Order

In March 2002, for the first time in 87 years, a whole new order of insects was discovered. Insects in this order look like a cross between stick insects, praying mantises, and grasshoppers. Upon its discovery, the order was nicknamed *gladiators.* Now called *Mantophasmatodea,* the "gladiator bugs" raised the total number of insect orders to 31.

EXPLORE

1. **ANALYZE** List some things about an insect that could be included in its species name. Tell why each is important.

2. **CHALLENGE** Scientists recently discovered a new centipede in New York's Central Park, the first new species in the park in over 100 years. Centipedes are related to insects. Find out what centipedes and insects have in common and how they differ.

RESOURCE CENTER
CLASSZONE.COM

Learn more about new insects

An adult Jerusalem cricket can reach 2 inches in length.

Classification systems change as scientists learn more.

◀ BEFORE, you learned	▶ NOW, you will learn
• Scientists give each species a unique scientific name	• About the connection between new discoveries and taxonomy
• There are seven levels of classification	• About three domains
• Dichotomous keys help us identify organisms	• About six kingdoms

VOCABULARY

domain p. 61
Plantae p. 63
Animalia p. 63
Protista p. 63
Fungi p .63
Archaea p. 63
Bacteria p. 63

THINK ABOUT

How do scientists define kingdoms?

Look at this photograph of a sea urchin. It lives its life buried in or slowly moving across the ocean floor. The sea urchin's mouth is located on its under-side. It feeds on food particles that settle on or are buried in

the ocean floor. The sea urchin doesn't appear to have much in common with a tiger, an alligator, even a human. Yet all of these organisms belong in the same kingdom, called Animalia. Why do you think scientists would group these organisms together?

Taxonomy changes as scientists make discoveries.

The list of species continues to grow as scientists discover new species. In addition, taxonomists are learning more about the evolutionary history of species. As you read in Section 1, new knowledge resulted in the reclassification of species such as the giant panda. Both the names of species and the groups into which they are arranged may change as a result of discoveries about the evolution of these species.

Early scientists described two large groups of organisms—plants and animals. Plants were described as green and nonmoving. Animals moved. Most scientists today use a system that includes six kingdoms. In addition, taxonomists have added a level of organization above the kingdom level.

Three Domains

Microscopes and other advances in technology have allowed scientists to observe that there are three fundamentally different types of cells. Based on this observation scientists have arranged kingdoms into larger groups called **domains.** For example, the domain Eukarya contains the protists, fungi, plants, and animals.

RESOURCE CENTER
CLASSZONE.COM

Find out more about modern classification.

The table below summarizes the relationships among the six kingdoms and the three domains. You will learn more about kingdoms in the rest of this section.

Domains and Kingdoms						
Domain	Bacteria	Archaea	Eukarya			
Kingdom	Bacteria	Archaea	Protista	Fungi	Plantae	Animalia
Cell type	No nucleus	No nucleus	With nucleus	With nucleus	With nucleus	With nucleus
Cell number	Unicellular	Unicellular	Unicellular	Mostly multicellular	Multicellular	Multicellular
How organisms get energy	Varies	Varies	Varies	Absorbs materials	Uses sunlight	Consumes food

The photographs below show examples of cells from each domain. One of the traits that distinguishes cells of Eukarya from cells of Bacteria and Archaea is the presence of a nucleus. Cells that contain a nucleus are called eukaryotic cells, and cells that do not contain a nucleus are called prokaryotic cells. The domains Bacteria and Archaea include prokaryotic cells. Organisms in the domain Eukarya include those having eukaryotic cells.

CHECK YOUR READING How are prokaryotic cells different from eukaryotic cells?

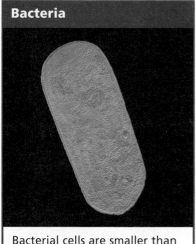

Bacteria

Bacterial cells are smaller than Eukarya cells and have no nucleus.

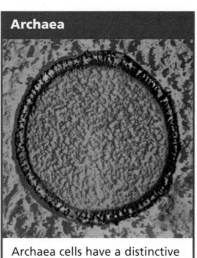

Archaea

Archaea cells have a distinctive chemistry and can survive extreme environments.

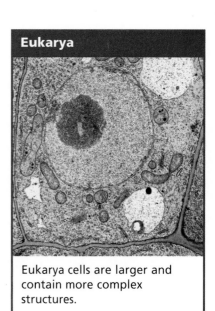

Eukarya

Eukarya cells are larger and contain more complex structures.

All living things on Earth can be classified in six kingdoms.

Plantae

- Plants are multicellular and live on land.
- Plants obtain energy from sunlight.
- A plant cell has a nucleus, a cell wall, and chloroplasts.

Animalia

- Animals are multicellular and able to move.
- Animals obtain energy by eating food.
- An animal cell has a nucleus but no cell wall or chloroplasts.

Protista

- Most protists are single-celled.
- Multicellular protists lack complex structure.
- A protist cell has a nucleus.

Fungi

- All fungi except yeasts are multicellular.
- Fungi obtain energy by absorbing materials.
- A fungus cell has a nucleus and a cell wall, but no chloroplasts.

Archaea

- Archaea are unicellular organisms without nuclei.
- Archaea cells have different chemicals than bacteria.
- Archaea can live in extreme conditions.

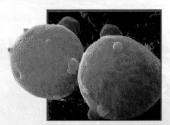

Bacteria

- Bacteria are unicellular organisms.
- A bacterial cell has no nucleus.
- Bacteria reproduce by dividing in two.

Six Kingdoms

The classification system that many scientists use today has six kingdoms. Every known species on Earth is included in one of these six kingdoms.

- Kingdom **Plantae** (PLAN-TEE) includes plants such as trees, grass, and moss.

- Kingdom **Animalia** (AN-uh-MAL-yuh) includes animals, from lions and tigers and bears to bugs and multicellular microbes.

- Kingdom **Protista** (pruh-TIHS-tuh) includes organisms that don't fit easily into animals, plants, or fungi. They are either unicellular organisms or have a simple multicellular structure.

- Kingdom **Fungi** (FUHN-jy) includes mushrooms, molds, and yeasts.

- Kingdom **Archaea** (AHR-kee-uh) contains organisms that are similar to bacteria, but have a cell structure that is so different that scientists separate them into their own kingdom.

- Kingdom **Bacteria** (bak-TIHR-ee-uh) are unicellular organisms with no nucleus.

This system may change as scientists learn more about the species in each kingdom. Before 1990, most scientists preferred a five-kingdom system that combined Archaea and Bacteria into a single kingdom. However, as scientists learned of chemical differences between the cells of the species, they arranged them into two kingdoms. Today, some scientists suggest that the kingdom Protista should be arranged into smaller kingdoms because of the many differences among its species. Many scientists agree on a system similar to the one summarized on page 62.

 CHECK YOUR READING Which of the six kingdoms include unicellular organisms?

The two most familiar kingdoms are plants and animals.

Carolus Linneaus divided all of the species he identified into two large groups: plants and animals. People still use these groups to describe most living things today. But these two kingdoms also include unfamiliar organisms.

It might seem odd that living things that are so different from each other—humans, elephants, termites, ducks, fish, worms—are all part of the same group. However, all of these organisms share some general traits, just as all plants share another set of general traits.

Plantae

About 250,000 plant species live on Earth. They range from tiny mosses to the largest organisms on the planet, giant sequoia trees. The oldest living organism on our planet is a plant called the bristlecone pine. Some living bristlecone pines were growing when the Egyptians built the pyramids, about 4000 years ago.

Clematis viticella
(Italian clematis)

All plants are multicellular and are eukaryotes, which means their DNA is stored in the nucleus of their cells. All plants are able to make sugars using the Sun's energy. Plants cannot move from place to place, but they can grow around objects, turn toward light, and grow upward. Plant cells are different from animal cells, because plant cells have tough walls outside their cell membranes.

Animalia

Scientists have already named a million species in the kingdom Animalia. Many different types of animals inhabit the planet, but more than 90 percent of the named species are insects. The animal kingdom also includes familiar animals such as whales, sharks, humans, bears, dogs, and fish.

All animals get their energy by eating other organisms or by eating food made by other organisms. Animals have the ability to move around for at least part of their life. Most animals have mouths and some type of nervous system. Plant and animal cells are both eukaryotic, but animal cells have no cell walls.

CHECK YOUR READING What is the most abundant type of species in the animal kingdom?

Abracadabrella birdsville
(jumping spider)

Giraffa camelopardalis
(giraffe)

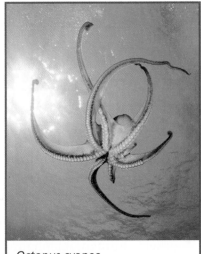

Octopus cyanea
(day octopus)

Other organisms make up four more kingdoms.

Carolus Linnaeus's classification systems included the organisms he knew about in the late 1700s. Some of the organisms Linnaeus called plants—the mushrooms, molds, and their relatives—turned out to have some characteristics very different from those of plants. Biologists now put fungi in a kingdom of their own.

Three other kingdoms consist mainly of microscopic organisms. These are Protista, Archaea, and Bacteria. Most organisms on Earth are classified as bacterial or archaea. These are prokaryotic organisms, which have small, simple cells and no nuclei.

CHECK YOUR READING What are the four kingdoms besides Plantae and Animalia?

Protista

The kingdom Protista includes a wide variety of organisms. Most protists are unicellular. Protists that are multicellular have structures that are too simple to be classified as animals, plants, or fungi. All protists have large, complex cells with a true nucleus (eukaryotes). Some eat other organisms as animals do, some get energy from sunlight as plants do. Some protists resemble fungi. However, protists that are multicellular do not have as many specialized cells or structures as plants, animals, and fungi.

Macrocystis pyrifera (giant kelp)

Many protists live in pond water or sea water. The largest of these unicellular species are barely visible without a microscope. However, large organisms such as seaweeds are also classified as Protista. Some seaweeds can grow hundreds of feet in a single year.

Different groups of protists evolved from different ancestors. Scientists still debate whether kingdom Protista should be classified as one kingdom or should be split into several kingdoms.

Fungi

Every time a loaf of bread is baked, a fungus is responsible for the rising dough. One group of fungi called yeasts makes it possible for us to make bread and many other food products. Another type of fungi that people eat includes some mushrooms. A mushroom grows in thin threads underground, and only the small cap breaks above the ground.

Fungi are usually divided into three categories: mushrooms, molds, and yeasts. The trait that separates fungi from other organisms is that fungi take in nutrients from their surroundings instead of eating other organisms or using sunlight. Both plants and fungi remain rooted in one place. Most fungi have cell walls similar to the cell walls of plants. Unlike plants, however, many fungi act as decomposers, breaking down dead or decaying material into simpler parts that can be absorbed or recycled by other organisms.

Penicillium
(bread mold)

Lepiota procera
(parasol mushroom)

Archaea

In the mid-1990s a researcher studying the genes of some bacteria discovered that although they resembled bacteria in size and cell type, some species had very specific genetic differences. After more study, scientists decided to call these organisms archaea. They differ so much that scientists now classify archaea in the separate kingdom of Archaea.

Archaea appear to be more related to eukaryotes—organisms with complex cells containing nuclei—than to bacteria. Archaea do not have nuclei, but their cell structure is different from that of bacteria. Like bacteria, archaeans live in many environments, especially in the ocean. But they also live in some very extreme environments, such as boiling mud near geysers, hot vents at the bottom of the ocean, salty ponds, and deep under the sand.

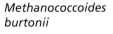
Methanococcoides
burtonii

CHECK YOUR READING Which traits classify an organism as part of the kingdom Archaea?

Bacteria

Bacteria live nearly everywhere on Earth. This kingdom includes organisms that cause human disease and spoil food, but most of these organisms are helpful members of biological communities.

All bacteria are unicellular organisms. They have small, simple cells without a nucleus. Most bacteria have a cell wall outside the cell membrane, but this wall is not the same as the cell wall of plants. Bacteria reproduce by dividing in two, which allows them to increase their numbers quickly.

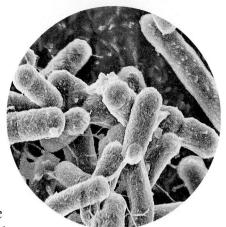

Escherichia coli
(E. coli)

Species and environments change.

In the last chapter you have read about the ways species change over time. You have also read how the evolutionary history of species helps scientists classify living things.

Scientists have named over a million species and placed them into six kingdoms. In addition, scientists estimate that there are millions—maybe tens of millions—more species that haven't been discovered. Scientists have also discovered forms of life preserved in the fossil record. Some of those organisms are the ancestors of organisms that live today.

Species evolve over time as individual organisms and environments change. Individual organisms are faced with many other pressures that affect daily lives. These pressures may come from changes in their living space, in the availability of food or other resources, or from other organisms. In the next chapter, you will read about how groups of species are affected by changes in their surroundings.

2.3 Review

KEY CONCEPTS

1. What are the names of the six kingdoms used in the classification system?

2. How are species sorted into the various kingdoms?

CRITICAL THINKING

3. **Communicate** Make a table with columns headed Characteristics, Animalia, and Plantae. Using as many rows as needed, list characteristics that differ between these two kingdoms.

4. **Analyze** Explain how fungi differ from plants.

● CHALLENGE

5. **Analyze** One bacterium has a membrane surrounding its DNA. Should this organism be classified with the eukaryotes? Why or why not?

CHAPTER INVESTIGATION

Making a Field Guide

OVERVIEW AND PURPOSE A field guide is an illustrated book that shows the differences and similarities among plant or animal organisms. In this activity you will
- observe and classify leaves
- prepare a field guide based on your observations

▶ Question

A field guide helps scientists identify organisms. Can you successfully prepare such a field guide? What would you like to know about how field guides are used and made? Write a question that begins with *Which, How, Why, When,* or *What.*

▶ Procedure

MATERIALS
- plastic gloves
- shoebox
- hand lens
- pencil
- paper
- tracing paper
- crayons

1. Make 5 or more tables like the one shown on the sample science notebook on page 69. Gather at least 5 samples of different leaves from an area that your teacher chooses. **CAUTION: Wear protective gloves when handling plants. Be aware of any poisonous plants in your area.** Place your samples in a shoebox and bring them back to the classroom for observation.

2. **CAUTION: Wear plastic gloves when handling leaf samples.** Use the hand lens to study the leaves that you gathered. Make a sketch of each of the leaves. Create leaf rubbings by placing each leaf between two sheets of tracing paper and rubbing the top paper with the side of a pencil or crayon. Record your observations about each leaf in one of the data tables.

step 2

3. Use the information in your table to prepare your field guide. Start by dividing your leaves into two groups on the basis of one of the characteristics you observed. Then compare the leaves in each group. How are they similar or different? Continue to observe and divide the samples in each group until each leaf is in a classification by itself.

4. Use scientific field guides or other sources to identify your sample leaves. Find out the common and scientific name for each leaf and add that information to your table.

5. Describe the location of each sample and what effect the plant it represents has on its environment. For example, does the plant provide food or shelter for animals? Does it have a commercial use, or is it simply a common weed?

6. Use your data tables, sketches, and leaf rubbings to prepare your field guide for the chosen area.

▶ Observe and Analyze

Write It Up

1. **CLASSIFY** What characteristics did you choose for classifying your leaf samples? Explain why you grouped the leaves the way you did.

2. **ANALYZE** Which characteristics of the leaves you gathered were most useful in finding their scientific names and in identifying them?

▶ Conclude

Write It Up

1. **INFER** Could you use the same characteristics you used to group your samples to classify leaves of other species?

2. **LIMITATIONS** Were there any leaves you could not classify? What would help you classify them?

3. **APPLY** How are field guides useful to scientists working on environmental studies? How are field guides useful to tourists or others who are exploring an environment?

▶ INVESTIGATE Further

CHALLENGE Combine your field guide with those made by all the other members of your class to make one large field guide. Use all the sketches and observations to classify leaves into several large groups.

Making a Field Guide: Leaf 1

Characteristic	Observations
Simple leaf or several leaflets	
Number of lobes	
Texture	
Leaf edge	
Vein patterns	

Common name
_____

Scientific name
_____

Location where found
_____

Uses/role in environment
_____

the **BIG** idea

Scientists have developed a system for classifying the great diversity of living things.

CONTENT REVIEW
CLASSZONE.COM

◀ KEY CONCEPTS SUMMARY

2.1 Scientists develop systems for classifying living things.

- Living things are arranged in groups based on similarities.
- Classification is the process of arranging organisms into groups.
- Taxonomy involves classifying as well as naming species.

VOCABULARY
classification p. 44
taxonomy p. 44

2.2 Biologists use seven levels of classification.

Spotted turtle
Clemmys guttata

Classification: Spotted turtle	
Kingdom	Animalia
Phylum	Chordata
Class	Reptilia
Order	Testudines
Family	Emydidae
Genus	*Clemmys*
Species	*guttata*

VOCABULARY
genus p. 52
binomial nomenclature p. 52
dichotomous key p. 56

2.3 Classification systems change as scientists learn more.

The most popular system of classification in use today is a three-domain system that includes six kingdoms of organisms.

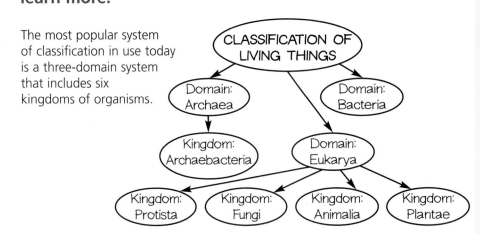

VOCABULARY
domain p. 61
Plantae p. 63
Animalia p. 63
Protista p. 63
Fungi p. 63
Archaea p. 63
Bacteria p. 63

Reviewing Vocabulary

Make a frame like the one shown for each vocabulary word listed below. Write the word in the center. Decide what information to frame it with. Use definitions, examples, descriptions, parts, or pictures.

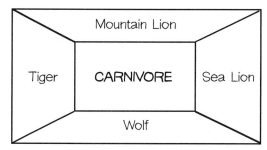

1. Plantae

2. Animalia

3. Protista

4. Fungi

Reviewing Key Concepts

Multiple Choice *Choose the letter of the best answer.*

5. The scientific process of arranging organisms into groups based on similarities is
   a. observation
   b. classification
   c. binomial nomenclature
   d. dichotomy

6. The system of naming organisms developed by Carolus Linnaeus is called
   a. binomial nomenclature
   b. taxonomy
   c. dichotomous nomenclature
   d. classification

7. Which group includes the most species?
   a. kingdom
   b. family
   c. domain
   d. phylum

8. The science of taxonomy allows scientists to
   a. identify unfamiliar organisms
   b. classify and name organisms
   c. refer to one specific type of organism
   d. determine similar traits of organisms

9. Which allows scientists to use genetic information to classify organisms?
   a. physical traits
   b. DNA
   c. fossil evidence
   d. habitats

10. A dichotomous key contains a series of questions that people use to
    a. find similar organisms
    b. identify organisms
    c. name organisms
    d. describe organisms

11. What are the names of the three domains?
    a. Plantae, Animalia, Protista
    b. Bacteria, Protista, Fungi
    c. Bacteria, Archaea, Eukarya
    d. Protista, Archaea, Eukarya

12. Which is an example of a trait?
    a. bone structure
    b. DNA information
    c. fossil records
    d. habitat

13. A group of species that have similar characteristics is called
    a. an order
    b. a family
    c. a phylum
    d. a genus

14. Which characteristic is common to animals, plants, protists, and fungi?
    a. ability to make their own food
    b. eukaryotic cells
    c. ability to move
    d. multicellular structure

Short Answer *Write a short answer to each question.*

15. What are the rules for creating a scientific name for an organism?

16. How is a field guide different from a dichotomous key?

17. What types of information caused scientists to add the level of domain to the system of classification?

Thinking Critically

18. ANALYZE How do scientists use fossils to classify organisms?

19. APPLY Scientists once classified American vultures and African vultures together in the falcon family. Now, scientists know that American vultures are more closely related to storks. What type of evidence might scientists have used to come to this conclusion? Explain your answer.

20. EVALUATE Which two of these species are more closely related: *Felis catus, Felis concolor, Picea concolor?* How do you know?

21. INFER A scientist is studying the following organisms. What conclusions can you draw about the organisms based on their scientific names?

- *Ursus americanus*
- *Ursus arctos*
- *Ursus maritimus*

Tremarctos Omatus
(spectacled bear)

22. ANALYZE Two organisms you are studying are in the same class, but in a different order. What does this information tell you about the two organisms?

23. RANK Which of these have more groups of organisms: phylum or family? Explain your answer.

24. SUMMARIZE Describe how you would use a dichotomous key to identify this leaf.

25. SYNTHESIZE Why was it necessary for scientists to create groups for classifying organisms other than the groups of plants and animals described by Linnaeus?

26. CLASSIFY Suppose you discover a new organism that is single celled, has a nucleus, lives in the water, and uses sunlight to produce its energy. In which kingdom would you classify this organism? Explain.

the BIG idea

27. INFER Look again at the picture on pages 40–41. Now that you have finished the chapter, how would you change or add details to your answer to the question on the photograph?

28. PROVIDE EXAMPLES Imagine that you are a scientist studying a variety of organisms in a South American rain forest. You have classified one organism in the kingdom Animalia and another organism in the kingdom Plantae. Give examples of the characteristics that would enable you to classify each organism in those kingdoms.

UNIT PROJECTS

Check your schedule for your unit project. How are you doing? Be sure that you've placed data or notes from your research in your project folder.

Analyzing Graphics

Choose the letter of the best response.

By following the steps in this chart, it is possible to find the type of tree to which a leaf belongs.

Step 1
1a) Leaves are needlelike.................Go to step 2
1b) Leaves are flat and scalelike.........Go to step 5

Step 2
2a) Needles are clustered...................Go to step 3
2b) Needles are not clustered.............Go to step 4

Step 3
3a) Clusters of 2–5 needles...............Pine
3b) Clusters greater than 10.............Go to step 4

Step 4
4a) Needles soft...............................Larch
4b) Needles stiff.............................True cedar

Step 5
5a) Needles are short and sharp........Giant sequoia
5b) Some leaves are not sharp..........Go to Step 6

1. Which has leaves with clusters of 2–5 needles?
   a. pine tree
   b. larch tree
   c. true cedar tree
   d. giant sequoia

2. If a tree has clusters of leaves greater than 10, you would go to
   a. step 1
   b. step 2
   c. step 3
   d. step 4

3. Each step on the key compares two
   a. species
   b. animals
   c. traits
   d. trees

4. A tree with soft needles that are not clustered is most likely a
   a. pine tree
   b. larch tree
   c. true cedar tree
   d. giant sequoia

5. Which statement best describes the characteristics of a giant sequoia?
   a. flat, scalelike needles that are short and sharp
   b. flat, scalelike needles that are stiff
   c. clustered needles that are soft
   d. clustered needles that are short and sharp

Extended Response

6. A biologist has discovered and collected a number of unknown plant species from a rain-forest environment. Explain what type of evidence a biologist would rely on to determine if the plant species were new. Give specific examples of what a biologist would look for. What process would scientists go through to name the new species?

7. As you learned in the chapter, there are scientists who classify and name organisms. Explain why it is important for these taxonomists to study biological relationships. What may these relationships indicate about early life and modern life?

TIMELINES in Science

LIFE Unearthed

How do scientists know about life on Earth millions of years ago? They dig, scratch, and hunt. The best clues they find are hidden in layers of rock. The rock-locked clues, called fossils, are traces or remains of living things from long ago. Some fossils show the actual bodies of organisms, while others, such as footprints, reveal behavior.

Before 1820, most fossil finds revealed the bodies of ocean life. Then large bones of lizardlike walking animals began turning up, and pictures of a new "terrible lizard," or dinosaur, took shape. Later, discoveries of tracks and nests showed behaviors such as flocking and caring for young. Even today, discoveries of "living fossils," modern relatives of prehistoric species, have offered us a rare glimpse of the activity of early life.

1824
Giant Lizards from Fragments

William Buckland describes *Megalosaurus*, a giant crocodilelike animal he studies from only a few bits of jaw, teeth, ribs, pelvis, and one leg. A year later Gideon Mantell assembles *Iguanodon*, a similar animal, from fossil bones.

EVENTS

| 1800 | 1810 | 1820 |

APPLICATIONS AND TECHNOLOGY

TECHNOLOGY

Removing Fossils with Care

The technology for removing fossils from rock beds has not changed much since the 1820s. Collectors still work by hand with hammers, chisels, trowels, dental picks, and sieves. Gideon Mantell used these when he chiseled out *Iguanodon* bones embedded in one large rock called the "Mantle piece."

Fossil hunters also use hand lenses and microscopes. Sometimes a protective layer is built up with glue, varnish, or another finish. For larger samples, a plaster cast often supports the fossil. Most fossils are packed using a technology found in any kitchen—a sealable plastic bag.

1909

Burgess Shale Shows Soft Bodies

In the Burgess Pass of the Canadian Rocky Mountains, Charles Walcott finds fossils preserved in shale, a soft rock that preserves lacelike details such as the soft tissues of the Marella. The glimpse of life 505 million years ago is the earliest yet seen.

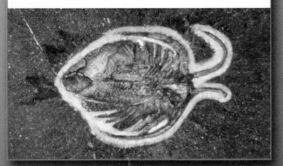

1944

New Dawn for the Dawn Redwood

Beside a small temple, a Chinese scientist discovers the dawn redwood, or metasequoia, growing. Common in fossil specimens 100 million years old, the tree had not been seen alive in recorded history. The 1944 find starts a search, and in 1948, scientists find a small wild grove in China as well.

1938

African Fisherman Hauls in History

A South African fisherman pulls up a five-foot fish he has never seen. He calls the local museum, whose curator, a naturalist, has also never seen the species. To her surprise, biologists identify it as a coelacanth, a prehistoric fish thought to be extinct for more than 50 million years.

1900	1910	1920	1930	1940

APPLICATION

Protecting Fossils and Dig Sites

The United States Antiquities Act of 1906 preserves and protects historic and prehistoric sites. The act requires collectors to have a permit to dig for or to pick up fossils on public lands such as national parks. It also requires that any major find be publicly and permanently preserved in a museum.

The United Nations also now designates World Heritage sites. For example, the original Burgess Shale find in Yoho National Park in Canada is now protected by international law. Since 1906, many states and provinces in Canada have enacted their own laws about land rights and the excavation and transport of fossils.

1974

"Lucy" and Upright Kin Found

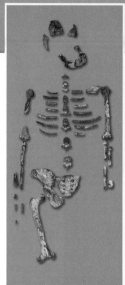

Digging in Ethiopia, Donald Johanson finds an almost complete hominid skeleton. He names the fossil "Lucy," after a Beatles' song. Lucy is over 3 million years old, is three and one-half feet tall, and has an upright stance or posture. A year later, Johanson's crew finds "The First Family," a group of 13 skeletons of the same species as Lucy.

1990

Largest Tyrannosaurus, "Sue"

Out on a walk with her dog in the South Dakota badlands, amateur fossil hunter Sue Hendrickson discovers three huge bones jutting out of a cliff. Hendrickson finds the largest and most complete *T. rex* skeleton yet. The 67-million-year-old "Sue" is now on display in the Field Museum of National History in Chicago, Illinois.

1953

Piltdown Man No Neanderthal

Scientists once applauded the discovery in 1912 of a "Neanderthal skull" in the Piltdown gravel pit, but a few had their doubts. In 1953, radioactive potassium dating proves the Piltdown man to be nothing more than the jaw of an orangutan placed beside human skull fragments.

1950   1960   1970   1980   1990

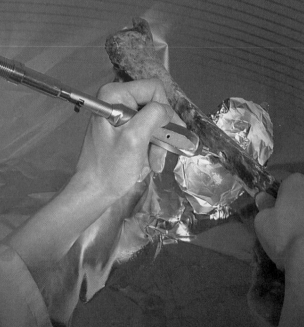

TECHNOLOGY

How Old Is a Fossil?

Before 1947, scientists used a method called relative dating. They assigned a date to a fossil according to the rock layer in which it was found. The deeper, or older, the layer, the older the fossil.

The discovery of radiometric dating in 1947 marked the first time a fossil's date could be pinpointed. Organic matter decays at a constant rate. So, by measuring the rate of decay, you can tell the age of the matter. Radiocarbon 14 is used to tell the age of a fossil that is less than 10,000 years old. Since most fossils are older than that, scientists use other methods. Potassium-argon decays more slowly than carbon. It is a more common method. All types of fossil dating have margins of error, or limits to accuracy.

1993

Oldest Fossils Are Too Small to See

Fossils discovered up to this point date back about 550 million years, to the dawn of the Cambrian Period. J. William Schopf identifies fossils of microorganisms scientifically dated to 3.4 billion years ago. This startling find near Australia's Marble Bar opens up a vast period of time and once again reshapes theories about life's beginnings.

 RESOURCE CENTER
CLASSZONE.COM
Discover more about the latest fossil and living-fossil finds.

2000

TECHNOLOGY

Fossil Classification and DNA

There are many ways to classify fossils. Scientists look at bone structure, body posture, evidence of behavior, and environment. Microscopes are used to identify organisms too small for the eye to see. Study of DNA molecules helps to identify species when soft tissues remain intact, such as in fossils formed in amber or crystallized tree sap. In 1983, polymerase chain reaction (PCR) became the simplest method to study the DNA extracted from fossils. In PCR, parts of DNA can be copied billions of times in a few hours.

INTO THE FUTURE

Technology is sure to play a role in future fossil finds. Scientists can communicate via laptop computers and satellites, which allow the public to follow excavations as they occur.

Computer modeling helps scientists determine what incomplete skeletons looked like. It also helps them determine how dinosaurs and other living things once moved. Fossil finds can be combined with digitized information about modern living organisms and about environmental conditions. The model can test hypotheses or even help to formulate them.

Another area of technology that may become increasingly applied to fossils is DNA testing to identify and help date fossils. This is more complicated in fossilized bone, as the genetic material can be fragmented. But with time, scientists may discover new techniques to extract better genetic information. DNA is also the basis for cloning, which as yet can only be applied to living organisms. Perhaps in the future it can be applied to preserved remains.

ACTIVITIES

Writing About Science: Film Script

Write your own version of the story of life on Earth. Include drawings, photographs, or video clips to illustrate your story.

Reliving History

Think about the equipment archaeologists and paleontologists use on excavations. Think about their goals. Write a proposal to a local university or museum asking them to fund your excavation.

3 Population Dynamics

the BIG idea

Populations are shaped by interactions between organisms and the environment.

Key Concepts

SECTION

3.1 Populations have many characteristics.
Learn about the stages and factors that all populations have in common.

SECTION

3.2 Populations respond to pressures.
Learn how change can affect populations.

SECTION

3.3 Human populations have unique responses to change.
Learn how the responses of human populations are different from responses of other populations.

 Internet Preview

CLASSZONE.COM

Chapter 3 online resources: Content Review, Visualization, three Resource Centers, Math Tutorial, Test Practice

This image was created by combining satellite shots of parts of Earth. What does it suggest about Earth's populations?

How Does Population Grow?

For every three human births there is one death. Use a bucket and water to represent the human population. For every 3 cups of water you add to the bucket, take away one cup.

Observe and Think
How did the water level rise—quickly, slowly, or steadily?

Large and Small Populations

Put about 40 marbles in a bowl. Remove any 10 marbles from the bowl and put them in another dish. Each dish of marbles represents a population.

Observe and Think
How would a chance event such as a fire affect these two populations differently?

Internet Activity: Population Dynamics

Go to **ClassZone.com** to learn more about the factors that describe a population. Find out how change in each of the factors can affect the population.

Observe and Think
How would a change in one factor affect the dynamics of a population?

NSTA
scilinks.org
SC/LINKS

Limiting Factors **Code: MDL038**

Getting Ready to Learn

◀ CONCEPT REVIEW

- Living things change over time.
- Species adapt to their environment or become extinct.

◀ VOCABULARY REVIEW

See Glossary for definitions.

ecosystem

habitat

species

CONTENT REVIEW
CLASSZONE.COM
Review concepts and vocabulary.

▶ TAKING NOTES

CHOOSE YOUR OWN STRATEGY

Take notes using one or more strategies from earlier chapters—**main idea and details** or **supporting main ideas.** You can also use other note-taking strategies that you might already know.

VOCABULARY STRATEGY

Think about a vocabulary term as a **magnet word** diagram. Write the other terms or ideas related to that term around it.

See the Note-Taking Handbook on pages R45–R51.

SCIENCE NOTEBOOK

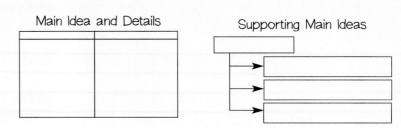

Main Idea and Details

Supporting Main Ideas

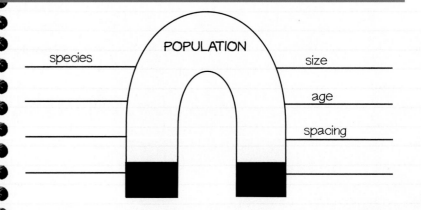

species   POPULATION   size

age

spacing

Populations have many characteristics.

 BEFORE, you learned

- Species change over time
- Evolution is a process of change
- A habitat is an area that provides organisms with resources

NOW, you will learn

- About stages in population dynamics
- About variables that define a population
- About changes that affect populations

VOCABULARY

population dynamics p. 81
carrying capacity p. 82
population size p. 84
population density p. 85

THINK ABOUT

How fast can a population grow?

How big can a population grow? Suppose you started with a pair of fruit flies. That single pair can lay and fertilize 200 eggs. In three weeks, each pair from that batch could produce 200 flies of its own—producing up to 20,000 flies. Assume all eggs hatch— an event highly unlikely in the real world. After three weeks, 2 million fruit flies would be buzzing around the area. After just 17 generations, given ideal conditions (for the fruit fly, that is), the mass of fruit flies would exceed the mass of planet Earth.

Populations go through three stages.

CHOOSE YOUR OWN STRATEGY
Begin taking notes on the three stages of populations. Use a strategy from an earlier chapter or one that you already know.

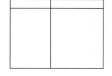

Look closely at the fruit flies above. As a group of the same species living together in a particular area, they represent a population. The particular area in which a scientist studies a population may be as large as a mountain range or as small as a puddle. Scientists study how populations of organisms change as they interact with each other and the environment. Over time, the number of individuals in a population changes by increasing or decreasing. **Population dynamics** is the study of why populations change and what causes them to change. In this chapter you will learn about some of the important observations scientists have made about populations.

 CHECK YOUR READING What is population dynamics?

One species of iguana may have several populations living on different islands. As a result, these iguana populations don't interact with each other. Yet there may be other populations of iguanas living on the islands made up of a different species.

Growth, Stability, and Decline

READING TiP

As you read about growth, stability, and decline, refer to the explanations on the graph.

As different as populations may be—whether cacti, finches, dragonflies, or iguanas—all populations go through the same three stages of change: growth, stability, and decline.

All living things need resources such as water, energy, and living space. Populations get their resources from the environment. However, the area a population occupies can support only so many individuals. **Carrying capacity** is the maximum number of individuals an ecosystem can support.

When a habitat contains enough resources to meet the needs of a population, the population grows rapidly. This growth stage of a population tends to be brief. On a graph, it looks like a sharp rise. The growth stage is followed by a period of stability, when the size of a population remains constant. For most populations, the stability stage is the longest stage of a population's existence. The stability stage is often followed by a decline in population size.

Population Change

The graph shows three stages of population change.

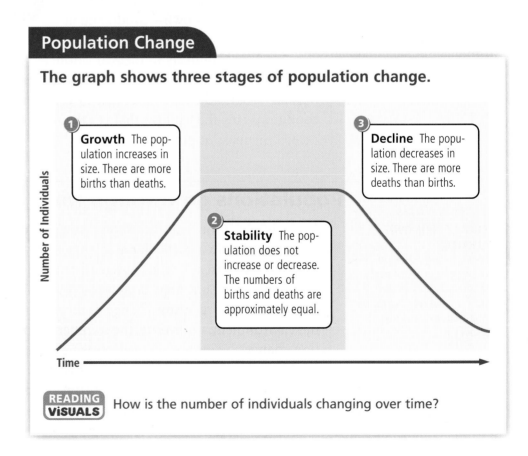

1 **Growth** The population increases in size. There are more births than deaths.

2 **Stability** The population does not increase or decrease. The numbers of births and deaths are approximately equal.

3 **Decline** The population decreases in size. There are more deaths than births.

Number of Individuals

Time

READING ViSUALS How is the number of individuals changing over time?

During the growth stage, populations can increase according to two general patterns. One pattern is rapid growth, which increases at a greater and greater rate. Another pattern is gradual growth, which increases at a fairly steady rate. The two graphs below show the two different types of growth.

Population Growth

The graphs show two patterns of population growth.

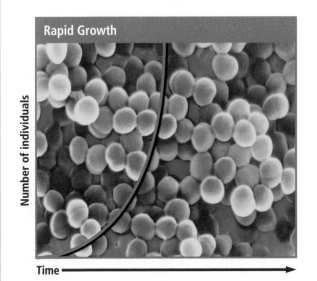

Rapid Growth

Number of individuals

Time

Gradual Growth

Number of individuals

Time

Darwin's Observations of Population Growth

In Chapter 1 you read about the observations and conclusions made by the naturalist Charles Darwin. In his book *On the Origin of Species* Darwin included important observations about population growth.

REMINDER

A species that is no longer living is considered extinct.

- All populations are able to grow rapidly.
- Populations tend to remain constant in size.
- There are limits to natural resources.
- Within a given population there is genetic variation.

Darwin recognized that organisms in most species have the ability to produce more than two surviving offspring. He knew that if there were no limits to growth, then populations would grow rapidly. However, Darwin also observed that in the real world there are natural limits to growth, so populations tend to stabilize. In order for a species to continue, individuals must be replaced as they die. This means that, on average, one member of a population must produce one surviving offspring. If the birth rate doesn't match the death rate, a population can decline until it becomes extinct.

Four characteristics define a population.

When scientists think about population dynamics, they consider four major characteristics. These characteristics include population size, population density, population spacing, and age structure.

Population Size

Population size is the number of individuals in a population at a given time. Even when the population size appears to be stable over time, changes can occur from year to year or from place to place. Population size varies from one habitat to another. It also varies within a single habitat.

An area where the summers are hot and the winters are cold is a good place to observe how population size might change at different times of year. For example, the population sizes of many insects change within a year. Mosquitoes that are all around you on warm summer evenings are nowhere in sight when the temperatures fall below freezing.

The size of plant populations can also change during the year. In the spring and summer you can see flowering plants across the deserts, woods, and mountains of North America. However, by fall and early winter, when there is less rainfall and temperatures drop, many of these plants die. Below is a picture of a southwestern desert in full bloom. During the springtime months of March through May, many deserts in the United States experience a change. There is a period of rapid growth as a variety of wildflowers begins to bloom.

When there is little rainfall a desert seems empty. After a rain, there is a brief time when plants bloom.

The availability of resources, such as water, increases plant growth. By summer the change in season brings higher temperatures and less rainfall. As a result, desert wildflowers experience a rapid decline in their population size.

 CHECK YOUR READING What are two factors that affect population size?

Population Density

Population density is a measure of the number of individuals in a certain space at a particular time. Population density is related to population size. If a population's size increases and all of the individuals remain in the same area, then population density increases, too. There are more individuals living in the same amount of space. If the size of a population in a particular area decreases, density also decreases. Some species, such as bumblebees or mice, live in populations with high densities. Other species, such as blue herons or wolves, live in populations with low densities.

 CHECK YOUR READING What is the difference between low density and high density?

Population Density

Density can change over time and over the entire area of the population.

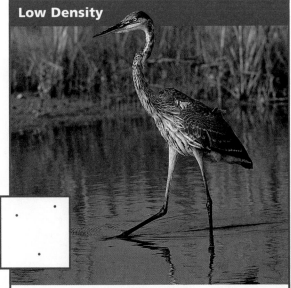

Low Density

Herons are usually found alone or in pairs in marshy areas. Herons are an example of a low-density population.

High Density

Bees in a beehive are an example of a high-density population—many individuals are packed into a small area.

READING VISUALS COMPARE How does the number of herons in an area compare with the number of bees?

The distribution of a population across a large geographic area is its range. Within that range, population density may vary. For example, there may be more grasshoppers in the middle of a prairie than there are at the edges. The population density tends to be higher where more resources are available. Habitats located in the middle of a population range tend to have a greater population density than habitats located at the edges.

 CHECK YOUR READING How might population density vary within a range?

Population Spacing

Take a look around you as you walk through a local park. You might notice many flowers growing in open, sunny spots but few beneath the shade of large trees. The pattern in which the flowers grow is an example of population spacing. Scientists have observed three distinct patterns of spacing: clumped, uniform, and random.

In clumped spacing, individuals form small groups within a habitat. Animals like elephants clump because of their social nature. Clumping can also result from the way resources are distributed throughout a habitat. Salamanders that prefer moist, rotten logs may be clumped where logs have fallen in their habitat.

Population Spacing

Population spacing describes how individuals arrange themselves within a population.

Clumped

Individuals that clump themselves often gather around resources.

Uniform

Individuals that are uniformly arranged often compete for resources.

Random

Random patterns are rare and occur without regard to other individuals.

READING VISUALS Compare and contrast the way populations are spaced.

Some individuals live at a distance from each other. These individuals are uniformly spaced. Many plants that grow too close together become evenly spaced as individuals die out. Uniform spacing can protect saguaro cacti from competing for important resources in the desert. Individuals that aren't uniform or clumped space themselves randomly. Dandelions, for instance, grow no matter where other dandelions are growing.

Age Structure

Scientists divide a population into three groups based on age.

- postreproductive: organisms can no longer reproduce
- reproductive: organisms capable of reproduction
- prereproductive: organisms not yet able to reproduce

The age structure of a population affects how much it can grow. On the graph below the postreproductive age range for humans is over 45, reproductive is 14 to 44 yearsof age, and prereproductive is 0-14.

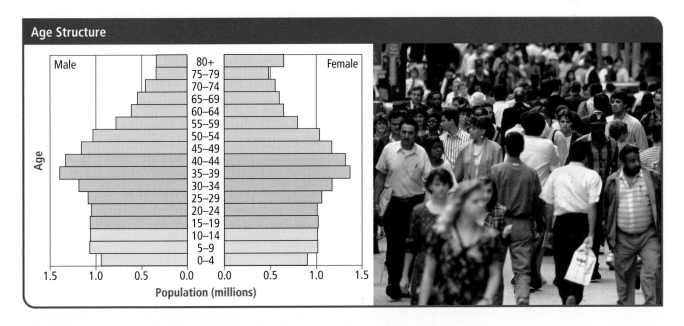

Age Structure

Scientists can predict population change.

Scientists use these four factors—size, density, spacing, and age structure—to describe a population and to predict how it might change over time. Sometimes a population changes when a particular factor changes.

A population can change in response to its surroundings. Suppose a population of frogs is living in a pond where the water becomes saltier. Only those frogs that can survive in an environment with more salt will survive. Thus the population size of frogs will probably decrease as a result of the changing conditions. By looking at population size, scientists can predict how changes affect the population.

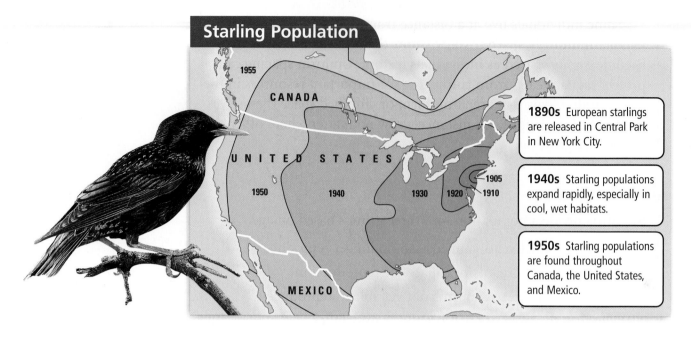

Starling Population

1890s European starlings are released in Central Park in New York City.

1940s Starling populations expand rapidly, especially in cool, wet habitats.

1950s Starling populations are found throughout Canada, the United States, and Mexico.

Scientists can also predict change by looking at the distribution of population. The story of the European starling provides a dramatic example of how the movement of organisms into or out of an area affects a population.

In 1890, the first starlings were introduced to the United States in New York City's Central Park. Their numbers went from 60 individuals to about 200 million in just over 100 years as they expanded on the North American continent. The population of starlings rose as starlings moved into new habitats that had the resources they needed.

Today large populations of starlings can still be found across the North American continent. Even within a given habitat, the population can vary. In Central Park for example, you can find starlings in clumps, uniformly spaced, or randomly spaced.

VISUALIZATION
CLASSZONE.COM

Watch how a change in the environment can effect a population.

3.1 Review

KEY CONCEPTS

1. Describe the three stages of population growth.

2. Make a chart showing the four factors that affect population dynamics and an example of each.

3. Give an example of how a shift in age distribution can affect population growth.

CRITICAL THINKING

4. **Apply** Choose a population in your neighborhood. Describe its population spacing. Is it clumped, uniformly spaced, or randomly spaced?

5. **Compare/Contrast** How is population size related to population density? Your answer should mention area.

⚠ CHALLENGE

6. **Predict** Explain how a heavy thunderstorm might affect the population density of birds living in the area.

Making Sense of Samples

In a pond study, a biologist takes samples of water from four locations in one pond every three months. Using a microscope, she examines the samples and calculates the protist population for each location. The data table shows the number of protists found per milliliter in each sample of pond water.

Data Table: Number of protists per milliliter (mL) of pond water				
Location	**Fall**	**Winter**	**Spring**	**Summer**
Under the pier	150	50	120	410
Among the water lilies	200	80	180	500
Shallow area	220	90	200	360
Deepest area	80	60	100	390
Seasonal Average				

Example

Suppose you want to find the average number of protists per milliliter of pond water for that fall.

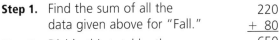

Step 1. Find the sum of all the data given above for "Fall."

$$\begin{array}{r} 150 \\ 200 \\ 220 \\ +\ 80 \\ \hline 650 \end{array}$$

Step 2. Divide this total by the number of data entries for "Fall."

$650 \div 4 = 162.5$

Step 3. Round to nearest whole number.

$162.5 \rightarrow 163$

ANSWER 163 protists per mL of pond water

For each season or location give the average number of protists.

1. Winter

2. Spring

3. Summer

4. Under the pier

5. Among the water lilies

6. Shallow area

7. Deepest area

8. Whole pond, yearlong

CHALLENGE Suppose the biologist only took samples from three areas in the pond. Which missing area would throw off the averages the most?

3.2 Populations respond to pressures.

 BEFORE, you learned

- Four characteristics are used to describe a population
- Scientists study these four characteristics to predict population change

 NOW, you will learn

- About limits to population growth
- How population density affects limiting factors
- About two reproductive strategies found within populations

VOCABULARY

immigration p. 91
emigration p. 91
limiting factor p. 92
opportunist p. 95
competitor p. 96

EXPLORE Population Density

How does population density vary?

PROCEDURE

MATERIALS
- stopwatch
- notebook

1. Choose three different locations in your school where you can observe how many people enter and leave an area during a specific time period.

2. Position three people at each location a counter, a timekeeper, and a recorder.

3. Count the number of people who pass through the area for at least 2 minutes. Record the number.

4. Compare your data with the data collected by other groups.

WHAT DO YOU THINK?
- Where was the number of people the highest? the lowest?
- Explain what may have affected population density at each location.

CHOOSE YOUR OWN STRATEGY
Use a strategy from an earlier chapter or one of your own to take notes on the main idea: *Population growth is limited.*

Population growth is limited.

No population can grow forever. Every population has a limit to its growth. For example, the cockroach has been around for more than 300 million years. This insect has outlived the dinosaurs and may persist long after humans have become extinct. Yet even if cockroaches became the only species on the planet, several factors would limit their population size.

Birth, Death, Immigration, and Emigration

When scientists study how a population changes, they must consider four things: birth, death, immigration, and emigration. There is even a simple formula to help scientists track population change.

Population change = (birth + immigration) − (death + emigration)

It is too simple to say that a high birth rate means population growth, or that many deaths mean population decline. **Immigration** is the movement of individuals into a population. For example, if a strong wind blows the seeds of a plant from one area into another, the new plant would be said to immigrate into the new area. Immigration can increase a population or help stabilize a declining population. Birth and immigration introduce individuals into a population.

Emigration is the movement of individuals out of a population. If resources become scarce within a habitat, some of the individuals might move to areas with greater supplies. Others may even die. Death and emigration remove individuals from a population.

⚠ **CHECK YOUR READING** List two factors that lead to population growth and two that lead to population decline.

Consider, for example, a flock of seagulls that flies inland during a storm. They stop at a city dump where food is plentiful. These incoming seagulls become part of the seagull population that is already living at the dump. A raccoon population living in the same area has been eating the seagulls' eggs, causing the number of seagull births to decrease. If enough seagulls immigrate to the dump, the seagull population would increase, making up for the decrease in births. Immigration would help keep the population stable. The seagull population would also increase if part of the raccoon population moved away.

Limiting Factors

When a population is growing at a rapid rate, the birth rate is much higher than the death rate. That means that more individuals are being born than are dying during a particular time period. There are plenty of resources available, and the population size is increasing rapidly. Eventually, however, the population will stop growing, because a habitat can support only a limited number of organisms.

A **limiting factor** is a factor that prevents the continuing growth of a population in an ecosystem. Abiotic, or nonliving, limiting factors include air, light, and water. Other limiting factors can be living things, such as other organisms in the same population or individuals belonging to different species within the same area.

CHECK YOUR READING What are two limiting factors?

Competition can occur between different populations sharing the same habitat. Competition can also occur among individuals of the same population. Suppose, for example, that a population of deer in a forest preserve were to increase, either through births or immigration. Population density at the forest preserve would go up. More and more deer in that area would be competing for the same amount of food.

Density-Dependent Factors

Density-dependent factors have a greater effect on populations with many individuals in a small area.

Factors may include
• Competition
• Disease
• Parasitism
• Predation

Effects of Population Density

In the situation described above, the seagull population could decrease as a result of competition for food. Competition is an example of a density-dependent factor—that is, a limiting factor that affects a population when density is high. Disease is another density-dependent factor. The more crowded an area becomes, the easier it is for disease to spread, so more individuals are affected. If population density is low, there is less contact between individuals, which means that disease will spread more slowly. Density-dependent factors have a greater effect on the population as it grows. They can bring a population under control, because they apply more pressure to a growing population.

There are also density-independent factors. These limiting factors have the same effect on a population, whether it has a high density or a low density. Freezing temperatures could be considered a density-independent factor. A freeze might kill all of the flowering plants in an area, whether or not the population density is high. A natural event such as a wildfire is another example of a density-independent factor. When a wildfire occurs in a forest, it can wipe out an entire ecosystem.

 CHECK YOUR READING How are limiting factors that are density-dependent different from limiting factors that are density-independent?

Density-Independent Factors

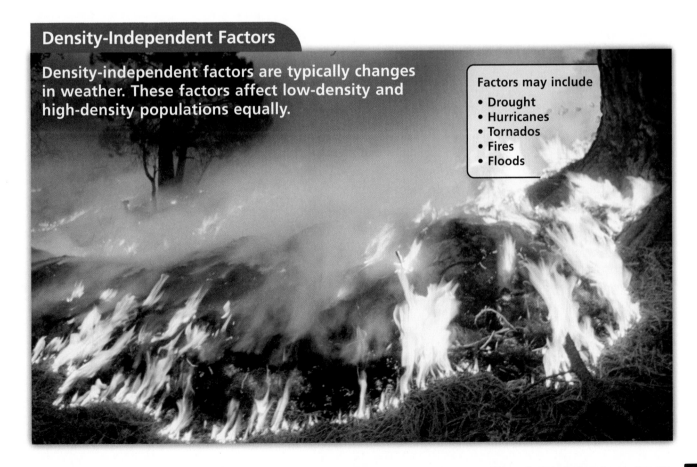

Density-independent factors are typically changes in weather. These factors affect low-density and high-density populations equally.

Factors may include
- Drought
- Hurricanes
- Tornados
- Fires
- Floods

Limiting factors include nonliving factors in the environment and natural events such as earthquakes, fires, and storms. During times of drought, there may not be enough food to meet the needs of all the organisms in an area. The quality of the food declines as well. For example, a lack of water may cause a population of trees to produce fewer pieces of fruit, and the fruit itself may be smaller. If there is little food available, a condition called famine arises. If the famine is severe, and if death rates exceed birth rates, then the population size will fall dramatically.

CHECK YOUR READING How do limiting factors affect populations? Remember a summary includes only the most important information.

Limiting factors affect human populations as well. However, humans have found different ways to help overcome many of these limits. In Section 3.3 you will read about how the human response to limits differs from that of other biological populations.

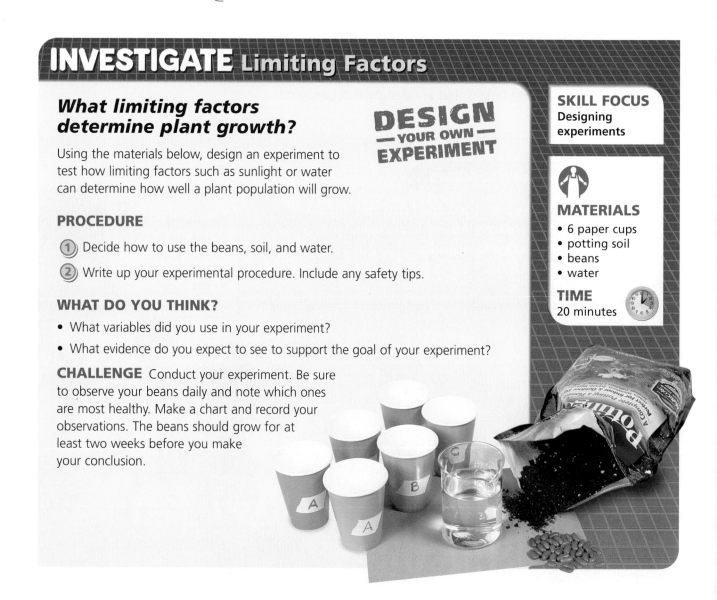

INVESTIGATE Limiting Factors

What limiting factors determine plant growth?

DESIGN — YOUR OWN — EXPERIMENT

Using the materials below, design an experiment to test how limiting factors such as sunlight or water can determine how well a plant population will grow.

PROCEDURE

1. Decide how to use the beans, soil, and water.
2. Write up your experimental procedure. Include any safety tips.

WHAT DO YOU THINK?

- What variables did you use in your experiment?
- What evidence do you expect to see to support the goal of your experiment?

CHALLENGE Conduct your experiment. Be sure to observe your beans daily and note which ones are most healthy. Make a chart and record your observations. The beans should grow for at least two weeks before you make your conclusion.

SKILL FOCUS
Designing experiments

MATERIALS
- 6 paper cups
- potting soil
- beans
- water

TIME
20 minutes

Populations have distinct reproductive survival strategies.

Although reproduction of offspring is not necessary for the survival of an individual organism, it is necessary for the survival of a species. Scientists studying populations observe patterns in the reproductive strategies used among species. There are two main strategies that many species use. There are also many species whose strategies fit somewhere in between.

Strategies of Opportunists

Opportunists are species that reproduce rapidly if their population falls below carrying capacity. They share many characteristics, including a short life span and the ability to reproduce large quantities of offspring. Their population size tends to change often, and opportunists live across many areas. Opportunists include algae, dandelions, bacteria, and insects. These species can reproduce and move across an area quickly. In addition, they can adapt quickly to environmental changes. Populations of opportunists often grow rapidly.

VOCABULARY
Remember to make a word magnet for the term *opportunist*. Include examples in your diagram.

Opportunists

Pine trees are opportunists that can spread across an area quickly.

Pine cones release huge amounts of pollen into the air.

Competitors

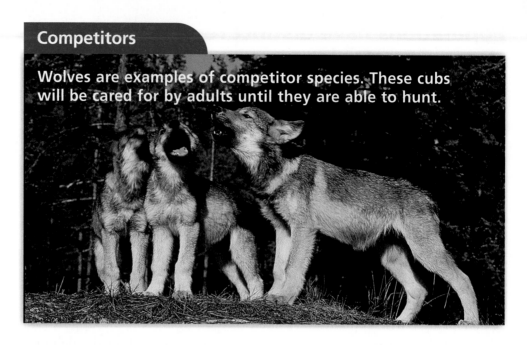

Wolves are examples of competitor species. These cubs will be cared for by adults until they are able to hunt.

Strategies of Competitors

You might be familiar with the term *competitor* as meaning an organism that struggles with another to get resources. Scientists who study population growth use the term *competitor* in another way. **Competitors** are species with adaptations that allow them to remain at or near their carrying capacity for long periods of time. Competitors have many characteristics that differ from those of opportunists.

Species that have a competitive reproductive strategy often live longer and have fewer offspring. Elephants and saguaro cacti are two examples of competitors. The offspring of competitors take longer to develop than those of opportunists. Also, organisms with this strategy tend to take care of their young for a longer period of time. Competitors are not distributed across areas as widely as opportunists, but greater numbers of their offspring survive to reproductive age.

3.2 Review

KEY CONCEPTS

1. What four factors do scientists consider when they measure population change?

2. Give two examples of density-dependent factors and two examples of density-independent factors.

3. Other than life span, how do opportunists and competitors differ?

CRITICAL THINKING

4. **Analyze** Why would it be a mistake to predict population growth based on birth rate alone?

5. **Apply** Give an example of a factor that limits a population near you.

○ **CHALLENGE**

6. **Synthesize** There has been an oil spill along a waterway famous for its populations of seals, dolphins, and sea birds. Six months later, all populations show a decline. Explain what factors might have caused such a change and whether the oil spill was a density-dependent or density-independent factor or both.

Studying the Schools

There's a lot more to catching fish than putting a net or a line into the ocean. More and more these days, finding fish means looking at the big and changing picture of fish populations. Once you start fishing, you need to know when to stop fishing, as well as how to protect the other organisms in the ocean environment.

Density

If there are too few fish of a particular species in one area, it is best to leave them and look for a place with greater population density. By using the most suitable gear, the captain avoids killing or injuring fish and other animals that shouldn't be part of the catch.

Distribution

Some fish live alone, and some live in big groups, called schools. Some, called ground fish, stay on the bottom, while others swim near the surface. One way to see the distribution of fish is with sonar. An image made from sonar shows that a school of hake swims at a depth of about 320 meters (1050 ft).

Partners in Research

Many boat captains set up partnerships with researchers to study fish and to help them to thrive. Sonar equipment is a tool shared by scientists and commercial fishers. Images are made by sending sound waves through the water and receiving the patterns of sound waves that bounce, or echo, back.

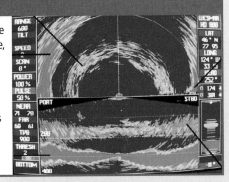

Single beam sound signal from ship

Signal echoes back to ship

Sea floor

EXPLORE

1. **INFER** Boat captains talk to each other about how many fish they catch and where and when they catch them. What are three reasons why this would be important?

2. **CHALLENGE** Suppose a fishing boat captain over fishes an organism that is a source of food for another organism. Describe what may happen to the other organism.

Human populations have unique responses to change.

 BEFORE, you learned

- Over time, all populations stop growing
- All populations are affected by limiting factors
- Reproductive strategies include opportunism and competition

▶ **NOW, you will learn**

- How human populations differ from other populations
- How humans adapt to the environment
- How human populations affect the environment

VOCABULARY

pollution p. 104

EXPLORE Population Change

How can you predict human population growth?

PROCEDURE

MATERIALS
- graph paper
- colored pencils

① Copy the graph on the right. The graph shows populaton growth expected in the United States with an increase in both birth and death rates and with steady immigration.

② The graph shows a medium rate of growth. Draw another line to show what low population growth might look like. Label it.

③ Explain the patterns of birth rates, death rates, and immigration that might be likely to result in low population growth.

WHAT DO YOU THINK?
- How would the projected U.S. population size change if there were no immigration?
- How might an increase in immigration affect expected birth rates?

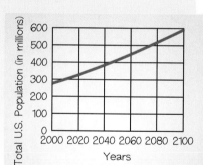

Human populations differ from populations of other species.

CHOOSE YOUR OWN STRATEGY
Begin taking notes on the differences between human populations and populations of other species.

Humans are not the fastest or the largest organisms on Earth. They must get food from other organisms. Humans have a limited sense of smell, and the vision of a human is inferior to that of a hawk. However, the human population now dominates our planet. Why? Humans are able to shape their environment. Humans are also able to determine their own biological reproduction. Because humans can control many factors that limit growth, Earth's carrying capacity for humans has increased. Two key factors that have increased Earth's carrying capacity for humans are habitat expansion and technology.

Habitat Expansion

Individuals who study the history of ancient peoples know that populations of humans have spread throughout the world. Discoveries of ancient human tools and skeletons indicate that the first human populations lived on the continent now known as Africa. Over time, human populations have spread over nearly the entire planet.

The word habitat refers to a place where an organism can live. Humans have expanded their habitats, and thus the population has grown. Humans can survive in many different environments by adding air conditioning or heat to regulate indoor temperature. They can design and build shelters that protect them from harsh environments.

Adapting to Climate

Humans have designed buildings that allow them to survive in different climates.

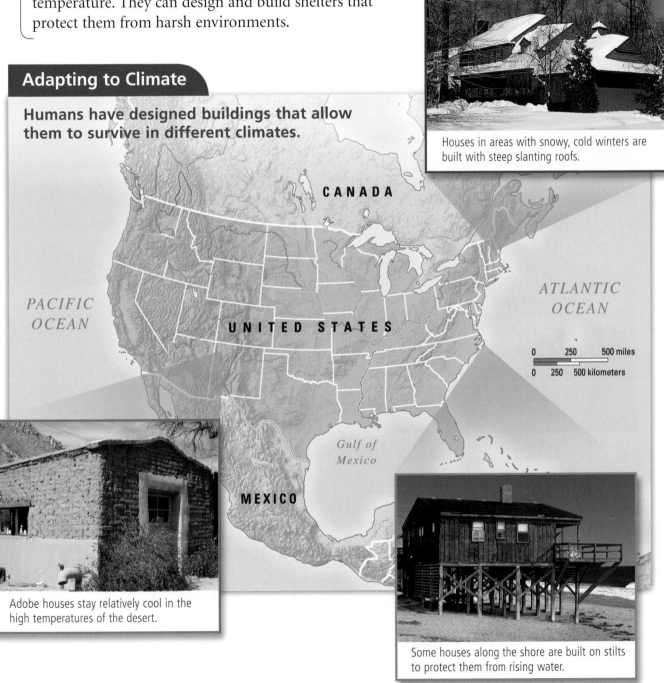

Houses in areas with snowy, cold winters are built with steep slanting roofs.

Adobe houses stay relatively cool in the high temperatures of the desert.

Some houses along the shore are built on stilts to protect them from rising water.

Technology

Limited resources and environmental conditions such as climate do not affect human population growth the way they do the growth of other biological populations. Humans have found ways to fit themselves into almost every climate by altering their clothing, shelter, diet, and means of transportation.

Scientific discoveries and the advances of technology—such as improved sanitation and medical care—have increased the standard of living and the life expectancy of many humans. Important goods such as food and shelter are manufactured and shipped around the world. Water which is a limited resource can be transported through pipes and dams to irrigate fields or reach normally dry areas. Water can also be purified for drinking or treated before it is released back into the environment.

CHECK YOUR READING How does technology help humans get resources they need for survival?

Technology

Transporting Water

Food is often grown on large farms. Humans have developed irrigation systems to carry water to the fields.

Purifying Water

Water that has been used by humans contains wastes that can be removed at large watertreatment plants.

Human populations are growing.

As you've read, humans have developed solutions to many limits on growth. These solutions have allowed the human population to grow rapidly. Scientists are studying the history of this growth and trying to predict whether it will continue or change.

History of Human Population Growth

Until about 300 years ago, the human population grew slowly. Disease, climate, and the availability of resources limited population size. Most offspring did not survive to adulthood. Even though birthrates were high, death rates were also high.

Notice the human population on the graph below. Many historical events have affected its growth. For example, the development of agriculture provided humans with a more stable food source. This in turn helped support human population growth. Today, populations across many parts of the world are increasing rapidly. Scientists identify three conditions that allow for rapid growth: the availability of resources, lack of predators, and survival of offspring to reproductive age. As these conditions change, so does the population.

RESOURCE CENTER
CLASSZONE.COM

Learn more about world-wide human population growth.

Population Projections

To help prepare for the future, scientists make predictions called population projections. Population projections forecast how a population will change, based on its present size and age structure. Population projections provide a picture of what the future might look like. Using population projections, government agencies, resource managers, and economists can plan to meet the future needs of a population.

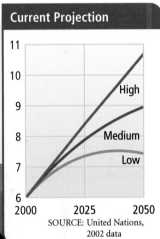

Current Projection

High

Medium

Low

SOURCE: United Nations, 2002 data

The blowout of the graph shows three projections for the human population size. Experts disagree about the rate at which the population will grow.

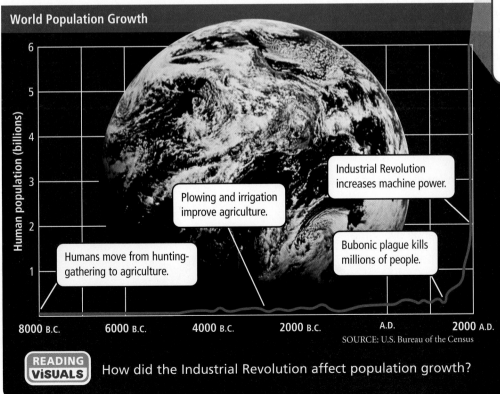

World Population Growth

Human population (billions)

Industrial Revolution increases machine power.

Plowing and irrigation improve agriculture.

Humans move from hunting-gathering to agriculture.

Bubonic plague kills millions of people.

8000 B.C.   6000 B.C.   4000 B.C.   2000 B.C.   A.D.   2000 A.D.

SOURCE: U.S. Bureau of the Census

READING VISUALS How did the Industrial Revolution affect population growth?

In addition to population size and age structure, scientists making population projections consider other factors. These factors include the ages of individuals having children. The average number of offspring produced by an individual also affects projections. In addition, life expectancy and health in a particular population affect population growth.

The factors affecting population growth vary from society to society. The human population in the African country Botswana provides an example of how disease and health can affect population growth.

In some African countries, death rates due to HIV/AIDS have lowered population projections for the year 2015 by almost 18 percent. Botswana's population will decline, because more than 30 percent of adults are infected with HIV/AIDS. So many people in Botswana have already died of HIV/AIDS that the average life expectancy has dropped from 63 years of age in the late 1980s to 32 years in 2003. Consider the impact this will have on the population's age structure. Because many people who die from HIV/AIDS are in their reproductive years, the long-term effects on population growth will be significant.

CHECK YOUR READING What factors do scientists consider when they make population projections?

INVESTIGATE Population

How can you graph population growth data for your area?

PROCEDURE

1. Use local population data taken from each census over five decades.

2. On graph paper, mark off five decades along the *x*–axis. Make a *y*–axis to show population size.

3. Plot the census information for each decade as a line graph.

WHAT DO YOU THINK?

- How did the local population change over time?
- What do you think accounted for the change?

CHALLENGE Based on the trend you see so far, how might the population change in the future? Use another color to extend the line on your graph to project population change over the next five decades. Explain why you think the population will change as you have predicted.

SKILL FOCUS
Graphing data

MATERIALS
- graph paper
- census data
- 2 colored pencils

TIME
30 minutes

Human population growth affects the environment.

You have read that extinction of species is a part of the history of life on Earth. The ways a population uses and disposes of resources have a great impact on local and global environments. As the human population continues to grow and use more resources, it contributes to the decline and extinction of other populations.

Some scientists estimate that over 99 percent of the species that have ever existed on Earth are now extinct. Most of these species vanished long before humans came on the scene. However, some experts are concerned that human activity is causing other species to become extinct at a much higher rate than they would naturally. Human populations put pressure on the environment in many ways, including

RESOURCE CENTER
CLASSZONE.COM

Find out more on introduced species in the United States.

- introduction of new species
- pollution
- overfishing

Introduction of New Species

Travelers have introduced new species to areas both on purpose and by accident. Many species introduced to an area provide benefits, such as food or beauty. Some species, however, cause harm to ecosystems. One example of an introduced species is the zebra mussel. An ocean vessel accidentally released zebra mussels from Asia into the Great Lakes region of the United States. With no natural predators that consume them, the mussels have reproduced quickly, invading all of the Great Lakes, the Mississippi River, and the Hudson River. The mussels compete with native species for food and reduce water quality, endangering the ecosystem.

Kudzu is another introduced species. In the 1930s, kudzu was used in the southeastern United States to keep soil from being washed away. The plants, which have beautiful purple flowers, were imported from Japan. Starch made from kudzu is also a popular ingredient in some Asian recipes. However, populations of the kudzu vines planted in the United States have grown too far and too fast. Kudzu grows as much as 0.3 meters (about a foot) per day, killing trees and other plants living in the same area.

The kudzu plant, though at one time considered beautiful, is threatening other species.

Pollution

While human activities might cause some populations to decline, they can also cause other populations to grow. Sometimes this population growth causes pollution and habitat disturbance. **Pollution** is the addition of harmful substances to the environment. One example of such an activity is large-scale hog farming.

Human demands for pork combined with a growing human population have caused the hog farming industry to expand. Between 1987 and 2001, the hog population in North Carolina grew from 2.6 million to 10 million. These 10 million hogs produced more than 50,000 tons of waste each day. Wastes from large populations of hogs affect water supplies, soil, and air quality.

Pollution has also affected the Salton Sea in southeastern California. The growing demand for goods and agriculture has led to chemical dumping from industries and pesticide runoff from nearby farms. The rivers that run into the lake carry high levels of harmful chemicals such as DDT. Local birds that live and feed in this area have weakened shells that cannot support baby birds. Pollution has also caused fish to become deformed.

Large-scale hog farms affect water, soil, and air quality.

Pollution

The Salton Sea in California is surrounded by farm fields and industries that contribute to pollution.

Used water from irrigation drains into the Salton Sea.

Overfishing

Fish and crustaceans such as shrimp and lobsters have long been an important food source for many people. In the 1900s, the techniques and equipment that fishers used allowed them to catch so many fish that fish populations began to decrease. As the human population has continued to grow, so has the demand for fish. However, if fish do not survive long enough in the wild, they do not have the chance to reproduce. Many species have been so overfished that their populations may not recover.

Lobster fishing in particular has supported coastal communities in the northeastern United States for generations. But the demand for this food source has caused populations to decline. Areas that fishers trapped for years may now have only a small population of lobsters. And the lobsters fishers are catching may not be as large as those from earlier decades.

In order to help lobster populations recover, laws have been enforced to protect their life cycle and reproduction. Today, people who trap lobsters are required to release females with eggs. They are also allowed to keep only mature lobsters. Younger lobsters are returned to the waters to mature and reproduce. Efforts like these help protect the lobster population and secure the jobs of fishers by helping fish populations remain stable.

Fishers harvesting lobster measure the tails of the animals they catch. A lobster that is too small is returned to the sea to allow it to grow.

 CHECK YOUR READING Describe how overfishing would affect resources.

3.3 Review

KEY CONCEPTS

1. What factors—other than birth, death, immigration, and emigration—must scientists consider when making projections of human population?

2. Give an example of how Earth's carrying capacity for humans has increased.

3. What are three ways that humans affect other populations?

CRITICAL THINKING

4. **Infer** Consider the effect of HIV/AIDS on Botswana's human population. How might age structure affect Botswana's population growth?

5. **Analyze** Do you think it is possible to predict the maximum number of humans that Earth can support? Why or why not?

CHALLENGE

6. **Apply** Identify a challenge faced by the human population in your state. Explain how the challenge is related to pollution, introduction of new species, habitat disturbance, or overfishing.

CHAPTER INVESTIGATION

Sustainable Resource Management

OVERVIEW AND PURPOSE Wood is a renewable resource, but the demand for wood is continuing to grow worldwide. Humans are harvesting trees more quickly than trees have the ability to grow and replace themselves. The result is a forest in decline. In this activity you will

- model what happens when trees are harvested to meet the needs of a growing population
- calculate the rate at which the population of a renewable resource declines

▶ Problem

How can people meet the ongoing human demand for wood without using all the trees?

▶ Hypothesize

Write a hypothesis to explain how you will use the increasing human demand for wood to determine how overuse of a resource might affect a population. Your hypothesis should take the form of an "If . . . , then . . . , because . . ." statement.

▶ Procedure

MATERIALS
- coffee can with 120 craft sticks
- bundle of 32 craft sticks
- stopwatch

1. Copy the data table on page 107 into your **Science Notebook.**

2. In your group of classmates, decide who will fill each of the following roles: forest, timer, forest manager, harvester/record keeper.

3. **Forest:** Get a coffee can of 120 craft sticks. These sticks represent the available tree supply.

4. **Timer:** Sound off each 15-second interval and each minute.

5 **Forest Manager:** Get 32 sticks from the teacher. You will add 1 new tree every 15 seconds by putting a stick in the coffee can.

6 **Harvester:** At the end of the first minute, cut down 1 tree by removing 1 stick from the coffee can. At the end of the second minute, cut down 2 trees; at the end of the third, cut down 4 trees. At the end of each additional minute cut down twice as many trees as you did before. This represents the doubling of the demand for trees based on human population growth.

Observe and Analyze | Write It Up

1. **CALCULATE** At the end of each minute, add 4 trees, but subtract twice as many trees as you subtracted the minute before.

2. **RECORD AND CALCULATE** Complete the chart. How many trees are left in the forest after 8 minutes of harvesting?

Conclude | Write It Up

1. **INFER** What effect does increasing human population growth have on forests?

2. **EVALUATE** Was the forest always shrinking?

3. **INTERPRET** Compare your results with your hypothesis. Do your data support your hypothesis?

4. **IDENTIFY LIMITS** What aspects of this investigation fail to model the natural habitat?

5. **APPLY** What other renewable resources need sustainable management?

INVESTIGATE Further

CHALLENGE Explain how you could use the data gathered in this investigation to develop methods of sustainable resource management.

Sustainable Resource Management

Table 1. Rate of Harvest

Minutes	Number of Trees at Start of Minute	Number of New Trees	Number of Trees Harvested	Number of Trees at End of Minute
1	120	+4	−1	123
2				
3				
4				
5				
6				
7				
8				

the BIG idea

Populations are shaped by interactions between organisms and the environment.

CONTENT REVIEW
CLASSZONE.COM

◀ KEY CONCEPTS SUMMARY

3.1) Populations have many characteristics.

- Populations go through three stages:
  growth
  stability
  decline
- Four characteristics define a population:
  size
  density
  spacing
  age structure
- Scientists can predict population changes.

VOCABULARY
population dynamics p. 81
carrying capacity p. 82
population density p. 85

3.2) Populations respond to pressures.

Populations change as they respond to pressures from limiting factors.

Two types of limiting factors are density dependent and density independent.

VOCABULARY
immigration p. 91
emigration p. 91
limiting factor p. 92
opportunist p. 95
competitor p. 96

3.3) Human populations have unique responses to change.

Humans can control many factors that limit most biological populations.

VOCABULARY
pollution p. 104

Reviewing Vocabulary

Describe how the vocabulary terms in the following pairs are related to each other. Explain the relationship in a one- or two-sentence answer. Underline each vocabulary term in your answers.

1. population dynamics and carrying capacity

2. immigration and emigration

3. limiting factor and population density

4. opportunists and competitors

Reviewing Key Concepts

Multiple Choice *Choose the letter of the best answer.*

5. The study of changes in a population over time and the factors that affect these changes is called population
  a. stability
  b. dynamics
  c. spacing
  d. density

6. A population that has reached its maximum size in a given area is said to have reached its
  a. population range
  b. gradual growth
  c. carrying capacity
  d. population projection

7. Assuming there is no immigration or emigration, a population size will remain constant if
  a. the birth rate equals the death rate
  b. the birth rate exceeds the death rate
  c. the death rate exceeds the birth rate
  d. the birth rate increases constantly

8. Distinct patterns in a population such as clumped, uniform, or random populations are examples of population
  a. density
  b. spacing
  c. growth
  d. dynamics

9. Which factors affect the size and growth of a population?
  a. number of births and deaths
  b. emigration and immigration
  c. competition between populations
  d. all of the above

10. A limiting factor that depends on the size of the population in a given area is a
  a. density-dependent factor
  b. density-independent factor
  c. reproduction survival strategy
  d. carrying capacity

11. Density-independent limiting factors include
  a. predators
  c. floods
  b. parasites
  d. competition

12. Which are abiotic factors in an environment?
  a. disease and parasites
  b. air, light, and water
  c. earthquakes and fires
  d. competition and predators

13. Which is an example of competition for resources?
  a. individuals in a population feeding on the same food sources
  b. movement of seagulls into a population of other seagulls
  c. an increase in the population of raccoons in a particular environment at a steady rate
  d. a population of fruit trees producing less fruit because of drought

14. Two factors that have increased Earth's carrying capacity for humans are habitat expansion, and
  a. habitat disturbance
  b. strategies of competitors
  c. strategies of opportunists
  d. technology

Short Answer *Write a short answer to each question.*

15. What factors might affect the density of a population?

16. What is the age structure of a population?

17. Describe three factors that account for the rapid growth of the human population during the past 500 years.

Thinking Critically

18. ANALYZE Under what conditions does gradual growth in a population occur?

19. COMMUNICATE Describe four observations that Darwin made about population growth.

20. PREDICT The graph below shows the exponential growth rate of a colony of unicellular organisms. If the population continues to grow at the same rate during the next 2 hours, what will the population be after 10 hours? Explain your answer.

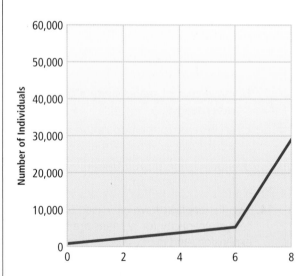

21. PREDICT In a certain population 35 percent of the individuals are under the age of 20. What predictions might you make about the size of the population in 10 years?

22. PROVIDE EXAMPLES What limiting factors might cause the carrying capacity of a population to change? Provide at least three examples. Describe how the population might change.

23. SYNTHESIZE What is an example of a density-independent factor that has affected a human population? Describe how this factor changed the population.

24. INFER Wolves are the natural predators of moose. Both populations are found on an island in the middle of Lake Superior. During one season, the population of moose increased dramatically. What could have caused the increase in the moose population?

25. EVALUATE Why do you suppose that the growth rate of human populations differs dramatically in different countries?

26. SYNTHESIZE Human activity has resulted in the decline of many populations of other species. Choose one example of how humans have put pressure on species around the world and describe ways that humans can avoid causing continued decreases in these populations.

the BIG idea

27. INFER Look again at the picture on pages 78–79. Now that you have finished the chapter, how would you change or add details to your answer to the question on the photograph?

28. SUMMARIZE Write one or more paragraphs describing the factors that affect population size, density, and age structure. Use the following terms in your descriptions.

immigration	density-dependent factors
emigration	density-independent factors
limiting factors	

UNIT PROJECTS

If you need to do an experiment for your unit project, gather the materials. Be sure to allow enough time to observe results before the project is due.

Analyzing Data

The graph below is an example of a population growth curve.

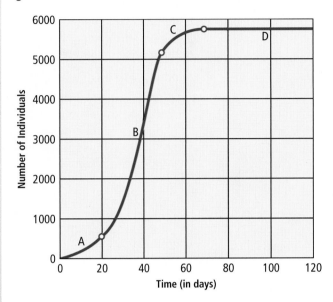

Use the graph to answer the questions below.

1. What does the time interval marked *D* represent?

a. Population is decreasing.

b. Carrying capacity has been reached.

c. Birth rates exceed death rates.

d. Population is growing.

2. Which time interval on the graph represents gradual growth?

a. interval A and interval B

b. interval C and interval D

c. interval C only

d. interval D only

3. During which time interval do limiting factors in a population begin to have an effect on the population growth?

a. interval A only

b. interval B only

c. interval C only

d. interval C and interval D

4. This graph represents a typical

a. gradual curve

b. rapid curve

c. slow curve

d. flat curve

5. What conclusion can you draw from the information in the graph?

a. Density-dependent factors have had no effect on the population shown on the graph.

b. The graph indicates an absence of disease and a supply of unlimited resources.

c. Resources have become more available, so the population continues to increase exponentially.

d. As resources become less available, the population rate slows or stops.

Extended Response

6. What part of the graph above shows the growth of the human population during the last 500 years? Explain. What are some factors that might allow the human population to reach its carrying capacity?

7. Choose a population of organisms in your area. Describe the limiting factors that may affect the growth of that population. Make sure you include both density-dependent and density-independent factors in your discussion.

UNIT C

Diversity of Living Things

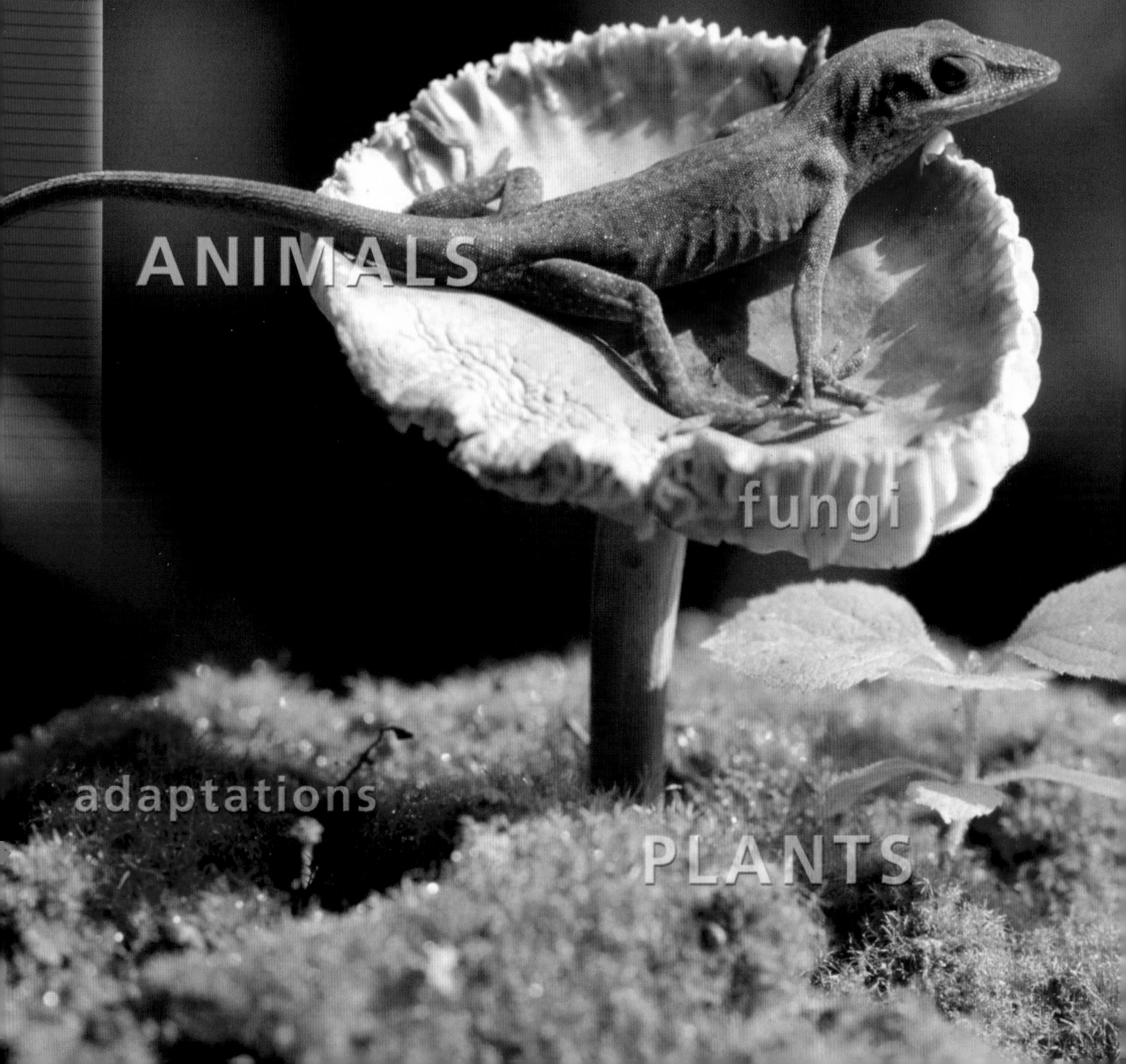
ANIMALS
fungi
adaptations
PLANTS

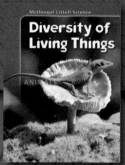

Diversity of Living Things
Contents Overview

Chilling Changes

How do organisms survive in this chilly Arctic landscape? Scientists are studying how organisms have adapted to the extreme cold of Earth's northern climates.

SCIENTIFIC AMERICAN FRONTIERS

Learn more about how living things respond to freezing temperatures in the video "Frozen Alive."

Caribou search for lichen and small plants to eat in northern Alaska.

Lichen find materials and living space on rocks in frozen environments.

When Life Chills Out

When faced with the approach of winter, some animals hurry up, and some slow down. You may have seen animals getting a move on, migrating to warmer places. Other animals stay alive at home by hibernating, or entering a sleep-like state. Hibernation conserves energy until spring by slowing down many body processes. But what happens when an organism's body temperature dips below freezing?

Ice formation inside an organism's body is one of the most serious, and potentially damaging, threats to winter survival. If ice forms inside cells, it can damage the cell's operation and tear holes in the cell membrane, almost certainly leading to death.

An arctic ground squirrel peers above snow-covered ground in Alaska.

Some animals and plants take cold weather survival to an extreme. Some frogs and insects can allow their bodies to freeze solid. Some fish have fluids in their bodies that can *cool* below the freezing point of water and still flow. How do they do it?

Scientists studying survivors of extreme cold are not just learning about the ways organisms respond in the wild. Research on cold weather survival helps scientists understand problems faced by human society. Growing crops year-round and using bacteria to clean up pollution in a frozen environment are two examples. There are two main responses that allow living things to live in a sub-freezing world.

Arctic woolly caterpillars may take many years to grow to full size.

When the caterpillar reaches full size, it forms a cocoon and changes into a moth.

Avoid Ice, or Tolerate It

Organisms can either avoid the forming of ice, or tolerate it. Some animals, like a fish called a flounder, produce antifreeze proteins in their bodies. The proteins keep ice from forming in the blood and other fluids. The fluids thicken, but still flow. They never turn to ice crystals. Scientists call this response "freeze-avoidance."

Others, like some frogs, many types of insects, and some trees do allow ice to form inside their bodies. In these organisms, ice forms, but only in the spaces outside the cells. "Freeze-tolerant" organisms pump fluid out of their cells. Specialized proteins located outside of the cells encourage ice to form there, rather than inside the cells.

Perhaps the champion of freeze tolerance is a small Arctic insect called the Arctic woolly caterpillar. It is only active for a few weeks out of the year, during the brief Arctic summer. It can take this caterpillar up to fifteen years to mature into a moth!

Temperatures during Arctic winters often fall as low as −70°C, and, because the ground is frozen year-round, the caterpillars cannot burrow. Instead, their bodies freeze solid in winter, shutting down nearly all of their cellular activity and

SCIENTIFIC AMERICAN FRONTIERS

View the "Frozen Alive" segment of your Scientific American Frontiers video to see how scientists studying fish and frogs have begun to solve the mysteries of life surviving a freeze.

IN THIS SCENE FROM THE VIDEO ▶ How do the frog's systems start up again, after being shut down during freezing. This scan shows activity in the liver.

WHAT BRINGS ON THE THAW? Ken Storey collects wood frogs. The frogs have an automatic response to cold temperatures, which allows Ken and his team to keep them in a freezer without killing them. Storey and his team know the "what" of freeze tolerance. They want to learn the "how." How does the frog stay alive during and after shutdown? Storey expects that the thawing process works in the usual way, that the frogs will begin to warm from the outside in. Instead he finds that internal organs begin the thaw. The liver is the first organ to activate. It produces glucose or sugar, which then gets other cells, those in the heart, to begin their work.

expending almost no energy. Scientists have known for centuries that some insects can freeze over the winter, but only recently have they begun to understand exactly how insects' bodies change to allow them to freeze and thaw.

Scientist Ken Storey has discovered a set of genes that turn on, like a switch, in response to freezing temperatures. These genes are called master control genes, because they have the ability to turn other genes in the body on or off. In the case of freeze-tolerant animals, master control genes first turn off nearly all the genes in the body. Arctic caterpillars have many thousands of genes, but during the winter most of those genes are turned off. Keeping genes turned off is an adaptation that helps the caterpillar conserve energy throughout the winter.

Is It Really Extreme?

Organisms have adapted to a wide variety of environments. The Arctic woolly caterpillar is suited to life near the Arctic Circle. Some organisms must be able to survive in the exact opposite—the extreme heat of deserts. Others thrive in extremely salty conditions. Some plants and bacteria can even live in places with dangerously high levels of poisonous chemicals.

An environment doesn't have to be extreme to present challenges to the organisms that live there. Animals in a forest or meadow still need to find food and shelter, avoid predators, and respond to changes. The organisms living in any environment face a unique set of challenges.

? UNANSWERED Questions

As scientists learn more about how animals survive in extremely cold climates, they also uncover additional questions:

- Do animals respond to temperature or a lack of light?
- How do cellular processes that halt during the winter get started up again?
- Can scientists grow freeze resistant crops?

UNIT PROJECTS

As you study this unit, work alone or in a group on one of the projects listed below. Use the bulleted steps to guide your project.

Museum Exhibit

Plan a museum exhibit showing different ways in which animals respond to extreme environments.

- Research three to five types of organisms and find out what kind of environmental changes these organisms face.
- Design, make visuals, and write text to accompany your exhibit.

Grow a Fast Plant

Observe the entire life cycle of a plant in less than six weeks. Record your observations in a journal.

- Gather information and any materials necessary to grow and care for fast plants. Obtain fast plant seeds and plant them.
- Observe the plant for a few minutes every day. Make notes in your journal, and write weekly summaries.

Local Field Study

Report on organisms that live in your local area.

Identify three organisms you see on a regular basis and learn more about how they survive throughout the year.

Pick one plant or animal and observe it for a few minutes once a week in the morning and in the late afternoon. How does it change over time?

CAREER CENTER
CLASSZONE.COM

Learn more about careers in biology.

1

Single-Celled Organisms and Viruses

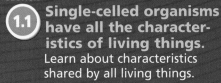

the BIG idea

Bacteria and protists have the characteristics of living things, while viruses are not alive.

Key Concepts

SECTION

1.1 Single-celled organisms have all the characteristics of living things.
Learn about characteristics shared by all living things.

SECTION

1.2 Bacteria are single-celled organisms without nuclei.
Learn about the characteristics of bacteria and archaea.

SECTION

1.3 Viruses are not alive but affect other living things.
Learn about virus structure and how they affect other cells.

SECTION

1.4 Protists are a diverse group of organisms.
Learn about protists and how they affect the environment.

Internet Preview

CLASSZONE.COM

Chapter 1 online resources: Content Review, two Visualizations, three Resource Centers, Math Tutorial, Test Practice.

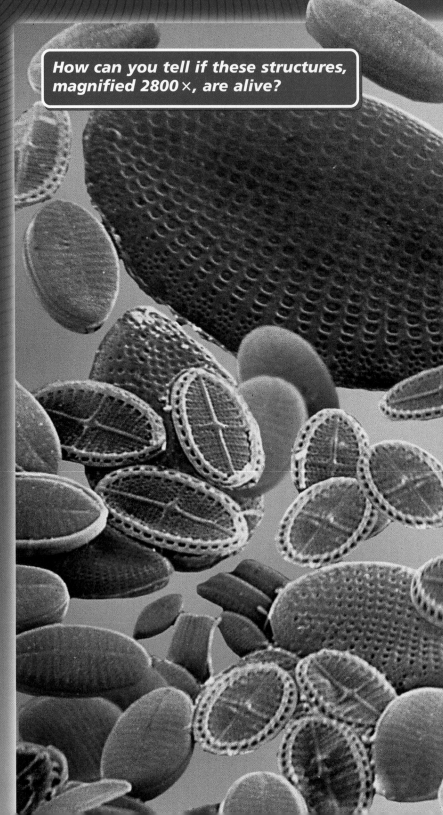

How can you tell if these structures, magnified 2800×, are alive?

EXPLORE (the **BIG** idea)

Where Can You Find Microscopic Life?

Make a list of places where you might find living things that are too small to be seen by your unaided eye. Then use a hand lens, magnifying glass, or microscope, to investigate some of the places on your list.

Observe and Think What do microscopic organisms look like. Why are there so many places where you can find microscopic life?

How Quickly Do Bacteria Multiply?

Tape a funnel to the top of a two-liter bottle. Place one bean in the funnel. After one minute, drop two more beans into the funnel. Continue adding beans to the bottle every minute, adding twice as many beans as you did before. When it is time to add 64 beans, use 1/8 of a cup, and then continue to double the amounts.

Observe and Think How long did it take to fill the bottle?

Internet Activity: Microscopic Life and You

Go to **ClassZone.com** to learn about the single-celled organisms.

Observe and Think What types of organism live in the human body?

NSTA
scilinks.org
SCI**LINKS**

Kingdom Protista **Code: MDL039**

Getting Ready to Learn

◀ CONCEPT REVIEW

- All living things interact with their environment to meet their needs.
- The cell is the fundamental unit of life.

◀ VOCABULARY REVIEW

See Glossary for definitions.

cell
matter
molecule
organism
species

CONTENT REVIEW
CLASSZONE.COM

Review concepts and vocabulary.

▶ TAKING NOTES

MAIN IDEA WEB

Write each new blue heading in a box. Then write notes in boxes around the center box that give important terms and details about that blue heading.

VOCABULARY STRATEGY

Place each vocabulary term at the center of a **description wheel diagram.** Write some words describing it on the spokes.

See the Note-Taking Handbook on pages R45–R51.

SCIENCE NOTEBOOK

They are organized, with an outside and an inside.

They increase in size.

Living things share common characteristics.

They reproduce and form other organisms like themselves.

They respond to changes in the environment.

some just one cell — MICROORGANISM — need microscope

very small

most living things

Single-celled organisms have all the characteristics of living things.

◀ **BEFORE,** you learned

- All living things are made of cells
- Organisms respond to their environment
- Species change over time

▶ **NOW,** you will learn

- About the various sizes of organisms
- About characteristics that are shared by all living things
- About needs shared by all organisms

VOCABULARY

microorganism p. 10
kingdom p. 11
binary fission p. 12
virus p. 14

EXPLORE Organisms

What living things are in the room with you?

PROCEDURE

1. Make a list of all the living things that are in your classroom.

2. Compare your list with the lists of your classmates. Make one list containing all the living things your class has identified.

WHAT DO YOU THINK?

- How did you identify something as living?
- Were you and your classmates able to see all the living things on your list?

MATERIALS
- paper
- pencil

Living things come in many shapes and sizes.

MAIN IDEA WEB
Make a web of the important terms and details about the main idea: *Living things come in many shapes and sizes.*

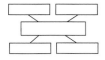

You can spot mushrooms in many places while walking through a forest. Scientists have discovered mushrooms that come from the same individual fungus more than 5 kilometers (3 miles) apart in an Oregon forest. Most of this honey mushroom fungus is below ground, stretching over an area covering more than 1600 football fields. This mushroom is one of the largest known living things on Earth.

Many other living things share the soil in the Oregon forest. Earthworms, insects, and many other organisms that are too small to be seen with a naked eye, also live there. For every living thing that is large enough to be seen, there are often countless numbers of smaller living things that share the same living space.

The honey mushroom fungus is one example of an organism. You, too, are an organism, and tiny bacteria living inside your body are also organisms. In fact, any living thing can be called an organism.

When you identify living things, you probably begin with those you can observe—plants, animals, and fungi such as mushrooms. However, most living things are too small to observe without a microscope. Even the tiniest organisms are made of cells. Very small organisms are called **microorganisms.** Some microorganisms are made of just one cell.

CHECK YOUR READING Compare and contrast the words *microorganism* and *organism*.

A visitor to a mangrove swamp forest can find an amazing variety of organisms. The mangrove trees themselves are the most obvious organisms. Roots from these trees grow above and below the muddy bottom of the forest. Other organisms live in almost every part of the mangrove tree.

READING TiP

The prefix *micro-* means "very small." Therefore, *microscope* means "very small scope" and *microorganism* means "very small organism."

Six Kingdoms of Life

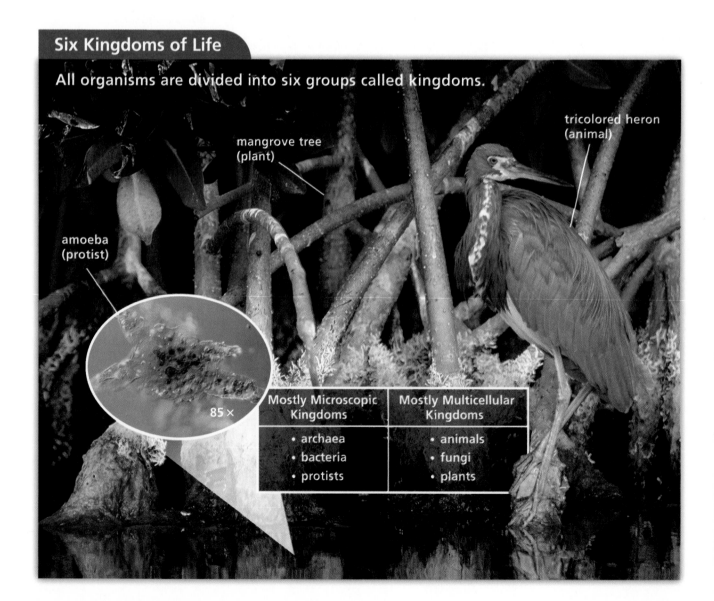

All organisms are divided into six groups called kingdoms.

tricolored heron (animal)

mangrove tree (plant)

amoeba (protist)

85×

Mostly Microscopic Kingdoms	Mostly Multicellular Kingdoms
• archaea	• animals
• bacteria	• fungi
• protists	• plants

A single drop of water from a mangrove swamp may be living space for many microorganisms. The circled photograph on page 10 was taken using a microscope, and shows an amoeba that may be found in the water of the swamp. Larger organisms, such as manatees and fish, swim around the roots of mangrove trees. Birds, such as tri-colored herons and roseate spoonbills, live on branches.

Scientists divide the organisms they identify into groups called **kingdoms.** This unit will cover all of the kingdoms of life, listed in the table on page 10. You are already familiar with plants and animals. Fungi are another kingdom. Fungi include mushrooms found in a forest. The other three kingdoms are composed of mostly microscopic life. You will learn more about microscopic organisms later in this chapter.

Living things share common characteristics.

All living things—from the microorganisms living in a mangrove swamp to the giant organisms living in the open ocean—share similar characteristics. Living things are organized, grow, reproduce, and respond to the environment.

Organization

Cells, like all living things, have an inside and an outside. The boundary separating the inside from the outside of an individual cell is called the cell membrane. Within some cells, another structure called the nucleus is also surrounded by a membrane. Cells perform one or more functions that the organism needs to survive

In this chapter, you will read about organisms made of a single cell. Some types of single-celled organisms contain a nucleus and some do not. All single-celled organisms contain every structure they need to survive within their one cell. They have structures to get energy from complex molecules, structures to help them move, and structures to help them sense their environment. All of the structures are part of their organizations.

Growth

Living things increase in size. Organisms made of one cell do not grow as large as organisms made of many cells. But all living things consume food or other materials to get energy. These materials are also used to build new structures inside cells or replace worn-out structures. As a result, individual cells grow larger over time.

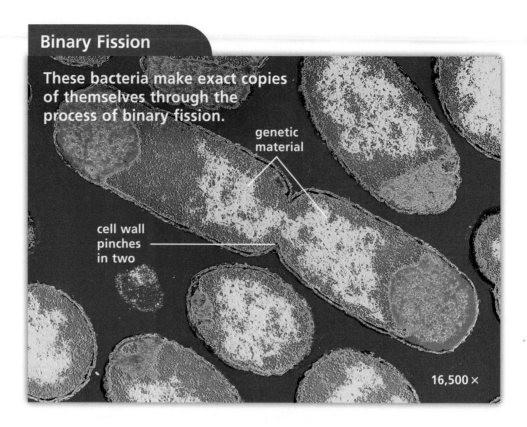

Binary Fission

These bacteria make exact copies of themselves through the process of binary fission.

genetic material

cell wall pinches in two

16,500 ×

Reproduction

Living things reproduce, forming other organisms like themselves. Every organism contains genetic material, which is a code contained in a special molecule called DNA. The code contains every characteristic of the individual organism. In order to reproduce, an organism must make a copy of this material, which is passed on to its offspring.

Single-celled organisms reproduce by a process called **binary fission.** In binary fission, material from one cell is broken apart into two cells. The genetic material of the original cell doubles so that each daughter cell has an exact copy of the DNA of the original cell. You might say that single-celled organisms multiply by dividing. One cell divides into 2 cells, 2 cells divide into 4, 4 into 8, 16, 32, 64, and so on. In some cells, binary fission can repeat in as little as 20 minutes.

CHECK YOUR READING   Describe how a single-celled organism is organized, grows, and reproduces.

VISUALIZATION
CLASSZONE.COM

Observe the process of binary fission.

Response

Organisms respond to changes in the environment. Even microscopic organisms respond to conditions such as light, temperature, and touch. The ability to respond allows organisms to find food, avoid being eaten, or perform other tasks necessary to survive.

INVESTIGATE Microorganisms

How do these organisms respond to their environment?

PROCEDURE

1. Place a drop of the hydra culture on a microscope slide. Using the microscope, find a hydra under medium power and sketch what you see.

2. Add a drop of warm water to the culture on the slide. How does the hydra respond? Record your observations.

3. Add a drop of the daphnia culture. Record your observations.

WHAT DO YOU THINK?

- Which observations, if any, indicate that hydras respond to their environment?

- Daphnia are organisms. What is the relationship between hydra and daphnia?

CHALLENGE What other experiments could you do to observe the responses of hydra or daphnia to their environment?

SKILL FOCUS
Observing

MATERIALS
- microscope
- slide
- hydra culture
- daphnia culture
- water

TIME
30 minutes

Living things need energy, materials, and living space.

Have you ever wondered why you need to eat food, breathe air, and drink water? All living things need energy and materials. For most organisms, water and air are the materials necessary for life.

Food supplies you with energy. You—like all living things—need energy to move, grow, and develop. All animals have systems for breaking down food into usable forms of energy and materials. Plants have structures that enable them to transform sunlight into usable energy. Some microorganisms transform sunlight, while others need to use other organisms as sources of energy.

Most of the activities of living things take place in water. Water is also an ingredient for many of the reactions that take place in cells. In addition, water helps support an organism's body. If you add water to the soil around a wilted plant, you will probably see the plant straighten up as water moves into its cells.

Materials in the air include gases such as carbon dioxide and oxygen. Many of the processes that capture and release energy involve these gases. Some organisms—such as those found around hydrothermal vents—use other chemicals to capture and release energy.

Viruses are not alive.

Sometimes it's not easy to tell the difference between a living and a nonliving thing. A **virus** is a small collection of genetic material enclosed in a protein shell. Viruses have many of the characteristics of living things, including DNA. However, a virus is not nearly as complex as an animal cell and is not considered a living thing.

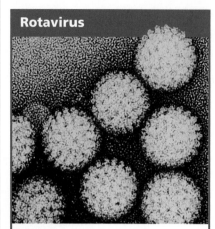

Rotavirus

These viruses contain DNA but do not grow or respond to their environment. 570,000×

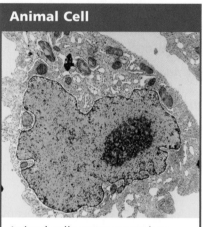

Animal Cell

Animal cells grow, reproduce, and respond to external conditions. 4800×

Animal cells have structures that allow them to get materials or energy from their environment. Viruses do not grow once they have formed, and they do not take in any energy. Animal cells can make copies of their genetic material and reproduce by dividing in two. Viruses are able to reproduce only by "taking over" another cell and using that cell to make new viruses. Animal cells also have many more internal structures than viruses. Viruses usually contain nothing more than their DNA.

1.1 Review

KEY CONCEPTS

1. Give examples of organisms that are very large and organisms that are very small.

2. Name four characteristics that all living things share.

3. Name three things that living things must obtain to survive.

CRITICAL THINKING

4. **Synthesize** Give examples of how a common animal, such as a dog, is organized, grows, responds, and reproduces.

5. **Predict** In a certain lake, would you expect there to be more organisms that are large enough to see or more organisms that are too small for you to see? Why?

● CHALLENGE

6. **Design** Try to imagine the different structures that a single-celled organism needs to survive in pond water. Then use your ideas to design your own single-celled organism.

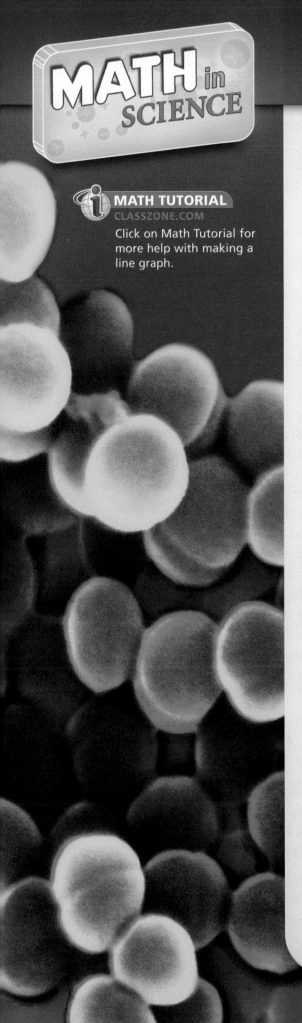

MATH in SCIENCE

MATH TUTORIAL
CLASSZONE.COM

Click on Math Tutorial for more help with making a line graph.

Graphing Growth

If you hold marbles in your hand and drop them into a bowl, each drop into the marble collection adds the same amount. If you plot this growth on a line graph, you will have a straight line.

By contrast, a bacterial colony's growth expands as it grows. All the bacteria divide in two. Every time all the bacteria divide, the colony doubles in size.

EXAMPLE

Compare the two types of growth on a graph.

Graph 1. Suppose the marble collection begins with one marble, and after every minute, one marble is added.

The graph shows: $x + 1 = y$
The slope of the line stays the same at each interval.

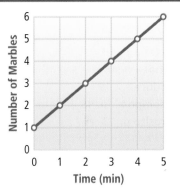

Graph 2. Suppose a bacterial colony begins with one bacterium, and every minute, a bacterial cell divides, forming two bacteria.

The graph shows: $2^x = y$
The slope gets steeper at each interval.

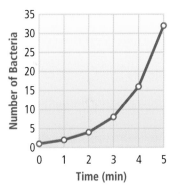

Examine the graphs and answer the questions.

1. How many marbles are in the collection after 3 min? How many bacteria are in the colony after 3 min?

2. After 7 min, what number of marbles would show in graph 1? Name the coordinates for this point. What number of bacteria would be shown in graph 2? Name the coordinates.

3. Copy the two graphs on graph paper. Extend each graph to 10 min. Plot the growth according to the pattern or formula given.

CHALLENGE Suppose the bacteria have a lifespan of 10 min. How many bacteria will be in the colony after 20 min?

Bacteria are single-celled organisms without nuclei.

◀ **BEFORE, you learned**

- Organisms come in all shapes and sizes
- All living things share common characteristics
- Living things may be divided into six kingdoms

▶ **NOW, you will learn**

- About the simplest living things
- About bacteria and archaea
- That bacteria may help or harm other organisms

VOCABULARY

bacteria p. 16
archaea p. 18
producer p. 19
decomposer p. 19
parasite p. 19

THINK ABOUT

Where are bacteria?

Bacteria are the simplest form of life. But that doesn't mean they're not important or numerous. As you look about the room you're sitting in, try to think of places where you might find bacteria. In fact, bacteria are on the walls, in the air, on the floor, and on your skin. It's hard to think of a place where you wouldn't find bacteria. The photograph shows a magnification of bacteria living on a sponge. The bacteria are magnified 580×. There are hundreds of millions of bacteria on your skin right now. And there are trillions of bacteria that live inside your intestines and help you digest food.

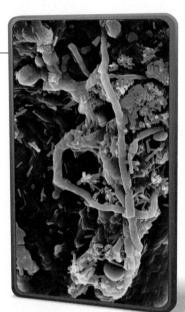

Bacteria and archaea are the smallest living things.

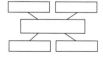

MAIN IDEA WEB
Make a web of the important terms and details about the main idea: *Bacteria and archaea are the smallest living things.* Be sure to include how bacteria are classified.

The names of the organisms belonging in the kingdoms Archaea and Bacteria are probably unfamiliar. Yet you actually encounter these organisms every day. Bacteria are everywhere: on your skin, in the ground, in puddles and ponds, in the soil, and in the sea. About 300 species of bacteria are living in your mouth right now.

Bacteria are the simplest kind of life known on Earth. All bacteria are composed of just one cell without a nucleus. Their genetic material is contained in a single loop within the cell. A bacterium reproduces using binary fission.

Bacteria

All bacteria are single cells without nuclei.

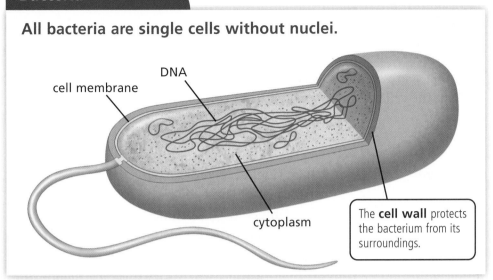

cell membrane

DNA

cytoplasm

The **cell wall** protects the bacterium from its surroundings.

Bacterial cells are different from the cells of other organisms. A bacterial cell is about 1/10 to 1/20 the size of a typical cell from organisms such as animals, plants, fungi, or protists. These four groups include organisms made up of cells with true nuclei. The nucleus is a structure that is enclosed by a membrane and that holds the genetic material.

Despite their small size, bacteria are simple only when compared with more complex cells. Bacteria are much more complex than viruses, because they have many internal structures that viruses do not have. For example, one important feature of most bacteria is a covering called a cell wall, which surrounds and protects the soft cell membrane like a rain jacket. Bacterial cells contain many large molecules and structures that are not found in viruses.

READING TiP

The plural of *bacterium* is *bacteria,* and the plural of *nucleus* is *nuclei.*

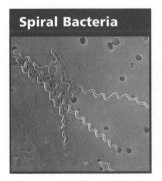
Spiral Bacteria

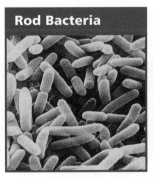
Rod Bacteria

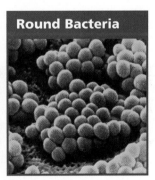
Round Bacteria

Scientists often classify bacteria by their external shapes.

- Spiral-shaped bacteria occur in single strands.
- Rod-shaped bacteria may occur singly or in chains.
- Round-shaped bacteria may occur singly or in pairs, chains, or clusters.

CHECK YOUR READING   Name two features that all bacteria share.

Archaea and bacteria are found in many environments.

RESOURCE CENTER
CLASSZONE.COM

Find out more about the many different types of bacteria.

Two types of single-celled organisms do not have nuclei. Bacteria are the most common and can be found in nearly every environment. Archaea are similar in size to bacteria, but share more characteristics with the cells of complex organisms like plants and animals.

Archaea

Archaea (AHR-kee-uh) are single-celled organisms that can survive in the largest range of environments. These environments may be very hot, very cold, or contain so much of a substance such as salt that most living things would be poisoned. As a result, scientists often group archaea according to where they live.

Methanogens take their name from methane, the natural gas they produce. These archaea die if they are exposed to oxygen. They may live in the dense mud of swamps and marshes, and in the guts of animals such as cows and termites.

READING TiP

The word halophile is formed using the root word *halo-* which means "salt," and the suffix *–phile* which means "love." Therefore, a *halophile* is a "salt lover."

Halophiles live in very salty lakes and ponds. Some halophiles die if their water is not salty enough. When a salty pond dries up, so do the halophiles. They can survive drying and begin dividing again when water returns to the pond.

Thermophiles are archaea that thrive in extreme heat or cold. They may live in hot environments such as hot springs, near hot vents deep under the sea, or buried many meters deep in the ice.

Archaea

Archaea are organisms that can live in extreme environments.

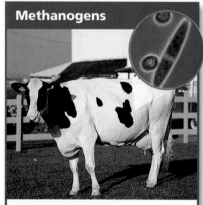

Methanogens

Methanogens maybe found in a cows' stomach where they help with digestion.

Halophiles

Halophiles can be found in extremely salty bodies of water such as the Dead Sea.

Thermophiles

Thermophiles may be found in hot geysers such as this one in Yellowstone National Park.

Bacteria

Most single-celled organisms without a nuclei are classified as bacteria. Bacteria are found in almost every environment and perform a variety of tasks. Some bacteria contain chlorophyll. Using sunlight for energy, these bacteria are an important food source in oceans. These bacteria also release oxygen gas, which animals need to breathe.

 CHECK YOUR READING What are some common traits of bacteria and archaea?

Bacteria without chlorophyll perform different tasks. Some bacteria break down parts of dead plants and animals to help recycle matter. Some bacteria release chemicals into the environment, providing a food source for other organisms. Scientists often group bacteria by the roles they play in the environment. Three of the most common roles are listed below.

Bacteria that transform energy from sunlight into energy that can be used by cells are called **producers.** These bacteria are a food source for organisms that cannot make their own food.

Decomposers get energy by breaking down materials in dead or decaying organisms. Decomposers help other organisms reuse materials found in decaying matter.

Parasites live in very close relationships either inside or on the surface of other organisms. Parasites harm their host organisms or host cells. Other bacteria live in close relationships with host organisms but are helpful to their hosts, or do not affect them.

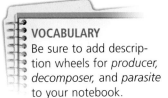

VOCABULARY
Be sure to add description wheels for *producer, decomposer,* and *parasite* to your notebook.

Bacteria

Three roles bacteria play in the environment are shown below.

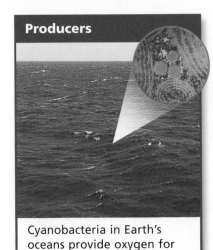

Producers

Cyanobacteria in Earth's oceans provide oxygen for animals to breathe.

Decomposers

Some bacteria break down dead wood into materials used by other organisms.

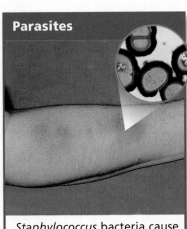

Parasites

Staphylococcus bacteria cause infections such as these boils in humans.

Bacteria may help or harm other organisms.

Some bacteria, such as producers and decomposers, are helpful to other organisms. But other bacteria can be harmful. These bacteria can causes diseases in animals and plants.

Helpful Bacteria

One shovelful of ordinary soil contains trillions of bacteria, and every fallen leaf or dead animal is covered with bacteria. These bacteria break down the matter in dead bodies and waste materials. Broken-down materials may become available for other organisms to build their bodies.

Cities use bacteria to break down sewage. Bacteria in sewage-treatment plants live on the material dissolved in liquid sewage. After the bacteria have finished, the water is clean enough to sterilize. Then water can be released into rivers or oceans. Other bacteria are used to clean up oil spills by decomposing oil suspended on the ocean's surface.

Bacteria can also change materials that do not come from living things and make them available for other organisms. For example, some bacteria can convert nitrogen gas to nitrogen compounds. This process, called nitrogen fixation, makes nitrogen available to plants in a form that is useful to them. Plants use this nitrogen in making proteins, which are an important part of every cell.

Helpful Bacteria

Bacteria inside the root nodules of soybean plants convert nitrogen into a form the plant can use.

bacteria inside nodules

nodules on roots

Like bacteria, certain types of archaea are helpful to other organisms. All animals that eat plants such as grass depend on archaea. Methanogens help break down the cellulose in cell walls. Termites and cows are two examples of animals that can digest cellulose because of the archaea in their stomachs.

 CHECK YOUR READING Name two helpful roles that bacteria can play in the environment.

Harmful Bacteria

Not all bacteria are helpful to other organisms. Scientists first discovered that bacteria cause some diseases in the late 1800s. Much of the scientific research into harmful bacteria developed because bacteria cause disease in humans. Tuberculosis, cholera, and infant diarrhea are examples of disease caused by bacteria. Bacteria also may cause disease in many animals and in plants.

Bacteria can cause the symptoms of disease in three ways.

- They can invade parts of the body, multiplying in body tissues and dissolving cells.
- They can poison the body with chemicals they produce and release.
- They can poison the body with chemicals that are part of the bacteria itself.

One way to fight bacterial disease is with vaccinations. Vaccines help individual organisms prepare to fight diseases they might encounter in the future. Humans, as well as cats and dogs, get vaccinations for bacterial diseases. A similar approach helps wildlife managers keep salmon safe from bacterial kidney disease.

Bacterial wilt causes disease in this pumpkin.

1.2 Review

KEY CONCEPTS

1. Explain why bacteria are classified as living cells but viruses are not.
2. Name two main groups of bacteria.
3. Describe three ways that bacteria affect other organisms.

CRITICAL THINKING

4. **Visualize** Draw a diagram of a bacterium. Label the parts of the cell.
5. **Predict** Where in your neighborhood would you find most of the bacteria that cause decomposition?

⚠ CHALLENGE

6. **Analyze** Parasitic bacteria do not usually kill their hosts, at least not for a long period of time. Why is it better for parasites not to kill their hosts?

CHAPTER INVESTIGATION

Bacteria

OVERVIEW AND PURPOSE People routinely wash themselves to keep clean. You probably take a bath or shower every day, and you also wash your hands. Your hands may appear to be perfectly clean, but appearances can be deceiving. Your hands pick up bacteria from the objects you touch. You cannot see or feel these microscopic organisms, but they are there, on your skin. In this activity you will

- sample bacteria in your environment
- sample bacteria on your hands

▶ Problem

Write It Up

Do you pick up bacteria from your environment?

▶ Hypothesize

Write It Up

Write a hypothesis about whether bacteria in your environment are transferred to your skin. Your hypothesis should take the form of an "If . . . , then . . . , because . . ." statement.

▶ Procedure

1. Make a data table in your **Science Notebook** like the one shown on page 23.

2. Obtain three agar petri dishes. Be careful not to open the dishes.

3. Remove the lid from one dish and gently press two fingers onto the surface of the agar. Close the lid immediately. Tape the dish closed. Mark the tape with the letter A. Include your initials and the date. Mark your hand as the source in Table 1. Wash your hands.

step 3

MATERIALS
- 3 covered petri dishes with sterile nutrient agar
- marker
- tape
- everyday object, like a coin or eraser
- sterile cotton swab
- hand lens
for Challenge:
- 1 covered petri dish with sterile nutrient agar
- sterile swab

4. Choose a small object you handle every day, such as a coin or an eraser. Remove the lid from the second petri dish and swipe the object across the agar. You can instead use a sterile swab to rub on the object, and then swipe the swab across the agar. Close the lid immediately. Tape and mark the dish B, as in step 3. Include the source in Table 1.

5. Choose an area of the classroom you have regular contact with, for example, the top of your desk or the classroom door. Use a clean swab to rub the area and then swipe the swab across the agar of the third petri dish. Tape and mark the dish as C, following the instructions in step 3. Dispose of the swab according to your teacher's instructions.

step 5

6. Place the agar plates upside down in a dark, warm place for two to three days. **CAUTION: Do not open the dishes. Wash your hands when you have finished.**

▶ Observe and Analyze

Write It Up

1. **OBSERVE** Observe the dishes with the hand lens. You may want to pull the tape aside, but do not remove the covers. Include a description of the bacteria in Table 1. Are the bacteria in one dish different from the others?

2. **OBSERVE** Observe the amounts of bacterial growth in each dish and record your observations in Table 1. Which dish has the most bacterial growth? the least growth?

3. Return the petri dishes to your teacher for disposal. **CAUTION: Do not open the dishes. Wash your hands thoroughly with warm water and soap when you have finished.**

▶ Conclude

Write It Up

1. **INFER** Why is it necessary for the agar to be sterile before you begin the experiment?

2. **INFER** What function does the agar serve?

3. **INTERPRET** Compare your results with your hypothesis. Do your observations support your hypothesis?

4. **IDENTIFY LIMITS** What limits are there in making a connection between the bacteria in dish A and those in dishes B and C?

5. **EVALUATE** Why is it important to keep the petri dishes covered?

6. **APPLY** Why is it important to use separate petri dishes for each sample?

▶ INVESTIGATE Further

CHALLENGE Contamination can be a problem in any experiment involving bacteria, because bacteria are everywhere. Obtain a petri dish from your teacher. Swipe a sterile swab on the agar and place the agar plate upside down in a dark, warm place for two to three days. Do the results of this test make you reevaluate your other lab results?

Bacteria

Table 1. Observations of Bacteria

Petri Dish	Source	Description of Bacteria	Amount of Bacteria
A	hand		
B			
C			

KEY CONCEPT

Viruses are not alive but affect all living things.

◀ **BEFORE,** you learned

- Most organisms are made of a single cell
- Living things share common characteristics
- Viruses are not living things

▶ **NOW,** you will learn

- About the structure of viruses
- How viruses use a cell's machinery to reproduce
- How viruses affect host cells

VOCABULARY

host cell p. 26

EXPLORE Viruses

How were viruses discovered?

PROCEDURE

① Fill a small container with mixed sesame seeds and salt.

② Holding the sieve over the paper plate, pour the mixture into the sieve.

③ Gently shake the sieve until nothing more falls through.

④ Using a hand lens, examine the material that fell through the sieve and the material that stayed in the sieve.

MATERIALS

- small container
- sesame seeds
- table salt
- small kitchen sieve
- paper plate
- hand lens

WHAT DO YOU THINK?

- What is the most important difference between the particles that got through the sieve and the particles that remained behind?
- How could you change your sieve to make it not let through both kinds of particles?

Viruses share some characteristics with living things.

MAIN IDEA WEB
Remember to make a web of the important terms and details about the main idea: *Viruses share some characteristics with living things.*

In the late 1800s, scientists such as Louis Pasteur showed that some small organisms can spoil food and cause disease. Once the cause was found, scientists looked for ways to prevent spoilage and disease. One method of prevention they found was removing these harmful organisms from liquids.

Bacteria may be removed from liquids by pouring the liquid through a filter, like a coffee filter or a sieve. To remove bacteria, a filter must have holes smaller than one millionth of a meter in diameter.

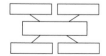

INVESTIGATE Viruses

How do infections spread?

SKILL FOCUS
Analyzing

PROCEDURE

1. Get a cup of sample liquid from your teacher. Pour half the liquid from your cup into the cup of a classmate, then pour the same amount back into the original cup. Your cup should then contain a mixture of the liquids from both cups.

2. Repeat step 1 with at least two other classmates.

3. Drop one drop of solution A into your paper cup. If it changes color, you are "infected." If you were "infected," add drops of solution B until your liquid turns clear again. Count how many drops it takes to "cure" you.

WHAT DO YOU THINK?

- If you were "infected," can you figure out who "infected" you?
- If you were not "infected," is it possible for anyone who poured liquid into your cup to be "infected"?

CHALLENGE Only one person in your class started out with an "infection." Try to figure out who it was.

MATERIALS
- paper cup
- sample liquid
- solution A
- solution B

TIME
30 minutes

When a filter had removed all of the harmful organisms from a liquid, the liquid no longer caused any illnesses. This method worked when there was only bacteria in the liquid. Sometimes filtering did not prevent disease. Something much smaller than bacteria was in the liquid. Scientists called these disease-causing particles viruses, from the Latin word for "slimy liquid" or "poison."

 **RESOURCE CENTER**
CLASSZONE.COM

Learn more about viruses.

 CHECK YOUR READING   How does the size of viruses compare with the size of bacteria?

Scientists have learned much about viruses, and can even make images of them with specialized microscopes. Viruses consist of genetic material contained inside a protective protein coat called a capsid. The protein coat may be a simple tube, such as the coat of an ebola virus, or have many layers, such as the smallpox virus shown on page 26.

Viruses may come in many shapes and sizes, but all viruses consist of a capsid and genetic material. The ability of viruses to make copies of their genetic material is one way that viruses are similar to living things. Also the protein coat is similar to a cell's outer membrane. But viruses do not grow, and viruses do not respond to changes in their environment. Therefore, viruses are not living organisms.

Virus

All viruses, including this smallpox virus, contain genetic material surrounded by a capsid.

The **genetic material** stores information the virus needs to make copies of itself.

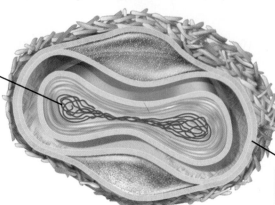

Smallpox Virus

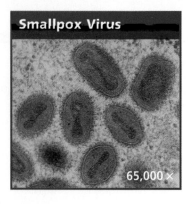

65,000×

The **capsid** protects the genetic material and gives shape to the virus.

Viruses multiply inside living cells.

VISUALIZATION
CLASSZONE.COM

See how viruses infect and multiply within bacteria.

Remember that all living things reproduce. Viruses cannot reproduce by themselves, which is one of the ways they are different from living things. However, viruses can use materials within living cells to make copies of themselves. The cells that viruses infect in order to make copies are called **host cells**. Despite their tiny size, viruses have the ability to cause a lot of damage to cells of other organisms.

One of the best studied viruses infects bacteria. It's called a bacteriophage (bak-TEER-ee-uh-FAYJ), which comes from the Latin for "bacteria eater." Some of the steps that a bacteriophage goes through to multiply are shown in the illustration.

❶ **Attachment** The virus attaches to the surface of a bacterium.

❷ **Injection** The virus injects its DNA into the bacterium.

❸ **Production** Using the same machinery used by the host cell for copying its own DNA, the host cell makes copies of the viral DNA.

❹ **Assembly** The viral DNA forces the infected cell to assemble new viruses from the parts it has created.

❺ **Release** The cell bursts open, releasing 100 or more new viruses.

Viruses have proteins on their surfaces that look like the proteins that the host cell normally needs. The virus attaches itself to special sites on the host that are usually reserved for these proteins.

Not every virus makes copies in exactly the same way as the bacteriophage. Some viruses are inside host cells. Others use the host cell as a factory that produces new viruses one at a time. These viruses may not be as harmful to the infected organism because the host cell is not destroyed.

Making New Viruses

Viruses, such as this bacteriophage, use other cells to make new viruses.

Virus (bacteriophage)

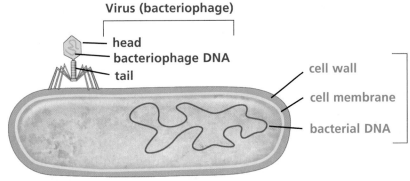

head
bacteriophage DNA
tail

cell wall
cell membrane
bacterial DNA

Host cell
(bacterium)

1 Attachment
The bacteriophage virus attaches to a bacterium.

injected DNA

bacterial DNA

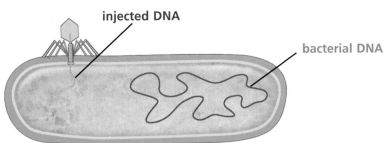

2 Injection
The virus breaks through the cell wall and cell membrane and injects its DNA into the host cell.

empty virus
copies of viral DNA

bacterial DNA pieces

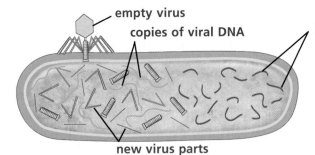

3 Production
The viral DNA breaks down the host cell's DNA and uses the host cell's machinery to produce the parts of new viruses.

new virus parts

new viruses

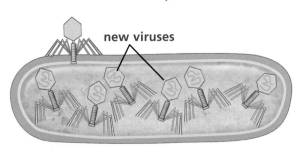

4 Assembly
The viral DNA uses the host cell's machinery to assemble new viruses.

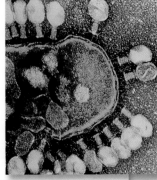

burst bacterium

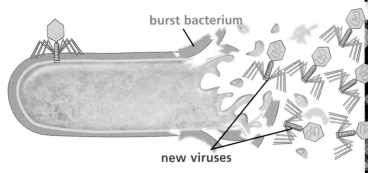

5 Release
The host cell breaks apart and new viruses that are able to infect other host cells are released .

new viruses

Rows of hospital beds are filled with Massachusetts influenza patients in 1918.

Viruses may harm host cells.

A host cell does not often benefit from providing living space for a virus. The virus uses the cell's material, energy, and processes. In many cases, after a virus has made many copies of itself, the new viruses burst out of the host cell and destroy it.

Harmful viruses cause huge problems. Viruses that cause diseases such as polio, smallpox, diphtheria, or AIDS have had a major impact on human history. About 25 million people died of influenza in an outbreak that occurred just after World War I.

In the photograph, nurses work to ease the symptoms of infected patients. The most infectious patients were enclosed in tents. Others were made as comfortable as possible on beds outside. Since viruses such as influenza can spread quickly, the camp was isolated from the rest of the community.

Plant viruses can stunt plant growth and kill plants. When plant viruses invade crop plants, they can cause much economic damage, decreasing food production. Plants, animals, bacteria, and all other living things are capable of being infected by viruses.

Today, scientists are discovering ways to use viruses in a positive way. Scientists use viruses to insert certain pieces of genetic material into living cells. For example, the portion of genetic material that allows some marine organisms to produce a chemical that glows can be inserted into tissue samples to help with their identification.

1.3 Review

KEY CONCEPTS

1. What are the two parts that every virus has?

2. Why are viruses not considered to be living things?

3. Explain how copies of viruses are produced.

CRITICAL THINKING

4. **Compare and Contrast** What features do viruses and cells have in common? How are they different?

5. **Explain** Summarize the steps by which a bacteriophage makes new viruses.

⬥ CHALLENGE

6. **Synthesize** What characteristics of viruses can make them so dangerous to humans and other living organisms?

The Virus and the Tulip

The people of Holland around the 1620s were trading fortunes and farmland for one beautiful flower. Tulips had arrived from Turkey by way of Vienna, and interest in the flower spread through Holland like a fever. In a frenzy called "tulipomania," collectors paid as much as 5400 guilders, the price of a city house, for just one tulip bulb—but not any ordinary tulip.

Broken Flower Bulbs

Tulip traders searched for tulips with patterns, stripes, or feathery petals. These plants were called broken bulbs. Within a field of colored tulips, suddenly an odd or patterned flower grew. Once a color break showed up, it stayed with that flower's line into each new generation, until the line died off. And die off it did. The patterned petals were caused by a virus inside the plant, and the virus caused the flowers to weaken. The blooms got smaller in each generation.

The Mystery Source

While the trade in tulips rose, growers tried many tricks to produce the crazy patterns. Still, the broken bulbs grew rarely and randomly, or so it seemed. Viruses weren't discovered until 300 years later. Scientists then figured out that a virus had caused the broken bulbs.

A small leaf-eating insect called an aphid had carried the virus from plant to plant.
© Dennis Kunkel/Dennis Kunkel Microscopy, Inc.

Back Down to the Ground

Like any goldrush, tulipomania crashed. People lost fortunes and fought over claims. In 1637, the government stopped all trading. Today, tulips with striped and feathery patterns grow around the world, but the patterns observed are not caused by viruses. Still, every now and then, a strange looking bulb appears. Instead of prizing it, growers remove it. They don't want a field of virus-infested, weakened plants.

EXPLORE

1. **OBSERVE** Look at tulips in a garden catalog, and find breeds with patterns. Observe the tulip closely. Draw or paint the modern flower and label its name.

2. **CHALLENGE** Viruses can produce sickness, but they have other effects too. Do research on viruses to list some effects of viruses that have value to scientists, doctors, or other people.

Patterns in these tulips are part of the genetic make-up of the flowers.

Protists are a diverse group of organisms.

- Organisms are grouped into six kingdoms
- Bacteria are single-celled organisms without a nucleus
- Viruses are not living things

- About characteristics of protists
- About the cell structure of protists
- How protists get their energy

VOCABULARY

algae p. 31
plankton p. 33
protozoa p. 34

THINK ABOUT

Where can protists be found?

Protists include the most complex single-celled organisms found on Earth. Fifty million years ago, a spiral-shelled protist called a nummulitid was

common in some oceans. Even though its shell was the size of a coin, the organism inside was microscopic and single celled. When the organism died, the shells accumulated on the ocean floor. Over millions of years, the shells were changed into the rock called limestone. This limestone was used to build the great pyramids of Egypt. Some of the most monumental structures on Earth would not exist without organisms made of just a single cell.

Most protists are single-celled.

When Anton van Leeuwenhoek began using one of the world's first microscopes, he looked at pond water, among other things. He described, in his words, many "very little animalcules." Some of the organisms he saw probably were animals, microscopic but multicellular animals. However, many of the organisms Leeuwenhoek saw moving through the pond water had only a single cell. Today, more than 300 years later, scientists call these single-celled organisms protists.

Protists include all organisms with cells having nuclei and not belonging to the animal, plant, or fungi kingdoms. In other words, protists may be considered a collection of leftover organisms. As a result, protists are the most diverse of all the kingdoms.

INVESTIGATE Protists

What lives in pond water?

PROCEDURE

(1) Using a dropper, place one small drop of pond water in the center of a slide. Try to include some of the material from the bottom of the container.

(2) Gently place a cover slip on the drop of water.

(3) Observe the slide with a hand lens first.

(4) Starting with low power, observe the slide with a microscope. Be sure to follow microscope safety procedures as outlined by your teacher. Carefully focus up and down on the water. If you see moving organisms, try to follow them by gently moving the slide.

WHAT DO YOU THINK?

• Describe and draw what you could see with the hand lens.

• Describe and draw what you could see with the microscope.

• Compare your observations with those of other students.

CHALLENGE Choose one organism that moves and observe it for some time. Describe its behavior.

Most protists are single-celled, microscopic organisms that live in water. However, protists also include some organisms with many cells. These many-celled organisms have simpler structures than animals, plants, or fungi. They also have fewer types of cells in their bodies.

 CHECK YOUR READING Why are protists considered the most diverse group of organisms?

The group of protists you're probably most familiar with is seaweeds. At first glance, seaweed looks like a plant. On closer inspection scientists see that it has a simpler structure. Some seaweeds called kelp can grow 100 meters long.

The name **algae** applies to both multicellular protists and single-celled protists that use sunlight as an energy source. Both seaweed and diatoms are types of algae. Slime molds are another type of multicellular protist.

VOCABULARY
Be sure to make a description wheel for *algae* and add to it as you read this section.

Given the many different types of organisms grouped together as protists, it is no surprise that protists play many roles in their environments. Algae are producers. They obtain energy from sunlight. Their cells provide food for many other organisms. These protists also produce oxygen, which is beneficial to many other organisms. Both of these roles are similar to those played by plants. Other protists act as parasites and can cause disease in many organisms, including humans.

Protists come in a variety of shapes and sizes.

Euglena

magnified 2800 ×

Diatoms

magnified 65 ×

Seaweed

Protists live in any moist environment, including both freshwater and saltwater, and on the forest floor. Some protists move around in the water, some simply float in place, and some stick to surfaces. The photographs above show a small sample of the large variety of organisms that are called protists.

Seaweed is a multicellular protist that floats in the water and can be found washed up on beaches. Slime molds are organisms that attach to surfaces, absorbing nutrients from them. Diatoms are single-celled algae that float in water and are covered by hard shells. Euglena are single-celled organisms that can move like animals but also get energy from sunlight.

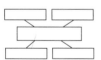

MAIN IDEA WEB
Remember to make a web of the important terms and details about the main idea: *Protists obtain their energy in three ways.* Include examples of each method of obtaining energy.

Protists obtain their energy in three ways.

Protists can be classified by their way of getting energy. Some protists capture sunlight and convert it to usable energy. Another group of protists gets its energy from other organisms. A third group absorbs materials that contain stored energy.

Some protists, such as the euglena in the upper left photograph, can even switch from one mode of life to another. They swim rapidly through pond water like animals. If they receive enough sunlight, they look green and make their own food like plants. But if they are left in the dark long enough, they absorb nutrients from their environment like fungi.

 CHECK YOUR READING Explain how the organisms in the photographs above get their energy.

Algae

Plantlike protists, called algae, get energy from sunlight. Like plants, they use the Sun's energy, water, and carbon dioxide from the air or water. Algae contain chlorophyll, a green pigment that is necessary to capture the Sun's energy. In the process of transforming energy from sunlight, algae release oxygen gas into the air. This important process, which is called photosynthesis, also takes place in plants and some bacteria. Organisms that perform photosynthesis also supply much of the food for other organisms.

Diatoms are examples of single-celled algae. Like all algae, a diatom contains a nucleus in which to store its genetic material. Diatoms also have chloroplasts, which are the energy-producing centers that contain chlorophyll.

Algae

Algae are plantlike protists. *Chlamydomonas* is an example of single-celled algae.

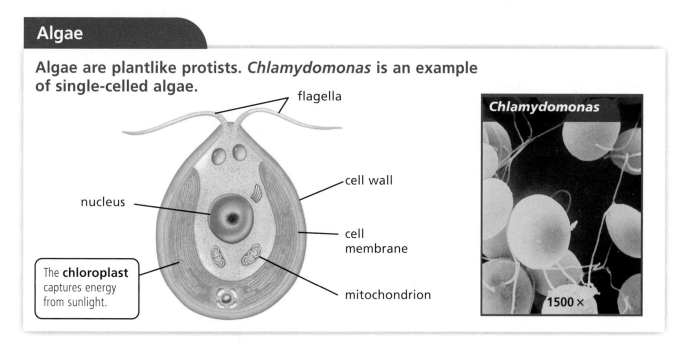

flagella

nucleus

cell wall

cell membrane

The **chloroplast** captures energy from sunlight.

mitochondrion

Chlamydomonas

1500×

Another type of algae are microscopic colonies of nearly identical cells called volvox. These cells, arranged in a hollow ball, look like some single-celled algae. Sometimes cells break off from the hollow ball to form new colonies. The new colonies will eventually escape the parent colony. Colonial organisms such as volvox are the simplest kind of multicellular organisms. Seaweed is another example of multicellular algae.

All organisms that drift in water are called **plankton.** Plankton includes the young of many animals and some adult animals, as well as protists. Plankton that perform photosynthesis are called phytoplankton (plantlike plankton). Phytoplankton include algae and the cyanobacteria you learned about earlier. Phytoplankton live in all of the world's oceans and produce most of the oxygen animals breathe.

Protozoa, such as this *Paramecium*, are animallike protists.

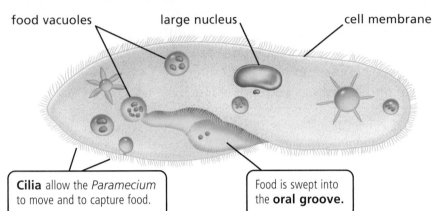

food vacuoles   large nucleus   cell membrane

Cilia allow the *Paramecium* to move and to capture food.

Food is swept into the **oral groove.**

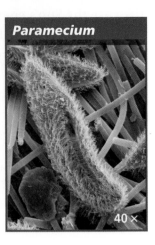

Paramecium

40×

Protozoa

Protists that eat other organisms, or decaying parts of other organisms, are animal-like protists, or **protozoa.** They include many forms, all single-celled. Protozoa cannot use sunlight as a source of energy and they must move around to obtain the energy they need to survive. Certain chemicals in protozoa can recognize when a particle of food is nearby. The food particle is usually another organism or a part of one. The protozoan ingests the food and breaks it down to obtain energy.

Some animal-like protists swim rapidly, sweeping bacteria or other protists into a groove that looks like a mouth. One example, called a paramecium, is shown above. A paramecium moves about using thousands of short wavy strands called cilia.

Another group of protozoa swim with one or more long whiplike structures called flagella. A third group of protozoa has very flexible cells. Organisms such as the amoeba oozes along surfaces. When it encounters prey, the amoeba spreads out and wraps around its food.

A number of protists live as parasites, some of which cause disease in animals and humans. One of the world's most significant human diseases, malaria, is caused by a protist. A single species of mosquito carries the parasite from human to human. When the mosquito bites an infected human, it sucks up some of the parasite along with the blood. When that same mosquito bites another human, it passes on some of the parasite. In the human blood stream, the parasite goes through a complex life cycle, eventually destroying red blood cells.

REMINDER

A parasite is an organism that lives inside or on another organism and causes the organism harm.

CHECK YOUR READING   How do protozoa and algae differ in the way they obtain energy?

Other Protists

Protists that absorb food from their environment can be called funguslike protists. These protists take in materials from the soil or from other organisms and break materials down in order to obtain energy. They are called decomposers.

The term *mold* refers to many organisms that produce a fuzzy-looking growth. Most of the molds you might be familiar with, like bread mold, are fungi. But three groups of protists are also called molds. These molds have structures that are too simple to be called fungi, and they are single celled for a portion of their lives. One example of a funguslike protist is water mold, which forms a fuzzy growth on food. This food may be decaying animal or plant tissue or living organisms. Water molds live mainly in fresh water.

Slime molds live on decaying plants on the forest floor. One kind of slime mold consists of microscopic single cells that ooze around, eating bacteria. When their food is scarce, however, many of the cells group together to produce a multicellular colony. The colony eventually produces a reproductive structure to release spores. Wind can carry spores about, and they sprout where they land.

A walk in a moist forest might give you a chance to see a third kind of mold. This organism looks like a fine net, like lace, several centimeters across, on rotting logs. These slime molds are not multicellular, but instead one giant cell with many nuclei. They are the plasmodial slime molds.

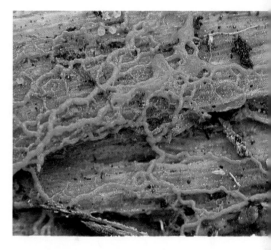

Plasmodial slime mold may grow on decaying wood after a period of rainy weather.

 CHECK YOUR READING   How do funguslike protists get energy?

1.4 Review

KEY CONCEPTS

1. What are two characteristics of protists?
2. What feature do all protists have in common?
3. What are the three different types of protists?

CRITICAL THINKING

4. **Provide Examples** Some protists are dependent on other organisms and cannot live independently. Other protists are independent and have organisms that depend on them. Give an example of each.

◯ CHALLENGE

5. **Hypothesize** Scientists are considering reclassifying protists into many kingdoms. How might they decide how many kingdoms to use and how to place organisms in these kingdoms?

Chapter Review

the **BIG** idea

Bacteria and protists have the characteristics of living things, while viruses are not alive.

CONTENT REVIEW
CLASSZONE.COM

◀ KEY CONCEPTS SUMMARY

1.1 Single-celled organisms have all the characteristics of living things.

Scientists divide organisms into six **kingdoms.** All living things, including **microorganisms,** are organized, grow, reproduce, and respond to the environment.

Plants   Animals   Protists   Fungi   Bacteria   Archaea

VOCABULARY
microorganism p. 10
kingdom p. 11
binary fission p. 12
virus p. 14

1.2 Bacteria are single-celled organisms without nuclei.

- Bacteria and archaea are the smallest living things.
- Archaea and bacteria are found in many environments.
- Bacteria may help or harm other organisms.

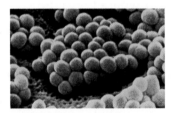

VOCABULARY
bacteria p. 16
archaea p. 17
producer p. 19
decomposer p. 19
parasite p. 19

1.3 Viruses are not alive but affect other living things.

A virus consists of genetic material enclosed in a protein coat. Viruses cannot reproduce on their own, but they use materials within living cells to make copies of themselves.

injected DNA   **bacterial DNA**

VOCABULARY
host cell p. 26

1.4 Protists are a diverse group of organisms.

 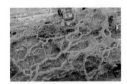

Plantlike **algae** get energy from sunlight.

Funguslike protists are decomposers.

Protozoa, animal-like protists, eat other organisms.

VOCABULARY
algae p. 31
plankton p. 33
protozoa p. 34

Reviewing Vocabulary

Draw a triangle for each of the terms listed below. Define the term, use it in a sentence, and draw a picture to help you remember the term. An example is completed for you.

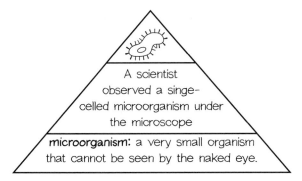

A scientist observed a singe-celled microorganism under the microscope

microorganism: a very small organism that cannot be seen by the naked eye.

1. binary fission

2. producer

3. virus

4. host cell

Describe how the vocabulary terms in the following pairs of words are related to each other. Explain the relationship in a one- or two-sentence answer. Underline each vocabulary term in your answers.

5. archaea, bacteria

6. microorganism, organism

7. decomposers, parasite

8. protists, algae

Reviewing Key Concepts

Multiple Choice *Choose the letter of the best answer.*

9. Which group is *not* a microscopic kingdom?
   a. fungi
   b. bacteria
   c. archaea
   d. protists

10. What happens in binary fission?
   a. DNA is combined into one cell.
   b. The daughter cells differ from the parent cell.
   c. Material from one cell is broken into two cells.
   d. One cell divides into four exact cells.

11. Which is a characteristic of a virus?
   a. obtains energy from sunlight
   b. responds to light and temperature
   c. doesn't contain DNA
   d. reproduces only within other cells

12. Which is the simplest type of organism on Earth?
   a. protists
   b. bacteria
   c. viruses
   d. parasites

13. Which statement about bacteria is *not* true?
   a. Bacteria reproduce using binary fission.
   b. Bacteria do not have a nucleus.
   c. Bacteria do not contain genetic material.
   d. Bacteria are either rod-, cone-, or spiral-shaped.

14. Archaea that can survive only in extreme temperatures are the
   a. methanogens
   b. halophiles
   c. thermophiles
   d. bacteria

15. A weakened viral or bacterial disease that is injected into the body is
   a. a filter
   b. a diatom
   c. a bacteriophage
   d. a vaccine

16. Which group of protists absorbs food from their environment?
   a. diatoms
   b. molds
   c. protozoa
   d. plankton

17. Which obtains energy by feeding on other organisms?

    a. amoeba   **c.** phytoplankton

    b. algae   **d.** mushroom

Short Answer *Write a short answer to each question.*

18. Briefly describe the characteristics that all living things share.

19. How are bacteria harmful to humans?

20. What are plankton?

Thinking Critically

21. APPLY Imagine you are a scientist on location in a rain forest in Brazil. You discover what you think might be a living organism. How would you be able to tell if the discovery is a living thing?

22. COMMUNICATE What process is shown in this photograph? Describe the sequence of events in the process shown.

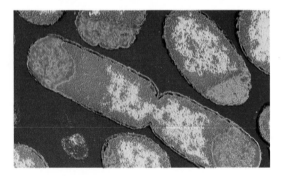

23. CLASSIFY Why are archaea classified in a separate kingdom from bacteria?

24. ANALYZE Why are some bacteria considered "nature's recyclers"? Explain the role that these bacteria play in the environment.

25. CALCULATE A bacterium reproduces every hour. Assuming the bacteria continue to reproduce at that rate, how many bacteria will there be after 10 hours? Explain how you know.

26. HYPOTHESIZE A student conducts an experiment to determine the effectiveness of washing hands on bacteria growth. He rubs an unwashed finger across an agar plate, then washes his hands and rubs the same finger across a second plate. What hypothesis might the student make for this experiment? Explain.

27. COMPARE AND CONTRAST Describe three ways that viruses differ from bacteria.

28. ANALYZE A scientist has grown cultures of bacteria on agar plates for study. Now the scientist wants to grow a culture of viruses in a laboratory for study. How might this be possible? Give an example.

29. PROVIDE EXAMPLES How are protists both helpful and harmful to humans? Give examples in your answer.

the BIG idea

31. INFER Look again at the picture on pages 6–7. Now that you have finished the chapter, how would you change or add details to your answer to the question on the photograph?

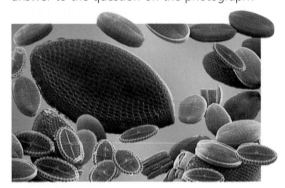

UNIT PROJECTS

If you are doing a unit project, make a folder for your project. Include in your folder a list of resources you will need, the date on which the project is due, and a schedule to track your progress. Begin gathering data.

Analyzing Data

The graph below shows growth rates of bacteria at different temperatures.

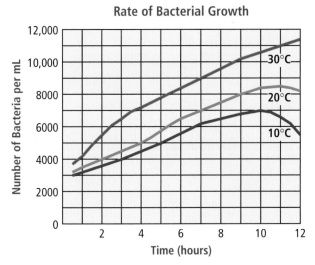

Rate of Bacterial Growth

Number of Bacteria per mL / Time (hours)

30°C
20°C
10°C

Choose the letter of the best answer.

1. At which temperature did growth of bacteria occur at the greatest rate?

a. 0°C   **c.** 20°C

b. 10°C   **d.** 30°C

2. Which statement is true about the growth rate of bacteria at 10°C?

a. Bacteria grew rapidly at first, then declined after 6 hours.

b. Bacteria growth increased at a steady rate.

c. Bacteria grew slowly, then declined rapidly after 8 hours.

d. Bacteria showed neither an increase nor decrease in growth rate.

3. What is the concentration of bacteria at a temperature of 20°C after 4 hours?

a. about 5000 per mL   **c.** about 7000 per mL

b. about 6000 per mL   **d.** about 8000 per mL

4. During which hour was the concentration of bacteria at 20°C the greatest?

a. hour 2   **c.** hour 6

b. hour 4   **d.** hour 8

5. Which conclusion can be drawn from the data in the graph?

a. The rate of bacterial growth is the greatest at the highest temperature.

b. The rate of bacterial growth is the least at the highest temperature.

c. The rate of bacterial growth is the greatest at the lowest temperature.

d. The rate of bacterial growth does not change depending on temperature.

6. How much did the rate of bacterial growth increase between 2 hours and 8 hours at 30°C?

a. 2000 per mL

b. 4000 per mL

c. 6000 per mL

d. 8000 per mL

Extended Response

7. A scientist wants to test the effect of temperature on the same bacteria shown in the graph at higher temperatures. The scientist tests the growth rate of bacteria at 50°C, 75°C, and 100°C. Based on the information in the graph and your knowledge of bacteria, what results might the scientist get? Explain your reasoning.

8. Antibiotics are drugs that are used to inhibit the growth of bacterial infections. A scientist wants to test the ability of three different antibiotics to control the growth of a certain type of bacteria. The scientist has isolated the bacteria in test tubes. Each antibiotic is prepared in a tablet form. Design an experiment that will test the effectiveness of the antibiotic tablets on the bacteria. Your experiment should include a hypothesis, a list of materials, a procedure, and a method of recording data.

CHAPTER

2 Introduction to Multicellular Organisms

the BIG idea

Multicellular organisms live in and get energy from a variety of environments.

How does an organism get energy and materials from its environment?

Key Concepts

SECTION

2.1 Multicellular organisms meet their needs in different ways.
Learn about specialized cells, tissues, and organs.

SECTION

2.2 Plants are producers.
Learn how plants get energy and respond to the environment.

SECTION

2.3 Animals are consumers.
Learn how animals get energy and how they interact with the environment.

SECTION

2.4 Most fungi are decomposers.
Learn about fungi and how they get energy.

Internet Preview

CLASSZONE.COM

Chapter 2 online resources: Content Review, Visualization, four Resource Centers, Math Tutorial, Test Practice

EXPLORE (the BIG idea)

Where Does It Come From?

Think about the things you use every day. Just like any other organism, you depend on the environment to meet your needs. The food you eat comes from plants and animals. Also, much of what you use is made of materials processed from living matter.

Observe and Think Identify three nonfood items you come into contact with every day. Where does the material for these products come from?

How Can a Multicellular Organism Reproduce on Its Own?

Take an old potato and cut it in half, making sure that there are eyes on both halves. Plant each half in a pot of soil. Water the pots once a day. After two weeks, remove the potato halves from the pots and examine.

Observe and Think What happened to the potato halves?

Internet Activity: Bee Dance

Go to **ClassZone.com** to explore how bees communicate.

Observe and Think What type of information can a bee communicate to other bees in a hive?

NSTA
scilinks.org

SCiLINKS

Animal Behavior **Code: MDL040**

Getting Ready to Learn

◄ CONCEPT REVIEW

- Living things are organized, grow, respond, and reproduce.
- Protists get energy in three different ways.
- Single-celled organisms reproduce when the cell divides.

◄ VOCABULARY REVIEW

kingdom p. 11
producer p. 19
decomposer p. 19
See Glossary for definitions.

adaptation, DNA, genetic material

 CONTENT REVIEW
CLASSZONE.COM
Review concepts and vocabulary.

▶ TAKING NOTES

MAIN IDEA AND DETAILS

Make a two-column chart. Write the main ideas, such as those in the blue headings, in the column on the left. Write details about each of those main ideas in the column on the right.

VOCABULARY STRATEGY

Write each new vocabulary term in the center of a **four square** diagram. Write notes in the squares around each term. Include a definition, some characteristics, and some examples of the term. If possible, write some things that are not examples of the term.

See the Note-Taking Handbook on pages R45–R51.

SCIENCE NOTEBOOK

MAIN IDEAS	DETAILS
Plants respond to their environment.	1. Plants respond to different stimuli. 2. A stimulus is something that produces a response.

Definition	Characteristics
Group of same type of cells performing similar functions	Cells are similar. Different tissues do different jobs.

TISSUE

Examples	Nonexamples
skin tissue nerve tissue muscle tissue	a simple cell

Multicellular organisms meet their needs in different ways.

◀ BEFORE, you learned	▶ NOW, you will learn
• Organisms get energy and materials from the environment • All organisms are organized, grow, respond, and reproduce • Differences in genetic material lead to diversity	• About the functions of cells in multicellular organisms • How multicellular organisms are adapted to different environments • About sexual reproduction

VOCABULARY

tissue p. 44
organ p. 44
sexual reproduction p. 48
meiosis p. 48
fertilization p. 48

THINK ABOUT

Why is teamwork important?

For any team to be successful, it is important for people to work well together. Within a team, each person has a different role. For example, the team in this restaurant includes people to greet diners and seat them, people to buy and cook the food, and people to take food orders and serve the food. By dividing different jobs among different people, a restaurant can serve more customers at the same time. What would happen in a large restaurant if the diners were seated, cooked for, and served by the same person?

Multicellular organisms have cells that are specialized.

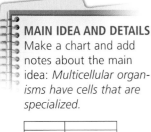

MAIN IDEA AND DETAILS
Make a chart and add notes about the main idea: *Multicellular organisms have cells that are specialized.*

In single-celled organisms, all the functions of life are performed by one cell. These functions include getting energy and materials, removing wastes, and responding to changes in the environment. In multicellular organisms, however, different jobs are done by different cells—the cells are specialized. A blood cell carries oxygen. A nerve cell sends or receives a signal. Just as the different jobs of running a restaurant are divided among different people, in multicellular organisms different functions are divided among different cells.

In this chapter, you will read about plants, animals, and fungi. These three kingdoms are made up almost entirely of multicellular organisms. The cells in multicellular organisms are organized in ways that enable them to survive and reproduce.

What are some advantages of specialization?

PROCEDURE

(1) Form into two teams, each representing an organism. The single-celled team will be made up of just one person; the multicellular team will be made up of three. Each team obtains a box of materials from the teacher.

(2) Each team must do the following tasks as quickly as possible: make a paper-clip chain, write the alphabet on both sides of one piece of paper, and make a paper airplane from the second piece of paper. The members of the three-person team must specialize, each person doing one task only.

WHAT DO YOU THINK?

- What are some advantages to having each person on the three-person team specialize in doing a different job?

- Why might time be a factor in the activities done by cells in a multicellular organism?

CHALLENGE Suppose the "life" of the multicellular team depended on the ability of one person to make a paper airplane. How would specialization be a disadvantage if that person were not at school?

SKILL FOCUS
Modeling

MATERIALS
- two boxes, each containing 20 paper clips, 2 pieces of paper, and 1 pencil

TIME
10 minutes

Levels of Organization

For any multicellular organism to survive, different cells must work together. The right type of cell must be in the right place to do the work that needs to be done.

Organization starts with the cell. Cells in multicellular organisms are specialized for a specific function. In animals, skin cells provide protection, nerve cells carry signals, and muscle cells produce movement. Cells of the same type are organized into **tissue,** a group of cells that work together. For example, what you think of as muscle is muscle tissue, made up of many muscle cells.

A structure that is made up of different tissues is called an **organ.** Organs have particular functions. The heart is an organ that functions as a pump. It has muscle tissue, which pumps the blood, and nerve tissue, which signals when to pump. Different organs that work together and have a common function are called an organ system. A heart and blood vessels are different organs that are both part of a circulatory system. These organs work together to deliver blood to all parts of a body. Together, cells, tissues, organs, and organ systems form an organism.

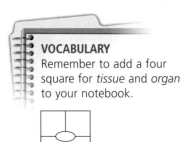

VOCABULARY
Remember to add a four square for *tissue* and *organ* to your notebook.

Organ Systems and the Organism

In almost all multicellular organisms, different organ systems take care of specific needs. Here are a few examples of organ systems found in many animals:

REMINDER

A system is a group of objects that interact, sharing energy and matter.

- nervous system enables a response to changing conditions
- muscular system produces movement and supplies heat
- respiratory system takes in oxygen and releases carbon dioxide
- circulatory system delivers oxygen and removes carbon dioxide
- digestive system breaks down food into a usable form

Organ systems allow multicellular organisms to obtain large amounts of energy, process large amounts of materials, respond to changes in the environment, and reproduce.

CHECK YOUR READING How are the functions of organ systems related to the needs of an organism? Give an example.

Different organ systems work together. For example, the respiratory system works with the circulatory system to deliver oxygen and remove carbon dioxide. When an animal such as a turtle breathes in, oxygen is brought into the lungs. Blood from the circulatory system picks up the oxygen, and the heart pumps the oxygen-rich blood out to the cells of the body. As oxygen is delivered, waste carbon dioxide is picked up. The blood is pumped back to the lungs. The carbon dioxide is released when the turtle breathes out. More oxygen is picked up when the turtle breathes in.

Organ Systems

Organ systems work together to meet the needs of an organism.

Blood vessels called **veins** return oxygen-poor blood to the lungs.

Each **lung** fills with air containing oxygen.

Blood vessels called **arteries** carry oxygen-rich blood to the body.

The **heart** pumps blood to the lungs.

Multicellular organisms are adapted to live in different environments.

All organisms have characteristics that allow them to survive in their environment. An adaptation is any inherited characteristic that increases the chance of an organism's surviving and producing offspring that also reproduce. An adaptation may have to do with the way an organism gets its energy or processes materials. An adaptation may relate to the shape or structure of an organism's body. An adaptation can even be a form of behavior.

CHECK YOUR READING The text above mentions different types of adaptations. Name three.

READING TiP

Offspring is a word used to describe the new organisms produced by reproduction in any organism. Think of it as meaning "to spring off."

When most multicellular organisms reproduce, the offspring are not exact copies of the parents. There are differences. If a particular difference gives an organism an advantage over other members in its group, then that difference is referred to as an adaptation. Over time, the organism and its offspring do better and reproduce more.

You are probably familiar with the furry animal called a fox. Different species of fox have different adaptations that enable them to survive in different environments. Here are three examples:

- **Fennec** The fennec is a desert fox. Its large ears are an adaptation that helps the fox keep cool in the hot desert. As blood flows through the vessels in each ear, heat is released. Another adaptation is the color of its fur, which blends in with the desert sand.

- **Arctic fox** The Arctic fox lives in the cold north. Its small ears, legs, and nose are adaptations that reduce the loss of heat from its body. Its bluish-gray summer fur is replaced by a thick coat of white fur as winter approaches. Its winter coat keeps the fox warm and enables it to blend in with the snow.

- **Red fox** The red fox is found in grasslands and woodlands. Its ears aren't as large as those of the fennec or as small as those of the Arctic fox. Its body fur is reddish brown tipped in white and black, coloring that helps it blend into its environment.

The diversity of life on Earth is due to the wide range of adaptations that have occurred in different species. An elephant has a trunk for grasping and sensing. A female kangaroo carries its young in a pouch. The largest flower in the world, the rafflesia flower, is almost a meter wide, blooms for just a few days, and smells like rotting meat.

Adaptations are the result of differences that can occur in genetic material. The way multicellular organisms reproduce allows for a mixing of genetic material. You will read about that next.

INFER The strong odor of the rafflesia flower attracts flies into the plant. How might this adaptation benefit the plant?

Adaptations in Different Environments

Fennec

Habitat: warm; Sahara Desert and Saudi Arabia

Size: about 40 cm (15 in.), 1.25 kg (2.7 lb)

large ears

light brown fur

Arctic Fox

Habitat: cold; Northern Eurasia and North America

Size: about 50 cm (20 in.), 4 kg (9 lb)

small ears

winter: thick white fur

summer: thin bluish-gray fur

Red Fox

Habitat: moderate; North and Central America, Eurasia

Size: about 65 cm (25 in.), 6 kg (13 lb)

ears of moderate size

reddish-brown fur

READING VISUALS Foxes are hunters that feed on small animals. How might the coat color of each fox contribute to its survival?

Sexual reproduction leads to diversity.

Most multicellular organisms reproduce sexually. In **sexual reproduction,** the genetic material of two parents comes together, and the resulting offspring have genetic material from both. Sexual reproduction leads to diversity because the DNA in the offspring is different from the DNA in the parents.

Two different cellular processes are involved in sexual reproduction. The first is **meiosis** (my-OH-sihs), a special form of cell division that produces sperm cells in a male and egg cells in a female. Each sperm or egg cell contains only one copy of DNA, the genetic material. Most cells contain two copies of DNA.

The second process in sexual reproduction is **fertilization.** Fertilization occurs when the sperm cell from the male parent combines with the egg cell from the female parent. A fertilized egg is a single cell with DNA from both parents. Once the egg is fertilized, it divides. One cell becomes two, two cells become four, and so on. As the cells divide, they start to specialize, and different tissues and organs form.

One copy of DNA in cell after meiosis

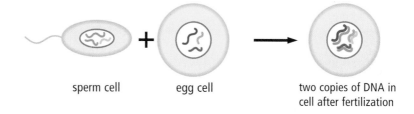

sperm cell   egg cell   two copies of DNA in cell after fertilization

Differences in genetic material and in the environment produce differences in offspring. Whether a tulip flower is red or yellow depends on the genetic material in its cells. How well the tulip grows depends on conditions in the environment as well as genetic materials.

eggs

buds

Sexual Reproduction The fertilized eggs of a sala-mander contain genetic material from two parents.

Asexual Reproduction The buds of a sea coral have the same genetic material as the parent.

Most reproduction that occurs in multicellular organisms is sexual reproduction. However, many multicellular organisms can reproduce by asexual reproduction. With asexual reproduction, a single parent produces offspring.

Budding is a form of asexual reproduction. In budding, a second organism grows off, or buds, from another. Organisms that reproduce asexually can reproduce more often. Asexual reproduction limits genetic diversity within a group because offspring have the same genetic material as the parent.

CHECK YOUR READING How do offspring produced by sexual reproduction compare with offspring produced by asexual reproduction?

With sexual reproduction, there is an opportunity for new combinations of characteristics to occur in the offspring. Perhaps these organisms process food more efficiently or reproduce more quickly. Or perhaps they have adaptations that allow them to survive a change in their environment. In the next three sections, you will read how plants, animals, and fungi have adapted to similar environments in very different ways.

2.1 Review

KEY CONCEPTS

1. How do specialized cells relate to the different levels of organization in a multicellular organism?

2. What is an adaptation? Give an example.

3. What two cellular processes are involved in sexual reproduction?

CRITICAL THINKING

4. **Compare and Contrast** How do the offspring produced by sexual reproduction compare to those produced by asexual reproduction?

5. **Predict** If fertilization occurred without meiosis, how many copies of DNA would be in the cells of the offspring?

CHALLENGE

6. **Synthesize** Do you consider the different levels of organization in a multicellular organism an adaptation? Explain your reasoning.

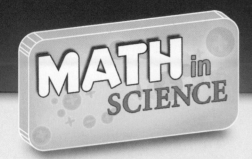

Making Data Visual

A circle graph is a good way to see part-to-whole relationships. To use data presented in a circle graph, do the following:

Example

Suppose, at a waterhole in a game preserve, researchers observed ten animals throughout the day. What fraction of the sightings were giraffes?

(1) The circle graph shows the data for the sightings. The whole circle represents the total sightings, 10.

(2) 3 of the 10 equal parts are shaded for giraffes.

(3) Write "3 out of 10" as a fraction $\frac{3}{10}$.

ANSWER Giraffes = $\frac{3}{10}$ of the sightings.

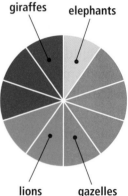

Answer the following questions.

1. What fraction of the sightings were lions?

2. What fraction of the sightings were gazelles?

3. Which animal did the researchers observe in greatest number?

4. Which animal did they observe in the least number? How many sightings occurred for that animal?

5. What fraction of the total does that animal represent?

6. If the researchers had seen one hundred animals, and the graph looked the same as it does, how many giraffe sightings would their graph represent?

CHALLENGE You also record the nighttime visitors: first, 2 young elephants; then a lioness with 2 thirsty cubs; then a giraffe, followed by a hyena and 3 gazelles. Calculate the fraction of the night's population that is represented by each type of animal. Use the fractions to draw a circle graph of the data on "Night Sightings at the Waterhole." Shade and label the graph with the types of animals.

KEY CONCEPT
2.2 Plants are producers.

 BEFORE, you learned

- Multicellular organisms have tissues, organs, and systems
- Organisms have adaptations that can make them suited to their environment
- Sexual reproduction leads to genetic diversity

 NOW, you will learn

- How plants obtain energy
- How plants store energy
- How plants respond to their environment

VOCABULARY

photosynthesis p. 52
autotroph p. 52
cellular respiration p. 53
stimulus p. 55

EXPLORE Stored Energy

In what form does a plant store energy?

PROCEDURE

1. Obtain pieces of potato, celery, and pear that have been placed in small plastic cups.

2. Place a few drops of the iodine solution onto the plant material in each cup. The iodine solution will turn dark blue in the presence of starch. It does not change color in the presence of sugar.

MATERIALS

- pieces of potato, celery, and pear
- 3 plastic cups
- iodine solution
- eye dropper

WHAT DO YOU THINK?

- Observing each sample, describe what happened to the color of the iodine solution after a few minutes.
- Starch and sugars are a source of energy for a plant. What do your observations suggest about how different plants store energy?

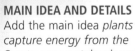
MAIN IDEA AND DETAILS
Add the main idea *plants capture energy from the Sun* to your notebook and fill in details on photosynthesis and stored energy.

Plants capture energy from the Sun.

If you stand outside on a warm, sunny day, you may see and feel energy from the Sun. Without the Sun's energy, Earth would be a cold, dark planet. The Sun's heat and light provide the energy almost all organisms need to live.

However, energy from the Sun cannot drive cell processes directly. Light energy must be changed into chemical energy. Chemical energy is the form of energy all organisms use to carry out the functions of life. Plants are an important part of the energy story because plants capture energy from the Sun and convert it to chemical energy.

 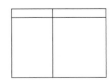

Producing Sugars

READING TiP

The roots for *photosynthesis* are *photo-,* which means "light," and *synthesis,* which means "to put together." Together they mean "put together by light."

Plants capture energy from sunlight and convert it to chemical energy through the process of **photosynthesis.** The plant takes in water and carbon dioxide from the environment and uses these simple materials to produce sugar, an energy-rich compound that contains carbon. Oxygen is also produced. Plants are referred to as producers because they produce energy-rich carbon compounds.

The cells, tissues, and organ systems in a plant work together to supply the materials needed for photosynthesis. Most photosynthesis takes place in the leaves. The leaves take in carbon dioxide from the air, and the stems support the leaves and hold them up toward the Sun. The roots of the plant anchor it in the soil and supply water. The sugars produced are used by the rest of the plant for energy and as materials for growth.

CHECK YOUR READING What is the product of photosynthesis?

Another name for a plant is **autotroph** (AW-tuh-TRAHF). Autotroph means self-feeder. Plants do not require food from other organisms. Plants will grow if they have energy from the Sun, carbon dioxide from the air, and water and nutrients from the soil.

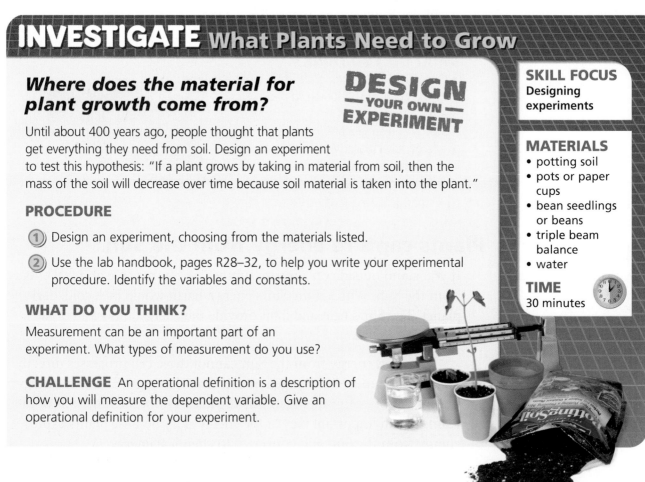

INVESTIGATE What Plants Need to Grow

Where does the material for plant growth come from?

DESIGN —YOUR OWN— EXPERIMENT

SKILL FOCUS
Designing experiments

Until about 400 years ago, people thought that plants get everything they need from soil. Design an experiment to test this hypothesis: "If a plant grows by taking in material from soil, then the mass of the soil will decrease over time because soil material is taken into the plant."

PROCEDURE

1. Design an experiment, choosing from the materials listed.

2. Use the lab handbook, pages R28–32, to help you write your experimental procedure. Identify the variables and constants.

WHAT DO YOU THINK?

Measurement can be an important part of an experiment. What types of measurement do you use?

CHALLENGE An operational definition is a description of how you will measure the dependent variable. Give an operational definition for your experiment.

MATERIALS
- potting soil
- pots or paper cups
- bean seedlings or beans
- triple beam balance
- water

TIME
30 minutes

Storing and Releasing Energy

Plants are not the only organisms that capture energy through photosynthesis. Algae and certain bacteria and protists also use photosynthesis. Plants are different from single-celled producers, however. Plants are multicellular organisms with parts of their bodies specialized for storing energy-rich material. Single-celled producers can store very little energy.

Only part of the energy captured by a plant is used as fuel for cellular processes. Some of the sugar produced is used as building material, enabling the plant to grow. The remaining sugar is stored. Often the sugars are stored as starches. Starch is an energy-rich compound made of many sugars. Starches can store a lot of chemical energy. When a plant needs energy, the starches are broken back down into sugars and energy is released. **Cellular respiration** is the process by which a cell uses oxygen to break down sugars to release the energy they hold.

Some plants, such as carrots and beets, store starch in their roots. Other plants, including celery and rhubarb, have stems adapted for storing starch. A potato is a swollen, underground stem called a tuber. Tubers have buds—the eyes of the potato—that can sprout into new plants. The starch stored in the tuber helps the new sprouts survive.

potato plant

tuber

plant cell

starch granules

 CHECK YOUR READING What is the original source of a plant's stored energy?

Plants are adapted to different environments.

Almost everywhere you look on land, you'll see plants. Leaves, stems, and roots are adaptations that enable plants, as producers, to live on land. Not all plants, however, look the same. Just as there are many different types of land environments, there are many different types of plants that have adapted to these environments.

Grasses are an example of plants that grow in several environments. Many grasses have deep roots, produce seeds quickly, and can grow in areas with a wide range of temperatures and different amounts of precipitation. Grasses can survive drought, fires, freezing temperatures, and grazing. As long as the roots of the plant survive, the grasses will grow again. Grasses are found in the Arctic tundra, as well as in temperate and tropical climates.

Now compare trees to grasses. If the leaves and stems of a tree die away because of fire or drought, often the plant will not survive. Because of their size, trees require a large amount of water for photosynthesis. A coniferous (koh-NIHF-uhr-uhs) tree, like the pine, does well in colder climates. It has needle-shaped leaves that stay green throughout the year, feeding the plant continually. A deciduous (dih-SIHJ-oo-uhs) tree, like the maple, loses its leaves when temperatures turn cold. The maple needs a long growing season and plenty of water for new leaves to grow.

Plants have reproductive adaptations. It may surprise you to learn that flowering plants living on cold, snowy mountaintops have something in common with desert plants. When rain falls in the desert, wildflower seeds sprout very quickly. Within a few weeks, the plants grow, flower, and produce new seeds that will be ready to sprout with the next rainy season. The same thing happens in the mountains, where the snow may thaw for only a few weeks every summer. Seeds sprout, flowers grow, and new seeds are produced—all before the snow returns. You will read more about plant reproduction in Chapter 3.

Some plants have adaptations that protect them. Plants in the mustard family give off odors that keep many plant-eating insects away. Other plants, such as poison ivy and poison oak, produce harmful chemicals. The nicotine in a tobacco plant is a poison that helps to keep the plant from being eaten.

CHECK YOUR READING Name two different types of adaptations plants have.

Some adaptations plants have relate to very specific needs. For example, the Venus flytrap is a plant that grows in areas where the soil lacks certain materials. The leaves of the Venus flytrap fold in the middle and have long teeth all around the edges. When an insect lands on an open leaf, the two sides of the leaf fold together. The teeth form a trap that prevents the captured insect from escaping. Fluids given off by the leaf digest the insect's body, providing materials the plant can't get from the soil.

RESOURCE CENTER
CLASSZONE.COM

Learn more about plant adaptations.

ANALYZE An insect provides nutrients that this Venus flytrap cannot get from the soil. Is this plant still a producer? Ask yourself where the plant gets its energy.

Gravity

Plant roots always grow downward and stems always grow upward. All plants respond to gravity as a stimulus.

Touch

The tendril of a climbing plant grows around a nearby object. The plant responds to touch as a stimulus.

Plants respond to their environment.

During a hot afternoon, parts of the flower known as the Mexican bird of paradise close. As the Sun goes down, the flower reopens. The plant is responding to a stimulus, in this case, sunlight. A **stimulus** is something that produces a response from an organism. Plants, like all organisms, respond to stimuli in their environment. This ability helps them to survive and grow.

VOCABULARY Make a four square for the term *stimulus* in your science notebook.

Gravity

Gravity is the force that keeps you bound to Earth and gives you a sense of up and down. All plants respond to gravity. They also have a sense of up and down—roots grow down and stems grow up. Suppose you place a young seedling on its side, so that its roots and stems stretch out to the side. In a very short time, the tip of the root will begin to turn down, and the tip of the stem will turn up.

Touch

Many plants also respond to touch as a stimulus. Peas, morning glories, tropical vines, and other climbing plants have special stems called tendrils. Tendrils respond to the touch of a nearby object. As the tendrils grow, they wrap around the object. The twining of tendrils around a fence or another plant helps raise a plant into the sunlight.

How Plants Respond to Light

Auxin, a hormone, is a chemical substance that stimulates cell growth and makes plant stems bend toward light.

1 The presence of sunlight stimulates the production of auxin at the tip of the stem.

2 Auxin moves to cells on the dark side of the plant.

3 Cells with high levels of auxin grow longer than other cells, causing the plant to bend.

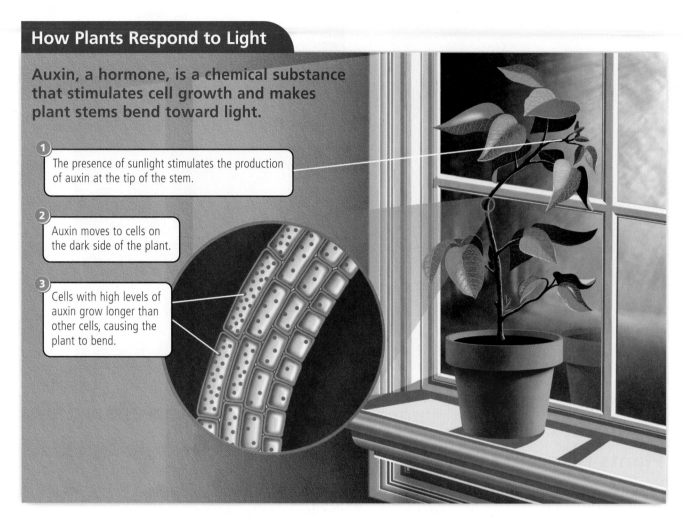

Light

READING TiP

The words *stimulus, stimuli,* and *stimulate* all have the same root, meaning "to provoke or encourage action."

VISUALIZATION
CLASSZONE.COM

Examine how plants respond to different stimuli.

Light is a powerful stimulus for plants. You can see that stems and leaves grow toward light by placing an indoor plant near a window. After several days, the tips of the stems start to bend toward the window. What happens if you turn the plant around so that those stems reach into the room? The stems will bend as they continue to grow, turning back toward the light.

Plants respond to light with the help of a hormone. A **hormone** is a chemical substance produced in one part of an organism and travels to a different part where it produces a reaction. Hormones act as chemical messengers. They allow an organism to respond to changes in its body or to changes in the environment around it.

Auxin (AWK-sihn), a plant hormone that stimulates cell growth, is produced at the tip of a plant stem. Auxin moves away from light. As a result, the cells on the darker side of a plant stem contain more auxin than those on the lighter side. Higher levels of auxin in plant cells on the darker side cause those cells to grow longer. The longer cells cause the plant stem to bend, moving the tip of the stem toward the light.

Plants respond to seasonal changes.

Most regions of the world go through seasonal changes every year. For example, during the summer in North America, temperatures rise and the days get longer. As winter approaches, temperatures go down and the days become shorter. These types of seasonal changes have an effect on plants.

For plants, a shorter period of daylight will affect the amount of sunlight available for photosynthesis. Shorter days cause many plants to go into a state of dormancy. When plants are dormant, they temporarily stop growing and so require less energy.

In temperate climates, the approach of winter causes the leaves of deciduous trees to die and drop to the ground. The trees enter a state of dormancy during which their growth is slowed. Other plants, such as wild cornflowers, do not survive the change. New cornflowers will grow the following season, from seeds left behind.

 CHECK YOUR READING What stimulus causes a deciduous plant to respond by dropping its leaves?

For many plants, reproduction is also affected by seasonal changes. For some plants, the amount of daylight is a factor. A few plants, such as rice and ragweed, produce flowers only in autumn or winter, when days are short. They are short-day plants. Long-day plants flower in late spring and summer, when days are long. Lettuce, spinach, and irises are long day-plants. You will read more about plants in Chapter 3.

2.2 Review

KEY CONCEPTS

1. What process makes a plant a producer, and what does a plant produce?

2. Name three stimuli that plants respond to, and give examples of how a plant responds.

3. How do seasonal changes affect plants? Give an example.

CRITICAL THINKING

4. **Give Examples** Give three examples of ways that plants are adapted to their environments. How do these adaptations benefit the plant?

● CHALLENGE

5. **Apply** Some experiments suggest that the hormone auxin is involved in the twining of tendrils. Use what you know about auxin to explain how it might cause tendrils to twine around anything they touch. Draw a diagram.

2.3 Animals are consumers.

◀ **BEFORE, you learned**

- Plants are producers
- Plants have adaptations for capturing and storing energy
- Plants respond to different stimuli

▶ **NOW, you will learn**

- How animals obtain energy
- How animals process food
- About different ways animals respond to their environment

VOCABULARY

consumer p. 58
heterotroph p. 58
behavior p. 62
predator p. 63
prey p. 63
migration p. 64
hibernation p. 64

THINK ABOUT

What can you tell from teeth?

Many animals have teeth. Teeth bite, grind, crush, and chew. A fox's sharp biting teeth capture small animals that it hunts on the run. A horse's teeth are flat and strong—for breaking down the grasses it eats. Run your tongue over your own teeth. How many different shapes do you notice? What can the shape of teeth suggest about the food an animal eats?

Animals obtain energy and materials from food.

You probably see nonhuman animals every day, whether you live in a rural area or a large city. If the animals are wild animals, not somebody's pet, then chances are that what you see these animals doing is moving about in search of food.

READING TiP

The meaning of *heterotroph* is opposite to that of *autotroph*. The root *hetero-* means "other." *Heterotroph* means "other-feeder," or "feeds on others."

Animals are consumers. A **consumer** is an organism that needs to get energy from another organism. Unlike plants, animals must consume food to get the energy and materials they need to survive. Animals are heterotrophs. A **heterotroph** (HEHT-uhr-uh-TRAHF) is an organism that feeds on, or consumes, other organisms. By definition, animals are, quite simply, multicellular organisms that have adaptations that allow them to take in and process food.

Obtaining Food

Food is a source of energy and materials for animals.

Simple feeding Some animals, such as corals, can filter food from their environment.

Complex feeding Many animals, such as bats, actively search for and capture food.

Animals need food. And animals have many different ways of getting it. For some animals, feeding is a relatively simple process. An adult coral simply filters food from the water as it moves through the coral's body. Most animals, however, must search for food. Grazing animals, such as horses, move along from one patch of grass to another. Other animals must capture food. Most bats use sound and hearing to detect the motion of insects flying at night. Its wings make the bat able to move through the air quickly and silently.

What Animals Eat

Just about any type of living or once-living material is a source of food for some animal. Animals can be grouped by the type of food they eat.

- Herbivores (HUR-buh-VAWRS) feed on plants or algae.
- Carnivores (KAHR-nuh-VAWRS) feed on other animals.
- Omnivores (AWM-nuh-VAWRS) feed on both plants and animals.

Another group are those animals that feed on the remains of once-living animals. Many insects do, as do some larger animals, such as vultures. Other animals, such as worms, act as decomposers.

 CHECK YOUR READING Describe how herbivores, carnivores, and omnivores get their energy.

MAIN IDEA AND DETAILS
Make a chart about the main idea: *Animals obtain energy and materials from food.* Include *herbivore, carnivore,* and *omnivore* in the details.

Different species of animals have adapted in different ways to take advantage of all the energy-rich material in the environment. To get energy and materials from food, all animals must first break the food down—that is, they must digest it.

Processing Food

RESOURCE CENTER
CLASSZONE.COM

Find out more about
animal adaptations.

Energy is stored in complex carbon compounds in food. For the cells
in an animal to make use of the energy and materials stored in this
food, the large complex compounds must be broken back down into
simpler compounds.

 CHECK YOUR READING How must food be changed so an animal gets energy?

Digestion is the process that breaks food down into pieces that are
small enough to be absorbed by cells. A few animals, such as sponges,
are able to take food particles directly into their cells. Most animals,
however, take the food into an area of their body where the materials
are broken down. Cells absorb the materials they need. Animals such
as jellyfish have a single opening in their bodies where food is brought
into a central cavity, or gut. The unused materials are released through
the same opening.

A digestive system uses both physical and chemical activity to
break down food. Many animals have a tubelike digestive system.
Food is brought in at one end of the animal, the mouth, and waste is
released at the other end. As food moves through the system, it is
continually broken down, releasing necessary materials called
nutrients to the cells.

INVESTIGATE Owl Pellets

What does an owl eat, and how well does it digest its food?

PROCEDURE

1. Get an owl pellet from your teacher. Open the foil and place the pellet in a tray.

2. Use a needle tool and tweezers to sort through the materials in the pellet and separate them.

3. When you have finished, dispose of the materials according to your teacher's instructions, and wash your hands.

WHAT DO YOU THINK?

- What can you tell about what an owl eats from looking at the remains in the pellet?

- What materials are not digested?

CHALLENGE Use the bone identification key to identify what the owl ate.

SKILL FOCUS
Inferring

MATERIALS
- owl pellet
- needle tool
- tweezers
- tray
- *for Challenge:* bone identification key

TIME
30 minutes

Obtaining Oxygen

Animals need oxygen to release the energy in food.

Grasshopper

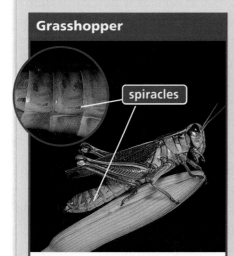

spiracles

Most insects take in oxygen through body openings called spiracles.

Bass

gills

Fish have gills, which pick up dissolved oxygen as water flows over them.

Tiger

lungs

This yawning tiger, like many animals, gets oxygen by inhaling air into its lungs.

Releasing and Storing Energy

Animals obtain energy from sugars and other carbon compounds the same way plants do, through the process of cellular respiration. As you read in Section 2.2, cellular respiration is a process in which energy is released when sugars are broken down inside a cell. The process requires both oxygen and water.

 CHECK YOUR READING   What is the function of cellular respiration?

Many animals take in water in the same way they take in food, through the digestive system. Oxygen, however, is often taken in through a respiratory system. In many animals, the respiratory system delivers oxygen to the blood, and the blood carries oxygen to the cells.

Animals have different structures for obtaining oxygen. Many insects take in oxygen through spiracles, tiny openings in their bodies. Fish have gills, structures that allow them to pick up oxygen dissolved in the water. Other air-breathing animals take in oxygen through organs called lungs.

Most animals do not feed continuously, so they need to be able to store materials from food in their tissues or organs. Many animals, including humans, take in large amounts of food at one time. This gives an animal time to do other activities, such as caring for young or looking for more food.

Animals interact with the environment and with other organisms.

Animals, as consumers, must obtain food, as well as water, from their environment. An animal's body has many adaptations that allow it to process food. These can include digestive, respiratory, and circulatory systems. Also important are the systems that allow animals to interact with their environment to obtain food. In many animals, muscle and skeletal systems provide movement and support. A nervous system allows the animal to sense and respond to stimuli.

Animals respond to many different types of stimuli. They respond to sights, sounds, odors, light, or a change in temperature. They respond to hunger and thirst. They also respond to other animals. Any observable response to a stimulus is described as a **behavior.** A bird's drinking water from a puddle is a behavior. A lion's chasing an antelope is a behavior, just as the antelope's running to escape the lion is a behavior.

CHECK YOUR READING   What is a behavior and how does it relate to a stimulus?

Some behaviors are inherited, which means they are present at birth. For example, a spider can weave a web without being shown. Other behaviors are learned. For example, the young lion in the photograph learns that a porcupine is not a good source of food.

All behaviors fall into one of three general categories:

- individual behaviors
- interactions between animals of the same species
- interactions between animals of different species

ANALYZE Do you consider the defensive behavior of a porcupine an adaptation?

Individual behaviors often involve meeting basic needs. Animals must find food, water, and shelter. They sleep. They groom themselves. Animals also respond to changes in their environment. A lizard may warm itself in the morning sunlight and then move into the shade when the Sun is high in the sky.

Interactions that occur between animals of the same species are often described as social behaviors. Basic social behaviors include those between parents and offspring and behaviors for attracting a mate. Within a group, animals of the same species may cooperate by working together. Wolves hunt in packs and bees maintain a hive. Behaviors among animals of the same species can also be competitive. Animals often compete for a mate or territory.

 CHECK YOUR READING What are some ways that animals of the same species cooperate and compete?

For macaques, grooming is both an individual and a social behavior. Here a mother grooms her young.

Interactions that occur between animals of different species often involve the search for food. A **predator** is an animal that hunts other animals for food. Predators have behaviors that allow them to search for and capture other organisms. A cheetah first stalks an antelope, then chases it down, moving as fast as 110 kilometers per hour.

An animal that is hunted by another animal as a source of food is the **prey.** Behaviors of prey animals often allow them to escape a predator. An antelope may not be able to outrun a cheetah, but antelopes move in herds. This provides protection for the group since a cheetah will kill only one animal. Other animals, such as the pufferfish and porcupine, have defensive behaviors and structures.

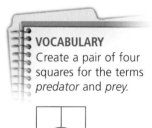

unthreatened pufferfish

threatened pufferfish

Animals of different species can also interact in cooperative ways. Tickbirds remove ticks from the skin of an impala. This behavior provides food for the bird and provides relief for the impala. Sometimes animals take advantage of the behavior of other animals. Many animals eat the remains of prey left over after a predator has finished feeding.

Animals respond to seasonal changes.

Animals, like plants, are affected by seasonal changes in their environment. Certain types of food may not be available all year round. A region might go through periods of drought. Some animals do not do well in extreme heat or cold. Unlike plants, animals can respond to seasonal changes by changing their location. **Migration** is the movement of animals to a different region in response to changes in the environment.

monarch butterfly

Each spring, millions of monarch butterflies begin to fly north from Mexico and parts of southern California. As they migrate, the females lay eggs among milkweed plants. This new generation, when it matures, will continue to travel north, moving into the northern United States and parts of Canada. This second generation of monarchs also lays eggs. Monarchs cannot survive the winter temperatures of the north, so the butterflies make the long journey back to Mexico and California in the fall. These butterflies are a different generation from the butterflies that migrated from the south. This suggests their behavior is inherited, not learned. The fall migration route is shown on the map.

Not all animals migrate in response to seasonal changes. Many nonmigratory animals do change their behaviors, however. For example, when winter cold reduces the food supply, some animals hibernate. **Hibernation** is a sleeplike state that lasts for an extended time period. The body systems of a hibernating animal slow down, so the animal needs less energy to survive. Many animals, including frogs, turtles, fish, and some types of insects, hibernate. You will learn more about different types of animals in Chapters 4 and 5.

Monarch butterflies migrate each winter to California and Mexico.

2.3 Review

KEY CONCEPTS

1. In what way are animals consumers?

2. Name three body systems that relate to how an animal gets its energy.

3. What is a behavior?

CRITICAL THINKING

4. **Give Examples** Identify three categories of animal behavior and give an example of each.

5. **Analyze** How is migration similar to hibernation? How is it different?

⬤ CHALLENGE

6. **Analyze** Scientists often look at feeding patterns as a flow of energy through the living parts of the environment. Describe the flow of energy as it relates to plants, herbivores, and carnivores.

WILDLIFE PHOTOGRAPHER

An Animal's World

Have you ever watched a TV documentary, or flipped through the pages of a magazine and wondered, "How did the photographer ever get that picture?" For a wildlife photographer, understanding animal biology is essential.

Cover and Protection

Photographers use camera traps and blinds. A blind, made of branches, is built upwind of an animal gathering place. Steve Winter has built camera traps, where a hidden camera emits a beam of light when an animal steps into it.

Habitat

Certain habitats—such as snow and cold, swamp and mud, or sea water—present challenges to a person with a camera. Underwater photographers need to use scuba gear to swim with animals like the Caribbean reef shark.

Behavior

To photograph an endangered species like the jaguar, a photographer must learn animal behavior. Steve Winter and a team of scientists used dogs with keen scent-tracking to find jaguars who are active mostly at night. They learned that jaguars have a favorite scratching tree for claw sharpening—perfect photo opportunity!

EXPLORE

1. **OBSERVE** With or without a camera, find a spot where you are likely to find wildlife. Sit as still as possible and wait. What animals do you observe? What do they do?

2. **CHALLENGE** Interview a photographer about digital photography, and ask how technology is changing photography.

Most fungi are decomposers.

BEFORE, you learned	NOW, you will learn
• Plants and animals interact with the environment • Plants transform sunlight into chemical energy • Animals get energy by eating other organisms	• How fungi get energy and materials • About different types of fungi • How fungi interact with other organisms

VOCABULARY

hyphae p. 67
spore p. 67
lichen p. 70

EXPLORE Mushrooms

What does a mushroom cap contain?

PROCEDURE

1. Carefully cut the stem away from the mushroom cap, as near the cap as possible.

2. Place the mushroom cap on white paper and cover it with a plastic cup. Leave overnight.

3. Carefully remove the cup and lift the mushroom cap straight up.

4. Use a hand lens to examine the mushroom cap and the print it leaves behind.

WHAT DO YOU THINK?

• How does the pattern in the mushroom cap compare with the mushroom print?
• What made the print?

MATERIALS

• fresh store-bought mushrooms
• sharp knife
• clear plastic cup
• paper
• hand lens

Fungi absorb materials from the environment.

MAIN IDEA AND DETAILS
Don't forget to make a main idea chart with detail notes on the main idea: *Fungi absorb materials from the environment.*

Plants are producers; they capture energy from the Sun and build complex carbon compounds. Animals are consumers; they take in complex carbon compounds and use them for energy and materials. Fungi (FUHN-jy), at least most fungi, are decomposers. Fungi break down, or decompose, the complex carbon compounds that are part of living matter. They absorb nutrients and leave behind simpler compounds.

Fungi are heterotrophs. They get their energy from living or once-living matter. They, along with bacteria, decompose the bodies of dead plants and animals. They also decompose materials left behind by organisms, such as fallen leaves, shed skin, and animal droppings.

Characteristics of Fungi

Except for yeasts, most fungi are multicellular. The cells of a fungus have a nucleus and a thick cell wall, which provides support. Fungi are different from plants and animals in their organization. Plants and animals have specialized cells, which are usually organized into tissues and organs. Multicellular fungi don't have tissues or organs. Instead, a typical fungus is made up of a reproductive body and network of cells that form threadlike structures called **hyphae** (HY-fee).

A mass of hyphae, like the one shown in the diagram below, is called a mycelium (my-SEE-lee-uhm). The hyphae are just one cell thick. This means the cells in the mycelium are close to the soil or whatever substance the fungus is living in. The cells release chemicals that digest the materials around them, and then absorb the nutrients they need. As hyphae grow, openings can form between the older cells and the new ones. This allows nutrients to flow back to the older cells, resulting in what seems like one huge cell with many nuclei.

READING TiP

The root of the word *hyphae* means "web." Look at the diagram below to see their weblike appearance.

Reproduction

Fungi reproduce with spores, which can be produced either asexually or sexually. A **spore** is a single reproductive cell that is capable of growing into a new organism. The mushrooms that you buy at the store are the spore-producing structures of certain types of fungi. These spore-producing structures are reproductive bodies of mushrooms. A single mushroom can produce a billion spores.

Parts of a Fungus

The mycelium makes up a large part of a multicellular fungus.

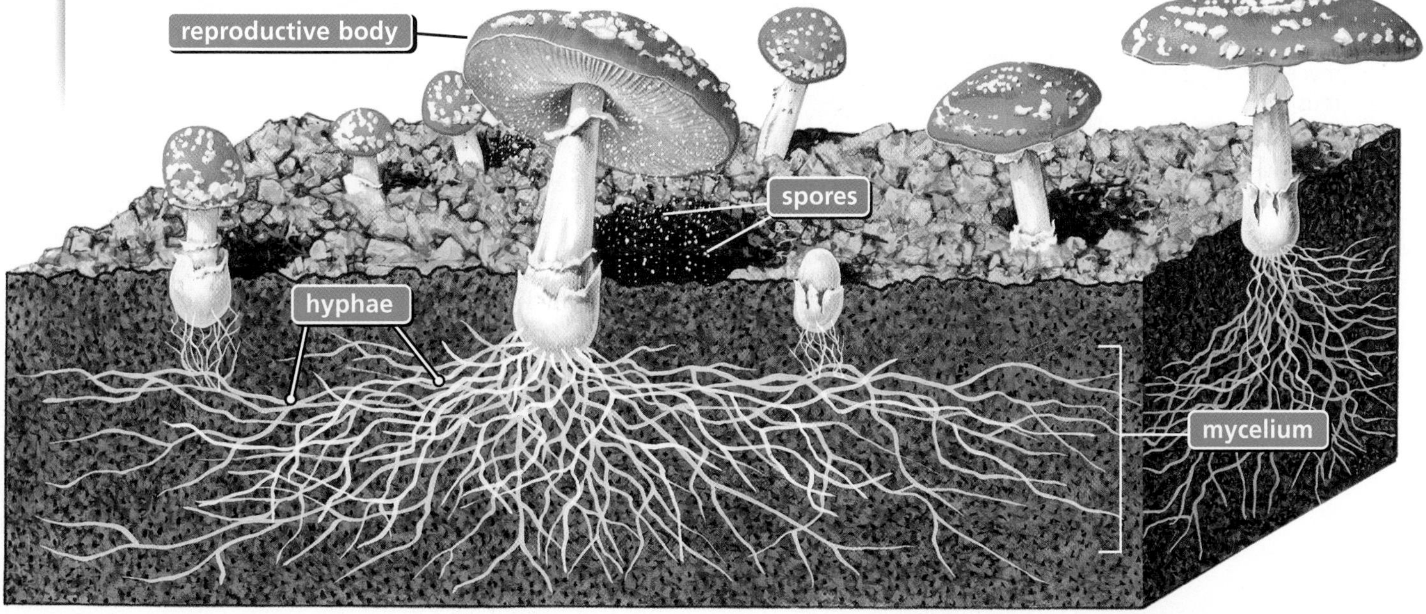

reproductive body

spores

hyphae

mycelium

Learn more about different types of fungi.

Spores are released into the air and spread by the wind. Because they're so small and light, the wind can carry spores long distances. Scientists have found spores 160 kilometers above Earth's surface. Some spores have a tough outer covering that keeps the reproductive cell from drying out. Such spores can survive for many years. If the parent fungus dies, the spores may remain and grow when conditions are right.

Fungi reproduce in other ways. For example, a multicellular fungi can reproduce asexually when hyphae break off and form a new mycelium. Yeasts, which are single-celled fungi, reproduce asexually by simple cell division or by budding. Yeasts can also produce spores.

Fungi include mushrooms, molds, and yeasts.

A convenient and simple way to study fungi is to look at their forms. They are mushrooms, molds, and yeasts. You are probably familiar with all of them. The mushrooms on your pizza are a fungus. So is the mold that grows if you leave a piece of pizza too long in the refrigerator. The crust of the pizza itself rises because of the activity of yeast.

Mushrooms

What we call a mushroom is only a small part of a fungus. A single mushroom you buy in the store could have grown from a mycelium that fills an area 30 meters across. When you see a patch of mushrooms, they are probably all part of a single fungus.

For humans, some mushrooms are edible and some are poisonous. A toadstool is a poisonous mushroom. The cap of a mushroom is where the spores are produced. Both the cap and the stalk it grows on are filled with hyphae.

 What is produced in a mushroom cap?

Molds

What we call mold, that fuzzy growth we sometimes see on food, is the spore-producing part of another form of fungus. The hyphae of the mold grow into the food, digesting it as they grow. Not all food molds are bad. Different species of the fungus *Penicillium* are used in the production of Brie, Camembert, and blue cheeses. Some species of the *Aspergillus* fungus are used to make soy sauce.

One interesting application of a mold is the use of the fungus *Trichoderma*. This mold grows in soil. The digestive chemicals it produces are used to give blue jeans a stonewashed look.

INFER Where is the mycelium of these mushrooms?

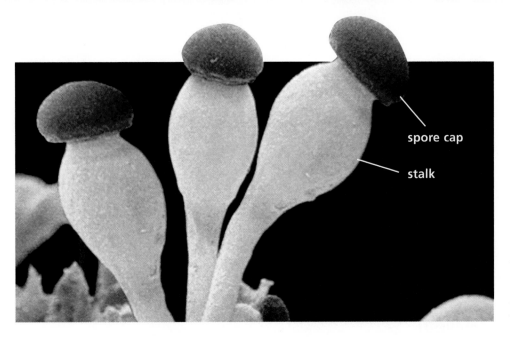

Pilobolus reacts to sunlight as a stimulus. The bend in the stalk will cause the spore cap to fly off.

Many molds cause disease. Fungal molds cause athlete's foot. Molds also affect plants. They are the cause of Dutch elm disease and the powdery white mildews that grow on plants. Compounds made from molds are also used to treat disease. Penicillin is an antibiotic that comes from the *Penicillium* fungus. It is used to fight bacterial diseases, such as pneumonia.

Molds reproduce with spores, which are typically carried by moving air. The "hat thrower" fungus *Pilobolus*, however, has an interesting adaptation for spreading spores. *Pilobolus* grows in animal droppings. It has a spore-containing cap—its hat—that grows on top of a stalk. The stalk responds to light as a stimulus and bends toward the Sun. As the stalk bends, water pressure builds up, causing the spore cap to shoot off, like a tiny cannonball. A spore cap can be thrown up to two meters away. If the spore caps land in grass, then cows and other grazing animals will eat the caps as they graze. A new cycle begins, with more *Pilobolus* being dispersed in the animal's droppings.

Yeasts

Yeasts are single-celled fungi. Some species of fungi exist in both yeast form and as multicellular hyphae. Yeasts grow in many moist environments, including the sap of plants and animal tissues. They also grow on moist surfaces, including shower curtains. Certain yeasts grow naturally on human skin. If the yeast begins to reproduce too rapidly, it can cause disease.

Yeasts are used in many food products. The activity of yeast cells breaking down sugars is what makes bread rise. The genetic material of the yeast *Saccharomyces cerevisiae* has been carefully studied by scientists. The study of this organism has helped scientists understand how genetic material controls the activities of a cell.

Yeasts are single-celled fungi.

Fungi can be helpful or harmful to other organisms.

Fungi have a close relationship to the environment and all living things in the environment. Fungi, along with bacteria, function as the main decomposers on Earth. The digestive chemicals that fungi release break down the complex compounds that come from living matter, dead matter, or the waste an organism leaves behind. A fungus absorbs what it needs to live and leaves behind simpler compounds and nutrients. These are then picked up again by plants, as producers, to start the cycle over again. Fungi also live in the sea, recycling materials for ocean-living organisms.

CHECK YOUR READING What beneficial role do fungi play in the environment?

The threadlike hyphae of a fungus can grow into and decompose the material produced by another organism. This means that fungi can be helpful, for example, by releasing the nutrients in a dead tree back into the soil. Or fungi can be harmful, for example, attacking the tissues of a plant, such as the Dutch elm.

Most plants interact with fungi in a way that is helpful. The hyphae surround the plant roots, providing nutrients for the plant. The plant provides food for the fungus. Some fungi live together with single-celled algae, a network referred to as a **lichen** (LY-kuhn). The hyphae form almost a sandwich around the algae, which produce sugars and other nutrients the fungus needs.

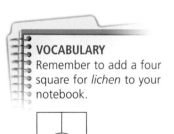

VOCABULARY
Remember to add a four square for *lichen* to your notebook.

Lichen

A lichen is formed by a close association between algae and fungi.

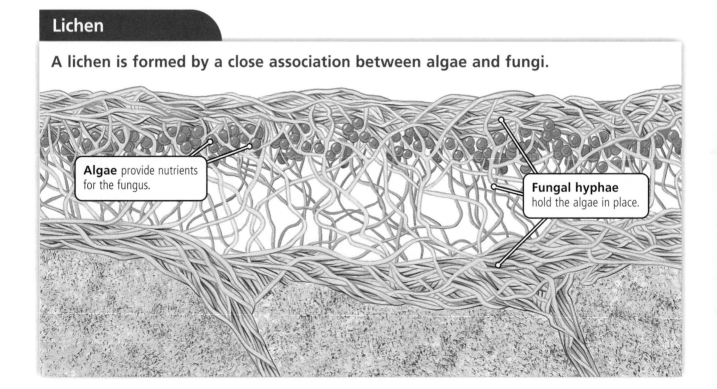

Algae provide nutrients for the fungus.

Fungal hyphae hold the algae in place.

Lichens can live just about anywhere. Lichens are found in the Arctic and in the desert. They can even grow on bare rock. The hyphae can break the rock down, slowly, and capture the particles of newly formed soil. This eventually prepares the ground for new plant growth.

On the harmful side, many fungi produce toxins, harmful chemicals. In 1845, a fungus infected Ireland's potato crop, causing the population of Ireland to drop from 8 million to about 4 million. Many people died from disease. Others died from starvation because of the loss of the important food crop. And hundreds of thousands of Irish left Ireland, many emigrating to the United States. Today, several fungal diseases are spreading through the worlds banana crops.

 CHECK YOUR READING Name some ways fungi can be harmful to organisms.

The toxic quality of a fungus can be put to good use, as in the case of the antibiotic penicillin. The photographs show what happens when a bacterium comes in contact with penicillin. The antibiotic prevents the bacterial cells from making new cell walls when they divide. This causes the cells to break open and the bacteria to die.

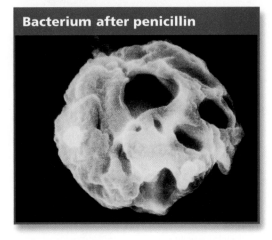

Bacterium before penicillin

Bacterium after penicillin

Penicillin is an antibiotic drug made from compounds taken from a species of the *Penicillium* fungus.

2.4 Review

KEY CONCEPTS

1. Describe the structure of a fungus.
2. How do fungi reproduce?
3. Describe two relationships between fungi and other organisms.

CRITICAL THINKING

4. **Analyze** Scientists used to classify fungi as plants. Today, scientists say that fungi are more like animals than plants. How are fungi like plants? How are they like animals?
5. **Predict** What might change in an environment where there were no fungi?

⬥ CHALLENGE

6. **Connect** Think of at least one way your life is affected by fungi in each of their three main forms: mushrooms, molds, and yeast. Are these effects beneficial or harmful to you?

CHAPTER INVESTIGATION

What Do Yeast Cells Use for Energy?

OVERVIEW AND PURPOSE Yeasts are tiny one-celled fungi that require food, water, and a warm place to grow. When they have a food source, they release carbon dioxide gas as a waste product. Yeast is used to make foods such as bread. In this activity, you will
- observe the activity of yeast
- draw conclusions about the effect of three materials on the activity of yeast

▶ **Problem**

How do sugar, salt, and sweetener affect the growth of yeast?

▶ **Hypothesize**

Write a hypothesis to explain how sugar, sweetener, and salt affect the activity of yeast in bread dough. Your hypothesis should take the form of an "If . . ., then . . ., because . . ." statement.

▶ **Procedure**

1. Make a data table like the one shown on page 73. Label four sheets of notebook paper *A, B, C,* and *D.*

2. Spread a very thin layer of flour over the baking sheet. Measure $\frac{1}{4}$ cup of flour and place it on the baking sheet as a mound. Repeat three times, forming separate mounds. Label the mounds *A, B, C,* and *D.*

MATERIALS
- baking sheet
- flour
- measuring cups
- measuring spoons
- sugar
- artificial sweetener
- salt
- quick-rise yeast
- warm water
- metric ruler
- marker
- clothespins
- clear plastic straws

3 Add 3 teaspoons of sugar to mound A. Add 3 tsp of sweetener to mound B. Add 3 tsp of salt to mound C. Add nothing to mound D.

4 Add $\frac{1}{4}$ tsp of the quick-rise yeast to each of the mounds. Slowly add 1 tsp of warm water to each mound to moisten the mixture. Spread a pinch of flour over your hands and knead the mounds by hand. Add water, 1 tsp at a time until the mixture has the consistency of dough. If the mixture gets too sticky, add more flour. Knead well and form each mound into a ball. Wash your hands thoroughly when you are finished. Do not taste or eat the dough.

5 Push 2 straws into each ball of dough, making sure the dough reaches at least 3 cm into the straws.

step 5

6 Squeeze the end of each straw to push the dough from the ends. Place a clothespin on the end of each straw closest to the dough. Fold and tape the other end. Mark both edges of the dough on the straw. Stand each straw upright on the appropriate piece of paper labeled *A, B, C,* or *D.*

step 6

7 Predict which mounds of dough will rise after 30 minutes. Write down your predictions in the data table.

8 After 30 minutes, measure the amount the dough has risen in each straw. Write down the results in the data table.

▶ **Observe and Analyze**

1. **OBSERVE** In which mounds did the dough rise?

2. **OBSERVE** Did any of the remaining mounds of dough change? Explain.

3. **INFER** What was the purpose of using two straws for each of the mounds?

▶ **Conclude**

1. **INTERPRET** Which is the most likely source of energy for yeast: salt, sugar, or sweetener? How do you know?

2. **INTERPRET** Compare your results with your hypothesis. How does your data support or disprove your hypothesis?

3. **LIMITATIONS** What limitations or sources of error could have affected your results?

4. **CONNECT** How would you account for the air spaces that are found in some breads?

5. **APPLY** Would you predict that breads made without yeast contain air spaces?

▶ **INVESTIGATE Further**

CHALLENGE Design an experiment in which you can observe the production of carbon dioxide by yeast.

What Do Yeast Cells Use for Energy?

Table 1. Observations of Dough Rising

Mound	Prediction	Results
A. sugar and yeast		
B. sweetener and yeast		
C. salt and yeast		
D. yeast		

the **BIG** idea

Multicellular organisms live in and get energy from a variety of environments.

◀ KEY CONCEPTS SUMMARY

 2.1 Multicellular organisms have many ways of meeting their needs.

- The bodies of multicellular organisms have different levels of organization.
- Multicellular organisms have a wide range of adaptations.
- Multicellular organisms reproduce by sexual reproduction. Some also reproduce asexually.

VOCABULARY
tissue p. 44
organ p. 44
sexual reproduction p. 48
meiosis p. 48
fertilization p. 48

2.2 Plants are producers.

Plants capture energy from the Sun and store it as sugar and starch. Plants are adapted to many environments. They respond to stimuli in the environment.

VOCABULARY
autotroph p. 52
photosynthesis p. 52
cellular respiration p. 53
stimulus p. 55

 2.3 Animals are consumers.

Animals consume food to get energy and materials. Animals are adapted to many enviroments. They interact with the environment and with other organisms.

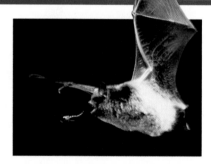

VOCABULARY
consumer p. 58
heterotroph p. 58
behavior p. 62
predator p. 63
prey p. 64
migration p. 64
hibernation p. 64

2.4 Most fungi are decomposers.

Fungi absorb energy from their surroundings. Fungi include mushrooms, molds, and yeasts. They affect people and other organisms in both helpful and harmful ways.

VOCABULARY
hyphae p. 67
spore p. 67
lichen p. 70

Reviewing Vocabulary

Draw a Venn diagram for each pair of terms. Put at least one shared characteristic in the overlap area, and put at least one difference in the outer circles.

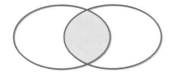

1. tissue, organ
2. autotroph, heterotroph
3. photosynthesis, cellular respiration
4. predator, prey
5. producer, consumer
6. migration, hibernation

Reviewing Key Concepts

Multiple Choice *Choose the letter of the best answer.*

7. Which body system transports materials such as nutrients and oxygen throughout an animal's body?
   a. respiratory system
   b. circulatory system
   c. digestive system
   d. nervous system

8. An example of an adaptation is
   a. a change in climate that increases plant growth
   b. the movement of a group of animals to an area that has more food and water
   c. a change in location of a squirrel's nest
   d. the ability of a plant to resist fungal disease better than other plants

9. Plants capture the Sun's energy through which process?
   a. reproduction   **c.** photosynthesis
   b. cellular respiration   **d.** digestion

10. Plants produce auxin in response to which stimulus?
    a. light
    b. gravity
    c. temperature
    d. touch

11. A plant is best described as
    a. a herbivore
    b. an omnivore
    c. a carnivore
    d. a producer

12. A carnivore is best described as an animal that
    a. eats plants
    b. eats plants and other animals
    c. eats other animals
    d. makes its own food

13. Mushrooms produce
    a. spores
    b. buds
    c. mold
    d. yeast

14. Fungi and algae together form
    a. hyphae
    b. mushrooms
    c. lichen
    d. mold

Short Answer *Write a short answer to each question.*

15. Write a short paragraph comparing sexual reproduction with asexual reproduction. How are they the same? How are they different?

16. Write a short paragraph to explain how the sugars and starches stored in plant tissue are important to the survival of animals.

17. Write a short paragraph to explain how fungi are dependent on plants and animals for their energy.

Thinking Critically

The diagram below shows a woodland food web. Each arrow starts with a food source and points to a consumer. Use the diagram to answer the next six questions.

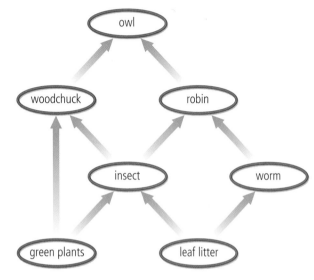

18. ANALYZE What is the original source of energy for all the animals in the food web? Explain your reasoning.

19. CLASSIFY Identify the consumers in this food web.

20. CLASSIFY Identify the animals in the food web as either herbivores, carnivores, omnivores, or decomposers.

21. EVALUATE Does an omnivore have an advantage over carnivores and herbivores in finding food?

22. ANALYZE What role does the worm play in the food web, and why it is important?

23. PREDICT How might this food web change over the course of a year, and how would that affect the feeding activity of animals in the food web?

24. CONNECT A woodchuck is sometimes referred to as a groundhog. Many people celebrate February 2 as groundhog day. The legend is that if a groundhog emerges from its burrow on this day and sees its shadow, then there will be six more weeks of winter. The groundhog is emerging from a long sleeplike state. What is this behavior, and how does it benefit the animal?

25. ANALYZE Do you think the defensive behavior of a porcupine or pufferfish is an adaptation? Explain your reasoning.

26. SYNTHESIZE A plant responds to gravity, touch, and light as stimuli. How does this relate to a plant being a producer?

27. SYNTHESIZE How are the cells of multicellular organisms like those of single-celled organisms? How are they different?

28. ANALYZE What quality of asexual reproduction makes a fungal disease spread so quickly.

the BIG idea

29. SYNTHESIZE Look again at the photograph on pages 40–41. Plants, animals, and fungi are pictured there. How do these organisms get energy and materials from the environment?

30. SUMMARIZE Write a short paragraph to describe how matter and energy move between members of the kingdoms of plants, animals, and fungi. Use the words in the box below. Underline the terms in your answer.

photosysnthesis	consumer
producer	decomposer

UNIT PROJECTS

By now you should have completed the following items for your unit project.

- questions that you have asked about the topic
- schedule showing when you will complete each step of your project
- list of resources including Web sites, print resources, and materials

Interpreting Diagrams

The diagram shows the feeding relationships between certain animals and plants in a forest environment. The size of the bars represent the relative numbers of each organism. The arrow shows the flow of energy between these groups of organisms.

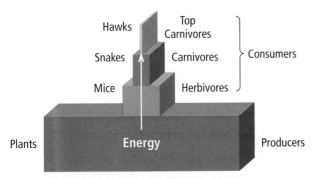

Feeding Relationships Among Plants and Animals

Use the diagram to answer the questions below.

1. Which is the largest group of organisms in the forest?

  a. plants

  b. mice

  c. snakes

  d. hawks

2. Most energy in the forest comes from

  a. top carnivores

  b. carnivores

  c. herbivores

  d. plants

3. Which description best fits the snake?

  a. a producer that feeds upon mice

  b. a consumer that is eaten by mice

  c. a consumer that feeds upon mice

  d. a consumer that feeds upon plants

4. A hawk is a top carnivore that feeds upon both snakes and mice. Which of the following best describes a top carnivore?

  a. a carnivore that feeds upon other carnivores

  b. a carnivore that feeds upon both carnivores and herbivores

  c. a consumer that gets its energy from producers

  d. a producer that supplies energy to consumers

5. Which statement best summarizes the diagram?

  a. The energy in a forest environment flows one way, from producers to consumers.

  b. Consumers don't need as much energy as producers.

  c. Energy in a forest environment goes from plants to animals and then back to plants.

  d. The number of producers depends on the number of consumers.

Extended Response

6 The diagram above shows the amount of energy available at each level of a forest environment. Describe what happens to the amount of energy going from the producer level into the different levels of consumers. Based on the diagram, not all the energy produced at a given level is available to organisms in the next level. What has happened to that energy? Use the words in the word box in your answer. Underline the words.

producer	energy
consumer	food

7. How would the number of plants, snakes, and hawks be affected if some disease were to reduce the numbers of mice in the forest?

TIMELINES in Science

DISCOVERIES IN Biodiversity

Scientists have discovered new species in the treetops of tropical forests and in the crannies of coral reefs. The quest to catalog the types and numbers of living things, the biodiversity of Earth, began in the late 1600s. A wave of naturalists set sail from Europe to the Americas and to Africa to find specimens of living things.

In the late 19th century, biologists reached agreement on a system for naming and classifying each new species. The mid-20th century brought an understanding of DNA and how it could be used to compare one species with another. Now new organisms could be pinpointed with precision. To this day, millions of undiscovered species lie deep in the unexplored ocean, in tropical forests, and even in heavily trafficked U.S. cities. A large concentration of Earth's known species now live in named and protected biodiversity "hotspots."

1670

Merian Illustrates from Life

In her day, it was typical to work from preserved specimens, but Maria Merian draws from life. Shown below is her illustration of the Legu Lizard she observes in South America. In 1670, she publishes a richly illustrated book of insects, the first to describe the process of metamorphosis.

EVENTS

1670

APPLICATIONS AND TECHNOLOGY

TECHNOLOGY

Improvements in Navigation

Since the Age of Exploration in the 1500s and 1600s, European shipbuilding and sailing had boomed. Vast improvements had been made, especially in charting and mapping. Travel from Europe to Africa, Asia, and the Americas became an important part of business and science. Still, ships often lost their way or wrecked in raging storms. The invention by John Harrison in 1765 of the marine chronometer, a clock that could work at sea, changed navigation forever. Nobody expected a landlocked clockmaker to solve the puzzle, but the sea clock provided an accurate way to record sightings of stars and planets, and thus plot longitude at sea. The ocean remained a dangerous passage, but now, if tossed off course, a captain could still steer clear.

1775

A Catalog of Living Things

In 1775 Carl Linnaeus completed a book called *Systema Naturae*. His book outlines a system to organize and name plants and animals. The naming system gave scientists a precise and consistent method for sharing discoveries.

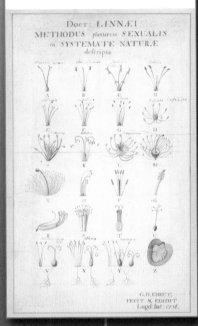

1859

Naturalists in the Amazon

Henry Walter Bates travels from England to the Amazon rainforest in South America with Alfred Russell Wallace. Bates sails home in 1859, bringing over 14,000 specimens, mostly insects. About 8000 of Bates's finds are new discoveries. Wallace loses his collection in a shipwreck.

1889

Naming Discoveries

At the height of discovering new species, conflicts arise over who gets to name living things. In 1889, a conference settles the matter. The first person to publish a description of an organism has the right to claim the discovery and to name it.

1770   **1780**   **1860**   **1870**   **1880**

TECHNOLOGY

Living Things Too Small to See

Before the 1600s, scientists were unable to see microorganisms. Antony van Leeuwenhoek, a drapery maker who made microscopes in his spare time, was one of the first to observe these tiny organisms. He made the first observation of bacteria, and viewed lake water through a microscope like the one shown to the far right. Others used microscopes to draw detailed close-ups, such as an insect's compound eye shown here.

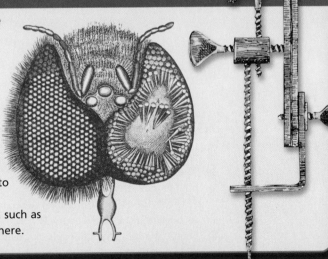

1970

The Bacteria Kingdom Divides

Dr. Carl Woese discovers that bacterialike organisms living in places with extremely high temperatures have genetic material very different from bacteria. Woese suggests a new kingdom or domain called archaebacteria, which is later shortened to Archaea.

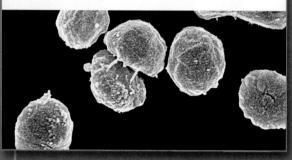

1974

Fogging the Rainforest

Terry Erwin spouts plumes of insecticide into trees and discovers thousands of new insects species in the rainforest canopy. Erwin uses an organism insecticide that does not harm other parts of the ecosystem. Erwin spreads ground sheets or big funnels around a tree, sprays, and, after an hour or so catches the fallen insects, which look like jewels.

1990

Diver, SCUBA Pioneer, Heads Research

Sylvia Earle is the first woman to serve as chief scientist at the National Oceanic and Atmospheric Administration (NOAA). Earle pioneers SCUBA diving and discovers many new fish and marine species—especially new seaweeds in the Gulf of Mexico. Here she shows a sample to a student in a submersible vehicle.

1970   **1980**   **1990**

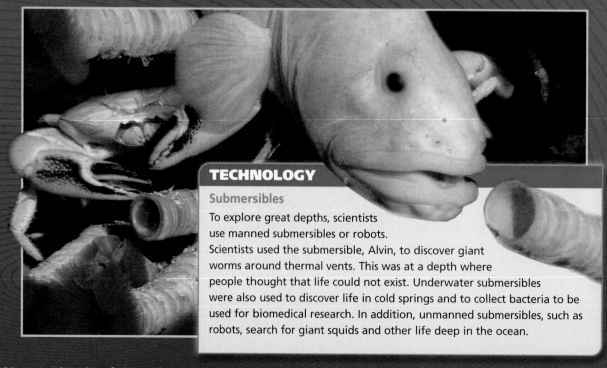

TECHNOLOGY

Submersibles

To explore great depths, scientists use manned submersibles or robots. Scientists used the submersible, Alvin, to discover giant worms around thermal vents. This was at a depth where people thought that life could not exist. Underwater submersibles were also used to discover life in cold springs and to collect bacteria to be used for biomedical research. In addition, unmanned submersibles, such as robots, search for giant squids and other life deep in the ocean.

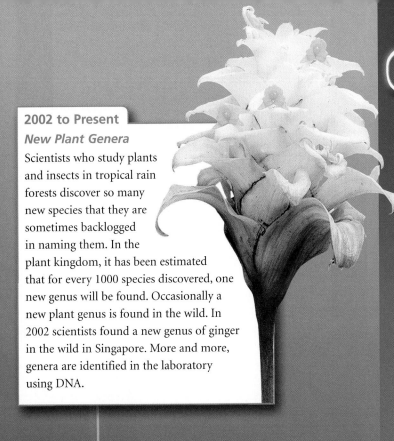

2002 to Present
New Plant Genera
Scientists who study plants and insects in tropical rain forests discover so many new species that they are sometimes backlogged in naming them. In the plant kingdom, it has been estimated that for every 1000 species discovered, one new genus will be found. Occasionally a new plant genus is found in the wild. In 2002 scientists found a new genus of ginger in the wild in Singapore. More and more, genera are identified in the laboratory using DNA.

RESOURCE CENTER
CLASSZONE.COM

Read about current biodiversity discoveries and research.

2000

INTO THE FUTURE

Although scientists have explored most of the continents, little is known about what life is like in the more remote areas. Deep-sea exploration, for example, is only just beginning, and big surprises surface with each expedition. Technology will continue to delve deeper toward the floor of deep oceans with underwater robotics, manned submersibles, and better mapping and imaging systems.

Science will increasingly rely on organizing the growing data on biodiversity. Currently, scientists who study one area of life mostly share data with others in the same field. For example, scientists studying plants share their data with other botanists. An effort to create global databases to share information about all species is beginning to bring together this data. Databases that catalogue the genes of living things are being created. The better we know the genetic profile of various species, the better we can identify and compare them.

In addition, the attention to the health of biodiversity hotspots and ecosystems everywhere may help stop extinction, the dying off of a whole species. Extinction decreases the diversity of living things, and scientists have recognized that Earth's biodiversity plays a big role in keeping ecosystems healthy.

APPLICATION

Biodiversity Hotspots
In 1988, environmentalist Mike Meyers creates a list of 18 areas that he calls biodiversity "hotspots." In 2000, Myers increases the number of hotspots to 25. How does an area get to be called a hotspot? It has to have a large number of species that exist only in that location and it has to be a region in great danger of habitat loss. Hotspots cover only 1.5 % of the Earth's surface yet they contain 44 percent of all species of higher plants and 35 percent of all land vertebrates. Scientists place most of their effort in discovering new species in these hotspots.

cold hot

ACTIVITIES

Writing About Science: Documentary
Research one hotspot and report on the diverse species living there. Note any legal steps or other efforts to conserve biodiversity in that area.

Reliving History
Devise an animal classification system based on a criterion such as habitat, diet, or behavior. What are the strengths and weaknesses of your system?

3

Plants

the BIG idea

Plants are a diverse group of organisms that live in many land environments.

Key Concepts

SECTION

3.1 Plants are adapted to living on land.
Learn about plant characteristics and structures.

SECTION

3.2 Most mosses and ferns live in moist environments.
Learn about how mosses and ferns live and reproduce.

SECTION

3.3 Seeds and pollen are reproductive adaptations.
Learn about seeds, pollen, and gymnosperms.

SECTION

3.4 Many plants reproduce with flowers and fruit.
Learn about flowers, fruit, and angiosperms.

Internet Preview

CLASSZONE.COM

Chapter 3 online resources: Content Review, Simulation, Visualization, four Resource Centers, Math Tutorial, Test Practice

How does such a large tree get what it needs to survive?

EXPLORE (the BIG idea)

How Are Plants Alike, How Are They Different?

Find samples of plants in your area. Draw or take pictures of them for your science notebook. Note each plant's shape, size, and the environment where you found it.

Observe and Think Do all plants have leaves? Do all plants have flowers?

How Are Seeds Dispersed?

Make a model of a seed with wings, such as a seed from a maple tree. Fold a strip of paper in half the long way and then unfold it. Cut a little less than halfway along the fold. Refold the uncut part of the paper and bend out the two cut strips so they look like wings. Put a paper clip on the bottom of the folded part. Drop your seed.

Observe and Think How does having seeds with wings benefit a plant?

Internet Activity: Sprouting Seeds

Go to **ClassZone.com** to watch a time-lapse video of a seed sprouting.

Observe and Think If plants come from seeds, where do seeds come from?

NSTA
scilinks.org
SCI LINKS

Plant Kingdom **Code: MDL041**

Getting Ready to Learn

◀ CONCEPT REVIEW

- All organisms get water and other materials from the environment.
- Plants have specialized tissues with specific functions.
- Plants are producers.

◀ VOCABULARY REVIEW

meiosis p. 48

fertilization p. 48

photosynthesis p. 52

spore p. 67

cycle *See Glossary.*

 **CONTENT REVIEW**
CLASSZONE.COM
Review concepts and vocabulary.

▶ TAKING NOTES

MIND MAP

Write each main idea, or blue heading, in an oval; then write details that relate to each other and to the main idea. Organize the details so that each spoke of the web has notes about one part of the main idea.

VOCABULARY STRATEGY

Draw a **word triangle** diagram for each new vocabulary term. On the bottom line, write and define the term. Above that, write a sentence that uses the term correctly.
At the top, draw a small picture to remind you of the definition.

See the Note-Taking Handbook on pages R45–R51.

SCIENCE NOTEBOOK

cells have a nucleus   two-part life cycle

cells have cell walls   producers

PLANTS SHARE COMMON CHARACTERISTICS

multicellular

live on land

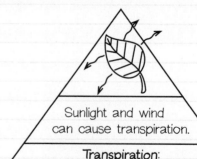

Sunlight and wind can cause transpiration.

Transpiration:
the movement of water vapor out of a plant and into the air

KEY CONCEPT

3.1 Plants are adapted to living on land.

◀ **BEFORE,** you learned

- All organisms have certain basic needs and characteristics
- The bodies of multicellular organisms are organized
- Plants are producers

▶ **NOW,** you will learn

- About plant diversity
- About common characteristics of plants
- How the bodies of plants are organized

VOCABULARY

vascular system p. 87
transpiration p. 88

EXPLORE Leaf Characteristics

What is a leaf?

PROCEDURE

1. Examine the leaf your teacher gives you carefully. Try to notice as many details as you can.

2. Make a drawing of both sides of your leaf in your notebook. Label as many parts as you can and write down your ideas describing each part's function.

3. Compare your diagram and notes with those of your classmates.

MATERIALS
- assorted leaves
- hand lens

WHAT DO YOU THINK?
- What characteristics did most or all of your leaves have?
- How would you describe your leaf to someone who could not see it?

Plants are a diverse group of organisms.

MIND MAP
Make a mind map for the first main idea:
Plants are a diverse group of organisms.

Plants are nearly everywhere. Walk through a forest, and you're surrounded by trees, ferns, and moss. Drive along a country road, and you pass fields planted with crops like cotton or wheat. Even a busy city has tree-lined sidewalks, grass-covered lawns, and weeds growing in vacant lots or poking through cracks in the pavement.

Earth is home to an amazing variety of plant life. Plants come in all shapes and sizes, from tiny flowers no bigger than the head of a pin to giant trees taller than a 12-story building. Plants are found in all types of environments, from the icy Arctic to the steamy tropics.

Plant species live in a variety of environments and have a wide range of features.

Orchids

Seed pods of the vanilla orchid are used to flavor food.

Horsetails

Horsetails have a distinctive shape and texture.

Bristlecone Pine

Bristlecone pines are some of the oldest trees on Earth.

Plants share common characteristics.

▼ REMINDER

A *species* is a classification used for a group of organisms that are so similar that members of the group can breed and produce offspring that can also reproduce.

Scientists estimate that at least 260,000 different species of plants live on Earth today. The photographs on this page show three examples of plants that are very different from one another.

Orchids are flowering plants that mostly grow in tropical rain forests. To get the sunlight they need, many orchids grow not in the soil but on the trunks of trees. Horsetails are plants that produce tiny grains of a very hard substance called silica. Sometimes called scouring rushes, these plants were once used to scrub clean, or scour, dishes and pots. Bristlecone pine trees live on high mountain slopes in North America where there is little soil and often high winds. These trees grow very slowly and can live for several thousand years.

You can see from these three examples that plant species show great diversity. Despite how different an orchid is from a horsetail and a bristlecone pine, all three plants share certain characteristics. These are the characteristics that define a plant as a plant:

• Plants are multicellular organisms.

• A plant cell has a nucleus and is surrounded by a cell wall.

• Plants are producers. They capture energy from the Sun.

• Plant life cycles are divided into two stages, or generations.

 CHECK YOUR READING   What characteristics are shared by all plants?

Plant parts have special functions.

You could say that a plant lives in two worlds. The roots anchor a plant in the ground. Aboveground, reaching toward the Sun, are stems and leaves. Together, stems and leaves make up a shoot system. These two systems work together to get a plant what it needs to survive.

A plant's root system can be as extensive as the stems and leaves that you see aboveground. Roots absorb water and nutrients from the soil. These materials are transported to the leaves through the stems. The leaves use the materials, along with carbon dioxide from the air, to make sugars and carbohydrates. The stems then deliver these energy-rich compounds back to the rest of the plant.

CHECK YOUR READING What are two plant systems, and what are their functions?

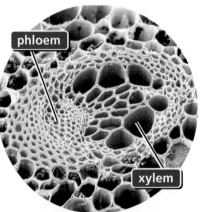

Transporting Water and Other Materials

Stems serve as the pathway for transporting water, nutrients, and energy-rich compounds from one part of a plant to another. In most plants, the materials move through a **vascular system** (VAS-kyuh-lur) that is made up of long, tubelike cells. These tissues are bundled together and run from the roots to the leaves. A vascular bundle from the stem of a buttercup plant is shown.

Transport is carried out by two types of tissue. Xylem (ZY-luhm) is a tissue that carries water and dissolved nutrients up from the roots. Phloem (FLOH-em) is a tissue that transports energy-rich materials down from the leaves. Xylem cells and phloem cells are long and hollow, like pipes. The xylem cells are a little larger than the phloem cells. Both tissues include long fibers that help support the plant body, as well as cells that can store extra carbohydrates for energy.

phloem

xylem

This vascular bundle has been magnified 113×.

> **REMINDER**
> Plants make sugar through *photosynthesis*. The sugars that are not used immediately are stored as carbohydrates, energy-rich compounds.

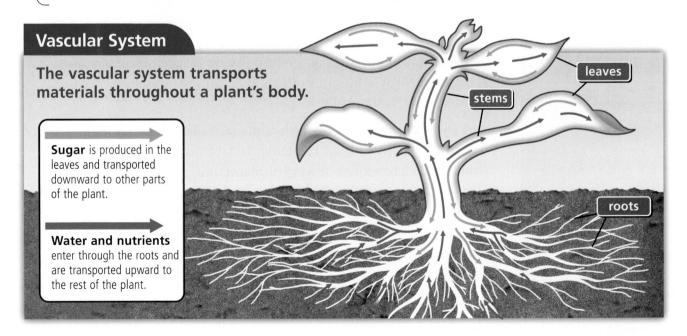

Vascular System

The vascular system transports materials throughout a plant's body.

leaves

stems

roots

Sugar is produced in the leaves and transported downward to other parts of the plant.

Water and nutrients enter through the roots and are transported upward to the rest of the plant.

Making Sugars

Plants produce sugars through the process of photosynthesis. Photosynthesis is a series of chemical reactions that capture light energy from the Sun and convert it into chemical energy stored in sugar molecules. The starting materials needed are carbon dioxide, water, and light. The end products are sugars and oxygen. The chemical reaction for photosynthesis can be written like this:

carbon dioxide + water + sunlight → sugars + oxygen

Photosynthesis takes place in chloroplasts, structures that contain chlorophyll. Chlorophyll, the chemical that gives plants their green color, produces the reaction. Most chloroplasts in a plant are located in leaf cells. As you can see from the illustration on page 89, the structure of the leaf is specialized for capturing light energy and producing sugar.

 CHECK YOUR READING What is photosynthesis, and why is it important?

The upper surface of the leaf, which is turned toward the Sun, has layers of cells filled with chloroplasts. Vascular tissue located toward the center of the leaf brings in water and nutrients and carries away sugars and carbohydrates. Tiny openings at the bottom of the leaf, called stomata (STOH-muh-tuh), lead to a network of tiny spaces where gases are stored. The carbon dioxide gas needed for photosynthesis comes in through the stomata, and oxygen gas moves out. This process is called gas exchange.

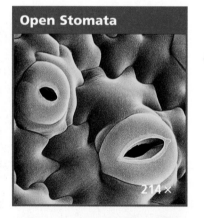

Open Stomata

214×

Closed Stomata

Controlling Gas Exchange and Water Loss

For photosynthesis to occur, a plant must maintain the balance of carbon dioxide and water in its body. Carbon dioxide gas from the air surrounding a plant enters through the stomata in its leaves. Open stomata allow carbon dioxide and oxygen to move into and out of the leaf. These openings also allow water to evaporate. The movement of water vapor out of a plant and into the air is called **transpiration** (TRAN-spuh-RAY-shuhn). Both sunlight and wind cause water in leaves to evaporate and transpire.

For photosynthesis to occur, a plant needs to have enough carbon dioxide come in without too much water evaporating and moving out. Plants have different ways of maintaining this balance. The surface of leaves and stems are covered by a waxy protective layer, called a cuticle. The cuticle keeps water from evaporating. Also, when the air is dry, the stomata can close. This can help to prevent water loss.

 CHECK YOUR READING What are two ways plants have to keep from losing too much water?

Inside a Leaf

The leaf is an organ that produces sugars. It is made up of different types of cells and tissues.

Cells at the surface produce a waxy cuticle that keeps the leaf from losing water.

Most chloroplasts are located in cells of the upper layer of the leaf.

Xylem transports water and nutrients up from the roots.

Phloem transports energy-rich compounds made in the leaf down to other parts of the plant.

Carbon dioxide, oxygen, and water vapor move into and out of the leaf through stomata.

READING VISUALS How is the top of a leaf different from the bottom of a leaf?

stem

spines

The stomata are an adaptation that allows a plant to adjust to daily changes in its environment. Plants can respond to hot, dry weather by keeping their stomata closed. Stomata can be open during the night, when evaporation is less likely to occur. Most plants have stomata.

Some species of plants have special adaptations for survival in a particular environment. For example, a cactus plant has adaptations that allow it to survive in a desert. The spines of a cactus are actually modified leaves. A plant with regular leaves would lose too much water through transpiration. In cacti, most photosynthesis occurs in the thick fleshy stem, where the cactus also stores water and carbon dioxide gas.

APPLY Plant stems branch as they grow. Do cactus plants have branches?

Plants grow throughout their lifetimes.

Plants grow for as long as they live. This is true for plants that live for only one season, such as sunflowers, and for plants that can live for many years, such as trees. Plants grow bigger when cells at the tips of their roots and stems divide and multiply more rapidly than other plant cells do. A plant's roots and stems can grow longer and thicker and can branch, or divide. However, only stems grow leaves. Leaves grow from buds produced by growth tissue in a plant's stems. The bud of an oak tree is shown on page 91.

Plant stems are structures with more than one function. You have read that a plant's stem includes its vascular system, which allows the plant to transport materials between its leaves and roots. Long stiff fibers in the tissues of the vascular system provide support and give the plant shape. Plant stems can also store the sugars produced by photosynthesis. Many plants, including broccoli, celery, and carrots, convert sugars into carbohydrates and then store this energy-rich material in their stems or roots.

 CHECK YOUR READING What are three functions of plant stems?

Plants with Soft Stems

RESOURCE CENTER
CLASSZONE.COM

Learn more about plant systems.

The soft stems and leaves of many weeds, wildflowers, garden flowers, and vegetables die when the environment they live in becomes too cold or too dry. This type of plant survives by using the carbohydrates stored in its roots. Then, when the environment provides it with enough warmth, water, and sunlight, the plant will grow new, soft, green stems and leaves.

Plant Growth

Plants, such as these oak trees, grow most when there is enough warmth, water, and sunlight.

Oak Bud

The tips of the shoots produce buds, which become new leaves and stems.

Plants with Woody Stems

Some plants, such as trees and shrubs, have tough, thick stems that do not die each year. These stems keep growing longer and thicker. As the stems grow, they develop a type of tough xylem tissue that is not found in soft stems. This tough xylem tissue is called wood. The growing tissues in woody stems are located near the outer surface of the stem, right under the bark. This means that, for a tree like one of the oaks in the photograph above, the center of the trunk is the oldest part of the plant.

3.1 Review

KEY CONCEPTS

1. What characteristics do all plants have in common?

2. How does the structure of a leaf relate to its function?

3. What tissues move materials throughout a plant?

CRITICAL THINKING

4. **Summarize** Describe how the structure of a leaf allows a plant to control the materials involved in photosynthesis.

5. **Analyze** Do you think the stems of soft-stemmed plants have chloroplasts? How about woody-stemmed plants? Explain your reasoning. Hint: Think about the color of each.

⬥ CHALLENGE

6. **Evaluate** Scientists who study the natural world say that there is unity in diversity. How does this idea apply to plants?

3.2 Most mosses and ferns live in moist environments.

 BEFORE, you learned

- All plants share common characteristics
- The body of a plant has specialized parts
- Plants grow throughout their lifetimes

 NOW, you will learn

- About the first plants
- About reproduction in nonvascular plants, such as mosses
- About reproduction in vascular plants such as ferns

EXPLORE Moss Plants

What do moss plants look like?

PROCEDURE

MATERIALS
- live moss plant
- hand lens

1. Use a hand lens to examine a moss plant. Look for different structures and parts you can identify.

2. Draw a diagram of the moss plant in your notebook. Label parts you identified and parts you would like to identify.

3. Write a brief description of each parts function.

WHAT DO YOU THINK?
- How would you describe a moss plant to someone who had never seen one?
- How does a moss plant compare with the other plants you are familiar with?

Plant species adapted to life on land.

Life first appeared on Earth about 3.8 billion years ago. Tiny single-celled and multicellular organisms lived in watery environments such as warm, shallow seas, deep ocean vents, and ponds. Fossil evidence suggests that plant life did not appear on land until about 475 million years ago. The ancestors of the first plants were among the first organisms to move onto land.

What did these plantlike organisms look like? Scientists think they looked much like the green algae you can find growing in watery ditches or shallow ponds today. Both green algae and plants are autotrophs, or producers. Their cells contain chloroplasts that enable them to convert the Sun's light energy into the chemical energy stored in sugars.

RESOURCE CENTER
CLASSZONE.COM

Explore plant evolution.

C 92 Unit: **Diversity of Living Things**

The First Plants

Suppose that hundreds of millions of years ago, the area now occupied by your school was a shallow pond full of tiny, floating organisms that could photosynthesize. The Sun overhead provided energy. The pond water was full of dissolved nutrients. The organisms thrived and reproduced, and over time the pond became crowded. Some were pushed to the very edges of the water. Then, after a period of dry weather, the pond shrank. Some organisms at the edge were no longer in the water. The ones that were able to survive were now living on land.

Scientists think the first plants shared a common ancestor with green algae, shown here magnified about 80×.

Scientists think that something like this took place in millions of watery environments over millions of years. Those few organisms that were stranded and were able to survive became ancestors to the first plants. Life on land is very different from life in water. The first plants needed to be able to get both nutrients and water from the land. There is no surrounding water to provide support for the body or to keep body tissues from drying out. However, for organisms that survived, life on land had many advantages. There is plenty carbon dioxide in the air and plenty of direct sunlight.

 CHECK YOUR READING Why is having plenty of sunlight and water an advantage for a plant? Your answer should mention photosynthesis.

Mosses and Ferns

Among the first plants to live on Earth were the ancestors of the mosses and ferns you see today. Both probably evolved from species of algae that lived in the sea and freshwater. Mosses are simpler in structure than ferns. Mosses, and two closely related groups of plants known as liverworts and hornworts, are descended from the first plants to spread onto the bare rock and soil of Earth. Ferns and their relatives appeared later.

This diorama shows what a forest on Earth might have looked like about 350 million years ago.

How much sunlight reaches an organism living in water?

PROCEDURE

(1) Thread the string through the holes in the button so that the button hangs flat. Fill the empty bottle with clean water.

(2) Look down through the top of the bottle. Lower the button into the water until it either disappears from view or reaches the bottom. Have a classmate measure how far the button is from the surface of the water.

(3) Add two spoonfuls of kelp granules to the water. Repeat step 2.

MATERIALS
- white button
- string
- empty clear plastic bottle
- water
- ruler
- kelp granules
- tablespoon

TIME
20 minutes

WHAT DO YOU THINK?

- How did the distance measured the second time compare with your first measurement?

- Why might a photosynthetic organism living on land get more sunlight than one living in water?

CHALLENGE What do the kelp granules in this experiment represent? What does that suggest about the advantages of living on land?

Mosses are nonvascular plants.

Moss plants have adaptations for life on land. Mosses have simple roots, stems, and leaves. Moss cells also have special areas for storing water and nutrients. Each moss cell, like all plant cells, is surrounded by a thick wall that provides it with support. Mosses do not grow very large, but there are many species of them, and over millions of years they have adapted to survive in many environments.

If you look closely at a clump of moss, you will see that it is actually made up of many tiny, dark green plants. Mosses belong to a group called the nonvascular plants. Nonvascular plants do not have vascular tissue. Water and nutrients simply move through nonvascular plants' bodies cell by cell. A plant can get enough water this way as long as its body is no more than a few cells thick.

 CHECK YOUR READING What limits the size of moss plants?

Water also plays a part in the reproductive cycle of a moss plant. In the first part of the cycle, the moss grows and maintains itself, producing the male and female structures needed for sexual reproduction. If conditions are right and there is enough water, the plant enters a spore-producing stage, the second part of the cycle.

Mosses reproduce with spores.

Mosses, ferns, and fungi all reproduce with spores. Spores are an important adaptation that allowed the ancestors of these organisms to reproduce on land. A spore is a single reproductive cell that is protected by a hard, watertight covering. The covering prevents the cell from drying out. Spores are small and can be transported through the air. This means offspring from spores can grow in places that are distant from the parent organisms.

The green moss plants you are familiar with have grown from spores. They represent the first generation. Within a clump of moss are both male and female reproductive structures. When conditions are right, these structures produce sperm and eggs. Fertilization can occur only if water is present because the tiny moss sperm move by swimming. A layer of water left by rain is one way sperm can move to the eggs on another part of the plant.

The fertilized egg grows into a stalk with a capsule on the end—the second generation of the plant. The stalk and capsule grow from the female moss plant. Inside the capsule, the process of meiosis produces thousands of tiny spores. When the spores are released, as shown in the photograph, the cycle can begin again.

REMINDER

Sexual reproduction involves two processes: fertilization and meiosis.

Moss Releasing Spores

capsule

stalk

spores

moss plant

IDENTIFY Point out the two generations of the moss plant shown here.

Mosses, like other plants, can also reproduce asexually. A small piece of a moss plant can separate and can grow into a new plant, or new plants can branch off from old ones. Asexual reproduction allows plants to spread more easily than sexual reproduction. However, the genetic material of the new plants is the same as that of the parent. Sexual reproduction increases genetic diversity and the possibility of new adaptations.

 CHECK YOUR READING Compare and contrast sexual and asexual reproduction. Your answer should mention *genetic material*.

Ferns are vascular plants.

Ferns, and two closely related groups of plants known as horsetails and club mosses, were the first plants on Earth with vascular systems. The tubelike tissue of a vascular system moves water through a plant's body more quickly than when water moves cell by cell. Because of this, vascular plants can grow much larger than nonvascular plants. Vascular tissue also provides support for the weight of a larger plant.

The presence of vascular tissue has an effect on the development of roots, stems, and leaves. The root system can branch out more, anchoring a larger plant as well as providing water and nutrients. Vascular tissue moves materials more efficiently and gives extra support. The stems can branch out and more leaves can grow. This results in more sugars and other materials needed for energy and growth.

Nonvascular

Liverworts are tiny nonvascular plants. The liverworts shown here are life-size.

Vascular

Ferns are vascular plants. Notice how tall a tree fern can grow.

READING VISUALS COMPARE AND CONTRAST How do the penny and the person help to show that the tree ferns are much larger than the liverworts?

Ferns reproduce with spores.

You may have seen ferns growing in the woods or in a garden. The leaves of ferns, called fronds, are often included in a flower bouquet. The next time you have a chance to look at a fern frond, take a look at the back. You will probably see many small clusters similar to those shown to the right. The clusters are full of spores.

spores
spore cluster

Ferns, like mosses, have a two-part life cycle. In ferns, spores grow into tiny structures that lie very close to the ground. You would have to look closely to find these structures on the ground, for they are usually smaller than the size of your thumbnail. Within these structures are the sperm- and egg-producing parts of the fern plant. This is the first generation of the plant. Like mosses, the sperm of a fern plant need water to swim to the egg. So fertilization occurs only when plenty of moisture is present.

The second part of a fern life cycle is the plant with fronds that grows from the fertilized egg. As the fronds grow, the small egg-bearing part of the plant dies away. The fronds produce clusters, and cells within those clusters undergo meiosis and produce spores. The more the fern grows, the more clusters and spores it produces. The spores, when they are released, spread through the air. If conditions are right where the spores land, they grow into new fern plants and a new cycle begins. This is sexual reproduction. Ferns, like mosses, also reproduce asexually. New ferns branch off old ones, or pieces separate from the plant and grow.

As fern fronds grow, they produce clusters of spores on the back of the fronds.

 CHECK YOUR READING Explain one way that sexual reproduction in ferns is similar to reproduction in mosses. Explain one way it is different.

3.2 Review

KEY CONCEPTS

1. For the ancestors of the first plants, what were some advantages to living on land?

2. What are three adaptations that make mosses able to live on land?

3. What are two characteristics you can observe that distinguish vascular plants from nonvascular plants?

CRITICAL THINKING

4. **Synthesize** Vascular plants such as ferns can grow bigger and taller than nonvascular plants such as mosses. Does this mean they can also capture more sunlight? Explain your answer.

5. **Compare** Make a chart that shows how the life cycles of mosses and ferns are different, and how they are similar.

CHALLENGE

6. **Evaluate** Consider the conditions that are needed for mosses and ferns to reproduce sexually. Sexual reproduction increases genetic diversity within a group of plants, while asexual reproduction does not. Explain why asexual reproduction is still important for both moss and fern plants.

3.3 Seeds and pollen are reproductive adaptations.

◀ BEFORE, you learned

- Plant species evolved from algaelike ancestors
- Mosses are nonvascular plants that reproduce with spores
- Ferns are vascular plants that reproduce with spores

▶ NOW, you will learn

- How some plants reproduce with pollen and seeds
- About the advantages of pollen and seeds

VOCABULARY

seed p. 98
embryo p. 98
germination p. 99
pollen p. 100
gymnosperm p. 102

THINK ABOUT

Is a seed alive?

A lotus is a type of pond lily that is commonly found in water gardens. The plants take root in the bottom of a pond. A plant scientist in California experimented with lotus seeds from China that were over 1000 years old. The scientist made a small opening in the hard covering of each seed and planted the seeds in wet soil. Some of the seeds sprouted and grew. What made it possible for these seeds to survive for such a long time? Is a seed alive?

Seeds are an important adaptation.

Spores are one adaptation that made it possible for plants to reproduce on land. Seeds are another. A **seed** is a young plant that is enclosed in a protective coating. Within the coating are enough nutrients to enable the plant to grow. Seeds and spores can both withstand harsh conditions. Seeds, however, have several survival advantages over spores. These advantages make it possible for seed plants to spread into environments where seedless plants are less likely to survive.

In seedless plants, such as mosses and ferns, fertilization brings about the growth of the next generation of the plant. In seed plants, there is a step in between. Fertilization brings about the growth of an embryo. An **embryo** (EHM-bree-OH) is the immature form of an organism that has the potential to grow and develop. The seed protects the plant embryo until conditions are right for it to grow.

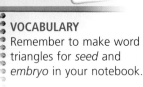

VOCABULARY
Remember to make word triangles for *seed* and *embryo* in your notebook.

An embryo can remain inside a seed for a long time without growing. When moisture, temperature, and other conditions are right, a seed will start to grow. **Germination** (JUR-muh-NAY-shuhn) is the beginning of growth of a new plant from a spore or a seed. If you've ever planted a seed that sprouted, you've observed germination.

 CHECK YOUR READING What is germination?

When a seed germinates, it takes in water from its surroundings. As the embryo begins to grow, it uses the stored nutrients in the seed for energy and materials. The nutrients need to last until the new plant's roots and shoots can start to function.

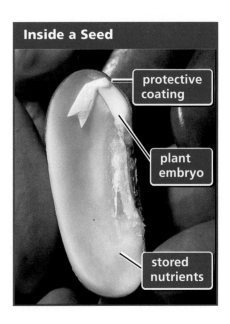

Inside a Seed

protective coating

plant embryo

stored nutrients

Some plants reproduce with seeds.

In most places, plants that reproduce with seeds are common and easy to see. Trees, bushes, flowers, and grasses are all seed plants. It's a bit harder to find plants that reproduce with spores, such as mosses or ferns. Why are there so many more seed plants in the world? The diagram below shows some of the differences and similarities between seeds and spores.

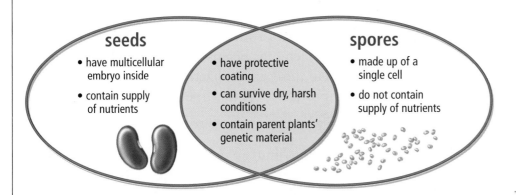

seeds
- have multicellular embryo inside
- contain supply of nutrients

- have protective coating
- can survive dry, harsh conditions
- contain parent plants' genetic material

spores
- made up of a single cell
- do not contain supply of nutrients

One important difference between a seed and a spore is that the seed contains a multicellular organism. If you look closely at the photograph above you can see the tiny leaves at the top of the embryo, with the root below. Spores are just a single cell. Seeds can be spread by wind, animals, or water. Spores are mostly carried by the wind. The sperm of seed plants, unlike the sperm of mosses and ferns, do not need water to reach the egg. One important similarity between a seed and a spore is that both can grow into a new plant.

 CHECK YOUR READING Name three ways seeds are different from spores.

 **RESOURCE CENTER** CLASSZONE.COM

Learn more about seeds.

Pine trees reproduce with pollen and seeds.

Seed plants, such as pine trees, do not have swimming sperm. Instead, they have pollen. A **pollen** grain is a small multicellular structure that holds a sperm cell. It has a hard outer covering to keep the sperm from drying out. Pollen grains can be carried from one plant to another by wind, water, or by animals such as insects, bats, or birds. The process of pollination is completed when a pollen grain attaches to the part of a plant that contains the egg and releases the sperm.

The life cycle of a pine tree provides an example of how seed plants reproduce. As you read the numbered paragraphs on this page, follow the numbers on the labels of the diagram on page 101.

follow the numbers on the labels of the diagram on page 101.

Pinecones release lots of pollen into the air.

1. The reproductive structures of a pine tree are the pinecones. Meiosis occurs in the pine cones, producing sperm and egg cells. Each tree has separate male and female cones.

2. In male cones, the sperm cells are contained in pollen grains, which are released into the air. In female cones, the egg cells are enclosed in protective compartments within the cone scales.

3. The female cone produces a sticky substance. When a pollen grain lands, it sticks. A pollen tube begins to grow from the pollen grain through the scale to the egg. Fertilization occurs when the pollen tube reaches the protective compartment and sperm travel through it to one of the eggs.

4. The fertilized egg grows into an embryo. The compartment, with its protective covering and supply of nutrients, becomes the seed. The pinecone eventually releases its seeds. The winged seeds can float through the air and may be carried long distances by the wind. If the seed lands on the ground and germinates, it can become a new pine tree.

In the life cycle of a pine tree, meiosis and fertilization occur completely within the tissue of the mature plant. Fertilization doesn't require an outside source of water. The sperm cells in a pollen grain and the egg cells in a cone scale represent the first generation of the plant. The seed and the tree that grows from the seed represent the second generation.

 What do pollen grains and cone scales contain?

> **REMINDER**
>
> A *cycle* is a series of events that repeat regularly.

Life Cycle of a Pine Tree

open female cone

④ Seeds

Each fertilized egg becomes an embryo in a seed. A female cone can contain many seeds. The cone opens and the seeds are released.

seed

① Meiosis

A mature pine tree has both male and female cones. Meiosis occurs inside the cones, producing sperm and egg cells.

Male Cones

Female Cone

③ Fertilization

Sperm move through the pollen tube to fertilize one of the egg cells at the base of the female cone scale.

pollen tube

sperm   fertilized egg

pollen grain

② Pollination

Male cones release pollen into the air. A pollen grain sticks to the scales of a female cone, and a pollen tube begins to grow.

scales

READING VISUALS Use the definition of a cycle to predict what happens after seeds are released from pinecones.

What conditions make a pinecone open?

PROCEDURE

① Place your pinecone in the beaker of water. Observe any changes that take place. Leave the cone in the water until the changes stop.

② Remove the cone from the water and place it on a paper towel to dry. Observe any changes that take place as the cone dries.

WHAT DO YOU THINK?

• What did you observe when the cone was in the water?

• What happened when the cone dried out?

CHALLENGE Try this procedure on cones from different plant species.

SKILL FOCUS
Observing

MATERIALS
• dried, open pinecones
• beaker of water
• paper towels

TIME
20 minutes

Gymnosperms are seed plants.

Pollen and seeds are reproductive adaptations. They did not appear in plants until millions of years after seedless plants such as mosses and ferns had already begun to live on land. Today, however, most of the plant species on Earth reproduce with seeds, and many species of seedless plants have become extinct. Some scientists think this is because over time Earth's climate has become drier and cooler. Seed plants are generally better adapted for reproducing in dry, cool environments than seedless plants are.

Fossil evidence shows that species of seed plants in the **gymnosperm** (JIHM-nuh-SPURM) group have existed on Earth for more than 250 million years. Plants classified as gymnosperms produce seeds, but the seeds are not enclosed in fruit. The word *gymnosperm* comes from the Greek words for "naked seed." There are four types of gymnosperms living on Earth today.

 CHECK YOUR READING What is distinctive about gymnosperm seeds?

MIND MAP
Make a mind map for the main idea that *gymnosperms are seed plants.* Don't forget to include the definition of a gymnosperm in your mind map.

Conifers

The conifers, or cone-bearing trees, are the type of gymnosperm you are probably most familiar with. The conifers include pine, fir, spruce, hemlock, cypress, and redwood trees. Many conifers are adapted for living in cold climates, where there is relatively little water available. Their leaves are needle-shaped and have a thick cuticle. This prevents the plant from losing much water to transpiration. Conifers can also keep their needles for several years, which means the plants can produce sugars all year.

Ginkgo trees like this one are gymnosperms that do not produce cones. Their seeds are exposed to the environment.

Other Gymnosperms

The other types of living gymnosperms are cycads, gnetophytes, and ginkgoes. These three types of gymnosperms appear to be quite different from one another. Cycads are palmlike plants that are found in tropical areas. They produce cones for seeds. Many cycads produce poisonous compounds. Gnetophytes are another type of tropical gymnosperm that produces cones. Chemicals taken from certain gnetophyte plants have been used to treat cold symptoms for thousands of years.

Ginkgoes are gymnosperms with fleshy seeds that hang from their branches. Ginkgoes are often grown in parks and along streets, but you will not often see them with seeds. People avoid putting male and female ginkgo trees together because the seed coat of a ginkgo produces a particularly foul smell.

3.3 Review

KEY CONCEPTS

1. How are seeds different from spores?

2. How does fertilization in seed plants differ from fertilization in seedless plants?

3. Seed plants are found in environments where seedless plants are not. List at least two reasons why.

CRITICAL THINKING

4. **Compare and Contrast** What is the difference between a spore and a pollen grain? In what ways are spores and pollen grains similar?

5. **Hypothesize** Gymnosperms produce a lot of pollen, and most of it blows away, never fertilizing an egg. Why might this characteristic help a plant species survive?

CHALLENGE

6. **Analyze** Like all plants, a pine tree has a two-part life cycle. Look again at the diagram on page 101, and then make a new version of it in your notebook. Your version should show where in the life cycle each generation begins and ends. Hint: reread the text on page 100.

CHAPTER INVESTIGATION

Which Seeds Will Grow?

OVERVIEW AND PURPOSE Many of the foods you eat come from seed plants. What seeds or parts of seed plants have you eaten lately? What seeds can you find outside in your neighborhood? What conditions do the seeds from these plants need to grow? In this investigation, you will

- plant a variety of seeds
- observe differences in germination and growth among seeds planted in similar conditions

▶ Problem

How successfully will a variety of seeds germinate in conditions that can be provided in your classroom?

▶ Hypothesize

Read through all of the steps of the procedure and then write a hypothesis. Your hypothesis should explain what you think will happen when your class plants its collection of seeds and observes their growth for at least ten days. Your hypothesis should take the form of an "If . . . , then . . . , because . . ." statement.

▶ Procedure

MATERIALS
- assorted seeds
- potting soil
- paper cups
- water
- paper towels
- labels

1. Make a data table in your **Science Notebook** like the one shown on page 105.

2. Examine the seeds you will use in this investigation. Try to identify them. Record your observations in the data table.

step 2

3 Use the materials provided to plant the seeds. Remember that the planting conditions should be the same for each of the seeds. Label each container.

4 Decide where you will keep your seeds while they are growing and how often you will check and water them. Be sure to keep the growing conditions for all of the seeds the same. Wash your hands.

5 Observe your seeds for at least ten days. Check and water them according to the plan you made.

step 5

Observe and Analyze
Write It Up

1. In your **Science Notebook**, draw and label a diagram showing how you planted the seeds, the materials you used, and the place where they are being kept.

2. Each time you check on your seeds, record your observations in your data table.

3. **IDENTIFY** Which seeds germinated? What differences in growth and development did you observe in the different types of seeds?

Conclude
Write It Up

1. **INTERPRET** Compare your results with your hypothesis. Did your data support your hypothesis?

2. **INFER** What patterns or similarities did you notice in the seeds that grew most successfully?

3. **IDENTIFY LIMITS** What unexpected factors or problems might have affected your results?

4. **APPLY** Use your experience to tell a young child how to grow a plant from a seed. What type of seeds would you suggest? Write directions for planting and caring for seeds that a younger child could understand.

INVESTIGATE Further

CHALLENGE Some seeds need special conditions, such as warmth or a certain amount of moisture, before they will germinate. Design an experiment in which you test just one type of seed in a variety of conditions to learn which results in the most growth. Include a hypothesis, a materials list, and a procedure when you write up your experiment.

Which Seeds Will Grow?

Table 1. Observations of Seeds

Seed	Observations
Kidney bean	sprouted March 3
Popcorn	
Sunflower	
Rice	

EXTREME SCIENCE

Forest Fires release jackpine seeds from their pinecones to sprout after the fire stops.

Seed Survivors

Seeds can not only survive some harsh conditions, but often, harsh conditions make it possible for seeds to grow into new plants.

Forest Fires

Jackpine seeds are locked inside pinecones by a sticky resin. The pinecones survive hot forest fires that melt the resin and release the seeds. In fact, without the high temperatures from fires, the seeds would never get the chance to sprout and grow into jackpine trees.

Bomb Damage

In 1940, during World War II, The British Museum was firebombed. People poured water over the burning museum and its contents. In the museum were silk-tree seeds collected in China and brought to the museum in 1793. After the firebombing 147 years later, the seeds sprouted.

Dodo Digestion

Seeds of Calvaria trees, which live on the island of Mauritius have very hard outer shells. The outer shell must be softened before the seeds can sprout. Hundreds of years ago, dodo birds ate the Calvaria fruits. Stones and acids in the birds' digestive tract helped soften the seed. After the dodo birds deposited them, the softened seeds would sprout. Dodo birds went extinct in 1681, and no young Calvaria trees grew. In 1975, only about 13 Calvaria trees remained. Recently, scientists have used artificial means to grind and break down the Calvaria seed cover and foster new tree growth.

EXPLORE

1. **INFER** Why do you think the silk tree seeds sprouted? Think about how the seeds' environment changed.

2. **CHALLENGE** If you were a scientist who wanted to help the Calvaria trees make a comeback, what methods might you try for softening the seeds?

RESOURCE CENTER
CLASSZONE.COM

Find out more about extreme seeds.

KEY CONCEPT

Many plants reproduce with flowers and fruit.

 BEFORE, you learned

- Seed plants do not have swimming sperm
- Gymnosperms reproduce with pollen and seeds

NOW, you will learn

- About flowers and fruit
- About the relationship between animals and flowering plants
- How humans need plants

VOCABULARY

angiosperm p. 107
flower p. 108
fruit p. 108

EXPLORE Fruit

What do you find inside fruit?

PROCEDURE

1. Place the apple on a paper towel. Carefully cut the apple in half. Find the seeds.

2. Place the pea pod on a paper towel. Carefully split open the pea pod. Find the seeds.

3. Both the apple and the pea pod are examples of fruits. In your notebook, draw a diagram of the two fruits you examined. Label the fruit and the seeds.

MATERIALS
- apple
- paper towel
- plastic knife
- pea pod

WHAT DO YOU THINK?
- How many seeds did you find?
- What part of an apple do you eat? What part of a pea?

MIND MAP
Make a mind map diagram for the main idea: *Angiosperms have flowers and fruit.*

Angiosperms have flowers and fruit.

Have you ever eaten peanuts, grapes, strawberries, or squash? Do you like the way roses smell, or how spider plants look? All of these plants are angiosperms, or flowering plants. An **angiosperm** (AN-jee-uh-SPURM) is a seed plant that produces flowers and fruit. Most of the species of plants living now are angiosperms. The grasses at your local park are angiosperms. Most trees whose leaves change color in the fall are angiosperms.

The sperm of a flowering plant are protected in a pollen grain and do not need an outside source of water to reach the eggs. The eggs develop into embryos that are enclosed within seeds. Both generations of angiosperms and gymnosperms occur within a single plant.

The reproductive cycles of angiosperms and gymnosperms are alike in many ways. Both angiosperms and gymnosperms have separate male and female reproductive structures. In some species, male and female parts grow on the same plant, but in others there are separate male and female plants.

An important difference between angiosperms and gymnosperms is that in angiosperms, the sperm and egg cells are contained in a flower. The **flower** is the reproductive structure of an angiosperm. Egg cells develop in a part of the flower called an ovary. Once the eggs are fertilized and the seed or seeds form, the ovary wall thickens and the ovary becomes a **fruit.**

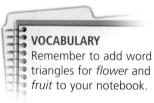

VOCABULARY
Remember to add word triangles for *flower* and *fruit* to your notebook.

 CHECK YOUR READING What reproductive structures do angiosperms have that gymnosperms do not?

The diagram on page 109 shows the life cycle of one type of angiosperm, a cherry tree. As you read the numbered paragraphs below, follow the numbers on the labels in the diagram.

 The reproductive structures of a cherry tree are its flowers. The anther is the male part. The pistil (PIHS-tuhl) is the female part. Meiosis in the anther produces sperm cells enclosed within pollen grains. Meiosis in the ovary of the pistil produces egg cells.

2 The pollen grains are released. When a pollen grain is caught on the pistil of a flower, a pollen tube starts to grow. Within the ovary one of the egg cells matures.

3 Fertilization occurs when the pollen tube reaches the ovary and sperm fertilizes the egg. The fertilized egg grows into an embryo and develops a seed coat. The ovary develops into a fruit.

4 The fruit may fall to the ground or it may be eaten by animals. If the seed inside lands in a place where it can germinate and survive, it will grow into a new cherry tree.

 CHECK YOUR READING What is the flower's role in the sexual reproduction of an angiosperm?

Many flowering plants also reproduce asexually. New shoots can grow out from the parent plant. For example, strawberries and spider plants can reproduce by sending out shoots called runners. New plants grow from the runners, getting nutrients from the parent until the roots of the new plant are established. Plants can spread quickly this way. This form of asexual reproduction allows plants to reproduce even when conditions are not right for the germination of seeds.

Life Cycle of a Cherry Tree

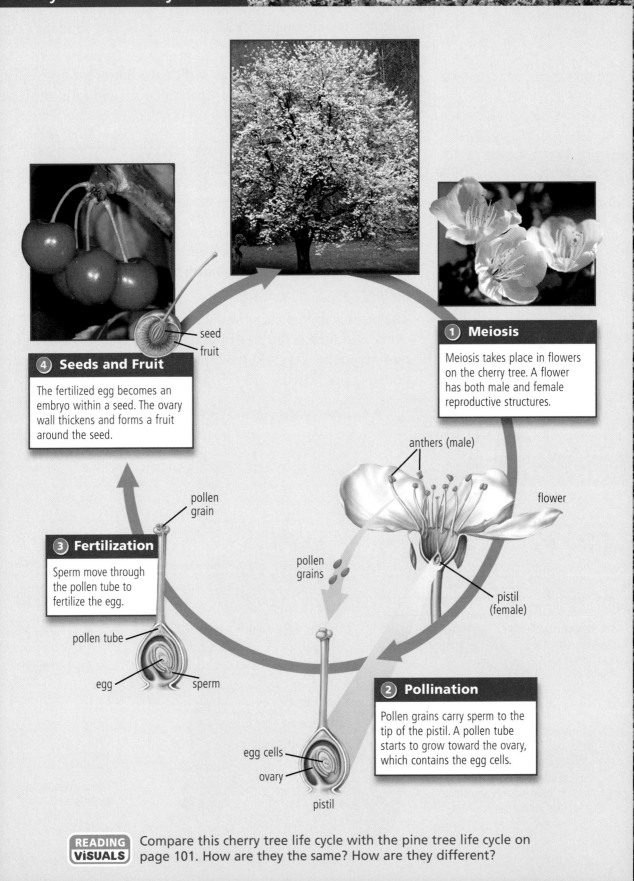

④ Seeds and Fruit

The fertilized egg becomes an embryo within a seed. The ovary wall thickens and forms a fruit around the seed.

seed
fruit

① Meiosis

Meiosis takes place in flowers on the cherry tree. A flower has both male and female reproductive structures.

anthers (male)

flower

pollen grain

③ Fertilization

Sperm move through the pollen tube to fertilize the egg.

pollen grains

pollen tube

egg   sperm

pistil (female)

② Pollination

Pollen grains carry sperm to the tip of the pistil. A pollen tube starts to grow toward the ovary, which contains the egg cells.

egg cells
ovary

pistil

READING ViSUALS Compare this cherry tree life cycle with the pine tree life cycle on page 101. How are they the same? How are they different?

Flowers

Flowers vary in size, shape, color, and fragrance. They all have some similar structures, although they are not always as easy to see as in the lily pictured below.

- Sepals are leafy structures that enclose the flower before it opens. When the flower blooms, the sepals fall open and form the base of the flower.

- Petals are leafy structures arranged in a circle around the pistil. The petals open as the reproductive structures of the plant mature. Petals are often the most colorful part of a flower. The petals help to attract animal pollinators.

- The stamen (STAY-muhn) is the male reproductive structure of a flower. It includes a stalk called a filament and the anther. The anther produces sperm cells, which are contained in pollen grains.

- The pistil is the female reproductive structure of the flower. The ovary is located at the base of the pistil and contains the egg cells that mature into eggs. At the top of the pistil is the stigma, where pollen grains attach.

CHECK YOUR READING What are the stamen and pistil?

Parts of a Flower

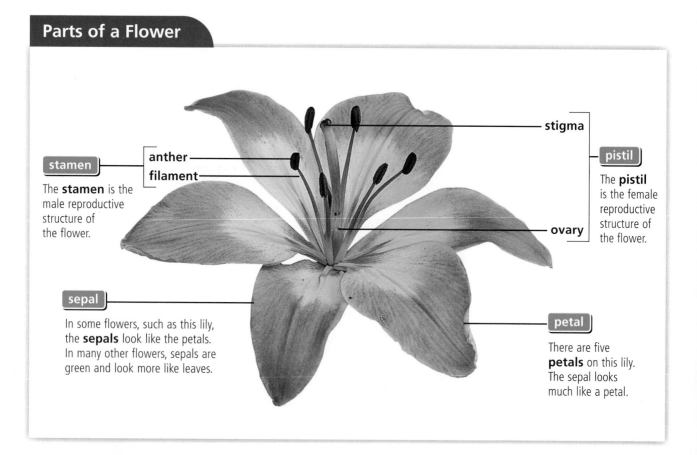

stigma

pistil
The **pistil** is the female reproductive structure of the flower.

anther
filament

stamen
The **stamen** is the male reproductive structure of the flower.

ovary

sepal
In some flowers, such as this lily, the **sepals** look like the petals. In many other flowers, sepals are green and look more like leaves.

petal
There are five **petals** on this lily. The sepal looks much like a petal.

INVESTIGATE Flower Parts

What parts of a flower can you identify?

PROCEDURE

① Examine the flower you are given. Try to notice as many details as you can. Draw a diagram of the flower in your notebook and label its parts.

② Carefully take your flower apart. Sort the parts. Draw and label one example of each part in your notebook.

WHAT DO YOU THINK?

• Which of the parts of a flower labeled in the diagram on page 110 did you find in your flower?

• Based on your experience, what would you look for if you were trying to decide whether a structure on an unfamiliar plant was a flower?

SKILL FOCUS
Observing

MATERIALS
• assorted flowers
• hand lens

TIME
15 minutes

Fruit

A fruit is a ripened plant ovary. Some ovaries contain more than one seed, such as an apple. Some contain only one seed, like a cherry. Apples and cherries are called fleshy fruits, because they have juicy flesh. The corn you eat as corn on the cob is a fleshy fruit. There are also dry fruits. The shells of peanuts, walnuts, and sunflowers are dry fruits. The structures of a dry fruit help protect the seed. Some dry fruits, like the winged fruit of a maple tree or the feathery tip of a dandelion seed, have structures that allow the seeds to be carried by the wind.

Animals spread both pollen and seeds.

Reproduction in many types of flowering plants includes interactions between plants and animals. The plants are a source of food for the animal. The animals provide a way to transport pollen and seeds. As they eat, animals move pollen from flower to flower and seeds from place to place.

Have you ever watched a honeybee collect nectar from a flower? Nectar is a sweet sugary liquid located at the bottom of the flower. As the bee crawls around in the flower, reaching down for the nectar, it rubs against the anthers and picks up pollen grains. When the bee travels to another flower, some of that pollen rubs off onto the pistil of the second flower.

pollen grains

 CHECK YOUR READING How do bees benefit from the flowers they pollinate?

An animal that pollinates a flower is called a pollinator. Bees and other insects are among the most important pollinators. Bees depend on nectar for food, and they collect pollen to feed their young. Bees recognize the colors, odors, and shapes of flowers. Bee-pollinated plants include sunflowers, rosemary, lavender, and thousands of other species.

The relationship between angiosperms and their pollinators can be highly specialized. Sometimes the nectar is located in a tube-shaped flower. Only certain animals, for example hummingbirds with long, slender beaks, can pollinate those flowers. Some flowers bloom at night. These flowers attract moths and bats as pollinators. Night-blooming flowers are usually pale, which means they are visible at night. Also, they may give off a strong scent to attract animal pollinators.

The advantage of animal pollination is that the pollen goes to where it is needed most. The pollen collected by a bee has a much better chance of being brought to another flower. By comparison, pollen grains that are spread by the wind are blown in all directions. Each grain has only a small chance of landing on another flower. Wind-pollinated plants produce a lot more pollen than plants that are pollinated by animals.

 CHECK YOUR READING What is the advantage of animal pollination over wind pollination?

 **SIMULATION** CLASSZONE.COM

Compare the different ways seeds are dispersed.

The fruits produced by angiosperms help to spread the seeds they contain. Some seeds, like dandelion and maple seeds, are carried by the wind. Many seeds are scattered by fruit-eating animals. The seeds go through the animal's digestive system and are eventually deposited on the ground with the animal's waste.

Animals eat fleshy fruit and distribute the seeds with their waste.

The burrs in this horse's mane are dry fruit that contain seeds.

Animals also help to scatter some types of dry fruits—not by eating them, but by catching them on their fur. Have you ever tried to pet a dog that has run through a grassy field? You might have noticed burrs stuck in the animal's fur. The seeds of many grasses and wildflowers produce dry fruits that are covered with spines or have pointed barbs. Seeds protected by these types of dry fruits stick to fur. The seeds travel along with the animal until the animal rubs them off.

Humans depend on plants for their survival.

Without plants, humans and all other animals would not be able to live on Earth. After plants adapted to life on land, it become possible for animals to live on land as well. Land animals rely on plants for food and oxygen. Many animals live in or near plants. Plants also supply materials humans use every day.

Food and Oxygen

All organisms must have energy to live. For animals, that energy comes from food. Plants, especially angiosperms, are the main source of food for all land animals. Plants capture energy from the Sun to make sugars and carbohydrates. Those same energy-rich materials are then consumed by animals as food. Even animals that eat other animals depend on plants for survival, because plants may provide food for the animals they eat.

Photosynthesis, the process that plants use to produce sugars and carbohydrates, also produces oxygen. The oxygen in the air you breathe is the product of the photosynthetic activity of plants and algae. Animals, including humans, need oxygen to release the energy stored in food.

Plants capture light energy from the Sun and store it in sugars and carbohydrates.

Energy Resources and Soil

Plants are an important source of many natural resources. Natural gas and coal are energy resources that formed deep underground from the remains of plants and other organisms. Natural gas and coal are important fuels for many purposes, including the generation of electricity.

Even the soil under your feet is a natural resource associated with plants. Plant roots can break down rock into smaller and smaller particles to form soil. When plants die, their bodies decay and add richness to the soil.

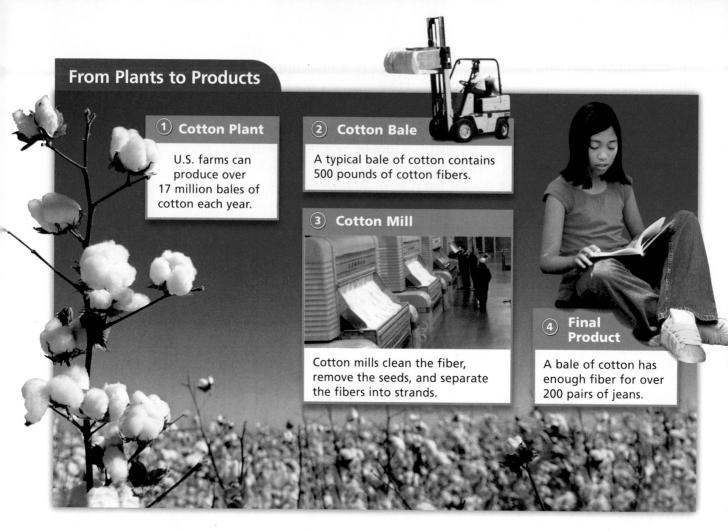

From Plants to Products

① Cotton Plant

U.S. farms can produce over 17 million bales of cotton each year.

② Cotton Bale

A typical bale of cotton contains 500 pounds of cotton fibers.

③ Cotton Mill

Cotton mills clean the fiber, remove the seeds, and separate the fibers into strands.

④ Final Product

A bale of cotton has enough fiber for over 200 pairs of jeans.

Other Products

Plant materials are part of many products people use every day. Plants provide the wood used to build houses and the wood pulp used to make paper for books like the one you are reading. The cotton in blue jeans comes from plants. So do many dyes that are used to add color to fabrics. Aspirin and many other medicines made by drug companies today are based on chemicals originally found in plants.

3.4 Review

KEY CONCEPTS

1. How do flowers relate to fruit?

2. How are animals involved in the life cycles of some flowering plants?

3. List three ways that humans depend upon plants.

CRITICAL THINKING

4. **Predict** If you observed three plants in a forest—a moss, a fern, and a flowering plant—which do you think would have the most insects nearby?

5. **Connect** Draw an apple like the one shown on page 107. Label three parts of the fruit and explain from which part of an apple flower each part grew.

○ CHALLENGE

6. **Synthesize** There are more species of flowering plants on Earth than species of mosses, ferns, or cone-bearing plants such as pine trees. How do you think the different ways spores, pollen, and seeds are spread affect the genetic diversity of different types of plants? Explain your reasoning.

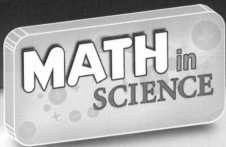

MATH TUTORIAL
CLASSZONE.COM

Click on Math Tutorial for
more help with perimeter
and area.

Chloroplast Math

You can't count the number of chloroplasts in a leaf very easily,
but you can estimate the number. For example, if you know the
number of chloroplasts in a small area, you can estimate the
number of chloroplasts in a whole leaf.

Example

Suppose you are studying how lilacs make food from sunlight. You
read that there are 50 million chloroplasts for every square centimeter of a leaf. You want to know the number in a whole leaf.

(1) Cover the leaf with centimeter grid paper.

(2) Count the number of whole
squares covering
the leaf.
7

(3) Match pairs or sets of
partly covered squares, that
add up to a whole square.
7 + 5 = 12

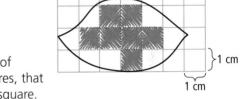

(4) Add on any remaining 0.5 (half), 0.025 (quarter), or 0.75
(three-quarters) of a square.
12 + .5 = 12.5

(5) Finally, multiply the number of squares by the number of
chloroplasts in one square.

ANSWER 50,000,000 × 12.5 = 625,000,000.

Give estimates for the following amounts.

1. Trace the beech leaf shown on this
page onto a sheet of centimeter
grid paper. What is the leaf's
approximate area in cm^2?

2. About how many chloroplasts are
in this beech leaf?

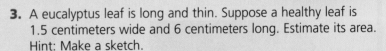

3. A eucalyptus leaf is long and thin. Suppose a healthy leaf is
1.5 centimeters wide and 6 centimeters long. Estimate its area.
Hint: Make a sketch.

4. What is the approximate number of chloroplasts in the
eucalyptus leaf described above?

CHALLENGE Collect two leaves. Trace the leaves on
centimeter grid paper. Label each tracing with its name,
estimated area, and its approximate number of chloroplasts.

Chapter Review

the BIG idea

Plants are a diverse group of organisms that live in many land environments.

CONTENT REVIEW
CLASSZONE.COM

KEY CONCEPTS SUMMARY

3.1 Plants are adapted to living on land.

All plants share common characteristics. The parts of a plant are specialized to get water and nutrients from the soil, gases from the air, and energy from the Sun. Plants have tissues, organs, and organ systems.

VOCABULARY
vascular system p. 87
transpiration p. 88

3.2 Most mosses and ferns live in moist environments.

The ancestors of present-day mosses and ferns were among the first land plants. Mosses are small nonvascular plants. Ferns are larger vascular plants. Both reproduce with spores and need moisture for a sperm to reach an egg.

3.3 Seeds and pollen are reproductive adaptations.

Gymnosperms, such as the pine tree, reproduce with **pollen** and seeds.

Seeds provide protection for the young plant as well as a supply of nutrients.

VOCABULARY
seed p. 98
embryo p. 98
germination p. 99
pollen p. 100
gymnosperm p. 102

3.4 Many plants reproduce with flowers and fruit.

Angiosperms use flowers and fruit to reproduce. **Flowers** produce pollen and contain the plant's reproductive structures.

Fruit develops after pollination and contains seeds. Animals eat fruit and transport seeds to new locations.

VOCABULARY
angiosperm p. 107
flower p. 108
fruit p. 108

Write a statement describing how the terms in each pair are related to each other.

1. transpiration, cuticle

2. spores, seeds

3. seed, embryo

4. flower, fruit

The table below shows Greek (G.) and Latin (L.) words that are roots of words used in this chapter.

angeion (G.)	vessel or holder
gymnos (G.)	naked
sperma (G.)	seed
germinatus (L.)	sprout
pollen (L.)	fine flour

Describe how these word roots relate to the definitions of the following words.

5. angiosperm

6. gymnosperm

7. germination

8. pollen

Reviewing Key Concepts

Multiple Choice *Choose the letter of the best answer.*

9. Which of these is a characteristic of only some plants?
   a. They produce sugars.
   b. They are multicellular.
   c. They have a vascular system.
   d. They have alternation of generations.

10. Which part of a plant anchors it in the soil?
   a. shoot system   **c.** vascular system
   b. root system   **d.** growth tissue

11. Which plant tissue transports water to different parts of the plant?
   a. vascular   **c.** stomata
   b. leaf   **d.** cuticle

12. Which part of a leaf does *not* allow transpiration?
   a. stomata   **c.** stem
   b. cell wall   **d.** cuticle

13. Which of these structures do mosses and ferns reproduce with?
   a. seeds   **c.** spores
   b. growth tissue   **d.** pollen

14. How are mosses different from ferns, pine trees, and flowering plants?
   a. Mosses reproduce through sexual reproduction.
   b. Mosses need moisture to reproduce.
   c. Mosses produce sugar through photosynthesis.
   d. Mosses have no vascular tissue.

15. What do seeds have that spores and pollen do not?
   a. a supply of nutrients
   b. a reproductive cell
   c. a protective covering
   d. a way to be transported

Short Answer *Write a short answer to each question.*

16. What are three ways plants are important to humans?

17. Explain how the bat in these photographs is interacting with the flower. How might the activity benefit the plant?

Thinking Critically

The next four questions refer to the labeled parts of the diagram of the leaf below.

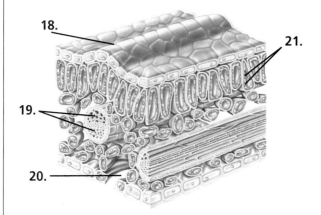

18.

21.

19.

20.

18. CLASSIFY Identify the layer that covers a leaf. What function does it serve, and why is that function important?

19. CLASSIFY What are the two tissues shown here, how do they function, and what system do they belong to?

20. HYPOTHESIZE Identify the structure and write a hypothesis about what would happen to this structure if the air around the plant was very hot and dry.

21. ANALYZE What are these structures? What is their function? Why are there more of them at the top of the leaf than at the bottom?

22. COMMUNICATE A leaf is made up of different tissues and specialized cells. What is the main function of a leaf? How does the organization of tissues and cells in a leaf help it to carry out this function? Include the following terms in your answer: *sunlight, energy, oxygen gas, carbon dioxide gas, water,* and *sugar*.

23. CLASSIFY What is the name of the group of plants pine trees belong to? What group of plants do cherry trees belong to? Which of the two groups is more widespread?

24. CONNECT You or someone you know may be allergic to pollen that is in the air during some plants' growing seasons. What is the advantage of a plant producing so much pollen?

25. SUMMARIZE Copy and complete the table below, indicating which reproductive structures are part of the life cycles of mosses, ferns, pine trees, and cherry trees. The first row is done.

	moss	fern	pine tree	cherry tree
sperm	✓	✓	✓	✓
egg				
pollen				
seed				
cone				
flower				
fruit				

26. SYNTHESIZE Plants were among the first organisms to live on land. Name at least two ways that plants made land habitable for animals. In what way did animals help plants to spread farther onto the land?

27. PROVIDE EXAMPLES Describe how a plant might reproduce asexually. Explain one advantage and one disadvantage asexual reproduction might have for the plant you described.

the BIG idea

28. SUMMARIZE Look again at the photograph on pages 82-83. Now that you have finished the chapter, how would you change or add details to your answer to the question on the photograph?

29. SYNTHESIZE Think of three different types of plants that you have seen. Use what you know about those plants as supporting evidence in a paragraph you write on one of these topics:

Plants are a diverse group of organisms.

Plants share common characteristics.

UNIT PROJECTS

Check your schedule for your unit project. How are you doing? Be sure that you have placed data or notes from your research in your project folder.

Analyzing Data

A pesticide is a material that kills pests, such as insects. A plant specialist wants to know if a new pesticide has any effect on the production of oranges. Grove A is planted using the same pesticide that was used in previous years. The new pesticide is used in grove B. Both groves have the same number of orange trees. The bar graph shows the data for one season.

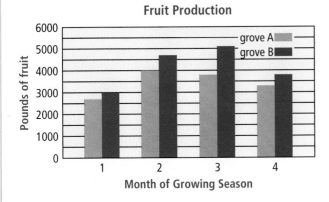

Fruit Production

Choose the letter of the best response.

1. About how many pounds of fruit were grown in grove A during month 1 of the growing season?

   a. about 2000 lb

   b. about 2700 lb

   c. about 3000 lb

   d. about 3500 lb

2. During which month in the growing season was the most fruit produced?

   a. month 1   **c.** month 3

   b. month 2   **d.** month 4

3. About how many pounds of fruit were produced altogether by both groves in month 2?

   a. about 4000 lb

   b. about 4700 lb

   c. about 5000 lb

   d. about 8700 lb

4. Comparing the production in both groves, during which month was there the least amount of difference in the number of pounds of fruit produced?

   a. month 1

   b. month 2

   c. month 3

   d. month 4

5. Based on the data in the graph, what might the plant specialist conclude about the effectiveness of the new pesticide used in grove B?

   a. The pesticide is effective only after three months of growth.

   b. The pesticide does not have any effect on orange production.

   c. The pesticide used in grove A is more effective than the pesticide used in grove B.

   d. The pesticide increases the overall production of oranges throughout the growing season.

Extended Response

6. Pesticides are intended to kill insects that harm the growth of a plant. However, not all insects are harmful. Insects often pollinate the flowers of fruit trees. Pollination leads to fertilization of the flower, and fruit grows from the fertilized flower. Describe what might happen if a pesticide kills insects that are pollinators. What effect might such a pesticide have on the flowers of the plant and on its fruit?

7. Pesticides are only one factor that affect the growth of plants and the number of flowers or fruit the plant produces. Write a paragraph that names some other factors that may affect plant growth. Include environmental factors and factors that are controlled by humans.

Invertebrate Animals

the **BIG** idea

Invertebrate animals have a variety of body plans and adaptations.

Key Concepts

SECTION
4.1 Most animals are invertebrates.
Learn about sponges and other invertebrates.

SECTION
4.2 Cnidarians and worms have different body plans.
Learn how the body plans of cnidarians are different from those of worms.

SECTION
4.3 Most mollusks have shells, and echinoderms have spiny skeletons.
Learn about how mollusks and echinoderms meet their needs.

SECTION
4.4 Arthropods have exoskeletons and joints.
Learn about insects, crustaceans, and arachnids.

Internet Preview

CLASSZONE.COM

Chapter 4 online resources: Content Review, Visualization, four Resource Centers, Math Tutorial, Test Practice

How does this jellyfish find food and eat?

EXPLORE (the BIG idea)

Worm-Watching

Find a worm and observe it for a while in its natural environment. How much can you learn about how a worm meets its needs by watching it for a short time? Record your observations in your notebook.

Observe and Think
What body parts can you identify on a worm? How would you describe a worm's activities and behavior?

Insects and You

Think about times when you have seen or noticed insects. Make a list of your experiences in your notebook. Then, start keeping a list of all the insects you see for the next week. How long do you think this list will be?

Observe and Think How many different types of insects did you see? Where did you see them? What characteristics do you think insects share?

Internet Activity: Invertebrate Diversity

Go to **ClassZone.com** to learn more about different types of invertebrates.

Observe and Think
Of every 20 animal species on Earth, 19 are invertebrates. How many types of invertebrates can you name?

scilinks.org

Sponges Code: MDL042

Getting Ready to Learn

◀ CONCEPT REVIEW

- All animals need energy, materials, and living space.
- Animals get energy and materials from food.
- Animals have different adaptations and behaviors for meeting their needs.

◀ VOCABULARY REVIEW

predator p. 63

prey p. 63

adaptation *See Glossary.*

CONTENT REVIEW
CLASSZONE.COM
Review concepts and vocabulary.

▶ TAKING NOTES

COMBINATION NOTES

To take notes about a new concept, first make an informal outline of the information. Then make a sketch of the concept and label it so you can study it later. Use arrows to connect parts of the concept when appropriate.

CHOOSE YOUR OWN STRATEGY

For each new vocabulary term, take notes by choosing one of the strategies from earlier chapters—**description wheel, four square,** or **word triangle.** You can also use other vocabulary strategies that you might already know.

See the Note-Taking Handbook on pages R45–R51.

SCIENCE NOTEBOOK

Notes

Sponges are simple animals
- no organs
- attached to one place
- remove food from water

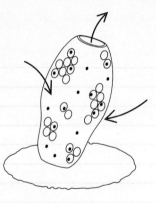

Description Wheel

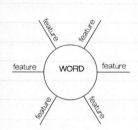

Four Square

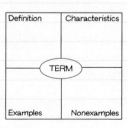

Word Triangle

Most animals are invertebrates.

 BEFORE, you learned

- Animals are consumers; they get food from the environment
- Most animals have body systems, including tissues and organs
- Animals interact with the environment and other animals

NOW, you will learn

- About the diversity of invertebrates
- About six groups of invertebrates
- How sponges get energy

VOCABULARY

invertebrate p. 123
sponge p. 125
sessile p. 125
larva p. 126

THINK ABOUT

What makes an animal an animal?

A sponge is an animal. It has no head, eyes, ears, arms, or legs. A sponge doesn't have a heart or a brain or a mouth. It doesn't move. Typically, it spends its life attached to the ocean floor. Many people used to think that sponges were plants that had adapted to life in the water. Scientists, however, classify them as animals. How might you decide if the organism in the photograph is an animal?

Invertebrates are a diverse group of organisms.

About one million invertebrate species live on Earth. **Invertebrates** are animals that do not have backbones. In fact, invertebrates do not have any bone tissue at all. Invertebrates can be found just about everywhere, from frozen tundra to tropical forests. Some invertebrates live in water, while others survive in deserts where there is almost no water. Many invertebrates live inside other organisms.

Most invertebrate animals are small. Crickets, oysters, sea stars, earthworms, ants, and spiders are some examples of invertebrates. The fact that invertebrates do not have backbones for support tends to limit their size. However, some ocean-dwelling invertebrates can be quite large. For example, the giant squid can grow to 18 meters (59 ft) in length and can weigh over 450 kilograms (992 lb).

INVESTIGATE Invertebrates

Which types of invertebrates live near you?

PROCEDURE

1. Cut the potato in half lengthwise. Scoop out a hole and carve a channel so it looks like the photograph below.

2. Put the two halves back together and wrap them with masking tape. Leave the channel uncovered. It is the entrance hole.

3. Take the potato trap outside and bury it upright in soil, with the entrance hole sticking out of the ground. Wash your hands.

4. Collect the potato the next day. Remove the masking tape and look inside.

WHAT DO YOU THINK?

- Observe the contents of the potato. Record your observations.

- Would you classify the contents of the potato as living or nonliving? Do you think they are animals or plants?

CHALLENGE Predict how your observations would be different if you buried the potato in a different place.

MATERIALS
- potato
- knife
- spoon
- masking tape

TIME
20 minutes

In this chapter, you will learn about six groups of invertebrates:

- **Sponges** are the simplest invertebrates. They live in water. They filter food from the water that surrounds them.

- **Cnidarians** also live in water. Animals in this group have a central opening surrounded by tentacles. They take in food and eliminate waste through this opening. Jellyfish, sea anemones, hydras, and corals are cnidarians.

- **Worms** are animals with soft, tube-shaped bodies and a distinct head. Some worms live inside other animals. Others live in the water or on land.

- **Mollusks** have a muscular foot that allows them to move and hunt for food. Some mollusks live on land. Others live in water. Clams, snails, and octopuses are mollusks.

- **Echinoderms** are water animals that have a central opening for taking in food. Sea stars and sand dollars are echinoderms.

- **Arthropods** are invertebrates that are found on land, in the water, and in the air. They have legs. Some have wings. Insects, spiders, crabs, and millipedes are arthropods.

Sponges are simple animals.

Sponges are the simplest multicellular animals on Earth. These invertebrates are **sessile** (SEHS-EEL) organisms, which means they live attached to one spot and do not move from place to place. Most live in the ocean, although some live in fresh water. Sponges have no tissues or organs. The body of a sponge is made up of a collection of cells. The cells are organized into a body wall, with an outside and an inside. Sponges are adapted to feed continuously. They feed on plankton and other tiny organisms that live in the water.

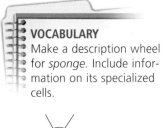

VOCABULARY
Make a description wheel for *sponge*. Include information on its specialized cells.

Specialized Cells

A sponge meets its needs with cells specialized for different functions. Pore cells along the body wall create tiny openings throughout the body. The pores lead into larger canals and sometimes a central opening, where cells with tiny hairs, or flagella, move water through the sponge. As water moves out, more water enters, as shown in the diagram below. Specialized cells filter out food particles and oxygen. Other specialized cells digest the food.

 CHECK YOUR READING What adaptations does a sponge have for obtaining food?

Feeding in Sponges

Structures in a sponge's body function to remove food from water.

1 Water flows into the sponge through pores in the body wall.

2 Flagella along the inside of the sponge move water through the sponge.

3 Specialized cells pick up food particles as the water moves by.

4 Specialized cells digest the food particles.

flow of water

inside of sponge

pores

Another adaptation sponges have are structures that make the body stiff. Most sponges have spicules (SPIHK-yoolz), which are needlelike spines made of hard minerals such as calcium or silicon. Spicules help give the sponge its shape and provide support. In some sponges, spicules stick out from the body. This may make the sponge less likely to become a source of food for other animals.

Reproduction

This basket sponge is releasing microscopic larvas into the water.

Sponges can reproduce asexually. Buds form alongside the parent sponge or the buds break off and float away. Tiny sponges can float quite a distance before they attach to the ocean floor or some underwater object and start to grow.

Sponges also reproduce sexually, as most multicellular organisms do. In sponges, sperm are released into the water. In some sponges, the eggs are released too. In this case, fertilization occurs in the water. In other sponges, the eggs are contained in specialized cells in the body wall. Sperm enter the sponge to fertilize the egg.

A fertilized egg becomes a larva. A **larva** is an immature form—an early stage—of an organism that is different from the parent. Sponge larvas are able to swim. They move away from the parent and will grow into a sponge once they attach to some underwater surface. Then they become sessile, like their parents.

Sponges provide a good starting point for studying other invertebrates. There are many different types of invertebrates, with a wide range of body structures and behaviors. Invertebrates have adapted to many different environments. By comparison, the sponge is a simple organism that has changed very little over time. Sponges today look very similar to fossil sponges that are millions of years old.

4.1 Review

KEY CONCEPTS

1. Make a table with six columns. Write the name of an invertebrate group above each column. Fill in the table with a characteristic and an example for each group.

2. What does it mean that sponges are sessile?

3. How do sponges meet their need for energy?

CRITICAL THINKING

4. **Apply** Give two examples of how structure in a sponge relates to function. You should use the words *flagella* and *spicule* in your answer.

5. **Infer** How is water involved in the reproductive cycle of a sponge?

CHALLENGE

6. **Analyze** Sponges have lived on Earth for hundreds of millions of years. Sponges today look very similar to fossil sponges. What does this suggest about how well the simple structure of a sponge meets its needs? Do species always change over time?

MATH in SCIENCE

MATH TUTORIAL
CLASSZONE.COM
Click on Math Tutorial for more help with line symmetry.

Mirror, Mirror

A pattern or shape that has *line symmetry* contains a mirror image of its parts on either side of a straight line. Think about the shapes of a starfish or a butterfly.

Example

If you were to cut these shapes out of flat paper, you could fold the paper along a line of symmetry. The two halves would match.

Some shapes have more than one line of symmetry. The shapes of most anemones, and starfish, like flowers, can fold along two, three, or more lines of symmetry.

Sketch each shape. Then draw any lines of symmetry. If there are none, write "zero."

1) 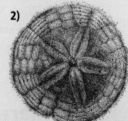 2)  3)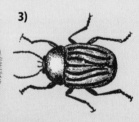

4)  5)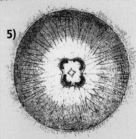

CHALLENGE Write out the uppercase letters of the alphabet *A* to *Z*. For each letter, write whether it has zero, one, or two lines of symmetry.

KEY CONCEPT
Cnidarians and worms have different body plans.

BEFORE, you learned

- Invertebrates are a diverse group of animals
- Sponges are sessile organisms
- Sponges meet their needs with simple bodies and specialized cells

NOW, you will learn

- About body systems in cnidarians
- About body symmetry and feeding patterns
- About body systems in worms

VOCABULARY

cnidarian p. 128
tentacle p. 128
mobile p. 130

EXPLORE Worm Movement

How does body shape affect movement?

PROCEDURE

1. Put a thin layer of soil on the tray and gently place the worm on it. Use the spray bottle to keep the soil and your hands moist.

2. Draw a sketch of the worm and try to identify the parts of its body.

3. Record your observations of its movement.

4. Follow your teacher's instructions in handling the worm and materials at the end of the lab. Wash your hands.

MATERIALS

- worm
- tray
- soil
- spray bottle filled with distilled water

WHAT DO YOU THINK?

- How does the shape of a worm's body affect its movement?
- How would you describe a worm to someone who has never seen one?

Cnidarians have simple body systems.

COMBINATION NOTES
Make notes and diagrams for the main idea: *Cnidarians have simple body systems.*

Cnidarians (ny-DAIR-ee-uhnz) are invertebrates. Like sponges, cnidarians are found only in water. This group includes jellyfish, corals, sea anemones, and small freshwater organisms called hydras. Most cnidarians feed on small plankton, fish, and clams. Many cnidarians are sessile for most of their lives. Like sponges, cnidarians have adaptations that allow them to pull food in from the water that surrounds them.

All cnidarians have **tentacles,** fingerlike extensions of their body that reach into the water. Other animals have tentacles, but the tentacles of cnidarians have specialized stinging cells. The tentacles, with their stinging cells, are an adaptation that enables cnidarians to capture prey.

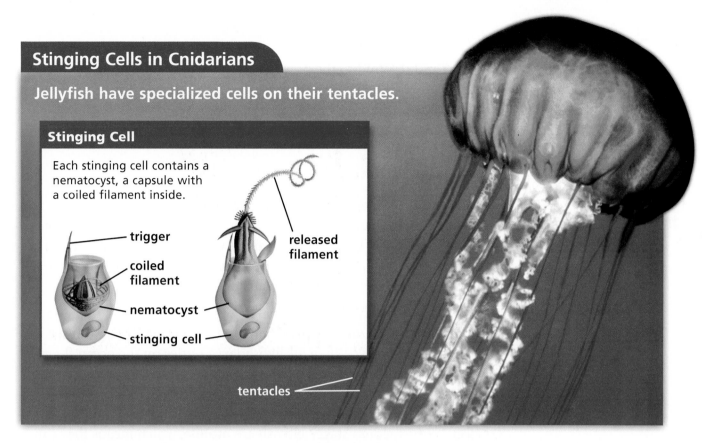

Stinging Cells in Cnidarians

Jellyfish have specialized cells on their tentacles.

Stinging Cell

Each stinging cell contains a nematocyst, a capsule with a coiled filament inside.

trigger

coiled filament

nematocyst

stinging cell

released filament

tentacles

Each stinging cell has a nematocyst (NEHM-uh-tuh-SIHST), a capsule that holds a barbed filament. The filament is like a tiny hollow tube coiled up inside the capsule. When prey comes into contact with the stinger cell, the filament is released. Sometimes this stinger wraps itself around the prey. In most species of cnidarians, the stinger stabs the prey and releases a poison from its tip. These stingers are what produce the sting of a jellyfish. Stinging cells have a second function. They protect cnidarians from predators.

 CHECK YOUR READING Describe how the structure of a nematocyst allows it to function in capturing food and providing protection.

Tissues and Body Systems

A cnidarian's body is made up of flexible layers of tissue. These tissues, along with specialized cells, make up its body systems. The tissues are organized around a central opening where food is taken in and wastes are released. The tentacles bring the prey into this opening. The opening leads into a cavity, a gut, where the food is digested.

Cnidarians have a simple muscle system for movement. Even though cnidarians are sessile during most of their lives, they still move their bodies. Cnidarians bend from side to side and extend their tentacles. Adult jellyfish swim. The movement is produced by muscle cells that run around and along the sides of its body. When the muscle cells shorten, or contract, they produce movement.

Cnidarians, when they move, interact with the environment. They sense and respond to the prey that come in contact with their tentacles. This behavior is the result of a simple nervous system. Cnidarians have a network of nerve cells, a nerve net that extends throughout their bodies.

Reproduction

Cnidarians reproduce both sexually and asexually, and water plays a role in both processes. Buds produced by asexual reproduction are carried away from the sessile parent by water. In sexual reproduction, sperm are carried to the egg. Fertilization results in a free-swimming larva. The larva, if it survives, develops into an adult.

Jellyfish are cnidarians with a life cycle that includes several stages. A jellyfish's body, or form, is different at each stage, as you can see in the diagram below. When a jellyfish larva settles on the ocean floor, it grows into a form called a polyp. The polyp, which is sessile, develops disk-shaped buds that stack up like a pile of plates. The buds, once they are released, are called medusas. Each medusa is an adult jellyfish. In the medusa stage, jellyfish are **mobile,** which means they can move their bodies from place to place.

Jellyfish Life Cycle

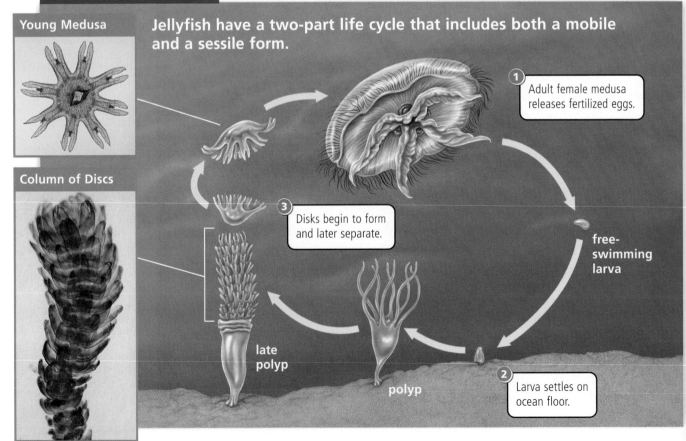

Young Medusa

Column of Discs

Jellyfish have a two-part life cycle that includes both a mobile and a sessile form.

1 Adult female medusa releases fertilized eggs.

3 Disks begin to form and later separate.

free-swimming larva

late polyp

polyp

2 Larva settles on ocean floor.

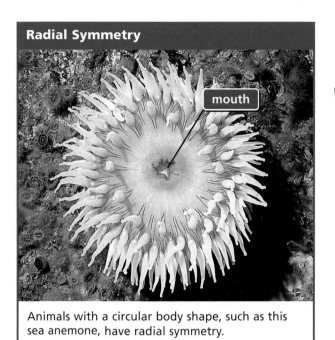

Radial Symmetry

mouth

Animals with a circular body shape, such as this sea anemone, have radial symmetry.

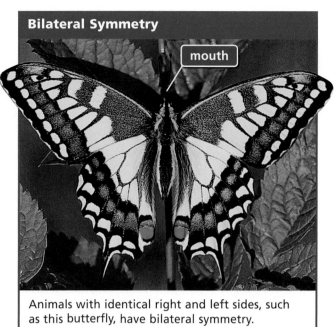

Bilateral Symmetry

mouth

Animals with identical right and left sides, such as this butterfly, have bilateral symmetry.

Animals have different body plans.

Scientists sometimes use the term body plan to describe the shape of an animal's body. Most cnidarians have a body plan with radial symmetry. This means the body is organized around a central point, a mouthlike opening that leads into a gut. You can see from the diagram of the jellyfish life cycle on page 30 that both the polyp and medusa have radial symmetry.

A radial body plan allows a sessile organism, such as the sea anenome shown in the photograph above, to capture food from any direction. A radial body plan also affects how a mobile animal moves. A jellyfish medusa moves forward by pushing down on the water. It has to stop moving to change direction.

Most animals, including worms, butterflies, birds, and humans, have a body plan with bilateral symmetry. One half looks just like the other, as you can see in the photograph of the butterfly above. You can recognize a bilaterally symmetrical shape because there is only one way to draw a line dividing it into two equal halves.

Animals with bilateral symmetry have a forward end where the mouth is located. This is the animal's head. The animal moves forward, head first, in search of food. A bilateral body shape works well in animals that are mobile. Food enters at one end, and is processed as it moves through the body. Once all the nutrients have been absorbed, the remaining wastes are released at the other end.

READING TiP

The root of the word *radial* means "ray," like the spoke of a wheel. The roots of the word *bilateral* are *bi-*, meaning "two," and *lateral*, meaning "side."

 CHECK YOUR READING Describe how radial symmetry and bilateral symmetry affect an animal's feeding behaviors.

Most worms have complex body systems.

RESOURCE CENTER
CLASSZONE.COM

Learn more about the many types of worms.

Some worms have simple bodies. Others have well-developed body systems. Worms have a tube-shaped body, with bilateral symmetry. In many worms, food enters at one end and is processed as it moves through a digestive tract. Worms take in oxygen, dissolved in water, through their skin. Because of this, worms must live moist environments. Many live in water.

Segmented Worms

Segmented worms have bodies that are divided into individual compartments, or segments. These worms are referred to as annelids (AN-uh-lihdz), which means "ringed animals." One annelid you might be familiar with is the earthworm. As the diagram below shows, an earthworm's segments can be seen on the outside of its body.

An earthworm has organs that are organized into body systems. The digestive system of an earthworm includes organs for digestion and food storage. It connects to the excretory system, which removes waste. Earthworms pass soil through their digestive system. They digest decayed pieces of plant and animal matter from the soil and excrete what's left over. A worm's feeding and burrowing activity adds nutrients and oxygen to the soil.

 CHECK YOUR READING Name two body systems found in earthworms.

Inside an Earthworm

An earthworm has organs and body systems.

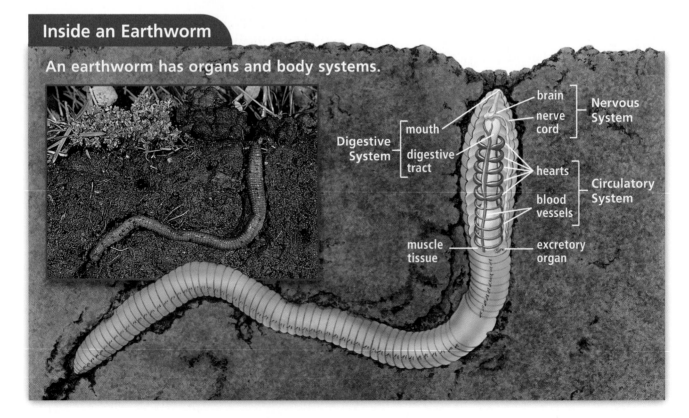

Digestive System — mouth, digestive tract

Nervous System — brain, nerve cord

Circulatory System — hearts, blood vessels

muscle tissue

excretory organ

Earthworms have several layers of muscle tissue in their body wall. Hairlike bristles on the segments help to anchor a worm in the soil as it moves. The nervous system includes a brain and a nerve cord that runs through the body. An earthworm can detect strong light and vibrations in the soil. These stimuli signal danger to a worm. An earthworm also has a circulatory system. It is made up of several hearts that pump blood through blood vessels.

Some annelids reproduce asexually, while others reproduce sexually. There are no distinct male or female worms. Earthworms, for example, carry both male and female reproductive structures. To reproduce, two worms exchange sperm. The sperm fertilize eggs the worms carry in their bodies. The eggs are laid and later hatch into larvas.

Flatworms and Roundworms

Flatworms are the worms with the simplest bodies. Some are so small and flat that they move with cilia, not muscles. These flatworms absorb nutrients directly through the skin. Many flatworms live as parasites, feeding off other organisms. For example, tapeworms are flatworms that infect humans and other animals. The tapeworm has no need for a digestive system because it gets digested nutrients from its host.

Roundworms are found just about everywhere on Earth. The bodies of roundworms are more complex than those of flatworms. They have muscles to move with, and a nervous system and digestive system. Some roundworms are important decomposers on land and in the water.

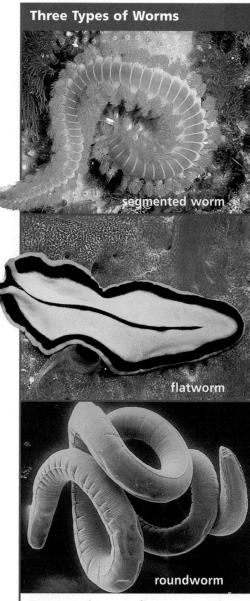

Three Types of Worms

segmented worm

flatworm

roundworm

Segmented worms, flatworms, and roundworms are the most common worms on Earth.

4.2 Review

KEY CONCEPTS

1. What adaptation do cnidarians have for capturing prey?

2. What is the difference between radial symmetry and bilateral symmetry?

3. Pick two systems found in an earthworm and describe how they work together.

CRITICAL THINKING

4. **Predict** How might having sense organs located at the front end of the body benefit an animal?

5. **Infer** Would the food of a jellyfish medusa be different from the food of a polyp? Support your answer.

⬆ CHALLENGE

6 **Compare and Contrast** Describe how the different body symmetries of cnidarians and segmented worms affect their movement and feeding behaviors.

CHAPTER INVESTIGATION

Worm Behavior

OVERVIEW AND PURPOSE Earthworms do not have eyes, so they cannot see. An earthworm needs an environment that provides it with moisture, food, and protection from predators. How do worms gather information about their surroundings? How do they respond to changes in their environment? In this investigation you will

- observe worm behavior
- predict how worms will respond to surfaces with different textures

▶ Problem

How is worm behavior affected by environmental conditions?

▶ Hypothesize

You should complete steps 1–9 in the procedure before writing your hypothesis. Write a hypothesis to explain how worms will respond to different surface textures in an environment. Your hypothesis should take the form of an "If . . . , then . . . , because . . ." statement.

▶ Procedure

1. Make a data table in your **Science Notebook** like the one shown on page 135.

2. Cover one half of the bottom of the aquarium with potting soil and the other half with sand.

3. Fill the beaker with 250 mL of distilled water and use it to fill the spray bottle. Spray all the water over the potting soil so it is evenly moistened.

MATERIALS
- aquarium
- potting soil
- coarse sand
- small beaker
- distilled water
- spray bottle
- filter paper
- 5 or more worms
- 2 containers, one for untested worms and one for tested worms
- stopwatch
- *for Challenge* flashlight

4 Repeat step 3, but this time moisten the sand. Refill the spray bottle.

5 Place a piece of filter paper in the middle of the aquarium so it is half on the soil and half on the sand, as shown.

step 5

6 Put on your gloves. Spray your hands with water. Gently remove one worm and observe it until you can tell which end is its head.

step 6

7 Start the stopwatch as you place the worm on the middle of the filter paper. Note which part of the aquarium the worm's head points toward.

8 Observe the worm's behavior for two minutes and then remove it carefully from the aquarium and place it in the container for tested worms.

9 Write your observations in your data table. State your hypothesis.

10 Fix the sand, soil, and paper in the aquarium so they are arranged as they were for the first worm. Then repeat steps 6–9 with at least four more worms.

11 Return the worms to their original living place. Wash your hands.

▶ Observe and Analyze
Write It Up

1. **OBSERVE** What behaviors suggest that worms gather information about their surroundings?

2. **OBSERVE** What evidence did you see to suggest that worms respond to information they get about their surroundings?

3. **INTERPRET DATA** What patterns did you notice in the behavior of the worms you tested?

▶ Conclude
Write It Up

1. **INTERPRET** Compare your results with your hypothesis. Does your data support your hypothesis?

2. **IDENTIFY LIMITS** What sources of error could have affected your investigation?

3. **EVALUATE** Based on your observations and evidence, what conclusions can you draw about the connection between worm behavior and environmental conditions?

▶ INVESTIGATE Further

CHALLENGE Worms respond to light as a stimulus. Design an experiment to test the reaction of worms to the presence of light.

Worm Behavior

Hypothesis

Table 1. Observations of Tested Worms

	Starting Position	Ending Position	Description of Behavior
Worm 1			
Worm 2			
Worm 3			
Worm 4			
Worm 5			

Most mollusks have shells, and echinoderms have spiny skeletons.

◀ BEFORE, you learned

- Body shape affects how animals move and behave
- Cnidarians have radial symmetry and simple body systems
- Worms have bilateral symmetry and complex body systems

▶ NOW, you will learn

- About different types of mollusks and their features
- About different types of echinoderms and their features

VOCABULARY

mollusk p. 136
gill p. 137
lung p. 137
echinoderm p. 139

THINK ABOUT

How does a snail move?

Snails belong to a group of mollusks called gastropods. The name means "belly foot." Snails are often put into aquariums to clean up the algae that can build up along the walls of the tank. If you get a chance, look at a snail moving along the glass walls of an aquarium, observe how it uses its foot to move. How would you describe the action of the snail's foot?

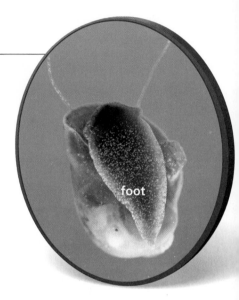

foot

Mollusks are soft-bodied animals.

VOCABULARY
Choose a strategy from earlier chapters, such as a word triangle, or one of your own to take notes on the term *mollusk*.

One characteristic that is shared by all **mollusks** is a soft body. Many of these invertebrate animals also have an outer shell to protect their body. Oysters, clams, snails, and mussels are all mollusks. So are octopuses, squids, and slugs. Mollusks live on land and in freshwater and saltwater environments. You will read about three groups of mollusks: bivalves, gastropods, and cephalopods.

Most mollusks have well-developed organ systems. They have muscles, a digestive system, a respiratory system, a circulatory system, and a nervous system with sensory organs. Mollusks reproduce sexually, and in most species there are distinct male and female organisms. Two adaptations distinguish mollusks as a group. First, all mollusks have a muscular foot. A mollusk's head is actually attached to its foot. Second, all mollusks have a mantle, a layer of folded skin that protects its internal organs.

Bivalves

Bivalves are named for a hard shell that is made up of two matching halves. Clams, mussels, scallops, and oysters are all bivalves. The shell, when it is closed, completely encloses the body. If you've ever seen a raw oyster, you know that a bivalve's body looks like a mass of tissue. Bivalves do not have a distinct head, but they do have a mouth and sensory organs. The scallop shown in the photograph has light-sensitive organs that look like tiny eyes.

Bivalves are filter feeders, they filter food from the surrounding water. To move, a bivalve balances upright, opens its shell, and extends its foot. The animal moves by pushing the foot in and out. The foot is also used for burrowing, digging down into the sand.

The invertebrates you've studied so far—sponges, cnidarians, and worms—take in oxygen all along the surface of their bodies. A bivalve takes in oxygen through a pair of gills. A **gill** is an organ that filters dissolved oxygen from water. The gill is an adaptation that allows an organism to take in a lot of oxygen in just one area of its body. It is made up of many folds of tissue that create a large surface area. Blood picks up the oxygen and moves it to the rest of the animal's body. In most bivalves, the gills also filter food from the water.

Bivalve

Most of this blue-eyed scallop's body is inside its two-part shell.

RESOURCE CENTER
CLASSZONE.COM
Discover more about mollusks.

 CHECK YOUR READING What are the two functions of gills and how do those functions relate to where bivalves live?

Gastropods

Gastropods are the most diverse group of mollusks. Some, such as snails and slugs, live on land. Many live in water, for example, conches, whelks, and periwinkles. Many gastropods are protected by a spiral-shaped shell. To protect itself, a gastropod withdraws into the shell.

The gastropod's head is located at the end of its foot. The head has eyes and specialized tentacles for sensing. Many gastropods have a cutting mouth part, called a radula, that shreds their food. Some gastropods eat animals, but most feed on plants and algae. Gastropods that live in water have gills. Some gastropods that live on land have lungs. A **lung** is an organ that absorbs oxygen from the air. Like gills, lungs have a large surface area.

Gastropod

This brown-lipped snail extends most of its body out of its shell when it moves.

INVESTIGATE Mollusks and Echinoderms

How do mollusk shells compare with echinoderm skeletons?

PROCEDURE

1. Closely observe the mollusk shells and skeletons of sea stars and sand dollars you are given.

2. Examine the shape and texture of each. Sort them by their characteristics.

WHAT DO YOU THINK?

How are the shells and skeletons the same? How are they different?

CHALLENGE Based on your observations, what can you infer about the bodies of living mollusks, sea stars, and sand dollars?

SKILL FOCUS
Observing

MATERIALS
Selection of mollusk shells, sea stars, and sand dollars

TIME
15 minutes

Cephalopods

Cephalopods (SEHF-uh-luh-PAHDZ) live in saltwater environments. Octopuses, squids, and chambered nautiluses are cephalopods. Among mollusks, cephalopods have the most well-developed body systems.

Cephalopods

This Maori octopus has a well-developed head attached to a foot with eight tentacles.

Cephalopods have a brain and well-developed nerves. They have a pair of eyes near their mouth. The foot, which surrounds the mouth, has tentacles for capturing prey. The mantle is adapted to push water forcefully through a tube-shaped structure called a siphon. This produces a jet of water that moves the animal. Gills take in oxygen, which is picked up by blood vessels and pumped through the body by three hearts.

Octopuses and squids do not have protective shells. They do have protective behaviors, however. Some can change body color to match their surroundings. Some release dark clouds of inklike fluid into the water, to confuse their predators. The lack of a shell lets them move freely through the water.

The nautilus is the only cephalopod that has a shell. The shell is made up of separate compartments, or chambers. The nautilus itself lives in the outermost chamber. The inner chambers are filled with gas, which makes the animal better able to float. The chambered shell also provides the soft-bodied nautilus with protection from predators.

VISUALIZATION
CLASSZONE.COM

Watch how different cephalopods move.

CHECK YOUR READING   How is the foot of a cephalopod adapted for hunting?

Mollusks show a range of adaptations.

You might not think that a clam would belong to the same group as an octopus. These organisms look very different from one another. They also interact with the environment in different ways. The great variety of mollusks on Earth today provides a good example of how adaptations within a group can lead to great diversity. A good example of this is the range of adaptations shown in the shape and function of a mollusk's foot.

The foot of the bivalve is a simple muscular structure that moves in and out of its shell. The foot allows a bivalve to crawl along the ocean floor and to bury itself in the sand. Gastropods have a head at the end of the foot, which runs the length of the body. Muscles in the foot produce ripples that allow the gastropod to glide over a surface as it searches for food. In cephalopods, the foot has tentacles to pull food into its mouth. The tentacles also help some cephalopods move along the ocean floor.

foot

COMPARE How does the foot of this clam compare with the foot of an octopus?

Echinoderms have unusual adaptations.

Echinoderms are a group of invertebrates that live in the ocean. In their adult form, their bodies have radial symmetry. Sea stars, sea urchins, sea cucumbers, and sand dollars belong to this group. Echinoderms feed off the ocean floor as they move along. An echinoderm's mouth is located at the center of the body, on the underside. Some echinoderms, such as sea urchins and sand dollars, filter food from their surroundings. Others, such as sea stars, are active predators that feed on clams, snails, and even other echinoderms.

COMBINATION NOTES
Remember to take notes and make sketches for the main idea: *Echinoderms have unusual adaptations.*

Spines and Skeletons

Echinoderm means "spiny-skinned." Some of the more familiar echinoderms have long, sharp spines, like the sea urchin in the photograph at the bottom of this page. However, some echinoderm species, such as sea cucumbers, have spines that are very small.

One unusual adaptation that echinoderms have is a type of skeleton. Remember that echinoderms are invertebrates, they have no bone tissue. The echinoderm skeleton is made up of a network of stiff, hard plates. The plates lie just under the surface of the echinoderm's skin. Some echinoderms, such as sea stars, have skeletons with loosely connected plates and flexible arms. In other echinoderms, such as sand dollars,the plates grow close together, so the skeleton does not allow for much flexibility.

This purple sea urchin has very obvious spines.

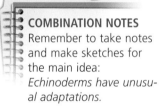

This sea star has captured a bivalve and is using its tube feet to open the shell.

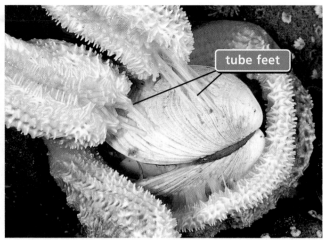

tube feet

This sea star's arms have been pulled up to show how its tube feet are attached to the bivalve's shell.

Water Vascular System and Tube Feet

Another adaptation that is unique to echinoderms is a water vascular system. This system is made up of water-filled tubes that radiate out from the center of the echinoderm's body. Tiny openings along the upper surface of the echinoderm's body feed water into these tubes. At the base of the tubes is a series of tube feet.

Muscles attached to the top of each tube can close the tube off, producing suction at the base of the tube. The tube feet stick to the ocean floor, allowing the echinoderm to pull itself along. The tube feet can also be used for hunting prey. For example, a sea star can surround a clam or oyster with its body, as shown in the photograph on the left. The tube feet pull the shell open. Then, the sea star's stomach is pushed out through its mouth and into the bivalve's shell, where it begins to digest the bivalve's body. Not all echinoderms eat other animals. Some, like sea urchins, feed off algae on the ocean floor.

4.3 Review

KEY CONCEPTS

1. What two features do all mollusks have?

2. What are two features all echinoderms have?

3. What are two functions of tube feet in echinoderms?

CRITICAL THINKING

4. **Analyze** For mollusks and echinoderms, what are the advantages and disadvantages of having a shell or spiny skeleton?

5. **Compare and Contrast** Compare the foot of mollusks with the tube feet of echinoderms.

CHALLENGE

6. **Analyze** Animals with lungs or gills can be larger than animals that take in oxygen through their skin. What feature do both lungs and gills have that affect the amount of oxygen they can absorb? What role does the circulatory system play?

Eating Well

Common sea stars have five arms. When one arm is missing, sea stars are, amazingly, able to grow another. Scientists interested in this amazing ability designed an experiment to see how having four arms instead of five affect a sea star's ability to consume prey. The sea stars use tube feet on each arm to pry open the shells of mussels and eat the animal's insides.

Scientists, working in 1999 and 2000, examined common sea stars caught in fishing gear. The study divided them into two groups: one group with five arms and one group with only four arms. Each sea star was tested to see how well it could open and eat a mussel.

◗ Observations

Scientists made these observations:

> a. Most of the sea stars with all five arms opened and ate a mussel.
> b. Fewer than half of the sea stars with four arms opened and ate a mussel.
> c. All the sea stars that opened a mussel took about 13 hours to finish eating it.

◗ Conclusions

Here are some conclusions about sea stars eating mussels:

> a. Common sea stars are most likely to feed successfully if they have all their arms.
> b. A common sea star with only four arms will starve.
> c. Common sea stars eat slowly regardless of how many arms they have.
> d. Common sea stars with only four arms choose mussels that are difficult to open.

◗ Evaluate the Conclusions

On Your Own Think about each observation that the scientists noted. Do they support the conclusions? Do some observations support one conclusion but not another? If a conclusion is not supported, what extra observations would you need to make?

With A Partner Compare your thinking with your partner's thinking. Do you both agree with the conclusions?

CHALLENGE Why do you think the sea stars with only four arms were less likely to open and eat a mussel?

The common sea star (Asterias rubeus) can regrow a missing arm. Its main prey is the mussel.

KEY CONCEPT

4.4 Arthropods have exoskeletons and joints.

◀ BEFORE, you learned

- Mollusks are invertebrates with soft bodies, some have shells
- Echinoderms have spiny skeletons
- Different species adapt to the same environment in different ways

▶ NOW, you will learn

- About different groups of arthropods
- About exoskeletons in arthropods
- About metamorphosis in arthropods

VOCABULARY

arthropod p. 142
exoskeleton p. 143
molting p. 143
insect p. 145
metamorphosis p. 146

EXPLORE Arthropods

What are some characteristics of arthropods?

PROCEDURE

1. Observe the pillbugs in their container. Draw a sketch of a pillbug.

2. Gently remove the pillbugs from their container and place them in the open end of the box. Observe and make notes on their behavior for several minutes.

3. Return the pillbugs to their container.

WHAT DO YOU THINK?

- Describe some of the characteristics you noticed about pillbugs.
- Are pillbugs radially or bilaterally symmetrical?

MATERIALS

- clear container
- shoebox with half of cover removed
- pillbugs
- hand lens

Most invertebrates are arthropods.

COMBINATION NOTES
Make notes and diagrams for the main idea: *Most invertebrates are arthropods.*

There are more species of arthropods than there are any other type of invertebrate. In fact, of all the animal species classified by scientists, over three-quarters are arthropods. An **arthropod** is an invertebrate that has a segmented body covered with a hard outer skeleton. Arthropods can have many pairs of legs and other parts that extend from their body. Insects are arthropods, so are crustaceans such as the shrimp, and arachnids such as the spider.

Fossil evidence shows that arthropods first appeared on land about 420 million years ago, around the same time as plants. Arthropods are active animals that feed on all types of food. Many arthropods live in water, but most live on land.

segmented body

jointed legs

RESOURCE CENTER
CLASSZONE.COM

Find out more about the diversity of arthropods.

The exoskeleton of this crayfish completely covers its body.

Exoskeletons and Jointed Parts

One adaptation that gives arthropods the ability to live in many different environments is the exoskeleton. An **exoskeleton** is a strong outer covering, made of a material called chitin. The exoskeleton completely covers the body of an arthropod. In a sense, an exoskeleton is like a suit of armor that protects the animal's soft body. For arthropods living on land, the exoskeleton keeps cells, tissues, and organs from drying out.

CHECK YOUR READING What are two functions of an exoskeleton?

A suit of armor is not much good unless you can move around in it. The arthropod's exoskeleton has joints, places where the exoskeleton is thin and flexible. There are joints along the different segments of the animal's body. An arthropod body typically has three sections: a head at one end, a thorax in the middle, and an abdomen at the other end. Legs are jointed, as are other parts attached to the body, such as antennae and claws. Muscles attach to the exoskeleton around the joints, enabling the arthropod to move.

The exoskeleton is like a suit of armor in one other way. It doesn't grow. An arthropod must shed its exoskeleton as it grows. This process is called **molting.** For an arthropod, the times when it molts are dangerous because its soft body is exposed to predators.

COMPARE How does the shape of this cicada's molted exoskeleton compare to the shape of its body?

Complex Body Systems

Arthropods have well-developed body systems. They have a nervous system with a brain and many different sensory organs. Their digestive system includes a stomach and intestines. Arthropods have an open circulatory system, which means the heart moves blood into the body directly. There are no blood vessels. Arthropods reproduce sexually. An arthropod has either a male or a female reproductive system.

Three Major Groups of Arthropods

Scientists have named at least ten groups of arthropods, but most arthropod species belong to one of three groups: insects, crustaceans, or arachnids.

Insects

- Includes beetles, bees, wasps, ants, butterflies, moths, and grasshoppers
- 3 pairs of legs, 3 body segments, 1 pair of antennae
- Most live on land

Crustaceans

- Includes shrimp, crabs, lobsters, barnacles, and pill bugs
- Number of body segments and pairs of legs varies, 2 pairs of antennae
- Most live in water; some live on land

Arachnids

- Includes spiders, ticks, mites, and scorpions
- 4 pairs of legs, 2 body segments, no antennae
- Most live on land

 READING VISUALS What body features can you see that are shared by all of these arthropods?

Parts of an Insect's Body

Adult insects have three body segments and six jointed legs.

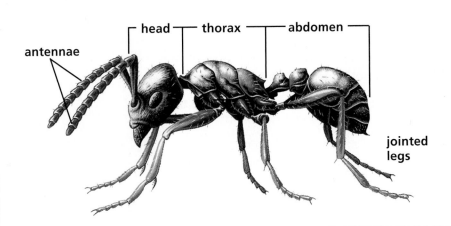

antennae

head thorax abdomen

jointed legs

READING TiP

The word *insect* relates to its body being **in sect**ions. Note the three sections in the diagram of the ant.

Insects are six-legged arthropods.

Scientists have so far identified over 700,000 insect species. **Insects** are arthropods that as adults have three body segments, a pair of antenna, and six legs attached to the middle segment, the thorax. Insect species have adapted to all sorts of environments and live on every continent. Most insects live on land. These insects obtain oxygen through spiracles, small openings in their exoskeleton.

 CHECK YOUR READING What are two characteristics all adult insects share?

VOCABULARY
Don't forget to take notes on the term *insect*, using a strategy from an earlier chapter or one that you already know.

Insects show great diversity in appearance. Many species have adaptations in color and shape that allow them to blend into their environments. For example, a stick insect is the same color and shape as a twig. Insect bodies also have different adaptations. Many insects have compound eyes and antennae, which are sensory organs. Many insects fly, having one or two pairs of wings.

Many insects are herbivores. And many insect species have mouth parts adapted for feeding on specific plants. A butterfly, for example, has a tubelike mouth that can reach into a flower to get nectar. Insects that feed on flowers often help the plants reproduce because the insects carry pollen from flower to flower. Other insects harm the plants they feed on. A grasshopper has jawlike mouth parts that crush parts of a plant. Many plants have defensive adaptations, such as poisons in leaves and stems, to keep insects away.

Some insects, for example, ants, termites, and some bees, are social insects. They must live in groups in order to survive. Members of the group work together to gather food, maintain the nest, and care for the offspring. Often with social insects, just one female, called a queen, produces and lays eggs.

INVESTIGATE Insect Metamorphosis

How often do mealworms molt?

PROCEDURE

1. Prepare the jar for the mealworms. Fill it halfway with oat bran for food. Place a slice of potato and a piece of carrot on top for moisture.

2. In your notebook, note how many mealworms you have. Carefully place the mealworms inside the jar and close the lid. Wash your hands.

3. Without opening the jar, look for signs of activity every day. Once a week, open the container and pour some of the contents into a tray. Examine this sample for molted exoskeletons. Then return it to the jar. Replace the vegetables and add new oats as needed. Wash your hands.

WHAT DO YOU THINK?

- What changes did you observe in the mealworms?
- Did you see any sign of other stages of development?

CHALLENGE Use tweezers and a petri dish to collect the molted exoskeletons. How do the number of molts compare to the number of worms? Estimate how often the worms molt.

All insects reproduce sexually. Females lay eggs, often a large number of eggs. The queen honey bee can lay over a million eggs in her lifetime. Many insect eggs have a hard outer covering. This adaptation protects the egg from drying out and can allow hatching to be delayed until conditions are right.

During their life cycle, insects undergo a process in which their appearance and body systems may change dramatically. This process is called **metamorphosis.** There are three stages to a complete metamorphosis. The first stage is the larva, which spends its time eating. The second stage is the pupa. During this stage, the insect body develops within a protective casing. The final stage is the adult, which is capable of going on to produce a new generation.

READING TiP

The word *metamorphosis* means "many changes."

CHECK YOUR READING What happens to an insect during metamorphosis?

Not all insects go through complete metamorphosis. Some insects, such as grasshoppers, have a simple metamorphosis. When a young grasshopper hatches from an egg, its form is similar to an adult's, just smaller. A grasshopper grows and molts several times before reaching adult size.

1. A female mosquito lays a mass of eggs on the surface of the water.

2. Each egg develops into a larva that swims head down, feeding on algae.

3. The larva develops into a pupa. Inside, the body of the insect matures.

4. At the adult stage, the mosquito leaves the water and flies away.

You have probably seen many insects in their larval form. A caterpillar is a larva, so is an inchworm. Often the larval form of an insect lives in a way very different from its adult form. A mosquito, for example, begins its life in the water. The larva swims about, feeding on algae. The pupa forms at the water's surface. The developing mosquito is encased in a protective covering. The adult form of the mosquito, the flying insect, leaves the water. It is a parasite that feeds off the blood of other animals.

Crustaceans live in water and on land.

Most crustacean species live in the water. Several of these, including the Atlantic lobster and the Dungeness crab, are used by people as a source of food. Crustaceans are important to the ocean food web. Tiny crustaceans such as krill and copepods are a food source for many other animals, including other invertebrates, fish, and whales. Some species of crustaceans live in freshwater and a few, such as pill bugs, live on land.

CHECK YOUR READING Where do most crustaceans live?

Crustaceans have three or more pairs of legs and two pairs of sensory antennae. Many of the larger, water-living crustaceans, such as crabs, have gills. Most crustaceans, like other arthropods, have a circulatory system that includes a heart but no blood vessels. Crustaceans reproduce sexually. Their young hatch from eggs.

The eating habits of crustaceans vary. Lobsters and shrimp eat plants and small animals. Many crustaceans are scavengers, feeding off the remains of other organisms. Some, such as barnacles, are filter feeders. The larval form of a barnacle is free swimming. However, as an adult this arthropod attaches itself to a rock or another hard surface, such as a mollusk's shell or the hull of a ship. It uses its tentacles to capture food from the surrounding water.

IDENTIFY How many pairs of legs does this crab have?

Arachnids are eight-legged arthropods.

Spiders, mites, ticks, and scorpions belong to a group called the arachnids. Like all arthropods, arachnids have an exoskeleton, jointed limbs, and segmented bodies. But the bodies of arachnids have some characteristics that distinguish them from other arthropods. Arachnids always have four pairs of legs and only two body segments. Arachnids do not have antennae.

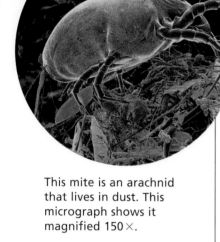

This mite is an arachnid that lives in dust. This micrograph shows it magnified 150×.

Some arachnids, including ticks and chigger mites, are parasites. Other arachnids, such as spiders and scorpions, are predators. Recall that predators get their food by capturing and consuming other animals. Predatory arachnids kill their prey by stinging them, biting them, or injecting them with venom.

The spiders are the largest group of arachnids. Many spiders have a unique adaptation for capturing their prey. They produce an extremely strong material, called silk, inside their bodies and use the silk to make webs for capturing food. The spider spins strands of silk out from tubes called spinnerets at the rear of its abdomen. It weaves the strands into a nearly invisible web. The web serves as a net for catching insects and other small organisms that the spider eats. This adaptation allows web-building spiders to wait for their prey to come to them. Other invertebrates, such as silkworms, produce silk, but they do not weave webs.

CHECK YOUR READING How is the way some spiders capture prey unusual?

Some arachnids obtain oxygen through spiracles, as insects do. However, certain species of spiders have a unique type of respiratory organ referred to as book lungs. Book lungs are like moist pockets with folds. They are located inside the animal's abdomen.

This spider has wrapped its prey in silk.

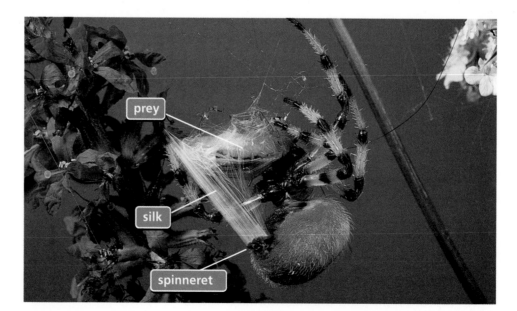

prey

silk

spinneret

Millipede

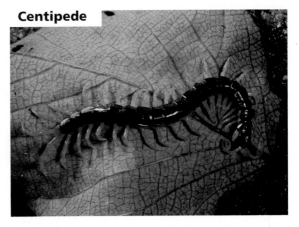
Centipede

READING VISUALS COMPARE AND CONTRAST With their long segmented bodies, a millipede and a centipede look very similar. How are they different?

Millipedes and centipedes are arthropods.

At first glance, the members of two other arthropod groups look similar. Both centipedes and millipedes have long, segmented bodies and many legs. However, animals from these groups differ in their body features and their behavior.

Millipedes are arthropods with two pairs of walking legs on each body segment. Millipedes move rather slowly and eat decaying leaves and plant matter. When disturbed, many millipedes emit a foul odor that can be harmful to predators.

Centipedes can move more quickly. They have one pair of walking legs per body segment. They have antennae and jawlike mouthparts. Many centipedes also have pincers on their rearmost segment. Centipedes are predators. They can use their jaws, and pincers to paralyze prey and protect themselves from predators.

Review

KEY CONCEPTS

1. Describe the characteristics of insects, crustaceans, and arachnids.

2. What is molting and how does it relate to an exoskeleton?

3. Name three arthropods and the adaptations they have for feeding.

CRITICAL THINKING

4. **Analyze** How does the form of an exoskeleton relate to its function?

5. **Connect** Mosquitoes can spread disease, such as the West Nile virus. People are advised not to leave open containers of water in the yard. How does standing water contribute to an increase in the number of mosquitoes?

○ CHALLENGE

6. **Evaluate** Many plant-eating insects live less than a year. An adult will lay eggs in the fall and then die as winter comes. The eggs hatch the next spring. How does the life cycle of the insect fit in with the life cycle of plants? What role does the egg play in the survival of the insect species in this case?

the BIG idea

Invertebrate animals have a variety of body plans and adaptations.

KEY CONCEPTS SUMMARY

 4.1 ## Most animals are invertebrates.

Invertebrates are a diverse group of animals. Species of invertebrates live in almost every environment.

Sponges are simple invertebrates that have several types of specialized cells.

VOCABULARY
invertebrate p. 123
sponge p. 125
sessile p. 125
larva p. 126

 4.2 ## Cnidarians and worms have different body plans.

Cnidarians have simple bodies with specialized cells and tissues.

Most **worms** have organs and complex body systems.

VOCABULARY
cnidarian p.128
tentacle p. 128
mobile p. 130

 4.3 ## Most mollusks have shells, and echinoderms have spiny skeletons.

Mollusks include bivalves, gastropods, and cephalopods.

Echinoderms have a water vascular system and tube feet.

VOCABULARY
mollusk p. 136
gill p. 137
lung p. 137
echinoderm p. 139

4.4 ## Arthropods have exoskeletons and joints.

Arthropods, which include insects, crustaceans, and arachnids, are the most abundant and diverse group of animals.

VOCABULARY
arthropod p. 142
exoskeleton p. 143
molting p. 143
insect p. 145
metamorphosis p. 146

Reviewing Vocabulary

Copy and complete the chart below.

Word	Definition	Example
1. mollusk		clam, snail, squid
2. arthropod	invertebrate with jointed legs, segmented body, and an exoskeleton	
3.	ocean-dwelling animal with spiny skeleton	sea star
4. sessile		sponge
5. larva		caterpillar
6. metamorphosis		caterpillar changing into a butterfly
7. molting	process by which an arthropod sheds its exoskeleton	
8.	arthropod with three body segments, one pair of antennae, and six legs	grasshopper, mosquito, beetle

Reviewing Key Concepts

Multiple Choice *Choose the letter of the best answer.*

9. Which of the following groups of animals is the most abundant?

    a. worms   **c.** echinoderms

    b. mollusks   **d.** arthropods

10. In what way are all invertebrates alike?

    a. They do not have backbones.

    b. They live in the ocean.

    c. They are predators.

    d. They have a closed circulatory system.

11. Sponges bring food into their bodies through a

    a. system of pores

    b. water vascular system

    c. mouth

    d. digestive tract

12. Which group of invertebrates has a mantle?

    a. echinoderms

    b. crustaceans

    c. cnidarians

    d. mollusks

13. Bivalves, cephalopods, and gastropods are all types of

    a. echinoderms

    b. mollusks

    c. crustaceans

    d. cnidarians

14. As they grow, arthropods shed their exoskeleton in a process called

    a. metamorphosis

    b. symmetry

    c. molting

    d. siphoning

15. Which invertebrate animals always have three body segments: a head, a thorax, and an abdomen?

    a. segmented worms

    b. adult insects

    c. arachnids

    d. echinoderms

16. Which group of invertebrates have a water vascular system and tube feet?

    a. echinoderms   **c.** cnidarians

    b. crustaceans   **d.** mollusks

Short Answer *Write a short answer to each question.*

17. Describe the stages in the life cycle of an insect that has complete metamorphosis.

18. Explain one advantage and one disadvantage an exoskeleton has for an organism.

19. Is a spider an insect? Explain.

Thinking Critically

20. **CLASSIFY** What characteristics does a sponge have that make it seem like a plant? What characteristic makes a sponge an animal?

21. **PROVIDE EXAMPLES** Arthropods are the most diverse and abundant group of animals on Earth. Give three examples of arthropod features that enable them to be active in their environment.

22. **INFER** Worms have a tube-shaped body with openings at either end. How does this body plan relate to the way a worm obtains its food and processes it?

23. **COMPARE** Jellyfish go through a life cycle that involves different stages of development. Insects also go through different stages of development in a process called metamorphosis. What are some similarities between metamorphosis in a mosquito, for example, and a jellyfish life cycle? Use the terms in the table below in your answer.

larva	polyp	medusa
pupa	adult	mobile
sessile		

Refer to the chart below as you answer the next three questions.

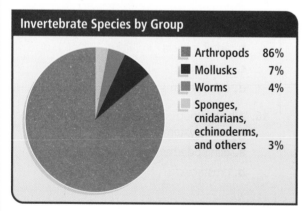

Invertebrate Species by Group

■ Arthropods	86%
■ Mollusks	7%
■ Worms	4%
■ Sponges, cnidarians, echinoderms, and others	3%

24. **APPLY** What percentage of invertebrate species are arthropods?

25. **CALCULATE** What is the combined percentage of all other invertebrate species, not including arthropods?

26. **APPLY** How could you modify this pie chart to show that insects, crustaceans, and arachnids are types of arthropods?

27. **APPLY** A sea star has a radial body plan. A spider has a bilateral body plan. How does the shape of these animal's bodies affect how they capture their food?

28. **COMPARE AND CONTRAST** How are the three main groups of arthropods similar? How are they different?

29. **SYNTHESIZE** Animal bodies need support as well as protection. What structures do the bodies of a sponge, a bivalve, and an insect have for protection and support? Use the terms in the table below in your answer.

| spicule | shell | exoskeleton |

30. **PREDICT** Many people think of insects as pests, but some species of insects are important pollinators for many flowering plants. Also, many animals eat insects. What problems would humans face if Earth's insect species became extinct?

the BIG idea

31. **INFER** How does a cnidarian such as the jellyfish in the photograph on pages 120–121 respond to its environment? Is the diver in the photograph in danger? Explain your answer.

32. **COMPARE AND CONTRAST** Make a chart showing the key features of the body plans of three different invertebrate animal groups. For each group, identify one characteristic that is an adaptation.

UNIT PROJECTS

If you need to create graphs or other visuals for your project, be sure you have grid paper, poster board, markers, or other supplies.

Analyzing Data

Reef-building corals are invertebrates that live in clear, warm ocean water. As a coral grows, it produces a hard external skeleton. If many generations of corals grow near each other over a long period of time, their accumulated skeletons form a structure called a reef. Many ocean life-forms live in and around coral reefs. This table shows the maximum growth rates of five species of reef-building corals.

Choose the letter of the best response

Species	Rate of Growth (mm per year)	Number of Years to Grow a 1400-m Reef
A	143	9,790
B	99	14,100
C	120	11,700
D	100	14,000
E	226	6,190

1. Which has the fastest rate of growth?

a. Species C

b. Species B

c. Species D

d. Species E

2. What is the growth rate for Species B ?

a. 99 mm per year

b. 120 mm per year

c. 143 mm per year

d. 14,100 mm per year

3. Which takes the shortest amount of time to grow to 1400 meters?

a. Species B

b. Species C

c. Species D

d. Species E

4. Which have about the same rate of growth?

a. Species A and C

b. Species B and D

c. Species C and E

d. Species D and E

5. How many years does it take Species A to grow into a 1400-m reef?

a. 143

b. 226

c. 9790

d. 14,000

6. Based on the information in the table, which statement is true?

a. Coral species with the fastest growth rates take the greatest amount of time to grow.

b. Coral species with the slowest growth rates take the least amount of time to grow.

c. Coral species have different rates of growth that affect how long it takes them to grow.

d. Coral species that grow more than 100 mm per year take the longest to grow.

Extended Response

7. Corals are cnidarians. They are sessile animals that live attached to one place. Other ocean-dwelling animals are mobile and can move about their environment. Crustaceans like the lobster are mobile, so are mollusks like the octopus. How does being sessile or mobile affect the feeding behaviors of an animal? Do you think the bodies and systems of sessile animals are going to be different from those of mobile animals? Use some of the terms in the word box in your answer.

digestive system	sessile	mobile
nervous system	filter	mouth
muscle tissue	food	sensory organs

Vertebrate Animals

the **BIG** idea

Vertebrate animals live in most of Earth's environments.

> **What do these penguins have in common with this seal?**

Key Concepts

SECTION

5.1 Vertebrates are animals with endoskeletons.
Learn how most of the vertebrates on Earth are fish.

SECTION

5.2 Amphibians and reptiles are adapted for life on land.
Learn how most amphibians hatch in water and most reptiles hatch on land.

SECTION

5.3 Birds meet their needs on land, in water, and in the air.
Learn how adaptations for flight affect how birds meet their needs.

SECTION

5.4 Mammals live in many environments.
Learn about mammals' many adaptations.

Internet Preview

CLASSZONE.COM

Chapter 5 online resources: Content Review, two Visualizations, four Resource Centers, Math Tutorial, Test Practice.

EXPLORE (the BIG idea)

What Animals Live Near You?

Make a list of animals you think live in your neighborhood. Remember that some animals are small! Organize the animals on your list into groups.

Observe and Think Where do you think you would see the most animals? What about the widest variety?

How Is a Bird Like a Frog?

Fish, frogs, snakes, birds, dogs, and humans are all vertebrate animals. Choose two vertebrates and quickly sketch their body plans, including their skeletons.

Observe and Think Where do you think each animal's brain, heart, and stomach are located?

Internet Activity: Where in the World?

Go to **ClassZone.com** to learn more about where different types of vertebrate animals are found in North America.

Observe and Think What sorts of adaptations would an animal need to live near the North Pole? What about in a desert?

NSTA
scilinks.org
SCiLINKS

Bird Characteristics **Code: MDL043**

Getting Ready to Learn

◀ CONCEPTS REVIEW

- All living things have common needs.
- Plants and some invertebrates have adaptations for life on land.
- Most multicellular organisms can reproduce sexually.

◀ VOCABULARY REVIEW

migration p. 64

embryo p. 98

gill p. 137

lung p. 137

exoskeleton p. 143

CONTENT REVIEW
CLASSZONE.COM

Review concepts and vocabulary.

▶ TAKING NOTES

CHOOSE YOUR OWN STRATEGY

Take notes using one or more of the strategies from earlier chapters – **main idea webs, main idea and details, mind maps,** or **combination notes**. You can also use other note-taking strategies that you may already know.

VOCABULARY STRATEGY

Think about a vocabulary term as a **magnet word** diagram. Write other terms and ideas related to that term around it.

See the Note-Taking Handbook on pages R45–R51.

SCIENCE NOTEBOOK

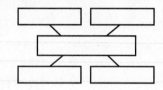

Main Idea Web

Main Idea and Details

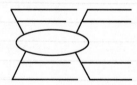

Mind Map

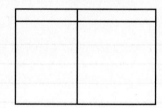

ENDOTHERM

bird

mammal

transforms food into heat

hair, feathers, blubber

shivers, sweats, pants

active in cold environments

Vertebrates are animals with endoskeletons.

◀ **BEFORE, you learned**

- Most animals are invertebrates
- Animals have adaptations that suit their environment
- Animals get energy by consuming food

▶ **NOW, you will learn**

- About the skeletons of vertebrate animals
- About the characteristics of fish
- About three groups of fish

VOCABULARY

vertebrate p. 157
endoskeleton p. 157
scale p. 161

EXPLORE Streamlined Shapes

How does a fish's shape help it move?

PROCEDURE

MATERIALS
tub of water

1. Place your hand straight up and down in a tub of water. Keep your fingers together and your palm flat.

2. Move your hand from one side of the tub to the other, using your palm to push the water.

3. Move your hand across the tub again, this time using the edge of your hand as if you were cutting the water.

WHAT DO YOU THINK?

- In which position was the shape of your hand most like the shape of a fish's body?
- How might the shape of a fish's body affect its ability to move through water?

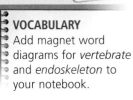

VOCABULARY
Add magnet word diagrams for *vertebrate* and *endoskeleton* to your notebook.

Vertebrate animals have backbones.

If you asked someone to name an animal, he or she would probably name a vertebrate. Fish, frogs, snakes, birds, dogs, and humans are all **vertebrates,** or animals with backbones. Even though only about 5 percent of animal species are vertebrates, they are among the most familiar and thoroughly studied organisms on Earth.

Vertebrate animals have muscles, a digestive system, a respiratory system, a circulatory system, and a nervous system with sensory organs. The characteristic that distinguishes vertebrates from other animals is the **endoskeleton,** an internal support system that grows along with the animal. Endoskeletons allow more flexibility and ways of moving than exoskeletons do.

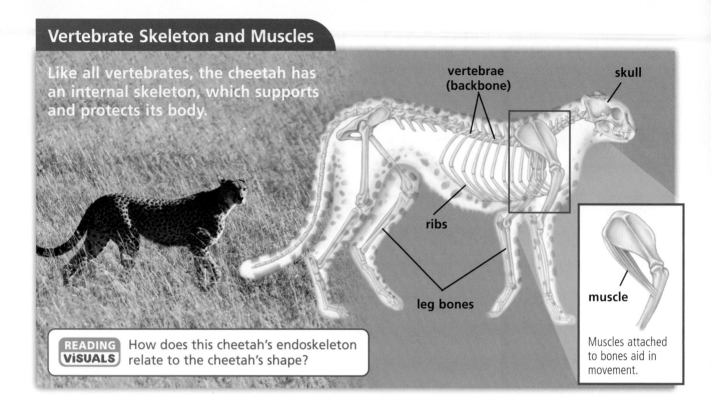

Vertebrate Skeleton and Muscles

Like all vertebrates, the cheetah has an internal skeleton, which supports and protects its body.

vertebrae (backbone)

skull

ribs

leg bones

muscle

Muscles attached to bones aid in movement.

READING VISUALS How does this cheetah's endoskeleton relate to the cheetah's shape?

Vertebrates are named for specialized bones called vertebrae. These bones are located in the middle of each vertebrate animal's central body segment. Together, the vertebrae are sometimes called a backbone. The vertebrae support muscles and surround the spinal cord, which connects the animal's brain to its nerves. Other bones, such as the ribs and skull, protect organs like the heart, lungs, and brain.

CHECK YOUR READING What is one function of the endoskeleton for vertebrate animals?

Most vertebrates are fish.

NOTETAKING STRATEGY Choose a strategy from an earlier chapter to take notes on the idea that most vertebrates are fish. Be sure to include information on adaptations to water.

Fish are the most diverse group of vertebrate animals. There are more than 20,000 species of fish, ranging in size from tiny minnows to huge whale sharks. Fish live in nearly every aquatic environment, from freshwater lakes to the bottom of the sea. Some fish even are able to survive below the ice in the Antarctic!

Fish are adapted for life in water. Like all living things, fish need to get materials from their environment. For example, fish must be able to get oxygen from water. Fish must also be able to move through water in order to find food. Fish that live in water where sunlight does not penetrate need special organs to help them find food.

Most fish move by using muscles and fins to push their stream-lined bodies through water. These muscles allow fish to move more quickly than most other invertebrates. Most fish also have an organ called a swim bladder, which allows them to control the depth at which they float.

Fish have sensory organs for taste, odor, and sound. Most fish species have eyes that allow them to see well underwater. Most fish also have a sensory system unlike other vertebrates. This system includes an organ called a lateral line, which allows fish to sense vibrations from objects nearby without touching or seeing them.

Fish, like some invertebrates, remove oxygen from water with specialized respiratory organs called gills. You can locate most fishs' gills by looking for the openings, called gill slits, on the sides of their head. You can see what gills look like in the diagram of a fish below.

VISUALIZATION
CLASSZONE.COM
Explore how fish breathe.

 CHECK YOUR READING How are gills similar to lungs?

Fish gills are made up of many folds of tissue and are filled with blood. When a fish swims, it takes water in through its mouth and then pushes the water back over its gills. In the gills, oxygen dissolved in the water moves into the fish's blood. Carbon dioxide, a waste product of respiration, moves from the blood into the water. Then the water is forced out of the fish's body through its gill slits. The oxygen is transported to the fish's cells. It is a necessary material for releasing energy.

Inside a Fish

Fish are vertebrates that live in water.

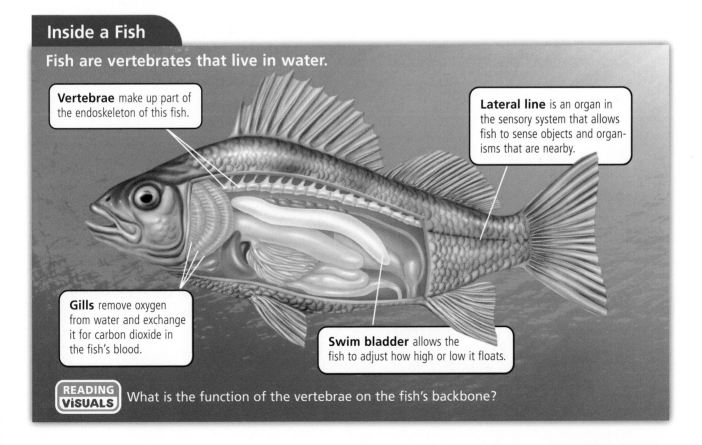

Vertebrae make up part of the endoskeleton of this fish.

Lateral line is an organ in the sensory system that allows fish to sense objects and organisms that are nearby.

Gills remove oxygen from water and exchange it for carbon dioxide in the fish's blood.

Swim bladder allows the fish to adjust how high or low it floats.

READING VISUALS What is the function of the vertebrae on the fish's backbone?

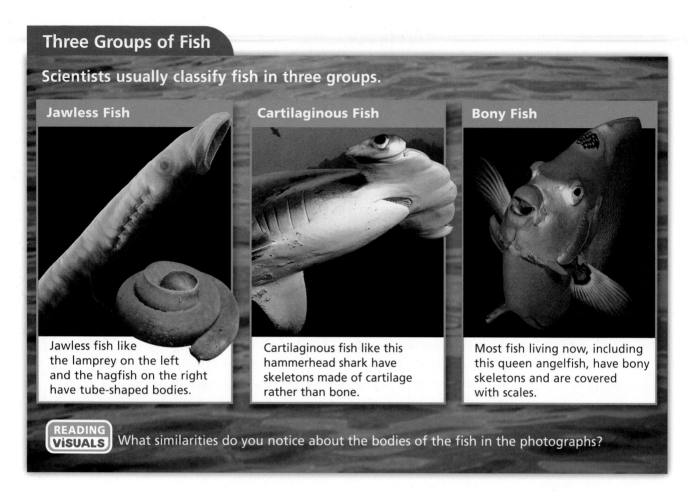

Three Groups of Fish

Scientists usually classify fish in three groups.

Jawless Fish

Jawless fish like the lamprey on the left and the hagfish on the right have tube-shaped bodies.

Cartilaginous Fish

Cartilaginous fish like this hammerhead shark have skeletons made of cartilage rather than bone.

Bony Fish

Most fish living now, including this queen angelfish, have bony skeletons and are covered with scales.

READING VISUALS What similarities do you notice about the bodies of the fish in the photographs?

Fish can be classified in three groups.

Scientists classify fish into three major groups: jawless fish, cartilaginous fish, and bony fish. Each group is characterized by body features. As you read on and learn about each group of fish, look at the photographs above.

Jawless Fish

Scientists think that fish in this group, which includes lampreys and hagfish, are the living animals most similar to the first fish that lived on Earth. Jawless fish have simpler bodies than the other fish. They have a slender tubelike shape and a digestive system without a stomach.

As the name of the group implies, these fish do not have jaw bones. Although they do have teeth, they cannot chew. Most jawless fish eat by biting into another animal's body and then sucking out flesh and fluids.

RESOURCE CENTER
CLASSZONE.COM
Learn more about fish.

CHECK YOUR READING What is a characteristic of jawless fish?

Cartilaginous Fish

This group includes sharks, rays, and skates. Their skeletons are not made of hard bone, but of a flexible tissue called cartilage (KAHR-tuhl-ihj). Some species of sharks are dangerous to humans, but most cartilaginous fish feed primarily on small animals such as mollusks and crustaceans. Whale sharks and basking sharks, which are the largest fish on Earth, feed by filtering small organisms from the water as they swim.

Rays are flat-bodied cartilaginous fish that live most of their lives on the ocean floor. Their mouths are on the underside of their bodies. Most rays eat by pulling small animals out of the sand. A ray's flat body has fins that extend on either side of its vertebrae like wings. When rays swim, these fins wave so it looks as if the fish is flying through the water.

 CHECK YOUR READING Describe three ways cartilaginous fish species obtain food.

Bony Fish

Most fish species, including tuna, flounder, goldfish, and eels, are classified in this large, diverse group. Of the nearly 20,000 fish species, about 96 percent are bony fish. Bony fish have skeletons made of hard bone, much like the skeleton in your body. Most bony fish are covered with overlapping bony structures called **scales.** They have jaws and teeth and several pairs of fins.

The range of body shapes and behavior in bony fish show how living things are adapted to their environments. Think of the bright colors and patterns of tropical fish in an aquarium. These eye-catching features are probably adaptations for survival in the fishes' natural environment. In a coral reef, for example, bright stripes and spots might provide camouflage or might advertise the fish's presence to other animals, including potential mates.

Most young fish develop inside an egg.

Most fish species reproduce sexually. The female produces eggs, and the male produces sperm. In many fish species, individual animals select a mate. For example, a female fish might release eggs into the water at a time and place where a male can fertilize them. After the eggs are fertilized, the parent fish usually leave the eggs to develop and hatch on their own. Most fish reproduce this way, but there are many exceptions.

 REMINDER

In sexual reproduction the genetic material from two parents is combined in their offspring.

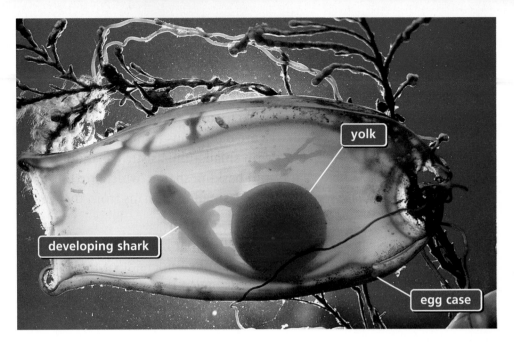

yolk

developing shark

egg case

This young shark is developing from an egg that is covered by an egg case. In this photograph, light shining through the egg case allows you to see the shark and the yolk inside.

All organisms that can reproduce sexually produce egg cells and sperm cells. However, the structure and size of eggs varies among species. In Chapter 3, you learned that the eggs of flowering plants are found inside the seeds in fruit. In Chapter 4, you read about the eggs of many different types of invertebrates. You learned that some eggs have a food supply and a protective covering. For animals, the food supply is called yolk, and the covering is called an egg case.

Most fish eggs are surrounded by a soft egg case that water can pass through. Since fish lay eggs in the water, this means that a fish embryo inside an egg gets the water and oxygen it needs directly from its surroundings. The egg's yolk provides the developing fish with food. Such eggs can develop on their own, without needing care from adults. However, many animals eat fish eggs. Fish often lay and fertilize many eggs, but few of them survive to maturity.

REMINDER

An embryo is the immature form of an organism that has the potential to grow to maturity.

 CHECK YOUR READING How are fish eggs different from invertebrate eggs?

5.1 Review

KEY CONCEPTS

1. Why are fish classified as vertebrate animals?

2. What are three adaptations that suit fish for life in water?

3. Name a feature for fish from each of these groups: jawless, cartilaginous, and bony.

CRITICAL THINKING

4. **Apply** If you wanted to choose tropical fish that could live comfortably in the same tank, what body features or behaviors might you look for?

5. **Infer** Some fish do not lay eggs. Their eggs develop inside the female fish. How might the offspring of one of these fish differ from those of an egg-laying fish?

CHALLENGE

6. **Synthesize** Fossils indicate that species of fish with bodies very similar to today's sharks have lived in aquatic environments for hundreds of millions of years. What can you infer about the adaptations of sharks from this?

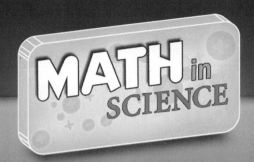

 MATH TUTORIAL
CLASSZONE.COM

Click on Math Tutorial
for more help dividing
by decimals.

Great Growth

The leatherback sea turtle is one of the largest reptiles alive. Full-grown, adult leatherbacks can weigh 880 kilograms. This huge turtle starts out life weighing just 44 grams.

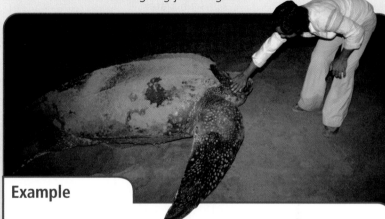

Example

How many times heavier is the 880 kg adult than the 44 g baby?

(1) Convert the units so they are all in kilograms.
44 g × 0.001 kg/g = 0.044 kg

(2) Divide 880 by 0.044 to get the answer.

(3) To divide by a decimal, multiply the divisor and the dividend by a multiple of 10. Since the decimal number is in thousandths, multiply by 1000.

$$0.044\overline{)880000} \qquad 44\overline{)\underset{}{\overset{20,000}{880000}}}$$

ANSWER The adult leatherback is 20,000 times heavier than the baby leatherback hatchling.

Answer the following questions.

1. An adult leatherback has been measured as 1.5 m from nose to tail. The same animal measured just 6 cm as a baby hatchling. How many times longer is the adult?

2. A typical box turtle grows to 12.5 cm long. How many times longer is the adult leatherback than the adult box turtle?

3. Suppose the box turtle hatched with a length of 2.5 cm. By how many times has its length grown at adulthood?

4. How many times longer is the leatherback hatchling than the box turtle hatchling?

CHALLENGE What fraction of its adult weight is the leatherback hatchling in the example?

KEY CONCEPT

Amphibians and reptiles are adapted for life on land.

 BEFORE, you learned

- Fish are vertebrates that live in water
- Fish gills remove oxygen from water
- Most young fish develop inside eggs laid in the water

NOW, you will learn

- About amphibians, vertebrates that can live on land for part of their lives
- About reptiles, vertebrates that can live on land for their whole lives
- About the body temperature of amphibians and reptiles

VOCABULARY

amphibian p. 167
reptile p. 168
ectotherm p. 170

EXPLORE Moving on Land

What good are legs?

PROCEDURE

MATERIALS
meter stick

1. Measure and record your height in meters.

2. Jump as far as you can, and have your partner record the distance.

3. Divide the distance you jumped by your height.

4. Some frogs can jump a distance that's equal to 10 times their body length. Calculate the distance you would be able to jump if you were a frog.

WHAT DO YOU THINK?
How might the ability to jump help a frog survive on land?

Vertebrates adapted to live on land.

Most of the groups of invertebrates and all of the vertebrates you have read about so far live in water. Organisms such as plants and insects became very diverse after adapting to live on land. Some vertebrate animals adapted to live on land as well. In this section you will learn about the first vertebrates to live on land, a group called the amphibians, and the group that came next, the reptiles.

Amphibians living today include frogs, toads, and salamanders. Reptiles include turtles, snakes, lizards, and crocodiles. Some people find it hard to tell animals from these two groups apart, but there are some important characteristics that distinguish them.

More than 350 million years ago, Earth was already inhabited by many species of vertebrate animals. All of them were fish. They

Amphibian

Reptile

READING VISUALS COMPARE AND CONTRAST Just by looking at these two animals, what physical differences can you see? What similarities do you see?

lived in salt water and fresh water, consumed other organisms as food, and obtained oxygen using specialized organs called gills.

Recall the pond you imagined in Chapter 3, when you learned that plants adapted to land. Now imagine the same pond a hundred million years later. The pond is crowded with invertebrates and fish, all competing for oxygen and food.

Suppose a period of dry weather makes the the pond start to dry up. Many animals die, and food and oxygen become scarce. On the banks of the pond it might be less crowded. Invertebrates living there are sources of food. Air on land contains more oxygen than water does. Fish that could survive on land would be better off than the fish in the pond in this situation.

However, the gills of fish work only when they are wet. Fins can function to make a fish move through water, but they are are not good for moving on land. Water provides more support for the body than air. Plus, fish sensory organs are specialized for detecting sounds and smells in water, not in air.

It took millions of years and many generations before different adaptations occurred and amphibians became a distinct group. These early amphibians were able to survive on land. Today there are fish that can breathe air and fish that can walk for short distances on land. There are also some modern amphibian species that have adapted to life only in water.

NOTETAKING STRATEGY
Choose a strategy from an earlier chapter or use one of your own to take notes on how vertebrates adapted to life on land.

 CHECK YOUR READING How are amphibians different from fish?

Wood Frog Life Cycle

Wood frogs live in moist forest environments and breed once a year, in early spring.

A female adult wood frog deposits a mass of eggs in a pool of fresh water.

The young wood frog climbs out of the water. From now on, it will live on land and breathe with lungs.

Some of the eggs hatch and become tadpoles. Tadpoles swim and breathe like fish.

The wood frog will grow until fall and slow its activity in winter. In spring females lay eggs and the cycle repeats.

The tadpole's legs develop, and its tail shrinks. Many changes occur inside the tadpole's body as well.

READING VISUALS What visible changes occur in a wood frog tadpole's body as it transforms into an adult wood frog?

Amphibians have moist skin and lay eggs without shells.

As adults, most **amphibians** have these characteristics:

- They have two pairs of legs, or a total of four limbs.
- They lay their eggs in water.
- They obtain oxygen through their smooth, moist skin. Many also have respiratory organs called lungs.
- Their sensory organs are adapted for sensing on land.

Most amphibians live in moist environments. Their skin is a respiratory organ that functions only when it is wet. Most species of amphibians live close to water or in damp places. Some are most active at night, when the ground is wet with dew. Others live mostly underground, beneath wet leaves, or under decaying trees.

Amphibians reproduce sexually. In most amphibian species, a female lays eggs in water, a male fertilizes them with sperm, and then the offspring develop and hatch on their own. Yolk inside the eggs provides developing embryos with nutrients. Like fish eggs, amphibian eggs do not have hard shells. This means developing amphibians can get water and oxygen directly from their surroundings.

 CHECK YOUR READING How is the way most amphibians reproduce similar to the way most fish reproduce?

 **RESOURCE CENTER**
CLASSZONE.COM

Learn more about amphibians.

Amphibian Life Cycle

The diagram shows the life cycle of one amphibian, the wood frog. When a young amphibian hatches, it is a larva. In Chapter 4 you learned that a larva is an early stage that is very different from the animal's adult form. For example, the larvae of frogs and toads are called tadpoles. Tadpoles look and behave like small fish. They breathe with gills, eat mostly algae, and move by pushing against the water with their tails.

After a few weeks, a tadpole's body begins to change. Inside, the lungs develop and parts of the digestive system transform. The tadpole begins to have some of the external features of a frog. It develops legs, its tail shrinks, and its head changes shape.

As a young wood frog's body changes, its gills stop functioning, and it begins breathing air with its lungs. The frog starts using its tongue to capture and eat small animals. It leaves the water and begins using its legs to move around on land. Some amphibians, such as sirens and bullfrogs, remain in or near water for all of their lives. Others, like wood frogs, most toads, and some salamanders, live in moist land environments as adults.

READING TIP

As you read about the amphibian life cycle in these paragraphs, look at the diagram on page 166 to see what a wood frog looks like at each stage.

Reptiles have dry, scaly skin and lay eggs with shells.

VOCABULARY
Add a magnet word diagram for *reptile* to your notebook.

Reptiles evolved soon after amphibians and are closely related to them. However, animals in the reptile group have adaptations that allow them to survive in hotter, drier places than amphibians. For many millions of years they were the largest and most diverse vertebrate animal group living on land. Most of the animals classified as reptiles have these characteristics:

- They have two pairs of legs, for a total of four limbs.
- They have tough, dry skin covered by scales.
- They obtain oxygen from air with respiratory organs called lungs.
- Their sensory organs are adapted for sensing on land.
- They lay their eggs, which have shells, on land.

CHECK YOUR READING What characteristics of reptiles are different from the characteristics of amphibians listed on page 167?

Lungs

Reptiles do not get oxygen through their skin the way amphibians do. They are born with lungs that provide their bodies with all the oxygen they need. Lungs, like gills, are internal organs made up of many folds of thin tissue filled with blood. When an animal with lungs inhales, it takes air in through its nostrils or mouth and moves the air into its lungs. There, oxygen is transported across the tissues and into the blood, and carbon dioxide is moved from the blood to the lungs and exhaled.

Reptiles like these garter snakes are covered with scales and breathe through their nostrils.

scales

nostril

dry, scaly skin

eggshell

CONTRAST How does the egg this gecko hatched from differ from the wood frog eggs shown on page 166?

Dry, Scaly Skin

Reptile skin is hard, dry, and covered with scales made of keratin, a substance much like your fingernails. The thick, waterproof skin of reptiles protects them from the environment and from predators. However, this means that reptiles cannot obtain water through their skin.

Eggs with Shells

The reptile egg is an important adaptation that allows vertebrate animals to survive in hot, dry environments. The eggs of reptiles contain everything an embryo needs: water, nutrients, a system for gas exchange, and a place to store waste. Membranes separate the internal parts of the egg, which is covered by a protective shell.

Reptiles reproduce sexually. The egg cell of the female joins with the sperm cell of the male in the process of fertilization. After fertilization, a protective case, or shell, forms around each egg while it is still inside the female's body. The female selects a place to lay the eggs on land. Many species of reptiles build or dig nests. Some female reptiles, including alligators, guard their nests and care for their offspring after they hatch. Most reptiles, however, leave soon after the eggs are laid. As you can see in the photograph above, when young reptiles hatch, they look like small adults.

RESOURCE CENTER
CLASSZONE.COM

Find out more about reptiles.

INVESTIGATE Eggs

What are some of the characteristics of eggs?

PROCEDURE

1. Carefully examine the outside of the hard-boiled egg. Try to notice as many details as you can. Write your observations in your notebook.

2. Gently crack the eggshell and remove it. Try to keep the shell in large pieces and the egg whole. Set the egg aside, and examine the pieces of shell. Look for details you could not see before. Write your observations in your notebook.

3. Examine the outside of the egg. Make notes about what you see. Include a sketch.

4. Use the knife to cut the egg in half. Take one half apart carefully, trying to notice as many parts as you can. Use the other half for comparison. Write up your observations.

WHAT DO YOU THINK?

- Reptiles, like birds, have eggs with hard shells. What structures does an egg with a shell contain?

- What might the function of each structure be?

CHALLENGE How might the egg's structures support a developing embryo?

The body temperatures of amphibians and reptiles change with the environment.

Amphibians and reptiles are **ectotherms,** animals whose body temperatures change with environmental conditions. You are not an ectotherm. Whether the air temperature of your environment is −4°C (25°F) or 43°C (110°F), your body temperature remains around 37°C (99°F). A tortoise's body temperature changes with the temperature of the air or water surrounding it. On a cool day, a tortoise's body will be cooler than it is on a hot one.

Many ectothermic animals can move and respond more quickly when their bodies are warm. Many ectotherms warm themselves in the Sun. You may have seen turtles or snakes sunning themselves. Ectothermic animals transform most of the food they consume directly into energy. Some ectotherms, even large ones such as alligators, or the Galápagos tortoise in the photograph, can survive for a long time without consuming much food.

This sand-diving lizard can reduce the amount of heat that transfers from the sand into its body by standing on two feet.

Although amphibians and reptiles do not have a constant body temperature, their bodies stop functioning well if they become too hot or too cold. Most amphibians and reptiles live in environments where the temperature of the surrounding air or water does not change too much. Others, like wood frogs and painted turtles, have adaptations that allow them to slow their body processes during the winter.

Amphibians and reptiles also have behaviors that allow them to adjust their body temperature in less extreme ways. The sand-diving lizard in the photograph above is able to control how much heat enters its body through the sand by standing on just two of its four feet. Many amphibians and reptiles live near water and use it to cool off their bodies.

5.2 Review

KEY CONCEPTS

1. What are three adaptations that allowed the first amphibians to survive on land?

2. What are two adaptations reptiles have that allow them to live their whole live on land?

3. A crocodile has been lying in the sun for hours. When it slides into the cool river, how will its body temperature change? Why?

CRITICAL THINKING

4. **Compare and Contrast** Make a diagram to show how amphibians and reptiles are different and how they are similar.

5. **Infer** Some reptiles, like sea turtles, live almost their whole lives in water. What differences would you expect to see between the bodies of a sea turtle and a land turtle?

⬤ CHALLENGE

6. **Hypothesize** For many millions of years, reptiles were the most diverse and successful vertebrate animals on land. Now many of these ancient reptiles are extinct. Give some reasons that might explain the extinction of these reptiles.

Sticky Feet

Imagine having the ability to walk up a polished glass window, across ceiling tiles, and down a mirror—without using suction or glue. Small tropical lizards called geckos have this unique ability, and scientists are beginning to understand what makes these animals stick.

A gecko's foot is covered in billions of tiny hairs. Each hair branches into hundreds of smaller hairs called spatulae, and the atoms in these spatulae are attracted to atoms in the surfaces the geckos walk on.

All atoms contain particles called electrons, which constantly move around. When two atoms get very close, the motion of their electrons can change, attracting the two atoms to one another.

Gecko toes

Spatulae 595 ×

Spatulae are over 200 times narrower than human hair. Because they are so small, many spatulae can get close enough to the surfaces geckoes walk on for their atoms to stick together.

Billions of these tiny atom-level forces combine with enough strength to suspend a gecko's body weight. Scientists call this property dry adhesion and have applied what they've learned from the soles of these small lizards to manufacturing renewable tape that never loses its ability to stick.

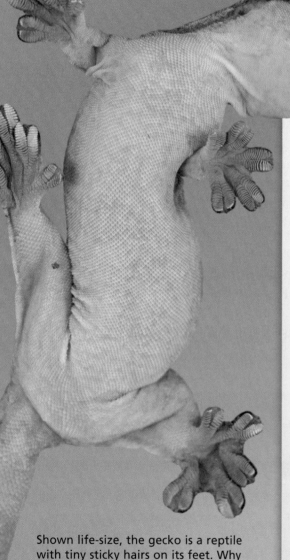

Shown life-size, the gecko is a reptile with tiny sticky hairs on its feet. Why are chemists and engineers interested in this adaptation?

EXPLORE

1. **CONNECT** What are some other animals that can walk up walls or across ceilings? How do you think they do this?

2. **CHALLENGE** Do you think geckos would be able to walk up wet surfaces as easily as dry ones? Why or why not?

Birds meet their needs on land, in water, and in the air.

◀ **BEFORE, you learned**

- Vertebrate animals have endoskeletons with backbones
- Amphibians and reptiles have adaptations for life on land
- Ectotherms do not maintain a constant body temperature

▶ **NOW, you will learn**

- About birds as endotherms
- How the adaptations of birds allow them to live in many environments
- About adaptations for flight

VOCABULARY

endotherm p. 174
incubation p. 179

EXPLORE Feathers

How do feathers differ?

PROCEDURE

① Examine several feathers.

② Make a list of ways some of your feathers differ from others.

③ Make a diagram of each feather, showing the characteristics you listed.

④ Compare your list and your diagram with those of your classmates.

MATERIALS
assorted feathers

WHAT DO YOU THINK?

- Of all the characteristics of feathers that you and your classmates listed, which do you think are the most important? Why?
- On the basis of your observations, what are some functions of feathers for birds?

NOTETAKING STRATEGY
Be sure to take notes on the main idea, *Bird species live in most environments.* Choose an earlier strategy or one of your own.

Bird species live in most environments.

Penguins live in Antarctica, and parrots inhabit the tropics. Pelicans scoop their food from the water, while cardinals crack open seeds and eat the insides. Swallows skim insects from above the surface of a pond. A soaring hawk swoops down, and a smaller animal becomes its prey. There are nearly 10,000 species of the vertebrate animals called birds. Their adaptations allow them to live all over the world.

Some bird species, such as pigeons, are adapted to live in a wide range of environments, while others have adaptations that limit them to living in one place. Many birds travel long distances during their lives. Some migrate as the seasons change, and others cover long distances while searching for food.

It probably seems easy for you to recognize which animals are birds. Birds are distinguished by these characteristics:

- They have feathers and a beak.
- They have four limbs: a pair of scaly legs and a pair of wings.
- Their eggs have hard shells.

Birds can maintain body temperature.

In the last section, you learned that the body temperature of ectotherms, such as amphibians and reptiles, changes with their environment. Birds are **endotherms,** or animals that maintain a constant body temperature. Maintaining temperature allows endotherms to live in some places where frogs, turtles, and alligators cannot.

This chickadee is an endotherm. This means its body remains warm, even in very cold weather.

When an ectothermic animal's body is cool, its systems slow down and it becomes less active. A less active animal consumes little or no food and is unlikely to reproduce. It moves slowly or not at all and breathes less often. Its nervous system becomes less responsive, and its heart pumps more slowly. An ectothermic animal that stays cool for too long will die. Even if it has enough food, its body lacks the energy needed to digest the food.

All animals are affected by the air temperature of their environment and will die if they become too cold. However, birds and other endotherms can stay active in colder climates than ectotherms. This is because endothermic animals have adaptations for generating more body heat and keeping it near their bodies.

 How can endotherms stay alive in colder climates than ectotherms?

Generating Heat

The energy birds produce as body heat comes from food. This means that birds and other endotherms need to eat a lot. An ectotherm such as a frog might be able to survive for days on the energy it gets from just one worm, while a bird on the same diet might starve. Also, the amount of food an endotherm needs is affected by climate. House sparrows and other birds that do not migrate need to eat more food and produce more energy to survive in winter than they do during warmer seasons.

Insulating with Down

Just as warm air trapped between down feathers helps keep geese warm, feathers in a jacket keep a student warm.

Down Feathers

Controlling Body Temperature

Birds have soft feathers, called down, that keep warm air close to their bodies. If you have ever slept with a down comforter or worn a down jacket, you know that these feathers are good insulation, even though they are not very heavy. Other feathers, called contour feathers, cover the down on birds. In most species, contour feathers are water-resistant and protect birds from getting wet.

Birds shiver when they are cold, and this muscular movement generates heat. They also have ways of cooling their bodies down when the weather is hot. Birds do not sweat, but they can fluff their feathers out to release heat. Birds, like other animals, have behaviors for maintaining body temperature, such as resting in a shady place during the hottest part of a summer day.

Most birds can fly.

Of all the animals on Earth today, only three groups have evolved adaptations for flight: insects, bats, and birds. Fossil evidence suggests that the first birds appeared on Earth about 150 million years ago and that they were reptiles with adaptations for flight. Scientists think that all birds are descended from these flying ancestors, even modern species such as ostriches and penguins, which cannot fly.

Adaptations for Flight

To lift its body into the air and fly, an animal's body has to be very strong, but also light. Many adaptations and many millions of years were needed before birds' body plans and systems became capable of flight. With these adaptations, birds lost the ability to do some things that other vertebrates can. As you read about birds' adaptations for flight, match the numbers with the diagram on the next page.

READING TiP

As you read the numbered text on this page, find the matching number on page 177.

1 Endoskeleton Some of the bones in a bird's body are fused, or connected without joints. This makes those parts of a bird's skeleton light and strong, but not as flexible. A specialized bone supports the bird's powerful flight muscles.

2 Wings and Feathers Birds do not have hands or paws on their wings. Contour feathers along the wing are called flight feathers, and are specialized for lifting and gliding. Feathers are a strong and adjustable surface for pushing against air.

3 Specialized Respiratory System Flying takes a lot of energy, so birds need a lot of oxygen. They breathe using a system of air sacs and lungs. Air follows a path through this system that allows oxygen to move constantly through a bird's body.

4 Hollow Bones Many of the bones in a bird's skeleton are hollow. Inside, crisscrossing structures provide strength without adding much weight.

Other body systems within birds are more suited for flight than systems in other invertebrates. Instead of heavy jaws and teeth, an internal organ called a gizzard grinds up food. This adaptation makes a bird lighter in weight and makes flight easier. Birds also have highly developed senses of hearing and vision, senses which are important for flight. Their senses of taste and smell are not as well developed.

 CHECK YOUR READING Give two examples of things that birds cannot do that relate to their adaptations for flight.

Benefits of Flight

Flight allows animals to get food from places where animals living on land or in water cannot. For example, some species of birds spend most of their lives flying over the ocean, hunting for fish. Also, a flying bird can search a large area for food more effectively than it could if it walked, ran, or swam.

For many species of birds, flight makes migration possible. In Chapter 2, you learned that some animals migrate to different living places in different seasons. Most migratory birds have two living places, one for the summer and one for the winter.

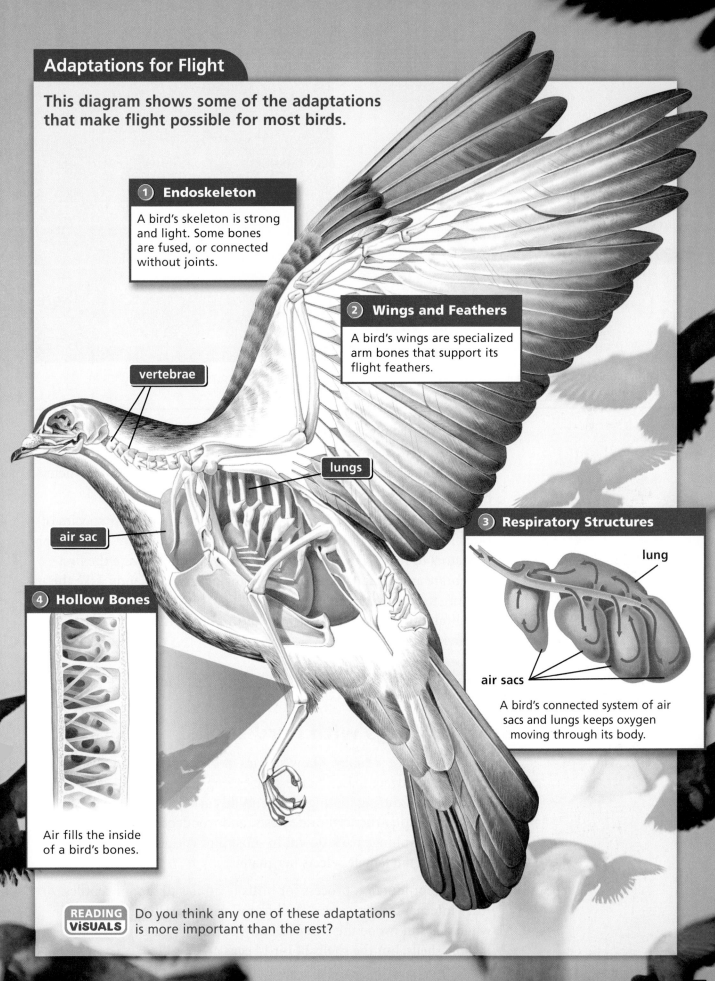

Adaptations for Flight

This diagram shows some of the adaptations that make flight possible for most birds.

① Endoskeleton

A bird's skeleton is strong and light. Some bones are fused, or connected without joints.

② Wings and Feathers

A bird's wings are specialized arm bones that support its flight feathers.

vertebrae

lungs

air sac

③ Respiratory Structures

lung

air sacs

A bird's connected system of air sacs and lungs keeps oxygen moving through its body.

④ Hollow Bones

Air fills the inside of a bird's bones.

READING VISUALS Do you think any one of these adaptations is more important than the rest?

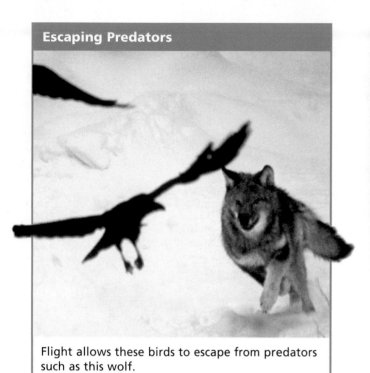

Flight allows these birds to escape from predators such as this wolf.

Flight allows this osprey to hunt for fish in bodies of water.

Some birds migrate very long distances. Ruby-throated hummingbirds, for example, migrate from Canada and the United States to Mexico and Central America each winter, flying nonstop 700 kilometers across the Gulf of Mexico.

By flying, birds can escape danger on the ground. Many species of birds lay their eggs and raise their young in places that are difficult for predators to reach. Fossil evidence suggests that birds were the first vertebrate animal species to live on many of Earth's islands. Like the first organisms that adapted to live on land, birds that were the first vertebrates on an island usually had little competition for food, water, and living space.

 CHECK YOUR READING How does flight benefit birds? Give three examples.

Birds lay eggs with hard shells.

Birds reproduce sexually. Many species of birds have distinctive ways of trying to attract mates. Some species sing, and others develop colorful feathers during mating season. Wild turkeys fight each other, bowerbirds construct elaborate nests, and woodcocks fly high in the air and then plunge back down. In most bird species, the male animals display and the female selects her mate.

The reproduction process for birds is similar to that of reptiles. After internal fertilization, a shell forms around each fertilized egg while it is still inside the female's body. Reptiles' eggs usually have flexible shells, but the shells of birds' eggs are hard.

The female bird chooses a place to lay the eggs. Often this is a nest. In some bird species either the male or the female builds the nest, while in others, mated birds build a nest together. Bird eggs have to be kept at a constant, warm temperature or they will not develop. Most birds use their body heat to keep the eggs warm. They sit on the eggs, which can support the adult birds' weight because the shells are hard. This process is called **incubation**. When the eggs hatch, the young birds are not yet able to fly. They must be cared for until they can meet their own needs.

These 3- to 8-day-old tanagers are being fed by both of their parents.

Most birds take care of their offspring.

In some bird species, male and female mates care for their offspring together. This is often the case for birds, such as the tanagers in the top photograph, whose young hatch before their eyes open or their feathers grow. It takes two adult birds to provide them with enough food, warmth, and protection.

The offspring of some species, like the ducks in the bottom photograph, hatch at a later state of development, with open eyes. They are already covered with down feathers and able to walk. In such species it's common for just one adult, usually the female, to incubate the eggs and care for the young.

These 7-day-old ducklings are able to find their own food while their mother watches over them.

5.3 Review

KEY CONCEPTS

1. What does an endothermic animal need to do in order to generate body heat?

2. What are two types of feathers, and what are their functions?

3. Describe three adaptations that make flight possible for birds.

CRITICAL THINKING

4. **Compare and Contrast** How is reproduction in birds similar to reproduction in reptiles? How does it different?

5. **Synthesize** Most flightless birds live on islands or in remote places where there are few predators. Explain why, in such an environment, flying birds' bodies might have adapted and become flightless.

⬥ CHALLENGE

6. **Hypothesize** Many species of birds begin migration while food is still plentiful in their current environment. Understanding what triggers migration in birds is an active area of scientific research. Develop a hypothesis about migration triggers in one species of bird. Describe how to test your hypothesis.

CHAPTER INVESTIGATION

Bird Beak Adaptations

OVERVIEW AND PURPOSE The beaks of most birds are adapted for eating particular types of food. In this lab you will

- use models to simulate how different types of beaks function
- infer how the shape of a bird's beak might affect the food a bird eats

▶ Question

For this lab, you will use a tool as a model of a specialized bird beak. You will try to obtain food with your beak at several different feeding stations. Each station will have a different type of food. Examine the tools that will be used for this lab, as well as the feeding stations. Then write a question about how beak shape might affect the food a bird eats. Your question should begin with *Which, How, When, Why,* or *What.* Keep in mind that you will be asked to answer this question at the end of the lab.

▶ Procedure

1. Make a data table like the one shown on page 181.

2. Complete the title of your data table by writing in the name of the tool you will be using.

3. Before you start collecting food at one of the feeding stations, write a prediction in your data table. Predict how well you think the tool will function and why.

MATERIALS
- tweezers
- eyedropper
- slotted spoon
- pliers
- test tubes in rack
- water
- dried pasta
- millet seeds
- jar of rubber bands
- empty containers
- stopwatch

4. See how much food you can collect in one minute. To collect food, you must move it from the feeding station into a different container, and you may only touch the food with the tool.

step 4

5. Describe your results in your data table.

6. Return the food you collected to the feeding station. Try to make it look just like it did when you started.

7. Repeat steps 3–6 at each of the other feeding stations.

Observe and Analyze
Write It Up

1. **INTERPRET DATA** At which feeding station did you have the best results? Why? Explain your answer.

2. **EVALUATE** How accurate were the predictions you made?

3. **APPLY** If you could visit each feeding station again, how would you change the way you used the tool to collect food? Explain your answer.

Conclude
Write It Up

1. **INFER** What answers do you have for the question you wrote at the beginning of this lab?

2. **INFER** In what ways do you think the experience you had during this lab is similar to the ways real birds obtain food?

3. **IDENTIFY LIMITATIONS** What unexpected factors or problems might have affected your results?

4. **SYNTHESIZE** What environmental and physical factors can a bird actually control when it is getting food?

5. **APPLY** Examine the beaks of the birds in the photographs below. Write a brief description of the shape of each bird's beak. Then, for each bird, name one type of food its beak might be suited for and one type of food each bird would probably not be able to eat.

INVESTIGATE Further

CHALLENGE How are other parts of birds' bodies specialized for the environments where they live? Investigate the feet of the following birds: ostrich, heron, woodpecker, pelican, and owl.

Bird Beak Adaptations

Question:

Table 1. Collecting Food with_____

Station	Prediction	Results
Water in test tubes		
Dried pasta		
Millet seeds		
Rubber bands in jar		

 Mammals live in many environments.

- Endotherms can stay active in cold environments
- Many bird adaptations are related to flight
- Birds lay hard-shelled eggs and usually take care of their young

- About mammals as endotherms
- About the diversity of adaptations in mammals
- That mammals produce milk, which is food for their young

VOCABULARY

mammal p. 183
placenta p. 186
gestation p. 186

THINK ABOUT

How diverse are mammals?

Mammals have adapted to survive in many environments and come in many shapes and sizes. Whales live in the ocean, and goats may live near mountain peaks. Some monkeys live in tropical forests, and polar bears survive in frozen areas. An elephant might not fit in your classroom, but the tiny shrew shown here could fit on your finger. As you read this chapter, think about the characteristics of mammals that help them to survive in such a variety of ways.

Mammals are a diverse group.

NOTETAKING STRATEGY
Using a strategy of your choice, take notes on the idea that mammals are a diverse group. Be sure to include mammal characteristics.

The group of vertebrates called mammals includes many familiar animals. Mice are mammals, and so are cows, elephants, and chimpanzees. You are a mammal, too. Bats are mammals that can fly. Some mammals, including whales, live in water.

Some mammal species, such as raccoons and skunks, have adapted to live in many sorts of environments, including cities. Others, such as cheetahs and polar bears, have adaptations for meeting their needs in just a few environments.

Mammals are a diverse animal group. Although there are less than 5000 species of mammals on Earth, mammal species come in many shapes and sizes, and have many different ways of moving, finding food, and eating. These are some of the characteristics that distinguish **mammals** from other animals:

- All mammals have hair during some part of their lives.
- Most mammal species have teeth specialized for consuming particular kinds of food.
- All mammal species produce milk, with which they feed their young.

RESOURCE CENTER
CLASSZONE.COM

Learn more about mammals.

Mammals are endotherms.

You have learned that endothermic animals are able to stay active in cold environments. This is because endotherms maintain a constant body temperature. Mammals are endotherms. This means that they use some of the food they consume to generate body heat. Mammals also have adaptations for controlling body temperature.

Hair

Many species of mammals have bodies covered with hair. Like birds' feathers, hair is an adaptation that allows mammals to have some control over the warmth or coldness of their bodies. Mammals that live in cold regions, like polar bears, have hair that keeps them warm. Desert mammals, such as camels, have hair that protects them from extreme heat.

Most mammals have at least two types of hair. Soft, fluffy underhairs keep heat close to their bodies, like the down feathers of birds. Water-resistant guard hairs cover the under-hairs and give the animal's fur its color.

Some species of mammals also have specialized hairs. A specialized structure is one that performs a particular function. For example, whiskers are sensory hairs that are part of an animal's sense of touch. Porcupines' quills are hairs that function in self defense.

 CHECK YOUR READING What are three functions of hair?

whiskers

Colored guard hairs give this tiger its stripes. Its whiskers are specialized sensory hairs. It also has underhairs, which you cannot see.

quills

This porcupine's quills are specialized guard hairs.

Body Fat

Some mammal species that live in water, such as dolphins, have very little hair. These mammals have a layer of fat, called blubber, that plays an important role in maintaining body temperature. The blubber is located between the animal's skin and muscles, and provides its organs with insulation from heat and cold.

Body fat can also be a storage place for energy. When a mammal consumes more food than it needs, the extra energy may be stored in its fat cells. Later, if the animal needs energy but cannot find food, it can use the energy stored in the fat.

For example, animals that hibernate, such as woodchucks, may eat a lot more than they need to survive at times when plenty of food is available. This makes them fat. Then, while they are hibernating, they do not have to eat, because their body fat provides them with the energy they need.

 CHECK YOUR READING What are two ways that body fat functions in mammals?

INVESTIGATE How Body Fat Insulates

How well does fat keep a mammal warm?

A layer of body fat between the muscles and the skin allows some mammals to survive in very cold places. In this investigation, you will experience how well that adaptation works by making a blubber glove model.

PROCEDURE

1. Half fill one large, zip-lip plastic bag with vegetable shortening. Turn another bag inside out and place it inside the bag with the shortening. Zip the edges of the two bags together so that the shortening is sealed between them.

2. Place one hand inside this "blubber glove." Then submerge both your gloved hand and your free hand in a tub of ice water. Which hand stays warmer? For how long? Record your observations.

WHAT DO YOU THINK?

How well did the layer of fat in your blubber glove insulate your hand?

CHALLENGE Would you expect an animal that lives in a very hot environment to have a thick layer of body fat?

SKILL FOCUS
Making models

MATERIALS
- 2 zip-lip plastic bags, 1/2-gallon size
- can of vegetable shortening
- bowl of ice water

TIME
15 minutes

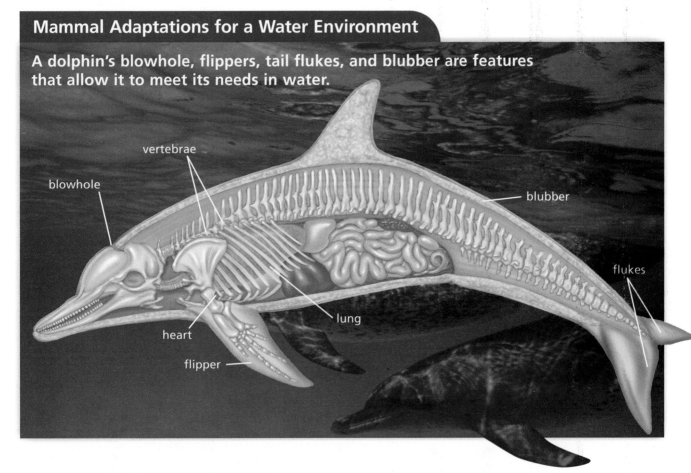

Mammal Adaptations for a Water Environment

A dolphin's blowhole, flippers, tail flukes, and blubber are features that allow it to meet its needs in water.

vertebrae

blowhole

blubber

flukes

lung

heart

flipper

Mammals have adapted to many environments.

Scientists think mammals appeared on Earth about 200 million years ago. Fossil evidence suggests that the first mammals were small land vertebrates with four limbs, a tail, and specialized teeth. They probably had fur and were most active at night.

Over millions of years, those early mammals adapted to live in many different environments and became the diverse group of species they are today. Moles, for example, live almost entirely underground. They have strong limbs for digging and organs specialized for sensing invertebrate prey in the dark. Spider monkeys, on the other hand, live mostly in trees. A spider monkey can use all four of its long limbs and its flexible, grasping tail to move through a forest without touching the ground.

The first mammals lived on land, but over time some species adapted to live in watery environments. Some of them, such as otters and walruses, live mostly in water but can also be found on land. Others, such as dolphins and whales, have bodies so completely adapted for life in the water that they no longer have a way of moving on land. If you look carefully at the diagram above, however, you will see that a dolphin's body plan differs in some important ways from that of a fish.

Mammals have reproductive adaptations.

Mammals reproduce sexually. Before a mammal can produce off-spring, it finds a mate. Some mammals, such as lions, live in groups that include both males and females. However, most mammals live alone most of the time. They find a mate when they are ready to reproduce. Some mammal species breed only at certain times of the year. Others can reproduce throughout the year.

Development Before Birth

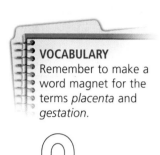

VOCABULARY
Remember to make a word magnet for the terms *placenta* and *gestation.*

Fertilization occurs internally in mammals. In almost every species of mammal, the offspring develop inside the female's body. Many mammals have a special organ called a **placenta** that transports nutrients, water, and oxygen from the mother's blood to the developing embryo. The embryo's waste materials leave through the placenta and are transported out of the mother's body along with her waste.

The time when a mammal is developing inside its mother is called **gestation**. As you can see in the diagram, the length of the gestation period is different for different species. Gestation ends when the young animal's body has grown and developed enough for it to survive outside the mother. Then it is born.

CHECK YOUR READING Where do the offspring of most mammals develop before they are born?

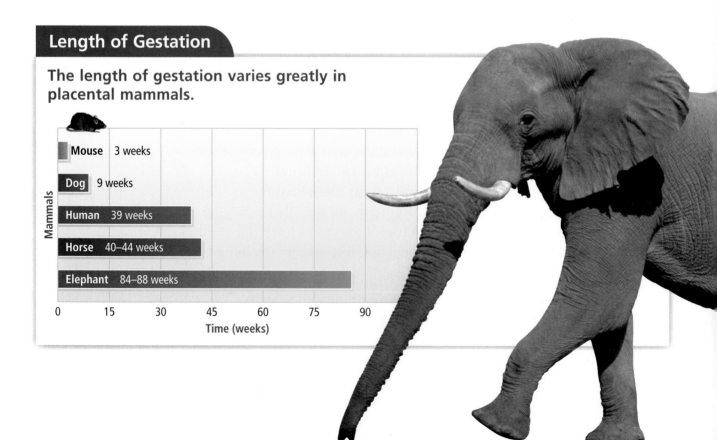

Length of Gestation

The length of gestation varies greatly in placental mammals.

Mammals	Time (weeks)
Mouse	3 weeks
Dog	9 weeks
Human	39 weeks
Horse	40–44 weeks
Elephant	84–88 weeks

Time (weeks): 0 15 30 45 60 75 90

Not all mammals fully develop inside their mothers. The duck-billed platypus and two species of spiny anteaters have young that hatch from eggs. Mammals in a group called the marsupials (mahr-SOO-pee-uhlz), which includes kangaroos, develop inside the mother at first but are born when they are still extremely small. Right after birth, a young marsupial climbs across its mother to a special pouch on the outside of her body. It completes its development there. Only one marsupial, the opossum, lives in North America.

Raising Young

Milk, a high-energy liquid food full of proteins, fats, sugars, and other nutrients, is the first food young mammals consume. Each species' milk has a different combination of these ingredients.

Mammals' bodies have special glands for producing milk, called mammary glands. In almost all mammal species, only females' mammary glands function. This means that only female mammals can feed the young with milk. In most mammal species, females gestate and care for the offspring alone. However, in some mammal species, the male helps raise the young.

This dog is feeding her puppies with milk.

Different species of mammals are born at varying stages of development. Most mice are helpless, blind, and naked at birth, while giraffes can walk soon after they are born. The length of time a young mammal needs care from an adult varies. Some seals nurse their young for less than a month before leaving them to survive on their own. Some whales live alongside their young for a much longer time. However, humans may be the mammal species that takes care of their offspring for the longest time of all.

5.4 Review

KEY CONCEPTS

1. Why is a bat classified as a mammal instead of a bird? Why are whales classified as mammals and not fish?

2. Name two adaptations that allow mammals to have control over body temperature.

3. How does the way that mammals feed their young differ from the ways other animals feed their young?

CRITICAL THINKING

4. **Apply** One day on your way home from school, you see an animal that you have never seen before. What clues would you look for to tell you what type of animal it is?

5. **Synthesize** Make a Venn diagram that shows how the vertebrate animal groups you learned about in this chapter are similar and different.

⬥ CHALLENGE

6. **Evaluate** This section begins with the statement "mammals are a diverse group." Explain what this means and why it is a true statement. How does the diversity of mammals compare to the diversity of other living things, such as bacteria, plants, arthropods, or fish?

the BIG idea

Vertebrate animals live in most of Earth's environments.

CONTENT REVIEW
CLASSZONE.COM

KEY CONCEPTS SUMMARY

5.1 **Vertebrates are animals with endoskeletons.**

All **vertebrate** animals have an **endoskeleton** which includes vertebrae, or backbones.

Most vertebrates are fish. Fish are adapted for life in a water environment.

vertebrae

VOCABULARY
vertebrate p. 157
endoskeleton p. 157
scale p. 161

5.2 **Amphibians and reptiles are adapted for life on land.**

Amphibians and **reptiles** have adaptations for moving, getting food, and breathing on land.

Most amphibians live in moist places.

Many reptiles live in hot, dry places.

VOCABULARY
ectotherm p. 170
amphibian p. 167
reptile p. 168

5.3 **Birds meet their needs on land, in water, and in the air.**

Birds have adaptations that allow them to survive in many environments. Many of the features and behaviors of birds relate to flight.

VOCABULARY
endotherm p. 174
incubation p. 179

Mammals live in many environments.

Mammal species live in many environments. Mammals have adaptations that allow them to survive in cold places. They also have distinctive reproductive adaptations.

VOCABULARY
mammal p. 183
placenta p. 186
gestation p. 186

Reviewing Vocabulary

Place each vocabulary term listed below at the center of a description wheel diagram. Write some words describing it on the spokes.

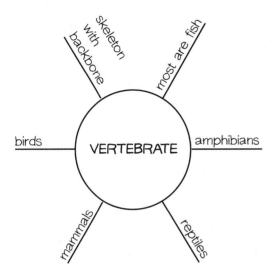

1. endotherm

2. migration

3. ectotherm

4. scale

5. incubation

6. gestation

Reviewing Key Concepts

Multiple Choice *Choose the letter of the best response.*

7. The vertebrate endoskeleton differs from an arthopod's exoskeleton because it

  a. supports muscles

  b. protects organs

  c. is inside the animal's body

  d. has joints

8. Most vertebrate species are

  a. fish   **c.** birds

  b. amphibians   **d.** mammals

9. Fish obtain oxygen from water with structures called

  a. vertebrae   **c.** lungs

  b. fins   **d.** gills

10. Down feathers provide insulation for a bird's body because they

  a. trap warm air between them

  b. are waterproof

  c. overlap each other

  d. are slightly oily

11. Which organ do both fish and amphibians have?

  a. lateral line

  b. lungs

  c. gills

  d. scaly skin

12. Mammals differ from other vertebrates because mammals can

  a. lay eggs

  b. produce milk

  c. are endotherms

  d. are able to swim

13. The two types of vertebrates that lay their eggs in water are

  a. amphibians and birds

  b. reptiles and fish

  c. fish and amphibians

  d. mollusks and fish

14. Which statement is true?

  a. All birds are ectotherms.

  b. All birds can fly.

  c. All birds have two wings and two legs.

  d. All birds have teeth and beaks.

15. The organ that transports materials between a female mammal and the offspring developing inside her body is called a

  a. yolk   **c.** blubber

  b. placenta   **d.** vertebrae

Short Answer *Write a short answer to the questions below.*

16. Describe how you would determine if an animal was a salamander or a lizard.

17. Why do bird eggs have to be incubated?

18. PREDICT Imagine that you live in Mexico and you have a pen pal who lives in Iceland. Both of you want to know about animals in the other person's country. Which of you will be more likely to have seen wild reptiles? Why?

19. APPLY Polar bears live in an arctic environment. Jaguars live in a rain forest environment. Which animal would you expect to have more body fat? Explain.

Refer to diagram below as you answer parts of the next two questions.

20. COMPARE Birds, like all vertebrates, have internal skeletons. What functions does a bird's skeleton have in common with all other vertebrates?

21. INFER This diagram shows only some of a bird's body systems. Name two systems that are not shown here, including organs that belong to them and their functions.

22. HYPOTHESIZE Not all birds migrate. Some birds, such as pigeons and house sparrows, stay in one living place through the winter. What do you think you would find if you compared the diets of birds that migrate with those of birds that do not?

23. MATH AND SCIENCE Scientists studying an endangered species of rainforest salamanders estimated that only 875 of these animals were still living in 2002. If this salamander population decreases by 50 animals per year, in what year will it become extinct? Explain how you found your answer.

24. CLASSIFY Imagine that you move to a new place and spend a year watching nearby animals. Read each description and identify each animal described below as a fish, amphibian, reptile, bird, or mammal.

a. A scaly animal warms itself on your sidewalk when the sun is out. It has dry skin, four legs, and a tail.

b. Small animals swim in a pond near your home. They have no legs, but they do have tails. As they grow older, their tails shrink and they develop four limbs. Then they disappear from the pond.

c. A furry animal chews a hole under your porch and seems to be living there. You later see it with smaller animals that appear to be its young.

d. A pair of flying, feathered animals collect objects and carry them into an opening under the gutter of your neighbor's house. At first you see them carrying twigs and grass, but later it looks as if they are carrying worms.

the BIG idea

25. DRAW CONCLUSIONS Look again at the picture on pages 154–155. What do penguins and seals have in common? What adaptations do some species of birds and mammals have that allow them to survive in cold environments like Antarctica?

26. PROVIDE EXAMPLES Think of an example of a species from each of the vertebrate animal groups you've learned about, and describe an adaptation that suits each to the environment where it lives. Explain your answers.

UNIT PROJECTS

Evaluate all the data, results, and information from your project folder. Prepare to present your project. Be ready to answer questions posed by your classmates about your results.

Analyzing Diagrams

*Read the text and study the diagram, and then choose the best response for
the questions that follow.*

Vertebrates, such as birds, fish, and mammals, have endoskeletons. This internal skeleton is made up of a system of bones that extends throughout the
body. Muscles can attach directly to the bones, around joints—the place where
two bones meet. As shown in the generalized diagram below, at least two
muscles are needed to produce movement. One of the muscles contracts, or
shortens, pulling on the bone, while the other muscle extends, or is stretched.

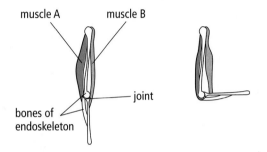

muscle A   muscle B

joint

bones of
endoskeleton

1. Endoskeletons are made up of
  a. contracting muscles
  b. extending muscles
  c. internal bones
  d. external bones

2. A muscle produces movement by
  a. pulling
  b. relaxing
  c. extending
  d. rotating

3. A joint is where
  a. one muscle connects to another
  b. one bone connects to another
  c. a muscle connects to a bone
  d. the bone ends

4. The leg in the diagram bends when
  a. muscle A contracts
  b. muscle A relaxes
  c. muscle B contracts
  d. muscles A and B contract

5. What is the main point of the diagram and the
text above?
  a. Two muscles are needed to produce movement
  in vertebrates.
  b. Vertebrates have internal skeletons.
  c. When one muscle shortens, another muscle
  gets longer.
  d. Movement in vertebrates is the result of the
  interaction of muscles and bones.

Extended Response

*Use terms from the word box to answer the next
question. Underline each term you use in your answer.*

6. Many fish go forward by moving their tails from
side to side. Describe the action of the muscles on
each side of the fish as the tail moves from one
side to the other.

contract	pull
extend	muscle

7. Using what you know about joints and muscles
and the diagram, describe what happens to muscles and bones as you bend your leg at the knee.

UNIT D

Ecology

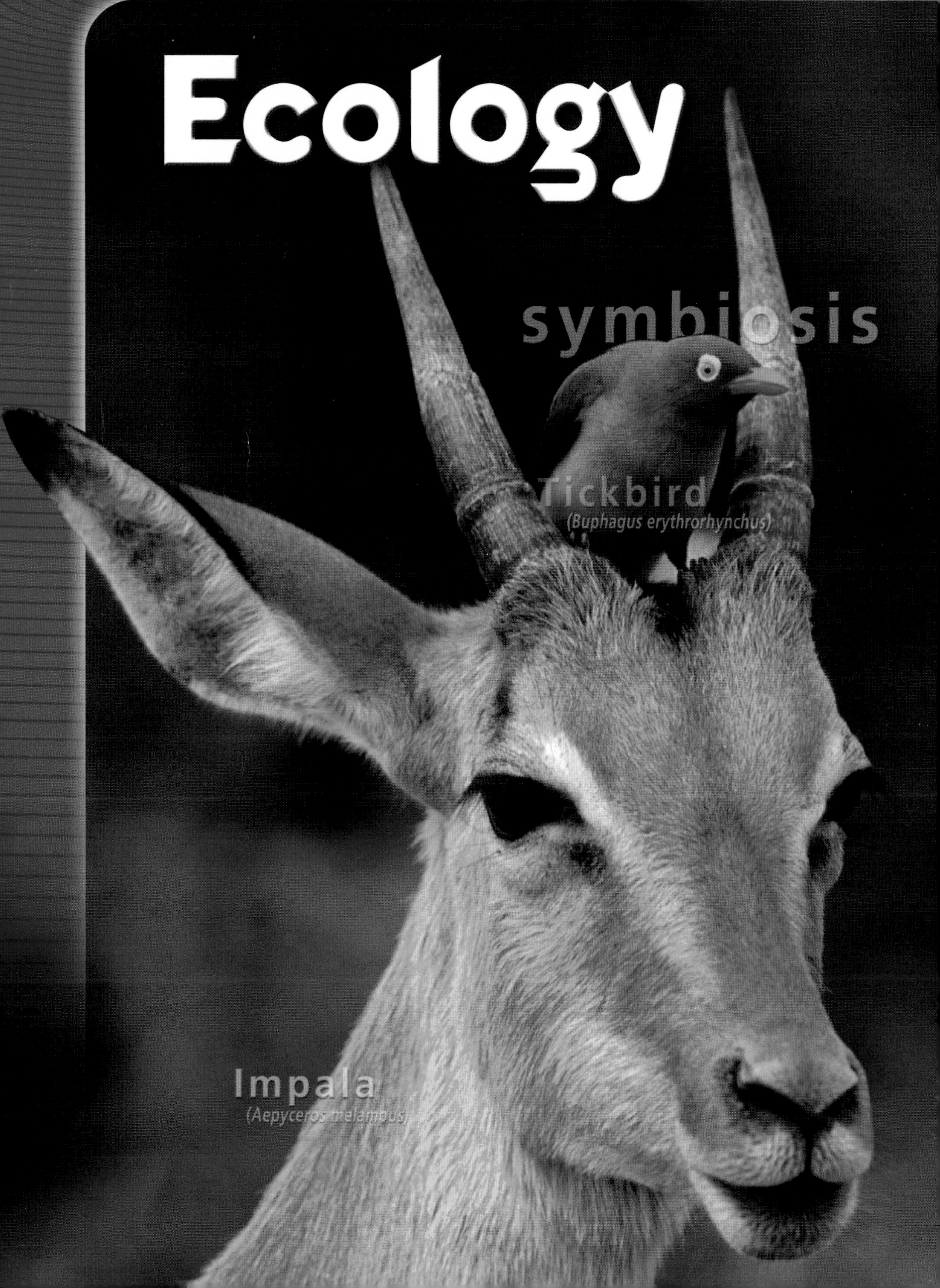
symbiosis
Tickbird
(Buphagus erythrorhynchus)
Impala
(Aepyceros melampus)

Ecology
Contents Overview

Unit Features

1 Ecosystems and Biomes   6

the **BIG** idea

Matter and energy together support life
within an environment.

2 Interactions Within Ecosystems   42

the **BIG** idea

Living things within an ecosystem interact with
each other and the environment.

3 Human Impact on Ecosystems   78

the **BIG** idea

Humans and human population growth
affect the environment.

ECOSYSTEMS ON FIRE

It may seem strange to set fire to a wilderness preserve, but fire brings health to some ecosystems.

SCIENTIFIC AMERICAN FRONTIERS

View the video "Prairie Comeback" to learn about the restoration of a prairie ecosystem.

An astonishing variety of plants blooms in this prairie in Missouri.

Fire and Life

Intense heat, smoke, the crackling of burning grasses, the crashing of flaming trees—all these characteristics of fire seem threatening. In recent years, forest fires have burned huge areas of forest and have endangered people and property nearby. But even though fire can be destructive, it can also be an agent of life. In fact, scientists are actively using fire to manage ecosystems—areas that contain specific groups of living and nonliving things. Prairies, forests, and woodlands are examples of ecosystems.

The fear of fire has led people to limit fires that are a natural part of some ecosystems. Preventing or putting out smaller fires in a forest ecosystem can mean trouble. Occasional small fires burn small amounts of material and cause only limited damage. Without these smaller fires, burnable materials may build up and lead to the outbreak of a catastrophic fire.

The species of living things in some ecosystems have adaptations that allow them to thrive on fire. In western forests in the United States trees such as lodgepole pine and jack pine depend upon flames to release seeds from their cones. Cape lilies lying under the forest floor blossom almost immediately after a forest fire. On prairies, flowers such as the rare coastal gayfeather in Texas or the fringed prairie orchid in Illinois benefit from prairie fires.

controlled burn

new growth

Seven months after a controlled burn, light shines on a new patch of wild hyacinth growing at the base of an oak tree.

Observing Patterns

Ecosystems include living things, such as plants and animals, and nonliving things, such as water and soil. Fires affect both the living and the nonliving. The photographs above show part of an oak woodland ecosystem. The photograph on the left shows a burn—a fire set deliberately by humans. The photograph on the right shows the same area seven months later.

Ashes left from fires add nutrients to the soil. Fire also opens space on the forest floor. Areas that were shaded by small trees, plants, and dead branches receive light. Over time, wild hyacinth and other new plants grow around the oak, and new insects and animals move into the area.

SCIENTIFIC AMERICAN FRONTIERS

View the "Prairie Comeback" segment of your Scientific American Frontiers video to see how understanding ecosystems can help bring a prairie into bloom.

IN THIS SCENE FROM THE VIDEO ▶ a bison grazes on new growth that appears after the prairie is burned.

BRINGING BACK THE PRAIRIE At one time natural events, such as lightning, along with human activity caused regular patterns of fire on the prairie. Bison grazed on tender young plants that grew up after fires, and the plants that weren't eaten by the bison had room to grow. In 1989, an organization called The Nature Conservancy turned the Chapman-Barnard Cattle Ranch in Northeast Oklahoma into the Tall Grass Prairie Restoration Preserve.

Scientists at the preserve are using controlled fire and reintroducing bison to the area. Today there are more than 750 species of plants and animals growing in the preserve.

In tall-grass prairie ecosystems, fire provides similar benefits. Fire burns away overgrown plants, enriches the soil, and clears the way for the growth of new plants. Bison prefer to graze on these new plants that appear after a fire.

A New Understanding

Although some of the benefits provided by ecosystems can't be measured, researchers are starting to measure the financial contributions of ecosystems. Ecosystems may help clean our water, balance gases in the atmosphere, and maintain temperature ranges.

Researchers today are studying these benefits. In fact, a new frontier in ecology, called ecosystem services, is emerging. This new study is gaining the attention of both scientists and economists.

Given our growing awareness of the importance of ecosystems, should humans deliberately set fire to areas in forests or prairies? The answer to this question requires an understanding of interactions among living and nonliving parts of ecosystems. Forest and prairie fires can be dangerous, but properly managed, they provide important benefits to society as well as to the natural world.

UNANSWERED Questions

Understanding the connections within ecosystems raises more questions. In the coming years, people will need to analyze the costs and benefits of ecosystem restoration.

- How will humans balance the need to feed the population with the cost of destroying ecosystems such as the prairie?
- How can scientists and wildlife managers protect people and property near forests while maintaining forest ecosystems?
- How do ecosystems protect natural resources, such as soil and water?

UNIT PROJECTS

As you study this unit, work alone or with a group on one of the projects listed below. Use the bulleted steps to guide your project.

Build an Ecosystem

Use an aquarium or other container to build an ecosystem such as an aquarium.

- Set up your ecosystem. Observe it daily, and record your observations.
- Bring your ecosystem into your classroom, or take photographs and make diagrams of it. Present the record of your observations along with the visual displays.

Conservation Campaign

Find out how much water, paper, and energy are used in a month at your school.

- Describe a plan for conserving resources.
- Present your plan. You might make posters, write announcements, perform a short skit.

Design a Park

You are part of a group that is planning a park near your school. Your group wants the park to include plants that lived in the area twenty-five years ago.

- Collect information from local museums, park districts, or botanic gardens. You can also visit Web sites sponsored by those organizations.
- Prepare a report and drawing of your park design.

CAREER CENTER
CLASSZONE.COM

Learn more about careers in ecology.

Ecosystems and Biomes

the BIG idea

Matter and energy together support life within an environment.

How many living and nonliving things can you identify in this photograph?

Key Concepts

SECTION 1.1
Ecosystems support life.
Learn about different factors that make up an ecosystem.

SECTION 1.2
Matter cycles through ecosystems.
Learn about the water, carbon, and nitrogen cycles.

SECTION 1.3
Energy flows through ecosystems.
Learn how energy moves through living things.

SECTION 1.4
Biomes contain many ecosystems.
Learn about different land and water biomes.

Internet Preview

CLASSZONE.COM

Chapter 1 online resources: Content Review, Simulation, Visualization, three Resource Centers, Math Tutorial, Test Practice

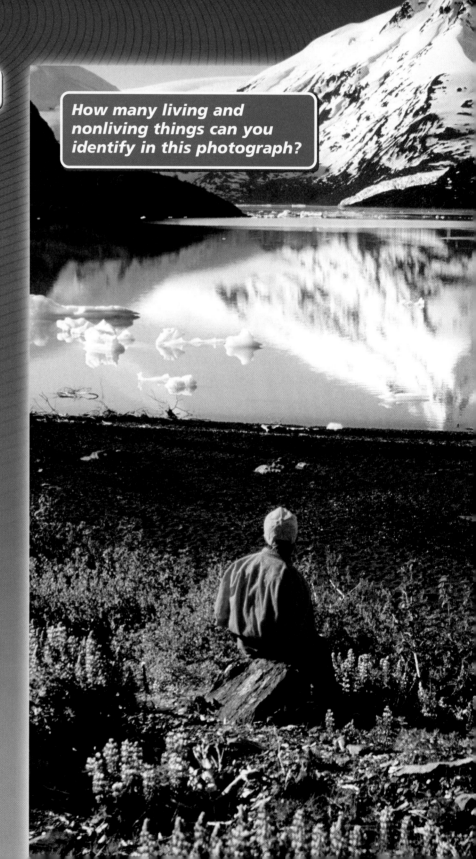

EXPLORE the BIG idea

How Do Plants React to Sunlight?

Move a potted plant so that the Sun shines on it from a different direction. Observe the plant each day for a week.

Observe and Think What change do you observe in the plant? What is it that plants get from the Sun?

What Is Soil?

Get a cupful of soil from outside and funnel it into a clear plastic bottle. Fill the bottle two-thirds full with water and place the bottle cap on tightly. Shake the bottle so that the soil and water mix completely. Place the bottle on a windowsill overnight. Wash your hands.

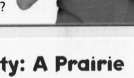

Observe and Think What has happened to the soil and water mixture? How many different types of material do you observe?

Internet Activity: A Prairie Ecosystem

Go to **ClassZone.com** to simulate the recovery of tall-grass and short-grass prairies. Discover the types of plants and animals best adapted for each type of prairie, and learn more about how to keep the prairie thriving.

Observe and Think What do all prairie plants have in common? How do prairie plants differ?

NSTA
scilinks.org
SCi LINKS

Food Chains and Food Webs **Code: MDL001**

Getting Ready to Learn

◀ CONCEPT REVIEW

- The natural world that surrounds all living things is called the environment.
- Most living things need water, air, food, and living space.
- All living things need a source of energy to stay alive and grow.

◀ VOCABULARY REVIEW

See Glossary for definitions.

biology	nutrient
energy	photosynthesis
environment	respiration
matter	system

CONTENT REVIEW
CLASSZONE.COM
Review concepts and vocabulary.

▶ TAKING NOTES

COMBINATION NOTES

To take notes about a new concept, first make an informal outline of the information. Then make a sketch of the concept and label it so you can study it later.

VOCABULARY STRATEGY

Write each new vocabulary term in the center of a **frame game** diagram. Decide what information to frame the term with. Use examples, descriptions, parts, sentences that use the term in context, or pictures. You can change the frame to fit each item.

See the Note-Taking Handbook on pages R45–R51.

SCIENCE NOTEBOOK

NOTES

Parts of an ecosystem:

- Animals
- Plants
- Soil
- Water
- Light
- Microorganisms

	nonliving factors	
physical or chemical	**ABIOTIC FACTOR**	water, light, soil, temperature
	affected by living factors	

Ecosystems support life.

◀ BEFORE, you learned

- Living things need to obtain matter and energy from the environment
- The Sun provides Earth with light and heat

▶ NOW, you will learn

- What factors define an ecosystem
- About living factors in an ecosystem
- About nonliving factors in an ecosystem

VOCABULARY

ecology p. 9
ecosystem p. 9
biotic factor p. 10
abiotic factor p. 10

EXPLORE Your Environment

How much can temperature vary in one place?

PROCEDURE

1. Choose three different locations inside your classroom where you can measure temperature.

2. Place a thermometer at each location. Wait for at least two minutes. Record the temperatures in your notebook.

3. Compare the data you and your classmates have collected.

WHAT DO YOU THINK?

- Which location was the warmest, and which was the coldest?
- Describe what factors may have affected the temperature at each location.

MATERIALS

- thermometer
- stopwatch

Living things depend on the environment.

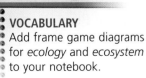

VOCABULARY
Add frame game diagrams for *ecology* and *ecosystem* to your notebook.

You wouldn't find a kangaroo in the Arctic and you won't see a polar bear in Australia. Each of these organisms is suited to a certain environment. The kangaroo and the polar bear are able to survive despite the harsh conditions of their surroundings. **Ecology** is the scientific study of how organisms interact with their environment and all the other organisms that live in that environment.

Scientists use the word **ecosystem** to describe a particular environment and all the living things that are supported by it. An ecosystem can be as small as a pond or as large as a desert. What is important in an ecosystem is how the living parts of the ecosystem relate to the nonliving parts.

Let's take a look at a pond. A pond ecosystem is more than just water and fish. Plants grow in and around the water, and animals feed on these plants. A variety of tiny microorganisms in the water are food for fish and for each other. These are just a few of the living parts, or **biotic factors** (by-AHT-ihk), of a pond ecosystem. The nonliving parts, or **abiotic factors** (AY-by-AHT-ihk), include the air that supplies oxygen and carbon dioxide, the soil that provides nutrients, the water in the pond, and the sunlight that plants need to grow.

CLASSIFY Name three living and three nonliving factors that are part of this pond ecosystem.

Biotic factors interact with an ecosystem.

Living things depend upon an ecosystem for food, air, and water, as well as other things they need for survival. In turn, living things have an impact on the ecosystem in which they live. Plants, as a biotic factor in land ecosystems, affect other biotic and abiotic parts of ecosystems. Plants are an important source of food. The types of plants found in a particular ecosystem will determine the types of animals that can live there. Plants can affect temperature by blocking sunlight. Plant roots hold soil in place. Even the atmosphere is affected by plants taking in carbon dioxide and releasing oxygen.

Animals, as biotic factors, also affect an ecosystem. A beaver that builds a dam changes the flow of a river and so affects the surrounding landscape. Large herds of cattle can overgraze a grassland ecosystem and cause the soil to erode. In an ocean biome, corals form giant reefs that provide food and shelter for marine organisms.

Many abiotic factors affect ecosystems.

Abiotic factors include both the physical and chemical parts of an ecosystem. Physical factors are factors that you can see or feel, such as the temperature or the amount of water or sunlight. Important chemical factors include the minerals and compounds found in the soil and whether the ecosystem's water is fresh or salty. It is the combination of different abiotic factors that determines the types of organisms that an ecosystem will support.

READING TiP

The word *biotic* means "living." The prefix *a-* in *abiotic* means "not," so *abiotic* means "not living."

 List four different abiotic factors that can affect an ecosystem.

Temperature

Temperature is an important abiotic factor in any ecosystem. In a land ecosystem, temperature affects the types of plants that will do well there. The types of plants available for food and shelter, in turn, determine the types of animals that can live there. For example, a tropical rain forest has not only a lot of rain but it has consistently warm temperatures. The wide variety of plants that grow in a tropical rain forest supports a wide variety of monkeys, birds, and other organisms.

Animals are as sensitive to temperature as plants are. Musk oxen with their thick coat of fur can survive in very cold environments, where temperatures of –40°C (–40°F) are normal. The water buffalo, with its light coat, is better suited to warm temperatures. The wild water buffalo lives where temperatures can reach 48°C (118°F).

This musk ox's thick fur keeps it warm in the cold temperatures of northern Canada.

A water buffalo cools itself in a shallow stream during a hot day in India.

 COMPARE AND CONTRAST How are these animals alike? How are they different?

Light

COMBINATION NOTES
Remember to make notes and diagrams to show how abiotic factors affect biotic factors in an ecosystem.

You can easily understand how abiotic factors work together when you think about sunlight and temperature. Sunlight warms Earth's surface and atmosphere. In addition, energy from sunlight supports all life on Earth. The Sun provides the energy that plants capture and use to produce food in a process called photosynthesis. The food produced by plants, and other photosynthetic organisms, feeds almost all the other living things found on Earth.

The strength of sunlight and the amount of sunlight available in a land ecosystem determine the types of plants in that ecosystem. A desert ecosystem will have plants like cacti, which can survive where sunlight is very strong. Meanwhile, mosses and ferns grow well on the forest floor, where much of the light is blocked by the trees above.

Light is a factor in ocean ecosystems as well. The deeper the water is, the less light there is available. In the shallow water near the shore, photosynthetic organisms can survive at the surface and on the ocean floor. In the open ocean, light is available for photosynthetic organisms only in the first hundred meters below the surface.

Soil

Soil, which is a mixture of small rock and mineral particles, is an important abiotic factor in land ecosystems. Organisms within the soil break down the remains of dead plants and animals. This process of decay provides important raw materials to the living plants and animals of an ecosystem.

The size of soil particles affects how much air and water the soil can hold.

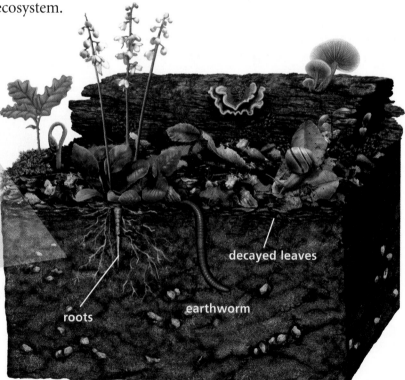

decayed leaves

roots

earthworm

Different ecosystems have different types of soil. The characteristics of the soil in an ecosystem affect plant growth. Soils that have a lot of decaying, or organic, matter can hold water well and allow air to reach the plant roots. Sandy soils usually do not hold water well because the water flows through too easily. Clay soil, which has small, tightly packed particles, will not allow water to move through easily at all. Minerals in the soil also affect plant growth.

 CHECK YOUR READING Explain how soil can affect plant life in an ecosystem.

Water

Another important abiotic factor in land ecosystems is the amount of water available to support life. All living things need water to carry out life processes. Plants need water as well as sunlight for photosynthesis. Animals need water to digest food and release the energy stored in the food. Look at the photograph to see the effect that an underground water source has on an otherwise dry, desert ecosystem. Trees could not survive there without a plentiful supply of water.

Ecosystems that have a lot of water can support a large number of different types of plants. These different types of plants can then support a large number of different types of animals. Tropical rain forests, the wettest of all ecosystems on land, are also the most diverse. Desert ecosystems, which are the driest land ecosystems, have far fewer types of plants and animals. The types and number of living things in a land ecosystem will always be related to the amount of fresh water available for its inhabitants.

INFER An oasis forms in the desert when underground water comes to the surface. How can you identify the boundary of this oasis?

1.1 Review

KEY CONCEPTS

1. Draw a diagram of an ecosystem near where you live. Label the factors "biotic" or "abiotic."

2. Give two examples of how plants and animals affect their environment.

3. Describe how temperature, light, and soil affect an ecosystem.

CRITICAL THINKING

4. **Predict** Think of a forest ecosystem. Now imagine that a large volcanic eruption throws large amounts of dust and ash into the air, blocking out sunlight. How might the forest ecosystem be affected if the sunlight is blocked for a day? For a year?

◯ CHALLENGE

5. **Apply** Think of how you fit into your local environment. List ways in which you interact with biotic and abiotic factors within your ecosystem.

CHAPTER INVESTIGATION

Soil Samples

OVERVIEW AND PURPOSE Nonliving, or abiotic, factors all have an effect on soil. The quality of the soil affects how well plants grow in a particular environment. In this investigation, you will

- observe and record how water travels through three soil samples
- predict how different types of soil would affect plant growth

▶ Problem

How does soil type affect how water moves through soil?

▶ Hypothesize

You should complete steps 1–5 in the procedure before writing your hypothesis. Write a hypothesis to explain how water moves through certain types of soil. Your hypothesis should take the form of an "If . . . , then . . . , because . . ." statement.

▶ Procedure

MATERIALS
- 3 pieces of paper
- spoon
- 50 mL each of clay, coarse sand, loam
- hand lens
- toothpick
- eyedropper
- water
- 3 pieces of filter paper
- 3 plastic funnels
- 3 large beakers
- small beaker
- stopwatch

1. Make a data table in your **Science Notebook** like the one shown on page 15.

2. Label three sheets of paper "Clay," "Sand," and "Loam." Carefully place a spoonful of each sample on the appropriately labeled paper.

3. Carefully examine each of the soils, with and without the hand lens. Describe the color of each, and record the information in your data table.

4. Use a toothpick to separate the particles of each sample of soil. Record the size of the particles in the data table.

5. Put a small amount of each soil sample in the palm of your hand. Add a drop of water and mix the soil around with your finger. Write a description of the texture of each sample in your data table. Be sure to wash your hands after you finish. After you have recorded your observations, write your hypothesis.

6. Fold each piece of filter paper to form cones as shown in the diagram. Place one filter inside each funnel. Place one funnel in each large beaker. Measure 50 mL of each soil sample and place the sample in one of the funnels.

7. Measure 150 mL of water and pour it into the funnel containing the clay. Start the stopwatch when the water begins to drip out of the funnel. Stop the watch when the water stops dripping. Record the time in seconds in the data table.

8. Repeat step 7 for the sand and the loam. When you have finished with the activity, dispose of the materials according to your teacher's directions, and wash your hands.

▶ Observe and Analyze

Write It Up

1. **INTERPRET DATA** Through which soil sample did the water move the fastest? The slowest?

2. **OBSERVE** What type of changes occurred in the soil as the water was added?

▶ Conclude

Write It Up

1. **INTERPRET** Compare your results with your hypothesis. Does your data support your hypothesis?

2. **IDENTIFY LIMITS** What sources of error could have affected this investigation?

3. **EVALUATE** Based on your observations, what can account for the differences in the times recorded for the three soil samples?

4. **PREDICT** Based on your results, which of the soil samples would you expect to be the best type of soil in which to grow plants? Explain.

▶ INVESTIGATE Further

CHALLENGE Design an experiment in which you test which of the three soil samples is best for growing plants. Include a materials list, hypothesis, and procedure for your experiment.

Soil Samples
Table 1. Soil Characteristics

Characteristics	Clay	Sand	Loam
Color			
Particle size			
Texture			
Time for water to stop dripping (sec)			

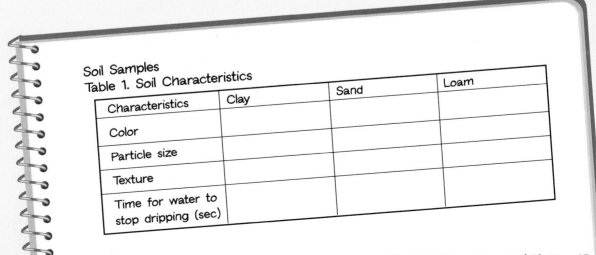

Matter cycles through ecosystems.

◀ **BEFORE,** you learned

- Ecosystems support life
- Living and nonliving factors interact in an ecosystem
- Temperature, light, soil, and water are important nonliving factors in ecosystems

▶ **NOW,** you will learn

- How matter is exchanged between organisms and their environment
- About the water, carbon, and nitrogen cycles

VOCABULARY

cycle p. 16
water cycle p. 17
carbon cycle p. 18
nitrogen cycle p. 19

EXPLORE The Water Cycle

Do plants release water?

PROCEDURE

① Cover a branch of the plant with a plastic bag. Tape the bag firmly around the stem.

② Water the plant and place it in a sunny window or under a lamp. Wash your hands.

③ Check the plant after ten minutes, at the end of class, and again the next day.

WHAT DO YOU THINK?

- What do you see inside the plastic bag?
- What purpose does the plastic bag serve?

MATERIALS

- 1 small potted plant
- 1 clear plastic bag
- tape
- water

All ecosystems need certain materials.

RESOURCE CENTER
CLASSZONE.COM

Explore cycles in nature.

Living things depend on their environment to meet their needs. You can think of those needs in terms of the material, or matter, required by all living things. For example, all organisms take in water and food in order to survive. All of the materials an organism takes in are returned to the ecosystem, while the organism lives or after it dies.

The movement of matter through the living and nonliving parts of an ecosystem is a continuous process, a cycle. A **cycle** is a series of events that happens over and over again. Matter in an ecosystem may change form, but it never leaves the ecosystem, so the matter is said to cycle through the ecosystem. Three of the most important cycles in ecosystems involve water, carbon, and nitrogen.

Water Cycle

Different processes combine to move water through the environment.

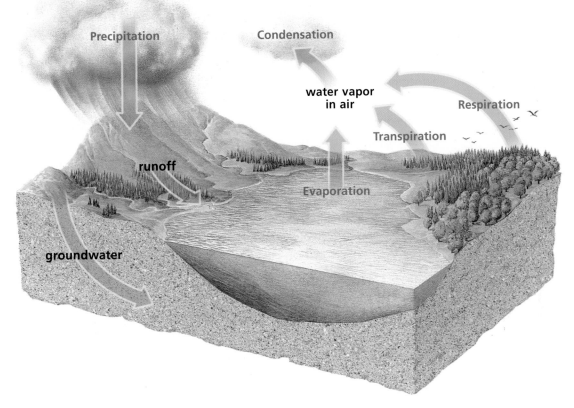

Precipitation

Condensation

water vapor in air

Respiration

Transpiration

runoff

Evaporation

groundwater

Water cycles through ecosystems.

Water is stored on Earth's surface in lakes, rivers, and oceans. Water is found underground, filling the spaces between soil particles and cracks in rocks. Large amounts of water are stored in glaciers and polar ice sheets. Water is also part of the bodies of living things. But water is not just stored, it is constantly moving. The movement of water through the environment is called the **water cycle.**

Water is made up of just two elements: oxygen and hydrogen. As water moves through an ecosystem, it changes in physical form, moving back and forth between gas, liquid, and solid. Water in the atmosphere is usually in gaseous form—water vapor. Water that falls to Earth's surface is referred to as precipitation. For precipitation to occur, water vapor must condense—it must change into a liquid or solid. This water can fall as rain, snow, sleet, mist, or hail.

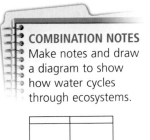

COMBINATION NOTES
Make notes and draw a diagram to show how water cycles through ecosystems.

 CHECK YOUR READING   What are the three physical forms of water in the water cycle?

Water returns to the atmosphere when heated, changing back into vapor, a process called evaporation. Living things also release water vapor. Animals release water vapor when they breathe, or respire. Plants release water vapor through a process called transpiration.

Carbon cycles through ecosystems.

Carbon is an element found in all living things. Carbon moves through Earth's ecosystems in a cycle referred to as the **carbon cycle.** It is through carbon dioxide gas found in Earth's atmosphere that carbon enters the living parts of an ecosystem.

Plants use carbon dioxide to produce sugar—a process called photosynthesis. Sugars are carbon compounds that are important building blocks in food and all living matter. Food supplies the energy and materials living things need to live and grow. To release the energy in food, organisms break down the carbon compounds—a process called respiration. Carbon is released and cycled back into the atmosphere as carbon dioxide. When living things die and decay, the rest of the carbon that makes up living matter is released.

READING **TiP**

Notice that photosynthesis is a process that brings carbon into living matter and respiration is a process that releases carbon.

CHECK YOUR READING Name three ways that living things are part of the carbon cycle.

Earth's oceans contain far more carbon than the air does. In water ecosystems—lakes, rivers, and oceans—carbon dioxide is dissolved in water. Algae and certain types of bacteria are the photosynthetic organisms that produce food in these ecosystems. Marine organisms, too, release carbon dioxide during respiration. Carbon is also deposited on the ocean floor when organisms die.

Carbon Cycle

Different processes combine to move carbon through the environment.

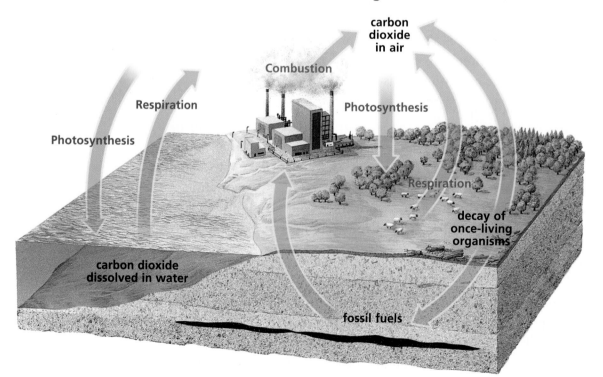

carbon dioxide in air

Combustion

Respiration

Photosynthesis

Photosynthesis

Respiration

decay of once-living organisms

carbon dioxide dissolved in water

fossil fuels

What is one form in which carbon is stored on the ocean floor?

PROCEDURE

1. Use the mortar and pestle to crush the seashell into a powder.
2. Pour the powder into a small beaker.
3. Add enough white vinegar to cover the powder.

WHAT DO YOU THINK?

- What happens when white vinegar is added to the crushed shell?
- What is the material produced in the reaction and where did it come from originally?

CHALLENGE What type of reaction have you observed?

SKILL FOCUS
Observing

MATERIALS
- mortar and pestle
- whole seashell or fragments
- small beaker
- white vinegar

TIME
15 minutes

Large amounts of carbon are stored underground. The remains of plants and animals buried for millions of years decay slowly and change into fossil fuels, such as coal and oil. The carbon in fossil fuels returns to ecosystems in a process called combustion. As humans burn fossil fuels to release energy, dust particles and gases containing carbon are also released into the environment.

Nitrogen cycles through ecosystems.

Nitrogen is another element important to life that cycles through Earth in the **nitrogen cycle.** Almost four-fifths of the air you breathe is clear, colorless nitrogen gas. Yet, you cannot get the nitrogen you need to live from the air. All animals must get nitrogen from plants.

Plants cannot use pure nitrogen gas either. However, plants can absorb certain compounds of nitrogen. Plants take in these nitrogen compounds through their roots, along with water and other nutrients. So how does the nitrogen from the atmosphere get into the soil? One source is lightning. Every lightning strike breaks apart, or fixes, pure nitrogen, changing it into a form that plants can use. This form of nitrogen falls to the ground when it rains.

Nitrogen Cycle

Different processes combine to move nitrogen through the environment.

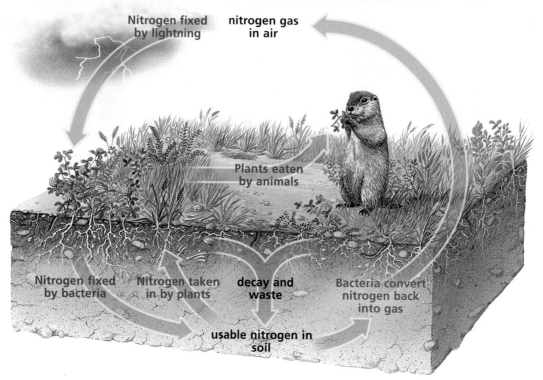

Nitrogen fixed by lightning

nitrogen gas in air

Plants eaten by animals

Nitrogen fixed by bacteria

Nitrogen taken in by plants

decay and waste

Bacteria convert nitrogen back into gas

usable nitrogen in soil

VISUALIZATION
CLASSZONE.COM

Watch the nitrogen cycle in action.

A far greater source of nitrogen is nitrogen-fixing bacteria. These bacteria live in the oceans as well as the soil. Some even attach themselves to the roots of certain plants, like alfalfa or soybeans. When organisms die, decomposers in the ocean or soil break them down. Nitrogen in the soil or water is used again by living things. A small amount is returned to the atmosphere by certain bacteria that can break down nitrogen compounds into nitrogen gas.

1.2 Review

KEY CONCEPTS

1. Draw a diagram of the water cycle. Show three ways in which water moves through the cycle.

2. Summarize the main parts of the carbon cycle.

3. Explain two ways that nitrogen gas in the atmosphere is changed into nitrogen compounds that plants can use.

CRITICAL THINKING

4. **Predict** When people burn fossil fuels, carbon dioxide gas is added to the atmosphere. How might increased carbon dioxide affect plant growth?

5. **Compare and Contrast** Review the nitrogen and carbon cycles. How are these two cycles similar and different?

⬤ CHALLENGE

6. **Apply** Draw a cycle diagram that shows how water is used in your household. Include activities that use water, sources of water, and ways that water leaves your house.

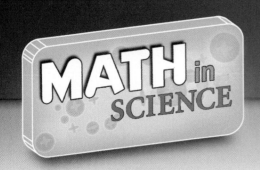

MATH TUTORIAL
CLASSZONE.COM

Click on Math Tutorial for more help with adding integers.

This iceberg is made up of fresh water, which freezes at 0°C. The surrounding ocean is salt water, which doesn't freeze at 0°C.

Temperature and the Water Cycle

Changes in temperature help water move through the environment. At freezing temperatures—below 32°F or 0°C for sea-level environments—water can begin to become solid ice. Ice starts to melt when the temperature rises above freezing, causing the water to become liquid again. Temperature change also causes water to become vapor, or gas, within the air.

Example

Suppose you are waiting for winter to come so you can skate on a small pond near your house. The weather turns cold. One day the temperature is 25°C, then the next day the air temperature drops by 35°C. What temperature is the air? If the air stays below 0°C, some of the water will begin to freeze.

(1) Write a verbal model:
25 degrees + a 35-degree drop = what temperature?

(2) Write an equation. Use negative and positive integers:
$25 + (-35) = ?$

(3) Solve the equation:
$25 - 35 = -10$

ANSWER −10°C.

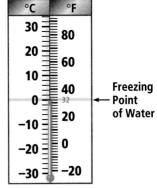

Answer the following questions.

1. A container of water is left out over night, when the temperature is −18°C. In the morning, the air temperature rises by 8°C. What temperature is the air? What will happen to the water?

2. An ice block sits in a field where the air is 0°C. The air temperature rises by 16°C, then it drops by 8°C. What temperature is the air in the field now? What will happen to the ice?

3. What happens to a block of ice after the temperature in the air follows this pattern: $-6 + 17 + 10 + 18 + (-5)$? What temperature has the air reached?

CHALLENGE Use a thermometer to measure the temperature of the air outside and indoors in degrees Celsius. Write two addition equations that show the temperature change between the two locations. One equation should show a rise, and one should show a drop.

KEY CONCEPT

1.3 Energy flows through ecosystems.

◀ **BEFORE, you learned**

- Matter cycles continuously through an ecosystem
- Living things are part of the water, carbon, and nitrogen cycles

▶ **NOW, you will learn**

- How living things move energy through an ecosystem
- How feeding relationships are important in ecosystems
- How the amount of energy changes as it flows through an ecosystem

VOCABULARY

producer p. 23
consumer p. 24
decomposer p. 25
food chain p. 26
food web p. 26
energy pyramid p. 28

EXPLORE Energy

How can you observe energy changing form?

PROCEDURE

① Mark and cut a spiral pattern in a square piece of paper.

② Cut a 15-cm piece of thread and tape one end to the center of the spiral.

③ Adjust the lamp to shine straight at the ceiling. Turn the lamp on.

④ Hold the spiral by the thread and let it hang 10 cm above the light bulb. CAUTION: Don't let the paper touch the bulb!

WHAT DO YOU THINK?

- What do you see happen to the spiral?
- In what sense has the energy changed form?

MATERIALS

- paper
- marker
- scissors
- thread
- tape
- desk lamp

Living things capture and release energy.

Everything you do—running, reading, and working—requires energy. The energy you use is chemical energy, which comes from the food you eat. When you go for a run, you use up energy. Some of that energy is released to the environment as heat, as you sweat. Eventually, you will need to replace the energy you've used.

Energy is vital to all living things. Most of that energy comes either directly or indirectly from the Sun. To use the Sun's energy, living things must first capture that energy and store it in some usable form. Because energy is continuously used by the activities of living things, it must be continuously replaced in the ecosystem.

All of these producers capture energy from sunlight.

Plants

This tomato plant uses energy from the Sun to produce food.

The food is used as a source of energy and material for the plant and all the organisms that eat the plant.

Seaweed

Seaweed is a producer found in Earth's oceans and coastal zones.

Phytoplankton

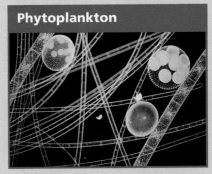

The most numerous producers are tiny organisms that live in water called phytoplankton.

 READING VISUALS What process do all of these producers have in common?

Producers

A **producer** is an organism that captures energy and stores it in food as chemical energy. The producers of an ecosystem make energy available to all the other living parts of an ecosystem. Most energy enters ecosystems through photosynthesis. Plants, and other photosynthetic organisms, take water and carbon dioxide from their environment and use energy from the Sun to produce sugars. The chemical energy stored in sugars can be released when sugars are broken down.

VOCABULARY
Remember to add a frame game for *producers* to your notebook.

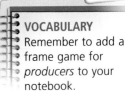

 CHECK YOUR READING How does energy enter into the living parts of an ecosystem?

Plants are the most common producers found in land ecosystems. In water ecosystems, most food is produced by photosynthetic bacteria and algae. A few examples of producers that use photosynthesis are shown in the photographs above.

The Sun provides most of the energy that is stored in food. One exception is the unusual case of a type of bacteria that lives in the deep ocean, where there is no sunlight. These bacteria produce food using heated chemicals released from underwater vents. This process is called chemosynthesis. Whether producers use photosynthesis or chemosynthesis, they do just as their name suggests—they produce food for themselves and for the rest of the ecosystem.

Consumers

A consumer is an organism that gets energy by eating producers or other consumers.

Primary consumer: caterpillar

Producer: tree

Secondary consumer: bird

READING VISUALS How does the energy inside the leaf get transferred to the bird?

Consumers

Organisms that cannot produce their own food must get their food from other sources. **Consumers** are organisms that get their energy by eating, or consuming, other organisms. To understand how energy flows through an ecosystem, you have to study feeding relationships. A feeding relationship starts with a producer, followed by one and often many more consumers.

 CHECK YOUR READING Describe the producer-consumer relationship in terms of energy.

READING TIP

Primary is a word that means "first in order," *secondary* means "second in order," and *tertiary* means "third in order."

Consumers are classified by their position in a feeding relationship. In a meadow ecosystem, animals such as antelopes and grasshoppers feed on grasses. They are primary consumers because they are the first link between the producers and the rest of the consumers in an ecosystem. The wolves that eat the antelopes and the meadowlarks that eat the grasshoppers are secondary consumers. There are also tertiary consumers, like the prairie falcon that eats the meadowlark. Ecosystems also have special consumers called scavengers, like the vulture or earthworm, which are consumers that feed on dead animals.

In the photograph above, energy enters the ecosystem through the tree, which is the producer. The caterpillar that gets its energy by feeding on the leaves is the first, or primary, consumer. The bird that gets its energy by feeding on the caterpillar is a secondary consumer.

Decomposers

If you've been for a hike through a forest, or a walk through a park, you have seen the interaction of producers and consumers. Tall trees and leafy shrubs are home to many insects and the birds that feed upon the insects. Also important to the maintenance of an ecosystem are decomposers, a group of organisms that often go unseen. **Decomposers** are organisms that break down dead plant and animal matter into simpler compounds.

mushrooms

Fungi, such as these mushrooms, are decomposers.

You can think of decomposers as the clean-up crew of an ecosystem. In a forest, consumers such as deer and insects eat a tiny fraction of the leaves on trees and shrubs. The leaves that are left on the forest floor, as well as dead roots and branches, are eventually digested by fungi and bacteria living in the soil. Decomposers also break down animal remains, including waste materials. A pinch of soil may contain almost half a million fungi and billions of bacteria.

The energy within an ecosystem gets used up as it flows from organism to organism. Decomposers are the organisms that release the last bit of energy from once-living matter. Decomposers also return matter to soil or water where it may be used again and again.

INVESTIGATE Decomposers

Where do decomposers come from?

SKILL FOCUS
Observing

PROCEDURE

1. Carefully use scissors to cut an opening across the middle of the bottle.

2. Place a handful of stones in the bottom of the bottle for drainage, and add enough soil to make a layer 10 cm deep.

3. Place some leaves and fruit slices on top of the soil.

4. Seal the cut you made with tape. Mark the date on the tape.

5. Add water through the top of the bottle to moisten the soil, and put the cap on the bottle. Wash your hands.

6. Observe the fruit slices each day for two weeks. Record your observations. Keep the soil moist.

October 3

MATERIALS
- clear soda bottle with cap
- scissors
- stones
- garden soil
- leaves
- slices of fruit
- masking tape
- marker
- water

TIME
30 minutes

WHAT DO YOU THINK?

- What do you observe happening to the fruit slices?
- Where do the decomposers in your bottle come from?

CHALLENGE Predict what would happen if you used potting soil instead of soil from outside.

Models help explain feeding relationships.

COMBINATION NOTES
Remember to take notes and draw a diagram for *food chain* and *food web*.

You have learned how energy is captured by producers and moved through ecosystems by consumers and decomposers. Scientists use two different models to show the feeding relationships that transfer energy from organism to organism. These models are food chains and food webs.

Food Chain

A chain is made of links that are connected one by one. Scientists use the idea of links in a chain as a model for simple feeding relationships. A **food chain** describes the feeding relationship between a producer and a single chain of consumers in an ecosystem.

The illustration in the white box on page 27 shows a wetland food chain. The first link in the chain is a cattail, a primary producer that captures the Sun's energy and stores it in food. The second link is a caterpillar, a primary consumer of the cattail. The frog is the next link, a secondary consumer that eats the caterpillar. The final link is a heron, a tertiary consumer that eats the frog. Energy is captured and released at each link in the chain. The arrows represent the flow of energy from organism to organism. You can see that some of the energy captured by the cattail makes its way through a whole chain of other organisms in the ecosystem.

Food Web

A **food web** is a model of the feeding relationships between many different consumers and producers in an ecosystem. A food web is more like a spiderweb, with many overlapping and interconnected food chains. It is a better model for the complex feeding relationships in an ecosystem, which usually has many different producers, with many primary and secondary consumers.

READING TiP

Notice that the food chain described above is also a part of the food web described here. Follow the blue arrows in the diagram on page 27.

The illustration on page 27 also shows a wetland food web. You can see that the feeding relationships can go in several directions. For example, the food web shows that ruddy ducks eat bulrushes, which are producers. That makes ruddy ducks primary consumers. Ruddy ducks are also secondary consumers because they eat snails. A food web shows how one consumer can play several roles in an ecosystem.

CHECK YOUR READING What is the difference between a food chain and a food web?

Both food chains and food webs show how different organisms receive their energy. They also show how different organisms depend on one another. If one organism is removed from the food web or food chain, it may affect many other organisms in the ecosystem.

Energy Flows Through Ecosystems

Energy is transferred from one organism to the next as organisms eat or are eaten.

A Wetland Food Chain

Flow of Energy
Energy flow starts at the bottom. Arrows represent energy moving from an organism that is eaten to the organism that eats it.

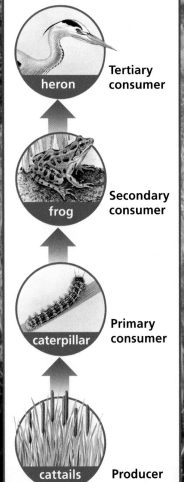

heron — **Tertiary consumer**

frog — **Secondary consumer**

caterpillar — **Primary consumer**

cattails — **Producer**

Decomposers
These tiny organisms recycle dead and decayed material.

A Wetland Food Web

heron

water snake

frog

blackbird

duck

beetle

caterpillar

snail

muskrat

bulrush

cattails

Available energy decreases as it moves through an ecosystem.

Another way to picture the flow of energy in an ecosystem is to use an energy pyramid. An **energy pyramid** is a model that shows the amount of energy available at each feeding level of an ecosystem. The first level includes the producers, the second level the primary consumers, and so on. Because energy is lost as it moves from producers to consumers, the bottom level is the largest. The available energy gets smaller and smaller the farther up the pyramid you go.

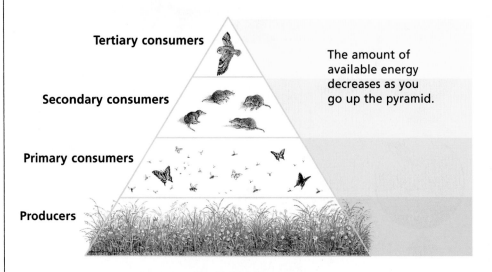

Tertiary consumers

Secondary consumers

Primary consumers

Producers

The amount of available energy decreases as you go up the pyramid.

READING TiP

Refer to the diagram above as you read the text. It is because some energy is lost at each level that the diagram takes the shape of a pyramid.

In the pyramid shown here, plants are the producers. They capture energy from the Sun, use some of it, then store the rest as food. The plants are eaten by insects, which also use up some of the energy before being eaten by shrews. The shrews use up energy before being eaten by the owl. You can see that it takes a lot of sunlight to support the producers and consumers in a food web that feeds an owl.

1.3 Review

KEY CONCEPTS

1. Describe the role of producers, consumers, and decomposers in an ecosystem.

2. Explain why a food web provides a better model of an ecosystem than a food chain does.

3. Explain how the amount of available energy changes as energy moves up a food chain.

CRITICAL THINKING

4. **Apply** Draw a food chain and a food web for an ecosystem near your home.

5. **Predict** Imagine that muskrats are removed from a wetland ecosystem. Predict what would happen both to producers and to secondary consumers.

�CHALLENGE

6. **Synthesize** Explain how the carbon cycle is related to a food web. Describe how energy and matter move through the food web and the carbon cycle.

Biomagnification

Matter moves through living things in an ecosystem. Some of it is used up, some of it is stored. Sometimes, a toxic, or poisonous, material can get into a food chain and be stored. The amount of poison increases over time, or is magnified. Biomagnification is the process by which matter becomes concentrated in living things in a food chain.

Moving up the Food Chain

DDT provides one example of the effects of biomagnification in an ecosystem. DDT is a chemical that was widely used to kill plant-eating insects. Some chemicals break down over time, but DDT does not. DDT collected in water and soil, was absorbed by living things, and moved up the food chain. The diagram shows how DDT became magnified in a wetland ecosystem. It entered through tiny organisms called zooplankton, which absorbed DDT from the water.

1 The DDT in zooplankton was about 800 times greater than the DDT in the environment.

2 Minnows fed on zooplankton. DDT was magnified 31 times so there was 24,800 times more DDT in minnows than in the environment: 800 x 31 = 24,800.

3 Trout ate minnows. DDT was magnified 1.7 times so there was 42,160 times more DDT in trout than in the environment.

4 Gulls ate trout. DDT was magnified 4.8 times so there was over 200,000 times more DDT in gulls than in the environment.

DDT is especially harmful to large birds such as osprey and eagles. The chemical made the shells of the eggs of these large birds so thin that the eggs did not survive long enough to hatch.

Moving up the Food Chain

This diagram shows how DDT moved up a food chain in Long Island Sound. The color in each circle below represents a certain level of DDT.

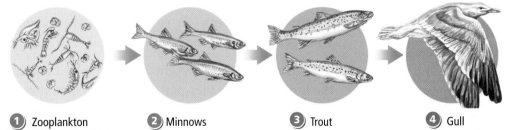

1 Zooplankton   2 Minnows   3 Trout   4 Gull

CHALLENGE Even though DDT was effective, some insects were not harmed by DDT. Predict what might happen to the numbers of those insects as a result of DDT use.

Biomes contain many ecosystems.

BEFORE, you learned

- Feeding relationships describe how energy flows through ecosystems
- The amount of available energy decreases as it flows through ecosystems

NOW, you will learn

- How biomes vary by region and by the plant life they support
- How different ecosystems make up a biome
- About the different land and water biomes on Earth

VOCABULARY

biome p. 30
coniferous p. 32
deciduous p. 33
estuary p. 36

THINK ABOUT

What do this plant's characteristics suggest about its environment?

A plant's overall shape and form help it to survive in its environment. Look closely at this plant in the photograph. Describe its shape. Does it have leaves? a stem? flowers? Look at the surrounding area. What do your observations suggest about the environment in general?

Regions of Earth are classified into biomes.

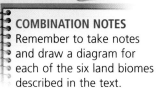

COMBINATION NOTES
Remember to take notes and draw a diagram for each of the six land biomes described in the text.

If you could travel along the 30° latitude line, either north or south of the equator, you'd notice an interesting pattern. You would see deserts give way to grasslands and grasslands give way to forests. Across Earth, there are large geographic areas that are similar in climate and that have similar types of plants and animals. Each of these regions is classified as a **biome** (BY-ohm). There are six major land biomes on Earth, as shown on the map on page 31.

Climate is an important factor in land biomes. Climate describes the long-term weather patterns of a region, such as average yearly rainfall and temperature ranges. Climate also affects soil type. Available water, temperature, and soil are abiotic factors important in ecosystems. The fact that the abiotic factors of a particular biome are similar helps to explain why the ecosystems found in these biomes are similar. Biomes represent very large areas, which means that there will be many ecosystems within a biome.

Land Biomes

Each land biome is characterized by a particular climate, the quality of the soil, and the plant life found there.

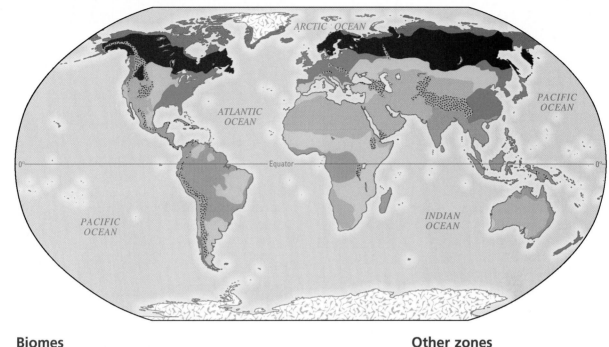

Biomes

■ Tundra   ■ Desert   ■ Temperate Forest

■ Taiga   ■ Grassland   ■ Tropical Forest

Other zones

▒ Mountain Zones

▨ Polar Ice

Taiga and Tundra

If you go to the northernmost regions of Earth, you will find two biomes—tundra and taiga—that are characterized by long cold winters and short cool summers. In the Arctic tundra, temperatures can go as low as –50°C, with a high of about 18°C. Temperature ranges in the taiga (TY-guh) are similar, –40°C to 20°C.

The tundra doesn't get much precipitation, less than 25 centimeters each year. Yet the area is wet because cold temperatures keep the water from evaporating. One of the important characteristics of tundra is permafrost, a deep layer of permanently frozen soil that lies just below the surface soil. Permafrost prevents trees from taking root in the tundra. Plants of the tundra are small and include mosses, grasses, and woody shrubs. Organisms called lichens also do well in the tundra.

The producers of tundra ecosystems support rodents, caribou, and musk oxen. Grizzly bears, white fox, and snowy owls are predators found there. Migrating birds come to nest in the tundra, feeding on insects that mature in summer.

snowy owl

Tundra Only small plants and lichens grow in the tundra because the soil below the surface is frozen.

Taiga Evergreen trees grow in the taiga, where the ground is cold but not frozen.

Even though the temperatures of the taiga are similar to those of the tundra, the taiga has more precipitation, 30 to 60 centimeters a year. The effect of this is that there is more snow on the ground, which insulates the soil below, keeping it from freezing.

Taiga ecosystems are characterized by evergreen trees called **coniferous** (koh-NIHF-uhr-uhs) trees. These trees have needlelike leaves that produce food all year long. This is an advantage in taiga ecosystems because decomposers work slowly in the cold, so the soil is low in nutrients. The wood and leaves of these trees feed insects and their seeds feed birds and squirrels. Taiga ecosystems support deer, elk, snowshoe hares, and beavers. Predators include lynx, owls, bears, and wolves.

Desert and Grassland

collared lizard

Deserts and grasslands are biomes found toward the middle latitudes. You can see from the map on page 31 that a desert biome often leads into a grassland biome. What deserts and grasslands have in common is that they do not get enough precipitation to support trees.

Some deserts are cold and some deserts are hot, but all deserts are characterized by their dry soil. Less than 25 centimeters of rain falls each year in a desert. Desert plants, like the cactus, and desert animals, like the collared lizard, can get by on very little water. Small burrowing animals like the kangaroo rat and ground squirrel are part of desert ecosystems. Desert predators include snakes, owls, and foxes.

Grassland ecosystems develop in areas of moderate rainfall, generally from 50 to 90 centimeters each year. There is enough rain to support grasses, but too little rain to support forests. Periodic wildfires and droughts keep smaller shrubs and tree seedlings from growing. Summers in grassland ecosystems are warm, up to 30°C, but winters are cold.

Grasses do well in large open areas. The more rain a grassland ecosystem gets, the higher the grasses grow. These ecosystems support seed-eating rodents that make their burrows in the grassland soil. There are also large grazing animals, like bison, wild horses, gazelle, and zebra. Predators include wolves, tigers, and lions.

Desert Plants of the desert are adapted to survive in dry soil. Many must also survive high daytime temperatures.

Grassland Grasslands receive enough rain to support grasses. Wildfires keep shrubs and trees from growing.

Temperate Forest and Tropical Forest

Trees need more water than smaller plants, shrubs, and grasses. So forest biomes are usually located in regions where more water is available. The taiga is a forest biome. There the coniferous trees survive on smaller amounts of precipitation because the cold weather limits evaporation. Across the middle latitudes, temperate forests grow where winters are short and 75 to 150 centimeters of precipitation fall each year. Near the equator, there are no winters. There, tropical forests grow where 200 to 450 centimeters of rain fall each year.

Most temperate forests are made up of deciduous trees, sometimes referred to as broadleaf trees. **Deciduous** (dih-SIHJ-oo-uhs) trees drop their leaves as winter approaches and grow new leaves in spring. The

Temperate Forest
Temperate forests contain many trees with leaves that change color and fall as winter approaches.

Tropical Forest
Tropical forests are warm enough that trees stay green during the entire year.

most common broadleaf trees in North American deciduous forests are oak, birch, beech, and maple. Temperate forests support a wide variety of animals. Animals like mice, chipmunks, squirrels, raccoons, and deer live off seeds, fruit, and insects. Predators include wolves, bobcats, foxes, and mountain lions.

Most temperate forests in North America are deciduous. However, the wet winters and dry summers in the Pacific Northwest support forests made up mostly of coniferous trees—redwoods, spruce, and fir. These forests are referred to as temperate rain forests. The largest trees in the United States are found in these temperate rain forests.

Tropical forests are located near the equator, where the weather is warm all year, around 25°C. The tropical rain forest is the wettest land biome, with a rainfall of 250 to 400 centimeters each year. The trees tend to have leaves year round. This provides an advantage because the soil is poor in nutrients. High temperatures cause materials to break down quickly, but there are so many plants the nutrients get used up just as quickly.

More types of animals, plants, and other organisms live in the tropical rain forest than anywhere else on Earth. The trees grow close together and support many tree-dwelling animals like monkeys, birds, insects, and snakes. There are even plants, like orchids and vines, that grow on top of the trees.

 CHECK YOUR READING How does the variety of plants in a biome affect the variety of animals in a biome?

INVESTIGATE Climate

How can you graph climate data for your area?

PROCEDURE

1. Gather local data on the average monthly precipitation and the average monthly temperature for a 12-month period.

2. On graph paper, mark off 12 months along the *x*-axis. Make a *y*-axis for each side of the graph, marking one "Temperature (°C)" and the other "Precipitation (mm)."

3. Plot the average precipitation for each month as a bar graph.

4. Plot the average temperature for each month as a line graph.

WHAT DO YOU THINK?

- How much precipitation did the area receive overall?
- What is the temperature range for the area?

CHALLENGE Collect data for the same location, going back 10, 20, and 30 years ago. Graph the data for each of these and compare these graphs to your original graph. Has the climate in your area changed? How might severe changes in climate affect the plant and animal life in your area?

SKILL FOCUS
Graphing data

MATERIALS
- graph data
- 2 colored pencils

TIME
20 minutes

Water covers most of Earth's surface.

leopard frog

Close to three-quarters of Earth's surface is covered by water. Water, or aquatic, biomes can be divided into two broad categories: freshwater biomes and saltwater biomes. Plants have a role as producers in the water biomes that are closely surrounded by land—in ponds and streams and wetlands, and in coastal areas. The food chains of deepwater ecosystems depend on tiny photosynthetic microorganisms called phytoplankton.

Freshwater Biomes

The ecosystems of freshwater biomes are affected by the qualities of the landscape in which they are found. For example, the running water of streams and rivers results from differences in elevation. In shallow rivers, green algae and plants grow in from the banks, providing food for insects and snails that feed fish, salamanders, turtles, and frogs. Plants in a freshwater biome, like a stream or river, may take root in the soil under the water if the water is not too deep or moving too fast. Phytoplankton are not part of river ecosystems because of the moving water.

Aquatic Biomes

Freshwater biomes include the still water of lakes, the running water of rivers, and estuaries where fresh and salt waters mix.

Lakes and Ponds

Estuaries

Rivers and Streams

Ponds and lakes have still water. Ponds are shallow and support many plants as producers. The deeper lakes depend much more on phytoplankton. Ponds and lakes support many different insects, shell-fish, snakes, fish, and the land animals that feed off them.

CHECK YOUR READING Name two types of freshwater biomes.

Estuaries are water ecosystems that mark a transition between freshwater and saltwater biomes. An **estuary** is the lower end of a river that feeds into the ocean, where fresh water and salt water mix. Marshes and wetlands are two types of estuaries. Estuaries are sometimes referred to as the nurseries of the sea because so many marine animals travel into the calm waters of an estuary to reproduce. Seaweed, marsh grasses, shellfish, and birds all thrive in estuaries.

Marine Biomes

Marine biomes are saltwater biomes. The three general marine biomes are coastal ocean, open ocean, and deep ocean. Beaches are part of the coastal ocean biome. Tidal pools also form along the coast as the tide comes in and goes out and the conditions constantly change. Organisms like crabs and clams are able to survive the ever-changing conditions to thrive in coastal areas.

Organisms in the open ocean receive less sunlight than in the coastal ocean, and the temperatures are colder. Many types of fish and

RESOURCE CENTER
CLASSZONE.COM

Find out more about land and aquatic biomes.

Coastal

Marine biomes include rocky and sandy shores as well as the open ocean and the deep waters below, where little or no light can reach.

Open Ocean

Deep Ocean

other marine animals and floating seaweed live in the upper ocean. There are no plants in the open ocean. The producers at the bottom of the food chain are different types of phytoplankton.

The deep-ocean regions are much colder and darker than the upper ocean. In the deep ocean there is no sunlight available for photosynthesis. The animals in the deep ocean either feed on each other or on material that falls down from upper levels of the ocean. Many organisms in deep ocean biomes can only be seen with a microscope.

1.4 Review

KEY CONCEPTS

1. In biomes located on land, abiotic factors are used to classify the different biome types. What are these abiotic factors?

2. Name a characteristic type of plant for each of the six land biomes.

3. Name six different aquatic biomes.

CRITICAL THINKING

4. **Predict** If an ecosystem in the grassland biome started to receive less and less rainfall every year, what new biome would be established?

5. **Infer** Name some abiotic factors that affect aquatic biomes and ecosystems.

⬥ CHALLENGE

6. **Apply** Use the map on page 31 to list the following four biomes in the order you would find them moving from the equator to the poles.

- desert
- taiga
- tropical Forest
- tundra

Chapter Review

the BIG idea

Matter and energy together support life within an environment.

CONTENT REVIEW
CLASSZONE.COM

KEY CONCEPTS SUMMARY

1.1 Ecosystems support life.

Ecosystems are made up of living things (biotic) and nonliving things (abiotic).

plants animals   temperature   Sun   soil   water

Biotic Factors   **Abiotic Factors**

VOCABULARY
ecology p. 9
ecosystem p. 9
biotic factor p. 10
abiotic factor p. 10

1.2 Matter cycles through ecosystems.

Water, carbon, and nitrogen are materials that are necessary for life. They move through ecosystems in continuous cycles.

VOCABULARY
cycle p. 16
water cycle p. 17
carbon cycle p. 18
nitrogen cycle p. 19

1.3 Energy flows through ecosystems.

Producers are the basis of feeding relationships in ecosystems.

cattails   caterpillar   frog

Producer   **Primary consumer**   **Secondary consumer**

Food chains and food webs help show how energy moves through living things.

VOCABULARY
producer p. 23
consumer p. 24
decomposer p. 25
food chain p. 26
food web p. 26
energy pyramid p. 28

1.4 Biomes contain many ecosystems.

Ecosystems of land biomes
- are affected by climate
- are affected by conditions of the soil
- are characterized by types of plants

Ecosystems of water biomes
- can be freshwater or saltwater
- are affected by landscape if freshwater
- are affected by depth if marine

VOCABULARY
biome p. 30
coniferous p. 32
deciduous p. 33
estuary p. 36

Reviewing Vocabulary

Write a statement describing how the terms in each pair are similar and different.

1. biotic, abiotic

2. producer, consumer

3. food chain, food web

The table shows the meanings of word roots that are used in many science terms.

Root	Meaning
bio–	life
ecos–	house
–ogy	study of

Use the information in the table to write definitions for the following terms.

4. ecology

5. biome

6. ecosystem

Reviewing Key Concepts

Multiple Choice *Choose the letter of the best answer.*

7. Which best describes the components of an ecosystem?
  a. light, water, soil, and temperature
  b. autotrophs and heterotrophs
  c. biotic and abiotic factors
  d. producers, consumers, and decomposers

8. What is the primary source of energy for most ecosystems?
  a. water   **c.** carbon
  b. nitrogen   **d.** sunlight

9. What is the process by which the water in rivers, lakes, and oceans is converted to a gas and moves into the atmosphere?
  a. precipitation   **c.** condensation
  b. evaporation   **d.** transpiration

10. The process called nitrogen fixation is essential for life on Earth. Which of the following is an example of nitrogen fixation?
  a. Plants take in nitrogen gas from the atmosphere.
  b. Animals take in nitrogen gas from the atmosphere.
  c. Water absorbs nitrogen.
  d. Bacteria convert nitrogen gas into a form that plants can use.

11. Which organism is a decomposer?
  a. vulture   **c.** musk ox
  b. sunflower   **d.** fungi

12. How are decomposers important in an ecosystem?
  a. They make atmospheric nitrogen available to plants in a usable form.
  b. They convert organic matter into more complex compounds.
  c. They are an important source of food for scavengers.
  d. They break down organic matter into simpler compounds.

13. What factor is least important in determining the plant life in a biome?
  a. average annual rainfall
  b. average annual temperature
  c. the type of soil
  d. the type of animals living there

Short Answer *Write a short answer to each question.*

14. Write a paragraph to describe how carbon dioxide gas in the atmosphere can become part of the carbon compounds found inside animals.

15. Write a paragraph to explain how the amount of available energy changes as you move from producers to consumers in a food web.

16. Write a paragraph to describe one important way in which the flow of energy through ecosystems is different from the cycling of matter.

Thinking Critically

Use the diagram to answer the next four questions.

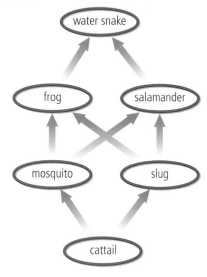

water snake

frog   salamander

mosquito   slug

cattail

17. CONNECT What does the diagram above represent and how does it relate to energy in an ecosystem?

18. CLASSIFY Identify each of the animals in the diagram above as a producer, primary consumer, or secondary consumer or tertiary consumer.

19. APPLY Another animal that is found in many wetlands ecosystems is the shrew. The shrew eats salamanders and slugs and is eaten by water snakes. Copy the diagram above and show how you would add the shrew to the diagram.

20. CONNECT Use the diagram above to make an energy pyramid. If only one-tenth of the energy available at each level is passed on to the next higher level, how much of the energy in a cattail is transferred to a salamander?

21. SYNTHESIZE Why would it be difficult to show a decomposer as part of an energy pyramid?

22. RANK Arrange the following list of biomes according to the relative amounts of precipitation in each, going from the least amount to the most: grassland, desert, deciduous forest, taiga, tropical rain forest.

23. SYNTHESIZE Why are plants but not animals considered an important factor in classifying a land biome?

24. SUMMARIZE Draw a diagram that illustrates aquatic biomes. On your diagram label the following: freshwater river, freshwater lake, estuary, coastal zone, open ocean zone. How do abiotic factors differ among these biomes?

25. COMPARE AND CONTRAST In what ways is your home like an ecosystem? In what ways is it different?

26. APPLY Describe a change in an abiotic factor that affected living factors in an ecosystem near you.

the BIG idea

27. CLASSIFY Look again at the photograph on pages 6–7. Now that you have finished the chapter, how would you change or add details to your answer to the question on the photograph?

28. SYNTHESIZE Write one or more paragraphs describing how matter and energy together support life in an ecosystem. You may use examples from one specific ecosystem if you wish. In your description, use each of the following terms. Underline each term in your answer.

ecosystem	decomposer
food web	nitrogen cycle
producer	carbon cycle
primary consumer	secondary consumer

UNIT PROJECTS

If you are doing a unit project, make a folder for your project. Include in your folder a list of the resources you will need, the date on which the project is due, and a schedule to track your progress. Begin gathering data.

Interpreting Graphs

Choose the letter of the best response.

The graphs below show average monthly temperature and precipitation for one year in Staunton, Virginia, an area located in a temperate deciduous forest biome.

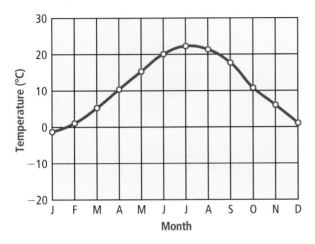

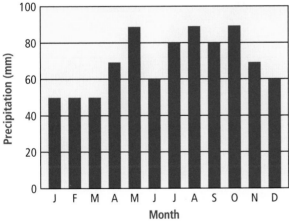

SOURCE: NASA

1. What was the average temperature during July?
  a. 20°
  b. 10°
  c. 23°
  d. 0°

2. Which months had the most precipitation?
  a. January, February, March
  b. May, August, October
  c. July, August, September
  d. December, January, February

3. What were conditions during May?
  a. warm and moist
  b. warm and dry
  c. cool and moist
  d. cool and dry

4. Which temperature is closest to the average temperature for the year shown?
  a. about 16°
  b. about 0°
  c. about 20°
  d. about 10°

5. How much precipitation would you estimate fell as snow in the year shown?
  a. less than 50 mm
  b. between 50 and 100 mm
  c. between 100 and 200 mm
  d. over 200 mm

Extended Response

6. Most of the United States is part of a temperate deciduous forest biome. The deciduous forest biome has four seasons. Trees in this biome lose their leaves yearly. Use this information, as well as the information in the graphs, to describe the seasons in the temperate deciduous forest biome.

7. Write a paragraph in which you describe a typical ecosystem in your city or town. In your answer include biotic factors such as plants, animals, and other organisms. Also include abiotic factors such as light, temperature, soil, and water. Finish your description by saying how you and other humans affect the ecosystem.

CHAPTER

Interactions Within Ecosystems

the **BIG** idea

Living things within an ecosystem interact with each other and the environment.

How do living things interact?

Key Concepts

SECTION

2.1 Groups of living things interact within ecosystems.
Learn about how different organisms share living areas, interact in larger communities, and show different patterns within those communities.

SECTION

2.2 Organisms can interact in different ways.
Learn about the different types of interactions in an ecosystem, including competition, cooperation, and symbiosis.

SECTION

2.3 Ecosystems are always changing.
Learn about the limits and boundaries of organisms within an ecosystem and how ecosystems may change over time.

Internet Preview

CLASSZONE.COM

Chapter 2 online resources: Content Review, Simulation, two Resource Centers, Math Tutorial, Test Practice

How Do Living Things Interact Where You Live?

Take your notebook outside. Observe how different living things interact. Record your observations.

Observe and Think Do the interactions you see benefit both living things or just one? Do they involve just animals or plants and animals?

How Many Roles Can a Living Thing Have in an Ecosystem?

While you are outside, choose an organism within your view and think about how it fits into the ecosystem.

Observe and Think In what way does the organism fit into feeding relationships in the ecosystem? What are some other roles the organism plays?

Internet Activity: Carrying Capacity

Go to **ClassZone.com** to simulate the carrying capacity of an area for a population of deer.

Observe and Think What factors other than available food might affect the carrying capacity for a popuation of deer?

NSTA
scilinks.org
SC*L*INKS

Populations and Communities Code: MDL002

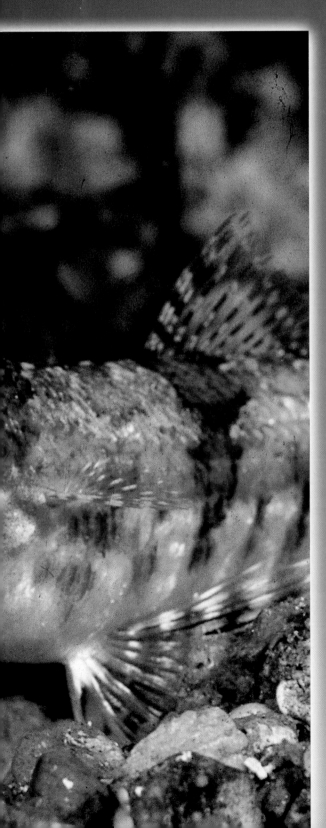

Getting Ready to Learn

◀ CONCEPT REVIEW

- Ecosystems support life.
- Different ecosystems make up a biome.

◀ VOCABULARY REVIEW

producer p. 23   **food chain** p. 26
consumer p. 24   **food web** p. 26
interaction *See Glossary.*

CONTENT REVIEW
CLASSZONE.COM
Review concepts and vocabulary.

▶ TAKING NOTES

OUTLINE

As you read, copy the headings on your paper in the form of an outline. Then add notes in your own words that summarize what you read.

VOCABULARY STRATEGY

Write each new vocabulary term in the center of a **four square** diagram. Write notes in the squares around each term. Include definition, some characteristics, and some examples of the term. If possible, write some things that are not examples of the terms.

See the Note-Taking Handbook on pages R45–R51.

SCIENCE NOTEBOOK

I. Groups of living things interact within ecosystems.

  A. Organisms occupy specific living areas.

    1. populations: same species in one area

    2. habitat and niche: place where organisms live; role of organisms

    3. community: several populations living together

Definition	Characteristics
where something lives	supplies shelter and food
HABITAT	
Examples	Nonexamples
a tree is a habitat for a bird	(you won't always use this square)

Groups of living things interact within ecosystems.

◀ **BEFORE, you learned**

- Abiotic and biotic factors interact in an ecosystem
- Matter and energy necessary for life move through the environment

▶ **NOW, you will learn**

- How groups of organisms interact in an ecosystem
- About levels of organization in an ecosystem
- About living patterns of different groups of organisms

VOCABULARY

species p. 45
population p. 46
habitat p. 46
niche p. 47
community p. 48

EXPLORE Counting Animals

How can you use a grid to estimate the number of animals in an area?

PROCEDURE

① Mark off an area on the graph paper as shown. Count the number of large squares in that area.

② Use a handful of rice to represent a group of animals. Spread the rice evenly within the area you marked. Count the number of "animals" inside one large square.

③ Use a calculator to multiply the counts from steps 1 and 2. This will give you an estimate of the total number of "animals." Check your answer by counting all the grains of rice.

WHAT DO YOU THINK?

- How close was your estimate to the actual number?
- What would prevent a scientist from making an actual count of animals in an area?

MATERIALS

- handful of rice
- large-grid graph paper
- marker
- calculator

Organisms occupy specific living areas.

On a walk through the woods, you may see many different plants and animals. These organisms, like all living things, depend on their environment to meet their needs. The particular types of living things you see will depend on the characteristics of the area you are visiting.

Scientists group living things according to their shared characteristics. The smallest grouping is the species. Scientists consider organisms to be members of the same **species** (SPEE-sheez) if the organisms are so similar that they can produce offspring that can also produce offspring. Members of a species can successfully reproduce.

READING TIP

The terms *species, specific,* and *special* come from the same Latin root meaning "kind." A species is a kind, or type, of organism.

Galápagos Island Populations

A population is a group of the same organisms that live in the same area.

Cacti

Crabs

Iguanas

Populations

VOCABULARY
Add a four square for *population* to your notebook. Include the word *habitat* in your diagram.

Scientists use the term **population** to mean a group of organisms of the same species that live in a particular area. In a way, this is similar to the population of people who live in a particular city or town. You can then think of those people who live in different cities or towns as belonging to different populations. It is the boundary of an area that defines a population. In the study of ecology, members of the same species that live in different areas belong to different populations.

A biological population can be a group of animals or a group of plants. It can be a group of bacteria or fungi or any other living thing. Populations of many different species will be found living in the same area. For example, the photographs above show different populations of organisms that all live in the same place—on one of the Galápagos Islands. The island has a population of cacti, a population of crabs, and a population of iguanas.

CHECK YOUR READING What is the difference between a species and a population?

Habitats and Niches

The Galápagos Islands are a small group of volcanic islands, off the coast of South America, that are famous for their unusual plant and animal life. These islands are the **habitat**—the physical location—where these plants and animals live. Island habitats have certain physical characteristics that describe them, including the amount of precipitation, a range of temperatures, and the quality of the soil. Different habitats have different characteristics.

Galápagos Island Habitat

This island habitat is home to many different populations.

Galápagos Islands

cacti

crabs

iguanas

READING VISUALS What resources are available in this habitat?

A habitat is filled with different species, each of which depends on the habitat's resources to meet its needs. The characteristics of a habitat determine the species of plants that can grow there. The species of plants found in a habitat, in turn, determine the species of animals and other organisms that will do well there.

Different populations within a habitat interact. They are part of the flow of energy and matter through an ecosystem. For example, in the Galápagos Island scene above, the cacti capture the Sun's energy and store fresh water. They also provide food for the iguana, who eats the cactus leaves. The cactus is a producer and the iguana is a primary consumer. The crabs of the Galápagos are secondary consumers that feed on other shellfish. Each of these organisms has a role to play in the habitat, a role which is referred to as its **niche** (nihch).

The niche an organism fills in a habitat is not limited to its place in a food web. Plants provide nesting sites as well as food. The droppings left behind by animals fertilize soil and often spread seed. Generally, no two species will fill exactly the same niche in a habitat.

Communities

Take a mental tour of your school. Note that you share space with people who do many different things—students, teachers, custodians, librarians, counselors, and many others. They all work together and help each other. We often say that a school is a community.

Scientists use the term *community* in a slightly different way. A biological **community** is a group of populations that live in a particular area and interact with one another. Cacti, iguanas, and crabs are part of the Galápagos Island community. This community also includes populations of tortoises, finches, fleas, bacteria, and many other species.

 How is a school community similar to a community of living things?

The environment can be organized into five levels.

OUTLINE
Add the different levels of the environment to your outline. Make sure to explain each term in the supporting details.

The five terms—biome, ecosystem, community, population, and organism—describe the environment at different levels.

1. **Biome** A biome describes in very general terms the climate and types of plants that are found in similar places around the world.

2. **Ecosystem** Within each biome are many ecosystems. Inside an ecosystem, living and nonliving factors interact to form a stable system. An ecosystem is smaller than a biome and includes only organisms and their local environment.

3. **Community** A community is made up of the living components of the ecosystem. In a community, different plants, animals, and other organisms interact with each other.

4. **Population** A population is a group of organisms of the same species that live in the same area.

5. **Organism** An organism is a single individual animal, plant, fungus, or other living thing. As the picture on page 49 shows, an organism plays a part in each level of the environment.

Patterns exist in populations.

Members of a population settle themselves into the available living space in different ways, forming a pattern. Populations may be crowded together, be spread far apart, or live in small groups. A population may also show a pattern over time. The number of individuals in the population may rise and fall, depending on the season or other conditions, or as a result of interactions with other organisms.

Levels in the Environment

Organisms living in an African savannah illustrate the different levels of the environment.

Grassland

① Biome
The African savannah is part of a grassland biome.

② Ecosystem
The community of organisms, along with water, soil, and other abiotic factors, make up an ecosystem.

③ Community
Populations of wildebeests, gazelles, lions, and grasses share the same living areas and resources. These and other populations form a savannah community.

④ Population
Gazelles travel together in herds looking for areas to graze in. The total number of gazelles in an ecosystem is called a population of gazelles.

⑤ Organism
The gazelle lives in various grassland habitats in eastern Africa and fills a particular niche.

READING VISUALS Describe the gazelle's place in each level of the environment.

Patterns in Living Space

The patterns formed by a population often show how the population meets its needs. For example, in California's Mojave desert the pale soil is dotted with dark-green shrubs called creosote bushes. A surprising thing about the bushes is their even spacing. No human shaped this habitat, however. The bushes are the same distance from each other because the roots of each bush release a toxin, a type of poison, that prevents the roots of other bushes from growing.

The distribution of animals in a habitat is often influenced by how they meet their needs. Animals must be able to reach their food supply and have places to raise their young. If you put up bird houses for bluebirds on your property, they must be spaced at least a hundred meters apart. Bluebirds need a large area of their own around their nest in order to collect enough insects to feed their young.

READING TiP

As you read this paragraph, note the pattern of wildebeests and elephants in the photograph.

Sometimes, the particular pattern of individuals in a living space helps a population survive. Herring swim in schools, with the individual fish spaced close together. Wildebeests roam African grasslands in closely packed herds. These animals rely on the group for their safety. Even if one member of the group is attacked, many more will survive.

CHECK YOUR READING What are some reasons for the spacing patterns observed in different populations?

elephant

wildebeest

READING VISUALS COMPARE AND CONTRAST How would you describe the spacing of these elephants and wildebeests?

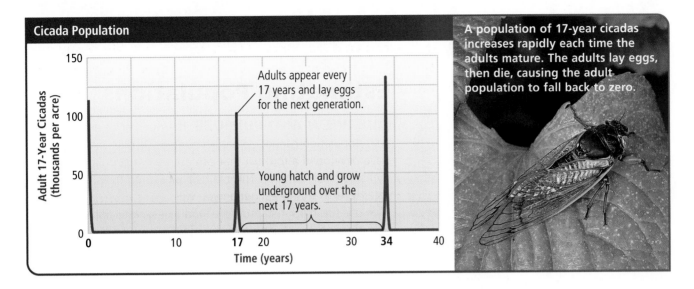

Cicada Population

Adult 17-Year Cicadas (thousands per acre)

Adults appear every 17 years and lay eggs for the next generation.

Young hatch and grow underground over the next 17 years.

Time (years)

A population of 17-year cicadas increases rapidly each time the adults mature. The adults lay eggs, then die, causing the adult population to fall back to zero.

Patterns in Time

At a spring picnic, you would rarely see the wasps called yellow jackets. At a fall picnic, however, they swarm to the food. This is an example of a population whose size changes with time. In spring, the queen wasp lays eggs and new wasps hatch. She continues to lay eggs all summer and the population grows. When winter comes, all the wasps except the queen die, and the population decreases.

Many birds that nest in North America in summer fly south to Central and South America in winter. There they find enough food and good nesting sites. In North America, this seasonal pattern leads to small bird populations in winter and large ones in summer.

The graph above shows an unusual pattern of population growth. Certain species of cicadas appear only every 17 years. Because no other species can rely on these insects as their main source of food, the cicadas survive long enough to lay eggs when they do appear.

2.1 Review

KEY CONCEPTS

1. What are two characteristics of a population?

2. Order these terms from the simplest to the most complex: biome, community, ecosystem, organism, population.

3. How do the terms *habitat* and *niche* relate to each other?

CRITICAL THINKING

4. **Apply** Choose a biological community in your region. Describe some of the populations that make up that community.

5. **Infer** How might the seasonal patterns of insect populations relate to the seasonal patterns of bird populations?

CHALLENGE

6. **Apply** The Explore activity on page 45 shows one way in which scientists sample a population to determine its total size. Would this method work for estimating the size of a population of 17-year cicadas? Why or why not?

CHAPTER INVESTIGATION

Estimating Populations

OVERVIEW AND PURPOSE The number of animals in a wild population cannot be easily counted. Wildlife biologists have developed a formula that can estimate a population's size by using small samples. This method is referred to as mark and recapture. In this investigation you will
- use the mark-recapture method to estimate population size
- test the effectiveness of the mark-recapture method by simulating an outbreak of disease in a population

▶ Problem

 Write It Up

How effective is the mark-recapture method in estimating population size?

▶ Hypothesize

 Write It Up

Write a hypothesis to explain how you will use a sudden change in population size to determine the effectiveness of the mark-recapture method. Your hypothesis should take the form of an "If . . . , then . . . , because . . ." statement.

▶ Procedure

1. Make two data tables in your **Science Notebook,** like the ones shown on page 53.

2. From your teacher, obtain a paper bag containing a "population" of white kidney beans.

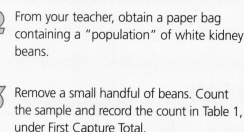

step 3

3. Remove a small handful of beans. Count the sample and record the count in Table 1, under First Capture Total.

4. Use a colored marker to mark your sample population. Return the beans to the bag, and gently shake the bag to mix all the beans.

5. Remove and count a second sample of beans. Record the count in Table 1, under Recapture Total.

6. Count the number of beans from this sample that were marked from the first capture. Record this number in Table 1, under Recapture Marked. Return all the beans to the bag.

MATERIALS
- paper bag
- white kidney beans
- 2 colored markers
- calculator

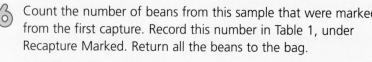

7 Use a calculator and the following formula to estimate the population size. Record the estimate in Table 1 as the Calculated Population Estimate.

$$\frac{\text{First Capture Total} \times \text{Recapture Total}}{\text{Recapture Marked}} = \frac{\text{Population}}{\text{Estimate}}$$

8 Disease strikes. Remove a small handful of beans from the bag. Count the beans, and record this count in Table 2, under Killed by Disease. Set these beans aside.

9 Repeat steps 3–7 to mark and recapture your survivor population. This time use a different colored marker to mark your sample population, and only include the beans marked in the second color in your counts.

10 Fill in Data Table 2 for the survivor population. Use the formula from step 7 to calculate your estimate of the survivor population.

11 Once you have calculated your estimate of survivors, dump out the paper bag and count all the beans that were inside. Record this count in Table 2, under Actual Survivors Total.

Observe and Analyze
Write It Up

1. CALCULATE From Table 2 add together the number of actual survivors and the number killed by disease. Put this in Table 1, under Actual Population Total.

2. CALCULATE Find the percentage of the population affected by disease using the following formula:

$$\frac{\text{Killed by disease} \times 100}{\text{Actual Population Total}} = \text{Percentage affected}$$

Conclude
Write It Up

1. INFER How did the estimated number of beans compare with the actual number?

2. IDENTIFY LIMITS What aspects of this investigation most likely would not be possible in a natural habitat? Why not?

3. EVALUATE Compare your results with your hypothesis. Do your data support your hypothesis?

INVESTIGATE Further

CHALLENGE Determine if using larger samples of a population gives better population estimates. Get another bag of unmarked beans from your teacher. Use a spreadsheet program, if available, to record your data and calculate the results.

Estimating Populations
Table 1. Population sampling before disease

First Capture Total	Recapture Total	Recapture Marked	Calculated Population Estimate	Actual Population Total

Table 2. Population sampling after disease

Survivors First Capture Total	Survivors Recapture Total	Survivors Recapture Marked	Calculated Survivors Estimate	Killed by Disease	Actual Survivors Total

2.2 Organisms can interact in different ways.

◀ **BEFORE,** you learned

- Different populations live together in a habitat
- Different species fill different niches in a habitat
- There are patterns in the ways organisms interact with each other and their environment

▶ **NOW,** you will learn

- About different types of interactions in an ecosystem
- How some species benefit from interactions
- How some species are harmed by interactions

VOCABULARY

predator p. 55
prey p. 55
competition p. 55
cooperation p. 57
symbiosis p. 58
mutualism p. 58
commensalism p. 59
parasitism p. 59

THINK ABOUT

What are some of the ways people interact?

People in a community interact with each other in many ways. An interaction is the way a person behaves toward or responds to another person. This photo-

graph shows groups of people at a soccer game. There are players from two teams and fans who are watching the game. How would you describe the interactions between the people in this photograph?

Organisms interact in different ways.

The photograph above shows how members of a human community both compete and cooperate. Different members of the populations of a biological community also compete and cooperate. They not only share a habitat, but they also share the resources in that habitat. How different organisms interact depends on their relationship to each other.

A robin in a meadow picks at the soil, pulls out an earthworm, and swallows it. This is one obvious way organisms in an ecosystem interact—one eats, and the other gets eaten. Organisms also compete. The robin may have to compete with a chickadee to get the earthworm. And organisms can cooperate. Ants work together to build a nest, collect food, and defend their colony.

 CHECK YOUR READING Name three ways organisms may interact with each other in an ecosystem.

Predator and Prey

Many interactions between organisms in an ecosystem involve food. A food chain shows the feeding relationships between different species. There are producers and consumers. Another way to look at a food chain is through the interactions of predators and prey. The **predator** is an animal that eats another. The **prey** is an animal that is eaten by a predator. In a food chain, an organism can be both predator and prey. A meadowlark that feeds on a grasshopper is, in turn, eaten by a prairie falcon.

Predators can affect how members of their prey populations are distributed. Herring move together in a school and wildebeests travel in herds to protect themselves. It is the sick or older members of the population that will most likely be eaten by predators. Species of prey may also have adaptations that relate to the behavior of predators. This is true of cicadas and their long reproductive cycles.

Prey populations, in turn, affect the location and number of predator populations. For example some birds are predators feeding on insects. One factor that may affect movement of birds from one location to another is the availability of insects.

> **REMINDER**
>
> A *producer* is an organism that makes its own food; a *consumer* is an organism that eats another organism for food.

Competition

In a team game, two teams compete against each other with the same goal in mind—to win the game. In a biological community, competition is for resources, not wins. **Competition** is the struggle between individuals or different populations for a limited resource.

In an ecosystem, competition may occur within the same species. Individual plants compete with each other for light, space, and nutrients. For example, creosote bushes compete with other creosote bushes for the same water supply. The toxins produced by the roots of one creosote bush prevent other creosote bushes from growing.

Competition also occurs between members of different species. In the tropical rain forests of Indonesia, vines called strangler figs compete with trees for water, light, and nutrients. The vine attaches itself to a host tree. As it grows, the vine surrounds and eventually kills the tree by blocking out sunlight and using up available water and nutrients.

INFER Do you think a strangler fig could survive on its own?

host tree

strangler fig

Competition

Competition between species
Two different species, hyenas and vultures, compete for the remains of a dead animal.

Competition within species Two male deer lock horns as they battle over territory.

Competition occurs between species and within species. For example, vultures and hyenas will compete over the food left in the remains of a dead animal. Wolves will compete with one another over territory. A wolf will mark its territory by urinating on trees and so warn off other wolves. Animals also compete over territory by fighting, using threatening sounds, and putting on aggressive displays.

Competition within species often occurs during the mating season. Male birds use mating songs and displays of feathers to compete for the attention of females. Male hippopotamuses fight to attract female hippopotamuses. Male crickets chirp to attract female crickets.

CHECK YOUR READING What sorts of resources do plants and animals compete for?

READING TiP

Compare and contrast the meanings of *competition* and *coexistence*.

Competition does not occur between all populations that share the same resources. Many populations can coexist in a habitat—different species can live together without causing harm to one another. Many different populations of plants coexist in a forest. Maple trees, beech trees, and birch trees can live side by side and still have enough water, nutrients, and sunlight to meet their needs.

INVESTIGATE Species Interactions

How do predator-prey populations interact?

Use these rules for predator-prey interaction for each round. If a predator card touches three or more prey cards, remove the prey cards touched. If the predator card does not touch at least three prey cards, remove the predator card and leave the prey cards. Predator cards are large, prey cards are small.

PROCEDURE

① Use masking tape to mark a boundary on a table top.

② Scatter five prey cards into the area. Take a predator card and toss it, trying to get it to land on the prey.

③ According to the rules above, remove the predators and prey that have "died." Record the number of predators and prey that have

"survived." This represents one generation.

④ Double the populations of predators and prey—they have "reproduced."

⑤ Scatter the prey cards into the area and then toss the predator cards as before. Repeat steps 3 and 4 for a total of 15 rounds (generations).

WHAT DO YOU THINK?

- How does the size of the prey population affect the predator population?
- How might the size of a habitat affect the interaction of predators and prey?

CHALLENGE Use graph paper and colored pencils to make a graph of your results. Or use a spreadsheet program if one is available to you.

SKILL FOCUS
Analyzing data

MATERIALS
- 20 10 × 10 cm cardboard squares— predators
- 200 3 × 3 cm paper squares— prey
- masking tape
  for Challenge:
- graph paper
- 2 colored pencils

TIME
30 minutes

predator

prey

Cooperation

Not all interactions in an ecosystem involve competition. **Cooperation** is an interaction in which organisms work in a way that benefits them all. Some predators cooperate when they hunt. Although individual lions may hunt on their own, they also hunt in packs to kill large prey.

Killer whales also cooperate when they hunt. The whales swim in packs called pods. The pod swims in circles around a school of fish, forcing the fish close together so they are easier to catch. Pod members may also take turns chasing a seal until it gets tired and is easily killed. The pod may even work together to attack larger species of whales.

Ants, bees, and termites are social insects. Members of a colony belong to different groups, called castes, and have different responsibilities. Some groups gather food while others defend the colony. Other animals, like apes and monkeys, live in family groups. Members of the family cooperate to care for their young.

Cooperation
Driver ants work together to bring food to their nest.

The survival of one species might depend on another species.

OUTLINE
Add a sentence about *symbiosis* to your outline and define the three types of symbiosis in the supporting details.

You have learned that many different organisms live together in a habitat. The fact that organisms live together forces them to interact in different ways. For example, an organism preys upon another for food. Or perhaps there is competition among organisms over resources such as food, water, and territory.

The actions of different organisms can be so closely related that the survival of one species depends on the action or presence of another. In such a relationship, at least one of the species is getting a resource that it needs to survive. Benefits of the relationship may include food, reproductive help, or protection.

The relationship between individuals of two different species who live together in a close relationship is called **symbiosis** (SIHM-bee-OH-sihs). This word means "living together." A symbiotic relationship may affect the partners in different ways.

- Both species benefit from the relationship.
- One species benefits while the other is not affected.
- One species benefits while the other is harmed.

Here are some examples for each of the three types of symbiosis.

Both Species Benefit

Stroll through a garden on a sunny day and notice the bees buzzing from flower to flower. Look closely at a single bee and you may see yellow pollen grains sticking to its hairy body. The relationship between the flower and the bee is an example of **mutualism** (MYOO-choo-uh-LIHZ-uhm)—an interaction between two species that benefits both. The bees get food in the form of nectar, and the flowers get pollen from other flowers, which they need to make seeds.

Many plants rely on mutualism to reproduce. The pollen needed to make seeds must be spread from flower to flower. The birds and insects that feed on the nectar in these flowers transfer pollen from one flower to the next. The seeds produced are then moved to new ground by animals that eat the seeds or the fruits that hold the seeds. This form of mutualism doesn't benefit the individual flower but instead ensures the survival of the species.

Mutualism The interaction between the hummingbird and the flower benefits both.

In some cases, mutualism is necessary for the survival of the organisms themselves. For example, termites are able to live off a food that most animals cannot digest: wood. The termites, in fact, can't digest wood either. However, they have living in their guts tiny single-celled organisms, protozoans, that can break the wood down into digestible components. The protozoans get a safe place to live, and the termites can take advantage of a plentiful food source.

Explore symbiotic relationships.

 CHECK YOUR READING Describe how a bee and a flower benefit from a symbiotic relationship.

One Species Benefits

Commensalism (kuh-MEHN-suh-LIHZ-uhm) is a relationship between two species in which one species benefits while the other is not affected. Orchids and mosses are plants that can have a commensal relationship with trees. The plants grow on the trunks or branches of trees. They get the light they need as well as nutrients that run down along the tree. As long as these plants do not grow too heavy, the tree is not affected.

Commensal relationships are very common in ocean ecosystems. Small fish called remoras use a type of built-in suction cup to stick to a shark's skin and hitch a ride. When the shark makes a kill, the remora eats the scraps. The shark makes no attempt to attack the remora. The remora benefits greatly from this commensal relationship; the shark is barely affected.

Not all commensal relationships involve food. Some fish protect themselves by swimming among the stinging tentacles of a moon jellyfish. The fish benefit from the relationship because the tentacles keep them safe from predators. The jellyfish is not helped or hurt by the presence of the fish. As in this example, it is common in commensal relationships for the species that benefits to be smaller than the species it partners with.

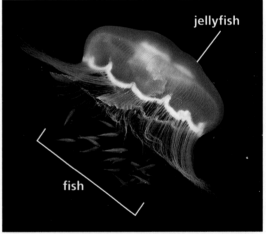

Commensalism The interaction between the jellyfish and the fish benefits the fish only.

One Species Is Harmed

There is one symbiotic relationship in which a small partner can harm a much larger host. **Parasitism** (PAR-uh-suh-TIHZ-uhm) is a relationship between two species in which one species benefits while the species it depends on, its host, is harmed. Parasites are often tiny organisms that feed off, and weaken, their hosts. Ticks, lice, and mites are external parasites that live on or attach to their host's skin. Other parasites, like tapeworms and ringworms, are internal parasites that live inside their hosts.

Symbiotic Relationships

Mutualism
Both species benefit from the relationship.

Commensalism
One species benefits while the other is not affected.

Parasitism
One species benefits while the other is harmed.

Parasitism
Mistletoe is a plant that takes nourishment from a tree, causing damage to the tree.

Mutualism
Aphids are insects that provide ants with a sweet liquid. Ants live alongside the aphids, protecting them from predators.

Commensalism
Lichens benefit from living on a tree, but the tree is not harmed.

Parasitism
Ticks are animals that attach to their hosts, feeding on the host's blood.

Mutualism
Nitrogen-fixing bacteria get their nourishment from the roots of certain plants, providing the plants with nitrogen in return.

Commensalism
Mice do well living near humans, living off the food scraps humans leave behind.

The relationship between cowbirds and warblers is an unusual type of association called nest or brood parasitism. Female cowbirds never build their own nests or rear their own young. Instead, they lay their eggs in warbler nests. Although nest parasitism does not harm the host warbler, it does harm the warbler species because either warblers eggs do not hatch, or the chicks do not survive. The warbler species is often harmed because cowbirds push most warbler eggs from the nest in order to make room for their own eggs. Once the cowbird chicks hatch, their larger size helps them to outcompete the smaller warbler chicks for food, so that the host's chicks starve.

host warbler

warbler chick   cowbird chick

Parasitism The larger cowbird chick is cared for by a warbler at the expense of the smaller warbler chick.

CHECK YOUR READING How is parasitism different from commensalism?

Interactions in an ecosystem are complex.

Different types of symbiosis occur throughout an ecosystem and often overlap. They may occur in the same locations, and the same species might be involved in more than one symbiotic relationship. The illustration on page 60 shows different symbiotic relationships that may occur in a backyard.

Symbiosis is just one of many interactions that take place in an ecosystem. The yard may have a garden, with individual tomato plants competing for water and nutrients; it may have ants cooperating to maintain a successful colony. An ecosystem is more than just a collection of biotic and abiotic factors. Interactions within an ecosystem help explain how resources are shared and used up and how energy flows through the system.

2.2 Review

KEY CONCEPTS

1. Name two ways in which members of the same species interact.

2. In what ways do members of different species interact?

3. Give an example of each type of symbiotic relationship: mutualism, commensalism, and parasitism.

CRITICAL THINKING

4. **Apply** Think of a biological community near you, and give an example of how one population has affected another.

5. **Compare and Contrast** Explain how symbiotic relationships are similar to and different from predator-prey interactions.

⚫ CHALLENGE

6. **Synthesize** Mutualism is more common in tropical ecosystems such as rain forests and coral reefs than in other ecosystems. Why do you think this is so?

SKILL: INFERRING

Where Are the Salamanders?

At the Cottonwood Lake Study Area in rural Stutsman County, North Dakota, U.S. Fish and Wildlife Service biologists have been studying wetland ecosystems for more than 30 years. Salamanders are one of the most abundant species in these wetlands. But in May 2000, the researchers started noticing sick salamanders in one wetland. By July, most salamanders had died. What killed them?

▶ Observations

a. In the past, cold winter weather and food shortages have killed salamanders at Cottonwood Lake.

b. The sick salamanders had discolored skin and enlarged livers.

c. The previous year, leopard frogs in a nearby wetland were found dying from a contagious fungal infection.

d. A viral disease has killed tiger salamanders elsewhere in the West.

e. Both large, well-fed salamanders and small, poorly nourished salamanders died.

▶ Inferences

The following statements are possible inferences:

a. A food shortage caused salamanders to starve.

b. The fungal disease that killed leopard frogs also killed the salamanders

c. Salamanders were killed by a viral disease.

▶ Evaluate Inferences

On Your Own Which of the inferences are supported by the observations? Write the observations that support each of the inferences you identify.

As a Group Discuss your decisions. Come up with a list of reasonable inferences.

CHALLENGE What further observations would you make to test any of these inferences?

This barred tiger salamander can be found in many wetlands in the Great Plains.

Ecosystems are always changing.

◀ **BEFORE, you learned**

- Populations in an ecosystem interact in different ways
- Organisms can benefit from interactions in an ecosystem
- Organisms can be harmed by interactions in an ecosystem

▶ **NOW, you will learn**

- How different factors affect the size of a population
- How biological communities get established
- How biological communities change over time

VOCABULARY

limiting factor p. 64
carrying capacity p. 65
succession p. 66
pioneer species p. 66

EXPLORE Population Growth

How does sugar affect the growth of yeast?

PROCEDURE

① Use a marker to label the cups A, B, C. Pour 150 mL of warm water into each cup. Mark the water level with the marker.

② Add 1/2 teaspoon of dry yeast to each plastic cup and stir.

③ Add 1/4 teaspoon of sugar to cup B. Add 1 teaspoon of sugar to cup C. Stir.

④ Wait 15 minutes. Measure the height of the foam layer that forms in each cup.

WHAT DO YOU THINK?

- Which cup had the most foam, which cup had the least?
- Describe the effect of sugar on a population of yeast.

MATERIALS

- 3 clear plastic cups
- warm water
- sugar
- dry yeast
- measuring spoons
- measuring cup
- stirring rod
- marker
- ruler

Populations change over time.

REMINDER

A *population* is a group of organisms of the same species that live together in the same habitat.

You may have a strong memory of a park you visited as a little child. You remember collecting pine cones, listening to woodpeckers, and catching frogs. Then you visit again, years later, and the park has changed. Maybe more land has been added, there are more birds and trees. Or maybe the area around the park has been developed. There seem to be fewer woodpeckers, and you can't find any frogs. The community has changed. There are a lot of factors that affect the populations within a biological community. Some have to do with the organisms themselves. Others relate to the habitat.

Population Growth and Decline

One factor that obviously affects population size is how often organisms reproduce. Birth rate is a measure of the number of births in an animal population. It can also be a measure of the stability of an ecosystem. For example, black bears reproduce once every two years. If there is not enough food available, however, the female bear's reproductive cycle is delayed, and the bear population does not grow.

Predator-prey interactions also affect population size. The graphs show how an increase in the moose population—the prey—in Isle Royale National Park was followed by an increase in the island's population of wolves—the predators. The wolves preyed upon the moose, the moose population decreased, then the wolf population decreased.

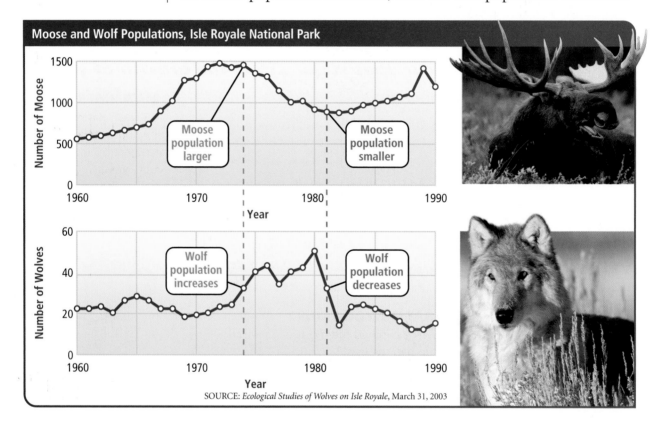

Moose and Wolf Populations, Isle Royale National Park

Moose population larger

Moose population smaller

Wolf population increases

Wolf population decreases

SOURCE: *Ecological Studies of Wolves on Isle Royale*, March 31, 2003

READING TiP

Note in the graphs above that it can take some time for the size of one population to affect the size of the other.

Any factor or condition that limits the growth of a population in an ecosystem is called a **limiting factor.** A large population of predators will limit the population of prey; a small population of prey will limit the population of predators. Too much or too little of any biotic or abiotic factor—like food, water, or light—makes an ecosystem unstable and brings about change.

A lack of nutrients in the soil is a limiting factor for plants. That is why farmers fertilize their crops. That same fertilizer, if it runs off into a lake, can increase the population of algae, another photosynthetic organism. A large population of algae can cover a lake with scum and use up oxygen needed by fish. This then limits the fish population.

INVESTIGATE Limiting Factors

What effect does spacing have upon a population of plants?

DESIGN —YOUR OWN— EXPERIMENT

Using the materials listed, design an experiment to test this hypothesis: "If plants grow too close together, the health of the population will be affected because the individual plants do not get enough of the nutrients and water that they need."

PROCEDURE

1. Decide how to use the seeds, cups, and soil to test the hypothesis.
2. Write up your experimental procedure. Include safety tips.

WHAT DO YOU THINK?

- What are the variables in your experiment?
- What evidence would you expect to see if your hypothesis is true?

CHALLENGE Conduct your experiment. Note that seeds must be planted near the top of the soil. A good measure for this is the tip of a pencil. Measure and record the growth of the seedlings. Allow the seedlings to grow for two weeks before drawing your conclusions.

SKILL FOCUS
Designing experiments

MATERIALS
- paper cups
- potting soil
- radish seeds
- water
- pencil
- ruler

TIME
20 minutes

Maintaining a Balance

Living things have certain minimum requirements for food, water, and living space. When a population reaches a state where it can no longer grow, the population has reached its **carrying capacity,** the maximum number of individuals that an ecosystem can support. You can see on page 64 that the graph for the moose population does appear to peak around 1500. Even if there were no wolves on the island of Isle Royale, the population of moose would still be limited because there is only so much food and space available.

 Explain the term *carrying capacity*.

> **VOCABULARY**
> Remember to make a four square diagram for *carrying capacity* in your notebook. Try to use *limiting factor* in your diagram.

An ecosystem's carrying capacity is different for each population. A meadow ecosystem will support many more bees and ants than bluebirds, for example. Isle Royale supports many more moose than wolves. The moose is a primary consumer of plants. It is at a lower level of the energy pyramid than the wolf, a secondary consumer.

Biotic factors can be limiting factors. These factors include the interactions between populations, such as competition, predation, and parasitism. Abiotic factors, such as temperature, availability of water or minerals, and exposure to wind, are also limiting.

Ecosystems change over time.

Take a walk in a New Hampshire woods and you may see the remains of old stone walls scattered about. A hundred years ago this land was mostly farmland. The farms were abandoned. And now, new trees have grown where farm animals once grazed.

Succession (suhk-SEHSH-uhn) is the gradual change in an ecosystem in which one biological community is replaced by another. The change from field to forest is an example of succession. Over time the grasses of open farmland are slowly replaced by small plants and shrubs, then trees.

Primary Succession

READING TiP

Succeed and *succession* come from the same Latin root word, *succedere*, meaning to go up or to follow after.

Very few places on Earth are without some form of life. Even when a lava flow covers an area or a glacier retreats and leaves behind an empty and barren environment, plants will move into the area and bring it back to life. These are examples of primary succession, the establishment of a new biological community.

Pioneer species are the first living things to move into a barren environment. In the illustration below, moss and lichen move in after a glacier retreats. There is little or no topsoil. Moss and lichen are common pioneers because they have tiny rootlike structures that can take hold on exposed rock.

Primary Succession

Primary succession can occur after a glacier retreats, when little topsoil is present.

1. Moss and lichen grow on rock with little or no soil. These pioneer species break apart the surface rock.

2. Over time, the rock breaks down further, forming soil. Larger plants take root. These support populations of animals.

3. Coniferous trees take root in a deep layer of soil. A diversity of plants and animals are supported in this habitat.

As the pioneers grow, they gradually weaken the rock surface. The rock breaks down and weathers over time. Decaying plant matter adds nutrients, forming soil. Now a variety of small plants and shrubs can take root. These plants, in turn, support insects, birds, and small rodents. Eventually there is enough soil to support coniferous trees. Forests grow, providing a stable habitat for larger animals.

 RESOURCE CENTER
CLASSZONE.COM

Learn more about succession.

Secondary Succession

Secondary succession takes place after a major disturbance to the biological community in a stable ecosystem. Despite the disturbance, the soil remains. A community can be disturbed by a natural event, like fire or flood, or it can be disturbed by human activity. A forest cleared or farmland abandoned can lead to secondary succession.

The illustration below shows secondary succession following a forest fire. The damage, as bad as it is, is surface damage. Below the surface, seeds and plant roots survive. After a time, grasses and small shrubs grow up among the decaying remains of the original plants. Birds, insects, and rodents return. Alder trees take root—alders are trees that put nutrients into the soil. Over time, a variety of trees and plants grow, providing food for a variety of animals.

 CHECK YOUR READING What is the difference between primary and secondary succession?

Secondary Succession

Secondary succession occurs if soil remains after a disturbance, such as a forest fire.

1 Plants at the surface are burned; however, below the surface seeds and some plant roots survive.

2 Grasses and small shrubs sprout among the charred trees and vegetation. Smaller animals return.

3 Deciduous trees like elm and maple grow and mature. A forest habitat is reestablished. More animals are supported.

Patterns of Change

All types of ecosystems go through succession. Succession can establish a forest community, a wetland community, a coastal community, or even an ocean community. Succession can happen over tens or hundreds of years. The pattern is the same, however. First a community of producers is established. These are followed by decomposers and consumers, then more producers, then more decomposers and consumers. Over time, a stable biological community develops.

In a way, the establishment of a biological community is like planting a garden. You first prepare the soil. Perhaps you add compost. This adds organic matter and nutrients to the soil, which helps the soil hold water. With the right preparation, your vegetables and flowers should grow well.

Pioneer species can function in one of two ways in an ecological succession. They can help other species to grow or they can prevent species from getting established.

READING TiP

As you read about the two ways plant species function in succession, think in terms of cooperation and competition.

- Some plant species function a bit like gardeners. Trees such as alders have nitrogen-fixing bacteria on their roots that improve the nutrient content of the soil and allow other tree seedlings to grow. Pioneering species may also stabilize the soil, shade the soil surface, or add nutrients to the soil when they die and decay.

- Other plant species produce conditions that keep out other plants. The plants may release chemicals that keep other plants from taking root. Or a new species may outcompete other species by using up resources or better resisting a disease.

Such interactions between living things help to determine succession in an ecosystem.

2.3 Review

KEY CONCEPTS

1. Describe three factors that could limit the size of a population in a habitat.

2. List two natural disturbances and two human-made disturbances that can lead to succession.

3. What role do pioneer species play in succession?

CRITICAL THINKING

4. **Infer** How and why would secondary succession in a tundra habitat differ from secondary succession in a rain-forest habitat?

5. **Predict** Suppose you are clearing an area in your yard to construct a small pond. Sketch the stages of succession that would follow this disturbance.

⚠ CHALLENGE

6. **Synthesize** Imagine you are the wildlife manager for a forest preserve that supports both moose and wolves. What types of information should you collect to determine the carrying capacity for each species?

MATH TUTORIAL
CLASSZONE.COM

Click on Math Tutorial for more help with multiplying fractions and whole numbers.

Birth Rates and Populations

Ecologists pay careful attention to the yearly birth rates of endangered species. A birth rate is usually expressed as a fraction. It is the number of births divided by the number of adult females. A 2/5 birth rate for a population means that there are 2 births for every 5 adult females.

Example

Suppose at a national park in Borneo, there is a 2/5 birth rate among orangutans. There are 150 adult females in the park. Estimate how many young will be born. To find out, multiply the fraction by the number of adult females.

(1) Multiply the numerator of the fraction by the whole number.

$$150 \text{ females} \times \frac{2 \text{ births}}{5 \text{ females}} = \frac{150 \times 2}{5} = \frac{300}{5}$$

(2) Divide by the denominator.

$$\frac{300}{5} = 300 \div 5 = 60$$

ANSWER 60 young

Answer the following questions.

1. In 2001, there were about 72 adult female right whales. Scientists observing the whales reported a 1/3 birth rate. About how many right whales were born in 2001?

2. Giant pandas are severely endangered. Currently about 140 giant pandas live in captivity, in zoos and parks. About 3/5 of these were born in captivity. How many is that?

3. The orangutan population of the world has decreased sharply. At one time there were over 100,000 ranging across Asia. Now there may be 21,000, of which, 2/3 live in Borneo. About how many orangutans live in Borneo?

CHALLENGE Suppose 1/1 is given as the desired birth rate to save an endangered population. If the population is currently at 4 births per 20 adult females, by how many times does the rate need to increase to reach the desired rate?

Chapter Review

the BIG idea

Living things within an ecosystem interact with each other and the environment.

CONTENT REVIEW
CLASSZONE.COM

◀ **KEY CONCEPTS SUMMARY**

2.1 Groups of living things interact within ecosystems.

- Members of the same species form a population within a habitat.

- Each species has a distinct role within a habitat. This is its niche.

Population of Crabs

Island Habitat for Crabs

VOCABULARY
species p. 45
population p. 46
habitat p. 46
niche p. 47
community p. 48

2.2 Organisms can interact in different ways.

Organisms within a community interact with each other in many ways. Some are predators, some are prey. Some compete with one another, some cooperate. Some species form symbiotic relationships with other species:

Mutualism
benefits both

Commensalism
benefits one, other unaffected

Parasitism
benefits one, harms other

VOCABULARY
predator p. 55
prey p. 55
competition p. 55
cooperation p. 57
symbiosis p. 58
mutualism p. 58
commensalism p. 59
parasitism p. 59

2.3 Ecosystems are always changing.

VOCABULARY
limiting factor p. 64
carrying capacity p. 65
succession p. 66
pioneer species p. 66

Primary Succession

In a barren area, a new community is established with pioneer species, like mosses, that do well with little or no soil. Mosses eventually give way to coniferous trees.

Secondary Succession

When a disturbance damages a community but soil remains, the community gets reestablished from seeds and roots left behind. Grasses grow, then small shrubs, and eventually trees.

Reviewing Vocabulary

Draw a Venn diagram for each pair of terms. Put shared characteristics in the overlap area, put differences to the outside. A sample diagram is provided.

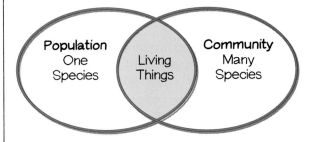

Population
One
Species

Living
Things

Community
Many
Species

1. habitat, niche

2. mutualism, commensalism

3. mutualism, parasitism

4. competition, cooperation

5. primary succession, secondary succession

Reviewing Key Concepts

Multiple Choice *Choose the letter of the best answer.*

6. What is carrying capacity?
- **a.** the largest population an ecosystem can support
- **b.** the smallest population an ecosystem can support
- **c.** the number of species an ecosystem can support
- **d.** the number of habitats in an ecosystem

7. A new species of bird moves into a habitat. The birds feed on a particular caterpillar, so that the resulting population of butterflies is small. What can be said of the relationship between the birds and the butterflies?
- **a.** The birds and the butterflies have a commensal relationship.
- **b.** The birds and butterflies compete.
- **c.** The birds are a limiting factor for the butterflies.
- **d.** The birds and butterflies coexist.

8. Certain types of worms live in the mud at the bottom of lakes. What does the mud represent for the worm?
- **a.** an ecosystem
- **c.** a community
- **b.** a niche
- **d.** a habitat

9. What is a pioneer species?
- **a.** a species that travels within an ecosystem
- **b.** a species that is among the first to move into an area after a natural disaster
- **c.** a species that depends upon animal life
- **d.** a species that cannot return after a natural disaster

10. Which is an example of competition within the same species?
- **a.** whales in a pod
- **b.** wildebeests in a herd
- **c.** creosote bushes in a desert
- **d.** birds that fly south

11. Which is an example of parasitism?
- **a.** dog and tick
- **b.** termite and protozoans
- **c.** shark and remora
- **d.** flower and hummingbird

12. Which is an example of secondary succession?
- **a.** succession after a forest fire
- **b.** succession after a large volcanic lava flow devastates an area
- **c.** succession after a glacier retreats, leaving bare rock
- **d.** succession after a hurricane washes away all the sand from a beach

Short Answer *Write a short answer to each question.*

13. Put the terms in order, starting with the term that includes the largest number of individuals and ending with the group containing the fewest individuals: community, population, ecosystem, biome.

14. List four ways in which members of the same species can cooperate with each other.

15. Describe three different types of symbiosis.

Thinking Critically

The data in the table below come from the records of a Canadian trading company that, in the late 1800s, bought lynx and hare pelts from hunters and trappers. The Canadian lynx and varying hare share the same habitat. The lynx relies on the hare as a food source. Use the table to answer the next three questions.

Year	Lynx	Hare
1	2	30
2	15	55
3	65	90
4	75	160
5	100	200
6	95	140
7	75	80
8	40	35
9	20	3
10	3	4
11	30	40
12	55	95

16. ANALYZE How would you describe the pattern that emerges between the two populations in years 1–7? How does the pattern change in years 8–10?

17. EVALUATE The data on the lynx and hare pelts have been used to suggest the sizes of the lynx and hare populations. Is this a reasonable approach to take? Why or why not?

18. ANALYZE Scientists have observed that hare populations will go through cycles of increasing and decreasing populations even when the lynx is not part of the habitat. How would you explain this observation?

19. APPLY A forest has pine trees, along with oak trees and birch trees. All the trees provide shelter and food for different animals in the habitat. Do these trees occupy the same niche? Explain.

20. INFER Explain why low-growing plants like mosses are eventually replaced by shrubs, and shrubs replaced by trees, in both primary and secondary successions.

21. PROVIDE EXAMPLES List three human activities that could lead to secondary succession.

22. ANALYZE Creosote bushes in the Mojave desert are spread out, so that each plant is about an equal distance from another. Write a short paragraph to describe the interaction of the creosote bushes, using the terms from the table.

competition	population pattern
limiting factor	community

23. APPLY How might building homes in a wooded area affect carrying capacity of different populations in the area?

the BIG idea

24. SUMMARIZE Look again at the photograph on pages 42–43. How would you change or add details to your answer to the question on the photograph?

25. APPLY Imagine that you are an ecologist from another galaxy who arrives on Earth. Describe a human community using the terms that an Earth ecologist would use to describe a natural community. Your description should include at least three examples of interactions between individuals (whether the same or different species). Identify the biotic or abiotic factors that serve as limiting factors to human population growth. Also state whether you think the human population is at or below its carrying capacity—and why.

UNIT PROJECTS

By now you should have completed the following items for your unit project.

- questions that you have asked about the topic
- schedule showing when you will complete each step of your project
- list of resources including Web sites, print resources, and materials

Standardized Test Practice

For practice on your
state test, go to . . .
TEST PRACTICE
CLASSZONE.COM

Understanding Symbiosis

Read the following description of the strangler fig and the relationship it has with other species in a rain forest. Then answer the questions that follow.

Strangler figs are part of many symbiotic relationships in a rain-forest ecosystem. In some cases, the symbiotic relationship benefits both the fig and an animal. Fig wasps lay their eggs in the fruit of the strangler fig and, in turn, pollinate it. Many birds feed on the fruit of the strangler fig and, in doing so, spread the seeds of the plant. The fig does not benefit from its interactions with all species. For example, certain butterflies feed on juice from the fruit without affecting the tree in any way.

The symbiotic relationship that gives the strangler fig its name is that between the strangler fig and its host tree. Birds drop seeds onto the top of a tree, and vines of the fig grow downward. Eventually, the vines of the strangler fig touch the ground and join with the roots of the host tree. The host tree is harmed because the leaves of the strangler fig block sunlight and its vines take root, using up nutrients the host tree needs.

1. Which feeding relationship is a form of mutualism in which both species benefit?
   a. the strangler fig and its host tree
   b. the strangler fig and the butterflies
   c. the strangler fig and the birds
   d. the strangler fig and the fig wasp

2. Which symbiotic relationship is a form of parasitism in which one species benefits and the other is harmed?
   a. the strangler fig and its host tree
   b. the strangler fig and the butterflies
   c. the strangler fig and the birds
   d. the strangler fig and the fig wasp

3. Which symbiotic relationship is a commensal relationship in which one species benefits without affecting the other?
   a. the strangler fig and its host tree
   b. the strangler fig and the butterflies
   c. the strangler fig and the birds
   d. the strangler fig and the fig wasp

4. Which word best describes the interaction between the strangler fig and its host?
   a. coexistence
   b. cooperation
   c. competition
   d. community

Extended Response

5. Strangler figs attach to trees that are sometimes cut for lumber. Write a paragraph that describes how removal of the host trees would affect these populations.
   • butterflies
   • birds
   • wasps
   • strangler figs

6. Write a paragraph describing some of the different roles played by a strangler fig in the rain forest. Use the vocabulary terms listed below in your answer.

habitat	niche	populations
community	ecosystem	

WILDERNESS CONSERVATION

The idea of wilderness conservation would have seemed strange to anyone living before the 1800s. The wilderness was vast and much of the wildlife in it dangerous to humans.

In the late 1800s, as smoke from railroads and factories rose in American skies, scientists, artists, even presidents began the work of setting aside land as parks and reservations to protect natural landscapes. Forestry, unpracticed in the U.S. before the 1890s, became a priority of the federal government as the new century dawned. Industries learned to harvest and nurture forests rather than clearing them. Next came the protection of animal species along with a call to control the pollution and depletion caused by human activity.

1872

National Parks Protect Resources

On March 1, 1872, President Ulysses S. Grant signs a law declaring Yellowstone's 2 million acres in northwest Wyoming as the country's first national park. Yellowstone serves as a model, and by 1887, about 45 million acres of forest have been set aside.

EVENTS

1870

APPLICATIONS and TECHNOLOGY

TECHNOLOGY

Seeing the Wilderness

The development of photography in 1839, and its spread during the Civil War, led to adventurous mobile photographers in the late 1800s. In the early 1860s Mathew Brady and other photographers took mobile studios to the battlefields to bring war news to the public. By the late 1860s and early 1870s the wagonload shrank to a pack load. In 1871, William Henry Jackson balanced his tripod in Yellowstone, as the official photographer of the region's first U.S. Geological Survey.

1905

U.S. Division of Forestry Formed

Gifford Pinchot becomes the first chief of the Forest Service. Pinchot warns lumberers to abandon clear-cutting, urging them to practice forestry, a more scientific approach. Pinchot instructs lumberers "to have trees harvested when they are ripe."

1892

Sierra Club Founded

The Sierra Club is formed to help people explore and enjoy the mountains of the Pacific region. The Club's goal, with John Muir the unanimous choice for President, is to help people and government preserve the forests of the Sierra Nevada.

1916

National Park Service (NPS) Founded

The system of protected forests grows so big that a federal agency is formed to oversee it. Stephen Mather serves as its first director. Today the NPS employs 20,000 staff; has 90,000 volunteers; and oversees 83.6 million acres.

1880   **1890**   **1900**   **1910**

APPLICATION

Protecting Animal Species

Fashions of the 1890s used feathers, furs, even whole birds. Out of concern for the extinction of many birds, including the Carolina parakeet and the heath hen, a movement to stop wearing rare feathers began at small tea parties. The U.S. Congress enacted the Lacey Act in 1899 to restore endangered species of game and wild birds. The landmark act became the first in a century of laws protecting animals. The Migratory Bird Treaty of 1917, the Bald Eagle Act of 1940, and the Endangered Species Act of 1973 set animal conservation as a national priority. The Endangered Species Act met its strongest test in protecting the northern spotted owl, whose entire range—in California, Oregon, Washington, and Canada—is protected.

1951

Nature Conservancy Established

The Nature Conservancy is formed to preserve plants, animals, and natural communities that represent Earth's biological diversity.

1962

Glen Canyon Destroyed

Completion of the Glen Canyon dam causes flooding in Glen Canyon, an immense area north of the Grand Canyon. Many groups fight to close the dam, but it is too late. The canyon is destroyed as Lake Powell forms.

1962

Silent Spring *Breaks Silence*

Biologist and science writer Rachel Carson publishes *Silent Spring.* Chemical pesticides have been widely used and publicized, but Carson uses scientific evidence to show that many of these chemicals harm people and the environment.

1968

Grand Canyon Dam Plans Squashed

Plans to dam the Grand Canyon are withdrawn as a result of public outcry. Recalling what happened to Glen Canyon, organizers ran national newspaper ads in 1966 making the public aware of plans to dam the Canyon.

1950   **1960**   **1970**

TECHNOLOGY

Maps to Save the Wilderness

Land and wildlife conservation has benefited from computer-based mapping technology called global information systems (GIS). GIS compiles satellite photographs, temperature readings, and other information into a central set of data. Scientists enter distributions of animals and overlay these data on existing maps. The resulting GIS maps show the gap in an animal's range and the quality of its habitat. Government efforts to restore the habitat of the endangered San Joaquin Kit Fox relied on GIS maps.

1990 to present
Reservation vs. Resource

In 1990, President George H.W. Bush expands the Arctic National Wildlife Refuge (ANWR) to more than twice its 1980 size. In 2001, President George W. Bush proposes limited oil drilling within the range. Today, debate continues over how to manage its resources and wildlife.

i RESOURCE CENTER
CLASSZONE.COM
Read more about current conservation efforts.

1990   **2000**

APPLICATION

Selling a Service

In New York City in 1996, the water department spent $1.5 billion to protect natural watersheds rather than build a $6 billion water treatment plant. In 2001, a group of scientists met to promote the value that ecosystems bring to society—benefits that include pest control, air purification, and water treatment. For example, dragonflies can eat 300 mosquitoes in a single day. Toads and bats can eat a thousand or more mosquitoes in a single day or night.

INTO THE FUTURE

Society has long put a price on natural resources—minerals, water, timber, and so on. But how much is an ecosystem worth? Communities have begun to look at the dollar values of "ecosystem services," the ongoing activities in nature that keep our environment healthy. Data is needed on ecosystem processes. Such data can be compared to the services of human-made treatment plants and agriculture.

Other questions arise with protecting species. Many species, such as wild turkeys and bald eagles, once endangered have come back in great numbers. When a protected species thrives it may endanger another species or bump up against the human landscape and human activity. How can managers of resources set priorities?

ACTIVITIES

Ecosystem Services Proposal

What services to the human population are provided by your local ecosystem? Choose one service and describe how natural processes and interactions within the ecosystem provide the benefits you've identified. What processes are involved?

Write a proposal for protecting the ecosystem. Include a comparison of the estimated cost of protecting the ecosystem and the cost of human services that provide a similar benefit.

Writing Project: The Story Behind the News

Research one of the events described on the timeline. Then write the story behind that event.

3 Human Impact on Ecosystems

the **BIG** idea

Humans and human population growth affect the environment.

How have humans affected this landscape?

Key Concepts

SECTION

3.1 Human population growth presents challenges.
Learn how the increasing human population must share land and resources and dispose of its wastes.

SECTION

3.2 Human activities affect the environment.
Learn how humans may affect natural resources, air and water quality, and biodiversity.

SECTION

3.3 People are working to protect ecosystems.
Learn about federal, local, and scientific efforts to improve resource use and protect ecosystems.

Internet Preview

CLASSZONE.COM

Chapter 3 online resources: Content Review, Visualization, four Resource Centers, Math Tutorial, Test Practice

EXPLORE (the BIG idea)

How Many Is Six Billion?

Use a piece of paper, scissors, and some tape to make a box that measures 1 cm by 1 cm by 1 cm. Fill the box with rice. Use the number of grains of rice in 1 cm^3 to calculate the volume of 6,000,000,000 grains of rice.

Observe and Think How many grains of rice are in a cubic centimeter? Do 6 billion grains take up more or less space than you expected?

How Easily Does Polluted Water Move Through Plants?

Place a few drops of food coloring in a half cup of water. Take a leafy stalk of celery and make a fresh cut across the bottom. Place the celery in the water overnight.

Observe and Think What do you observe about the celery and its leaves? What do your observations suggest about plants growing near polluted water?

Internet Activity: The Environment

Go to **ClassZone.com** to explore the effects of human activities on the environment.

Observe and Think How are people working to protect the environment?

NSTA
scilinks.org
SCi LINKS

Population Growth **Code: MDL003**

Getting Ready to Learn

◀ CONCEPT REVIEW

- Both living and nonliving factors affect ecosystems.
- Populations can grow or decline over time.
- Matter and energy move through the environment.

◀ VOCABULARY REVIEW

species p. 45
habitat p. 46

See Glossary for definitions.

diversity, urban

CONTENT REVIEW
CLASSZONE.COM
Review concepts and vocabulary.

▶ TAKING NOTES

SUPPORTING MAIN IDEAS

Make a chart to show main ideas and the information that supports them. Copy each blue heading; then add supporting information, such as reasons, explanations, and examples.

VOCABULARY STRATEGY

Think about a vocabulary term as a **magnet word** diagram. Write the other terms or ideas related to that term around it.

See the Note-Taking Handbook on pages R45–R51.

SCIENCE NOTEBOOK

Human populations can put pressure on ecosystems.

→ Humans produce waste that must be disposed of.

→ Resources must be shared among a growing human population.

→ Human population centers are expanding.

diversity   BIODIVERSITY   habitats

populations   variety

life   species

Human population growth presents challenges.

 BEFORE, you learned

- Populations have boundaries and are affected by limiting factors
- Living things form communities

 NOW, you will learn

- How a growing human population puts pressure on ecosystems
- How sharing resources can be difficult

VOCABULARY

natural resource p. 84
population density p. 86

EXPLORE Sharing Resources

How can you model resource distribution?

PROCEDURE

1. You will work in a group of several classmates. One member of your group gets a bag of objects from your teacher.

2. Each object in the bag represents a necessary resource. Divide the objects so that each member of the group gets the resources he or she needs.

3. After 10 minutes, you may trade resources with other groups.

WHAT DO YOU THINK?

- Did you get a fair share of your group's objects?
- How does the number of people in each group affect the outcome?
- Was the job made easier when trading occurred across groups?

MATERIALS
bag containing an assortment of objects

SUPPORTING MAIN IDEAS
Make a chart to show information that supports the first main idea presented: *The human population is increasing.*

The human population is increasing.

According to the United Nations, on October 12, 1999, Earth's human population reached 6 billion. Until 300 years ago, it had never grown beyond a few hundred million people. Only 200 years ago, the population reached 1 billion. So the increase to 6 billion people has occurred in a very short time. About one-third of all humans alive today are 14 years old or younger. Partly for this reason, experts predict Earth's population will keep growing—to 9 billion or more by the year 2050.

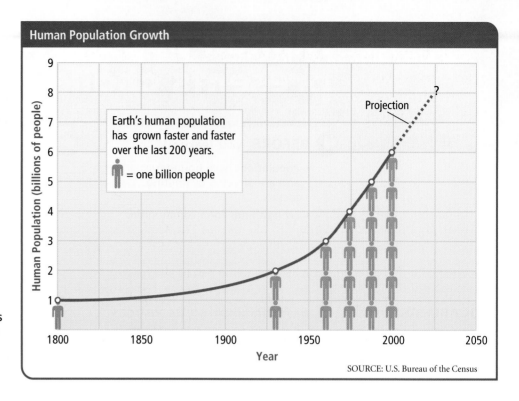

Human Population Growth

Human Population (billions of people)

Earth's human population has grown faster and faster over the last 200 years.

 = one billion people

Projection

?

SOURCE: U.S. Bureau of the Census

PREDICT The graph shows actual population growth through 2000. Predict how the population will grow in the future.

The graph above shows how the human population has grown in the last 200 years. You can see from the way the graph gets noticeably steeper after 1950 how quickly the population has increased in just the last 50 years. It is not just the number of babies being born that contributes to Earth's large human population. People are living longer as a result of improving health care and nutrition.

The dotted line on the graph shows a projection, which helps us predict what the population would be if it continues to grow at the rate it is growing today. However, remember that an ecosystem has a carrying capacity for any given population. At some point, Earth will reach its carrying capacity for the human population. Today, many people think that our planet is close to—if not already at—its carrying capacity for humans.

CHECK YOUR READING How might Earth's carrying capacity affect human population growth?

Human populations can put pressure on ecosystems.

VISUALIZATION
CLASSZONE.COM

Examine how the human population has grown.

If your family has guests for the weekend, you may find that you run out of hot water for showers or do not have enough milk for everyone's breakfast. The resources that would ordinarily be enough for your family are no longer enough.

You read in Chapter 2 that resources such as food, water, and space can be limiting factors for biological populations. These same resources limit Earth's human population. As the human population grows, it uses more resources—just as your weekend visitors used more of your home's resources. The activities of the growing human population are putting pressure on Earth's ecosystems.

▽ **REMINDER**

A *limiting factor* is something that prevents a population from continuing to grow.

Pressures of Waste Disposal

As Earth's human population grows, so does the amount of waste produced by humans. Humans, like all living things, produce natural waste. Often, the water that carries this waste is treated to remove harmful chemicals before being cycled back to the environment. However, some of these materials still make it into lakes, rivers, and oceans, harming these ecosystems.

Much of the waste material produced by humans is the result of human activity. Some of this waste is garbage, or food waste. The rest of it is trash, or nonfood waste. In the United States, huge amounts of trash are thrown out each year. Most garbage and trash ends up in landfills.

Landfills take up a lot of space. The Fresh Kills Landfill in Staten Island, New York, is 60 meters (197 ft) high and covers an area as big as 2200 football fields. Decomposing trash and garbage can release dangerous gases into the air as well as harmful chemicals into the ground. Liners, which are layers of plastic or packed clay, are used to keep chemicals from leaking into surrounding land and water.

Waste is deposited in one area at a time.

Each layer is covered with soil and clay.

Liners at the base of the landfill keep harmful materials from leaking.

clay

groundwater

Another way to get rid of trash and garbage is to incinerate it—burn it. The problem with incineration is that it releases harmful gases and chemicals into the air. To prevent the release of these harmful substances, incinerator smokestacks have filters. To prevent further environmental contamination, used filters must be disposed of safely.

Pressures on Resources

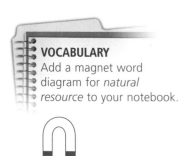

VOCABULARY
Add a magnet word diagram for *natural resource* to your notebook.

You have seen that a growing human population puts pressure on ecosystems by the amount of waste it leaves behind. Human populations also put pressure on ecosystems by what they take away. Humans depend on the environment for resources. A **natural resource** is any type of material or energy that humans use to meet their needs. Natural resources that humans take from their environment include water, food, wood, stone, metal, and minerals.

Clean fresh water is an important resource. Only 3 percent of Earth's water supply is fresh water—and two-thirds of that small amount is locked up in polar ice caps, glaciers, and permanent snow. As the human population grows, sharing this important resource will become more difficult.

INVESTIGATE Resources

How does your community meet its needs?

PROCEDURE

1. Obtain a recent map of your county, city, or town.

2. Using the map, try to identify where your community gets its electricity and water and how it disposes of trash and garbage.

3. Identify locations where food is grown.

WHAT DO YOU THINK?

- How much does your community rely on other communities for resources?
- What resources does your community share with other communities?
- Where does your community dispose of its own waste materials?

CHALLENGE Draw a grid on a piece of tracing paper and place it on top of the map. Use your grid to estimate what percentage of land in your city or town is used for housing and what percentage is used for governmental, agricultural, and commercial purposes.

SKILL FOCUS
Interpreting

MATERIALS
- map of your county, city, or town
For Challenge:
- tracing paper
- pencil
- ruler

TIME
30 minutes

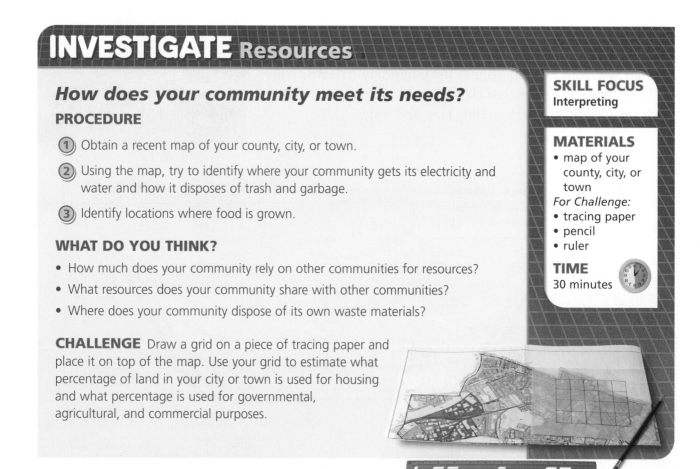

Case Study: The Colorado River

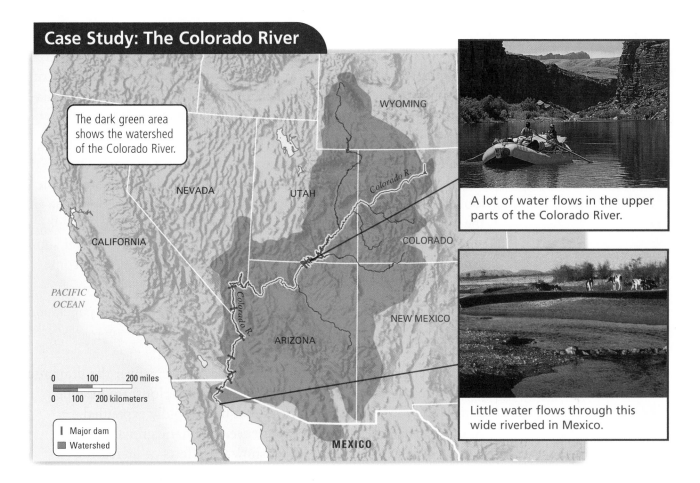

The dark green area shows the watershed of the Colorado River.

A lot of water flows in the upper parts of the Colorado River.

Little water flows through this wide riverbed in Mexico.

WYOMING

NEVADA

UTAH

Colorado R.

COLORADO

CALIFORNIA

PACIFIC OCEAN

NEW MEXICO

ARIZONA

Colorado R.

MEXICO

0   100   200 miles
0   100   200 kilometers

| Major dam
■ Watershed

A case study that involves the Colorado River shows how a growing human population puts pressures on natural resources. This example also shows that sharing resources isn't easy. The watershed of this major Western river extends into seven U.S. states and parts of Mexico. The watershed includes all the smaller rivers and streams that flow into the Colorado River. In a region where little rain falls each year, these streams and rivers are an important source of water for drinking and agriculture.

As the West was settled, people in the downstream states of California, Arizona, and Nevada worried that the people in the upstream states of Colorado, Utah, Wyoming, and New Mexico would drain too much water from the river. In 1922 the seven states signed an agreement that divided the water between the two groups.

Problems with this agreement soon became apparent. First, the needs of Native American and Mexican populations were not considered. Second, the dams and channels built to prevent floods and transport water harmed river ecosystems. And third, the seven states planned to use more water than the river usually holds. As a result, the river often runs nearly dry at its mouth, in Mexico.

READING TiP

As you read about the Colorado River, refer to the map above to see where the river flows and the states that use the Colorado River's water.

CHECK YOUR READING List three problems that developed after people made a plan to share Colorado River water.

Pressures of Urban Growth

RESOURCE CENTER
CLASSZONE.COM

Learn more about urban
expansion.

Until recently, the majority of Earth's population was spread out, so the population density was low. **Population density** is the measure of the number of people in a given area. Generally, the lower the population density, the less pressure there is on the environment.

Today, about half of the world's population lives in urban, or city, areas. People are attracted to these areas to live and to work. Over time, suburban areas around a city develop as more and more people look for a place to live. In cities, buildings are spaced close together, so the population density is high. A large number of people in a small area changes the landscape. The local environment can no longer support the number of people living there, and so resources must come from outside.

CHECK YOUR READING How does population density in a city differ from the population density of a suburb?

In recent years, some people have raised concern over the dramatic growth in and around urban areas. Los Angeles; Houston; Atlanta; and Washington, D.C. are all cities that have rapidly expanded. Another urban area that has experienced dramatic growth is Las Vegas, Nevada. The images below show the effects of increasing

Las Vegas, 1972

The darker colors distinguish the developed land of Las Vegas from the surrounding desert.

Las Vegas, 1997

city center

Over 25 years, the city expanded in all directions. The population went from 273,000 to 1,124,000.

population density around the city between 1972 and 1997. Located in the middle of the desert, Las Vegas depends upon the Colorado River for water and energy. As the population grows, so does the need for natural resources.

Pressures of Expanding Land Use

An increasing demand for resources in a particular area is one consequence of urban growth. But as communities around cities expand onto surrounding land, the environment is affected. Natural habitats, such as forests, are destroyed. Because forests cycle carbon through the environment, cutting down trees affects the carbon cycle. Soil that was held in place by tree roots may wash into lakes and rivers.

INFER What do you think this ecosystem looked like a hundred years ago? two hundred years ago?

Another consequence of widespread development is the loss of productive farmland. Development replaces more than 2.5 million acres of farmland each year in the United States. This means less land is available locally to produce food for the growing population. The result is that food is often transported great distances.

Unlike compact city development, widespread suburban development also increases the need for residents to have cars. This is because most people in suburban areas live farther from where they work, shop, or go to school. A greater number of cars decreases the air quality in communities and requires additional road construction, which can interrupt natural habitats and endanger wildlife.

CHECK YOUR READING Describe some ways that development harms natural ecosystems.

3.1 Review

KEY CONCEPTS

1. Identify four pressures placed on ecosystems by an increasing human population.

2. Give an example that shows how resources can be difficult to share.

CRITICAL THINKING

3. **Apply** Describe an example of sharing resources that occurs in your home.

4. **Infer** How would a city's population density change if the city increased in area and the number of people in it remained the same?

⬥ CHALLENGE

5. **Evaluate** Imagine that you lived along the Colorado River. What information would you need if you wanted to evaluate a water-sharing agreement.

Ecology in Urban Planning

Urban planners design and locate buildings, transportation systems, and green spaces in cities. One important thing they consider is how their proposal for development will affect the ecosystem. With the help of ecology, urban planners can balance the needs of humans and the environment.

❶ GATHERING DATA Urban planners use maps to gather information about the layout of a city, where populations of plants and animals exist, and where water and land resources are located.

❷ ANALYZING DATA Scientists help urban planners determine how the location and density of buildings, roads, or parks can affect natural habitats.

❸ APPLYING DATA By understanding the ecosystem, urban planners can develop areas to support different needs.

This habitat is left untouched because it supports rare migrating birds. Development would disturb the ecosystem and put the birds at risk.

This area has a stable population of native species. Park benches and trails encourage human recreation in well defined areas.

EXPLORE

1. **APPLY** Both ecologists and urban planners have to understand the ways that biotic and abiotic factors are interconnected. List some biotic and abiotic factors in a human community.

2. **CHALLENGE** Use the Internet to find out more about the planning board or planning office in your community. Is your community growing? In what ways? What are some decisions that planners are helping to make?

3.2 Human activities affect the environment.

D

◀ **BEFORE,** you learned	▶ **NOW,** you will learn
• Human populations are increasing	• How natural resources are classified
• Human population growth causes problems	• How pollution affects the environment
	• How a loss of diversity affects the environment

VOCABULARY

pollution p. 91
biodiversity p. 91

THINK ABOUT

How do you use water?

Think of the number of times you use water every day. Like all living things, you need water. In fact, more than half of the material that makes up your body is water.

No matter where you live, most of the time you can turn on a faucet and clean water flows out the spout. You use water when you take a shower, fix a snack, or wash a dish. If you've ever lost water service to your home, you've probably been reminded how much you depend upon it. No doubt about it, our need for water is serious.

SUPPORTING MAIN IDEAS
Make a chart to show information that supports the main idea: *Humans use many resources.*

Humans use many resources.

Throughout history, people around the world have relied on natural resources for survival. Ancient civilizations used stone to create tools and weapons. And wood was an important fuel for cooking and keeping warm. Today, humans continue to rely on the environment and have discovered additional resources to meet their needs. In Section 3.1 you read about sharing natural resources. Scientists classify these resources into two categories:

• renewable resources

• nonrenewable resources

Renewable Resources

RESOURCE CENTER
CLASSZONE.COM

Find out more about natural resources.

Two hundred years ago, most small towns in the Northeastern part of the United States included farm fields, pasture, and woods. The wooded areas that weren't farmed were used as wood lots. The wood from these lots supplied firewood for towns and was often exported for income.

Trees are an example of a renewable resource—a resource that can be used over and over again. The Sun's energy is another important renewable resource. Because the Sun is expected to supply energy for another five billion years, its energy is considered essentially unlimited. As you read earlier in your study of the water cycle, water can be classified as a renewable resource. Renewable resources can be replaced naturally or by humans in a short amount of time, but they may run out if they are overused or managed poorly.

CHECK YOUR READING Give three examples of renewable resources. Explain why each one is considered renewable.

Nonrenewable Resources

Nonrenewable resources are resources that cannot be replaced. In some cases, they may be replenished by natural processes, but not quickly enough for human purposes. Nonrenewable resources are often underground, making them more difficult to reach. But technology has enabled humans to locate and remove nonrenewable resources from places that used to be impossible to reach.

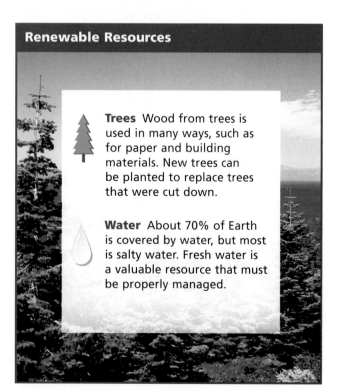

Renewable Resources

Trees Wood from trees is used in many ways, such as for paper and building materials. New trees can be planted to replace trees that were cut down.

Water About 70% of Earth is covered by water, but most is salty water. Fresh water is a valuable resource that must be properly managed.

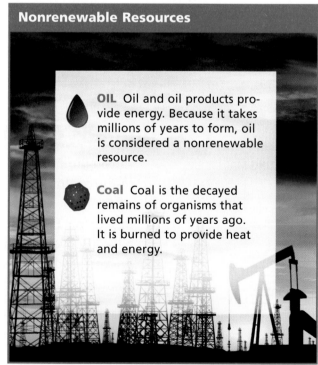

Nonrenewable Resources

OIL Oil and oil products provide energy. Because it takes millions of years to form, oil is considered a nonrenewable resource.

Coal Coal is the decayed remains of organisms that lived millions of years ago. It is burned to provide heat and energy.

Coal, petroleum, and natural gas are nonrenewable resources that are removed from underground by mining or drilling. Also called fossil fuels, they are the main energy source for heating, industry, and transportation and are used to make many products. Many minerals, like copper and gold, are also considered nonrenewable resources.

Pollution endangers biodiversity.

As you walk along a city street, you may smell exhaust or see litter. These are examples of pollution. **Pollution** is the addition of harmful substances to the environment. Many of the ways humans use natural resources cause pollution to be released into the soil, air, and water. Pollutants include chemicals, bacteria, and dirt. Even materials that are ordinarily not harmful can cause pollution when they build up in one location.

As pollution becomes common in an ecosystem, living things may be threatened. Plant and animal populations may decrease and biodiversity may decline. **Biodiversity** is the number and variety of life forms within an ecosystem. Healthy ecosystems support a variety of species. An ecosystem with a variety of organisms can recover more easily from disturbances than an ecosystem that has fewer species.

VOCABULARY
Don't forget to add magnet diagrams for the words *pollution* and *biodiversity*.

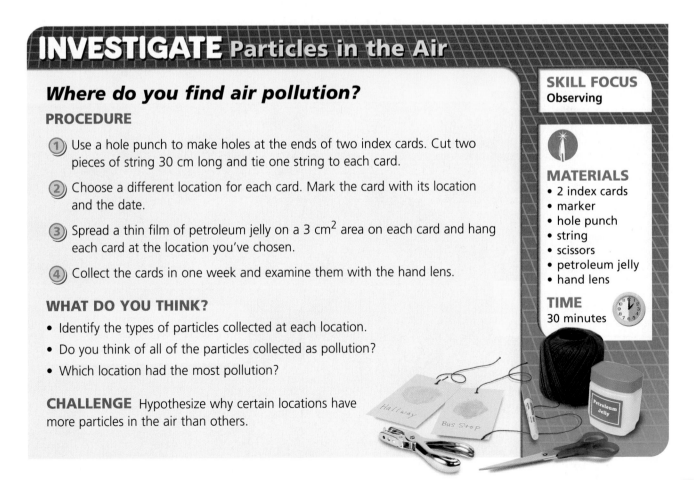

INVESTIGATE Particles in the Air

Where do you find air pollution?

PROCEDURE

(1) Use a hole punch to make holes at the ends of two index cards. Cut two pieces of string 30 cm long and tie one string to each card.

(2) Choose a different location for each card. Mark the card with its location and the date.

(3) Spread a thin film of petroleum jelly on a 3 cm^2 area on each card and hang each card at the location you've chosen.

(4) Collect the cards in one week and examine them with the hand lens.

WHAT DO YOU THINK?
- Identify the types of particles collected at each location.
- Do you think of all of the particles collected as pollution?
- Which location had the most pollution?

CHALLENGE Hypothesize why certain locations have more particles in the air than others.

SKILL FOCUS
Observing

MATERIALS
- 2 index cards
- marker
- hole punch
- string
- scissors
- petroleum jelly
- hand lens

TIME
30 minutes

Air Quality

Air quality affects entire ecosystems. For example, in 1980, Mount St. Helens erupted on the West Coast of the United States. Hot ash was blown 15 miles up into the air. Three days later some of that ash reached the East Coast. Although natural events occasionally release air pollutants, human activities pollute every day.

Today in the United States, motor vehicles, factories, and power plants are the main sources of air pollution. The fossil fuels they burn release sulfur dioxide, nitrogen dioxide, and carbon monoxide into the air. These pollutants affect humans and animals and are the main cause of acid rain, a serious problem affecting ecosystems.

READING TiP

Pollute and *pollutant* are in the same word family as pollution.

CHECK YOUR READING What air pollutants contribute to acid rain problems in the United States?

Acid rain occurs when air pollutants such as sulfur dioxide and nitrogen dioxide mix with water in the atmosphere to form acid droplets of rain, ice, snow, or mist. Just as the wind carried ash from Mount St. Helens, wind can carry these droplets for very long distances before they fall as rain.

Acid rain has been very harmful in areas without rich soil to help correct the rain's acidity. In New York's Adirondack Mountains, acid rain has killed all the fish in some lakes. The photograph below shows the impact of acid rain on trees in the Adirondacks. Where acid rain falls, it damages leaves and soil. This damage destroys both habitats and food sources for many animals, eventually reducing biodiversity.

Acid-Rain Damage

A close look at the branch reveals that some of the needles are turning brown.

Air Quality Spruce trees in the Adirondacks show damage caused when pollutants in the air mix with rain.

Water Quality

Water quality is another factor that affects biodiversity in ecosystems. Forty years ago, newspaper headlines announced that Lake Erie was "dead" because of pollution. Almost every living thing in the lake had died. Lake Erie suffered for years from pollution by neighborhoods, industries, and farms along its banks. Rivers that emptied into the lake also carried pollution with them.

The pollution found in Lake Erie is common in communities across the United States. Chemicals or waste that drain off of farm fields, animal feedlots, and landfills all cause water pollution. So do oil spills, soil erosion, and the discharging of wastewater from towns and industries.

 CHECK YOUR READING Name four different sources of water pollution.

Like air pollution, water pollution affects entire ecosystems. One river that suffers from heavy pollution is the Duwamish River in Washington. Over 600 million gallons of untreated waste and storm water drain off the land into the river. As a result, large amounts of bacteria and harmful chemicals contaminate the water, killing fish and putting humans at risk.

When fish and amphibians in aquatic ecosystems are exposed to pollution, the entire food web is affected. If fish become scarce, some birds may no longer find enough food. The bird population may decrease as birds die or move to a new habitat. The result is that biodiversity in the ecosystem decreases.

Water Quality A scientist tests the water of the Duwamish River after chemicals were released into the river.

Chemical Pollution

Pollution that flows into aquatic ecosystems can harm—even kill—organisms like these fish.

Pollution Across Systems

As you have learned, pollution can be spread among ecosystems by abiotic factors. For example, wind carried ash from Mount St. Helens to different ecosystems. Wind also carries acid rain to forest ecosystems. Pollution can also move between air and water. For example, some chemical pollutants can run off land and into a body of water. As this polluted water evaporates and cycles through the environment, some of the pollutants may be transported with it.

1 Runoff containing harmful chemicals flows into this pond.

air pollution

2 Water evaporates, taking some of the harmful chemicals into the air.

Habitat loss endangers biodiversity.

Scientists know that an ecosystem with many different species of plants and animals can withstand the effects of flooding, drought, and disease more effectively than an ecosystem with fewer species. But for biodiversity to be maintained, a habitat must be able to support a large number of different species. If living space is limited or a food source is removed, then the number of species in a biological community will be reduced.

Removing Habitat

One way human activities affect habitats is by reducing the amounts of natural resources available to living things. When this occurs, populations that rely on those resources are less likely to survive. For example, if you trim all the dead branches off the trees in your yard and remove them, insects that live in rotting wood will not settle in your yard. As a result, woodpeckers that may have nested in the area will lose their source of food. By removing this food source, you might affect the biodiversity in your backyard.

Now consider altering an ecosystem much larger than your backyard. Instead of removing a single resource, imagine removing a large area of land that is a habitat to many different species. Disturbing habitats removes not only food but space, shelter, and protection for living things.

Removing Habitat

A clear-cut forest provides a dramatic example of habitat loss.

Forest Habitat The forest provides food and shelter for many organisms.

Deforestation Removing all the trees from an area removes habitat that other species depend on.

Because of land development, forests that once stretched for hundreds of miles have been fragmented, or broken apart into small patches. Organisms that depend on trees cannot live in woods that have large areas that have been clear-cut. Their habitat is removed or reduced so there is a greater risk of attack by predators. Skunks, raccoons, and crows, which eat the eggs of forest songbirds, will not travel deep into large forests. However, they can reach nests more easily when forests are broken into small areas.

 CHECK YOUR READING Why is biodiversity important and how can human activities affect it?

Changing Habitat

Another kind of habitat loss occurs when humans move species into new habitats, either on purpose or by accident. Some species, when released in a new place, successfully compete against the native species, crowding them out. Over time, these species, called invasive species, may replace the native species.

One example of an invasive plant is purple loosestrife. In the 1800s loosestrife from Europe was brought to the United States to use as a garden plant and medicinal herb. One loosestrife plant can make about 2 million seeds a year. These seeds are carried long distances by wind, water, animals, and humans. Loosestrife sprouts in wetlands, where it can fill in open-water habitat or replace native plants such as goldenrod. Most ducks and fish do not feed on purple loosestrife.

Changing Habitat

Habitat loss occurs when purple loosestrife fills in open water or crowds out goldenrod.

Invasive Species Purple loosestrife fills in wetlands and crowds out native species, disturbing organisms that rely on native species for food or living space.

Native Species Goldenrod is a native species that is a food source for many wetland populations.

When the native plants that wetland animals depend on are crowded out by loosestrife, the animals disappear, too.

Scientists estimate that Earth supports more than 10 million different species. They also estimate that thousands of species are threatened, and over a hundred species of plants and animals become extinct every year. By protecting biodiversity we can help ecosystems thrive and even recover more quickly after a natural disturbance such as a hurricane. And biodiversity directly benefits humans. For example, many medications are based on natural compounds from plants that only grow in certain types of ecosystems.

3.2 Review

KEY CONCEPTS

1. List some renewable and nonrenewable resources that you need to survive.

2. Describe two ways in which pollution can move through ecosystems.

3. Explain what scientists mean by *biodiversity*.

CRITICAL THINKING

4. **Explain** Under some circumstances, valuable natural resources can be considered pollutants. Explain this statement, giving two examples.

5. **Compare** Identify two natural habitats in your area, one with high biodiversity and one with low biodiversity. Describe the biodiversity of each.

⬤ CHALLENGE

6. **Hypothesize** When lakes are polluted by acid rain, the water appears to become clearer, not cloudier. Why do you think this is the case?

CLASSZONE.COM

Click on Math Tutorial for more help with finding the volume of a rectangular prism.

How Much Water?

When you take a 10-minute shower, you are using about 190 liters of water. How much is that? Liters are a metric unit of capacity—the amount of liquid that can fit into a container of a certain size. The liter is based on a metric unit of volume. One liter is equal to 1000 cubic centimeters.

Example

A rectangular tank holds the amount of water used for a 10-minute shower. The dimensions of the tank are 250 cm × 40 cm × 19 cm. What is the volume of the tank?

Volume = **length** × **width** × **height**

$V = \mathbf{l} \times \mathbf{w} \times h$

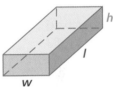

(1) Use the formula for volume.
Replace variables with actual dimensions.

$V = 250 \text{ cm} \times 40 \text{ cm} \times 19 \text{ cm}$

(2) Calculate by multiplying.

$(250 \times 40) \times 19$

$10{,}000 \quad \times 19 = 190{,}000$

(3) Check units:
$\text{cm} \times \text{cm} \times \text{cm} = \text{cm}^3$ (cubic centimeters)

ANSWER $250 \text{ cm} \times 40 \text{ cm} \times 19 \text{ cm} = 19{,}000 \text{ cm}^3$

Find the following volumes or dimensions.

1. Brushing your teeth with the water running uses the water in a tank 14 cm by 45 cm by 12 cm. Sketch an aquarium that holds exactly this amount. Label the dimensions. What is the volume?

2. If you turn off the water while you brush, you use only about half as much water. Sketch a rectangular tank that holds this volume. Label the dimensions. What is the volume?

3. A typical toilet flush uses the water in a 50 cm by 20 cm by 20 cm space. Find the volume in cubic centimeters. Sketch a model of this volume.

CHALLENGE An Olympic swimming pool is 50 m by 25 m by 3 m. What is its volume? There are approximately 5678 cubic meters of water in the water tower shown. How many Olympic pools of water would it take to fill the tower?

People are working to protect ecosystems.

◀ **BEFORE,** you learned	▶ **NOW,** you will learn
• Human activities produce pollutants • Human activity is depleting some natural resources	• About some of the laws that have been passed to help protect the environment • About efforts that are being made to conserve natural resources

VOCABULARY

conservation p. 99
sustainable p. 102

EXPLORE Environmental Impacts

What happens when soil is compressed?

PROCEDURE

1. Fill two pots with 1 cup each of potting soil.

2. Compress the soil in the second pot by pushing down hard upon it with your hand.

3. Pour 1 cup of water into the first pot. Start the stopwatch as soon as you start pouring. Stop the watch as soon as all the water has been absorbed. Record the time.

4. Pour 1 cup of water into the second pot and again record how long it takes for the water to be absorbed. Wash your hands.

WHAT DO YOU THINK?

• What effect does compressing the soil have upon how quickly the water is absorbed?

• What might happen to water that is not absorbed quickly by soil?

MATERIALS

• 2 plant pots with trays
• measuring cups
• potting soil
• water
• stopwatch

Environmental awareness is growing.

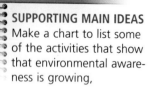

SUPPORTING MAIN IDEAS
Make a chart to list some of the activities that show that environmental awareness is growing.

As people moved westward across grassy plains and steep mountain ranges of the United States, many believed our nation's resources were endless. Midwestern prairies were converted to farmland. Forests were clear-cut for lumber. Land was mined for coal.

By the 1800s, foresters and naturalists began to take interest in preserving the wild areas they saw rapidly disappearing. In 1872 our nation's outlook started to change when Yellowstone, the world's first national park, was established. It wasn't long before conservation of wild places became a goal. **Conservation** is the process of saving or protecting a natural resource.

The movement to protect our environment grew rapidly in the 1960s. *Silent Spring,* a book that raised public awareness of the effect of harmful chemicals in the environment, sparked debate about serious pollution problems. As local efforts for environmental protection grew, the United States government responded. Throughout the 1970s important laws were passed to preserve and protect the environment. Today small groups of citizens, along with local and national government efforts, protect America's natural resources.

CHECK YOUR READING List three events in the history of the environmental movement in the United States.

RESOURCE CENTER
CLASSZONE.COM
Discover how people help ecosystems recover.

Volunteers work to clean up a stream.

Local Efforts

Maybe you have heard the expression "Think globally, act locally." It urges people to consider the health of the entire planet and to take action in their own communities. Long before federal and state agencies began enforcing environmental laws, individuals were coming together to protect habitats and the organisms that depend on them. These efforts are often referred to as grassroots efforts. They occur on a local level and are primarily run by volunteers.

Often the efforts of a few citizens gather the support and interest of so many people that they form a larger organization. These groups work to bring about change by communicating with politicians, publishing articles, or talking to the news media. Some groups purchase land and set it aside for preservation.

Federal Efforts

You have probably heard of the Endangered Species Act or the Clean Air Act. You might wonder, though, exactly what these laws do. The United States government works with scientists to write laws that ensure that companies and individuals work together to conserve natural resources and maintain healthy ecosystems.

In the late 1960s the National Environmental Policy Act, known as NEPA, made the protection of natural ecosystems a national goal. Several important laws followed. For example, the Clean Air Act and Clean Water Act improved the control of different kinds and amounts of pollutants that can be put into the air and water. The Environmental Protection Agency (EPA) enforces all federal environmental laws.

 CHECK YOUR READING Identify two federal environmental laws.

Over the past decades, chemical waste from factories has piled up in landfills and polluted water sources. These wastes can threaten ecosystems and human health. In 1980, citizen awareness of the dangers led to the Superfund Program. The goal of the program is to identify dangerous areas and to clean up the worst sites.

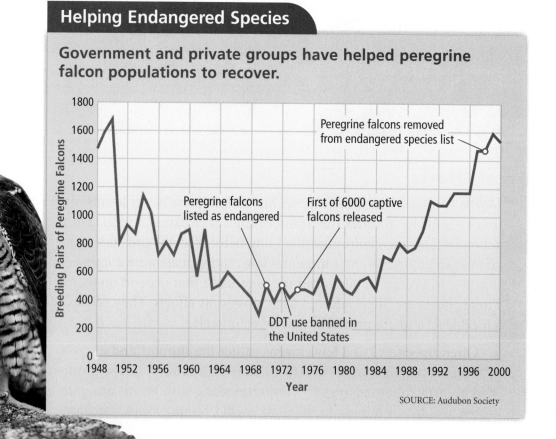

Helping Endangered Species

Government and private groups have helped peregrine falcon populations to recover.

Peregrine falcons listed as endangered

First of 6000 captive falcons released

Peregrine falcons removed from endangered species list

DDT use banned in the United States

(y-axis) Breeding Pairs of Peregrine Falcons: 0, 200, 400, 600, 800, 1000, 1200, 1400, 1600, 1800

(x-axis) Year: 1948, 1952, 1956, 1960, 1964, 1968, 1972, 1976, 1980, 1984, 1988, 1992, 1996, 2000

SOURCE: Audubon Society

Ecosystem Recovery

A growing awareness of the importance of healthy ecosystems is inspiring restoration projects.

Wetland

Restoration efforts in Galveston Bay, Texas, focus on bringing back the sea-grass meadows near the coast.

Volunteers help replant sea grass around Galveston Island State Park. Sea grass is a major habitat for birds, fish, and crabs and helps prevent erosion by holding bottom sediments in place.

Desert

Members of a restoration group work to restore desert plants and soil in Red Rock Canyon State Park, California.

1 A power auger is used to break up severely compacted soil and prepare it for planting.

2 Seedlings of native species, like the saltbush, are grown off site. Once they reach a more mature size, they are brought in to be planted.

3 Plastic cones are used to protect plants from being disturbed by severe weather or predators.

Federal agencies oversee the Superfund Program and other environmental laws. In addition to federal laws protecting the environment, there are state laws. Companies must follow all the laws that apply in each state where they do business. The same company may need to follow different laws in different states.

The United States is just one of many countries learning to deal with the effects of their human population on the environment. Dozens of countries have already met to discuss concerns about clear-cutting, water pollution, and endangered species. At this international level, the United Nations Environment Programme encourages sound environmental practices worldwide.

INFER At this Superfund site, the chemical cadmium pollutes the soil. Why does this worker need to wear a face mask?

Conserving resources protects ecosystems.

Around the world, individuals and companies are expressing more interest in **sustainable** practices—ways of living and doing business that use natural resources without using them up. Sustainable development allows people to enjoy a high quality of life while limiting harm to ecosystems. Developing new technologies, reducing resource use, and creating less waste are three ways to practice sustainability.

 CHECK YOUR READING What are sustainable practices?

Improving Resource Use

As you read in Chapter 2, many different interactions take place in ecosystems. Some organisms form close relationships with one other and their environment. Humans are like other organisms. We depend on the environment to help meet our requirements for life. Because many of the resources we rely on are limited, businesses and governments are changing the way they manage farms, forests, and energy resources. They are adopting sustainable practices.

Some farmers are practicing sustainable methods that protect land and provide nutritious food. Nearly one-third of U.S. farms practice conservation tillage, a method that involves planting seeds without plowing the soil. This technique can cut soil erosion by more than 90 percent. Organic farmers reject fertilizers and pesticides made from fossil fuels. Instead they use natural fertilizers, like compost, and natural pest controls, like ladybugs, which eat aphids.

Forestry practices are also changing. Cutting selectively instead of clear-cutting reduces soil erosion and encourages rapid regrowth. The U.S. Forest Service has adopted an ecosystem-management approach that tries to balance the need for timber with the need to conserve soil and water and preserve wildlife and biodiversity.

CHECK YOUR READING Give two examples of sustainable practices.

Energy companies are also promoting sustainability by developing alternative energy sources that do not come from fossil fuels. By the time you buy your first car, it may run on fuel cells, and the electricity in your house may be generated by a solar power plant.

Commercial geothermal power plants are a renewable energy source that uses the heat of molten rock in the Earth's interior. Geothermal power already supplies electricity to households in New Zealand, Japan, the United States, and elsewhere.

The energy of falling or flowing water can also be used to generate electricity in a hydropower plant. Commercial hydropower plants generate over half of the alternative energy used in the United States. Like solar and geothermal power, hydropower releases no pollutants. But hydropower often requires dams, which are expensive to build and can flood wildlife habitats and interfere with fish migration.

Wind is another source of energy that is clean and renewable. Large open areas with relatively constant winds are used as wind farms. Wind turbines are spread across these farms and convert the energy of moving air into electricity. Wind-generating capacity has increased steadily around the world in just the last ten years.

Solar Energy These mirrors collect and concentrate sunlight, which will be used to generate electricity.

INFER What benefits do people get from using mass transit? Why might some people be reluctant to use mass transit?

Reducing Waste and Pollution

Perhaps you are one of the many students who take a bus to school. Buses and trains are examples of mass transit, which move large groups of people at the same time. When you travel by mass transit, you are working to reduce waste and pollution. The photograph to the left shows a light rail train that carries commuters from downtown Portland, Oregon, into suburbs an hour away. In Portland, mass transit like this light rail helps reduce traffic congestion, air pollution, and noise pollution.

Another way to reduce pollution is by carpooling. Many states encourage carpools by reducing tolls or reserving highway lanes for cars carrying more than one person. Traffic is also reduced when workers telecommute, or work from home, using computers and telephones. Of course a telecommuter uses energy at home. But there are many ways to reduce home energy use. You can install compact fluorescent light bulbs, which use less electricity than a regular light bulb. And you can choose energy-efficient appliances.

CHECK YOUR READING   How does mass transit benefit the environment?

Most homes are heated with oil or natural gas, two nonrenewable resources. To use less of these resources, you lower your thermostat in winter or add insulation around doors and windows to keep heat inside. Many power companies offer a free energy audit, to show how you can use less energy at home.

Recycling is a fairly new idea in human communities, but if you think about it, it's what biological communities have always done to reduce waste and pollution. Resources are used again and again as they move through the water, nitrogen, and carbon cycles. Materials

READING TiP

The prefix re– means again, so to recycle a resource is to use it again.

These students are participating in a local recycling program.

that people now commonly recycle include glass, aluminum, certain types of plastic, office paper, newspaper, and cardboard.

Sometimes materials are recycled into the same product. Cans and glass bottles are melted down to make new cans and bottles. Materials can also be recycled into new products. Your warm fleece jacket might be made from recycled soda bottles. The cereal box on your breakfast table might be made from recycled paper.

 CHECK YOUR READING Name three things people can do at home that reduce waste and pollution.

Think globally, act locally.

Visitors to an ocean beach may find signs like the one on the right. Such signs remind people that small actions—like protecting the nests of sandpipers—make a difference in the preservation of ecosystems.

The challenges facing society are great. Providing Earth's growing population with clean water and air and with energy for warmth and transportation are only some of the many tasks. Scientists continue to learn about the interactions in ecosystems and how important ecosystems are to humans. As you have read about the interactions in ecosystems, you have probably realized that humans—including you—have a large effect on the natural world.

In the coming years, protection of ecosystems will remain a major challenge. By thinking globally, you will be able to understand the effects of society's decisions about resources, development, and transportation. By acting locally you can become involved in efforts to reduce the use of limited resources and to restore ecosystems.

3.3 Review

KEY CONCEPTS

1. List at least five ways that you can reduce your use of natural resources.

2. Describe three ways that resources can be managed in a sustainable way.

CRITICAL THINKING

3. **Infer** Controlling air and water pollution and protecting endangered species usually require the involvement of the federal government. Why can't state or local governments do this on their own?

CHALLENGE

4. **Apply** Explain how efforts to protect endangered species relate to restoration of ecosystems.

CHAPTER INVESTIGATION

Cleaning Oil Spills

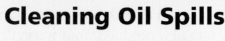

OVERVIEW AND PURPOSE

One example of a harmful effect of human activity is an oil spill. You've probably heard about oil spills in the news. Damage to an oil-carrying ship or barge can cause thick black oil to spill into the water. The oil floats on the water, and waves can carry the oil to shore. Oil gets caught on sand and living things that are part of a coastal ecosystem. These spills are especially difficult to clean up. In this investigation you will

- simulate an oil spill and test the effectiveness of various materials used to remove oil
- evaluate materials and processes used to clean up oil spills

▶ Problem

Write It Up

What materials are effective at removing oil spilled near a coastal ecosystem?

▶ Hypothesize

Write It Up

Write a hypothesis to propose a material or materials that might best remove oil from a coastal area. Your hypothesis should take the form of an "If . . . , then . . . , because . . ." statement.

▶ Procedure

MATERIALS
- small beaker
- 40 mL vegetable oil
- turmeric
- spoon
- aluminum baking pan
- sand
- large beaker
- water
- sponge
- dish soap
- rubbing alcohol
- paper towels
- cotton balls
- cotton rag
- cornstarch
- yarn
- feather
- seaweed

1 Measure out 40 mL of vegetable oil in a small beaker. Stir in turmeric to make the oil yellow.

2 Pour sand into one end of the pan as shown to model a beach.

3 Carefully pour enough water into the pan so that it forms a model ocean at least 2 cm deep. Try not to disturb the sand pile.

4 Use the yellow-colored oil to model an oil spill. Pour the oil onto the slope of the sand so that it runs off into the water.

step 4

Observe and Analyze
Write It Up

1. **RECORD** Write up your procedure for cleaning oil from sand and water. You may want to include a diagram.

2. **EVALUATE** What, if any, difficulties did you encounter in carrying out this experiment?

Conclude
Write It Up

1. **INTERPRET** How do your results compare with your hypothesis? Answer the problem statement.

2. **EVALUATE** Which materials were most useful for cleaning the water? Were they the same materials that were most useful for cleaning the sand?

3. **EVALUATE** Suppose you are trying to clean oil off of living things, such as a bird or seaweed. What process would you use?

4. **IDENTIFY LIMITS** In which ways did this demonstration fail to model a real oil spill?

INVESTIGATE Further

CHALLENGE Explain how the observations you made in this investigation might be useful in designing treatments for an actual oil spill.

5 Test the materials for effectiveness in removing the oil from the sand and the water.

6 Place the feather and the seaweed on the beach or in the water, where the oil is. Test materials for effectiveness in removing oil from the feather and seaweed.

7 Make a table in your **Science Notebook** like the one below. Record your observations on the effectiveness of each material.

8 Using your observations from step 7, design a process for removing oil from sand and water. This process may involve several materials and require a series of steps.

Cleaning Oil Spills

Problem What material or method is most effective in containing or cleaning up oil spills?

Hypothesis

Observations

	water	sand	feather	seaweed
paper towel				
cotton				

Chapter Review

the BIG idea

Humans and human population growth affect the environment.

 CONTENT REVIEW
CLASSZONE.COM

 KEY CONCEPTS SUMMARY

3.1 Human population growth presents challenges.

As the population continues to grow, there is a greater demand for natural resources. Cities and countries share many resources. Increasing populations put pressure on ecosystems.

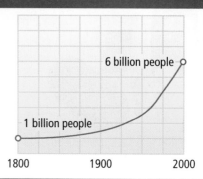

VOCABULARY
natural resource p. 84
population density p. 86

3.2 Human activities affect the environment.

Pollution and habitat loss make it difficult for plants and animals to survive. Without the necessary resources, biodiversity of living things decreases, and ecosystems become less stable.

Pollution

Habitat Loss

VOCABULARY
pollution p. 91
biodiversity p. 91

3.3 Humans are working to protect ecosystems.

Working at local and governmental levels, humans are helping ecosystems recover.

Laws protect endangered species.

Researchers are investigating alternative resources.

VOCABULARY
conservation p. 99
sustainable p. 102

Reviewing Vocabulary

Place each vocabulary term at the center of a description wheel diagram. Write some words describing it on the spokes.

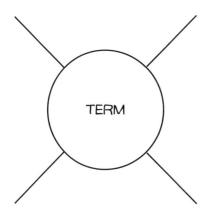

TERM

1. population density

2. natural resources

3. pollution

4. biodiversity

5. sustainable

6. conservation

Reviewing Key Concepts

Multiple Choice *Choose the letter of the best answer.*

7. In 2000, how big was Earth's human population?

   a. 1 billion   **c.** 6 billion

   b. 3 billion   **d.** 9 billion

8. Experts predict that by the year 2050, Earth's population will reach what number?

   a. 3 billion   **c.** 9 billion

   b. 6 billion   **d.** 12 billion

9. Which statement best explains why Earth's population has grown very rapidly in the last 100 years?

   a. On average, women are having children at an older age.

   b. People live longer because of improved health care and nutrition.

   c. Global warming has enabled farmers to grow more food.

   d. More land has been developed for housing.

10. Which of the four natural resources listed is likely to be used up the soonest?

    a. petroleum   **c.** sunlight

    b. water   **d.** wood

11. Which of the following is an example of increasing biodiversity?

    a. A forest is clear-cut for its wood, leaving land available for new uses.

    b. New species of animals and plants appear in a wildlife preserve.

    c. A new species of plant outcompetes all of the others around a lake.

    d. A cleared rain forest results in a change to a habitat.

12. Which represents a sustainable practice?

    a. conservation tillage and use of natural fertilizers

    b. more efficient removal of oil

    c. allowing unlimited use of water for higher fees

    d. restocking a lake with fish every year

13. What environmental problem does the Superfund Program address?

    a. habitat loss

    b. land development

    c. biodiversity

    d. pollution

Short Answer *Write a short answer to each question.*

14. List four ways increased population density affects ecosystem.

15. Three ways that humans dispose of waste are landfills, incineration, and wastewater treatment plants. List one advantage and one disadvantage of each.

16. Write a paragraph to describe how an increase in population density affects land development.

Thinking Critically

Use the graph to answer the next three questions.

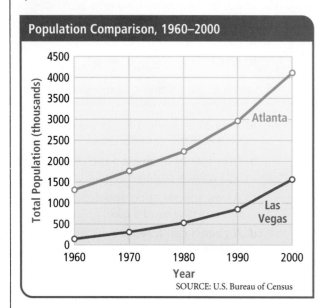

Population Comparison, 1960–2000

Total Population (thousands) vs. Year

Atlanta

Las Vegas

SOURCE: U.S. Bureau of Census

17. **COMPARE AND CONTRAST** Describe the population size and rate of growth for the cities of Atlanta and Las Vegas. Would you expect the population of Las Vegas to ever get bigger than that of Atlanta based on the data supplied?

18. **EVALUATE** Is it possible to determine from the data shown whether the population density is higher in Atlanta than Las Vegas? What other information would you need?

19. **CONNECT** Atlanta is located in a temperate-forest biome and Las Vegas is located in a desert biome. How might the characteristics of these biomes affect the carrying capacity of the human populations in these cities?

20. **PREDICT** If states in the U.S. used less water from the Colorado River, how would the depth of the river in Mexico be affected?

21. **COMPARE AND CONTRAST** Explain why trees are generally considered a renewable resource. Now describe circumstances under which they could be considered a nonrenewable resource.

22. **CLASSIFY** Sort the resources below into the correct categories:

Resource	Renewable	Nonrenewable
Water		
Coal		
Soil		
Wood		
Copper		
Petroleum		
Aluminum		
Sunlight		

23. **CALCULATE** A compact fluorescent bulb uses less energy than a regular bulb. It is estimated that a coal-burning power plant would release 72 kilograms more carbon dioxide (CO_2) a year to power one regular bulb than it would to power one fluorescent bulb. If you replace five regular bulbs with five compact bulbs, how much less CO_2 would be released in a 10-year period?

the **BIG** idea

24. **PROVIDE EXAMPLES** Look again at the photograph on pages 78–79. How would you change or add details to your answer to the question on the photograph?

25. **APPLY** You are on the town council of a community located on a small island. The council has decided to make a brochure for the town's citizens. In your brochure, describe the island habitat. Include information about natural resources, such as water and soil. List the plants and animals that live there. Establish four rules that the community should follow to preserve the local habitat.

UNIT PROJECTS

Evaluate the materials in your project folder. Finish your project and get ready to present it to your class.

Analyzing Data

Nowhere is the impact of human population growth more obvious than in the growth of urbanized areas. Buildings, parking lots, and roads are replacing forests, farmland, and wetlands. The table below shows the growth of urbanized areas around 10 cities in the United States during a 20-year period.

1. What patterns can you see in the way information is presented from the top of the table to the bottom?
   a. Cities are arranged alphabetically.
   b. Cities are arranged by growth in population over 20 years.
   c. Cities are arranged by the growth in land area over 20 years.
   d. Cities are arranged by size of urban area.

2. How would you describe the change in the land around Atlanta between 1970 and 1990?
   a. In 1990, more land was used for farming.
   b. The number of buildings and roads increased.
   c. The urbanized area decreased.
   d. Natural habitats for birds increased.

3. Which type of graph would be best for displaying the data in the table?
   a. a bar graph
   b. a circle graph
   c. a line graph
   d. a double bar graph

4. How many square kilometers around Philadelphia were affected by urbanization between 1970 and 1990?
   a. 1116 km^2
   b. 1166 km^2
   c. 1068 km^2
   d. 1020 km^2

Growth in land area, 1970-1990

Location	Growth in Land Area (km^2)
Atlanta, GA	1816
Houston, TX	1654
New York City-N.E. New Jersey	1402
Washington, D.C.-MD-VA	1166
Philadelphia, PA	1068
Los Angeles, CA	1020
Dallas-Fort Worth, TX	964
Tampa-St. Petersburg-Clearwater, FL	929
Phoenix, AZ	916
Minneapolis-Saint Paul, MN	885

SOURCE: U.S. Bureau of Census data on Urbanized Areas

Extended Response

5. Write a paragraph to describe how a rural area would change if the land were developed and the area became more urban. Use the vocabulary words listed below in your answer.

population density	biodiversity
renewable resources	nonrenewable resources

6. If you were an urban designer working for a small city that expected to expand rapidly in the next 10 years, what recommendations would you make to the city council on how the land should be developed?

UNIT E

Human Biology

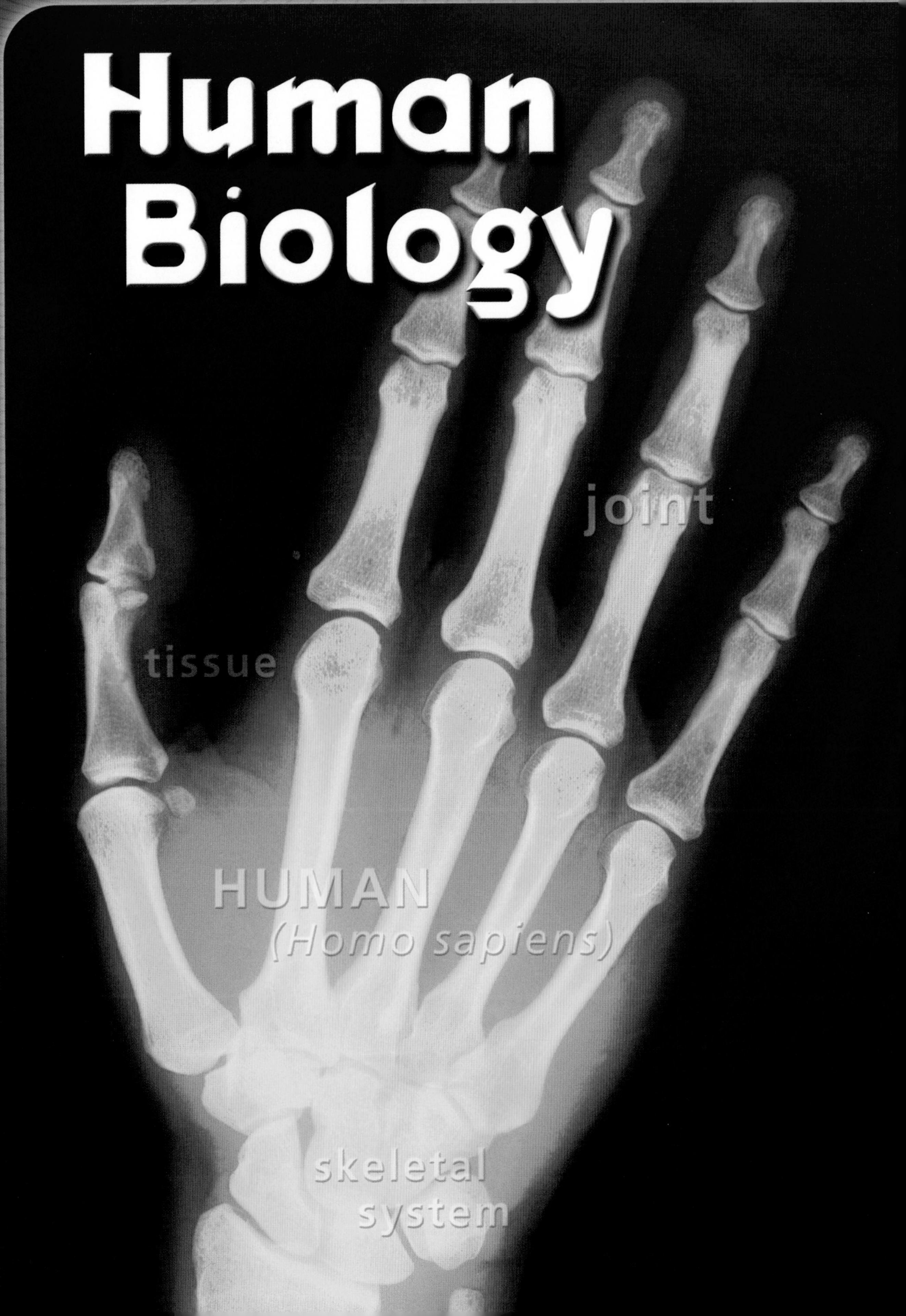
joint
tissue
HUMAN
(Homo sapiens)
skeletal
system

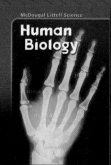

Human Biology
Contents Overview

E

Unit Features

1 Systems, Support, and Movement 6

the **BIG** idea

The human body is made up of
systems that work together to
perform necessary functions.

2 Absorption, Digestion, and Exchange 34

the **BIG** idea

Systems in the body obtain and process materials and remove waste.

3 Transport and Protection 62

the **BIG** idea

Systems function to transport materials and to defend and protect the
body.

4 Control and Reproduction 98

the **BIG** idea

The nervous and endocrine systems
allow the body to respond to internal and external conditions.

5 Growth, Development, and Health 130

the **BIG** idea

The body develops and maintains
itself over time.

Surprising Senses

SCIENTIFIC AMERICAN FRONTIERS

Learn more about how the brain and senses work. See the video "Sight of Touch."

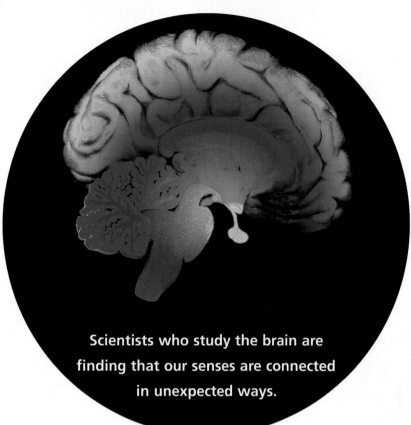

Scientists who study the brain are finding that our senses are connected in unexpected ways.

Senses and the Brain

One of the great mysteries still unsolved in science is what happens inside the brain. What is a thought? How is it formed? Where is it stored? How do our senses shape our thoughts? There are far more questions than answers. One way to approach questions about the brain is to study brain activity at times when the body is performing different functions.

Most advanced brain functions happen in the part of the brain called the cerebral cortex (suh-REE-bruhl KOR-tehks). That's where the brain interprets information from the senses. The cerebral cortex has many specialized areas. Each area controls one type of brain activity. Scientists are mapping these areas. At first, they studied people with brain injuries. A person with an injury to one area might not be able to speak. Someone with a different injury might have trouble seeing or hearing. Scientists mapped the areas in which damage seemed to cause each kind of problem.

Now scientists have even more tools to study the brain. One tool is called functional magnetic resonance imaging, or FMRI. Scientists put a person into a machine that uses radio waves to produce images of the person's brain. Scientists then ask the person to do specific activities, such as looking at pictures of faces or listening for specific sounds. The FMRI images show what parts of the person's brain are most active during each activity.

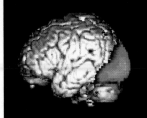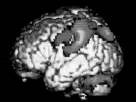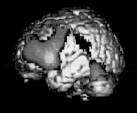

From left to right, these PET scans show brain activity during sight, hearing, Braille reading, and thought. Braille is a textured alphabet which is read by the fingers.

Double Duty

Using FMRI and other tools, scientists have identified the parts of the cerebral cortex that are responsible for each of the senses. The vision area is located at the back of the brain. The smell, taste, touch, and hearing areas are all close together in the middle part of the brain.

People don't usually use just one sense at a time. Scientists have found some unexpected connections. In one study, Marisa Taylor-Clarke poked the arms of some volunteers with either one or two pins. Then she asked them how many pins they felt. Taylor-Clarke found that people who looked at their arms before the test did better than those who didn't. FMRI showed that the part of their brains responsible for touch was also more active when they used their sense of sight.

These connections in the brain show up even when one sense doesn't work. Many people who have hearing impairments read lips to understand what other people are saying. Scientists using FMRI discovered that these people use the part of the brain normally used for hearing to help them understand what they see. This is even true for people who have never been able to hear.

Scrambled Senses

Some people have more connections between their senses than most people have. They may look at numbers and see colors, or associate smells with shapes. Some even get a taste in their mouths when they touch something. All these are examples of synesthesia (sin-uhs-THEE-zhuh). About 1 in 200 people have some kind of synesthesia.

SCIENTIFIC AMERICAN FRONTIERS

View the "Sight of Touch" segment of your Scientific American Frontiers video to learn about another example of connections between the senses.

IN THIS SCENE FROM THE VIDEO ▶ Michelle, a research subject, reads Braille with her fingers after wearing a blindfold for three days.

SEEING BY TOUCHING Many blind people read using Braille, a system of raised dots used to represent letters. Some, such as Braille proofreader Gil Busch, can read Braille at astonishing speeds. Scientist Alvaro Pascual-Leone used MRI to study

Gil's brain. The visual area of Gil's brain was active while he read Braille.

Gil has been blind since birth, so his brain has had a long time to adjust. Pascual-Leone wanted to know whether the brain could rewire itself in a shorter time. He asked volunteer Michelle Geronimo to wear a blindfold for a week. During that time, she learned to read Braille and experienced the world as a blind person does. At the end of the week, Pascual-Leone did an MRI of Michelle. The activity of her brain had changed too. Her visual center was active while she read Braille.

FMRI has made it possible for scientists to learn more about synesthesia. One group of scientists studied people who saw colors when they heard words. FMRI showed that the visual areas of their brains were active along with the hearing areas. (For most people, only the hearing area would be active.)

But why does synesthesia happen? Some scientists think that people with synesthesia have more connections between areas of their brains. Every person has extra connections when they're born, but most people lose many of them in childhood. Perhaps people with synesthesia keep theirs. Another theory suggests that their brains are "cross-wired," so information goes in unusual directions.

Some people with synesthesia see this colorful pattern when they hear a dog bark.

As scientists explore synesthesia and other connections between the senses, they learn more about how the parts of the brain work together. The human body is complex. And the brain along with the rest of the nervous system, has yet to be fully understood.

? UNANSWERED Questions

Scientists have learned a lot about how senses are connected. Their research leads to new questions.

- How does information move between different areas of the brain?
- How and why does the brain rewire itself?
- How does cross-wired sensing (synesthesia) happen?

UNIT PROJECTS

As you study this unit, work alone or in a group on one of the projects below.

Your Body System

Create one or several models showing important body systems.

- Draw the outline of your own body on a large piece of craft paper.
- Use reference materials to help you place everything correctly. Label each part.

The Brain: "Then and Now"

Compare and contrast past and present understandings of the brain.

- One understanding is that each part of the brain is responsible for different body functions. This understanding has changed over time.
- Research the history of this idea.
- Prepare diagrams of then and now. Share your presentation.

Design an Experiment

Design an experiment that will test one of the five senses. You should first identify a problem question you want to explore.

- The experiment may include a written introduction, materials procedure, and a plan for recording and presenting outcomes.
- Prepare a blank written experiment datasheet for your classmates to use.

CAREER CENTER
CLASSZONE.COM

Learn more about careers in neurobiology.

Systems, Support, and Movement

the **BIG** idea

The human body is made up of systems that work together to perform necessary functions.

Key Concepts

SECTION
1.1 The human body is complex.
Learn about the parts and systems in the human body.

SECTION
1.2 The skeletal system provides support and protection.
Learn how the skeletal system is organized and what it does.

SECTION
1.3 The muscular system makes movement possible.
Learn about the different types of muscles and how they work.

What systems make it possible for this racer to move so fast?

Internet Preview

CLASSZONE.COM

Chapter 1 online resources: Content Review, two Simulations, two Resource Centers, Math Tutorial, Test Practice

EXPLORE (the BIG idea)

How Many Bones Are in Your Hand?

Use a pencil to trace an outline of your hand on a piece of paper. Feel the bones in your fingers and the palm of your hand. At points where you can bend your fingers and hand, draw a circle. Each circle represents a joint where two bones meet. Draw lines to represent the bones in your hand.

Observe and Think How many bones did you find? How many joints?

How Does It Move?

The bones in your body are hard and stiff, yet they move smoothly. The point where two bones meet and move is called a joint. There are probably many objects in your home that have hard parts that move against each other: a joystick, a hinge, a pair of scissors.

Observe and Think What types of movement are possible when two hard objects are attached to each other? What parts of your body produce similar movements?

Internet Activity: The Human Body

Go to **ClassZone.com** to explore the different systems in the human body.

Observe and Think How are the systems in the middle of the body different from those that extend to the outer parts of the body?

NSTA
scilinks.org
SC*L*INKS

Tissues and Organs **Code: MDL044**

Getting Ready to Learn

◀ CONCEPT REVIEW

- The cell is the basic unit of living things.
- Systems are made up of interacting parts that share matter and energy.
- In multicellular organisms cells work together to support life.

◀ VOCABULARY REVIEW

See Glossary for definitions.

cell
system

CONTENT REVIEW
CLASSZONE.COM
Review concepts and vocabulary.

▶ TAKING NOTES

MAIN IDEA WEB

Write each new blue heading in a box. Then write notes in boxes around the center box that give important terms and details about that blue heading.

VOCABULARY STRATEGY

Write each new vocabulary term in the center of a **four square** diagram. Write notes in the squares around each term. Include a definition, some features, and some examples of the term. If possible, write some things that are not examples of the term.

See the Note-Taking Handbook on pages R45–R51.

SCIENCE NOTEBOOK

The cell is the basic unit of living things.

Tissues are groups of similar cells that function together.

The body has cells, tissues, and organs.

Organs are groups of tissues working together.

Definition	Features
Group of cells that work together	A level of organization in the body

TISSUE

Examples	Nonexamples
connective tissue, like bone	individual bone cells

The human body is complex.

 BEFORE, you learned

- All living things are made of cells
- All living things need energy
- Living things meet their needs through interactions with the environment

 NOW, you will learn

- About the organization of the human body
- About different types of tissues
- About the functions of organ systems

VOCABULARY

tissue p. 10
organ p. 11
organ system p. 12
homeostasis p. 12

THINK ABOUT

How is the human body like a city?

A city is made up of many parts that perform different functions. Buildings provide places to live and work. Transportation systems move people around. Electrical energy provides light and heat. Similarly, the human body is made of several systems. The skeletal system, like the framework of a building, provides support. The digestive system works with the respiratory system to provide energy and materials. What other systems in your body can you compare to a system in the city?

The body has cells, tissues, and organs.

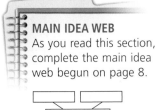

MAIN IDEA WEB
As you read this section, complete the main idea web begun on page 8.

Your body is made of many parts that work together as a system to help you grow and stay healthy. The simplest level of organization in your body is the cell. Next come tissues, then individual organs, and then systems that are made up of organs. The highest level of organization is the organism itself. You can think of the body as having five levels of organization: cells, tissues, organs, organ systems, and the organism. Although these levels seem separate from one another, they all work together.

 CHECK YOUR READING What are five levels of organization in your body?

How do the systems in your body interact?

PROCEDURE

1. Work with other classmates to make a list of everyday activities.

2. Discuss how your body responds to each task. Record your ideas.

3. Identify and count the systems in your body that you think are used to perform the task.

4. Have someone from your group make a chart of the different activities.

WHAT DO YOU THINK?

• Which systems did you name, and how did they work together to perform each activity?

• When you are asleep, what activities does your body perform?

CHALLENGE How could you make an experiment that would test your predictions?

SKILL FOCUS
Predicting

MATERIALS
large sheet of paper

TIME
20 minutes

Cells

The cell is the basic unit of life. Cells make up all living things. Some organisms, such as bacteria, are made of only a single cell. In these organisms the single cell performs all of the tasks necessary for survival. That individual cell captures and releases energy, uses materials, and grows. In more complex organisms, such as humans and many other animals and plants, cells are specialized. Specialized cells perform special jobs. A red blood cell, for example, carries oxygen and other nutrients from the lungs throughout the body.

Tissues

A **tissue** is a group of similar cells that work together to perform a particular function. Think of a tissue as a brick wall and the cells within it as the individual bricks. Taken together, the bricks form something larger and more functional. But just as the bricks need to be placed in a certain way to form the wall, cells must be organized in a tissue.

 CHECK YOUR READING How are cells related to tissues?

The human body contains several types of tissues. These tissues are classified into four main groups according to their function: epithelial tissue, nerve tissue, muscle tissue, and connective tissue.

Epithelial (EHP-uh-THEE-lee-uhl) tissue functions as a boundary. It covers all of the inner and outer surfaces of your body. Each of your internal organs is covered with a layer of epithelial tissue. Another type of tissue, nerve tissue, functions as a messaging system. Cells in nerve tissue carry electrical impulses between your brain and the various parts of your body in response to changing conditions.

Muscle tissue functions in movement. Movement results when muscle cells contract, or shorten, and then relax. In some cases, such as throwing a ball, you control the movement. In other cases, such as the beating of your heart, the movement occurs without conscious control. Connective tissue functions to hold parts of the body together, providing support, protection, strength, padding, and insulation. Tendons and ligaments are connective tissues that hold bones and muscles together. Bone itself is another connective tissue. It supports and protects the soft parts of your body.

Organs

Groups of different tissues make up organs. An **organ** is a structure that is made up of two or more types of tissue that work together to carry out a function in the body. For example, the structures that carry blood around your body contain all four types of tissues. As in cells and tissues, the structure of an organ relates to its function. The stomach's bag-shaped structure and strong muscular walls make it suited for breaking down food. The walls of the heart are also muscular, allowing it to function as a pump.

Levels of Organization

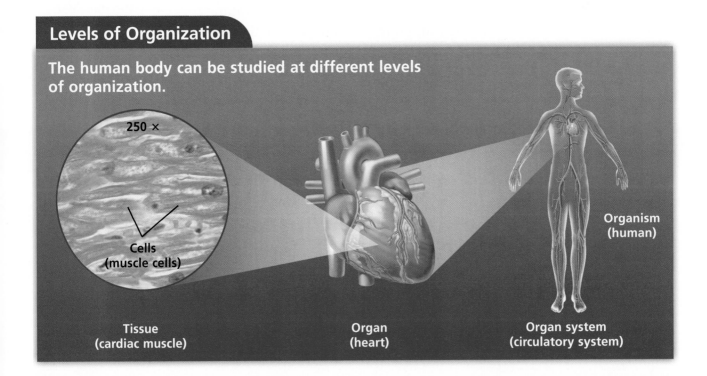

The human body can be studied at different levels of organization.

250 ×

Cells
(muscle cells)

Tissue
(cardiac muscle)

Organ
(heart)

Organ system
(circulatory system)

Organism
(human)

Organ Systems

An **organ system** is a group of organs that together perform a function that helps the body meet its needs for energy and materials. For example, your stomach, mouth, throat, large and small intestines, liver, and pancreas are all part of the organ system called the digestive system. The body is made up of many organ systems. In this unit, you will read about these systems. They include the skeletal, muscular, respiratory, digestive, urinary, circulatory, immune, nervous, and reproductive systems. Together, these systems allow the human organism to grow, reproduce, and maintain life.

The body's systems interact with one another.

READING TiP

VOCABULARY
The word *homeostasis* contains two word roots. *Homeo* comes from a root meaning "same." *Stasis* comes from a root meaning "stand still" or "stay."

The ability of your body to maintain internal conditions is called **homeostasis** (HOH-mee-oh-STAY-sihs). Your body is constantly regulating such things as your body temperature, the amount of sugar in your blood, even your posture. The processes that take place in your body occur within a particular set of conditions.

The body's many levels of organization, from cells to organ systems, work constantly to maintain the balance needed for the survival of the organism. For example, on a hot day, you may sweat. Sweating keeps the temperature inside your body constant, even though the temperature of your surroundings changes.

INFER This student is drinking water after exercising. Why is it important to drink fluids after you sweat?

1.1 Review

KEY CONCEPTS

1. Draw a diagram that shows the relationship among cells, tissues, organs, and organ systems.

2. Make a chart of the four basic tissue groups that includes names, functions, and examples.

3. Identify three functions performed by organ systems.

CRITICAL THINKING

4. **Apply** How does drinking water after you sweat help maintain homeostasis?

5. **Compare and Contrast** Compare and contrast the four basic tissue groups. How would all four types of tissue be involved in a simple activity, like raising your hand?

○ CHALLENGE

6. **Apply** Describe an object, such as a car, that can be used as a model of the human body. Explain how the parts of the model relate to the body.

Think SCIENCE

What Does the Body Need to Survive?

In 1914, Ernest Shackleton and 27 men set sail for Antarctica. Their goal was to cross the continent by foot and sled. The crew never set foot on Antarctica. Instead, the winter sea froze around their ship, crushing it until it sank. They were stranded on floating ice, over 100 miles from land. How long could they survive? How would their bodies respond? What would they need to stay alive?

You can make inferences in answer to any of these questions. First you need to recall what you know. Then you need new evidence. What was available to the explorers? Did they save supplies from their ship? What resources existed in the environment?

▶ Prior Knowledge

- The human body needs air, water, and food.
- The human body needs to maintain its temperature. The body can be harmed if it loses too much heat.

▶ Observations

Several of Shackleton's explorers kept diaries. From the diaries we know that the following:

- The crew hunted seals and penguins for fresh meat.
- The temperature was usually below freezing.
- Tents and overturned lifeboats sheltered the crew from the wind.
- Their clothes were made of thick fabric and animal skins and furs.
- They melted snow and ice in order to have fresh water.

▶ Make Inferences

On Your Own Describe how the explorers met each of the needs of the human body.

As a Group How long do you think these 28 men could have survived these conditions? Use evidence and inferences in your answer.

CHALLENGE How might survival needs differ for sailors shipwrecked in the tropics compared to the Antarctic?

RESOURCE CENTER
CLASSZONE.COM

Learn more about Shackleton's expedition.

The skeletal system provides support and protection.

BEFORE, you learned

- The body is made of cells, tissues, organs, and systems
- Cells, tissues, organs, and organ systems work together
- Systems in the body interact

NOW, you will learn

- About different types of bone tissue
- How the human skeleton is organized
- How joints allow movement

VOCABULARY

skeletal system p. 14
compact bone p. 15
spongy bone p. 15
axial skeleton p. 16
appendicular skeleton p. 16

EXPLORE Levers

How can a bone act as a lever?

PROCEDURE

MATERIALS
sports bag

1. A lever is a stiff rod that pivots about a fixed point. Hold the bag in your hand and keep your arm straight, like a lever. Move the bag up and down.

2. Move the handles of the bag over your elbow. Again hold your arm straight and move the bag up and down.

3. Now move the bag to the top of your arm and repeat the procedure.

WHAT DO YOU THINK?

- At which position is it easiest to move the bag?
- At which position does the bag move the farthest?
- How does the position of a load affect the action of a lever?

Bones are living tissue.

MAIN IDEA WEB
Make a web of the important terms and details about the main idea: *Bones are living tissue.*

Every movement of the human body is possible because of the interaction of muscles with the **skeletal system.** Made up of a strong connective tissue called bone, the skeletal system serves as the anchor for all of the body's movement, provides support, and protects soft organs inside the body. Bones can be classified as long bones, short bones, irregular bones, and flat bones. Long bones are found in the arms and legs. Short bones are found in the feet and hands. Irregular bones are found in the spine. Flat bones are found in the ribs and skull.

You might think that bones are completely solid and made up of dead tissue. They actually are made of both hard and soft materials.

Like your heart or skin, bones are living tissue. Bones are not completely solid, either; they have spaces inside. The spaces allow blood cells carrying nutrients to travel throughout the bones. Because bones have spaces, they weigh much less than they would if they were solid.

RESOURCE CENTER
CLASSZONE.COM

Explore the skeletal system.

Two Types of Bone Tissue

Every bone is made of two types of bone tissue: compact bone and spongy bone. The hard compact bone surrounds the soft spongy bone. Each individual bone cell lies within a bony web. This web is made up mostly of the mineral calcium.

Compact Bone Surrounding the spongy, inner layer of the bone is a hard layer called **compact bone.** Compact bone functions as the basic supportive tissue of the body, the part of the body you call the skeleton. The outer layer of compact bone is very hard and tough. It covers the outside of most bones.

Spongy Bone Inside the bone, the calcium network is less dense. This tissue is called **spongy bone.** Spongy bone is strong but lightweight. It makes up most of the short and the irregular bones found in your body. It also makes up the ends of long bones.

Marrow and Blood Cells

Within the spongy bone tissue is marrow, the part of the bone that produces red blood cells. The new red blood cells travel from the marrow into the blood vessels that run throughout the bone. The blood cells bring nutrients to the bone cells and carry waste materials away.

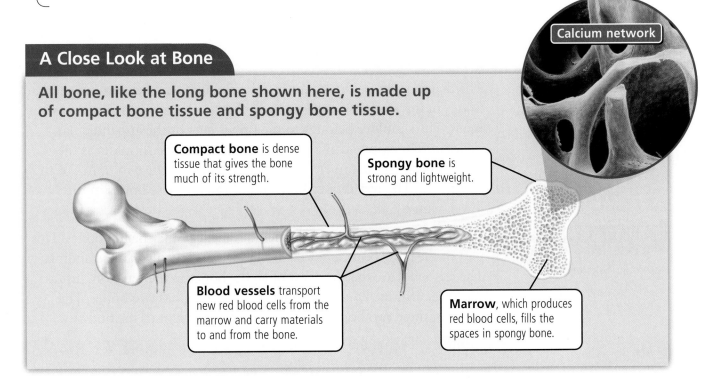

A Close Look at Bone

All bone, like the long bone shown here, is made up of compact bone tissue and spongy bone tissue.

Compact bone is dense tissue that gives the bone much of its strength.

Spongy bone is strong and lightweight.

Calcium network

Blood vessels transport new red blood cells from the marrow and carry materials to and from the bone.

Marrow, which produces red blood cells, fills the spaces in spongy bone.

The skeleton is the body's framework.

Like the frame of a building, the skeleton provides the body's shape. The skeleton also works with other systems to allow movement. Scientists have identified two main divisions in the skeleton. These are the axial (AK-see-uhl) skeleton, which is the central part of the skeleton, and the appendicular (AP-uhn-DIHK-yuh-luhr) skeleton. Bones in the appendicular skeleton are attached to the axial skeleton. The diagram on page 17 labels some of the important bones in your skeleton.

The Axial Skeleton

Imagine a line straight down your back. You can think of that line as an axis. Sitting, standing, and twisting are some of the motions that turn around the axis. The **axial skeleton** is the part of the skeleton that forms the axis. It provides support and protection. In the diagram, parts of the axial skeleton are colored in red.

The axial skeleton includes the skull, or the cranium (KRAY-nee-uhm). The major function of the cranium is protection of the brain. Most of the bones in the cranium do not move. The skull connects to the spinal column in a way that allows the head to move up and down as well as right to left.

Your spinal column makes up the main portion of the axial skeleton. The spinal column is made up of many bones called vertebrae. The many bones allow flexibility. If you run your finger along your back you will feel the vertebrae. Another set of bones belonging to the axial skeleton are the rib bones. The ribs function to protect the soft internal organs, such as the heart and lungs.

The Appendicular Skeleton

The diagram shows the bones in the appendicular skeleton in yellow. Bones in the **appendicular skeleton** function mainly to allow movement. The shoulder belongs to the upper part of the appendicular skeleton. The upper arm bone that connects to the shoulder is the longest bone in the upper body. It connects with the two bones of the lower arm. The wristbone is the end of one of these bones in the lower arm.

The lower part of the body includes the legs and the hip bones. This part of the body bears all of the body's weight when you are standing. The leg bones are the strongest of all the bones in the skeleton. Just as the lower arm includes two bones, the lower leg has two bones. The larger of these two bones carries most of the weight of the body.

CHECK YOUR READING How are the axial and appendicular skeletons alike? How are they different?

The Skeletal System

The skeletal system interacts with other body systems to allow this soccer player to stand, run, and kick.

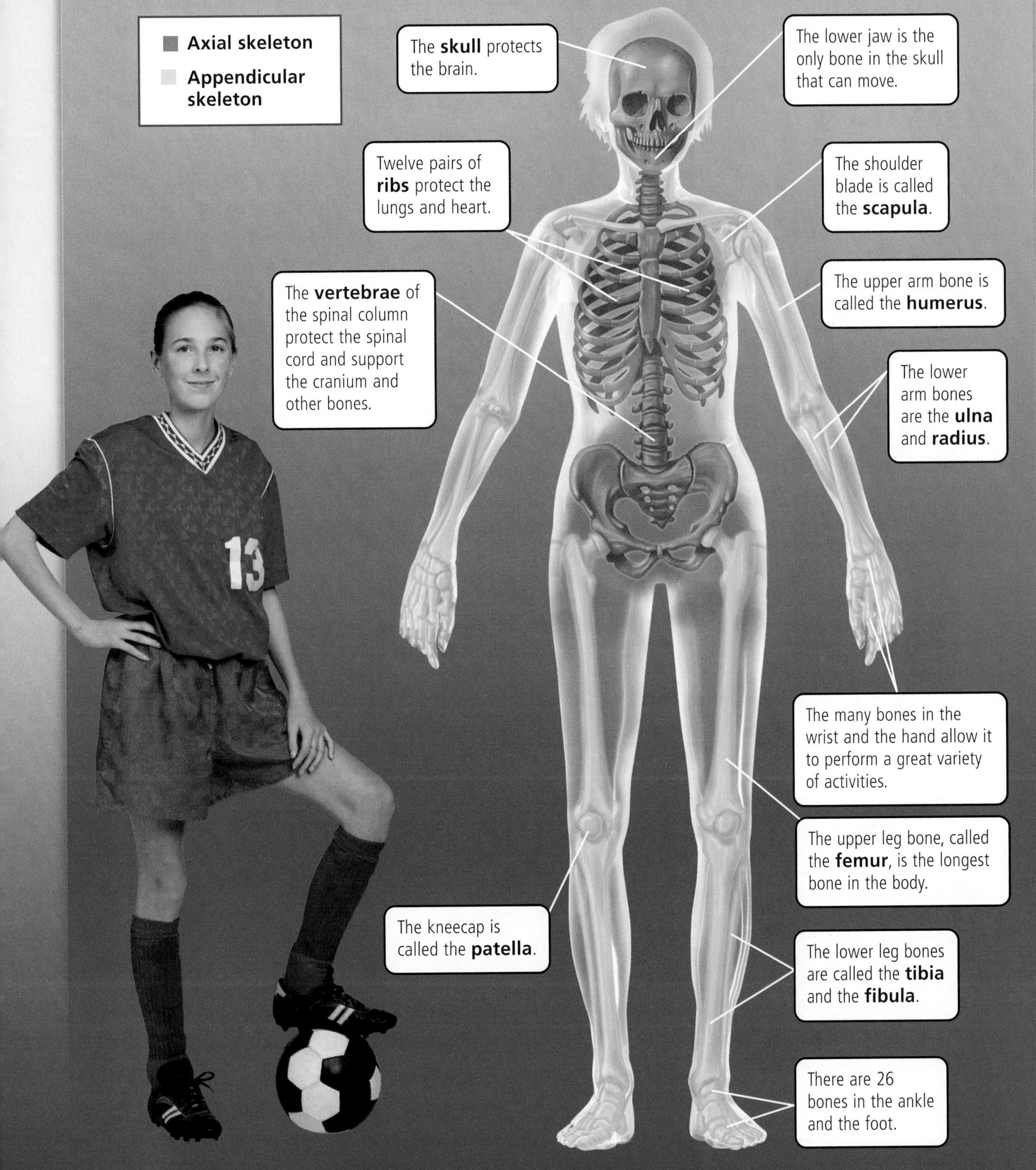

■ Axial skeleton

□ Appendicular skeleton

The **skull** protects the brain.

The lower jaw is the only bone in the skull that can move.

Twelve pairs of **ribs** protect the lungs and heart.

The shoulder blade is called the **scapula**.

The **vertebrae** of the spinal column protect the spinal cord and support the cranium and other bones.

The upper arm bone is called the **humerus**.

The lower arm bones are the **ulna** and **radius**.

The many bones in the wrist and the hand allow it to perform a great variety of activities.

The upper leg bone, called the **femur**, is the longest bone in the body.

The kneecap is called the **patella**.

The lower leg bones are called the **tibia** and the **fibula**.

There are 26 bones in the ankle and the foot.

READING VISUALS The word *appendicular* has the same root as the word *append,* which means to attach. How do you think this word applies to the appendicular skeleton?

The skeleton changes as the body develops and ages.

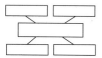

MAIN IDEA WEB Make a web of the important terms and details about the main idea: *The skeleton changes as the body develops and ages.*

You will remember that bones are living tissue. During infancy and childhood, bones grow as the rest of the body grows. Bones become harder as they stop growing. In adulthood, bones continue to change.

Infancy The skull of a newborn is made up of several bones that have spaces between them. As the brain grows, the skull also grows. During the growth of the skull, the spaces between the bones close.

Childhood Bone growth occurs at areas called growth plates. These growth plates are made of cartilage, a flexible bone tissue. The length and shape of bones is determined by growth plates. Long bones grow at the ends of the bone surrounding growth plates.

Adolescence Toward the end of adolescence (AD-uhl-EHS-uhns) bones stop growing. The growth plate is the last portion of the bone to become hard. Once growth plates become hard, arms and legs stop growing.

Adulthood Even after bones stop growing, they go through cycles in which old bone is broken down and new bone is formed. As people age, more bone is broken down than is formed. This can lead to a decrease in bone mass, which causes a decrease in bone density. The strength of bones depends upon their density. As people age, their bone density may decrease. Bones that are less dense may break more easily. Many doctors recommend that adults over a certain age get regular bone density tests.

REMINDER

Density is the ratio of mass over volume. Bone density is a measure of the mass of a bone divided by the bone's volume.

Test of Bone Density

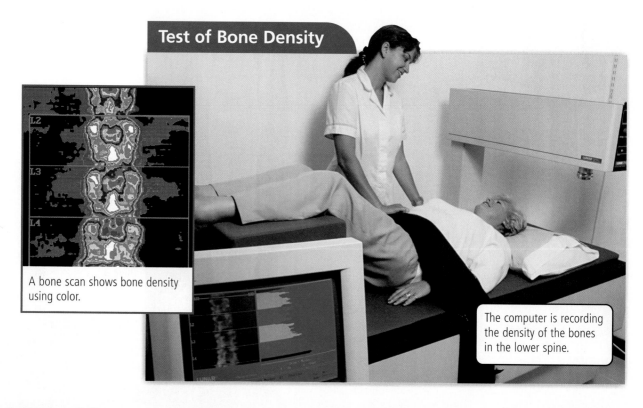

A bone scan shows bone density using color.

The computer is recording the density of the bones in the lower spine.

Joints connect parts of the skeletal system.

A joint is a place at which two parts of the skeletal system meet. There are three types of joints: immovable, slightly movable, and freely movable.

Immovable and Slightly Movable Joints An immovable joint locks bones together like puzzle pieces. The bones of your skull are connected by immovable joints. Slightly movable joints are able to flex slightly. Your ribs are connected to your sternum by slightly movable joints.

Freely Movable Joints Freely movable joints allow your body to bend and to move. Tissues called ligaments hold the bones together at movable joints. Other structures inside the joint cushion the bones and keep them from rubbing together. The entire joint also is surrounded by connective tissue.

Movable joints can be classified by the type of movement they produce. Think about the movement of your arm when you eat an apple. Your arm moves up, then down, changing the angle between your upper and lower arms. This is angular movement. The joint that produces this movement is called a hinge joint.

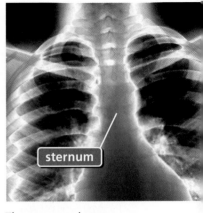

sternum

The sternum is an example of a slightly movable joint.

INVESTIGATE Movable Joints

How can you move at joints?

PROCEDURE

1. Perform several activities that involve your joints. Twist at the waist. Bend from your waist to one side. Reach into the air with one arm. Open and close your mouth. Push a book across your desk. Lift the book.

2. Record each activity and write a note describing the motion that you feel at each joint.

3. Try to see how many different ways you can move at joints.

WHAT DO YOU THINK?

- How was the motion you felt similar for each activity? How was it different?

- Based on your observations, identify two or more ways that joints move.

CHALLENGE Draw a diagram showing how you think each joint moves. How might you classify different types of joints based upon the way they move?

SKILL FOCUS
Observing

MATERIALS
book

TIME
20 minutes

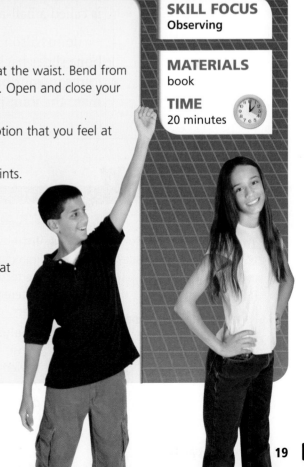

Movable Joints

The joints in the elbow and hip allow different types of movement.

Angular movement (elbow)

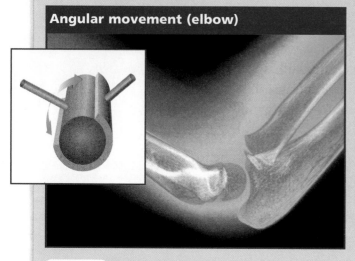

Rotational movement (hip)

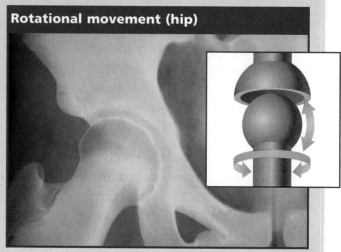

READING VISUALS **INFER** How do the structure and shape of each joint allow bones to move?

Your arm can also rotate from side to side, as it does when you turn a doorknob. Rotational movement like this is produced by a pivot joint in the elbow. You can also rotate your arm in a circle, like the motion of a softball pitcher winding up and releasing a ball. The joint in the shoulder that produces this type of rotational movement is called a ball-and-socket joint.

Joints also produce gliding movement. All joints glide, that is, one bone slides back and forth across another. In some cases, as with the joints in your backbone, a small gliding movement is the only movement the joint produces.

1.2 Review

KEY CONCEPTS

1. What are the functions of the two types of bone tissue?

2. What are the main divisions of the human skeleton?

3. Name three types of movement produced by movable joints and give an example of each.

CRITICAL THINKING

4. **Infer** What function do immovable joints in the skull perform? Think about the different stages of development in the human body.

5. **Analyze** Which type of movable joint allows the most movement? How does the joint's shape and structure contribute to this?

○ CHALLENGE

6. **Classify** The joints in your hand and wrist produce three different types of movement. Using your own wrist, classify the joint movement of the fingers, palm, and wrist. Support your answer.

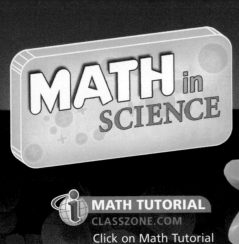

MATH in SCIENCE

MATH TUTORIAL
CLASSZONE.COM

Click on Math Tutorial for more help with comparing rates.

Rates of Production

Where do red blood cells come from? They are produced inside bone marrow at the center of long bones. About 200 billion red blood cells per day are produced by a healthy adult. When a person produces too few red blood cells, a condition called anemia may occur. Doctors study rates of blood cell production to diagnose and treat anemia.

A rate is a ratio that compares two quantities of different units. The number of cells produced per 24 hours is an example of a rate.

Example

A healthy adult produces red blood cells at a rate greater than 166 billion cells / 24 hours. Suppose a man's body produces 8 billion red blood cells / 1 hour. Would he be considered anemic?

(1) Write the two rates as fractions.

$$\frac{166}{24} \qquad \frac{8}{1}$$

(2) Simplify the fractions, so that the denominators are both 1. To simplify, divide the numerator by the denominator.

$$\frac{6.9}{1} \qquad \frac{8}{1}$$

(3) Compare the two whole numbers. Is the first number $<$, $>$, or $=$ to the second number?

$$6.9 \quad < \quad 8$$

ANSWER The rate is greater than 6.9. The patient is not anemic.

Compare the following rates to see if they indicate that a person is anemic or normal.

1. For women, a normal rate is about 178 billion red blood cells per day. A certain woman produces 6 billion red blood cells per hour. Is her rate low or healthy?

2. Suppose a different woman produces 150 million (not billion) red blood cells per minute. How does that rate compare to 178 billion cells per day? Is it $<$, $>$, or $=$ to it?

3. Suppose a certain man is producing 135 million red blood cells per minute. Is that rate low or healthy?

CHALLENGE In the example above of a man producing 166 billion cells per day, calculate the percentage by which the rate would need to increase to bring it up to the normal count.

1.3 The muscular system makes movement possible.

 BEFORE, you learned

- There are different types of bone tissue
- The human skeleton has two separate divisions
- Joints function in several different ways

 NOW, you will learn

- About the functions of muscles
- About the different types of muscles and how they work
- How muscles grow and heal

VOCABULARY

muscular system p. 23
skeletal muscle p. 24
voluntary muscle p. 24
smooth muscle p. 24
involuntary muscle p. 24
cardiac muscle p. 24

EXPLORE Muscles

How do muscles change as you move?

PROCEDURE

1. Sit on a chair with your feet on the floor.

2. Place your hand around your leg. Straighten one leg as shown in the photograph.

3. Repeat step 2 several times.

WHAT DO YOU THINK?

- How did your muscles change during the activity?
- Record your observations.
- What questions do you have about the muscular system?

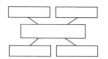

MAIN IDEA WEB
Make a web for the main idea: *Muscles perform important functions.*

Muscles perform important functions.

Every movement of your body—from the beating of your heart to the movement of food down your throat, to the blinking of your eyes— occurs because of muscles. Some movements are under your control, and other movements seem to happen automatically. However, muscles do more than produce movement. They perform other functions as well. Keeping body temperature stable and maintaining posture are two additional functions of muscles.

 What are three functions that muscles perform?

Movement

The **muscular system** works with the skeletal system to allow movement. Like all muscles, the muscles that produce movement are made up of individual cells called muscle fibers. These fibers contract and relax.

Most of the muscles involved in moving the body work in pairs. As they contract, muscles shorten, pulling against bones. It may surprise you to know that muscles do not push. Rather, a muscle on one side of a bone pulls in one direction, while another muscle relaxes. Muscles are attached to bones by stretchy connective tissue.

RESOURCE CENTER
CLASSZONE.COM

Discover more about muscles.

Maintaining Body Temperature

Earlier you read that processes within the body require certain conditions, such as temperature and the right amount of water and other materials. The balance of conditions is called homeostasis. One of the functions of the muscular system is related to homeostasis. Muscles function to maintain body temperature.

When muscles contract, they release heat. Without this heat from muscle contraction, the body could not maintain its normal temperature. You may have observed the way your muscles affect your body temperature when you shiver. The quick muscle contractions that occur when you shiver release heat and raise your body temperature.

 CHECK YOUR READING How do muscles help maintain homeostasis?

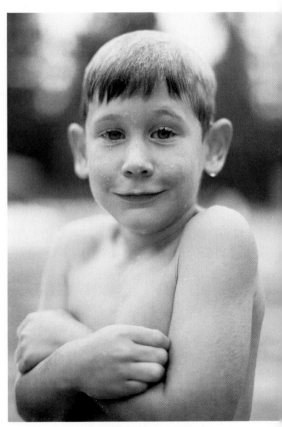

Muscles contract during shivering, raising body temperature.

Maintaining Posture

Have you ever noticed that you stand up straight without thinking about it, even though gravity is pulling your body down? Most muscles in your body are always a little bit contracted. This tension, or muscle tone, is present even when you are sleeping. The muscles that maintain posture relax completely only when you are unconscious.

Try standing on the balls of your feet for a few moments, or on one leg. When you are trying to balance or hold one position for any length of time, you can feel different muscles contracting and relaxing. Your muscles make constant adjustments to keep you sitting or standing upright. You don't have to think about these tiny adjustments; they happen automatically.

Your body has different types of muscle.

Your body has three types of muscle. All three types of muscle tissue share certain characteristics. For example, each type of muscle contracts and relaxes. Yet all three muscle types have different functions, and different types of muscle are found in different locations.

Skeletal Muscle

The muscles that are attached to your skeleton are called **skeletal muscles.** Skeletal muscle performs voluntary movement—that is, movement that you choose to make. Because they are involved in voluntary movement, skeletal muscles are also called **voluntary muscles.**

READING TIP

The root of the word *voluntary* comes from the Latin root *vol-*, meaning "wish." In the word *involuntary* the prefix *in-* suggests the meaning "unwished for." *Involuntary movement* means movement you can't control.

Skeletal muscle, like all muscle, is made of long fibers. The fibers are made up of many smaller bundles, as a piece of yarn is made up of strands of wool. One type of bundle allows your muscles to move slowly. Those muscles are called slow-twitch muscles. Another type of bundle allows your muscles to move quickly. These are called fast-twitch muscles. If you were a sprinter, you would want to develop your fast-twitch muscles. If you were a long distance runner, you would develop your slow-twitch muscles.

 CHECK YOUR READING What does it mean that skeletal muscles are voluntary muscles?

Smooth Muscle

VOCABULARY
Remember to add four squares for *involuntary muscles* and *voluntary muscles* to your notebook. Note differences in the two diagrams.

Smooth muscle is found inside some organs, such as the intestines and the stomach. Smooth muscles perform automatic movement and are called **involuntary muscles.** In other words, smooth muscles work without your knowing it. You have no control over their movement. For example, smooth muscles line your stomach wall and push food through your digestive system. Smooth muscle fibers are not as long as skeletal muscle fibers. Also, unlike skeletal muscles, smooth muscles are not fast-twitch. Smooth muscles contract slowly.

Cardiac Muscle

Your heart is made of **cardiac muscle.** Like smooth muscle, cardiac muscle moves without conscious control. Each cardiac muscle cell has a branched shape. The cells of the heart connect in a chain. These chains form webs of layered tissue that allow cardiac cells to contract together and make the heart beat. Just like the smooth muscle cells, the cardiac muscle cells contract slowly.

 CHECK YOUR READING Compare and contrast the three types of muscle described: skeletal, smooth, and cardiac.

Muscle Tissue

The marchers in this band are using all three different types of muscle tissue.

250×

Cardiac muscle allows the hearts of the band members to pump blood as they march to the beat of the music.

150×

Smooth muscle in the lungs allows the band members to breathe as they play their instruments.

360×

Skeletal muscle moves the legs of these marchers.

READING VISUALS Which movements of these band members are voluntary, and which are involuntary?

Skeletal muscles and tendons allow bones to move.

Skeletal muscles are attached to your bones by strong tissues called tendons. The tendons on the end of the muscle attach firmly to the bone. As the fibers in a muscle contract, they shorten and pull the tendon. The tendon, in turn, pulls the bone and makes it move.

You can feel your muscles moving your bones. Place your left arm, stretched out flat, in front of you on a table. Place the fingers of your right hand just above your left elbow. Bend your elbow and raise and lower your left arm. You are contracting your biceps. Can you feel the muscle pull on the tendon?

The dancers in the photograph are using many sets of muscles. The diagrams show how muscles and tendons work together to move bones. Muscles are shown in red. Notice how each muscle crosses a joint. Most skeletal muscles do. One end of the muscle attaches to one bone, crosses a joint, then attaches to a second bone. As the muscle contracts, it pulls on both bones. This pulling produces movement—in the case of these dancers, very exciting movement.

tendon

muscle relaxes

muscle contracts

bones

tendons

Skeletal muscles contract by shortening and pulling the tendon.

tendon

muscle relaxes

muscle relaxes

bones

tendons

Muscle fibers can return to their original length after being shortened.

Muscles grow and heal.

Developing Muscles An infant's muscles cannot do very much. A baby cannot lift its head, because the neck muscles are not strong enough to support it. For the first few months of life, a baby needs extra support, until the neck muscles grow strong and can hold up the baby's head.

The rest of the skeletal muscles also have to develop and strengthen. During infancy and childhood and into adolescence, humans develop muscular coordination and become more graceful in their movements. Coordination reaches its natural peak in adolescence but can be further improved by additional training.

Exercise and Muscles When you exercise regularly, your muscles get bigger. Muscles increase in size with exercise, because their cells reproduce more rapidly in response to the increased activity. Exercise also stimulates growth of individual muscle cells, making them larger.

Stretching your muscles before exercise helps prevent injury.

You may have experienced sore muscles during or after exercising. During exercise, chemicals can build up in the muscles and make them cramp or ache. The muscle soreness you feel a day or so after exercise is caused by damage to the muscle fibers. The muscle fibers have been overstretched or torn. Such injuries take time to heal, because the body must remove injured cells, and new ones must form.

1.3 Review

KEY CONCEPTS

1. What are the three main functions of the muscular system?
2. Make a rough outline of a human body and label places where you could find each of the three types of muscles.
3. Explain why you may be sore after exercise.

CRITICAL THINKING

4. **Apply** You are exercising and you begin to feel hot. Explain what is happening in your muscles.
5. **Analyze** Describe what happens in your neck muscles when you nod your head.

○ CHALLENGE

6. **Infer** The digestive system breaks down food and transports materials. How are the short length and slow movement of smooth muscle tissues in the stomach and intestines related to the functions of these organs?

CHAPTER INVESTIGATION

A Closer Look at Muscles

OVERVIEW AND PURPOSE You use the muscles in your body to do a variety of things. Walking, talking, reading the words on this page, and scratching your head are all actions that require muscles. How do your muscles interact with your bones? In this investigation you will

- examine chicken wings to see how the muscles and the bones interact
- compare the movement of the chicken wing with the movement of your own bones and muscles

▶ Problem

Write It Up

What are some characteristics of muscles?

▶ Hypothesize

Write It Up

Write a hypothesis to propose how muscles interact with bones. Your hypothesis should take the form of an "If . . . , then . . . , because . . ." statement.

▶ Procedure

MATERIALS
- uncooked chicken wing and leg (soaked in bleach)
- paper towels
- dissection tray
- scissors

1. Make a data table like the one shown on the sample notebook page. Put on your protective gloves. Be sure you are wearing gloves whenever you touch the chicken.

2. Obtain a chicken wing from your teacher. Rinse it in water and pat dry with a paper towel. Place it in the tray.

3. Extend the wing. In your notebook, draw a diagram of the extended wing. Be sure to include any visible external structures. Label the following on your diagram: lower limb, upper joint, and the wing tip.

step 3

4. Use scissors to remove the skin. Use caution so that you cut only through the skin. Peel back the skin and any fat so you can examine the muscles.

step 4

5. The muscles are the pink tissues that extend from one end of the bone to the other. Locate these in the upper wing and observe the way they move when you move the wing. Record your observations in your notebook.

6. Repeat this procedure for the muscles in the lower wing. In your notebook, draw a diagram of the muscles in the chicken wing.

7. There are also tendons in the chicken wing. These are the shiny white tissues at the end of the muscles. Add the tendons to your diagram.

8. Dispose of the chicken wing and parts according to your teacher's instructions. **Be sure to wash your hands well.**

▶ Observe and Analyze
Write It Up

1. **RECORD** Write a brief description of how the bones and muscles work together to allow movement.

2. **EVALUATE** What difficulties, if any, did you encounter in carrying out this experiment?

▶ Conclude
Write It Up

1. **INTERPRET** How does the chicken wing move when you bend it at the joint?

2. **OBSERVE** What happens when you pull on one of the wing muscles?

3. **COMPARE** Using your diagram of the chicken wing as an example, locate the same muscle groups in your own arm. How do they react when you bend your elbow?

4. **APPLY** What role do the tendons play in the movement of the muscles or bones?

▶ INVESTIGATE Further

CHALLENGE Using scissors, carefully remove the muscles and the tendons from the bones. Next find the ligaments, which are located between the bones. Add these to your diagram. Describe how you think ligaments function.

A Closer Look at Muscles

Problem What are some characteristics of muscles?

Table 1. Observations

Draw your diagrams	Write your observations
Extended wing	Muscles in the upper wing
Muscles in the wing	Muscles in the lower wing

Chapter Review

the BIG idea

The human body is made up of systems that work together to perform necessary functions.

CONTENT REVIEW
CLASSZONE.COM

KEY CONCEPTS SUMMARY

 1.1 The human body is complex.

You can think of the body as having five levels of organization: cells, tissues, organs, organ systems, and the whole organism itself. The different systems of the human body work together to maintain homeostasis.

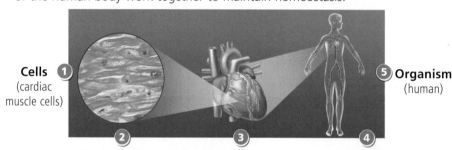

Cells (1) (cardiac muscle cells)

(5) **Organism** (human)

Tissue (2) (cardiac muscle)   **Organ** (3) (heart)   **Organ system** (4) (circulatory system)

VOCABULARY
tissue p. 12
organ p. 12
organ system p. 12
homeostasis p. 12

1.2 The skeletal system provides support and protection.

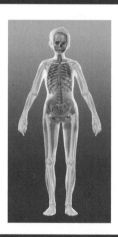

Bones are living tissue. The skeleton is the body's framework and has two main divisions, the **axial skeleton** and the **appendicular skeleton**. Bones come together at joints.

VOCABULARY
skeletal system p. 14
compact bone p. 14
spongy bone p. 15
axial skeleton p. 15
appendicular skeleton
  p. 16

1.3 The muscular system makes movement possible.

Types of muscle	Function
skeletal muscle, voluntary	moves bones, maintains posture, maintains body temperature
smooth muscle, involuntary	moves internal organs, such as the intestines
cardiac muscle, involuntary	pumps blood throughout the body

VOCABULARY
muscular system p. 24
skeletal muscle p. 24
voluntary muscle 24
smooth muscle p. 24
involuntary muscle
  p. 24
cardiac muscle p. 24

Reviewing Vocabulary

In one or two sentences describe how the vocabulary terms in each of the following pairs of words are related. Underline each vocabulary term in your answer.

1. cells, tissues

2. organs, organ systems

3. axial skeleton, appendicular skeleton

4. skeletal muscle, voluntary muscle

5. smooth muscle, involuntary muscle

6. compact bone, spongy bone

Reviewing Key Concepts

Multiple Choice *Choose the letter of the best answer.*

7. Which type of tissue carries electrical impulses from your brain?
   a. epithelial tissue
   b. muscle tissue
   c. nerve tissue
   d connective tissue

8. Connective tissue functions to provide
   a. support and strength
   b. messaging system
   c. movement
   d. heart muscle

9. Inside bone cells is a network made of
   a. tendons
   b. calcium
   c. marrow
   d. joints

10. The marrow produces
   a. spongy bone
   b. red blood cells
   c. compact bone
   d. calcium

11. Which bones make up the axial skeleton?
   a. skull, shoulder blades, arm bones
   b. skull, spinal column, leg bones
   c. shoulder blades, spinal column, and hip bones
   d. skull, spinal column, ribs

12. Bones of the skeleton connect to each other at

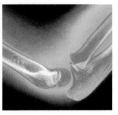

   a. tendons
   b. ligaments
   c. joints
   d. muscles

13. How do muscles contribute to homeostasis?
   a. They keep parts of the body together.
   b. They control the amount of water in the body.
   c. They help you move.
   d. They produce heat when they contract.

14. Cardiac muscle is found in the
   a. heart
   b. stomach
   c. intestines
   d. arms and legs

15. The stomach is made up of
   a. cardiac muscle
   b. skeletal muscle
   c. smooth muscle
   d. voluntary muscle

Short Answer *Write a short answer to each question.*

16. What is the difference between spongy bone and compact bone?

17. The root word *homeo* means "same," and the root word *stasis* means "to stay." How do these root words relate to the definition of *homeostasis*?

18. Hold the upper part of one arm between your elbow and shoulder with your opposite hand. Feel the muscles there. What happens to those muscles as you bend your arm?

Thinking Critically

19. **PROVIDE EXAMPLES** What are the levels of organization of the human body from simple to most complex? Give an example of each.

20. **CLASSIFY** There are four types of tissue in the human body: epithelial, nerve, muscles, and connective. How would you classify blood? Explain your reasoning.

21. **CONNECT** A clam shell is made of a calcium compound. The material is hard, providing protection to the soft body of a clam. It is also lightweight. Describe three ways in which the human skeleton is similar to a seashell. What is one important way in which it is different?

Use the diagram below to answer the next two questions

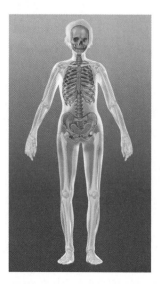

22. **SYNTHESIZE** Identify the type of joints that hold together the bones of the skull and sternum. How does this type of joint relate to the function of the skull and sternum?

23. **SYNTHESIZE** The human skeleton has two main divisions. Which skeleton do the arms and legs belong to? How do the joints that connect the arms to the shoulders and the legs to the hips relate to the function of this skeleton?

24. **COMPARE AND CONTRAST** How is the skeletal system of your body like the framework of a house or building? How is it different?

25. **SUMMARIZE** Describe three important functions of the skeleton.

26. **APPLY** The joints in the human body can be described as producing three types of movement. Relate these three types of movement to the action of brushing your teeth.

27. **COMPARE AND CONTRAST** When you stand, the muscles in you legs help to keep you balanced. Some of the muscles on both sides of your leg bones contract. How does this differ from how the muscles behave when you start to walk?

28. **INFER** Muscles are tissues that are made up of many muscle fibers. A muscle fiber can either be relaxed or contracted. Some movements you do require very little effort, like picking up a piece of paper. Others require a lot of effort, like picking up a book bag. How do you think a muscle produces the effort needed for a small task compared with a big task?

the **BIG** idea

29. **INFER** Look again at the picture on pages 6–7. Now that you have finished the chapter, how would you change or add details to your answer to the question on the photograph?

30. **SUMMARIZE** Write a paragraph explaining how skeletal muscles, bones, and joints work together to allow the body to move and be flexible. Underline the terms in your paragraph.

UNIT PROJECTS

If you are doing a unit project, make a folder for your project. Include in your folder a list of resources you will need, the date on which the project is due, and a schedule to track your progress. Begin gathering data.

Interpreting Diagrams

The action of a muscle pulling on a bone can be compared to a simple machine called a lever. A lever is a rod that moves about a fixed point called the fulcrum. Effort at one end of the rod can move a load at the other end. In the human body, a muscle supplies the effort needed to move a bone—the lever. The joint is the fulcrum, and the load is the weight of the body part being moved. There are three types of levers, which are classified according to the position of the fulcrum, the effort, and the load.

Read the text and study the diagrams, and then choose the best answer for the questions that follow.

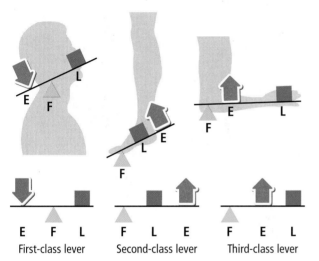

First-class lever   Second-class lever   Third-class lever

1. In a first-class lever
  a. the load is at end of the lever opposite the fulcrum
  b. the load is between the effort and the fulcrum
  c. the fulcrum is between the load and the effort
  d. the effort and load are on the same side

2. What is true of all levers?
  a. The fulcrum must be located at the center of a lever.
  b. The force of the load and effort point in the same direction.
  c. The load and effort are on the same side of the fulcrum.
  d. The force of the effort points in a direction opposite that of the load.

3. The fulcrum represents what structure in the human body?
  a. a joint   **c.** a muscle
  b. a bone   **d.** a part of the body

4. The main point of the diagram is to show
  a. how bones work
  b. that there are three types of levers and how they are classified
  c. where to apply a force
  d. the forces involved in moving parts of the body

Extended Response

Use the diagrams above and terms from the word box below to answer the next question. Underline each term you use in your answer.

fulcrum	load	effort	rod
bone	muscle	joint	

5. Suppose you had a heavy box to lift. Your first thought might be to bend over, stretch out your arms, and grab the box. Your body would be acting as a simple machine. Identify the type of lever this is and the parts of this machine.

6. A doctor would advise you not to lift a heavy object, like a box, simply by bending over and picking it up. That action puts too much strain on your back. It is better to bend your knees, hold the box close to your body, and then lift. How does this way of lifting change how you are using your body?

CHAPTER

2 Absorption, Digestion, and Exchange

the **BIG** idea

Systems in the body obtain and process materials and remove waste.

Key Concepts

SECTION 2.1 The respiratory system gets oxygen and removes carbon dioxide.
Learn how the respiratory system functions.

SECTION 2.2 The digestive system breaks down food.
Learn how the digestive system provides cells with necessary materials.

SECTION 2.3 The urinary system removes waste materials.
Learn how the urinary system removes wastes.

What materials does your body need to function properly?

Internet Preview

CLASSZONE.COM

Chapter 2 online resources: Content Review, two Visualizations, two Resource Centers, Math Tutorial, Test Practice.

EXPLORE (the **BIG** idea)

Mirror, Mirror

Hold a small hand mirror in front of your mouth. Slowly exhale onto the surface of the mirror. What do you see? Exhale a few more times onto the mirror, observing the interaction of your breath with the cool surface of the mirror.

Observe and Think What did you see on the surface of the mirror? What does this tell you about the content of the air that you exhale?

Water Everywhere

Keep track of how much liquid you drink in a 24-hour period of time. Do not include carbonated or caffeinated beverages. Water, juice, and milk can count. Add up the number of ounces of liquid you drink in that period of time.

Observe and Think How many ounces did you drink in one day? Do you drink fluids only when you feel thirsty?

Internet Activity: Lung Movement

Go to **ClassZone.com** to watch a visualization of lung and diaphragm movement during respiration. Observe how movements of the diaphragm and other muscles affect the lungs.

Observe and Think How do the diaphragm and lungs move during inhalation? during exhalation? Why do movements of the diaphragm cause the lungs to move?

NSTA
scilinks.org
SCI LINKS

Digestion **Code:** MDL045

Getting Ready to Learn

◀ CONCEPT REVIEW

- Cells make up tissues, and tissues make up organs.
- The body's systems interact.
- The body's systems work to maintain internal conditions.

◀ VOCABULARY REVIEW

cell p. 10

homeostasis p. 12

smooth muscle p. 24

energy *See Glossary.*

CONTENT REVIEW
CLASSZONE.COM

Review concepts and vocabulary.

▶ TAKING NOTES

OUTLINE

As you read, copy the blue headings on your paper in the form of an outline. Then add notes in your own words that summarize what you read.

VOCABULARY STRATEGY

Think about a vocabulary term as a **magnet word** diagram. Write the other terms or ideas related to that term around it.

See the Note-Taking Handbook on pages R45–R51.

SCIENCE NOTEBOOK

THE RESPIRATORY SYSTEM GETS OXYGEN AND REMOVES CARBON DIOXIDE.

  A. Your body needs oxygen.
    1. Oxygen is used to release energy
    2. Oxygen is in air you breathe

  B. Structures in the respiratory system function together
    1. nose, throat, trachea
    2. lungs

includes lungs   RESPIRATORY SYSTEM   breathing

gets oxygen

2.1

KEY CONCEPT

The respiratory system gets oxygen and removes carbon dioxide.

◀ **BEFORE, you learned**

- Cells, tissues, organs, and organ systems work together
- Organ systems provide for the body's needs
- Organ systems are important to the body's survival

▶ **NOW, you will learn**

- About the structures of the respiratory system that function to exchange gases
- About the process of cellular respiration
- About other functions of the respiratory system

VOCABULARY

respiratory system p. 37
cellular respiration p. 38

EXPLORE Breathing

How do your ribs move when you breathe?

PROCEDURE

① Place your hands on your ribs.

② Breathe in and out several times, focusing on what happens when you inhale and exhale.

③ Record your observations in your notebook.

WHAT DO YOU THINK?

- What movement did you observe?
- Think about your observations. What questions do you have as a result of your observations?

VOCABULARY
Make a word magnet diagram for the term *respiration*.

Your body needs oxygen.

During the day, you eat and drink only a few times, but you breathe thousands of times. In fact, breathing is a sign of life. The body is able to store food and liquid, but it is unable to store very much oxygen. The **respiratory system** is the body system that functions to get oxygen from the environment and remove carbon dioxide and other waste products from your body. The respiratory system interacts with the environment and with other body systems.

The continuous process of moving and using oxygen involves mechanical movement and chemical reactions. Air is transported into your lungs by mechanical movements and oxygen is used during chemical reactions that release energy in your cells.

 CHECK YOUR READING What are the two main functions of your respiratory system?

Exchanging Oxygen and Carbon Dioxide

Like almost all living things, the human body needs oxygen to survive. Without oxygen, cells in the body die quickly. How does the oxygen you need get to your cells? Oxygen, along with other gases, enters the body when you inhale. Oxygen is then transported to cells throughout the body.

The air that you breathe contains only about 20 percent oxygen and less than 1 percent carbon dioxide. Almost 80 percent of air is nitrogen gas. The air that you exhale contains more carbon dioxide and less oxygen than the air that you inhale. It's important that you exhale carbon dioxide because high levels of it will damage, even destroy, cells.

In cells and tissues, proper levels of both oxygen and carbon dioxide are essential. Recall that systems in the body work together to maintain homeostasis. If levels of oxygen or carbon dioxide change, your brain or blood vessels signal the body to breathe faster or slower.

The photograph shows how someone underwater maintains proper levels of carbon dioxide and oxygen. The scuba diver needs to inhale oxygen from a tank. She removes carbon dioxide wastes with other gases when she exhales into the water. The bubbles you see in the water are formed when she exhales.

 CHECK YOUR READING What gases are in the air that you breathe?

Gas Exchange

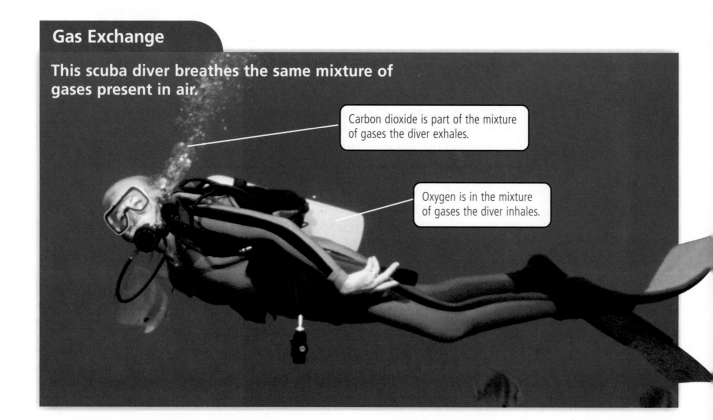

This scuba diver breathes the same mixture of gases present in air.

Carbon dioxide is part of the mixture of gases the diver exhales.

Oxygen is in the mixture of gases the diver inhales.

INVESTIGATE Lungs

How does air move in and out of lungs?

PROCEDURE

① Create a model of your lungs as shown. Insert an uninflated balloon into the top of the plastic bottle. While squeezing the bottle to force out some air, stretch the end of the balloon over the lip of the bottle. The balloon should still be open to the outside air. Tape the balloon in place with duct tape to make a tight seal

② Release the bottle so that it expands back to its normal shape. Observe what happens to the balloon. Squeeze and release the bottle several times while observing the balloon. Record your observations.

WHAT DO YOU THINK?

• Describe, in words, what happens when you squeeze and release the bottle.

• How do you think your lungs move when you inhale? when you exhale?

CHALLENGE Design an addition to your model that could represent a muscle called the diaphragm. What materials do you need? How would this work? Your teacher may be able to provide additional materials so you can test your model. Be sure to come up with a comprehensive list of materials as well as a specific diagram.l as a specific diagram.

MATERIALS
• one medium balloon
• 1-L clear plastic bottle with labels removed

TIME
15 minutes

Cellular Respiration

Inside your cells, a process called **cellular respiration** uses oxygen in chemical reactions that release energy. The respiratory system works with the digestive and circulatory systems to make cellular respiration possible. Cellular respiration requires glucose, or sugars, which you get from food, in addition to oxygen, which you get from breathing. These materials are transported to every cell in your body through blood vessels. You will learn more about the digestive and circulatory systems later in this unit.

During cellular respiration, your cells use oxygen and glucose to release energy. Carbon dioxide is a waste product of the process. Carbon dioxide must be removed from cells.

VOCABULARY
Add a magnet diagram for *cellular respiration* to your notebook. Include the word *energy* in your diagram.

 What three body systems are involved in cellular respiration?

Structures in the respiratory system function together.

OUTLINE

Add *Structures in the respiratory system function together* to your outline. Be sure to include the six respiratory structures in your outline.

I. Main idea
   A. Supporting idea
      1. Detail
      2. Detail
   B. Supporting idea

The respiratory system is made up of many structures that allow you to move air in and out of your body, communicate, and keep out harmful materials.

Nose, Throat, and Trachea When you inhale, air enters your body through your nose or mouth. Inside your nose, tiny hairs called cilia filter dirt and other particles out of the air. Mucus, a sticky liquid in your nasal cavity, also helps filter air by trapping particles such as dirt and pollen as air passes by. The nasal cavity warms the air slightly before it moves down your throat toward a tubelike structure called the windpipe, or trachea (TRAY-kee-uh). A structure called the epiglottis (EHP-ih-GLAHT-ihs) keeps air from entering your stomach.

Lungs The lungs are two large organs located on either side of your heart. When you breathe, air enters the throat, passes through the trachea, and moves to the lungs through structures called bronchial tubes. Bronchial tubes branch throughout the lungs into smaller and smaller tubes. At the ends of the smallest tubes air enters tiny air sacs called alveoli. The walls of the alveoli are only one cell thick. In fact, one page in this book is much thicker than the walls of the alveoli. Oxygen passes from inside the alveoli through the thin walls and is dissolved into the blood. At the same time, carbon dioxide waste passes from the blood into the alveoli.

 Through which structures does oxygen move into the lungs?

Ribs and Diaphragm If you put your hands on your ribs and take a deep breath, you can feel your ribs expand. The rib cage encloses a space inside your body called the thoracic (thu-RHAS-ihk) cavity. Some ribs are connected by cartilage to the breastbone or to each other, which makes the rib cage flexible. This flexibility allows the rib cage to expand when you breathe and make room for the lungs to expand and fill with air.

A large muscle called the diaphragm (DY-uh-FRAM) stretches across the floor of the thoracic cavity. When you inhale, your diaphragm contracts and pulls downward, which makes the thoracic cavity expand. This movement causes the lungs to push downward, filling the extra space. At the same time, other muscles draw the ribs outward and expand the lungs. Air rushes into the lungs, and inhalation is complete. When the diaphragm and other muscles relax, the process reverses and you exhale.

Explore the respiratory system.

 Describe how the diaphragm and the rib cage move.

Respiratory System

The structures in the respiratory system allow this flutist to play music.

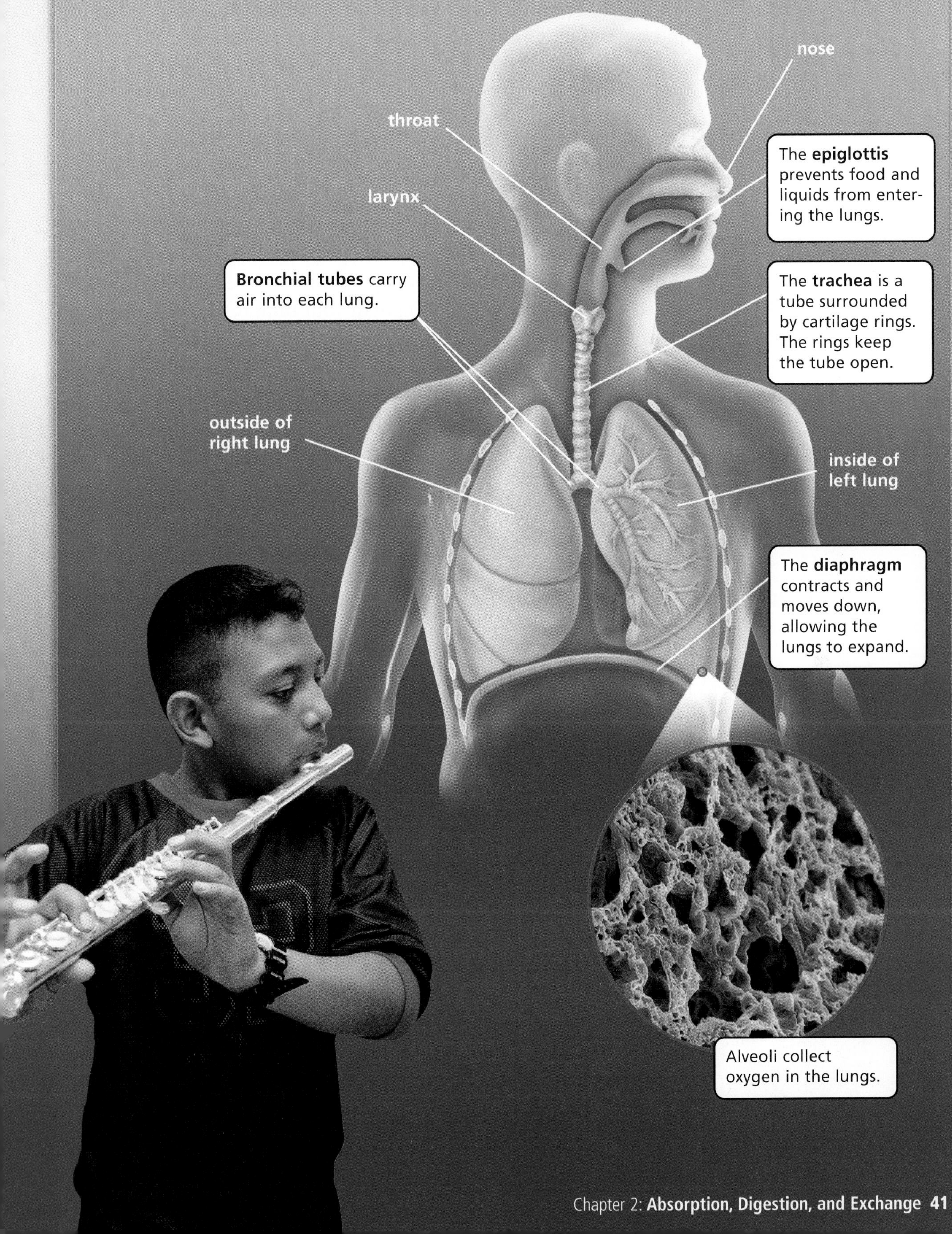

nose

throat

larynx

The **epiglottis** prevents food and liquids from entering the lungs.

Bronchial tubes carry air into each lung.

The **trachea** is a tube surrounded by cartilage rings. The rings keep the tube open.

outside of right lung

inside of left lung

The **diaphragm** contracts and moves down, allowing the lungs to expand.

Alveoli collect oxygen in the lungs.

The respiratory system is also involved in other activities.

In addition to providing oxygen and removing carbon dioxide, the respiratory system is involved in other activities of the body. Speaking and singing, along with actions such as sneezing, can be explained in terms of how the parts of the respiratory system work together.

Speech and Other Respiratory Movements

If you place your hand on your throat and hum softly, you can feel your vocal cords vibrating. Air moving over your vocal cords allows you to produce sound, and the muscles in your throat, mouth, cheeks, and lips allow you to form sound into words. The vocal cords are folds of tissue in the larynx. The larynx, sometimes called the voice box, is a two-inch, tube-shaped organ about the length of your thumb, located in the neck, at the top of the trachea. When you speak, the vocal cords become tight, squeeze together, and force air from the lungs to move between them. The air causes the vocal cords to vibrate and produce sound.

How Speech Works

Sound is formed by structures in the respiratory system.

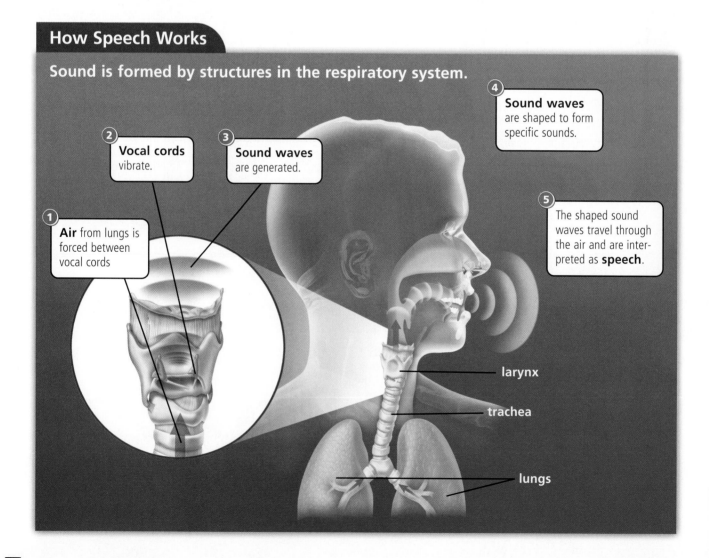

2 Vocal cords vibrate.

3 Sound waves are generated.

4 Sound waves are shaped to form specific sounds.

5 The shaped sound waves travel through the air and are interpreted as **speech**.

1 **Air** from lungs is forced between vocal cords

larynx

trachea

lungs

Some movements of the respiratory system allow you to clear particles out of your nose and throat or to express emotion. The respiratory system is involved when you cough or sneeze. Sighing, yawning, laughing, and crying also involve the respiratory system.

Sighing and yawning both involve taking deep breaths. A sigh is a long breath followed by a shorter exhalation. A yawn is a long breath taken through a wide-open mouth. Laughing and crying are movements that are very similar to each other. In fact, sometimes it's difficult to see the difference between laughing and crying.

The respiratory system also allows you to hiccup. A hiccup is a sudden inhalation that makes the diaphragm contract. Several systems are involved when you hiccup. Air rushes into the throat, causing the diaphragm to contract. When the diaphragm contracts, the air passageway between the vocal cords closes. The closing of this passageway produces the sound of the hiccup. Hiccups can be caused by eating too fast, sudden temperature changes, and stress.

Water Removal

Hiccups, coughs, yawns, and all other respiratory movements, including speaking and breathing, release water from your body into the environment. Water is lost through sweat, urine, and exhalations of air. When it is cold enough outside, you can see your breath in the air. That is because the water vapor you exhale condenses into larger droplets when it moves from your warm body to the cold air.

Water leaves your body through your breath every time you exhale.

2.1 Review

KEY CONCEPTS

1. How is oxygen used by your body's cells?

2. What are the structures in the respiratory system and what do they do?

3. In addition to breathing, what functions does the respiratory system perform?

CRITICAL THINKING

4. **Sequence** List in order the steps that occur when you exhale.

5. **Compare and Contrast** How is the air you inhale different from the air you exhale?

○ CHALLENGE

6. **Hypothesize** Why do you think a person breathes more quickly when exercising?

YOGA INSTRUCTOR

Breathing and Yoga

If you're reading this, you must be breathing. Are you thinking about how you are breathing? Yoga instructors help their students learn deep, slow breathing. The practice of yoga uses an understanding of the respiratory system as a tool for healthy exercise.

Nostril Breathing

An important aspect of breathing is removing wastes from the body:
- Yoga instructors teach students to inhale through the nostrils and exhale through the mouth.
- The nostrils filter dust and other particles, keeping dirt out of the lungs.
- The nostrils also warm the air as it enters the body.

Abdominal Breathing

Yoga instructors tell students to slowly expand and release the diaphragm:
- The diaphragm is a muscle below the lungs.
- When the muscle expands, air enters into the lungs.
- When it contracts, or relaxes, air is pushed out of the lungs.

nostrils

lungs

diaphragm muscle

Full Lung Breathing

Yoga instructors help students breathe in slowly so that first the abdomen expands, then the rib cage area, and finally the upper chest by the shoulders. When students exhale, they collapse the diaphragm, then release the chest, and lastly relax the shoulders.

EXPLORE

1. **APPLY** Try one of the three breathing methods described. Start by taking a few slow deep breaths; then try the yoga breathing. Count to 4 as you inhale, and to 4 again breathing out. How do you feel after each breath?

2. **CHALLENGE** Choose one of the breathing methods above. Describe what happens to air each time you inhale and exhale. Draw or write your answer.

2.2 The digestive system breaks down food.

◀ BEFORE, you learned

- The respiratory system takes in oxygen and expels waste
- Oxygen is necessary for cellular respiration
- The respiratory system is involved in speech and water removal

▶ NOW, you will learn

- About the role of digestion in providing energy and materials
- About the chemical and mechanical process of digestion
- How materials change as they move through the digestive system

VOCABULARY

nutrient p. 45
digestion p. 46
digestive system p. 46
peristalsis p. 46

EXPLORE Digestion

How does the digestive system break down fat?

PROCEDURE

1. Using a dropper, place 5 mL of water into a test tube. Add 5 mL of vegetable oil. Seal the test tube with a screw-on top. Shake the test tube for 10 seconds, then place it in a test tube stand. Record your observations.

2. Drop 5 mL of dish detergent into the test tube. Seal the tube. Shake the test tube for 10 seconds, then place in the stand. Observe the mixture for 2 minutes. Record your observations.

WHAT DO YOU THINK?

- What effect does detergent have on the mixture of oil and water?
- How do you think your digestive system might break down fat?

MATERIALS
- water
- dropper
- test tube
- vegetable oil
- test tube stand
- liquid dish detergent

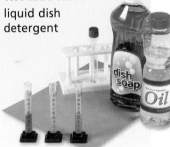

The body needs energy and materials.

After not eating for a while, have you ever noticed how little energy you have to do the simplest things? You need food to provide energy for your body. You also need materials from food. Most of what you need comes from nutrients within food. **Nutrients** are important substances that enable the body to move, grow, and maintain homeostasis. Proteins, carbohydrates, fats, and water are some of the nutrients your body needs.

You might not think of water as a nutrient, but it is necessary for all living things. In fact, more than half of your body is made up of water. Protein is another essential nutrient; it is the material that the body uses for growth and repair. Cells in your body—such as those composing muscles, bones, and skin—are built of proteins. Carbohydrates are nutrients that provide cells with energy. Carbohydrates make up cellulose, which helps move materials through the digestive system. Another nutrient, fat, stores energy.

Before your body can use these nutrients, they must be broken into smaller substances. **Digestion** is the process of breaking down food into usable materials. Your digestive system transforms the energy and materials in food into forms your body can use.

The digestive system moves and breaks down food.

VISUALIZATION
CLASSZONE.COM

Observe the process of peristalsis.

Your **digestive system** performs the complex jobs of moving and breaking down food. Material is moved through the digestive system by wavelike contractions of smooth muscles. This muscular action is called **peristalsis** (PEHR-ih-STAWL-sihs). Mucous glands throughout the system keep the material moist so it can be moved easily, and the muscles contract to push the material along. The muscles move food along in much the same way as you move toothpaste from the bottom of the tube with your thumbs. The body has complicated ways of moving food, and it also has complicated ways of breaking down food. The digestive system processes food in two ways: physically and chemically.

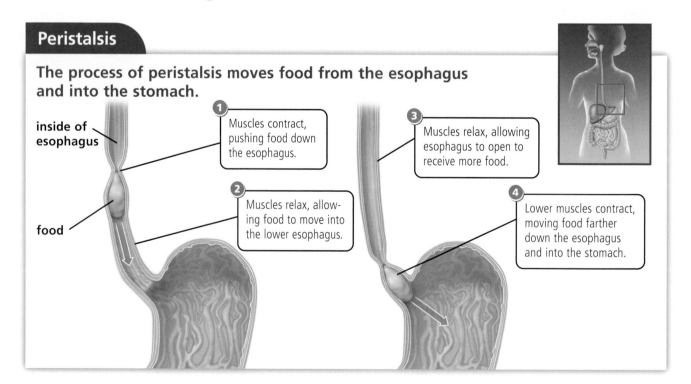

Peristalsis

The process of peristalsis moves food from the esophagus and into the stomach.

inside of esophagus

food

1. Muscles contract, pushing food down the esophagus.

2. Muscles relax, allowing food to move into the lower esophagus.

3. Muscles relax, allowing esophagus to open to receive more food.

4. Lower muscles contract, moving food farther down the esophagus and into the stomach.

INVESTIGATE Chemical Digestion

How does saliva break down starch?

PROCEDURE

① Cut two slices of the same thickness from the center of a potato. Lay the slices on a plate or tray.

② Using a dropper, add 15 drops of solution A to one potato slice. Add 15 drops of water to the other potato slice. Observe both potato slices for several minutes. Record your observations.

WHAT DO YOU THINK?

- What evidence did you see that starch is being broken down?
- How would you identify the substance left by the breakdown of starch?
- What is the purpose of the water in this activity?

CHALLENGE How could you change your experiment to model mechanical digestion? What structures in your mouth mechanically break down food?

SKILL FOCUS
Modeling

MATERIALS
- knife
- potato
- droppers
- solution A
- water

TIME
25 minutes

Mechanical Digestion

Physical changes, which are sometimes called mechanical changes, break food into smaller pieces. Your teeth chew your food so you are able to swallow it. Infants without teeth need an adult to cut up or mash food for them. Otherwise they need soft food that they can swallow without chewing. Your stomach also breaks down food mechanically by mashing and pounding it during peristalsis.

Chemical Digestion

Chemical changes actually change food into different substances. For example, chewing a cracker produces a physical change—the cracker is broken into small pieces. At the same time, liquid in the mouth called saliva produces a chemical change—starches in the cracker are changed to sugars. If you chew a cracker, you may notice that after you have chewed it for a few seconds, it begins to taste sweet. The change in taste is a sign of a chemical reaction.

VOCABULARY
Don't forget to add magnet word diagrams for *digestion, digestive system,* and *peristalsis* to your notebook.

 CHECK YOUR READING What are the two types of changes that take place during digestion?

Materials are broken down as they move through the digestive tract.

The digestive system contains several organs. Food travels through organs in the digestive tract: the mouth, esophagus, stomach, small intestine, and large intestine. Other organs, such as the pancreas, liver, and gall bladder, release chemicals that are necessary for chemical digestion. The diagram on page 49 shows the major parts of the entire digestive system.

READING TiP

As you read about the digestive tract, look at the structures on page 49.

Mouth and Esophagus Both mechanical and chemical digestion begin in the mouth. The teeth break food into small pieces. The lips and tongue position food so that you can chew. When food is in your mouth, salivary glands in your mouth release saliva, which softens the food and begins chemical reactions. The tongue pushes the food to the back of the mouth and down the throat while swallowing.

CHECK YOUR READING What part does the mouth play in digestion?

When you swallow, your tongue pushes food down into your throat. Food then travels down the esophagus to the stomach. The muscle contractions of peristalsis move solid food from the throat to the stomach in about eight seconds. Liquid foods take about two seconds.

Stomach Strong muscles in the stomach further mix and mash food particles. The stomach also uses chemicals to break down food. Some of the chemicals made by the stomach are acids. These acids are so strong that they could eat through the stomach itself. To prevent this, the stomach's lining is replaced about every three days.

Small Intestine Partially digested food moves from the stomach to the small intestine. There, chemicals released by the pancreas, liver, and gallbladder break down nutrients. Most of the nutrients broken down in digestion are absorbed in the small intestine. Structures called villi are found throughout the small intestine. These structures contain folds that absorb nutrients from proteins, carbohydrates, and fats. Once absorbed by the villi, nutrients are transported by the circulatory system around the body. You will read more about the circulatory system in Chapter 3.

Villi allow broken-down nutrients to be absorbed into your bloodstream.

Large Intestine In the large intestine, water and some other nutrients are absorbed from the digested material. Most of the solid material then remaining is waste material, which is compacted and stored. Eventually it is eliminated through the rectum.

CHECK YOUR READING Where in your digestive system does mechanical digestion occur?

Digestive System

As food moves through the digestive tract, structures of the digestive system break it down and absorb necessary materials.

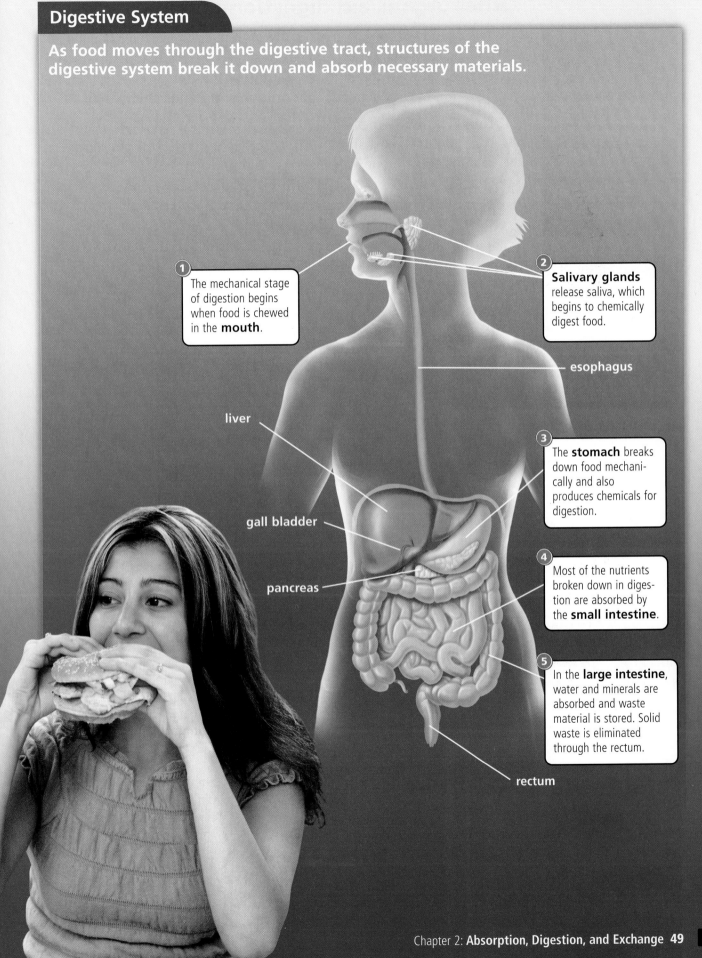

1 The mechanical stage of digestion begins when food is chewed in the **mouth**.

2 **Salivary glands** release saliva, which begins to chemically digest food.

esophagus

liver

gall bladder

pancreas

3 The **stomach** breaks down food mechanically and also produces chemicals for digestion.

4 Most of the nutrients broken down in digestion are absorbed by the **small intestine**.

5 In the **large intestine**, water and minerals are absorbed and waste material is stored. Solid waste is eliminated through the rectum.

rectum

Other organs aid digestion and absorption.

The digestive organs not in the digestive tract—the liver, gallbladder, and pancreas—also play crucial roles in your body. Although food does not move through them, all three of these organs aid in chemical digestion by producing or concentrating important chemicals.

Liver The liver—the largest internal organ of the body—is located in your abdomen, just above your stomach. Although you can survive losing a portion of your liver, it is an important organ. The liver filters blood, cleansing it of harmful substances, and stores unneeded nutrients for later use in the body. It produces a golden yellow substance called bile, which is able to break down fats, much like to the way soap breaks down oils. The liver also breaks down medicines and produces important proteins, such as those that help clot blood if you get a cut.

Gallbladder The gallbladder is a tiny pear-shaped sac connected to the liver. Bile produced in the the liver is stored and concentrated in the gallbladder. The bile is then secreted into the small intestine.

Pancreas Located between the stomach and the small intestine, the pancreas produces chemicals that are needed as materials move between the two. The pancreas quickly lowers the acidity in the small intestine and breaks down proteins, fats, and starch. The chemicals produced by the pancreas are extremely important for digesting and absorbing food substances. Without these chemicals, you could die of starvation, even with plenty of food in your system. Your body would not be able to process and use the food for energy without the pancreas.

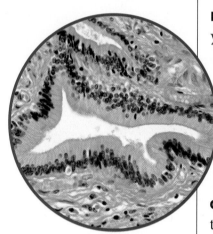

Bile is transferred from the liver to the gallbladder and small intestines through the bile duct.

 CHECK YOUR READING How does the pancreas aid in digestion?

2.2 Review

KEY CONCEPTS

1. List three of the functions of the digestive system.
2. Give one example each of mechanical digestion and chemical digestion.
3. How does your stomach process food?

CRITICAL THINKING

4. **Apply** Does an antacid deal with physical or chemical digestion?
5. **Apply** You have just swallowed a bite of apple. Describe what happens as the apple moves through your digestive system. Include information about what happens to the material in the apple.

○ CHALLENGE

6. **Compare and Contrast** Describe the roles of the large and the small intestines. How are they similar? How are they different?

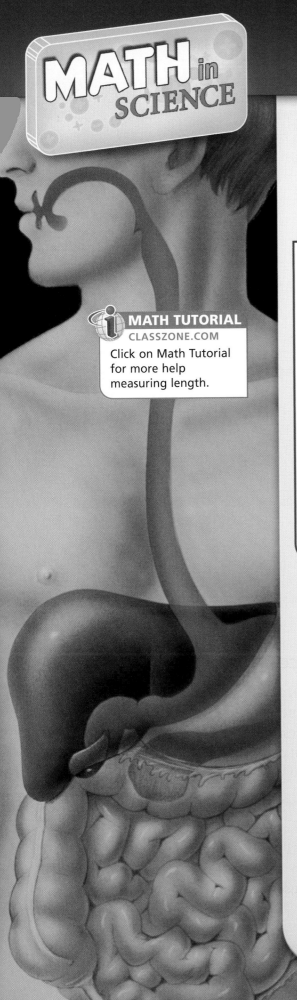

Internal Measurement

It wouldn't be useful if someone told you the length of your tongue in meters, or the length of a tooth in centimeters. To be meaningful, these measurements must be given in appropriate units.

MATH TUTORIAL
CLASSZONE.COM

Click on Math Tutorial for more help measuring length.

Example

Your esophagus is about the length of your forearm. Choose the appropriate units to measure its length. Would meters, centimeters, or millimeters be most appropriate?

(1) Look at your arm from your wrist to your elbow. It is about the same as a rolling pin. You don't need to measure your stomach to see that a meter would be too large a unit. One meter is about the height of a lab table.

(2) Look at the ruler in the picture. Compare your arm to the centimeters shown and the millimeters.

(3) You can measure your arm with either unit, but if you wiggle a bit, the count of millimeters is thrown off.

ANSWER Centimeters are the most appropriate units.

Answer the following questions.

1. If you uncoiled a human intestine, its length would be about equal to that of 2 cars parked end to end. What would be appropriate units to use to measure that?

2. What units would you use to measure the length of your tongue? The length of a tooth?

3. The large intestine is actually shorter than the small intestine. The small intestine is about the length of a small bus, and the large is about as long as a car's back seat. Tell the units you would choose for each. Explain why.

CHALLENGE Your stomach when empty is about the size of your clenched fist. To measure its volume (the space it takes up), what units would you use?

The ruler shows 20 centimeters (cm). 1 cm
There are 10 millimeters (mm) in each centimeter.

2.3 The urinary system removes waste materials.

 BEFORE, you learned

- The digestive system breaks down food
- Organs in the digestive system have different roles

NOW, you will learn

- How different body systems remove different types of waste
- Why the kidneys are important organs
- About the role of the kidney in homeostasis

VOCABULARY

urinary system p. 53
urine p. 53

EXPLORE Waste Removal

How does the skin get rid of body waste?

PROCEDURE

1. Place a plastic bag over the hand you do not use for writing and tape it loosely around your wrist.

2. Leave the bag on for five minutes. Write down the changes you see in conditions within the bag.

WHAT DO YOU THINK?

- What do you see happen to the bag?
- How does what you observe help explain the body's method of waste removal?

MATERIALS
- plastic bag
- tape
- stopwatch

Life processes produce wastes.

OUTLINE
Add *Life processes produce wastes* to your outline. Include four ways the body disposes of waste products.

I. Main idea
  A. Supporting idea
    1. Detail
    2. Detail
  B. Supporting idea

You have read that the respiratory system and the digestive system provide the body with energy and materials necessary for important processes. During these processes waste materials are produced. The removal of these wastes is essential for the continuing function of body systems. Several systems in your body remove wastes.

- The urinary system disposes of liquid waste products removed from the blood.
- The respiratory system disposes of water vapor and waste gases from the blood.
- The digestive system disposes of solid waste products from food.
- The skin releases wastes through sweat glands.

 CHECK YOUR READING What are four ways the body disposes of waste products?

The urinary system removes waste from the blood.

If you have observed an aquarium, you have seen a filter at work. Water moves through the filter, which removes waste materials from the water. Just as the filter in a fish tank removes wastes from the water, structures in your urinary system filter wastes from your blood.

As shown in the diagram, the **urinary system** contains several structures. The kidneys are two organs located high up and toward the rear of the abdomen, one on each side of the spine. Kidneys function much as the filter in the fish tank does. In fact, the kidneys are often called the body's filters. Materials travel in your blood to the kidneys. There, some substances are removed, and others are returned to the blood.

After the kidneys filter chemical waste from the blood, the liquid travels down two tubes called ureters (yu-REE-tuhrz). The ureters bring the waste to the bladder, a storage sac with a wall of smooth muscle. The lower neck of the bladder leads into the urethra, a tube that carries the liquid waste outside the body. Voluntary muscles at one end of the bladder allow a person to hold the urethra closed until he or she is ready to release the muscles. At that time, the bladder contracts and sends the liquid waste, or **urine,** out of the body.

> **VOCABULARY**
> Add a magnet diagram for *urinary system* to your notebook. Include in your diagram information about how kidneys function.

Urinary System

The urinary system transports wastes out of the body.

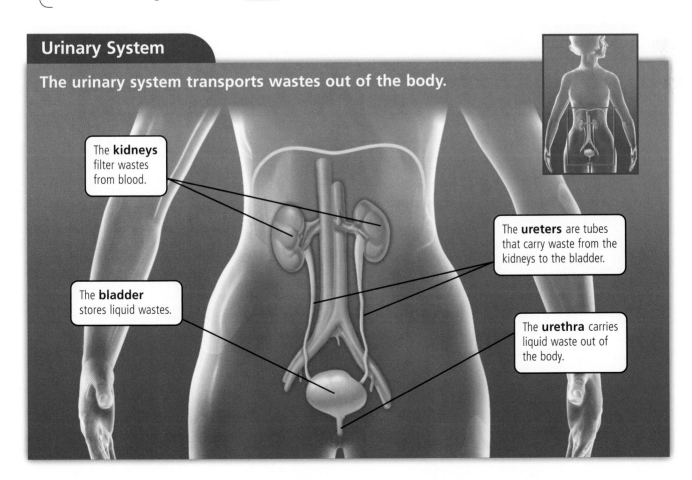

The **kidneys** filter wastes from blood.

The **ureters** are tubes that carry waste from the kidneys to the bladder.

The **bladder** stores liquid wastes.

The **urethra** carries liquid waste out of the body.

The kidneys act as filters.

RESOURCE CENTER
CLASSZONE.COM

Find out more about the urinary system.

At any moment, about one quarter of the blood leaving your heart is headed toward your kidneys to be filtered. The kidneys, which are about as long as your index finger—only 10 centimeters (3.9 in.) long—filter all the blood in your body many times a day.

The Nephron

Inside each kidney are approximately one million looping tubes called nephrons. The nephron regulates the makeup of the blood.

① Fluid is filtered from the blood into the nephron through a structure called the glomerulus (gloh-MEHR-yuh-luhs). Filtered blood leaves the glomerulus and circulates around the tubes that make up the nephron.

② As the filtered fluid passes through the nephron, some nutrients are absorbed back into the blood surrounding the tubes. Some water is also filtered out in the glomerulus, but most water is returned to the blood.

③ Waste products travel to the end of the nephron into the collecting duct. The remaining liquid, now called urine, passes out of the kidney and into the ureters.

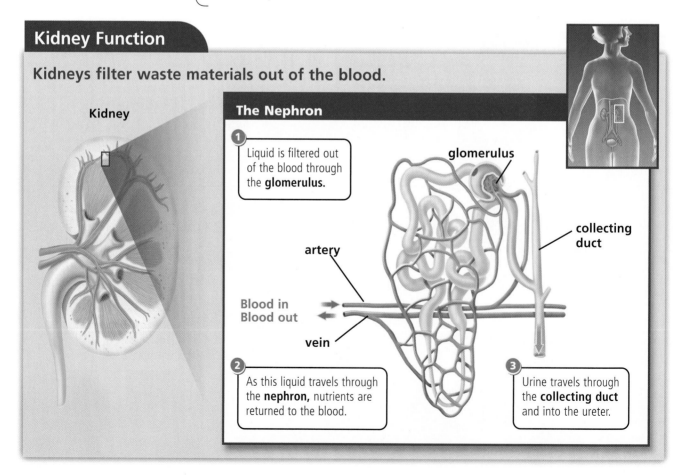

Kidney Function

Kidneys filter waste materials out of the blood.

Kidney

The Nephron

① Liquid is filtered out of the blood through the **glomerulus.**

glomerulus

collecting duct

artery

Blood in
Blood out

vein

② As this liquid travels through the **nephron,** nutrients are returned to the blood.

③ Urine travels through the **collecting duct** and into the ureter.

The amount of water in your body affects your blood pressure. Excess water increases blood pressure.

Water Balance

The kidneys not only remove wastes from blood, they also regulate the amount of water in the body. You read in Chapter 1 about the importance of homeostasis—a stable environment within your body. The amount of water in your cells affects homeostasis. If your body contains too much water, parts of your body may swell. Having too little water interferes with cell processes.

About one liter of water leaves the body every day. The kidneys control the amount of water that leaves the body in urine. Depending on how much water your body uses, the kidneys produce urine with more or less water.

 CHECK YOUR READING How do your kidneys regulate the amount of water in your body?

2.3 Review

KEY CONCEPTS

1. Describe the four organ systems that remove wastes and explain how each removes waste.

2. Describe the function of four organs in the urinary system.

3. Describe homeostasis and explain why the kidney is important to homeostasis.

CRITICAL THINKING

4. **Connect** Make a word web with the term *kidney* in the center. Add details about kidney function to the web.

⬤ CHALLENGE

5. **Synthesize** Explain why you may become thirsty on a hot day. Include the term *homeostasis* in your explanation.

CHAPTER INVESTIGATION

Modeling a Kidney

OVERVIEW AND PURPOSE Your kidneys are your body's filters. Every 20 to 30 minutes, every drop of your blood passes through the kidneys and is filtered. What types of materials are filtered by the kidneys? In this investigation you will
- model the filtering process of the kidneys
- determine what types of materials are filtered by your kidneys

▶ Problem

What types of materials can be removed from the blood by the kidneys?

▶ Hypothesize

Write a hypothesis to explain how substances are filtered out of the blood by the kidneys. Your hypothesis should take the form of an "If . . . , then . . . , because . . ." statement.

▶ Procedure

MATERIALS
- fine filter paper
- small funnel
- graduated cylinder
- 100 mL beaker
- solution A
- solution B
- solution C
- salinity test strips
- glucose test strips
- protein test strips

1. Make a data table like the one shown on the sample notebook page. Fold the filter paper as shown. Place the filter paper in the funnel, and place the funnel in the graduated cylinder.

2. Pour 20 mL of solution A into a beaker. Test the solution for salt concentration using a test strip for salinity. Record the results in your notebook. Slowly pour the solution into the funnel. Wait for it all to drip through the filter paper.

step 2

3 Test the filtered liquid for salt concentration again. Record the results.

4 Repeat steps 1, 2, and 3 for solution B using glucose test strips. Record the results in your notebook.

5 Repeat steps 1, 2, and 3 for solution C using protein test strips. Record the results in your notebook.

step 5

Observe and Analyze

Write It Up

1. **RECORD** Be sure your data table is complete.

2. **OBSERVE** What substances were present in solutions A, B, and C?

3. **IDENTIFY VARIABLES** Identify the variables and constants in the experiment. List them in your notebook.

Conclude

Write It Up

1. **COMPARE AND CONTRAST** In what ways does your model function like a kidney? How is your model not like a kidney?

2. **INTERPRET** Which materials were able to pass through the filter and which could not?

3. **INFER** What materials end up in the urine? How might materials be filtered out of the blood but not appear in the urine?

4. **APPLY** How is a filtering device useful in your body?

INVESTIGATE Further

CHALLENGE Your blood contains many chemicals. Some of these chemicals are waste products, but some are in the blood to be transported to different parts of the body. What other substances are filtered out of the blood by the kidneys? Which of the filtered substances are normally present in the urine? Use a variety of reference materials to research the chemicals found in urine. Revise your experiment to test the ability of your model kidney to filter other substances.

Modeling a Kidney

Table 1. Test-strip results

	Before filtering	After filtering
Solution A		
Solution B		
Solution C		

the BIG idea

Systems in the body obtain and process materials and remove waste.

◀ KEY CONCEPTS SUMMARY

2.1 **The respiratory system gets oxygen and removes carbon dioxide.**

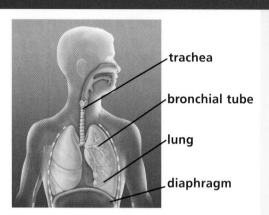

- trachea
- bronchial tube
- lung
- diaphragm

- Your body needs oxygen
- Structures in the respiratory system function together
- Your respiratory system is involved in other functions

VOCABULARY
respiratory system
  p. 37
cellular respiration
  p. 38

2.2 **The digestive system breaks down food.**

Structure	Function
Mouth	chemical and mechanical digestion
Esophagus	movement of food by peristalsis from mouth to stomach
Stomach	chemical and mechanical digestion; absorption of broken-down nutrients
Small intestine	chemical digestion; absorption of broken-down nutrients
Large intestine	absorption of water and broken-down nutrients, elimination of wastes

VOCABULARY
nutrient p. 45
digestion p. 46
digestive system p. 46
peristalsis p. 46

2.3 **The urinary system removes waste materials.**

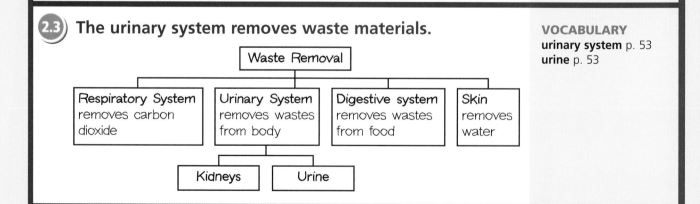

Waste Removal

| Respiratory System removes carbon dioxide | Urinary System removes wastes from body | Digestive system removes wastes from food | Skin removes water |

Kidneys — Urine

VOCABULARY
urinary system p. 53
urine p. 53

Reviewing Vocabulary

Copy the chart below and write the definition for each word. Use the meaning of the word's root to help you.

Word	Root meaning	Definition
EXAMPLE: rib cage	to arch over	bones enclosing the internal organs of the body
1. respiration	to breathe	
2. nutrient	to nourish	
3. digestion	to separate	
4. urine	to moisten, to flow	

Reviewing Key Concepts

Multiple Choice *Choose the letter of the best answer.*

5. Which system brings oxygen to your body and removes carbon dioxide?
   a. digestive system
   b. urinary system
   c. respiratory system
   d. muscular system

6. Which body structure in the throat keeps air from entering the stomach?
   a. trachea
   b. epiglottis
   c. lungs
   d. alveoli

7. Oxygen and carbon dioxide are exchanged through structures in the lungs called
   a. bronchial tubes
   b. alveoli
   c. cartilage
   d. villi

8. Carbon dioxide is a waste product that is formed during which process?
   a. cellular respiration
   b. peristalsis
   c. urination
   d. circulation

9. Carbohydrates are nutrients that
   a. make up most of the human body
   b. make up cell membranes
   c. enable cells to grow and repair themselves
   d. provide cells with energy

10. Which is *not* a function of the digestive system?
    a. absorb water from food
    b. absorb nutrients from food
    c. filter wastes from blood
    d. break down food

11. Which is an example of a physical change?
    a. teeth grind cracker into smaller pieces
    b. liquids in mouth change starches to sugars
    c. bile breaks down fats
    d. stomach breaks down proteins

12. Where in the digestive system is water absorbed?
    a. small intestine
    b. stomach
    c. large intestine
    d. esophagus

13. Chemical waste is filtered from the body in which structure?
    a. alveoli
    b. kidney
    c. stomach
    d. villi

14. The kidneys control the amount of
    a. oxygen that enters the blood
    b. water that is absorbed by the body
    c. urine that leaves the body
    d. water that leaves the body

Short Answer *Write a short answer to each question.*

15. Draw a sketch that shows how the thoracic cavity changes as the diaphragm contracts and pulls downward.

16. What are two products that are released into the body as a result of cellular respiration?

17. Through which organs does food pass as it travels through the digestive system?

18. What is the function of the urinary system?

Thinking Critically

19. SUMMARIZE Describe how gas exchange takes place inside the lungs.

20. SYNTHESIZE Summarize what happens during cellular respiration. Explain how the digestive system and the respiratory system are involved.

21. ANALYZE When there is a lot of dust or pollen in the air, people may cough and sneeze. What function of the respiratory system is involved?

22. INFER When you exhale onto a glass surface, the surface becomes cloudy with a thin film of moisture. Explain why this happens.

23. COMPARE AND CONTRAST Where does mechanical digestion take place? How is it different from chemical digestion?

24. PREDICT People with stomach disease often have their entire stomachs removed and are able to live normally. Explain how this is possible. Would a person be able to live normally without the small intestine? Explain your answer.

25. APPLY An athlete drinks a liter of water before a basketball game and continues to drink water during the game. Describe how the athlete's body is able to maintain homeostasis during the course of the game.

26. INTERPRET Use the diagram of the nephron shown below to describe what happens to the blood as it travels through the vessels surrounding the nephron.

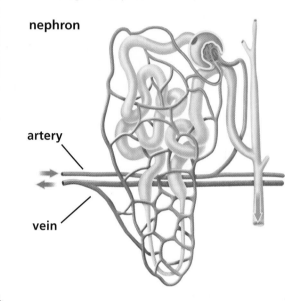

nephron

artery

vein

the BIG idea

27. INFER Look again at the picture on pages 34–35. Now that you have finished the chapter, how would you change or add details to your answer to the question on the photograph?

28. SYNTHESIZE Write a paragraph explaining how the respiratory system, the digestive system, and the urinary system work together with the circulatory system to eliminate waste materials from the body. Underline these terms in your paragraph.

UNIT PROJECTS

Check your schedule for your unit project. How are you doing? Be sure that you've placed data or notes from your research in your project folder.

Analyzing Data

The bar graph below shows respiration rates.

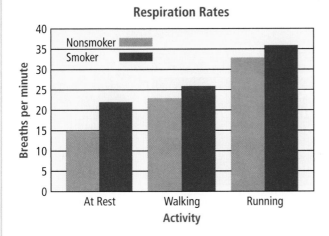

Respiration Rates

Use the graph to answer the questions below.

1. What is the best title for this graph?

a. Respiration Rates of Smokers and Nonsmokers

b. Cigarettes Smoked During Exercise

c. Activities Performed by Smokers and Nonsmokers

d. Blood Pressure Levels of Smokers and Nonsmokers.

2. How many breaths per minute were taken by a nonsmoker at rest?

a. 15 breaths per minute

b. 22 breaths per minute

c. 23 breaths per minute

d. 33 breaths per minute

3. For the nonsmokers, by how much did the respiration rate increase between resting and running?

a. 15 breaths per minute

b. 18 breaths per minute

c. 23 breaths per minute

d. 33 breaths per minute

4. Which statement is *not* true?

a. The nonsmoker at rest took more breaths per minute than the smoker at rest.

b. The nonsmoker took more breaths per minute running than walking.

c. The smoker took more breaths per minute than the nonsmoker while walking.

d. The nonsmoker took fewer breaths per minute than the smoker while running.

5. Which statement is the most logical conclusion to draw from the data in the chart?

a. Smoking has no effect on respiration rate.

b. Increased activity has no effect on respiration rate.

c. There is no difference in the respiration rates between the smoker and the nonsmoker.

d. Smoking and activity cause an increase in respiration rate.

Extended Response

6. Tar, which is a harmful substance found in tobacco smoke, coats the lining of the lungs over time. Based on the information in the graph and what you know about the respiratory system, write a paragraph describing how smoking cigarettes affects the functioning of the respiratory system.

7. Ads for cigarettes and other tobacco products have been banned from television. However, they still appear in newspapers and magazines. These ads make tobacco use look glamorous and exciting. Using your knowledge of the respiratory system, design an ad that discourages the use of tobacco products. Create a slogan that will help people remember how tobacco affects the health of the respiratory system.

Transport and Protection

the BIG idea

Systems function to transport materials and to defend and protect the body.

Key Concepts

SECTION 3.1
The circulatory system transports materials.
Learn how materials move through blood vessels.

SECTION 3.2
The immune system defends the body.
Learn about the body's defenses and responses to foreign materials.

SECTION 3.3
The integumentary system shields the body.
Learn about the structure of skin and how it protects the body.

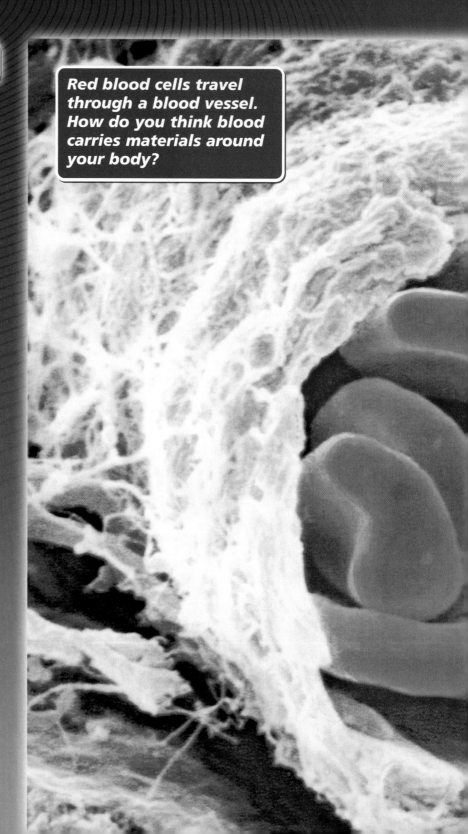

Red blood cells travel through a blood vessel. How do you think blood carries materials around your body?

Internet Preview

CLASSZONE.COM

Chapter 3 online resources: Content Review, two Visualizations, four Resource Centers, Math Tutorial, Test Practice

Blood Pressure

Fill a small, round balloon halfway full with air. Tie off the end. Gently squeeze the balloon in your hand. Release the pressure. Squeeze again.

Observe and Think As you squeeze your hand, what happens to the air in the balloon? What happens as you release the pressure?

Wet Fingers

Dip your finger into a cup of room-temperature water. Then hold the finger up in the air and note how it feels.

Observe and Think How does your finger feel now compared with the way it felt before you dipped it?

Internet Activity: Heart Pumping

Go to **ClassZone.com** to learn about how the heart pumps blood. See how the circulatory system interacts with the respiratory system.

Observe and Think Where does the blood go after it leaves the right side of the heart? the left side of the heart?

NSTA
scilinks.org

Immune System **Code:** MDL046

Getting Ready to Learn

◀ CONCEPT REVIEW

- The body's systems interact.
- The body's systems work to maintain internal conditions.
- The digestive system breaks down food.
- The respiratory system gets oxygen and removes carbon dioxide.

◀ VOCABULARY REVIEW

organ p. 11

organ system p. 12

homeostasis p. 12

nutrient p. 45

ⓘ CONTENT REVIEW
CLASSZONE.COM

Review concepts and vocabulary.

▶ TAKING NOTES

MAIN IDEA AND DETAIL NOTES

Make a two-column chart. Write the main ideas, such as those in the blue headings, in the column on the left. Write details about each of those main heads in the column on the right.

VOCABULARY STRATEGY

Write each new vocabulary term in the center of a **frame game** diagram. Decide what information to frame it with. Use examples, descriptions, parts, sentences that use the term in context, or pictures. You can change the frame to fit each term.

See the Note-Taking Handbook on pages R45–R51.

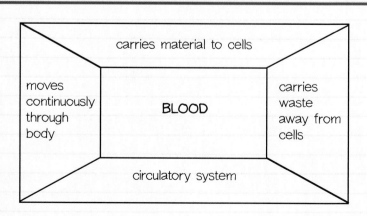

SCIENCE NOTEBOOK

MAIN IDEAS	DETAIL NOTES
1. The circulatory system works with other body systems.	1. Transports materials from digestive and respiratory systems to cells 2. Blood is fluid that carries materials and wastes 3. Blood is always moving through the body 4. Blood delivers oxygen and takes away carbon dioxide

carries material to cells

moves continuously through body

BLOOD

carries waste away from cells

circulatory system

The circulatory system transports materials.

◀ **BEFORE, you learned**

- The urinary system removes waste
- The kidneys play a role in homeostasis

▶ **NOW, you will learn**

- How different structures of the circulatory system work together
- About the structure and function of blood
- What blood pressure is and why it is important

VOCABULARY

circulatory system p. 65
blood p. 65
red blood cell p. 67
artery p. 69
vein p. 69
capillary p. 69

EXPLORE The Circulatory System

How fast does your heart beat?

PROCEDURE

① Hold out your left hand with your palm facing up.

② Place the first two fingers of your right hand on your left wrist below your thumb. Move your fingertips slightly until you can feel your pulse.

③ Use the stopwatch to determine how many times your heart beats in one minute.

WHAT DO YOU THINK?
- How many times did your heart beat?
- What do you think you would find if you took your pulse after exercising?

MATERIALS
stopwatch

VOCABULARY
Add a frame game diagram for the term *circulatory system* to your notebook.

The circulatory system works with other body systems.

You have read that the systems in your body provide materials and energy. The digestive system breaks down food and nutrients, and the respiratory system provides the oxygen that cells need to release energy. Another system, called the **circulatory system,** transports products from the digestive and the respiratory systems to the cells.

Materials and wastes are carried in a fluid called **blood**. Blood moves continuously through the body, delivering oxygen and other materials to cells and removing carbon dioxide and other wastes from cells.

Structures in the circulatory system function together.

RESOURCE CENTER
CLASSZONE.COM

Find out more about the circulatory system.

In order to provide the essential nutrients and other materials that your cells need, your blood must keep moving through your body. The circulatory system, which is made up of the heart and blood vessels, allows blood to flow to all parts of the body. The circulatory system works with other systems to provide the body with this continuous flow of life-giving blood.

The Heart

The heart is the organ that pushes blood throughout the circulatory system. The human heart actually functions as two pumps—one pump on the right side and one on the left side. The right side of the heart pumps blood to the lungs, and the left side pumps blood to the rest of the body. The lungs receive oxygen when you inhale and remove carbon dioxide when you exhale. Inside the lungs, the respiratory system interacts with the circulatory system.

The Heart

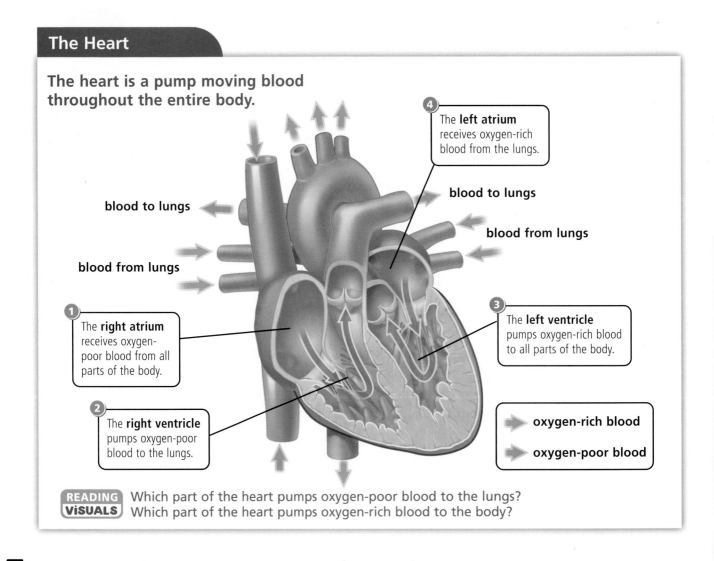

The heart is a pump moving blood throughout the entire body.

4 The **left atrium** receives oxygen-rich blood from the lungs.

blood to lungs

blood to lungs

blood from lungs

blood from lungs

1 The **right atrium** receives oxygen-poor blood from all parts of the body.

3 The **left ventricle** pumps oxygen-rich blood to all parts of the body.

2 The **right ventricle** pumps oxygen-poor blood to the lungs.

oxygen-rich blood

oxygen-poor blood

READING VISUALS Which part of the heart pumps oxygen-poor blood to the lungs? Which part of the heart pumps oxygen-rich blood to the body?

Each side of the heart is divided into two areas called chambers. Oxygen-poor blood, which is, blood from the body with less oxygen, flows to the right side of your heart, into a filling chamber called the right atrium. With each heartbeat, blood flows into a pumping chamber, the right ventricle, and then into the lungs, where it releases carbon dioxide waste and absorbs oxygen.

After picking up oxygen, blood is pushed back to the heart, filling another chamber, which is called the left atrium. Blood moves from the left atrium to the left ventricle, a pumping chamber, and again begins its trip out to the rest of the body. Both oxygen-poor blood and oxygen-rich blood are red. However, oxygen-rich blood is a much brighter and lighter shade of red than is oxygen-poor blood. The diagram on page 66 shows oxygen-poor blood in blue, so that you can tell where in the circulatory system oxygen-poor and oxygen-rich blood are found.

 Summarize the way blood moves through the heart. Remember, a summary contains only the most important information.

Blood

The oxygen that your cells need in order to release energy must be present in blood to travel through your body. Blood is a tissue made up of plasma, red blood cells, white blood cells, and platelets. About 60 percent of blood is plasma, a fluid that contains proteins, glucose, hormones, gases, and other substances dissolved in water.

White blood cells help your body fight infection by attacking disease-causing organisms. **Red blood cells** are more numerous than white blood cells and have a different function. They pick up oxygen in the lungs and transport it throughout the body. As red blood cells travel through the circulatory system, they deliver oxygen to other cells.

Platelets are large cell fragments that help form blood clots when a blood vessel is injured. You know what a blood clot is if you've observed a cut or a scrape. The scab that forms around a cut or scrape is made of clotted blood. After an injury such as a cut, platelets nearby begin to enlarge and become sticky. They stick to the injured area of the blood vessels and release chemicals that result in blood clotting. Blood clotting keeps blood vessels from losing too much blood.

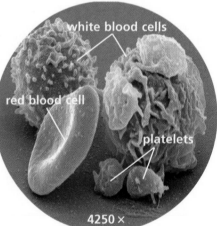

Blood is made mostly of red blood cells, white blood cells, and platelets.

 What are the four components that make up blood?

Circulatory System

The circulatory system allows blood to flow continuously throughout the body. The runner depends on a constant flow of oxygen-rich blood to fuel his cells.

oxygen-rich blood
oxygen-poor blood

The **heart** pumps oxygen-poor blood to the lungs and oxygen-rich blood to all parts of the body.

In the vessels of the **lungs**, oxygen-poor blood becomes oxygen-rich blood.

This major **vein** carries oxygen-poor blood from all parts of the body to the heart.

This major **artery** and its branches deliver oxygen-rich blood to all parts of the body.

This runner depends on a constant flow of oxygen-rich blood to fuel his cells.

As blood travels through blood vessels, some fluid is lost. This fluid, called lymph, is collected in lymph vessels and returned to veins and arteries. As you will read in the next section, lymph and lymph vessels are associated with your immune system. Sometimes scientists refer to the lymph and lymph vessels as the lymphatic system. The lymphatic system helps you fight disease.

Blood Vessels

Blood moves through a network of structures called blood vessels. Blood vessels are tube-shaped structures that are similar to flexible drinking straws. The structure of blood vessels suits them for particular functions. **Arteries**, which are the vessels that take blood away from the heart, have strong walls. An artery wall is thick and elastic and can handle the tremendous force produced when the heart pumps. **Veins** are blood vessels that carry blood back to the heart. The walls of veins are thinner than those of arteries. However, veins are generally of greater diameter than are arteries.

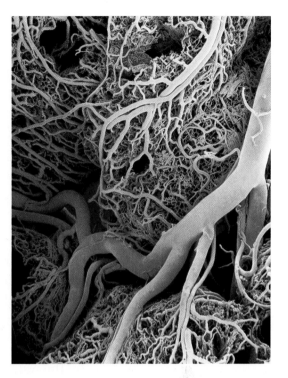

Arteries, capillaries, and veins form a complex web to carry blood to all the cells in the body (30×).

Most arteries carry oxygen-rich blood away from the heart, and most veins carry oxygen-poor blood back to the heart. However, the pulmonary blood vessels are exceptions. Oxygen-poor blood travels through the two pulmonary arteries, one of which goes to each lung. The two pulmonary veins carry oxygen-rich blood from the lungs to the heart.

Veins and arteries branch off into very narrow blood vessels called capillaries. **Capillaries** connect arteries with veins. Through capillaries materials are exchanged between blood and tissues. Oxygen and materials from nutrients move from the blood cells of arteries to the body's tissues through tiny openings in the capillary walls. Waste materials and carbon dioxide move from the tissues' cells through the capillary walls and into the blood in the veins.

 CHECK YOUR READING Compare and contrast arteries, veins, and capillaries.

Blood exerts pressure on blood vessels.

As you have read, the contractions of the heart push blood through blood vessels. The force produced when the heart contracts travels through the blood and exerts pressure on the blood vessels. This force is called blood pressure. To get an idea of how force affects pressure,

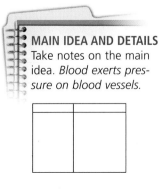

MAIN IDEA AND DETAILS
Take notes on the main idea. *Blood exerts pressure on blood vessels.*

consider a sealed plastic bag filled with water. If you push down at the center of the bag, you can see the water push against the sides.

The heart pushes blood in a similar way, exerting pressure on the arteries, veins, and capillaries in the circulatory system. It is important to maintain healthy blood pressure so that materials in blood get to all parts of your body. If blood pressure is too low, some of the cells will not get oxygen and other materials. On the other hand, if blood pressure is too high, the force may weaken the blood vessels and require the heart to work harder to push blood through the blood vessels. High blood pressure is a serious medical condition, but it can be treated.

The circulatory system can be considered as two smaller systems: one, the pulmonary system, moves blood to the lungs; the other, the systemic system, moves blood to the rest of the body. Blood pressure is measured in the systemic part of the circulatory system.

You can think of blood pressure as the pressure that blood exerts on the walls of your arteries when the heart contracts. Health professionals measure blood pressure indirectly with a device called a sphygmomanometer (SFIHG-moh-muh-NAHM-ih-tuhr).

Blood pressure is expressed with two numbers—one number over another number. The first number refers to the pressure in the arteries when the heart contracts. The second number refers to the pressure in the arteries when the heart relaxes and receives blood from the veins.

Blood Pressure

Blood pressure allows materials to travel to all parts of your body.

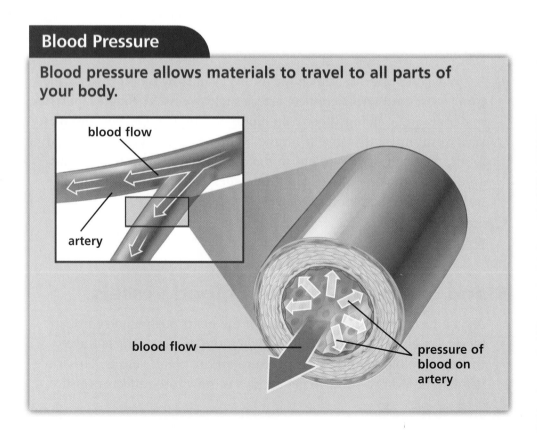

blood flow

artery

blood flow

pressure of blood on artery

Blood comes in four different types

Each red blood cell has special structures on its surface called antigens. There are two types of antigens, A and B. If your blood cells have A antigens, you have type A blood. If you have B antigens on your blood cells, you have type B blood. Some people have both antigens on their blood cells; they are said to have type AB blood. Some people have neither antigen and have type O blood. In the United States, O is the most common blood type, and AB is the least common.

Antibodies are present in the blood's liquid plasma. The antibodies will react with antigens of another blood type. Someone with type A blood has antibodies that react with type B blood; a person with type B blood has anti–type-A antibodies. Type O people have both types of antibodies; type AB people have none. Thus, people with type O blood are known as "universal donors," while those with AB blood are "universal recipients."

Knowing blood type is important, because one person can donate blood to another. However the blood types between donor and receiver must be compatible. If someone receives a blood of a type that triggers the antibodies in the plasma, his or her blood may clot. Such clotting can be fatal. The diagram shows which blood types are compatible. A person with blood type A can receive blood only from a person who has blood type O. Blood type O is said to be compatible with type A.

 CHECK YOUR READING Why is it important to know your blood type?

Blood Type Compatibility		
Blood Type	**Can Donate Blood To**	**Can Receive Blood From**
A	A, AB	A, O
B	B, AB	B, O
AB	AB	A, B, AB, O
O	A, B, AB, O	O

People can donate blood to others.

 RESOURCE CENTER
CLASSZONE.COM

Learn more about blood types.

3.1 Review

KEY CONCEPTS

1. What are the functions of the two sides of the heart?

2. What is the primary function of red blood cells?

3. Why can both high and low blood pressure be a problem?

CRITICAL THINKING

4. **Apply** List three examples of the circulatory system working with another system in your body.

5. **Compare and Contrast** Explain why blood pressure is expressed with two numbers.

○ CHALLENGE

6. **Identify Cause and Effect** You can feel the speed at which your heart is pumping by pressing two fingers to the inside of your wrist. This is your pulse. If you run for a few minutes, your pulse rate is faster for a little while, then it slows down again. Why did your pulse rate speed up and slow down?

CHAPTER INVESTIGATION

Heart Rate and Exercise

OVERVIEW AND PURPOSE In this activity, you will calculate your resting, maximum, and target heart rates. Then you will examine the effect of exercise on heart rate. Before you begin, read through the entire investigation.

▶ Procedure

MATERIALS
• notebook
• stopwatch
• calculator
• graph paper

1. Make a data table like the one shown on the sample notebook page.

2. Measure your resting heart rate. Find the pulse in the artery of your neck, just below and in front of the bottom of your ear, with the first two fingers of one hand. Do not use your thumb to measure pulse since the thumb has a pulse of its own. Once you have found the pulse, count the beats for 30 seconds and multiply the result by 2. The number you get is your resting heart rate in beats per minute. Record this number in your notebook.

step 2

3. Calculate your maximum heart rate by subtracting your age from 220. Record this number in your notebook. Your target heart rate should be 60 to 75 percent of your maximum heart rate. Calculate and record this range in your notebook.

4. Someone who is very athletic or has been exercising regularly for 6 months or more can safely exercise up to 85 percent of his or her maximum heart rate. Calculate and record this rate in your notebook.

5. Observe how quickly you reach your target heart rate during exercise. Begin by running in place at an intensity that makes you breathe harder but does not make you breathless. As with any exercise, remember that if you experience difficulty breathing, dizziness, or chest discomfort, stop exercising immediately.

step 5

⑥ Every 2 minutes, measure your heart rate for 10 seconds. Multiply this number by 6 to find your heart rate in beats per minute and record it in your notebook. Try to exercise for a total of 10 minutes. After you stop exercising, continue recording your heart rate every 2 minutes until it returns to the resting rate you measured in step 2.

▶ Observe and Analyze [Write It Up]

1. **GRAPH DATA** Make a line graph of your heart rate during and after the exercise. Graph the values in beats per minute versus time in minutes. Your graph should start at your resting heart rate and continue until your heart rate has returned to its resting rate. Using a colored pencil, shade in the area that represents your target heart-rate range.

2. **ANALYZE DATA** How many minutes of exercising were needed for you to reach your target heart rate of 60 to 75 percent of maximum? Did your heart rate go over your target range?

3. **INTERPRET DATA** How many minutes after you stopped exercising did it take for your heart rate to return to its resting rate? Why do you think your heart rate did not return to its resting rate immediately after you stopped exercising?

▶ Conclude [Write It Up]

1. **INFER** Why do you think that heart rate increases during exercise?

2. **IDENTIFY** What other body systems are affected when the heart rate increases?

3. **PREDICT** Why do you think that target heart rate changes with age?

4. **CLASSIFY** Create a table comparing the intensity of different types of exercise, such as walking, skating, bicycling, weight lifting, and any others you might enjoy.

▶ INVESTIGATE Further

CHALLENGE Determine how other exercises affect your heart rate. Repeat this investigation by performing one or two of the other exercises from your table. Present your data, with a graph, to the class.

Heart Rate and Exercise

Resting heart rate:

Maximum heart rate:

Target heart rate (60-75% of maximum):

Target heart rate (85% of maximum):

Table 1. Heart Rate During and After Exercise

Time (minutes)	0	2	4	6	8	10	12	14	16	18	20
Heart rate (beats per minute)											

3.2 The immune system defends the body.

 BEFORE, you learned

- The circulatory system works with other systems to fuel the body cells
- Structures in the circulatory system work together
- Blood pressure allows materials to reach all parts of the body

 NOW, you will learn

- How foreign material enters the body
- How the immune system responds to foreign material
- Ways that the body can become immune to a disease

VOCABULARY

pathogen p. 74
immune system p. 75
antibody p. 75
antigen p. 78
immunity p. 80
vaccine p. 80
antibiotic p. 81

EXPLORE Membranes

How does the body keep foreign particles out?

PROCEDURE

1. Place a white cloth into a sandwich bag and seal it. Fill a bowl with water and stir in several drops of food coloring.

2. Submerge the sandwich bag in the water. After five minutes, remove the bag and note the condition of the cloth.

3. Puncture the bag with a pin. Put the bag back in the water for five minutes. Remove the bag and note the condition of the cloth.

WHAT DO YOU THINK?

- How does a puncture in the bag affect its ability to protect the cloth?

MATERIALS
- white cloth
- zippered sandwich bag
- large bowl
- water
- food coloring
- small pin

Many systems defend the body from harmful materials.

MAIN IDEA AND DETAILS
Add the main idea *Many systems defend the body from harmful materials* to your chart along with detail notes.

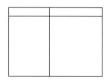

You might not realize it, but you come into contact with harmful substances constantly. Your body has ways to defend itself, and that is why you don't even notice. One of the body's best defenses is to keep foreign materials from entering in the first place. The integumentary (ihn-TEHG-yu-MEHN-tuh-ree), respiratory, and digestive systems are the first line of defense against **pathogens,** or disease-causing agents. Pathogens can enter through your skin, the air you breathe, and even the food you eat or liquids you drink.

 CHECK YOUR READING Which systems are your first line of defense against pathogens?

Integumentary System Defenses Most of the time, your skin functions as a barrier between you and the outside world. The physical barrier the skin forms is just one obstacle for pathogens. The growth of pathogens on your eyes can be slowed by other substances contained in tears. The millions of bacteria cells that live on the skin can also kill pathogens. The only way most pathogens can enter the body through the skin is through a cut. The circulatory system is then able to help defend the body because blood contains cells that destroy pathogens.

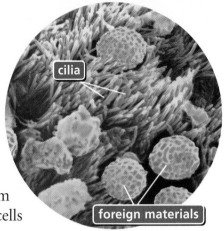

Cilia are hairlike protrusions that trap materials entering your respiratory system (600×).

Respiratory System Defenses Sneezing and coughing are two ways the respiratory system defends the body from harmful substances. Cilia and mucus also protect the body. Cilia are tiny, hairlike protrusions in the nose and the lungs that trap dust particles present in the air. Mucus is a thick and slippery substance found in the nose, throat, and lungs. Like the cilia, mucus traps dirt and other particles. Mucus contains substances similar to those in tears that can slow the growth of pathogens.

Digestive System Defenses Some foreign materials manage to enter your digestive system, but many are destroyed by saliva, mucus, enzymes, and stomach acids. Saliva in your mouth helps kill bacteria. Mucus protects the digestive organs by coating them. Pathogens can also be destroyed by enzymes produced in the liver and pancreas or by the acids in the stomach.

The immune system has response structures.

Sometimes foreign materials do manage to get past the first line of defense. When this happens, the body relies on the **immune system** to respond. This system functions in several ways:

- Tissues in the bone marrow, the thymus gland, the spleen, and the lymph nodes produce white blood cells, which are specialized cells that function to destroy foreign organisms.
- Some white blood cells produce a nonspecific response to injury or infection that is the second line of defense.
- Some white blood cells produce proteins called **antibodies,** which are part of a specific immune response to foreign materials.

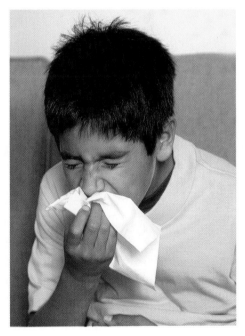

Sneezing helps to expel harmful substances from the body.

White Blood Cells

The immune system has specialized cells called white blood cells. There are five major types of white blood cells. The number of white blood cells in the blood can increase during an immune response. These cells travel through the circulatory system and the lymphatic system to an injured or infected area of the body. White blood cells leave the blood vessels and travel into the damaged tissue where the immune response takes place.

The Lymphatic System

RESOURCE CENTER
CLASSZONE.COM

Learn more about the lymphatic system.

The lymphatic system transports pathogen-fighting white blood cells throughout the body, much as the circulatory system does. The two systems are very similar. The lymphatic system carries lymph, and the circulatory system carries blood. Both fluids transport similar materials, such as white blood cells.

Lymph is the fluid left behind by the circulatory system. It moves through lymph vessels, which are similar to blood vessels. However, the lymphatic system has no pump like the heart to move fluid. Lymph drifts through the lymph vessels when your skeletal muscles contract or by gravity when your body changes position. As it moves, it passes through lymph nodes, which filter out pathogens and store white blood cells and antibodies. Because they filter out pathogens, infections are often fought in your lymph nodes, causing them to swell when you get sick.

CHECK YOUR READING How does the lymphatic system help the immune system?

The immune system responds to attack.

Certain illnesses can cause you to cough, sneeze, or have a fever. These signs of illness, or symptoms, make you uncomfortable when you are sick. But in fact, most symptoms are the result of the immune system's response to disease.

The immune system responds in two ways. The white blood cells that first respond to the site of injury or infection attack pathogens in a nonspecific response. These cells attack pathogens by engulfing them and also produce chemicals that help other white blood cells work better. The second part of the response is very specific to the types of pathogens invading the body. These white blood cells produce antibodies specific to each pathogen and provide your body with immunity.

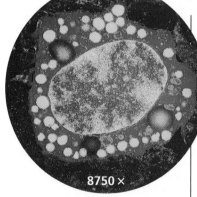

8750 ×

The mast cell above is an important part of the immune system.

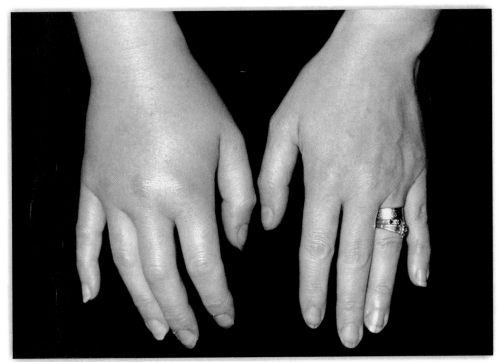

Wasp stings cause an immediate immune response. The area of the sting swells up and increases in temperature while your body battles the injury.

Nonspecific Response

Swelling, redness, and heat are some of the symptoms that tell you that a cut or scrape has become infected by foreign materials. They are all signs of inflammation, your body's first defense reaction against injuries and infections.

When tissue becomes irritated or damaged, it releases large amounts of histamine (HIHS-tuh-meen). Histamine raises the temperature of the tissues and increases blood flow to the area. Increased blood flow, which makes the injured area appear red, allows antibodies and white blood cells to arrive more quickly for battle. Higher temperatures improve the speed and power of white blood cells. Some pathogens cannot tolerate heat, so they grow weaker. The swelling caused by the production of histamine can be a small price to pay for this chemical's important work.

Histamine may also be produced when an illness affects more than one area of your body. In these cases, many tissues produce histamine. As a result, the temperature of your whole body rises. Any temperature above 37 degrees Celsius (98.6°F) is considered a fever, but only temperatures hot enough to damage tissues are dangerous. Trying to lower a high fever with medication is advisable in order to avoid tissue damage. When you have a small fever, lowering your body temperature might make you more comfortable, but it will not affect how long you stay sick.

 CHECK YOUR READING   What causes a fever when you are sick?

Specific Response

If a pathogen is not destroyed by the nonspecific response of the immune system, then a specific immune response occurs. T cells and B cells are the two major types of white blood cells that produce the immune response. They have different roles.

T Cells T cells identify and distinguish between pathogens because they recognize a marker called an **antigen,** which is carried by each pathogen. Each pathogen has a different type of antigen that only one type of T cell can recognize. When a T cell finds a pathogen with an antigen it recognizes, it begins to reproduce rapidly, making a large army of T cells that are also capable of identifying the antigen. Some T cells then attack cells that have been infected by the pathogen.

Immune Response

When pathogens invade the body, it uses white blood cells to fight back. T cells and B cells are two types of white blood cells that, together, identify and attack pathogens.

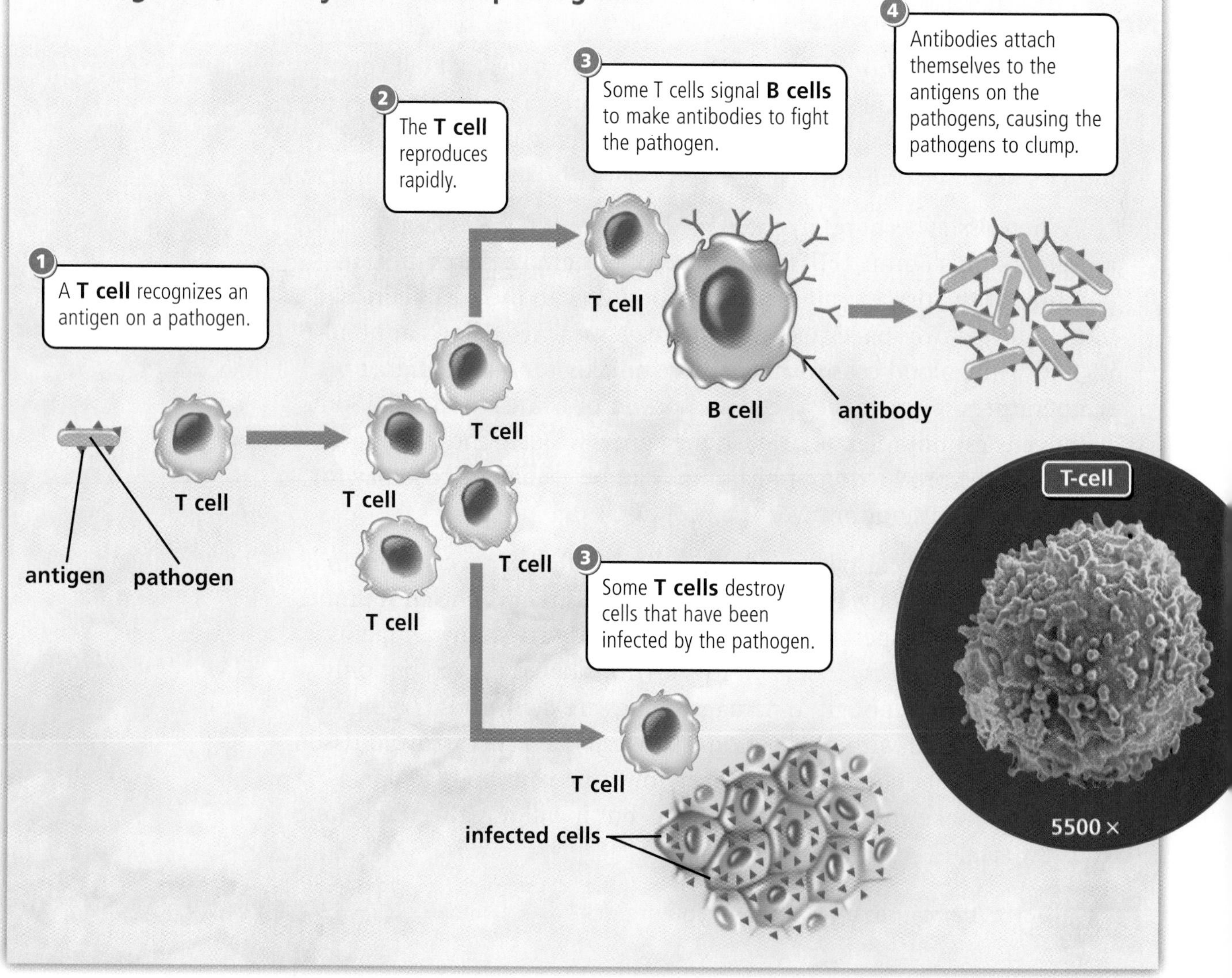

2 The **T cell** reproduces rapidly.

3 Some T cells signal **B cells** to make antibodies to fight the pathogen.

4 Antibodies attach themselves to the antigens on the pathogens, causing the pathogens to clump.

1 A **T cell** recognizes an antigen on a pathogen.

T cell

B cell   antibody

T cell

T cell

T cell

T cell

antigen   pathogen

T cell

3 Some **T cells** destroy cells that have been infected by the pathogen.

T cell

infected cells

T-cell

5500×

INVESTIGATE Antibodies

How do antibodies stop pathogens from spreading?

PROCEDURE

1. Your teacher will hand out plastic lids, each labeled with the name of a different pathogen. You will see plastic containers spread throughout the room. There is one container in the room with the same label as your lid.

2. At the signal, find the plastic container with the pathogen that has the same label as your lid and wait in place for the teacher to tell you to stop. If you still haven't found the matching container when time is called, your model pathogen has spread.

3. If your pathogen has spread, write its name on the board.

WHAT DO YOU THINK?

Which pathogens spread?

- What do you think the lid and container represent? Why?
- How do antibodies identify pathogens?

CHALLENGE Why do you think it is important for your body to identify pathogens?

SKILL FOCUS
Making models

MATERIALS
- plastic containers with lids
- index cards

TIME
15 minutes

B Cells After the T cells recognize an antigen, B cells are signaled to make antibodies to destroy the pathogen. Once a B cell finds the antigen, it releases antibodies, which attach themselves to the antigen. This causes pathogens to clump, making them unable to cause damage. In some cases, antigens and antibodies mark pathogens for attack by T cells.

Some of the antibodies remain in the body as a form of immune system memory. If the same type of foreign material appears, the system can respond much more quickly, because B cells do not have to produce a new antibody. Structures in the lymphatic system called lymph nodes store masses of white blood cells and antibodies until a large number are needed at one location.

> **READING TiP**
> *Antigen* and *antibody* are words that look very similar. Antigens are markers on pathogens. Antibodies fight pathogens.

 Why is it important for the body to store antibodies?

Development of Immunity

After your body has won out against a specific pathogen, antibodies designed to fight that pathogen remain in your system. If the same pathogen were to attack again, your immune system would almost certainly destroy it before you became ill. This resistance to a sickness is called **immunity.**

Immunity takes two forms: passive and active. When babies are first born, they have only the immune defenses given to them by their mothers. They have not had the chance to develop antibodies on their own. This type of immunity is called passive immunity. Antibodies are not produced by the person's own body but given to the body from another source. Babies must develop their own antibodies after a few months.

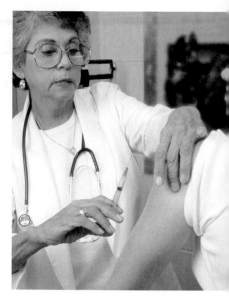

COMPARE A doctor gives a girl a vaccination. Is getting a vaccination an example of passive or active immunity?

You have active immunity whenever your body makes its own antibodies. Your body will again fight against any specific pathogen you have developed antibodies against. For example, it is most unlikely that you will get the same cold twice.

 What is the difference between active and passive immunity?

Most diseases can be prevented or treated.

Given enough time, your body will fight off most diseases. However, some infections can cause significant and lasting damage before they are defeated by the body's defenses. Other infections are so strong that the immune system cannot fight them. Medical advances in the prevention and treatment of diseases have reduced the risks of serious illness.

Vaccination

Another way to develop an immunity is to receive a **vaccine.** Vaccines contain small amounts of weakened pathogens that stimulate your immune response. Your B cells are called into action to create antibodies as if you were fighting the real illness. The pathogens are usually weakened, so that you will not get sick, yet they still enable your body to develop an active immunity.

Today we have vaccines for many common pathogens. Most children who are vaccinated will not get many diseases that their great grandparents, grandparents, and even parents had. Vaccinations can be administered by injection or by mouth. Babies are not the only ones who get them, either. You can be vaccinated at any age.

 CHECK YOUR READING Why don't vaccinations usually make you sick?

Treatment

Not all diseases can be prevented, but many of them can be treated. In some cases, treatments can only reduce the symptoms of the disease while the immune system fights the disease-causing pathogens. Other treatments attack the pathogens directly.

In some cases, treatment can only prevent further damage to body tissues by a pathogen that cannot be cured or defeated by the immune system. The way in which a disease is treated depends on what pathogen causes it. Most bacterial infections can be treated with antibiotics. **Antibiotics** are medicines that block the growth and reproduction of bacteria. You may have taken antibiotics when you have had a disease such as strep throat or an ear infection.

Types of Pathogens	
Disease	**Pathogen**
Colds, chicken pox, hepatitis, AIDS, influenza, mumps, measles, rabies	virus
Food poisoning, strep throat, tetanus, tuberculosis, acne, ulcers, Lyme disease	bacteria
Athlete's foot, thrush, ringworm	fungus
Malaria, parasitic pneumonia, pinworm, lice, scabies	parasites

3.2 Review

KEY CONCEPTS

1. Make a chart showing three ways that foreign material enters the body and how the immune system defends against each type of attack.

2. What are white blood cells and what is their function in the body?

3. What are two ways to develop immunity?

CRITICAL THINKING

4. **Compare and Contrast** Make a chart comparing B cells and T cells. Include an explanation of the function of antibodies.

5. **Apply** Describe how your immune system responds when you scrape your knee.

⚠ CHALLENGE

6. **Hypothesize** Explain why, even if a person recovers from a cold, that person could get a cold again.

MATH in SCIENCE

MATH TUTORIAL
CLASSZONE.COM
Click on Math Tutorial
for more help making
line graphs.

Pollen Counts

Every year, sometime between July and October, in nearly every state in the United States, the air will fill with ragweed pollen. For a person who has a pollen allergy, these months blur with tears. Linn County, Iowa, takes weekly counts of ragweed and non-ragweed pollen.

Weekly Pollen Counts, Linn County, Iowa											
	Jul. 29	Aug. 5	Aug. 12	Aug. 19	Aug. 26	Sept. 2	Sept. 9	Sept. 16	Sept. 23	Sept. 30	Oct. 7
Ragweed (Grain/m^3)	0	9	10	250	130	240	140	25	20	75	0
Non-Ragweed (Grain/m^3)	10	45	15	50	100	50	40	10	20	25	0

Example

A line graph of the data will show the pattern of increase and decrease of ragweed pollen in the air.

(1) Begin with a quadrant with horizontal and vertical axes.

(2) Mark the weekly dates at even intervals on the horizontal axis.

(3) Starting at 0 on the vertical axis, mark even intervals of 50 units.

(4) Graph each point. Connect the points with line segments.

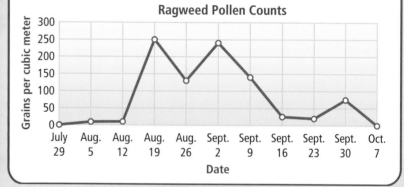

Complete and present your graph as directed below.

1. Use graph paper to make your own line graph of the non-ragweed pollen in Linn County.

2. Write some questions that can be answered by comparing the two graphs. Trade questions with a partner.

3. Which weeks have the highest pollen counts in Linn County?

CHALLENGE Try making a double line graph combining both sets of data in one graph.

The pollen of *Ambrosia artemisiifolia* (common ragweed) sets off a sneeze.

The integumentary system shields the body.

 BEFORE, you learned

- The body is defended from harmful materials
- Response structures fight disease
- The immune system responds in many ways to illness

 NOW, you will learn

- About the functions of the skin
- How the skin helps protect the body
- How the skin grows and heals

VOCABULARY

integumentary system p. 83
epidermis p. 84
dermis p. 84

EXPLORE The Skin

What are the functions of skin?

PROCEDURE

① Using a vegetable peeler, remove the skin from an apple. Take notes on the characteristics of the apple's peeled surface. Include observations on its color, moisture level, and texture.

② Place the apple on a dry surface. After fifteen minutes, note any changes in its characteristics.

WHAT DO YOU THINK?

- What is the function of an apple's skin? What does it prevent?
- What does this experiment suggest about how skin might function in the human body?

MATERIALS

- vegetable peeler
- apple

Skin performs important functions.

MAIN IDEA AND DETAILS
Start a two-column chart with the main idea *Skin performs important functions*. Add detail notes about those functions.

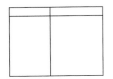

Just as an apple's skin protects the fruit inside, your skin protects the rest of your body. Made up of flat sheets of cells, your skin protects the inside of your body from harmful materials outside. The skin is part of your body's **integumentary system** (ihn-TEHG-yu-MEHN-tuh-ree), which also includes your hair and nails.

Your skin fulfills several vital functions:

- Skin repels water.
- Skin guards against infection.
- Skin helps maintain homeostasis.
- Skin senses the environment.

When you look at your hand, you only see the outer layer of skin. The skin has many structures to protect your body.

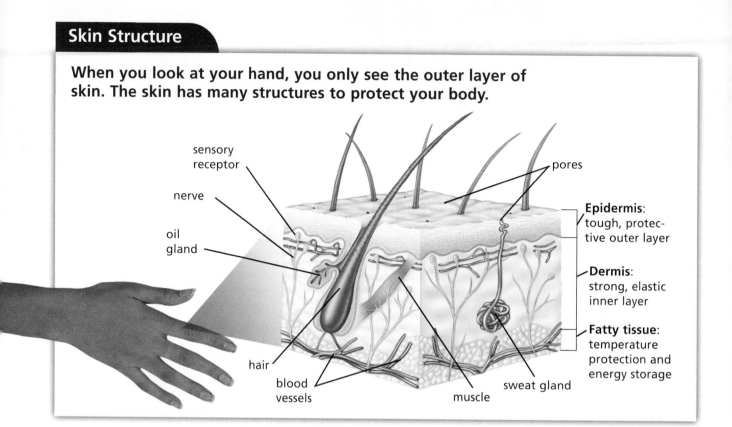

sensory receptor

nerve

oil gland

hair

blood vessels

muscle

sweat gland

pores

Epidermis: tough, protective outer layer

Dermis: strong, elastic inner layer

Fatty tissue: temperature protection and energy storage

The structure of skin is complex.

Have you ever looked closely at your skin? Your skin is more complex than it might at first seem. It does more than just cover your body. The skin is made up of many structures, which perform many different jobs.

Dermis and Epidermis

VOCABULARY
Add frame games for *epidermis* and *dermis* to your notebook.

As you can see in the diagram above, human skin is composed of two layers: an outer layer, called the **epidermis,** and an inner layer, called the **dermis.** The cells of the epidermis contain many protein fibers that give the skin tough, protective qualities. These cells are formed in the deepest part of the epidermis. Skin cells move upward slowly as new cells form below them. Above new cells, older cells rub off. The surface cells in the epidermis are dead but form a thick, waterproof layer about 30 cells deep.

The dermis, the inner layer of skin, is made of tissue that is strong and elastic. The structure of the dermis allows it to change shape instead of tear when it moves against surfaces. The dermis is rich in blood vessels, which supply oxygen and nutrients to the skin's living cells. Just beneath the dermis lies a layer of fatty tissue. This layer protects the body from extremes in temperature, and it stores energy for future use. Also in the dermis are structures that have special functions, including sweat and oil glands, hair, nails, and sensory receptors.

Sweat and Oil Glands

RESOURCE CENTER
CLASSZONE.COM

Explore the structure of skin.

Deep within the dermis are structures that help maintain your body's internal environment. Sweat glands help control body temperature, and oil glands protect the skin by keeping it moist. Both types of glands open to the surface through tiny openings in the skin called pores. Pores allow important substances to pass to the skin's surface. Pores can become clogged with dirt and oil. Keeping the skin clean can prevent blockages.

Sweat glands, which are present almost everywhere on the body's surface, help maintain homeostasis. When you become too warm, the sweat glands secrete sweat, a fluid that is 99% water. This fluid travels from the sweat glands, through the pores, and onto the skin's surface. You probably know already about evaporation. Evaporation is the process by which a liquid becomes a gas. During evaporation, heat is released. Thus, sweating cools the skin's surface and the body.

Like sweat glands, oil glands are present almost everywhere on the body. They secrete an oil that moistens skin and hair and keeps them from becoming dry. Skin oils add flexibility and provide part, but not all, of the skin's waterproofing.

 CHECK YOUR READING What are the functions of oil glands?

INVESTIGATE Skin Protection

How does oil protect your skin?

PROCEDURE

1. Rub a cotton ball dampened with alcohol across one of your palms.

2. Drip a couple of drops of water onto the palm with alcohol. Observe what happens. Record your observations.

3. Drip a couple of drops of water onto your other palm. Observe what happens. Record your observations.

WHAT DO YOU THINK?

• Compare the observations for each palm.

• What does this investigation suggest about the importance of oil and oil glands?

CHALLENGE Predict what might happen to your skin if you removed every trace of oil several times a day.

SKILL FOCUS
Observing

MATERIALS
• cotton ball
• rubbing alcohol
• dropper
• water

TIME
10 minutes

Hair and Nails

In addition to your skin, your integumentary system includes your hair and nails. Many cells in your hair and nails are actually dead but continue to perform important functions.

The hair on your head helps your body in many ways. When you are outside, it shields your head from the Sun. In cold weather, it traps heat close to your head to keep you warmer. Your body hair works the same way, but it is much less effective at protecting your skin and keeping you warm.

Fingernails and toenails protect the tips of the fingers and toes from injury. Both are made of epidermal cells that are thick and tough. They grow from the nail bed, which continues to manufacture cells as the cells that form the nail bed bond together and grow.

CHECK YOUR READING What are the functions of hair and nails?

145 ×

Hair

220 ×

Nails

Your hair and nails are made of dead cells, which continue to protect you.

Sensory Receptors

How does your body know when you are touching something too hot or too cold? You get that information from sensory receptors attached to the nerves. These receptors are actually part of the nervous system, but they are located in your skin. Your skin contains receptors that sense pressure, temperature, pain, touch, and vibration. These sensors help protect the body. For example, temperature receptors sense when an object is hot. If it is too hot and you touch it, pain receptors send signals to your brain telling you that you have been burned.

CHECK YOUR READING What are the five types of sensory receptors in skin?

The skin grows and heals.

As a person grows, skin also grows. As you have noticed if you have ever had a bruise or a cut, your skin is capable of healing. Skin can often repair itself after injury or illness.

Growth

As your bones grow, you get taller. As your muscles develop, your arms and legs become thicker. Through all your body's growth and change, your skin has to grow, too.

Most of the growth of your skin occurs at the base of the epidermis, just above the dermis. The cells there grow and divide to form new cells, constantly replacing older epidermal cells as they die and are brushed off during daily activity. Cells are lost from the skin's surface all the time: every 2 to 4 weeks, your skin surface is entirely new. In fact, a percentage of household dust is actually dead skin cells.

Healing Skin

Small injuries to the skin heal by themselves over time.

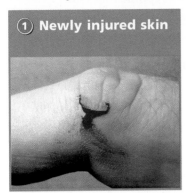
① **Newly injured skin**

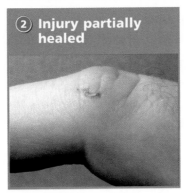
② **Injury partially healed**

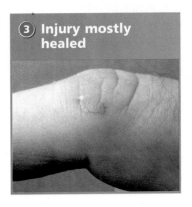
③ **Injury mostly healed**

READING VISUALS How do you think small injuries to the skin heal?

Injuries and Healing

You have probably experienced some injuries to your skin, such as blisters, burns, cuts, and bruises. Most such injuries result from the skin's contact with the outside world, such as a concrete sidewalk. In simple injuries, the skin can usually repair itself.

Burns can be serious injuries. They can be caused by heat, electricity, radiation, or certain chemicals. In mild cases—those of first-degree burns—skin merely becomes red, and the burn heals in a day or two. In severe cases—those of second-degree and third-degree burns—the body loses fluids, and death can result from fluid loss, infection, and other complications.

VISUALIZATION
CLASSZONE.COM

Explore how the skin heals.

Sunburns are usually minor first-degree burns, but that does not mean they cannot be serious. Rays from the Sun can burn and blister the skin much as a hot object can. Repeated burning can increase the chance of skin cancer. Specialized cells in the skin absorb the Sun's ultraviolet rays and help prevent tissue damage. These cells produce the skin pigment melanin when exposed to the Sun. The amount of melanin in your skin determines how dark your skin is.

Severe cold can damage skin as well. Skin exposed to cold weather can get frostbite, a condition in which the cells are damaged by freezing. Mild frostbite often heals just as well as a minor cut. In extreme cases, frostbitten limbs become diseased and have to be amputated.

 CHECK YOUR READING What types of weather can damage your skin?

Protection

Your skin is constantly losing old cells and gaining new cells. Although your skin is always changing, it is still important to take care of it.

- Good nutrition supplies materials the skin uses to maintain and repair itself. By drinking water, you help your body, and thus your skin, to remain moist and able to replace lost cells.
- Appropriate coverings, such as sunblock in summer and warm clothes in winter, can protect the skin from weather damage.
- Skin also needs to be kept clean. Many harmful bacteria cannot enter the body through healthy skin, but they should be washed off regularly. This prevents them from multiplying and then entering the body through small cuts or scrapes.

Wearing sunblock when you are outside protects your skin from harmful rays from the Sun.

3.3 Review

KEY CONCEPTS

1. List four functions of the skin.
2. How do the epidermis and dermis protect the body?
3. Make your own diagram with *How skin grows and repairs itself* at the center. Around the center, write at least five facts about skin growth and healing.

CRITICAL THINKING

4. **Apply** Give three examples from everyday life of sensory receptors in your skin reacting to changes in your environment.
5. **Connect** Describe a situation in which sensory receptors could be critical to survival.

CHALLENGE

6. **Infer** Exposure to sunlight may increase the number of freckles on a person's skin. Explain the connection between sunlight, melanin, and freckles.

EXTREME SCIENCE

Artificial Skin

Skin acts like a barrier, keeping our insides in and infections out. Nobody can survive without skin. But when a large amount of skin is severely damaged, the body cannot work fast enough to replace it. In some cases there isn't enough undamaged skin left on the body for transplanting. Using skin from another person risks introducing infections or rejection by the body. The answer? Artificial skin.

Here's the Skinny

To make artificial skin, scientists start with cells in a tiny skin sample. Cells from infants are used because infant skin-cell molecules are still developing, and scientists can manipulate the molecules to avoid transplant rejection. The cells from just one small sample of skin can be grown into enough artificial skin to cover 15 basketball courts. Before artificial skin, badly burned victims didn't have much chance to live. Today, 96 out of 100 burn victims survive.

A surgeon lifts a layer of artificial skin. The skin is so thin, a newspaper could be read behind it.

What's Next?

- Scientists are hoping to be able to grow organs using this technology. Someday artificially grown livers, kidneys, and hearts may take the place of transplants and mechanical devices.

- A self-repairing plastic skin that knits itself back together when cracked has been developed. It may someday be used to create organs or even self-repairing rocket and spacecraft parts.

- Artificial polymer "skin" for robots is being developed to help robots do delicate work such as microsurgery or space exploration.

Robot designer David Hanson has developed the K-bot, a lifelike face that uses 24 motors to create expressions.

EXPLORE

1. **COMPARE AND CONTRAST** Detail the advantages and disadvantages of skin transplanted from another place on the body and artificial skin.

2. **CHALLENGE** Artificial skin is being considered for applications beyond those originally envisioned. Research and present a new potential application.

A spray-on polymer creates an artificial outer skin to help heal surface wounds on an arm.

the **BIG** idea

Systems function to transport materials and to defend and protect the body.

CONTENT REVIEW
CLASSZONE.COM

◀ KEY CONCEPTS SUMMARY

(3.1) The circulatory system transports materials.

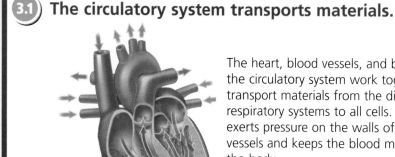

The heart, blood vessels, and blood of the circulatory system work together to transport materials from the digestive and respiratory systems to all cells. The blood exerts pressure on the walls of the blood vessels and keeps the blood moving around the body.

VOCABULARY
circulatory system
  p. 65
blood p. 65
red blood cell p. 67
artery p. 69
vein p. 69
capillary p. 69

(3.2) The immune system defends the body.

The immune system defends the body from pathogens. White blood cells identify and attack pathogens that find their way inside the body. The immune system responds to attack with inflammation, fever, and development of immunity.

Types of Pathogens	
Disease	**Pathogen**
colds, chicken pox, hepatitis, AIDS, influenza, mumps, measles, rabies	virus
food poisoning, strep throat, tetanus, tuberculosis, acne, ulcers, Lyme disease	bacteria
athlete's foot, thrush, ring worm	fungus
malaria, parasitic pneumonia, pinworm, lice, scabies	parasites

VOCABULARY
pathogen p. 74
immune system p. 75
antibody p. 75
antigen p. 78
immunity p. 80
vaccine p. 80
antibiotic p. 81

(3.3) The integumentary system shields the body.

The skin protects the body from harmful materials in the environment, and allows you to sense temperature, pain, touch, and vibration. In most cases the skin is able to heal itself after injury.

VOCABULARY
integumentary system
  p. 83
epidermis p. 84
dermis p. 84

Draw a word triangle for each of the terms below. Write a term and its definition in the bottom section. In the middle section, write a sentence in which you use the term correctly. In the top section, draw a small picture to illustrate the term.

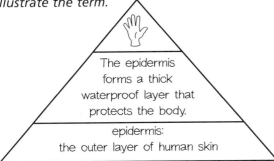

The epidermis forms a thick waterproof layer that protects the body.

epidermis: the outer layer of human skin

1. capillary

2. blood

3. dermis

4. antigen

Write a sentence describing the relationship between each pair of terms.

5. pathogen, antibody

6. artery, vein

7. immunity, vaccine

Reviewing Key Concepts

Multiple Choice *Choose the letter of the best answer.*

8. Which chamber of the heart pumps oxygen-poor blood into the lungs?
  a. right atrium
  b. right ventricle
  c. left atrium
  d. left ventricle

9. Which blood structures carry blood back to the heart?
  a. veins   **c.** arteries
  b. capillaries   **d.** platelets

10. The structures in the blood that carry oxygen to the cells of the body are the
  a. plasma   **c.** white blood cells
  b. platelets   **d.** red blood cells

11. High blood pressure is unhealthy because it
  a. does not exert enough pressure on your arteries
  b. causes your heart to work harder
  c. does not allow enough oxygen to get to the cells in your body
  d. causes your veins to collapse

12. Which category of pathogens causes strep throat?
  a. virus   **c.** fungus
  b. bacteria   **d.** parasite

13. Which of the following is a function of white blood cells?
  a. destroying foreign organisms
  b. providing your body with nutrients
  c. carrying oxygen to the body's cells
  d. forming a blood clot

14. Which makes up the integumentary system?
  a. a network of nerves
  b. white blood cells and antibodies
  c. the brain and spinal cord
  d. the skin, hair, and nails

15. Which structure is found in the epidermis layer of the skin?
  a. pores   **c.** surface cells
  b. sweat glands   **d.** oil glands

16. The layer of fatty tissue below the dermis protects the body from
  a. cold temperatures **c.** sunburn
  b. bacteria   **d.** infection

Short Answer *Write a short answer to each question.*

17. What are platelets? Where are they found?

18. What are antibodies? Where are they found?

19. What special structures are found in the dermis layer of the skin?

Thinking Critically

20. COMPARE AND CONTRAST How do the functions of the atria and ventricles of the heart differ? How are they alike? Use this diagram of the heart as a guide.

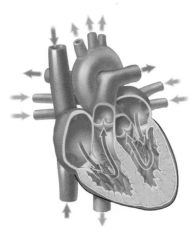

21. APPLY Veins have one-way valves that push the blood back to the heart. Most arteries do not have valves. Explain how these structures help the circulatory system function.

22. PROVIDE EXAMPLES Describe three structures in the body that help prevent harmful foreign substances from entering the body.

23. IDENTIFY CAUSE HIV is a virus that attacks and destroys the body's T cells. Why is a person who is infected with the HIV virus more susceptible to infection and disease?

24. APPLY You fall and scrape your knee. How does the production of histamines aid the healing of this injury?

25. ANALYZE Describe how the structure of the epidermis helps protect the body from disease.

25. SYNTHESIZE Explain how sweat glands, oil glands, and hair help your body maintain homeostasis.

27. HYPOTHESIZE People with greater concentrations of melanin in their skin are less likely to get skin cancer than people who have lesser concentrations of melanin. Write a hypothesis explaining why this is so.

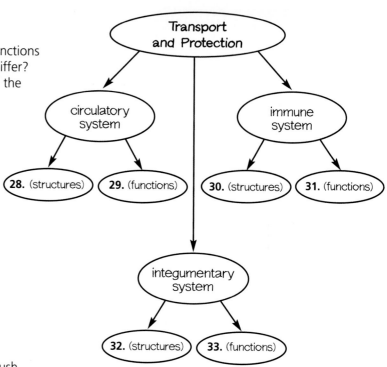

the BIG idea

34. INFER Look again at the picture on pages 62–63. Now that you have finished the chapter, how would you change or add details to your answer to the question on the photograph?

35. SYNTHESIZE Write a paragraph explaining how the integumentary system and the immune system work together to help your body maintain its homeostasis. Underline these terms in your paragraph.

UNIT PROJECTS

If you need to create graphs or other visuals for your project, be sure you have grid paper, poster board, markers, and other supplies.

Standardized Test Practice

For practice on your state test, go to . . .
TEST PRACTICE
CLASSZONE.COM

Analyzing Data

Choose the letter of the best answer.

This chart shows the amount of time a person can stay in the sun without burning, based on skin type and use of a sunscreen with the SPF shown.

Recommended Sun Protection Factors (SPF)

Skin Type	1 hr	2hr	3 hr	4hr	5hr
Very Fair/ Sensitive	15	30	30	45	45
Fair/Sensitive	15	15	30	30	45
Fair	15	15	15	30	30
Medium	8	8	15	15	30
Dark	4	8	8	15	15

1. What is the least SPF that a person with very fair skin should use while exposed to the sun?

a. 8
b. 15
c. 30
d. 45

2. If a person with a medium skin type is exposed to the sun for 5 hours, which SPF should be used?

a. 4
b. 8
c. 15
d. 30

3. Which skin type requires SPF 30 for three hours of sun exposure?

a. fair/sensitive
b. fair
c. medium
d. dark

4. Based on the data in the chart, which statement is a reasonable conclusion?

a. People with a fair skin type are less prone to UV damage than those with a dark skin type.
b. The darker the skin type, the more SPF protection a person needs.
c. A person with a medium skin type does not need as much SPF protection as a person with a fair skin type.
d. If exposure to the sun is longer, then a person needs a higher SPF for protection.

5. If a person normally burns after 10 minutes with no protection, an SPF 2 would protect that person for 20 minutes. How long would the same person be protected with SPF 15?

a. 1 hour
b. $1\frac{1}{2}$ hours
c. 2 hours
d. $2\frac{1}{2}$ hours

Extended Response

6. UV index levels are often broadcast with daily weather reports. A UV index of 0 to 2 indicates that it would take an average person about 60 minutes to burn. A UV index level of 10 indicates that it would take the average person about 10 minutes to burn. Write a paragraph describing some variable conditions that would affect this rate. Include both environmental as well as conditions that would apply to an individual.

7. Sun protection factors are numbers on a scale that rate the effectiveness of sunscreen. Without the use of sunscreen, UV rays from the Sun can cause sunburns. People who spend time in the sun without protection, or who get repeated burns are at a higher risk of developing deadly forms of skin cancer. Based on the information in the table and your knowledge of the layers of the skin, design a brochure encouraging people to protect their skin from the sun. Include in your brochure the harmful effects on your skin and ways to protect your skin from harmful UV rays.

TIMELINES in Science

SEEING INSIDE the Body

What began as a chance accident in a darkened room was only the beginning. Today, technology allows people to produce clear and complete pictures of the human body. From X-rays to ultrasound to the latest computerized scans, accidental discoveries have enabled us to study and diagnose the inner workings of the human body.

Being able to see inside the body without cutting it open would have seemed unthinkable in the early 1890s. But within a year of the discovery of the X-ray in 1895, doctors were using technology to see through flesh to bones. In the time since then, techniques for making images have advanced to allow doctors to see soft tissue, muscle, and even to see how body systems work in real time. Many modern employ X-ray technology, while others employ sound waves or magnetic fields.

1895

Accidental X-Ray Shows Bones

Working alone in a darkened lab to study electric currents passing through vacuum tubes, William Conrad Roentgen sees a mysterious light. He puts his hand between the tubes and a screen, and an image appears on the screen—a skeletal hand! He names his discovery the X-ray, since the images are produced by rays behaving like none known before them. Roentgen uses photographic paper to take the first X-ray picture, his wife's hand.

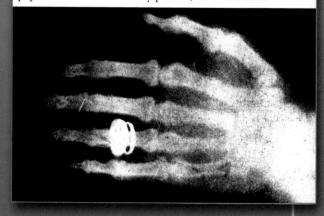

EVENTS

1880   1890

APPLICATIONS AND TECHNOLOGY

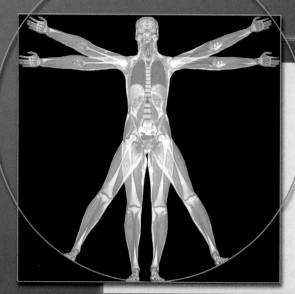

APPLICATION

Doctor Detectives

Within a year of Roentgen's discovery, X-rays were used in medicine for examining patients. By the 1920s, their use was wide-spread. Modern day X-ray tubes are based on the design of William Coolidge. Around 1913, Coolidge developed a new X-ray tube which, unlike the old gas tube, provides consistent exposure and quality. X-ray imaging changed the practice of medicine by allowing doctors to look inside the body without using surgery. Today, X-ray images, and other technologies, like the MRI used to produce the image at the left, show bones, organs, and tissues.

1914–1918

Radiologists in the Trenches

In World War I field hospitals, French physicians use X-ray technology to quickly diagnose war injuries. Marie Curie trains the majority of the female X-ray technicians. Following the War, doctors return to their practices with new expertise.

1898

Radioactivity

Building on the work of Henri Becquerel, who in 1897 discovers "rays" from uranium, physicist, Marie Curie discovers radioactivity. She wins a Nobel Prize in Chemistry in 1911 for her work in radiology.

1955

See-Through Smile

X-ray images of the entire jaw and teeth allow dentist to check the roots of teeth and wisdom teeth growing below the gum line.

1900   **1910**   **1950**

APPLICATION

Better Dental Work

Throughout the 1940s and 1950s dentists began to use X-rays. Photographing teeth with an X-ray allows cavities or decay to show up as dark spots on a white tooth. Photographing below the gum line shows dentists the pattern of growth of new teeth. By 1955, dentists could take a panoramic X-ray, one which shows the entire jaw. In the early years of dental X-rays, little was known about the dangers of radiation. Today, dentists cover a patient with a lead apron to protect them from harmful rays.

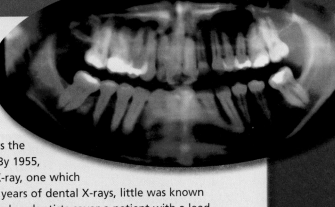

1976

New Scans Show Blood Vessels

The first computerized tomography (CT) systems scan only the head, but whole-body scanners follow by 1976. With the CT scan, doctors see clear details of blood vessels, bones, and soft organs. Instead of sending out a single X-ray, a CT scan sends several beams from different angles. Then a computer joins the images, as shown in this image of a heart.

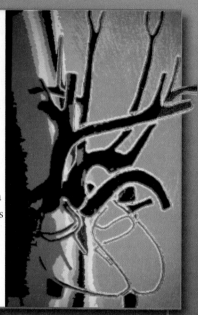

1977

Minus the Radiation

Doctors Raymond Damadian, Larry Minkoff, and Michael Goldsmith, develop the first magnetic resonance imaging (MRI). They nick-name the new machine "The Indomitable," as everyone told them it couldn't be done. MRI allows doctors to "see" soft tissue, like the knee below, in sharp detail without the use of radiation.

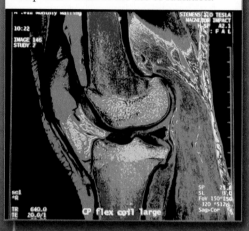

1973

PET Shows What's Working

The first positron emission tomography machine is called PET Scanner 1. It uses small doses of radioactive dye which travel through a patient's bloodstream. A PET scan then shows the distribution of the dye. This image of a face is made with PET scan technology.

1960   **1970**   **1980**

TECHNOLOGY

Ultrasound: Moving Images in Real Time

Since the late 1950s, Ian Donald's team in Scotland had been viewing internal organs on a TV monitor using vibrations faster than sound. In 1961, while examining a female patient, Donald noticed a developing embryo. Following the discovery, ultrasound imaging became widely used to monitor the growth and health of fetuses. Ultrasound captures images in real-time, showing movement of internal tissues and organs. Ultrasound uses high frequency sound waves to create images of organs or structures inside the body. Sound waves are bounced back from organs, and a computer converts the sound waves into moving images on a television monitor.

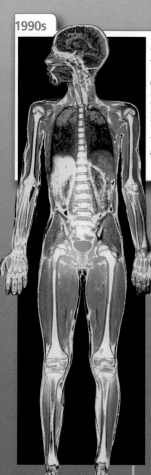

1990s

Filmless Images
With digital imaging, everything from X-rays to MRIs is now filmless. Data moves directly into 3D computer programs and shared databases.

2003
Multi-Slice CT
By 2003, 8- and 16-slice CT scanners offer detail and speed. A multi-slice scanner reduces exam time from 45 minutes to under 10 seconds.

RESOURCE CENTER
CLASSZONE.COM
Find more on advances in medical imaging.

1990   **2000**

TECHNOLOGY

3-D Images and Brain Surgery

In operating rooms, surgeons are beginning to use another type of 3D ultrasound known as interventional MRI. They watch 3-D images in real time and observe details of tissues while they operate. These integrated technologies now allow scientists to conduct entirely new types of studies. For example, 3-D brain images of many patients with one disease—can now be integrated into a composite image of a "typical" brain of someone with that disease.

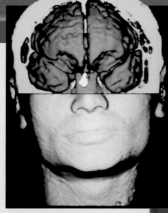

INTO THE FUTURE

Although discovered over 100 years ago X-rays are certain to remain a key tool of health workers for many years. What will be different in the future? Dentists have begun the trend to stop using film images, and rely on digital X-rays instead. In the future, all scans may be viewed and stored on computers. Going digital allows doctors across the globe to share images quickly by email.

Magnetic resonance imaging has only been in widespread use for about 20 years. Look for increased brain mapping—ability to scan the brain during a certain task. The greater the collective data on brain-mapping, the better scientists will understand how the brain works. To produce such an image requires thousands of patients and trillions of bytes of computer memory.

Also look for increased speed and mobile MRI scanners, which will be used in emergency rooms and doctor's offices to quickly assess internal damage after an accident or injury.

ACTIVITIES

Writing About Science: Brochure
Make a chart of the different types of medical imaging used to diagnose one body system. Include an explanation of how the technique works and list the pros and cons of using it.

Reliving History
X-rays use radioactivity which can be dangerous. You can use visible light to shine through thin materials that you don't normally see through. Try using a flashlight to illuminate a leaf. Discuss or draw what you see.

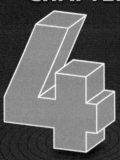

CHAPTER 4

Control and Reproduction

the **BIG** idea

The nervous and endocrine systems allow the body to respond to internal and external conditions.

Key Concepts

SECTION
4.1 The nervous system responds and controls.
Learn how the senses help the body get information about the environment.

SECTION
4.2 The endocrine system helps regulate conditions inside the body.
Learn the functions of different hormones.

SECTION
4.3 The reproductive system allows the body to produce offspring.
Learn about the process of reproduction.

Internet Preview

CLASSZONE.COM

Chapter 4 online resources: Content Review, Visualization, three Resource Centers, Math Tutorial, Test Practice

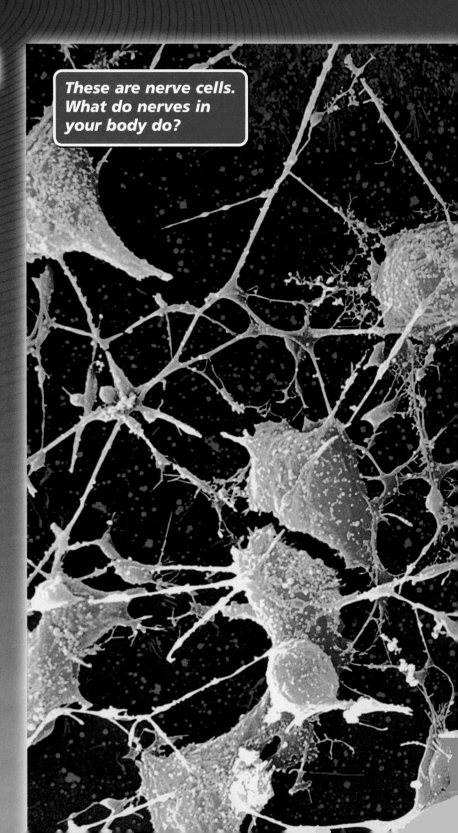

These are nerve cells. What do nerves in your body do?

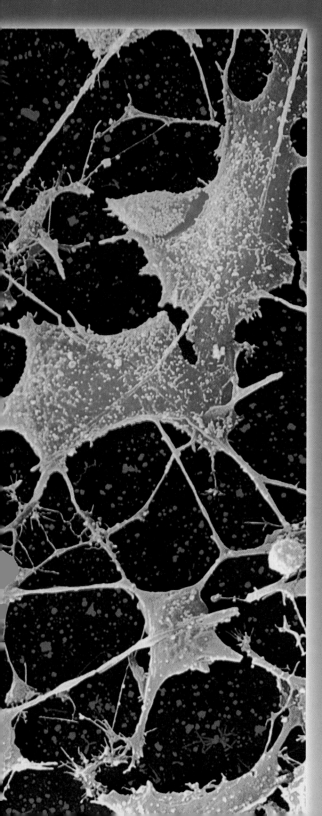

EXPLORE (the BIG idea)

Color Confusion

Make a list of six colors using a different color marker or colored pencil to write each one. Make sure not to write the color name with the same color marker or pencil. Read the list out loud as fast as you can. Now try quickly saying the color of each word out loud.

Observe and Think Did you notice a difference between reading the words in the list and saying the colors? If so, why do you think that is?

Eggs

Examine a raw chicken egg. Describe the appearance of the outside shell. Break it open into a small dish and note the different parts inside. Wash your hands when you have finished.

Observe and Think If this egg had been fertilized, which part do you think would have served as the food for the growing chicken embryo? Which part would protect the embryo from impact and serve to cushion it?

Internet Activity: The Senses

Go to **ClassZone.com** to learn how the senses allow the body to respond to external conditions. See how each sense sends specific information to the brain.

Observe and Think How do the different senses interact with one another?

NSTA
scilinks.org
SCiLINKS

Reproductive System **Code: MDL047**

CHAPTER 4

Getting Ready to Learn

◖ CONCEPT REVIEW

- The circulatory system transports materials.
- The immune system responds to foreign materials.
- The integumentary system protects the body.

◖ VOCABULARY REVIEW

homeostasis p. 12

circulatory system p. 65

immune system p. 75

integumentary system p. 83

CONTENT REVIEW
CLASSZONE.COM
Review concepts and vocabulary.

▶ TAKING NOTES

CHOOSE YOUR OWN STRATEGY

Take notes using one or more of the strategies from earlier chapters—**main idea webs, outlines,** or **main idea and detail notes.** You can also use other note-taking strategies that you might already know.

VOCABULARY STRATEGY

Place each vocabulary term at the center of a **description wheel** diagram. Write some words describing it on the spokes.

See the Note-Taking Handbook on pages R45–R51.

SCIENCE NOTEBOOK

Main Idea Web

Main Idea and Detail Notes

Outline
I. Main Idea
   A. Supporting idea
      1. Detail
      2. Detail
   B. Supporting idea

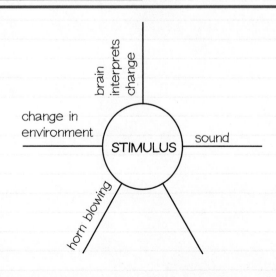

brain interprets change

change in environment

sound

STIMULUS

horn blowing

The nervous system responds and controls.

◀ BEFORE, you learned

- The body is defended from harmful materials
- Response structures fight disease
- The immune system responds to illness in many ways

▶ NOW, you will learn

- How the body's senses help monitor the environment
- How the sensory organs respond to stimuli
- How the nervous system works with other body systems

VOCABULARY

stimulus p. 102
central nervous system p. 104
neuron p. 105
peripheral nervous system p. 106
autonomic nervous system p. 107
voluntary nervous system p. 107

EXPLORE Smell

Can you name the scent?

PROCEDURE

1. With a small group, take turns smelling the 3 mystery bags given to you by your teacher.

2. In your notebook, write down what you think is inside each bag without showing the people in your group.

3. Compare your answers with those in your group and then look inside the bags.

MATERIALS
three small paper bags

WHAT DO YOU THINK?

- Did you know what was in the bags before looking inside? If so, how did you know?
- What are some objects that would require more than a sense of smell to identify?

Senses connect the human body to its environment.

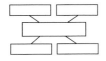

CHOOSE YOUR OWN STRATEGY
Use a strategy from an earlier chapter to take notes on the main idea. *Senses connect the human body to its environment.*

To maintain homeostasis and to survive, your body must constantly monitor the environment in which you live. This involves organs that interact so closely with the nervous system that they are often considered extensions of the nervous system. These are your sense organs. They give you the ability to see, smell, touch, hear, and taste.

Each of the senses can detect a specific type of change in the environment. For example, if you have begun to cross the street but suddenly hear a horn blowing, you may stop and step back onto the curb. Your sense of hearing allowed your brain to perceive that a car was coming and thus helped you to protect yourself.

The sound of the horn is a **stimulus.** A stimulus is a change in your environment that you react to, such as a smell, taste, sound, feeling, or sight. Your brain interprets any such change. If it did not, the information perceived by the senses would be meaningless.

Sight

If you have ever tried to find your way in the dark, you know how important light is for seeing. Light is a stimulus. You are able to detect it because your eyes, the sense organs of sight, capture light and help turn it into an image, which is processed by the brain.

Light enters the eye through the lens, a structure made of transparent tissue. Muscles surrounding the lens change its shape so the lens focuses light. Other muscles control the amount of light that enters the eye by altering the size of the pupil, a dark circle in the center of the eye. To reduce the amount of light, the area around the pupil, called the iris, contracts, making the pupil smaller thus allowing less light to enter. When the iris relaxes, more light can enter the eye.

At the back of the eye, the light strikes a layer called the retina. Among the many cells of the retina are two types of receptors, called rods and cones. Rods detect changes in brightness, while cones are sensitive to color.

Sight

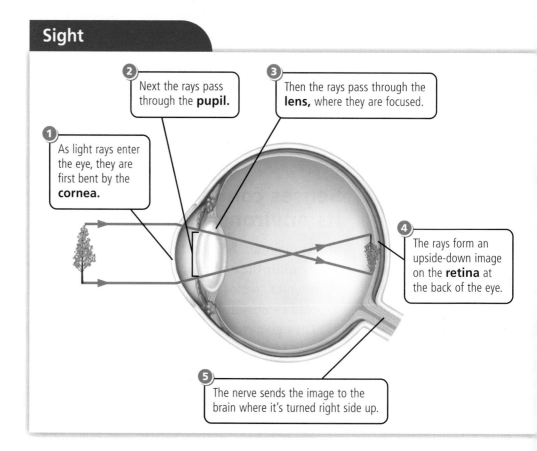

2. Next the rays pass through the **pupil.**

3. Then the rays pass through the **lens,** where they are focused.

1. As light rays enter the eye, they are first bent by the **cornea.**

4. The rays form an upside-down image on the **retina** at the back of the eye.

5. The nerve sends the image to the brain where it's turned right side up.

Hearing

Your eyes perceive light waves, but your ears perceive and interpret a different type of stimulus, sound waves. Sound waves are produced by vibrations. A reed on a clarinet vibrates, and so do your vocal cords. So does a bell after it has been hit by a mallet. The motion causes changes in the air that surrounds the bell. These changes can often be processed by the ear as sound, although many vibrations are too low or high to be heard by humans.

Sound waves enter the ear and are funneled into the auditory canal, a tube-shaped structure that ends at the eardrum. The eardrum vibrates when the sound waves strike it, and it transmits some of the vibrations to a tiny bone called the stirrup. Pressure caused by vibrations from the stirrup causes fluid in the ear to move. The movement of the fluid sends signals to the brain that are interpreted as sound.

 CHECK YOUR READING How are vibrations involved in hearing?

Hearing

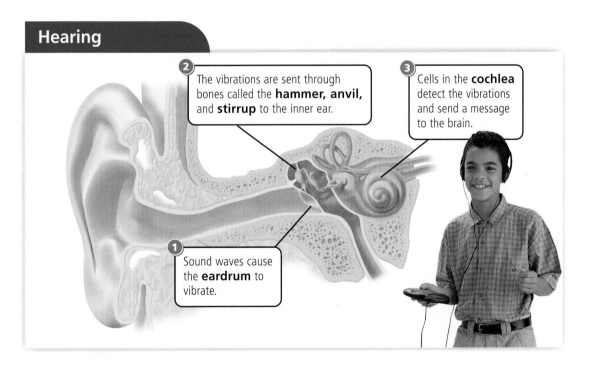

2 The vibrations are sent through bones called the **hammer, anvil, and stirrup** to the inner ear.

3 Cells in the **cochlea** detect the vibrations and send a message to the brain.

1 Sound waves cause the **eardrum** to vibrate.

Touch

The sense of touch depends on tiny sensory receptors in the skin. Without these you wouldn't be able to feel pressure, temperature, or pain. Nerves in the outer layer of your skin, or epidermis, sense textures, like smooth glass or rough concrete. Nerves deeper in the skin, in the dermis, sense pressure. Receptors also sense how hot or cold an object is and can thus help protect you from burning yourself. The sense of touch is important in alerting your brain to danger. Though you might wish that you couldn't feel pain it serves a critical purpose. Without it, you could harm your body without realizing it.

Smell

Whereas sight, touch, and hearing involve processing physical information from the environment, the senses of smell and taste involve processing chemical information. Much as taste receptors sense chemicals in food, smelling receptors sense chemicals in the air. High in the back of your nose, a patch of tissue grows hairlike fibers covered in mucus. Scent molecules enter your nose, stick to the mucus, and then bind to receptors in the hairlike fibers. The receptors send an impulse to your brain, and you smell the scent.

Taste

Your tongue is covered with small sensory structures called taste buds, which are also found in the throat and on the roof of the mouth. Each taste bud includes about 100 sensory cells that are specialized to detect chemicals in foods. The thousands of tastes you experience are combinations of just four basic types of taste: sweet, sour, bitter, and salty.

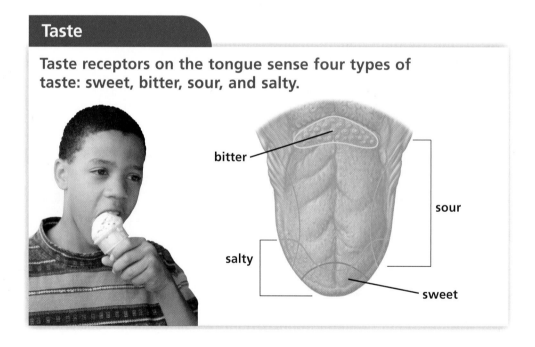

Taste

Taste receptors on the tongue sense four types of taste: sweet, bitter, sour, and salty.

bitter

sour

salty

sweet

The central nervous system controls functions.

RESOURCE CENTER
CLASSZONE.COM

Explore the nervous system.

The **central nervous system** consists of the brain and spinal cord. The brain is located in and protected by the skull, and the spinal cord is located in and protected by the spine. The central nervous system communicates with the rest of the nervous system through electrical signals sent to and from neurons. Impulses travel very quickly, some as fast as 90 meters (295 ft) per second. That's like running almost the entire length of a soccer field in one second!

Different areas of the brain control different functions.

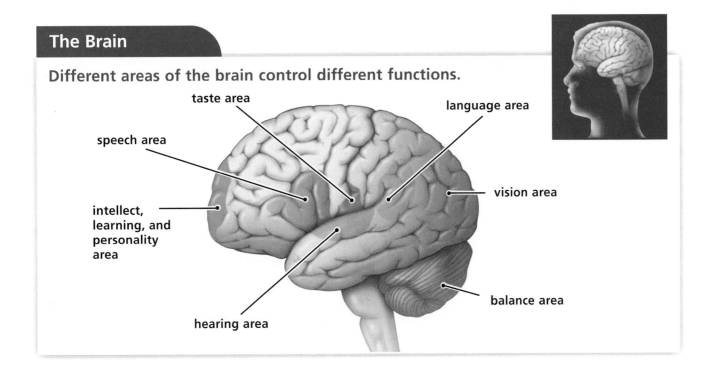

taste area

language area

speech area

vision area

intellect, learning, and personality area

balance area

hearing area

Brain

The average adult brain contains nearly 100 billion nerve cells, called **neurons.** The brain directly controls voluntary behavior, such as walking and thinking. It also allows the body to control most involuntary responses such as heartbeat, blood pressure, fluid balance, and posture.

As you can see in the diagram, every area of the brain has a specific function, although many functions may involve more than one area. For example, certain areas in the brain control the senses, while other areas help you stand up straight. The lower part of the brain, called the brain stem, controls activities such as breathing and vomiting.

VOCABULARY
Be sure to make a description wheel for the term *neuron*.

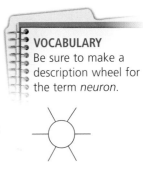

Spinal Cord

The spinal cord is about 44 centimeters (17 in.) long and weighs about 35–40 grams (1.25–1.4 oz). It is the main pathway for information, connecting the brain and the nerves throughout your body. The spinal cord is protected and supported by the vertebral column, which is made up of small bones called vertebrae. The spinal cord itself is a double-layered tube with an outer layer of nerve fibers wrapped in tissue, an inner layer of nerve cell bodies, and a central canal that runs the entire length of the cord. Connected to the spinal cord are 31 pairs of nerves, which send sensory impulses into the spinal cord, which in turn sends them to the brain. In a similar way, spinal nerves send impulses to muscles and glands.

 CHECK YOUR READING Describe the functions performed by the central nervous system.

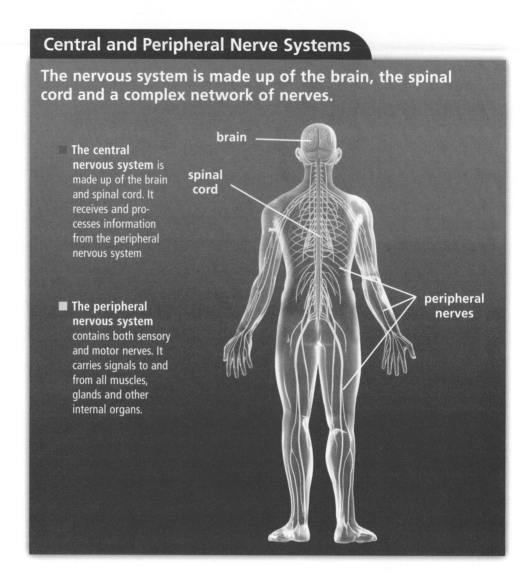

Central and Peripheral Nerve Systems

The nervous system is made up of the brain, the spinal cord and a complex network of nerves.

■ **The central nervous system** is made up of the brain and spinal cord. It receives and processes information from the peripheral nervous system

■ **The peripheral nervous system** contains both sensory and motor nerves. It carries signals to and from all muscles, glands and other internal organs.

brain

spinal cord

peripheral nerves

The peripheral nervous system is a network of nerves.

Nerves, which are found throughout the body, are often referred to altogether as the **peripheral nervous system.** Both sensory and motor nerves are parts of the peripheral nervous system. Sensory nerves receive information from the environment—such as heat or cold—and pass the information to the central nervous system. Motor nerves send signals to your muscles that allow you to move. The peripheral nervous system includes both voluntary motor nerves and involuntary responses.

Another type of motor nerves controls the involuntary responses of the body. In times of danger, there is no time to think. The body must respond immediately. In less stressful situations, the body maintains activities like breathing and digesting food. These functions go on without conscious thought. They are controlled by part of the peripheral nervous system called the the autonomic (AW-tuh-NAHM-ihk) nervous system.

The **autonomic nervous system** controls the movement of the heart, the smooth muscles in the stomach, the intestines, and the glands. The autonomic nervous system has two distinct functions: to conserve and store energy and to respond quickly to changes. You can think of the autonomic nervous system as having a division that performs each of these two main functions.

Each division is controlled by different locations on the spinal cord, or within the brain and the brain stem. The cerebellum, which is located at the rear of the brain, coordinates balance and related muscle activity. The brain stem, which lies between the spinal cord and the rest of the brain, controls heartbeat, respiration, and the smooth muscles in the blood vessels.

When you are under stress, one part of the autonomic nervous system causes what is called the "fight or flight response." Rapid changes in your body prepare you either to fight the danger or to take flight and run away from the danger. The response of your nervous system is the same, whether the stress is a real danger, like falling off a skateboard, or a perceived danger, like being worried or embarrassed.

The **voluntary nervous system** monitors movement and functions that can be controlled consciously. Every movement you think about is voluntary. The voluntary nervous system controls the skeletal muscles of the arms, the legs, and the rest of the body. It also controls the muscles that are responsible for speech and the senses.

The autonomic nervous system responds quickly to changes in balance.

 CHECK YOUR READING What is the difference between the voluntary and the autonomic nervous systems?

4.1 Review

KEY CONCEPTS

1. Make a chart of the five senses that includes a definition and a stimulus for each sense.

2. Explain the process by which you hear a sound.

3. What are two body systems with which the nervous system interacts? How do these interactions take place?

CRITICAL THINKING

4. **Classify** Determine if the following actions involve the autonomic or the voluntary nervous system: chewing, eye blinking, jumping at a loud noise, and riding a bike.

5. **Apply** Describe what messages are sent by the nervous system when you go outside wearing a sweater on a hot day.

○ CHALLENGE

6. **Hypothesize** When people lose their sense of smell, their sense of taste is often affected as well. Why do you think the ability to taste would be decreased by the loss of the ability to smell?

CHAPTER INVESTIGATION

Are You a Supertaster?

OVERVIEW AND PURPOSE Do you think broccoli tastes bitter? If so, you might be extra sensitive to bitter tastes. In this investigation you will

- examine the surface of your tongue to find a possible connection between the bumps you find there and your sensitivity to bitter flavors
- calculate the average number of papillae in your class

Make sure to do this investigation in the cafeteria since you will be placing food coloring on your tongue.

MATERIALS
- blue food coloring
- paper cup
- 1 cotton swab
- 1 reinforcement circle for ring-binder paper
- paper towel or napkin
- 1 sheet of white paper

▶ Problem
 Write It Up

How can you tell if you are a supertaster?

▶ Hypothesize
Write It Up

Write a hypothesis to explain how you might tell if you are a supertaster. Your hypothesis should take the form of an "If . . . , then . . . , because . . ." statement.

▶ Procedure

1. Make a data table in your **Science Notebook** like the one shown on page 109.

2. Put a few drops of blue food coloring into a paper cup.

3. Use a paper towel or a napkin to pat your tongue thoroughly dry.

4. Dip the tip of a cotton swab into the blue food coloring, and use it to paint the first 2 centimeters of your tongue.

5. Press a piece of white paper firmly onto the painted surface of your tongue, and then place the paper on your desk.

step 5

6. Place a notebook reinforcement circle on the blue area.

7. You should see white circles in a field of blue. The white circles are the bumps on your tongue called fungiform papillae. Count the number of white circles inside the reinforcement circle. There may be many white circles crammed together that vary in size, or just a few. If there are just a few, they may be larger than the ones on someone who has many white circles close together. If there are too many to count, try to count the number in half of the circle and multiply this number by 2. Record your total count in your data table.

▶ Observe and Analyze   Write It Up

1. **OBSERVE** What did you observe while looking at the tongue print? Is the surface the same all over your tongue?

2. **CALCULATE** Record the number of papillae within the reinforcement circle of all the students in your class.

   AVERAGE Calculate the average number of papillae counted in the class.

   $$\text{average} = \frac{\text{sum of papillae in class}}{\text{number of students}}$$

▶ Conclude   Write It Up

1. **INTERPRET** How do the number of fungiform papillae on your tongue compare with the number your partner counted?

2. **INFER** Do you think there is a relationship between the number of fungiform papillae and taste? If so, what is it?

3. **IDENTIFY** What foods might a supertaster not like?

4. **APPLY** Do you think that there are other taste perceptions besides bitterness that might be influenced by the number of fungiform papillae that an individual has? Why do you think so?

▶ INVESTIGATE Further

CHALLENGE Calculate the area in square millimeters inside the reinforcement circle, and use this value to express each person's papillae count as a density (number of papillae per square millimeter).

Are You a Supertaster?

Table 1. Papillae

Name	Number of papillae

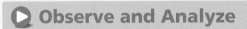

4.2 The endocrine system helps regulate body conditions.

◀ BEFORE, you learned

- Many body systems function without conscious control
- The body systems work automatically to maintain homeostasis
- Homeostasis is important to an organism's survival

▶ NOW, you will learn

- About the role of hormones
- About the functions of glands
- How the body uses feedback mechanisms to help maintain homeostasis

VOCABULARY

endocrine system p.110
hormone p.111
gland p.111

THINK ABOUT

How does your body react to surprise?

In a small group, determine how your body responds to a surprising situation. Have one student in the group pretend he or she is responding to a surprise. The other group members should determine how the body reacts physically to that event. How do your respiratory system, digestive system, circulatory system, muscle system, and skeletal system react?

CHOOSE YOUR OWN STRATEGY
Begin taking notes on the main idea: *Hormones are the body's messengers.* Use a strategy from an earlier chapter or one of your own. Include a definition of *hormone* in your notes.

Hormones are the body's chemical messengers.

Imagine you're seated on a roller coaster climbing to the top of a steep incline. In a matter of moments your car drops hundreds of feet. You might notice that your heart starts beating faster. You grab the seat and notice that your palms are sweaty. These are normal physical responses to scary situations. The **endocrine system** controls the conditions in your body by making and sending chemicals from one part of the body to another. Most responses of the endocrine system are controlled by the nervous system.

Hormones are chemicals that are made in one organ and travel through the blood to a second organ. The second organ, often called the target organ, responds to the chemical. Most hormones have more than one target organ. Many hormones, as you can see in the table below, affect all the cells in the body.

Because hormones are made at one location and function at another, they are often called chemical messengers. When the hormone reaches its target organ, it binds to receptors on the surface of or inside the organ's cells. There the hormone begins the chemical changes that cause the target organ to function in a specific way. All of the functions of the endocrine system work automatically, without your conscious control.

Different types of hormones perform different jobs. Some of these jobs are to control the production of other hormones, to regulate the balance of chemicals such as glucose and salt in your blood, or to produce responses to changes in the environment. Some hormones are made only during specific times in a person's life. For example, hormones that control the development of sexual characteristics are not produced during childhood. When production begins in adolescence, these hormones cause major changes in a person's body.

The individuals on this roller coaster are experiencing a burst of the hormone adrenaline.

 CHECK YOUR READING How are hormones like messengers?

Hormones		
Name	**Where produced**	**Where travels to**
Growth hormone	pituitary gland	all body cells
Antidiuretic hormone	pituitary gland	kidneys
Thyroxine	thyroid gland	all body cells
Cortisol	adrenal glands	all body cells
Adrenaline	adrenal glands	heart, lungs, stomach, intestines, glands
Insulin	pancreas	all body cells
Testosterone (males)	testes	all body cells
Estrogen (females)	ovaries	all body cells

Glands produce and release hormones.

The main structures of the endocrine system are organs called **glands.** Many glands in the body produce hormones and release them into your circulatory system. As you can see in the illustration on page 113, endocrine glands can be found in many parts of your body. However, all hormones move from the organ in which they are produced to target organs.

 **RESOURCE CENTER**
CLASSZONE.COM

Learn more about the endocrine system.

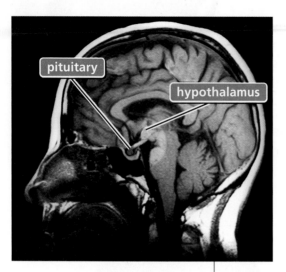

The hypothalamus and the pituitary are important endocrine glands.

Pituitary Gland The pituitary (pih-TOO-ih-TEHR-ee) gland can be thought of as the director of the endocrine system. The pituitary gland is the size of a pea and is located at the base of the brain—right above the roof of your mouth. Many important hormones are produced in the pituitary gland, including hormones that control growth, sexual development, and the absorption of water into the blood by the kidneys.

Hypothalamus The hypothalamus (HY-poh-THAL-uh-muhs) is attached to the pituitary gland and is the primary connection between the nervous and endocrine systems. All of the secretions of the pituitary gland are controlled by the hypothalamus which produces releasing hormones.

Pineal Gland The pineal (PIHN-ee-uhl) gland is a tiny organ about the size of a pea. It is buried deep in the brain. The pineal gland is sensitive to different levels of light and is essential to rhythms such as sleep, body temperature, reproduction, and aging.

Thyroid Gland You can feel your thyroid gland if you place your hand on the part of your throat called the Adam's apple and swallow. What you feel is the cartilage surrounding your thyroid gland. The thyroid releases hormones necessary for growth and metabolism. The tissue of the thyroid is made of millions of tiny pouches, which store the thyroid hormone. The thyroid gland also produces the hormone calcitonin, which is involved in the regulation of calcium in the body.

Thymus The thymus is located in your chest. It is relatively large in the newborn baby and continues to grow until puberty. Following puberty, it gradually decreases in size. The thymus helps the body fight disease by controlling the production of white blood cells called T-cells.

Adrenal Glands The adrenal glands are located on top of your kidneys. The adrenal glands secrete about 30 different hormones that regulate carbohydrate, protein, and fat metabolism and water and salt levels in your body. Some other hormones produced by the adrenal glands help you fight allergies or infections. Roller coaster rides, loud noises, or stress can activate your adrenal glands to produce adrenaline, the hormone that makes your heart beat faster.

Pancreas The pancreas is part of both the digestive and the endocrine systems. The pancreas secretes two hormones, insulin and glucagon. These hormones regulate the level of glucose in your blood. The pancreas sits beneath the stomach and is connected to the small intestine.

Ovaries and Testes The ovaries and testes also secrete hormones that control sexual development.

Other Organs Some organs that are not considered part of the endocrine system do produce important hormones. The kidneys secrete a hormone that regulates the production of red blood cells. This hormone is secreted whenever the oxygen level in your blood decreases. By stimulating the red bone marrow to produce more red blood cells, the ability of the blood to carry oxygen increases. The heart produces two hormones that help regulate blood pressure. These hormones, secreted by one of the chambers of the heart, stimulate the kidneys to remove more salt.

CHECK YOUR READING   Which organs are part of the endocrine system?

Endocrine System

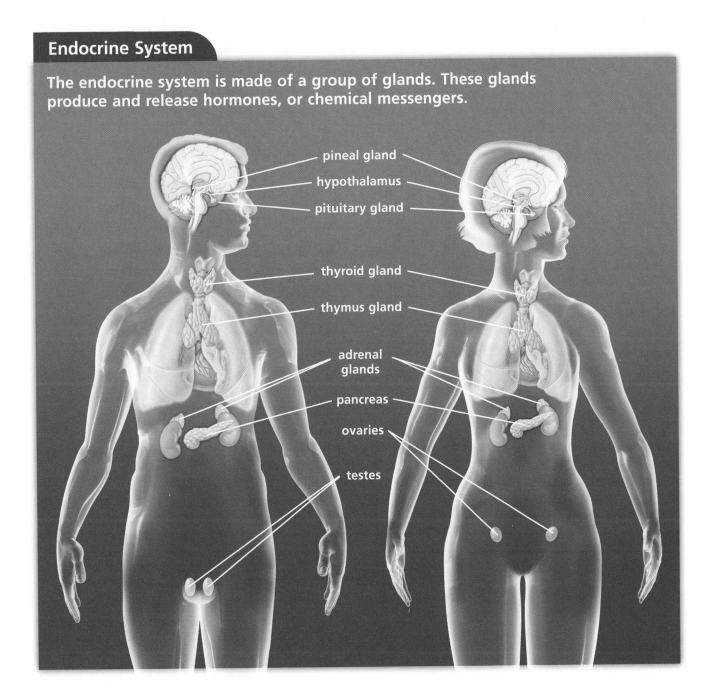

The endocrine system is made of a group of glands. These glands produce and release hormones, or chemical messengers.

pineal gland
hypothalamus
pituitary gland

thyroid gland

thymus gland

adrenal glands

pancreas

ovaries

testes

INVESTIGATE Response to Exercise

How does your body temperature change when you exercise?

PROCEDURE

1. Working in groups of two, read all the instructions in this activity first. Appoint one person to be the subject and one person to be the timer and note taker. Using a mercury-free thermometer, have the subject take his or her temperature. Record the temperature in your notebook.

2. While staying seated the subject begins to do sitting-down jumping jacks. The subjects does the jumping jacks for 1 minute and then immediately takes his or her temperature. Continue this procedure for a total of 3 times, measuring the temperature after each minute of exercise.

WHAT DO YOU THINK?

- How did the subject's temperature change while exercising?
- What factors may contribute to the rate at which the temperature changed in each person?
- How did the subject's physical appearance change from the beginning of the activity to the end?

CHALLENGE Graph the results on a line graph, with temperature on the *x*-axis and time on the *y*-axis.

Control of the endocrine system includes feedback mechanisms.

As you might recall, the cells in the human body function best within a specific set of conditions. Homeostasis (HOH-mee-oh-STAY-sihs) is the process by which the body maintains these internal conditions, even though conditions outside the body may change. The endocrine system is very important in maintaining homeostasis.

 CHECK YOUR READING Why is homeostasis important?

Because hormones are powerful chemicals capable of producing dramatic changes, their levels in the body must be carefully regulated. The endocrine system has several levels of control. Most glands are regulated by the pituitary gland, which in turn is controlled by the hypothalamus, part of the brain. The endocrine system helps maintain homeostasis through the action of negative feedback mechanisms.

Negative Feedback

Most feedback mechanisms in the body are called negative mechanisms, because the final effect of the response is to turn off the response. An increase in the amount of a hormone in the body feeds back to inhibit the further production of that hormone.

The production of the hormone thyroxine by the thyroid gland is an example of a negative feedback mechanism. Thyroxine controls the body's metabolism, or the rate at which the cells in the body release energy by cellular respiration. When the body needs energy, the thyroid gland releases thyroxine into the blood to increase cellular respiration. However, the thyroid gland is controlled by the pituitary gland, which in turn is controlled by the hypothalamus. Increased levels of thyroxine in the blood inhibit the signals from the hypothalamus and the pituitary gland to the thyroid gland. Production of thyroxine in the thyroid gland decreases.

Negative and Positive Feedback

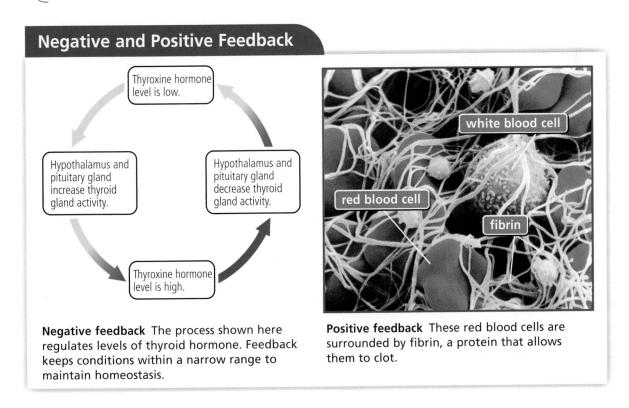

Negative feedback The process shown here regulates levels of thyroid hormone. Feedback keeps conditions within a narrow range to maintain homeostasis.

Positive feedback These red blood cells are surrounded by fibrin, a protein that allows them to clot.

Positive Feedback

Some responses of the endocrine system, as well as other body systems, are controlled by positive feedback. The outcome of positive feedback mechanism is not to maintain homeostasis, but to produce a response that continues to increase. Most positive feedback mechanisms result in extreme responses that are necessary under extreme conditions.

For example, when you cut yourself, chemicals are released from the damaged tissue that signal the blood to clot. The process of clotting causes more chemicals to form that increase the clotting action of the blood in the area of the injury. The upward spiral increases until a clot is formed that fills the injured area. Other examples of positive feedback include fever, the immune response, puberty, and labor.

CHECK YOUR READING What is the difference between negative and positive feedback?

Balanced Hormone Action

In the body, the action of one hormone is often balanced by the action of another. When you ride a bicycle, you are able to ride in a straight line, despite bumps and dips in the road, by making constant steering adjustments. If the bicycle is pulled to the right, you adjust the handlebars by turning a tiny bit to the left.

Some hormones maintain homeostasis in the same way that you steer your bicycle. The pancreas, for example, produces two hormones. One hormone, insulin, decreases the level of sugar in the blood. The other hormone, glucagon, increases sugar levels in the blood. The balance of the levels of these hormones maintains stable blood sugar between meals.

Hormone Imbalance

Because hormones regulate critical functions in the body, too little or too much of any hormone can cause serious disease. When the pancreas produces too little insulin, sugar levels in the blood can rise to dangerous levels. Very high levels of blood sugar can damage the circulatory system and the kidneys. This condition, known as diabetes mellitus, is often treated by injecting synthetic insulin into the body to replace the insulin not being made by the pancreas.

4.2 Review

KEY CONCEPTS

1. List three different jobs that hormones perform.

2. Draw an outline of the human body. Add the locations and functions of the pituitary, thyroid, adrenal, and pineal glands to your drawing.

3. What is the function of a negative feedback mechanism?

CRITICAL THINKING

4. **Analyze** Explain why hormones are called chemical messengers.

5. **Analyze** List two sets of hormones that have opposing actions. How do the actions of these hormones help maintain homeostasis?

CHALLENGE

6. **Connect** Copy the diagram below and add three more stimuli and the resulting feedback mechanisms.

CONNECTING SCIENCES

Heating and Cooling

The cells in our bodies can survive only within a limited temperature range. The body must maintain a constant core temperature at about 37°C (98.6°F). Body temperature is a measure of the average thermal energy in the body. To keep a constant temperature range, our bodies either lose or gain thermal energy.

Energy cannot be created or destroyed, but it can be transferred from one form or place to another. The major source of thermal energy in our bodies is food. When our bodies break down nutrients, some of the chemical energy is released as thermal energy that heats our bodies. Also, some of the kinetic energy from muscle movement is converted into thermal energy.

Body temperature is controlled by the hypothalamus region of the brain. The hypothalamus controls the rate of nutrient use. The hypothalamus also controls shivering and sweating.

Heat is the flow of energy from a warmer to a cooler object. Heat transfer between the body and its surroundings occurs in four ways.

1. **Evaporation:** When water evaporates, or changes from liquid to gas, energy is required. When perspiration evaporates from the surface of our skin, we lose thermal energy as heat.

2. **Radiation:** Heat transfer also occurs through waves that radiate out from a warm object or area. Sitting in the sunshine warms us because we gain thermal energy from the Sun's radiation. Our warm bodies can also radiate energy into cooler air.

3. **Conduction:** When two objects are in direct contact, heat flows by conduction from the warmer to the cooler object. If you stand barefoot on hot sand, heat quickly flows into your feet by conduction.

4. **Convection:** In convection, heat transfer occurs through the movement of particles in a gas or liquid. Your body loses some thermal energy because of convection in the air around you.

EXPLORE

1. **CONNECT** What are some behaviors that help you lose or gain thermal energy?

2. **CHALLENGE** Choose a behavior that either warms or cools your body. Draw a diagram and label it with the types of heat transfer that are occurring.

4.3 The reproductive system allows the production of offspring.

◀ **BEFORE**, you learned

- Some hormones regulate sexual development
- Glands release hormones

▶ **NOW**, you will learn

- About specialized cells and organs in male and female reproductive systems
- About fertilization
- About the development of the embryo and fetus during pregnancy

VOCABULARY

menstruation p. 119
fertilization p. 121
embryo p. 121
fetus p. 122

EXPLORE Reproduction

How are sperm and egg cells different?

PROCEDURE

① From your teacher, gather slides of egg cells and sperm cells.

② Put each slide under a microscope.

③ Draw a sketch of each cell.

④ With a partner, discuss the differences that you observed.

WHAT DO YOU THINK?

- What were the differences that you observed?
- What are the benefits of the different characteristics for each cell?

MATERIALS

- slides of egg and sperm cells
- microscope
- paper
- pencil

The reproductive system produces specialized cells.

CHOOSE YOUR OWN STRATEGY
Begin taking notes on the idea that the reproductive system produces specialized cells. You might use an outline or another strategy of your choice.

Like all living organisms, humans reproduce. The reproductive system allows adults to produce offspring. Although males and females have different reproductive systems, both systems share an important characteristic. They both make specialized cells. In any organism or any system, a specialized cell is a cell that takes on a special job.

In the female these specialized cells are called egg cells. In the male they are called sperm cells. In the reproductive system, each specialized cell provides genetic material. Genetic material contains the information that an organism needs to form, develop, and grow.

Both the male and female reproductive systems rely on hormones from the endocrine system. The hormones act as chemical messengers that signal the process of sexual development. Sexual development includes the growth of reproductive organs and the development of sexual characteristics. Once mature, the reproductive organs produce hormones to maintain secondary sexual characteristics.

The Female Reproductive System

The female reproductive system has two functions. The first is to produce egg cells, and the second is to protect and nourish the offspring until birth. The female has two reproductive organs called ovaries. Each ovary contains on average hundreds of egg cells. Every 28 days, the pituitary gland releases a hormone that stimulates some of the eggs to develop and grow.

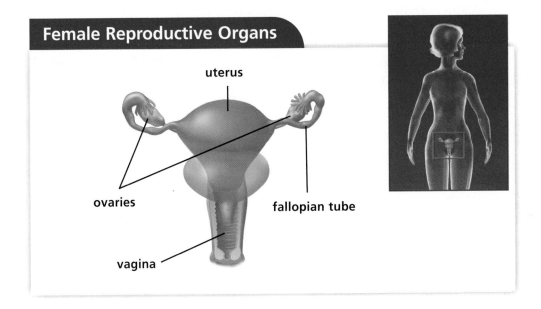

Female Reproductive Organs

uterus

ovaries

fallopian tube

vagina

Menstruation

After an egg cell develops fully, another hormone signals the ovary to release the egg. The egg moves from the ovary into a fallopian tube. Within ten to twelve hours, the egg cell is fertilized by a sperm cell and moves to the uterus. Once inside the thick lining of the uterus, the fertilized egg cell rapidly grows and divides.

However, if fertilization does not occur within 24 hours after the egg cell leaves the ovary, both the egg and the lining of the uterus begin to break down. The muscles in the uterus contract in a process called **menstruation.** Menstruation is the flow of blood and tissue from the body through a canal called the vagina over a period of about five days.

CHECK YOUR READING Where does the egg travel to after it leaves the ovary?

The Male Reproductive System

Testes The organs that produce sperm are called the testes (TEHS-teez). Inside the testes are tiny, coiled tubes hundreds of feet long. Sperm are produced inside these coiled tubes. The testes release a hormone that controls the development of sperm. This hormone is also responsible for the development of physical characteristics in men such as facial hair and a deep voice.

Sperm Sperm cells are the specialized cells of the male reproductive system. Males start producing sperm cells sometime during adolescence. The sperm is a single cell with a head and a tail. The sperm's head is filled with chromosomes, and the tail functions as a whip, making the sperm highly mobile. The sperm travel from the site of production, the testes, through several different structures of the reproductive system. While they travel, the sperm mix with fluids. This fluid is called semen and contains nutrients for the sperm cells. One drop of semen contains up to several million sperm cells.

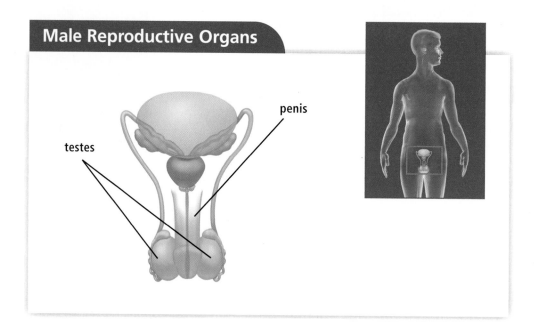

Male Reproductive Organs

penis

testes

The reproduction of offspring includes fertilization, pregnancy, and birth.

Each sperm cell, like each egg cell, has half of the genetic material needed for a human being to grow and develop. During sexual intercourse, millions of sperm cells leave the testes. The sperm cells exit the male's body through the urethra, a tube that leads out of the penis. The sperm cells enter the female's body through the vagina. Next they travel into the uterus and continue on to the fallopian tube.

VISUALIZATION
CLASSZONE.COM

Follow an egg from fertilization to implantation.

Fertilization

Fertilization occurs when one sperm cell joins the egg cell. The fallopian tube is the site of fertilization. Immediately, chemical changes in the egg's surface prevent any more sperm from entering. Once inside the egg, the genetic material from the sperm combines with the genetic material of the egg cell. Fertilization is complete.

The fertilized egg cell then moves down the fallopian tube toward the uterus. You can trace the path of the egg cell in the diagram on this page. It divides into two cells. Each of those cells divides again, to form a total of four cells. Cell division continues, and a ball of cells forms, called an **embryo.** Within a few days, the embryo attaches itself to the thickened, spongy lining of the uterus in a process called implantation.

Fertilization

The egg cell moves down the fallopian tube following fertilization. Its final destination is the uterus.

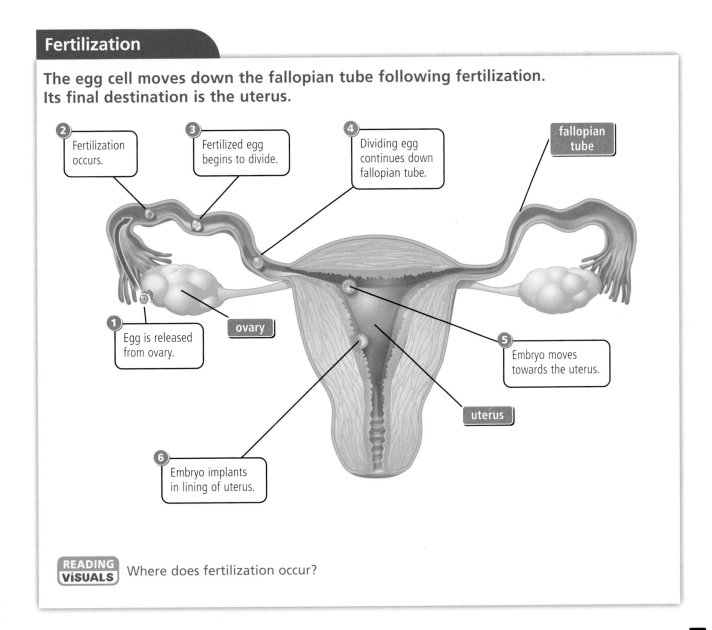

2 Fertilization occurs.

3 Fertilized egg begins to divide.

4 Dividing egg continues down fallopian tube.

fallopian tube

1 Egg is released from ovary.

ovary

5 Embryo moves towards the uterus.

uterus

6 Embryo implants in lining of uterus.

READING VISUALS Where does fertilization occur?

Pregnancy

The nine months of pregnancy can be divided into three periods of about the same length. Each period marks specific stages of development. In the first week following implantation, the embryo continues to grow rapidly. Both the embryo and the uterus contribute cells to a new, shared organ called the placenta. The placenta has blood vessels that lead from the mother's circulatory system to the embryo through a large tube called the umbilical cord. Oxygen and nutrients from the mother's body will move through the placenta and umbilical cord to the growing embryo.

Around the eighth week of pregnancy, the developing embryo is called a **fetus.** The fetus begins to have facial features, major organ systems, and the beginnings of a skeleton. The fetus develops the sexual traits that are either male or female. In the twelfth week, the fetus continues to grow and its bones develop further. In the last twelve weeks the fetus and all its organ systems develop fully.

Uterus and Placenta

By the fifth week of pregnancy, the placenta is fully developed.

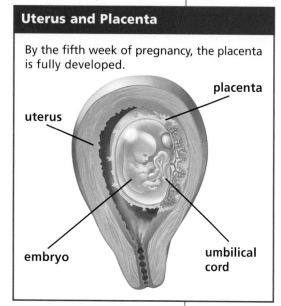

placenta

uterus

embryo

umbilical cord

 Describe the development of an embryo and fetus at two weeks, eight weeks, and twelve weeks.

Labor and Delivery

At the end of pregnancy, the fetus is fully developed and is ready to be born. The birth of a fetus is divided into three stages; labor, delivery, and birth of the placenta.

The first stage of birth begins with muscular contractions of the uterus. These contractions occur at intervals of 10 to 30 minutes and last about 40 seconds. They happen continually until the muscular contractions are occurring about every 2 minutes.

The second stage of birth is delivery. With each contraction the cervix dilates until it becomes wide enough for the mother's muscles to push the fetus out. During delivery the fetus is pushed out of the uterus, through the vagina, and out of the body. The fetus is still connected to the mother by the umbilical cord.

The umbilical cord is cut shortly after the fetus is delivered. Within minutes after birth, the placenta separates from the uterine wall and the mother pushes it out with more muscular contractions.

 What happens during each of the three stages of birth?

Growth of the Fetus

An embryo grows and develops from a ball of cells to a fully formed fetus.

4-day blastula

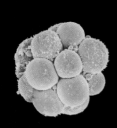

magnification 620x

- Embryo has 16 cells
- Not yet implanted in the uterus

5-week embryo

size < 1 cm

- Heart is beating
- Beginning of eyes, arms and legs are visible

8-week fetus

size 2–3 cm

- Embryo is now called a fetus
- Has all basic organs and systems

16-week fetus

size 13 cm

- Can move around in the womb
- Hair, eyelashes and eyebrows are growing

7–8 month fetus shown in this composite image is about 35–40 cm in length and weighs about 1.5–2.3 kg. The fetus usually gains at least 1 kg during the final month of pregnancy.

These twins provide an example of offspring born in a multiple birth.

Multiple Births

Do you have any friends who are twins or triplets? Perhaps you and your brothers or sisters are twins or triplets. The birth of more than one offspring is called a multiple birth. Multiple births are relatively uncommon in humans.

Identical twins are produced when a single fertilized egg divides in half. Each half then forms two complete organisms, or twins. Such twins are always of the same sex, look alike, and have identical blood types. Identical twins form early in pregnancy. Approximately 1 in 29 births is a set of identical twins.

Twins that are not identical are called fraternal twins. Fraternal twins are produced when two eggs are released at the same time and are fertilized by two different sperm. Consequently, fraternal twins may be very different from each other. Fraternal twins can be the same sex or different sexes.

 CHECK YOUR READING Why are some twins identical and some are not?

4.3 Review

KEY CONCEPTS

1. Describe the function of the male reproductive system and the two main functions of the female reproductive system.

2. Explain how an egg travels from the ovary to the uterus.

3. How is an embryo different from a fetus?

CRITICAL THINKING

4. **Sequence** Describe the sequence of events that occurs between fertilization and the stage called implantation.

5. **Analyze** Detail two examples of hormones interacting with the reproductive system, one involving the male system and one involving the female system.

◯ CHALLENGE

6. **Synthesize** Describe the interaction between the endocrine system and the reproductive system.

MATH TUTORIAL
CLASSZONE.COM
Click on Math Tutorial for
more help with solving
proportions.

SKILL: SOLVING PROPORTIONS

Twins and Triplets

Is the number of twins and triplets on the rise? Between 1980 and
1990, twin births in The United States rose from roughly 68,000 to
about 105,000. In 1980, there were about 3,600,000 births total.
To convert the data to birth rates, you can use proportions. A
proportion is an equation. It shows two ratios that are equivalent.

Example

Find the birth rate of twins born in The United States for 1980.
The rate is the number of twin births per 1000 births.

(1) Write the ratio of twin births to total births for that year.

$$\frac{68,000 \text{ twin births}}{3,600,000 \text{ total births}}$$

(2) Write a proportion, using x for the number you need to find.

$$\frac{68,000}{3,600,000} = \frac{x}{1000}$$

(3) In a proportion, the cross products are equal, so

$$68,000 \cdot 1000 = x \cdot 3,600,000$$

(4) Solve for x:

$$\frac{68,000,000}{3,600,000} = 18.9$$

ANSWER There were 18.9 twin births for every 1000 births in 1980.

Find the following birth rates.

1. In 1990, there were about 105,000 twin births and about
3,900,000 total births. What was the birth rate of twins?

2. In 1980, about 1,350 sets of triplets were born, and by 1990,
this number had risen to about 6,750. What were the birth
rates of triplets in 1987 and in 1990?

3. How much did the birth rate increase for twins between 1980
and 1990? for triplets?

4. Find the overall birth rate of twins and triplets in 1980.

5. Find the overall rate of twin and triplet births in 1990.
How much did it increase between 1980 and 1990?

CHALLENGE In 1989, there
were about 4 million total
births, and the rate of triplets
born per million births was
about 700. How many triplets
were born?

the BIG idea

The nervous and endocrine systems allow the body to respond to internal and external conditions.

CONTENT REVIEW
CLASSZONE.COM

◀ KEY CONCEPTS SUMMARY

4.1 The nervous system responds and controls.

- The nervous system connects the body with its environment using five senses: sight, touch, hearing, smell, and taste. Central nervous system includes the brain, the control center, and the spinal cord.
- The peripheral nervous system includes the autonomic and voluntary systems

VOCABULARY
stimulus p. 102
central nervous
  system p. 104
neuron p.105
peripheral nervous
  system p. 106
autonomic nervous
  system p. 107
voluntary nervous
  system p. 107

4.2 The endocrine system helps regulate conditions inside the body.

The body has chemical messengers called **hormones** that are regulated by the **endocrine system. Glands** produce and release hormones. The endocrine system includes feedback systems that maintain homeostasis.

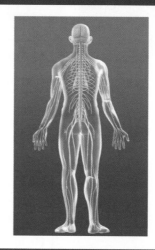

Thyroxine hormone level is low.

Hypothalamus and pituitary gland increase thyroid gland activity.

Hypothalamus and pituitary gland decrease thyroid gland activity.

Thyroxine hormone level is high.

VOCABULARY
endocrine system
  p. 110
hormone p. 111
gland p. 111

4.3 The reproductive system allows the body to produce offspring.

The female produces eggs, and the male produces sperm. Following **fertilization** the egg develops over a period of about nine months.

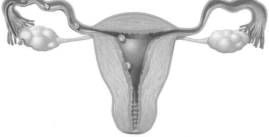

VOCABULARY
menstruation p. 119
fertilization p. 121
embryo p. 121
fetus p. 122

Reviewing Vocabulary

Make a frame for each of the vocabulary words listed. Write the word in the center. Decide what information to frame it with. Use definitions, examples, descriptions, parts, or pictures.

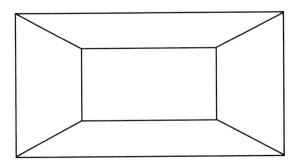

1. stimulus

2. neurons

3. hormones

4. fertilization

5. embryo

Reviewing Key Concepts

Multiple Choice *Choose the letter of the best answer.*

6. Which is a stimulus?
   a. a car horn blowing
   b. jumping at a loud noise
   c. taste buds on the tongue
   d. turning on a lamp

7. Light enters the eye through
   a. the lens
   b. the auditory canal
   c. the olfactory epithelium
   d. the taste buds

8. Which senses allow you to process chemical information?
   a. sight and smell
   b. taste and smell
   c. touch and hearing
   d. hearing and taste

9. What conserves energy and responds quickly to change?
   a. central nervous system
   b. peripheral nervous system
   c. autonomic nervous system
   d. voluntary nervous system

10. Which is <u>not</u> regulated by hormones?
   a. production of red blood cells
   b. physical growth
   c. blood pressure
   d. sexual development

11. Which gland releases hormones that are necessary for growth and metabolism?
   a. thyroid gland   **c.** adrenal gland
   b. pituitary gland   **d.** pineal gland

12. Eggs develop in the female reproductive organ called
   a. an ovary   **c.** a uterus
   b. a fallopian tube   **d.** a vagina

13. The joining of one sperm cell and one egg cell is an event called
   a. menstruation   **c.** implantation
   b. fertilization   **d.** birth

14. A ball of cells that is formed by fertilization is called the
   a. testes   **c.** ovary
   b. urethra   **d.** embryo

15. The period in which a fetus and all of its systems develop fully is the
   a. first three months
   b. second three months
   c. third three months
   d. pregnancy

Short Answer *Write a short answer to each question.*

16. List the parts of the body that are controlled by the autonomic nervous system.

17. What is a negative feedback mechanism? Give an example.

18. How are fertilization and menstruation related?

Thinking Critically

Use the diagram to answer the following two questions.

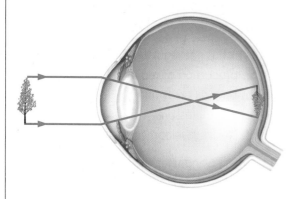

19. SUMMARIZE Use the diagram of the eye to describe how images are formed on the retina.

20. COMPARE AND CONTRAST How is the image that forms on the retina like the object? How is it different? Explain how the viewer interprets the image that forms on the retina.

21. APPLY A person steps on a sharp object with a bare foot and quickly pulls the foot back in pain. Describe the parts of the nervous system that are involved in this action.

22. ANALYZE Explain why positive feedback mechanisms do not help the body maintain homeostasis. Give an example.

23. CONNECT Copy the concept map and add the following terms to the correct box: brain, spinal cord, autonomic.

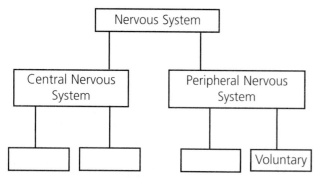

24. DRAW CONCLUSIONS A person who is normally very active begins to notice a significant decrease in energy level. After visiting a doctor, tests results show that one of the endocrine glands is not secreting enough of its hormone. Which gland could this be? Explain your answer.

25. SUMMARIZE Describe the events that occur during the female's 28-day menstrual cycle. Include in your answer how hormones are involved in the cycle.

26. COMPARE AND CONTRAST How are the functions of the ovaries and the testes alike? How are their functions different?

the BIG idea

27. INFER Look again at the picture on pages 98–99. Now that you have finished the chapter, how would you change or add details to your answer to the question on the photograph?

28. SYNTHESIZE How does the nervous system interact with the endocrine and reproductive systems? Give examples that support your answer.

UNIT PROJECTS

If you need to do an experiment for your unit project, gather the materials. Be sure to allow enough time to observe results before the project is due.

Analyzing Data

This chart shows some of the stages of development of a typical fetus.

Week of Pregnancy	Average Length of Fetus	Developmental Changes in the Fetus
6	0.5 cm	Primitive heartbeat
10	2.5 cm	Face, fingers, and toes are formed
14	7.5 cm	Muscle and bone tissue have developed
18	12.5 cm	Fetus makes active movements
24	28 cm	Fingerprints and footprints forming
28	37 cm	Rapid brain development
36	45 cm	Increase in body fat
38	50 cm	Fetus is considered full term

Use the chart to answer the questions below.

1. What is the average length the fetus at 10 weeks?

  a. 0.5 cm   **c.** 2.5 cm

  b. 0.5 in.   **d.** 2.5 in.

2. At about which week of development does the fetus begin to make active movements?

  a. week 10   **c.** week 18

  b. week 14   **d.** week 24

3. At about which week of development does the fetus reach a length of about 28 cm?

  a. week 18   **c.** week 36

  b. week 24   **d.** week 38

4. Which statement is true?

  a. The fetus grows about 5 cm in length during the last 2 weeks of development.

  b. The fetus begins to develop fingerprints at about week 28.

  c. During week 10, the average length of the fetus is about 7.5 cm

  d. The fetus is about 12.5 cm long when muscle and bone tissue develop.

5. Between which two weeks of development does the greatest increase in length usually take place?

  a. weeks 6 and 10

  b. weeks 10 and 14

  c. weeks 14 and 18

  d. weeks 24 and 28

Extended Response

6. Describe the changes in length and development that occur during each trimester of pregnancy.

7. The endocrine system and the nervous system have similar functions. Compare and contrast the two systems including the terms in the box. Underline each term in your answer.

homeostasis	autonomic system	hormones
feedback	smooth muscles	

5

Growth, Development, and Health

the **BIG** idea

The body develops and maintains itself over time.

Key Concepts

SECTION

5.1 **The human body changes over time.**
Learn about the different stages of human development.

SECTION

5.2 **Diet, exercise, and behaviors affect health.**
Learn about what a body needs to be healthy.

SECTION

5.3 **Science helps people prevent and treat disease.**
Learn how to help prevent the spread of disease.

 **Internet Preview**

CLASSZONE.COM

Chapter 5 online resources: Content Review, Visualization, three Resource Centers, Math Tutorial, Test Practice

How do people change as they grow?

EXPLORE (the BIG idea)

How Much Do You Exercise?

In your notebook, create a chart to keep track of your exercise for a week. Each time you exercise, write down the type of activity and the amount of time you spend. If possible, measure your heart rate during the activity.

Observe and Think How does the exercise affect your heart rate? If you exercised regularly, what would be the effect on your heart rate while you were resting?

How Safe Is Your Food?

Almost all food that you buy in a store is dated for freshness. Look at the labels of various foods including cereal, juice, milk, eggs, cheese, and meats.

Observe and Think Why do you think some foods have a longer freshness period than others? What types of problems could you have from eating food that is past date?

Internet Activity: Human Development

Go to **ClassZone.com** to watch a movie of a person aging.

Observe and Think In what ways does a person's face change as he or she ages?

NSTA scilinks.org
SCiLINKS

Human Development **Code: MDL048**

Getting Ready to Learn

◀ CONCEPT REVIEW

- The integumentary system protects the body.
- The immune system fights disease.
- A microscope is an instrument used to observe very small objects.

◀ VOCABULARY REVIEW

nutrient p. 45

pathogen p. 74

antibiotic p. 81

hormone p. 111

CONTENT REVIEW
CLASSZONE.COM
Review concepts and vocabulary.

▶ TAKING NOTES

CONTENT FRAME

Make a content frame for each main idea. Include the following columns: *Topic, Definition, Detail,* and *Connection.* In the first column, list topics about the title. In the second column, define the topic. In the third column, include a detail about the topic. In the fourth column, add a sentence that connects that topic to another topic in the chart.

CHOOSE YOUR OWN STRATEGY

For each new vocabulary term, take notes by choosing a strategy from earlier chapters—**four square, magnet word, frame game,** or **description wheel.** Or, use a strategy of your own.

See the Note-Taking Handbook on pages R45–R51.

SCIENCE NOTEBOOK

The human body develops and grows.

Topic	Definition	Detail	Connection
Childhood	Period after infancy and before sexual maturity.	Children depend on parents, but learn to do things for themselves, such as get dressed.	Adults do not have to depend on parents; they are independent and can care for others.

Four Square

Frame Game

Magnet Word

Description Wheel

5.1 The human body changes over time.

- Living things grow and develop
- The digestive system breaks down nutrients in food
- Organ systems interact to keep the body healthy

- About four stages of human development
- About the changes that occur as the body develops
- How every body system interacts constantly with other systems to keep the body healthy

VOCABULARY

infancy p. 134
childhood p. 134
adolescence p. 135
adulthood p. 136

EXPLORE Growth

Are there patterns of growth?

PROCEDURE

1. Measure the circumference of your wrist by using the measuring tape as shown. Record the length. Now measure the length from your elbow to the tip of your middle finger. Record the length.

2. Create a table and enter all the data from each person in the class.

WHAT DO YOU THINK?

- How does the distance between the elbow and the fingertip compare with wrist circumference?
- Do you see a pattern between the size of one's wrist and the length of one's forearm?

MATERIALS

- flexible tape measure
- graph paper

CONTENT FRAME
Make a content frame for the first main idea: *The human body develops and grows.* List the red headings in this section in the topics column.

The human body develops and grows.

Have you noticed how rapidly your body has changed over the past few years? Only five years ago you were a young child in grade school. Today you are in middle school. How has your body changed? Growth is both physical and emotional. You are becoming more responsible and socially mature. What are some emotional changes that you have noticed?

Human development continues long after birth. Although humans develop at different rates, there are several stages of development common to human life. In this section we will describe some of the stages, including infancy, childhood, adolescence, and later adulthood

Infancy

The stage of life that begins at birth and ends when a baby begins to walk is called **infancy.** An infant's physical development is rapid. As the infant's body grows larger and stronger, it also learns physical skills. When you were first born, you could not lift your head. But as your muscles developed, you learned to lift your head, to roll over, to sit, to crawl, to stand, and finally to walk. You also learned to use your hands to grasp and hold objects.

Infants also develop thinking skills and social skills. At first, they simply cry when they are uncomfortable. Over time, they learn that people respond to those cries. They begin to expect help when they cry. They learn to recognize the people who care for them. Smiling, cooing, and eventually saying a few words are all part of an infant's social development.

Nearly every body system changes and grows during infancy. For example, as the digestive system matures, an infant becomes able to process solid foods. Changes in the nervous system, including the brain, allow an infant to see more clearly and to control parts of her or his body.

The Apgar score is used to evaluate the newborn's condition after delivery.

Apgar Score			
Quality	0 points	1 point	2 points
Appearance	Completely blue or pale	Good color in body, blue hands or feet	Completely pink or good color
Pulse	No heart rate	<100 beats per minute	>100 beats per minute
Grimace	No response to airway suction	Grimace during suctioning	Grimace, cough/ sneeze with suction
Activity	Limp	Some arm and leg movement	Active motion
Respiration	Not breathing	Weak cry	Good, strong cry

Childhood

The stage called **childhood** lasts for several years. Childhood is the period after infancy and before the beginning of sexual maturity. During childhood children still depend very much upon their parents. As their bodies and body systems grow, children become more able to care for themselves. Although parents still provide food and other needs, children perform tasks such as eating and getting dressed. In addition, children are able to do more complex physical tasks such as running, jumping, and riding a bicycle.

Childhood is also a time of mental and social growth. During childhood a human being learns to talk, read, write, and communicate in other ways. Along with the ability to communicate come social skills such as cooperation and sharing. A child learns to interact with others.

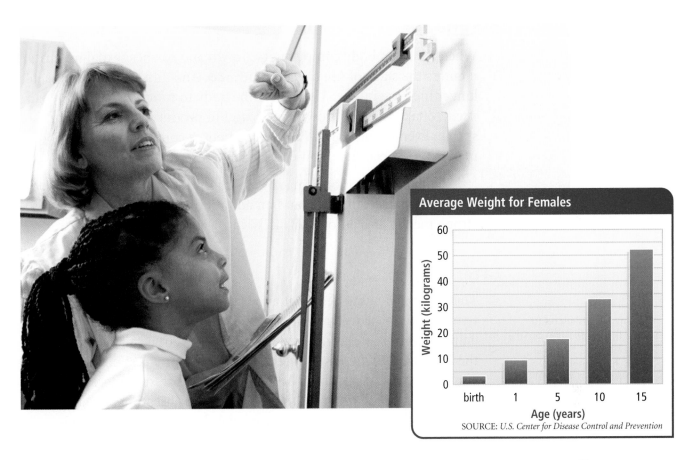

Average Weight for Females

SOURCE: *U.S. Center for Disease Control and Prevention*

Adolescence

The years from puberty to adulthood are called **adolescence** (AD-uhl-EHS-uhns). You and your classmates are adolescents. Childhood ends when the body begins to mature sexually. This process of physical change is called puberty. Not all people reach puberty at the same age. For girls, the changes usually start between ages eight and fourteen; for boys, puberty often begins between ages ten and sixteen.

VOCABULARY
Choose a strategy from earlier chapters or one of your own to take notes on the term *adolescence*.

The human body changes greatly during adolescence. As you learned in Chapter 4, the endocrine system produces chemicals called hormones. During adolescence, hormones signal parts of the reproductive system to mature. At this stage a person's sexual organs become ready for reproduction. These changes are accompanied by other changes. Adolescents develop secondary sexual characteristics. Boys may notice their voices changing. Girls begin developing breasts. Boys and girls both begin growing more body hair.

Probably the change that is the most obvious is a change in height. Boys and girls grow taller by as much as 10 centimeters (3.9 in.) during adolescence. Most adolescents eat more as they grow. Food provides materials necessary for growth.

CHECK YOUR READING What are some of the ways the body changes during adolescence?

Adulthood

When a human body completes its growth and reaches sexual maturity, it enters the stage of life called **adulthood.** An adult's body systems no longer increase in size. They allow the body to function fully, to repair itself, to take care of its own needs, and to produce and care for offspring. Even though physical development is complete at adulthood, mental and social development continue throughout life.

Mental and emotional maturity are important parts of adulthood. To maintain an adult body and an adult lifestyle, an individual needs strong mental and emotional skills.

Later Adulthood

READING TiP

You may find it helpful to review the information on the skeletal and muscular system in Chapter 1.

The process of aging begins at about the age of 30. Skin begins to wrinkle and loose its elasticity. Eyesight becomes increasingly poor, hair loss begins, and muscles decrease in strength. After the age of 65, the rate of aging increases. Internal organs become less efficient. Blood vessels become less elastic. The average blood pressure increases and may remain slightly high. Although the rate of breathing usually does not change, lung function decreases slightly. Body temperature is harder to regulate. However, one can slow the process of aging by a lifestyle of exercise and healthy diet.

Systems interact to maintain the human body.

It's easy to observe the external changes to the body during growth and development. Inside the body, every system interacts constantly with other systems to keep the whole person healthy throughout his or her lifetime. For example, the respiratory system constantly sends oxygen to the blood cells of the circulatory system. The circulatory system transports hormones produced by the endocrine system.

Your body systems also interact with the environment outside your body. Your nervous system monitors the outside world through your senses of taste, smell, hearing, vision, and touch. It allows you to respond to your environment. For example, your nervous system allows you to squint if the sun is too bright or to move indoors if the weather is cold. Your endocrine system releases hormones that allow you to have an increased heart rate and send more blood to your muscles if you have to respond to an emergency.

INVESTIGATE Life Expectancy

How has life expectancy changed over time?

In this activity, you will look for trends in the changes in average life expectancy over the past 100 years.

SKILL FOCUS
Graphing

MATERIALS
• graph paper
• computer graph-ing program

TIME
30 minutes

PROCEDURE

① Using the following data, create a bar graph to chart changes in life expectancy over the last 100 years.

Life Expectancy 1900–2000											
Year	1900	1910	1920	1930	1940	1950	1960	1970	1980	1990	2000
Average Life Expectancy (years)	47.3	50.0	54.1	59.7	62.9	68.2	69.7	70.8	73.7	75.4	76.9

SOURCE: National Center for Health Statistics

② Study the graph. Observe any trends that you see. Record them in your notebook.

WHAT DO YOU THINK?

• In general, what do these data demonstrate about life expectancy?

• Between which decades did average life expectancy increase the most?

CHALLENGE Using a computer program, create a table and bar graph to chart the data shown above.

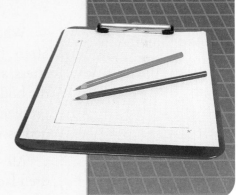

Every part of your daily life requires interactions among your body systems. Even during sleep several body systems cooperate. When you sleep, your nervous system allows your muscular system to keep your heart pumping and your lungs breathing. The heart pumps blood through your circulatory system, which has received oxygen from your respiratory system. All this cooperation takes place even while you are sleeping. Your endocrine system releases growth hormone during your sleep allowing your bones and muscles to grow. The neurons in your brain change when you fall asleep.

Keeping the body healthy is complex. The digestive and urinary systems eliminate solid and liquid wastes from the body. The circulatory and respiratory systems remove carbon dioxide gas. As you will learn in the next section, a healthy diet and regular exercise help the body to stay strong and function properly.

 Name three systems that interact as your body grows and maintains itself.

READING VISUALS COMPARE AND CONTRAST How do the interactions of your body system change when you are active and when you rest?

When body systems fail to work together, the body can become ill. Stress, for example, can affect all the body systems. Some types of stress, such as fear, can be a healthy response to danger. However, if the body experiences stress over long periods of time, serious health problems such as heart disease, ulcers, headaches, muscle tension, and depression can arise.

All stages of life include different types of stress. Infants and children face stresses as they learn to become more independent and gain better control over their bodies. Adolescents can be challenged by school, by the changes of puberty, or by being socially accepted by their peers. Adults may encounter stress in their jobs or with their families. The stress of aging can be very difficult for some older adults.

5.1 Review

KEY CONCEPTS

1. Make a development timeline with four sections. Write the names of the stages in order under each section. Include a definition and two details.

2. List a physical characteristic of each stage of development.

3. Give an example of an activity that involves two or more body systems.

CRITICAL THINKING

4. **Compare and Contrast** Make a chart to compare and contrast the infancy and childhood stages of development.

5. **Identify Cause and Effect** How is the endocrine system involved in adolescence?

⚠ CHALLENGE

6. **Synthesis** How does each of the body systems described change as a human being develops from infancy to older adulthood?

Aging the Face

In a movie, characters may go through development stages of a whole lifetime in just over an hour. An actor playing such a role will need to look both older and younger than he or she really is. Stage makeup artists have a toolbox full of techniques to make the actor look the part.

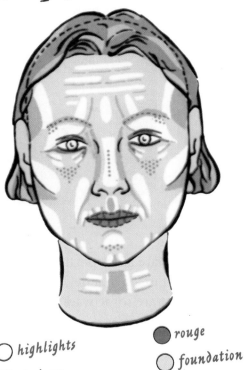

Makeup Guide for Aging

○ highlights
○ shadows
● rouge
○ foundation

Hair

As humans go through adulthood, their hair may lose the pigments that make it dark. Makeup artists color hair with dyes or even talcum powder. Wigs and bald caps, made of latex rubber, cover an actor's real hair. Eyebrows can be colored or aged by rubbing them with makeup.

Features

For a bigger-looking nose or extra skin around the neck, makeup artists use foam rubber, or layers of liquid rubber, and sometimes, wads of paper tissue to build up facial features. For example, building up the cheekbones with layers of latex makes the cheeks appear sharper, less rounded, and more hollow.

Skin

To make wrinkles or scars, makeup artists use light-colored makeup to for the raised highlights and dark-colored makeup for lower shadows and spots.

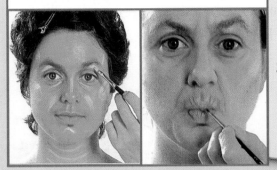

EXPLORE

1. **COMPARE** Look at photos of an older relative at three different stages of life, at about ten years apart. Describe how you might apply makeup to your own face if you were to portray this person's life in three movie scenes. What changes do you need to show?

2. **CHALLENGE** Research to find an image of a character portrayed in a movie, who needed to look very different than real life. From the picture, describe how the effect was achieved.

Systems in the body function to maintain health.

 BEFORE, you learned

- Human development involves all the body systems
- The human body continues to develop until adulthood
- Every body system interacts constantly with other systems to keep the body healthy

 NOW, you will learn

- About the role of nutrients in health
- Why exercise is needed to keep body systems healthy
- How drug abuse, eating disorders, and addiction can affect the body

VOCABULARY

nutrition p. 140
addiction p. 145

THINK ABOUT

What is health?

If you went online and searched under the word *health,* you would find millions of links. Clearly, health is important to most people. You may be most aware of your health when you aren't feeling well. But you know that clean water, food, exercise, and sleep are all important for health. Preventing illness is also part of staying healthy. How would you define health? What are some ways that you protect your health?

Diet affects the body's health.

VOCABULARY
Choose a strategy from an earlier chapter, such as a magnet word diagram, for taking notes on the term *nutrition*. Or use any strategy that you think works well.

What makes a meal healthy? The choices you make about what you eat are important. Nutrients from food are distributed to every cell in your body. You use those nutrients for energy and to maintain and build new body tissues. **Nutrition** is the study of the materials that nourish your body. It also refers to the process in which the different parts of food are used for maintenance, growth, and reproduction. When a vitamin or other nutrient is missing from your diet, illness can occur. Your body's systems can function only when they get the nutrients they need.

 **CHECK YOUR READING** How is nutrition important to health?

This family is enjoying a healthy meal of proteins, carbohydrates, and fats.

Getting Nutrients

Discover more about human health.

In order to eat a healthy diet, you must first understand what good nutrition is. There are six classes of nutrients: carbohydrates, proteins, fats, vitamins, minerals, and water. All of these nutrients are necessary as sources of energy for your body. Also, they each contribute to the chemical reactions that must take place within your cells.

Proteins are molecules that build tissues used for growth and repair. Proteins also stabilize blood sugar levels by stimulating important hormones. Good sources of proteins are poultry, red meat, fish, eggs, nuts, beans, grains, soy, and milk. Protein should make up at least 20 percent of your diet.

Carbohydrates are the body's most important energy source and are found in starch, sugar, and fiber. Fiber provides little energy, but is important for regular elimination. Natural sugars such as those found in fruits and vegetables are the best kinds of sugars for your body. Carbohydrates are found in bread and pasta, fruits, and vegetables. Carbohydrates should make up about 40 to 50 percent of your diet.

Fats are essential for energy and should account for about 10 to 15 percent of your diet. Many people eliminate fats from their diets in order to lose weight. But a certain amount of fat is necessary. Fats made from plants have the greatest health benefits. For example, olive oil is better for you than the oil found in butter.

Vitamins and minerals are needed by your body in small amounts. Vitamins are small molecules that regulate body growth and development. Minerals help build body tissues. While some vitamins can be made by your body, most of them are supplied to the body in food.

Water is necessary to for life. A human being could live for less than a month without food, but only about one week without water. Water has several functions. Water helps regulate your body temperature through evaporation when you sweat and breathe. Without water, important materials such as vitamins and other nutrients, could not be transported around the body. Water helps your body get rid of the waste products that move through the kidneys and pass out of the body in urine. Urine is composed mostly of water.

To make sure your body can function and maintain itself, you need to drink about two and one half liters or about eight glasses of water every day. You also get water when you eat foods with water in them, such as fresh fruit and vegetables.

Vitamins and Minerals	
Vitamin or Mineral	**Recommended Daily Allowance**
Vitamin A	0.3 to 1.3 mg
Niacin	6–18 mg
Vitamin B_2	0.5–1.6 mg
Vitamin B_6	0.5–2.0 mg
Vitamin C	15–120 mg
Vitamin E	6–19 mg
Calcium	500–1300 mg
Phosphorus	460–1250 mg
Potassium	1600–2000 mg
Zinc	3–13 mg
Magnesium	80–420 mg
Iron	7–27 mg

Source: National Institutes of Health

Understanding Nutrition

RESOURCE CENTER
CLASSZONE.COM

Examine the basic principles of nutrition.

Ever wonder what the word *lite* really means? What do labels saying that food is fresh or natural or organic mean? Not all advertising about nutrition is reliable. It is important to know what the labels on food really mean. Groups within the government, such as the United States Department of Agriculture, have defined terms that are used to describe food products. For example, if a food label says the food is "all natural," that means it does not contain any artificial flavor, color, or preservative.

Another example is the term *low-fat*. That label means that the food provides no more than 3 grams of fat per serving. The word *organic* means that the produce has been grown using no human-made fertilizers or chemicals that kill pests or weeds. It also means that livestock has been raised on organic feed and has not been given antibiotics or growth hormones. It takes some effort and a lot of reading to stay informed, but the more you know, the better the choices you can make.

What are you eating?

PROCEDURE

1. Gather nutrition labels from the following products: a carbonated soft drink, a bag of fresh carrots, canned spaghetti in sauce, potato chips, plain popcorn kernels, unsweetened applesauce, and fruit juice. Look at the percent of daily values of the major nutrients, as shown on the label for each food.

2. Make a list of ways to evaluate a food for high nutritional value. Include such criteria as nutrient levels and calories per serving.

3. Examine the nutrition labels and compare them with your list. Decide which of these foods would make a healthy snack.

WHAT DO YOU THINK?

- How does serving size affect the way you evaluate a nutritional label?

- What are some ways to snack and get nutrients at the same time?

CHALLENGE Design a full day's food menu that will give you all the nutrients you need. Use snacks as some of the foods that contribute these nutrients.

SKILL FOCUS
Analyzing

MATERIALS
nutrition labels

TIME
30 minutes

Exercise is part of a healthy lifestyle.

Regular exercise allows all your body systems to stay strong and healthy. You learned that your lymphatic system doesn't include a structure like the heart to pump its fluid through the body. Instead, it relies on body movement and strong muscles to help it move antibodies and white blood cells. Exercise is good for the lymphatic system.

Exercise

When you exercise, you breathe harder and more quickly. You inhale and exhale more air, which exercises the muscles of your respiratory system and makes them stronger. Exercise also brings in extra oxygen. Oxygen is necessary for cellular respiration, which provides energy to other body systems. The circulatory system is strengthened by exercise. Your heart becomes stronger the more it is used. The skeletal system grows stronger with exercise as well. Studies show that older adults who lift weights have stronger bones than those who do not. In addition, physical activity can flush out skin pores by making you sweat, and it reduces the symptoms of depression.

By eating healthy meals and exercising, you help your body to grow and develop.

Lifestyle

The lifestyles of many people involve regular exercise. Some lifestyles, however, include more sitting still than moving. A lifestyle that is sedentary, associated mostly with sitting down, can harm a person's health. Muscles and bones that are not exercised regularly can begin to break down. Your body stores unused energy from food as fat. The extra weight of body fat can make it harder for you to exercise. Therefore, it is harder to use up energy or to strengthen your skeletal, muscular, and immune systems. Researchers have also made connections between excess body fat and heart disease and diabetes.

 CHECK YOUR READING How does lifestyle affect health?

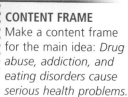
CONTENT FRAME
Make a content frame for the main idea: *Drug abuse, addiction, and eating disorders cause serious health problems.*

Drug abuse, addiction, and eating disorders cause serious health problems.

Every day, you make choices that influence your health. Some choices can have more serious health risks, or possibilities for harm, than others. You have the option to make healthy choices for yourself. Making unhealthy decisions about what you put into your body can lead to drug abuse, addiction, or eating disorders.

Drug Abuse

A drug is any chemical substance that you take in to change your body's functions. Doctors use drugs to treat and prevent disease and illness. The use of a drug for any other reason is an abuse of that drug. Abuse can also include using too much of a substance that is not harmful in small amounts. People abuse different drugs for different reasons. Drugs often do allow an individual to feel better for the moment. But they can also cause serious harm to an individual's health.

Tobacco Nicotine, the drug in tobacco, increases heart rate and blood pressure and makes it seem as if the user has more energy. Nicotine is also a poison; in fact, some farmers use it to kill insects. Tobacco smoke contains thousands of chemicals. Tar and carbon monoxide are two harmful chemicals in smoke. Tar is a sticky substance that is commonly used to pave roads. Carbon monoxide is one of the gases that cars release in their exhaust. People who smoke or chew tobacco have a high risk of cancer, and smokers are also at risk for heart disease.

Compounds Found in Unfiltered Tobacco Smoke		
Compound	Amount in First-Hand Smoke (per cigarette)	Amount in Second-Hand Smoke (per cigarette)
Nicotine	1–3 mg	2.1–46 mg
Tar	15–40 mg	14–30 mg
Carbon monoxide	14–23 mg	27–61 mg
Benzene	0.012–0.05 mg	0.4 mg
Formaldehyde	0.07–0.1 mg	1.5 mg
Hydrogen cyanide	0.4–0.5 mg	0.014–11 mg
Phenol	0.08–0.16 mg	0.07–0.25 mg

Source: U.S. Department of Health and Human Services

Alcohol Even a small amount of alcohol can affect a person's ability to think and reason. Alcohol can affect behavior and the ability to make decisions. Many people are killed every year, especially in automobile accidents, because of choices they made while drinking alcohol. Alcohol abuse damages the heart, the liver, the nervous system, and the digestive system.

Other Drugs Some drugs, such as cocaine and amphetamines, can make people feel more energetic and even powerful because they stimulate the nervous system and speed up the heart. These drugs are very dangerous. They can cause nervous disorders and heart attacks.

Drugs called narcotics also affect the nervous system. Instead of stimulating it, however, they decrease its activity. Narcotics are prescribed by doctors to relieve pain and to help people sleep. Abuse of narcotics can lead to addiction. More and more narcotics are then needed to gain the same effect. Because narcotics work by decreasing nerve function, large amounts of these drugs can cause the heart and lungs to stop.

Students can be active in protesting drug abuse.

Addiction

Drug abuse can often lead to addiction. **Addiction** is an illness in which a person becomes dependent on a substance or behavior. Repeated use of drugs such as alcohol, tobacco, and narcotics can cause the body to become physically dependent. When a person is dependent on a drug, taking away that drug can cause withdrawal. If affected by withdrawal, a person may become physically ill, sometimes within a very short period of time. Symptoms of withdrawal can include fever, muscle cramps, vomiting, and hallucinations.

Another type of addiction can result from the effect a drug, or even a behavior, produces. Although physical dependency may not occur, a person can become emotionally dependent. Gambling, overeating, and risk-taking are some examples of addictive behaviors. With both physical and emotional addictions, increasing amounts of a drug or behavior are necessary to achieve the effects. Someone who suffers from an addiction can be treated and can work to live a healthy life, but most addictions never go away completely.

Eating Disorders

An eating disorder is a condition in which people continually eat too much or too little food. One example of an eating disorder is anorexia nervosa. People with this disorder eat so little and exercise so hard that they become unhealthy. No matter how thin they are, they believe they need to be thinner. People with anorexia do not receive necessary nutrients because they don't eat. When the energy used by the body exceeds the energy taken in from food, tissues in the body are broken down to provide fuel. Bones and muscles, including the heart, can be damaged, and the person can die.

5.2 Review

KEY CONCEPTS

1. How do nutrients affect health?

2. Explain the effects of exercise on the respiratory and circulatory systems.

3. Make a chart showing the effects of tobacco, alcohol, and other drugs on the body.

CRITICAL THINKING

4. **Explain** How would you define health? Write your own definition.

5. **Synthesize** Explain how water can be considered a nutrient. Include a definition of *nutrient* in your explanation.

◯ CHALLENGE

6. **Apply** You have heard about a popular new diet. All of the foods in the diet are fat-free, and the diet promises fast weight loss. How might this diet affect health? Explain your answer.

MATH TUTORIAL
CLASSZONE.COM

Click on Math Tutorial for more help with choosing a data display.

Pumping Up the Heart

Heart rates differ with age, level of activity, and fitness. To communicate the differences clearly, you need to display the data visually. Choosing the appropriate display is important.

Example

The fitness trainer at a gym wants to display the following data:

Maximum heart rate while exercising (beats per minute)		
Age 21	Men	197
	Women	194
Age 45	Men	178
	Women	177
Age 65	Men	162
	Women	164

Here are some different displays the trainer could use:

• A bar graph shows how different categories of data compare. Data can be broken into 2 or even 3 bars per category.

• A line graph shows how data changes over time.

• A circle graph represents data as parts of a whole.

ANSWER The fitness trainer wants to show heart rate according to both age and gender, so a double bar graph would be the clearest.

What would be an appropriate way to display data in the following situations?

1. A doctor wants to display how a child's average heart rate changes as the child grows.

2. A doctor wants to display data showing how a person's resting heart rate changes the more the person exercises.

3. A scientist is studying each type of diet that the people in an experiment follow. She will show what percentage of the people with each diet had heart disease.

CHALLENGE Describe a situation in which a double line graph is the most appropriate data display.

Science helps people prevent and treat disease.

◀ **BEFORE, you learned**

- Good nutrition and exercise help keep the body healthy
- Drug abuse can endanger health
- Eating disorders can affect the body's health

▶ **NOW, you will learn**

- About some of the causes of disease
- How diseases can be treated
- How to help prevent the spread of disease

VOCABULARY

microorganism p. 148
bacteria p. 149
virus p. 149
resistance p. 153

EXPLORE The Immune System

How easily do germs spread?

PROCEDURE

MATERIALS
glitter

① Early in the day, place a small amount of glitter in the palm of one hand. Rub your hands together to spread the glitter to both palms. Go about your day normally.

② At the end of the day, examine your environment, including the people around you. Where does the glitter show up?

WHAT DO YOU THINK?

- How easily did the glitter transfer to other people and objects?
- What do you think this might mean about how diseases might spread?

Scientific understanding helps people fight disease.

Disease is a change that disturbs the normal functioning of the body's systems. If you have ever had a cold, you have experienced a disease that affected your respiratory system. What are the causes of disease? Many diseases are classified as infectious diseases, or diseases that can be spread. Viruses, bacteria and other materials cause infectious disease. The organisms that cause sickness are called **microorganisms.**

Before the invention of the microscope, people didn't know about microorganisms that cause disease. They observed that people who lived near each other sometimes caught the same illness, but they didn't understand why. Understanding disease has helped people prevent and treat many illnesses.

VOCABULARY
Remember to choose a strategy from earlier chapters or one of your own to take notes on the term *microorganism.*

The germ theory describes some causes of disease.

In the 1800s, questions about the causes of some diseases were answered. Scientists showed through experiments that diseases could be caused by very small living things. In 1857, French chemist Louis Pasteur did experiments that showed that microorganisms caused food to decay. Later, Pasteur's work and the work of Robert Koch and Robert Lister contributed to the germ theory. Pasteur's germ theory states that some diseases, called infectious diseases, are caused by germs.

Bacteria and Viruses

Germs are the general name given to organisms that cause disease. Germs include **bacteria** (bak-TEER-ee-uh), single-celled organisms that live almost everywhere. Within your intestines, bacteria function to digest food. Some bacteria, however, cause disease. Pneumonia (nu-MOHN-yuh), ear infections (ihn-FEHK-shuhnz), and strep throat can be caused by bacteria.

Most scientists do not consider **viruses** living things. However, viruses have many characteristics of living things. Viruses must exist within organisms. Once inside organisms, they use the materials inside cells to reproduce. Stomach flu, chicken pox, and colds are sicknesses caused by viruses. Both bacteria and viruses are examples of pathogens, agents that cause disease. The word *pathogen* comes from the Greek *pathos*, which means "suffering." Other pathogens include yeasts, fungi, and protists.

RESOURCE CENTER
CLASSZONE.COM

Explore ways to fight disease.

Treating Infectious Diseases

Diseases caused by bacteria can be treated with medicines that contain antibiotics. An antibiotic is a substance that can destroy bacteria. The first antibiotics were discovered in 1928 when a scientist named Alexander Fleming was performing experiments on bacteria. Fleming found mold growing on his bacteria samples. While most of the bacteria samples looked cloudy, the area around the mold was clear. From this observation, Fleming concluded that a substance in the mold had killed the bacteria.

Fleming had not intended to grow mold in his laboratory, but the accident led to the discovery of penicillin. Since the discovery of penicillin, many antibiotics have been developed. Antibiotics have saved the lives of millions of people.

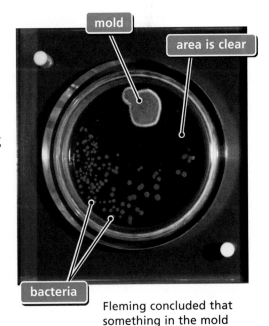

mold

area is clear

bacteria

Fleming concluded that something in the mold had killed the bacteria.

Infectious diseases spread in many ways.

READING TiP

As you read the text on this page, notice how each pathogen shown on p. 151 spreads.

One of the best ways to protect your health is by being informed and by avoiding pathogens. Pathogens can be found in many places, including air, water, and on the surfaces of objects. By knowing how pathogens travel, people are able to limit the spreading of disease.

Food, Air, and Water

Sometimes people get sick when they breathe in pathogens from the air. The viruses that cause colds can travel through air. If you cover your mouth when you sneeze or cough, you can avoid sending pathogens through the air. Pathogens also enter the body in food or water. Washing fruits and vegetables and cooking meats and eggs kills bacteria. Most cities in the United States add substances, such as chlorine, to the supply of public water. These substances kill pathogens. Boiling water also kills pathogens. People sometimes boil water if their community loses power or experiences a flood. Campers often need to boil or filter water before they use it.

Contact with Insects and Other Animals

Animals and insects can also carry organisms that cause disease. The animal itself does not cause the illness, but you can become sick if you take in the pathogen that the animal carries. Lyme disease, for example, is caused by bacteria that inhabit ticks. The ticks are not the illness, but if an infected tick bites you, you will get Lyme disease.

A deadly central nervous system infection called rabies can also come from animal contact. The virus that causes rabies is found in the saliva of an infected animal, such as a bat, raccoon, or opossum. If that animal bites you, you may get the disease. A veterinarian can give your pet an injection to prevent rabies. You can get other infections from pets. These infections include worms that enter through your mouth or nose and live in your intestines. You can also get a skin infection called ringworm, which is actually a fungus rather than a worm.

Person-to-Person Contact

Most of the illnesses you have had have probably been passed to you by another person. Even someone who does not feel sick can have pathogens on his or her skin. If you touch that person or if that person touches something and then you touch it, the pathogens will move to your skin. If the pathogens then enter your body through a cut or through your nose, mouth, or eyes, they can infect your body. The simplest way to avoid giving or receiving pathogens is to wash your hands often and well.

Pathogens and Disease

Infectious diseases are caused by microorganisms.

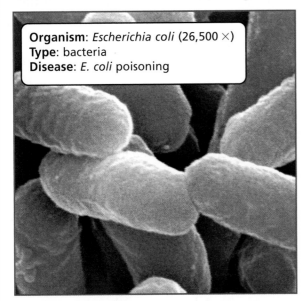

Organism: *Escherichia coli* (26,500 ×)
Type: bacteria
Disease: *E. coli* poisoning

Spread: contaminated food or water

Prevention: handwashing, thoroughly cooking meat, boiling contaminated water, washing fruits and vegetables, drinking only pasteurized milk, juice, or cider

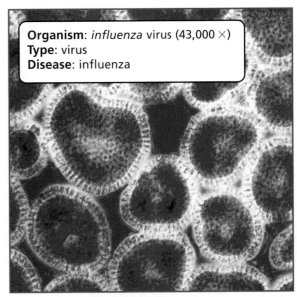

Organism: *influenza* virus (43,000 ×)
Type: virus
Disease: influenza

Spread: inhaling virus from sneezes or coughs of infected person

Prevention: vaccination

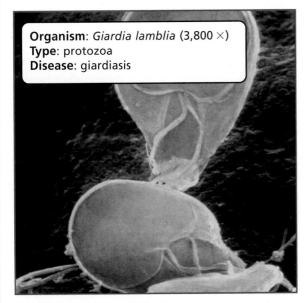

Organism: *Giardia lamblia* (3,800 ×)
Type: protozoa
Disease: giardiasis

Spread: contaminated food or water, close contact with infected person

Prevention: handwashing, thoroughly cooking meat, boiling contaminated water, washing fruits and vegetables, drinking only pasteurized milk, juice, or cider

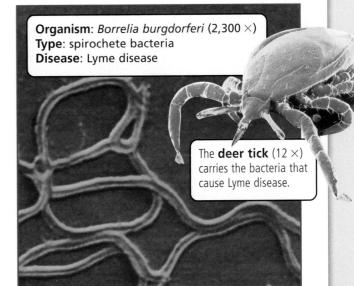

Organism: *Borrelia burgdorferi* (2,300 ×)
Type: spirochete bacteria
Disease: Lyme disease

The **deer tick** (12 ×) carries the bacteria that cause Lyme disease.

Spread: tick bite

Prevention: wear light-colored clothing, tuck pants into socks or shoes, check for ticks after outdoor activities, use repellents containing DEET

READING VISUALS How can people prevent each of these pathogens from spreading?

Noninfectious diseases are not contagious.

Noninfectious diseases are diseases that cannot be spread by pathogens. They are not contagious. You are born with some of these, and others can develop during life.

Diseases Present at Birth

Some diseases present at birth are inherited. Genes, which act as instructions for your cells, are inherited from your parents. Some forms of a gene produce cells that do not function properly. Most genetic disorders are due to recessive forms of a gene, which means that while both parents carry the defective form, neither one has the disorder. Cystic fibrosis, sickle cell anemia, and hemophilia are diseases inherited this way.

Asthma is a noncontagious disease often present at birth.

The symptoms of some genetic diseases may not be present immediately at birth. Huntington's chorea, even though it is an inherited condition, does not begin to produce symptoms until a person reaches adulthood. Other genes can increase the chances of developing a disease later in life, such as cancer or diabetes, but the pattern of inheritance is not totally understood.

The process of human development is complex. Some diseases present at birth may involve both inherited factors and development. Talipes, a disorder commonly known as clubfoot, is due to the improper development of the bones of the leg and foot. Talipes can be corrected by surgery after birth.

Diseases in Later Life

Some diseases, including heart disease, certain forms of cancer, and many respiratory disorders, have much less to do with genetics and more to do with environment and lifestyle. You have learned about the ways in which you can lead a healthy lifestyle. Good nutrition, exercise, and avoiding substances that can damage the body systems not only increase the length of life, but also the quality of life.

While people with family histories of cancer are at higher risk of getting it, environmental factors can influence risk as well. Tar and other chemicals from cigarettes can damage the lungs, in addition to causing cancer. Much is still not known about the causes of cancer.

 CHECK YOUR READING Name a noninfectious disease that is present at birth and one that may occur later in life.

Scientists continue efforts to prevent and treat illness.

In spite of all that scientists have learned, disease is still a problem all over the world. Illnesses such as AIDS and cancer are better understood than they used to be, but researchers must still find ways to cure them.

Even though progress is sometimes slow, it does occur. Better education has led to better nutrition. The use of vaccines has made some diseases nearly extinct. However, new types of illness sometimes appear. AIDS was first identified in the 1980s and spread quickly before it was identified. More recently, the West Nile virus appeared in the United States. This virus is transmitted by infected mosquitoes and can cause the brain to become inflamed. Efforts to control the disease continue.

Scientists work hard to fight disease.

Antibiotics fight pathogens, but they can also lead to changes in them. When an antibiotic is used too often, bacteria can develop **resistance,** or become partially immune, to its effects. This means that the next time those bacteria invade, that particular antibiotic will not stop the infection. For this reason, it is best not to use pathogen-killing drugs or chemicals unless you really need them.

 CHECK YOUR READING Describe the advantages and disadvantages of using an antibiotic when you are sick.

 **Review**

KEY CONCEPTS	CRITICAL THINKING	⬤ CHALLENGE

KEY CONCEPTS

1. Define microorganism and explain how microorganisms can affect health.

2. What is an antibiotic?

3. Make a chart showing ways that infectious diseases spread and ways to keep them from spreading.

CRITICAL THINKING

4. **Connect** Make a list of things you can do to avoid getting Lyme disease or the West Nile virus.

5. **Apply** How does washing your hands before eating help protect your health?

⬤ CHALLENGE

6. **Synthesize** How can nutrition help in the prevention of disease? Use these terms in your answer: *nutrients, pathogens,* and *white blood cells.*

CHAPTER INVESTIGATION

Cleaning Your Hands

OVERVIEW AND PURPOSE Your skin cells produce oils that keep the skin moist. This same layer of oil provides a nutrient surface for bacteria to grow. When you wash your hands with soap, the soap dissolves the oil and the water carries it away, along with the bacteria. In this activity you will
- sample your hands for the presence of bacteria
- test the effectiveness of washing your hands with water compared with washing them with soap and water

▶ Problem
Write It Up

Is soap effective at removing bacteria?

▶ Hypothesize
Write It Up

Write a hypothesis explaining how using soap affects the amount of bacteria on your hands. Your hypothesis should take the form of an "If . . . , then . . . , because . . ." statement.

▶ Procedure

MATERIALS
- 3 covered petri dishes with sterile nutrient agar
- soap
- marker
- tape
- hand lens

1. Make a data table in your **Science Notebook** like the one shown on page 155.

2. Obtain three agar petri dishes. Be careful not to open the dishes.

3. Remove the lid from one dish and gently press two fingers from your right hand onto the surface of the agar. Close the lid immediately. Tape the dish closed. Mark the tape with the letter *A*. Include your initials and the date.

step 3

4. Wash your hands in water and let them air-dry. Open the second dish with your right hand and press two fingers of your left hand into the agar. Close the lid immediately. Tape and mark the dish *B*, as in step 3.

5. Wash your hands in soap and water and let them air-dry. Open the third dish with one hand and press two fingers of the other hand into the agar. Close the lid immediately. Tape and mark the dish *C*, as in step 3.

6. Place the agar plates upside down in a dark, warm place for two to three days. **Caution:** Do not open the dishes. Wash your hands.

▶ Observe and Analyze
Write It Up

1. **OBSERVE** Use a hand lens to observe the amounts of bacterial growth in each dish, and record your observations in Table 1. Which dish has the most bacterial growth? the least growth?

2. **OBSERVE** Is there anything you notice about the bacterial growth in each dish other than the amount of bacterial growth?

3. Return the petri dishes to your teacher for disposal. **Caution:** Do not open the dishes. Wash your hands thoroughly with warm water and soap when you have finished.

▶ Conclude
Write It Up

1. **INFER** Why is it necessary to air-dry your hands instead of using a towel?

2. **INFER** Why is it important to use your right hand in step 3 and your left hand in step 4?

3. **INTERPRET** Compare your results with your hypothesis. Do your observations support your hypothesis?

4. **EVALUATE** Is there much value in washing your hands simply in water?

5. **EVALUATE** How might the temperature of the water you used when you washed your hands affect the results of your experiment?

6. **EVALUATE** Given the setup of your experiment, could you have prepared a fourth sample, for example to test the effectiveness of antibacterial soap?

▶ INVESTIGATE Further

CHALLENGE It is hard to tell which products are best for washing hands without testing them. Design an experiment to determine which cleans your hands best: baby wipes, hand sanitizer, regular soap, or antibacterial soap.

Cleaning Your Hands

Table 1. Observations

Petri Dish	Source	Amount of Bacteria
A	hand	
B	hand washed with water	
C	hand washed with soap and water	

Chapter Review

the BIG idea

The body develops and maintains itself over time.

CONTENT REVIEW
CLASSZONE.COM

◀ KEY CONCEPTS SUMMARY

5.1 **The human body changes over time.**

Your body develops and grows throughout your entire life. Some changes are physical and some are emotional. The stages of life are infancy, childhood, adolescence, adulthood, and later adulthood. All the different systems in the body interact to maintain your health.

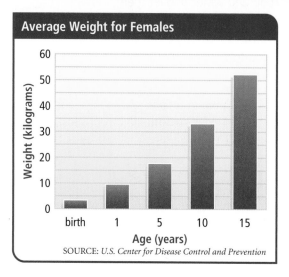

Average Weight for Females

Weight (kilograms) vs Age (years)

SOURCE: *U.S. Center for Disease Control and Prevention*

VOCABULARY
infancy p. 134
childhood p. 134
adolescence p. 135
adulthood p. 136

5.2 **Diet, exercise, and behaviors affect health.**

Your diet affects your health. Important nutrients include proteins, carbohydrates, fats vitamins, minerals, and water. Water is also essential to healthy living. Exercise is the final ingredient to a healthy life. Problems that can interfere with a healthy life are drug abuse, addiction, and eating disorders.

Spaghetti
IN TOMATO SAUCE WITH CHEESE
Nutrition Facts
Serving Size: 1 cup (252g)
Servings Per Container: about 2
Amount Per Serving
Calories 210   Calories from Fat 20
             % Daily Value*
Total Fat 2g
  Saturated Fat 1g   3%
Cholesterol 5mg   5%

VOCABULARY
nutrition p. 140
addiction p. 146

5.3 **Science helps people prevent and treat disease.**

- Science helps people fight disease.
- Antibiotics are used to fight diseases caused by bacteria.
- Infectious disease can spread in many ways including food, air, water, insects, animals, and person-to-person contact.
- Noninfectious diseases are not contagious. Some of these noninfectious diseases are present at birth and others occur in later life.

VOCABULARY
microorganism p. 148
bacteria p. 149
virus p. 149
resistance p. 153

Reviewing Vocabulary

Make a frame for each of the vocabulary words listed below. Write the word in the center. Decide what information to frame it with. Use definitions, examples, descriptions, parts, or pictures.

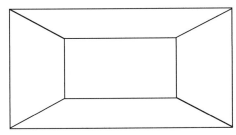

1. infancy
2. childhood
3. adolescence
4. adulthood

Reviewing Key Concepts

Multiple Choice *Choose the letter of the best answer.*

5. The stage of life known as infancy ends when an infant
   a. begins to cry
   b. learns to walk
   c. holds up his head
   d. sees more clearly

6. The process in which the body begins to mature sexually is called
   a. adolescence   c. nutrition
   b. adulthood   d. puberty

7. Which nutrients are sources of energy for the body?
   a. fats and carbohydrates
   b. water and protein
   c. fats and proteins
   d. water and carbohydrates

8. Which is *not* a benefit of regular exercise?
   a. flushed-out skin pores
   b. stronger skeletal system
   c. increased body fat
   d. strengthened heart

9. A sedentary life style is associated with
   a. a stronger immune system
   b. more sitting than moving
   c. regular exercise
   d. an eating disorder

10. The chemical found in tobacco that increases heart rate and blood pressure is
    a. cocaine   c. tar
    b. carbon monoxide   d. nicotine

11. Which term includes all of the others?
    a. bacteria   c. virus
    b. germ   d. pathogen

12. An example of a disease caused by bacteria is
    a. an ear infection
    b. stomach flu
    c. chicken pox
    d. a cold

13. Which statement about viruses is true?
    a. Viruses function to digest food.
    b. Viruses are one-celled organisms.
    c. Viruses are not living.
    d. Examples of viruses are fungi and yeasts.

14. A substance that can destroy bacteria is called
    a. a virus   c. an antibiotic
    b. a pathogen   d. a mold

15. Lyme disease is spread through
    a. drinking unfiltered water
    b. uncooked meats
    c. the bite of a dog
    d. the bite of a tick

Short Answer *Write a short answer to each question.*

16. In your own words, define *nutrition*.

17. What are pathogens? Give three examples.

18. Explain what happens if antibiotics are used too often.

Thinking Critically

19. **ANALYZE** Why do you think crying is an example of a social skill that develops during infancy?

20. **ANALYZE** Describe one physical, one mental, and one social change that a ten-year-old boy might experience over the next five years.

21. **EVALUATE** Explain why a diet that doesn't contain any fat would be unhealthy for most people?

22. **APPLY** Explain why people who live sedentary lifestyles should get more exercise.

23. **SYNTHESIZE** Discuss why doctors recommend that women avoid alcohol and tobacco use during pregnancy.

24. **COMPARE AND CONTRAST** How are anorexia and bulimia alike? How do they differ?

25. **ANALYZE** Explain why the work of Louis Pasteur was important in the understanding of infectious disease.

26. **HYPOTHESIZE** In 1854 a disease called cholera spread through the city of London. Most of the people who contracted the disease lived near the city's various water pumps. What might you hypothesize about the cause of the disease? How could you prevent people from contracting the disease in the future?

27. **PROVIDE EXAMPLES** What are some ways that a person can prevent noninfectious diseases such as cancer or diabetes?

the BIG idea

28. **INFER** Look again at the picture on pages 130–131. Now that you have finished the chapter, how would you change or add details to your answer to the question on the photograph?

29. **SUMMARIZE** Write one or more paragraphs explaining how lifestyle can lead to a healthy body and a longer life. Include these terms in your description.

nutrition	alcohol
exercise	infectious disease
germs	noninfectious disease
tobacco	

UNIT PROJECTS

Evaluate all the data, results, and information from your project folder. Prepare to present your project.

Average Weight for Females

SOURCE: *U.S. Center for Disease Control and Prevention*

Analyzing Data

The table below presents information about causes of death in the United States.

Leading Causes of Death in the United States

2000		1900	
Cause of Death	Percent of Deaths	Cause of Death	Percent of Deaths
heart disease	31%	pneumonia*	12%
cancer	23%	tuberculosis*	11%
stroke	9%	diarrhea*	11%
lung disease	5%	heart disease	6%
accident	4%	liver disease	5%
pneumonia*	4%	accident	4%
diabetes	3%	cancer	4%
kidney disease	1%	senility	2%
liver disease	1%	diphtheria*	2%

* infectious disease

Use the table to answer the questions below.

1. What was the leading cause of death in 1900?
   a. heart disease
   b. cancer
   c. pneumonia
   d. tuberculosis

2. Which infectious disease was a leading cause of death both in 1900 and 2000?
   a. tuberculosis
   b. diphtheria
   c. stroke
   d. pneumonia

3. Which was the leading noninfectious cause of death in both 1900 and 2000?
   a. pneumonia
   b. cancer
   c. heart disease
   d. accidents

4. Which cause of death showed the greatest increase between 1900 and 2000?
   a. heart disease
   b. cancer
   c. liver disease
   d. pneumonia

5. Which statement is true?
   a. The rate of infectious disease as a leading cause of death increased from 1900 to 2000.
   b. The rate of infectious disease as a leading cause of death decreased from 1900 to 2000.
   c. The rate of noninfectious disease as a leading cause of death decreased from 1900 to 2000.
   d. The rate of noninfectious disease as a leading cause of death remained the same.

6. How much did the rate of heart disease increase from 1900 to 2000?
   a. 37%
   b. 31%
   c. 25%
   d. 6%

Extended Response

7. Write a paragraph explaining the change in the number of deaths due to infectious diseases from 1900 to 2000. Use the information in the data and what you know about infectious disease in your description. Use the vocabulary words in the box in your answer.

bacterium	virus	pathogen
antibiotic	resistance	microorganism

8. The spread of infectious disease can be controlled in many different ways. Write a paragraph describing how the spread of infectious disease may be limited. Give at least two examples and describe how these diseases can be prevented or contained.

Student Resource Handbooks

Scientific Thinking Handbook

Making Observations

An **observation** is an act of noting and recording an event, characteristic, behavior, or anything else detected with an instrument or with the senses.

Observations allow you to make informed hypotheses and to gather data for experiments. Careful observations often lead to ideas for new experiments. There are two categories of observations:

- **Quantitative observations** can be expressed in numbers and include records of time, temperature, mass, distance, and volume.

- **Qualitative observations** include descriptions of sights, sounds, smells, and textures.

EXAMPLE

A student dissolved 30 grams of Epsom salts in water, poured the solution into a dish, and let the dish sit out uncovered overnight. The next day, she made the following observations of the Epsom salt crystals that grew in the dish.

Table 1. Observations of Epsom Salt Crystals

Quantitative Observations	Qualitative Observations
• mass = 30 g • mean crystal length = 0.5 cm • longest crystal length = 2 cm	• Crystals are clear. • Crystals are long, thin, and rectangular. • White crust has formed around edge of dish.

> To determine the mass, the student found the mass of the dish before and after growing the crystals and then used subtraction to find the difference.

> The student measured several crystals and calculated the mean length. (To learn how to calculate the mean of a data set, see page R36.)

> Photographs or sketches are useful for recording qualitative observations.

Epsom salt crystals

MORE ABOUT OBSERVING

- Make quantitative observations whenever possible. That way, others will know exactly what you observed and be able to compare their results with yours.

- It is always a good idea to make qualitative observations too. You never know when you might observe something unexpected.

Predicting and Hypothesizing

A **prediction** is an expectation of what will be observed or what will happen. A **hypothesis** is a tentative explanation for an observation or scientific problem that can be tested by further investigation.

EXAMPLE

Suppose you have made two paper airplanes and you wonder why one of them tends to glide farther than the other one.

1. Start by asking a question.

2. Make an educated guess. After examination, you notice that the wings of the airplane that flies farther are slightly larger than the wings of the other airplane.

3. Write a prediction based upon your educated guess, in the form of an "If . . . , then . . ." statement. Write the independent variable after the word *if*, and the dependent variable after the word *then*.

4. To make a hypothesis, explain why you think what you predicted will occur. Write the explanation after the word *because*.

1. Why does one of the paper airplanes glide farther than the other?

2. The size of an airplane's wings may affect how far the airplane will glide.

3. Prediction: If I make a paper airplane with larger wings, then the airplane will glide farther.

> To read about independent and dependent variables, see page R30.

4. Hypothesis: If I make a paper airplane with larger wings, then the airplane will glide farther, because the additional surface area of the wing will produce more lift.

> Notice that the part of the hypothesis after *because* adds an explanation of why the airplane will glide farther.

MORE ABOUT HYPOTHESES

- The results of an experiment cannot prove that a hypothesis is correct. Rather, the results either support or do not support the hypothesis.

- Valuable information is gained even when your hypothesis is not supported by your results. For example, it would be an important discovery to find that wing size is not related to how far an airplane glides.

- In science, a hypothesis is supported only after many scientists have conducted many experiments and produced consistent results.

Inferring

An **inference** is a logical conclusion drawn from the available evidence and prior knowledge. Inferences are often made from observations.

EXAMPLE

A student observing a set of acorns noticed something unexpected about one of them. He noticed a white, soft-bodied insect eating its way out of the acorn.

The student recorded these observations.

Observations

- There is a hole in the acorn, about 0.5 cm in diameter, where the insect crawled out.
- There is a second hole, which is about the size of a pinhole, on the other side of the acorn.
- The inside of the acorn is hollow.

Here are some inferences that can be made on the basis of the observations.

Inferences

- The insect formed from the material inside the acorn, grew to its present size, and ate its way out of the acorn.
- The insect crawled through the smaller hole, ate the inside of the acorn, grew to its present size, and ate its way out of the acorn.
- An egg was laid in the acorn through the smaller hole. The egg hatched into a larva that ate the inside of the acorn, grew to its present size, and ate its way out of the acorn.

When you make inferences, be sure to look at all of the evidence available and combine it with what you already know.

MORE ABOUT INFERENCES

Inferences depend both on observations and on the knowledge of the people making the inferences. Ancient people who did not know that organisms are produced only by similar organisms might have made an inference like the first one. A student today might look at the same observations and make the second inference. A third student might have knowledge about this particular insect and know that it is never small enough to fit through the smaller hole, leading her to the third inference.

Identifying Cause and Effect

In a **cause-and-effect relationship,** one event or characteristic is the result of another. Usually an effect follows its cause in time.

There are many examples of cause-and-effect relationships in everyday life.

Cause	Effect
Turn off a light.	Room gets dark.
Drop a glass.	Glass breaks.
Blow a whistle.	Sound is heard.

Scientists must be careful not to infer a cause-and-effect relationship just because one event happens after another event. When one event occurs after another, you cannot infer a cause-and-effect relationship on the basis of that information alone. You also cannot conclude that one event caused another if there are alternative ways to explain the second event. A scientist must demonstrate through experimentation or continued observation that an event was truly caused by another event.

EXAMPLE

Make an Observation

Suppose you have a few plants growing outside. When the weather starts getting colder, you bring one of the plants indoors. You notice that the plant you brought indoors is growing faster than the others are growing. You cannot conclude from your observation that the change in temperature was the cause of the increased plant growth, because there are alternative explanations for the observation. Some possible explanations are given below.

- The humidity indoors caused the plant to grow faster.

- The level of sunlight indoors caused the plant to grow faster.

- The indoor plant's being noticed more often and watered more often than the outdoor plants caused it to grow faster.

- The plant that was brought indoors was healthier than the other plants to begin with.

To determine which of these factors, if any, caused the indoor plant to grow faster than the outdoor plants, you would need to design and conduct an experiment.

See pages R28–R35 for information about designing experiments.

Recognizing Bias

Television, newspapers, and the Internet are full of experts claiming to have scientific evidence to back up their claims. How do you know whether the claims are really backed up by good science?

Bias is a slanted point of view, or personal prejudice. The goal of scientists is to be as objective as possible and to base their findings on facts instead of opinions. However, bias often affects the conclusions of researchers, and it is important to learn to recognize bias.

When scientific results are reported, you should consider the source of the information as well as the information itself. It is important to critically analyze the information that you see and read.

SOURCES OF BIAS

There are several ways in which a report of scientific information may be biased. Here are some questions that you can ask yourself:

1. Who is sponsoring the research?

   Sometimes, the results of an investigation are biased because an organization paying for the research is looking for a specific answer. This type of bias can affect how data are gathered and interpreted.

2. Is the research sample large enough?

   Sometimes research does not include enough data. The larger the sample size, the more likely that the results are accurate, assuming a truly random sample.

3. In a survey, who is answering the questions?

   The results of a survey or poll can be biased. The people taking part in the survey may have been specifically chosen because of how they would answer. They may have the same ideas or lifestyles. A survey or poll should make use of a random sample of people.

4. Are the people who take part in a survey biased?

   People who take part in surveys sometimes try to answer the questions the way they think the researcher wants them to answer. Also, in surveys or polls that ask for personal information, people may be unwilling to answer questions truthfully.

SCIENTIFIC BIAS

It is also important to realize that scientists have their own biases because of the types of research they do and because of their scientific viewpoints. Two scientists may look at the same set of data and come to completely different conclusions because of these biases. However, such disagreements are not necessarily bad. In fact, a critical analysis of disagreements is often responsible for moving science forward.

Identifying Faulty Reasoning

Faulty reasoning is wrong or incorrect thinking. It leads to mistakes and to wrong conclusions. Scientists are careful not to draw unreasonable conclusions from experimental data. Without such caution, the results of scientific investigations may be misleading.

EXAMPLE

Scientists try to make generalizations based on their data to explain as much about nature as possible. If only a small sample of data is looked at, however, a conclusion may be faulty. Suppose a scientist has studied the effects of the El Niño and La Niña weather patterns on flood damage in California from 1989 to 1995. The scientist organized the data in the bar graph below.

The scientist drew the following conclusions:

1. The La Niña weather pattern has no effect on flooding in California.

2. When neither weather pattern occurs, there is almost no flood damage.

3. A weak or moderate El Niño produces a small or moderate amount of flooding.

4. A strong El Niño produces a lot of flooding.

Flood and Storm Damage in California

Estimated damage (millions of dollars)

2000, 1500, 1000, 500, 0

1989   1992   1995

Starting year of season
(July 1–June 30)

■ Weak–moderate El Niño
■ Strong El Niño

SOURCE: *Governor's Office of Emergency Services, California*

For the six-year period of the scientist's investigation, these conclusions may seem to be reasonable. However, a six-year study of weather patterns may be too small of a sample for the conclusions to be supported. Consider the following graph, which shows information that was gathered from 1949 to 1997.

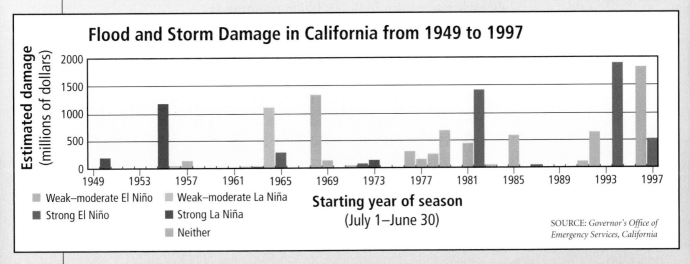

Flood and Storm Damage in California from 1949 to 1997

Estimated damage (millions of dollars)

2000, 1500, 1000, 500, 0

1949   1953   1957   1961   1965   1969   1973   1977   1981   1985   1989   1993   1997

■ Weak–moderate El Niño   ■ Weak–moderate La Niña
■ Strong El Niño   ■ Strong La Niña
■ Neither

Starting year of season
(July 1–June 30)

SOURCE: *Governor's Office of Emergency Services, California*

The only one of the conclusions that all of this information supports is number 3: a weak or moderate El Niño produces a small or moderate amount of flooding. By collecting more data, scientists can be more certain of their conclusions and can avoid faulty reasoning.

Analyzing Statements

To **analyze** a statement is to examine its parts carefully. Scientific findings are often reported through media such as television or the Internet. A report that is made public often focuses on only a small part of research. As a result, it is important to question the sources of information.

Evaluate Media Claims

To **evaluate** a statement is to judge it on the basis of criteria you've established. Sometimes evaluating means deciding whether a statement is true.

Reports of scientific research and findings in the media may be misleading or incomplete. When you are exposed to this information, you should ask yourself some questions so that you can make informed judgments about the information.

1. **Does the information come from a credible source?**

   Suppose you learn about a new product and it is stated that scientific evidence proves that the product works. A report from a respected news source may be more believable than an advertisement paid for by the product's manufacturer.

2. **How much evidence supports the claim?**

   Often, it may seem that there is new evidence every day of something in the world that either causes or cures an illness. However, information that is the result of several years of work by several different scientists is more credible than an advertisement that does not even cite the subjects of the experiment.

3. **How much information is being presented?**

   Science cannot solve all questions, and scientific experiments often have flaws. A report that discusses problems in a scientific study may be more believable than a report that addresses only positive experimental findings.

4. **Is scientific evidence being presented by a specific source?**

   Sometimes scientific findings are reported by people who are called experts or leaders in a scientific field. But if their names are not given or their scientific credentials are not reported, their statements may be less credible than those of recognized experts.

Differentiate Between Fact and Opinion

Sometimes information is presented as a fact when it may be an opinion. When scientific conclusions are reported, it is important to recognize whether they are based on solid evidence. Again, you may find it helpful to ask yourself some questions.

1. **What is the difference between a fact and an opinion?**

   A **fact** is a piece of information that can be strictly defined and proved true. An **opinion** is a statement that expresses a belief, value, or feeling. An opinion cannot be proved true or false. For example, a person's age is a fact, but if someone is asked how old they feel, it is impossible to prove the person's answer to be true or false.

2. **Can opinions be measured?**

   Yes, opinions can be measured. In fact, surveys often ask for people's opinions on a topic. But there is no way to know whether or not an opinion is the truth.

HOW TO DIFFERENTIATE FACT FROM OPINION

Opinions

Notice words or phrases that express beliefs or feelings. The words *unfortunately* and *careless* show that opinions are being expressed.

Opinion

Look for statements that speculate about events. These statements are opinions, because they cannot be proved.

Human Activities and the Environment

Unfortunately, human use of fossil fuels is one of the most significant developments of the past few centuries. Humans rely on fossil fuels, a non-renewable energy resource, for more than 90 percent of their energy needs.

This careless misuse of our planet's resources has resulted in pollution, global warming, and the destruction of fragile ecosystems. For example, oil pipelines carry more than one million barrels of oil each day across tundra regions. Transporting oil across such areas can only result in oil spills that poison the land for decades.

Facts

Statements that contain statistics tend to be facts. Writers often use facts to support their opinions.

Lab Handbook

Safety Rules

Before you work in the laboratory, read these safety rules twice. Ask your teacher to explain any rules that you do not completely understand. Refer to these rules later on if you have questions about safety in the science classroom.

Directions

- Read all directions and make sure that you understand them before starting an investigation or lab activity. If you do not understand how to do a procedure or how to use a piece of equipment, ask your teacher.
- Do not begin any investigation or touch any equipment until your teacher has told you to start.
- Never experiment on your own. If you want to try a procedure that the directions do not call for, ask your teacher for permission first.
- If you are hurt or injured in any way, tell your teacher immediately.

Dress Code

goggles

apron

gloves

- Wear goggles when
  — using glassware, sharp objects, or chemicals
  — heating an object
  — working with anything that can easily fly up into the air and hurt someone's eye
- Tie back long hair or hair that hangs in front of your eyes.
- Remove any article of clothing—such as a loose sweater or a scarf—that hangs down and may touch a flame, chemical, or piece of equipment.
- Observe all safety icons calling for the wearing of eye protection, gloves, and aprons.

Heating and Fire Safety

fire safety

heating safety

- Keep your work area neat, clean, and free of extra materials.
- Never reach over a flame or heat source.
- Point objects being heated away from you and others.
- Never heat a substance or an object in a closed container.
- Never touch an object that has been heated. If you are unsure whether something is hot, treat it as though it is. Use oven mitts, clamps, tongs, or a test-tube holder.
- Know where the fire extinguisher and fire blanket are kept in your classroom.
- Do not throw hot substances into the trash. Wait for them to cool or use the container your teacher puts out for disposal.

LAB HANDBOOK

Electrical Safety

electrical
safety

- Never use lamps or other electrical equipment with frayed cords.
- Make sure no cord is lying on the floor where someone can trip over it.
- Do not let a cord hang over the side of a counter or table so that the equipment can easily be pulled or knocked to the floor.
- Never let cords hang into sinks or other places where water can be found.
- Never try to fix electrical problems. Inform your teacher of any problems immediately.
- Unplug an electrical cord by pulling on the plug, not the cord.

Chemical Safety

chemical
safety

poison

fumes

- If you spill a chemical or get one on your skin or in your eyes, tell your teacher right away.
- Never touch, taste, or sniff any chemicals in the lab. If you need to determine odor, waft. Wafting consists of holding the chemical in its container 15 centimeters (6 in.) away from your nose, and using your fingers to bring fumes from the container to your nose.
- Keep lids on all chemicals you are not using.
- Never put unused chemicals back into the original containers. Throw away extra chemicals where your teacher tells you to.
- Pour chemicals over a sink or your work area, not over the floor.
- If you get a chemical in your eye, use the eyewash right away.
- Always wash your hands after handling chemicals, plants, or soil.

Wafting

Glassware and Sharp-Object Safety

sharp
objects

- If you break glassware, tell your teacher right away.
- Do not use broken or chipped glassware. Give these to your teacher.
- Use knives and other cutting instruments carefully. Always wear eye protection and cut away from you.

Animal Safety

- Never hurt an animal.
- Touch animals only when necessary. Follow your teacher's instructions for handling animals.
- Always wash your hands after working with animals.

Cleanup

disposal

- Follow your teacher's instructions for throwing away or putting away supplies.
- Clean your work area and pick up anything that has dropped to the floor.
- Wash your hands.

Using Lab Equipment

Different experiments require different types of equipment. But even though experiments differ, the ways in which the equipment is used are the same.

Beakers

- Use beakers for holding and pouring liquids.
- Do not use a beaker to measure the volume of a liquid. Use a graduated cylinder instead. (See page R16.)
- Use a beaker that holds about twice as much liquid as you need. For example, if you need 100 milliliters of water, you should use a 200- or 250-milliliter beaker.

Test Tubes

- Use test tubes to hold small amounts of substances.
- Do not use a test tube to measure the volume of a liquid.
- Use a test tube when heating a substance over a flame. Aim the mouth of the tube away from yourself and other people.
- Liquids easily spill or splash from test tubes, so it is important to use only small amounts of liquids.

Test-Tube Holder

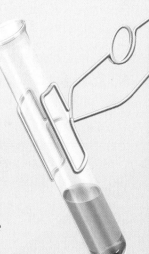

- Use a test-tube holder when heating a substance in a test tube.
- Use a test-tube holder if the substance in a test tube is dangerous to touch.
- Make sure the test-tube holder tightly grips the test tube so that the test tube will not slide out of the holder.
- Make sure that the test-tube holder is above the surface of the substance in the test tube so that you can observe the substance.

Test-Tube Rack

- Use a test-tube rack to organize test tubes before, during, and after an experiment.

- Use a test-tube rack to keep test tubes upright so that they do not fall over and spill their contents.

- Use a test-tube rack that is the correct size for the test tubes that you are using. If the rack is too small, a test tube may become stuck. If the rack is too large, a test tube may lean over, and some of its contents may spill or splash.

Forceps

- Use forceps when you need to pick up or hold a very small object that should not be touched with your hands.

- Do not use forceps to hold anything over a flame, because forceps are not long enough to keep your hand safely away from the flame. Plastic forceps will melt, and metal forceps will conduct heat and burn your hand.

Hot Plate

- Use a hot plate when a substance needs to be kept warmer than room temperature for a long period of time.

- Use a hot plate instead of a Bunsen burner or a candle when you need to carefully control temperature.

- Do not use a hot plate when a substance needs to be burned in an experiment.

- Always use "hot hands" safety mitts or oven mitts when handling anything that has been heated on a hot plate.

Microscope

Scientists use microscopes to see very small objects that cannot easily be seen with the eye alone. A microscope magnifies the image of an object so that small details may be observed. A microscope that you may use can magnify an object 400 times—the object will appear 400 times larger than its actual size.

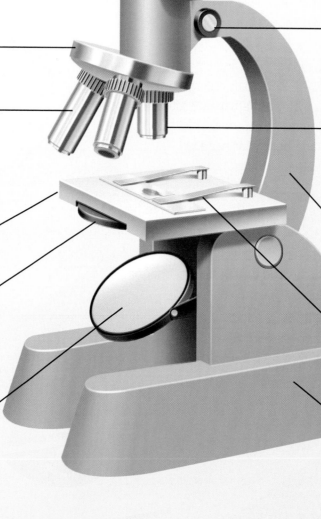

Body The body separates the lens in the eyepiece from the objective lenses below.

Nosepiece The nosepiece holds the objective lenses above the stage and rotates so that all lenses may be used.

High-Power Objective Lens This is the largest lens on the nosepiece. It magnifies an image approximately 40 times.

Stage The stage supports the object being viewed.

Diaphragm The diaphragm is used to adjust the amount of light passing through the slide and into an objective lens.

Mirror or Light Source Some microscopes use light that is reflected through the stage by a mirror. Other microscopes have their own light sources.

Eyepiece Objects are viewed through the eyepiece. The eyepiece contains a lens that commonly magnifies an image 10 times.

Coarse Adjustment This knob is used to focus the image of an object when it is viewed through the low-power lens.

Fine Adjustment This knob is used to focus the image of an object when it is viewed through the high-power lens.

Low-Power Objective Lens This is the smallest lens on the nosepiece. It magnifies an image approximately 10 times.

Arm The arm supports the body above the stage. Always carry a microscope by the arm and base.

Stage Clip The stage clip holds a slide in place on the stage.

Base The base supports the microscope.

VIEWING AN OBJECT

1. Use the coarse adjustment knob to raise the body tube.

2. Adjust the diaphragm so that you can see a bright circle of light through the eyepiece.

3. Place the object or slide on the stage. Be sure that it is centered over the hole in the stage.

4. Turn the nosepiece to click the low-power lens into place.

5. Using the coarse adjustment knob, slowly lower the lens and focus on the specimen being viewed. Be sure not to touch the slide or object with the lens.

6. When switching from the low-power lens to the high-power lens, first raise the body tube with the coarse adjustment knob so that the high-power lens will not hit the slide.

7. Turn the nosepiece to click the high-power lens into place.

8. Use the fine adjustment knob to focus on the specimen being viewed. Again, be sure not to touch the slide or object with the lens.

MAKING A SLIDE, OR WET MOUNT

1 Place the specimen in the center of a clean slide.

2 Place a drop of water on the specimen.

3 Place a cover slip on the slide. Put one edge of the cover slip into the drop of water and slowly lower it over the specimen.

4 Remove any air bubbles from under the cover slip by gently tapping the cover slip.

5 Dry any excess water before placing the slide on the microscope stage for viewing.

Spring Scale (Force Meter)

- Use a spring scale to measure a force pulling on the scale.
- Use a spring scale to measure the force of gravity exerted on an object by Earth.
- To measure a force accurately, a spring scale must be zeroed before it is used. The scale is zeroed when no weight is attached and the indicator is positioned at zero.
- Do not attach a weight that is either too heavy or too light to a spring scale. A weight that is too heavy could break the scale or exert too great a force for the scale to measure. A weight that is too light may not exert enough force to be measured accurately.

Graduated Cylinder

- Use a graduated cylinder to measure the volume of a liquid.
- Be sure that the graduated cylinder is on a flat surface so that your measurement will be accurate.
- When reading the scale on a graduated cylinder, be sure to have your eyes at the level of the surface of the liquid.
- The surface of the liquid will be curved in the graduated cylinder. Read the volume of the liquid at the bottom of the curve, or meniscus (muh-NIHS-kuhs).
- You can use a graduated cylinder to find the volume of a solid object by measuring the increase in a liquid's level after you add the object to the cylinder.

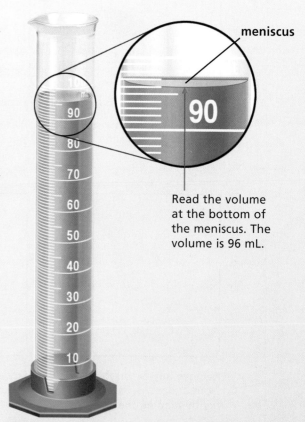

meniscus

Read the volume at the bottom of the meniscus. The volume is 96 mL.

Metric Rulers

- Use metric rulers or meter sticks to measure objects' lengths.

- Do not measure an object from the end of a metric ruler or meter stick, because the end is often imperfect. Instead, measure from the 1-centimeter mark, but remember to subtract a centimeter from the apparent measurement.

- Estimate any lengths that extend between marked units. For example, if a meter stick shows centimeters but not millimeters, you can estimate the length that an object extends between centimeter marks to measure it to the nearest millimeter.

- **Controlling Variables** If you are taking repeated measurements, always measure from the same point each time. For example, if you're measuring how high two different balls bounce when dropped from the same height, measure both bounces at the same point on the balls—either the top or the bottom. Do not measure at the top of one ball and the bottom of the other.

EXAMPLE

How to Measure a Leaf

1. Lay a ruler flat on top of the leaf so that the 1-centimeter mark lines up with one end. Make sure the ruler and the leaf do not move between the time you line them up and the time you take the measurement.

2. Look straight down on the ruler so that you can see exactly how the marks line up with the other end of the leaf.

3. Estimate the length by which the leaf extends beyond a marking. For example, the leaf below extends about halfway between the 4.2-centimeter and 4.3-centimeter marks, so the apparent measurement is about 4.25 centimeters.

4. Remember to subtract 1 centimeter from your apparent measurement, since you started at the 1-centimeter mark on the ruler and not at the end. The leaf is about 3.25 centimeters long (4.25 cm – 1 cm = 3.25 cm).

Triple-Beam Balance

This balance has a pan and three beams with sliding masses, called riders. At one end of the beams is a pointer that indicates whether the mass on the pan is equal to the masses shown on the beams.

1.   Make sure the balance is zeroed before measuring the mass of an object. The balance is zeroed if the pointer is at zero when nothing is on the pan and the riders are at their zero points. Use the adjustment knob at the base of the balance to zero it.

2.   Place the object to be measured on the pan.

3.   Move the riders one notch at a time away from the pan. Begin with the largest rider. If moving the largest rider one notch brings the pointer below zero, begin measuring the mass of the object with the next smaller rider.

4.   Change the positions of the riders until they balance the mass on the pan and the pointer is at zero. Then add the readings from the three beams to determine the mass of the object.

300 g	position of largest rider
90 g	position of middle rider
+ 3 g	position of smallest rider
393 g	mass of beaker

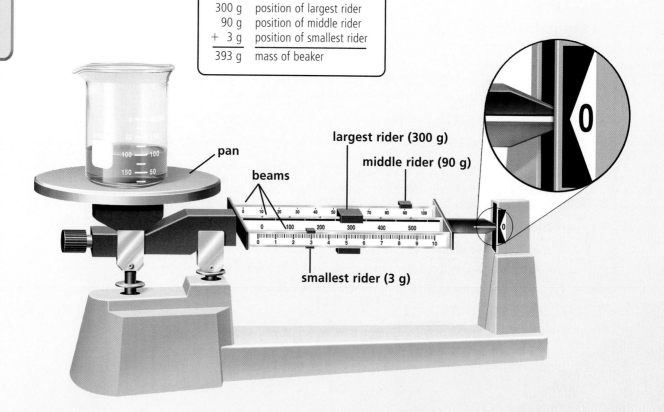

pan

beams

largest rider (300 g)

middle rider (90 g)

smallest rider (3 g)

Double-Pan Balance

This type of balance has two pans. Between the pans is a pointer that indicates whether the masses on the pans are equal.

1. Make sure the balance is zeroed before measuring the mass of an object. The balance is zeroed if the pointer is at zero when there is nothing on either of the pans. Many double-pan balances have sliding knobs that can be used to zero them.

2. Place the object to be measured on one of the pans.

3. Begin adding standard masses to the other pan. Begin with the largest standard mass. If this adds too much mass to the balance, begin measuring the mass of the object with the next smaller standard mass.

4. Add standard masses until the masses on both pans are balanced and the pointer is at zero. Then add the standard masses together to determine the mass of the object being measured.

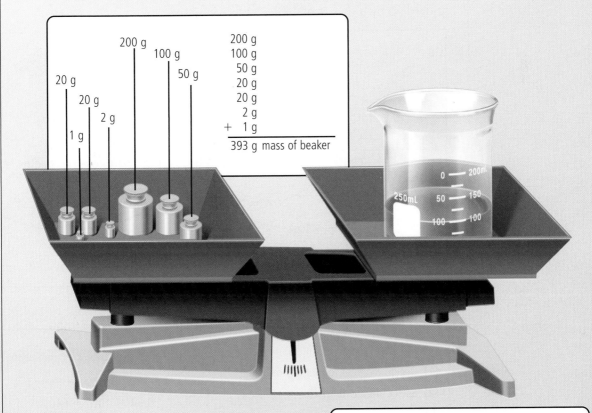

20 g	200 g
20 g	100 g
	50 g
200 g	20 g
100 g	20 g
50 g	2 g
2 g	+ 1 g
1 g	393 g mass of beaker

Never place chemicals or liquids directly on a pan. Instead, use the following procedure:

1. Determine the mass of an empty container, such as a beaker.

2. Pour the substance into the container, and measure the total mass of the substance and the container.

3. Subtract the mass of the empty container from the total mass to find the mass of the substance.

The Metric System and SI Units

Scientists use International System (SI) units for measurements of distance, volume, mass, and temperature. The International System is based on multiples of ten and the metric system of measurement.

Basic SI Units		
Property	**Name**	**Symbol**
length	meter	m
volume	liter	L
mass	kilogram	kg
temperature	kelvin	K

SI Prefixes		
Prefix	**Symbol**	**Multiple of 10**
kilo-	k	1000
hecto-	h	100
deca-	da	10
deci-	d	$0.1 \left(\frac{1}{10}\right)$
centi-	c	$0.01 \left(\frac{1}{100}\right)$
milli-	m	$0.001 \left(\frac{1}{1000}\right)$

Changing Metric Units

You can change from one unit to another in the metric system by multiplying or dividing by a power of 10.

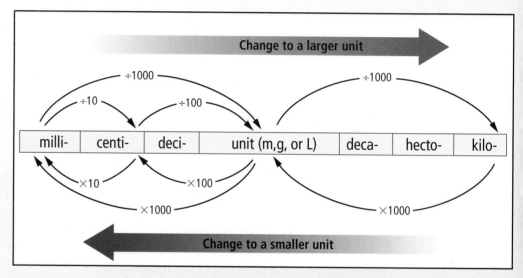

Example

Change 0.64 liters to milliliters.

(1) Decide whether to multiply or divide.

(2) Select the power of 10.

ANSWER 0.64 L = 640 mL

Change to a smaller unit by multiplying.

mL ◄——— × 1000 ——— L

0.64 × 1000 = **640.**

Example

Change 23.6 grams to kilograms.

(1) Decide whether to multiply or divide.

(2) Select the power of 10.

ANSWER 23.6 g = 0.0236 kg

Change to a larger unit by dividing.

g ——— ÷ 1000 ——► kg

23.6 ÷ 1000 = **0.0236**

Temperature Conversions

Even though the kelvin is the SI base unit of temperature, the degree Celsius will be the unit you use most often in your science studies. The formulas below show the relationships between temperatures in degrees Fahrenheit (°F), degrees Celsius (°C), and kelvins (K).

$$°C = \frac{5}{9}(°F - 32)$$

$$°F = \frac{9}{5}°C + 32$$

$$K = °C + 273$$

See page R42 for help with using formulas.

Examples of Temperature Conversions		
Condition	Degrees Celsius	Degrees Fahrenheit
Freezing point of water	0	32
Cool day	10	50
Mild day	20	68
Warm day	30	86
Normal body temperature	37	98.6
Very hot day	40	104
Boiling point of water	100	212

Converting Between SI and U.S. Customary Units

Use the chart below when you need to convert between SI units and U.S. customary units.

SI Unit	From SI to U.S. Customary			From U.S. Customary to SI		
Length	When you know	multiply by	to find	When you know	multiply by	to find
kilometer (km) = 1000 m	kilometers	0.62	miles	miles	1.61	kilometers
meter (m) = 100 cm	meters	3.28	feet	feet	0.3048	meters
centimeter (cm) = 10 mm	centimeters	0.39	inches	inches	2.54	centimeters
millimeter (mm) = 0.1 cm	millimeters	0.04	inches	inches	25.4	millimeters
Area	When you know	multiply by	to find	When you know	multiply by	to find
square kilometer (km^2)	square kilometers	0.39	square miles	square miles	2.59	square kilometers
square meter (m^2)	square meters	1.2	square yards	square yards	0.84	square meters
square centimeter (cm^2)	square centimeters	0.155	square inches	square inches	6.45	square centimeters
Volume	When you know	multiply by	to find	When you know	multiply by	to find
liter (L) = 1000 mL	liters	1.06	quarts	quarts	0.95	liters
	liters	0.26	gallons	gallons	3.79	liters
	liters	4.23	cups	cups	0.24	liters
	liters	2.12	pints	pints	0.47	liters
milliliter (mL) = 0.001 L	milliliters	0.20	teaspoons	teaspoons	4.93	milliliters
	milliliters	0.07	tablespoons	tablespoons	14.79	milliliters
	milliliters	0.03	fluid ounces	fluid ounces	29.57	milliliters
Mass	When you know	multiply by	to find	When you know	multiply by	to find
kilogram (kg) = 1000 g	kilograms	2.2	pounds	pounds	0.45	kilograms
gram (g) = 1000 mg	grams	0.035	ounces	ounces	28.35	grams

Precision and Accuracy

When you do an experiment, it is important that your methods, observations, and data be both precise and accurate.

low precision

precision, but not accuracy

precision and accuracy

Precision

In science, **precision** is the exactness and consistency of measurements. For example, measurements made with a ruler that has both centimeter and millimeter markings would be more precise than measurements made with a ruler that has only centimeter markings. Another indicator of precision is the care taken to make sure that methods and observations are as exact and consistent as possible. Every time a particular experiment is done, the same procedure should be used. Precision is necessary because experiments are repeated several times and if the procedure changes, the results will change.

EXAMPLE

Suppose you are measuring temperatures over a two-week period. Your precision will be greater if you measure each temperature at the same place, at the same time of day, and with the same thermometer than if you change any of these factors from one day to the next.

Accuracy

In science, it is possible to be precise but not accurate. **Accuracy** depends on the difference between a measurement and an actual value. The smaller the difference, the more accurate the measurement.

EXAMPLE

Suppose you look at a stream and estimate that it is about 1 meter wide at a particular place. You decide to check your estimate by measuring the stream with a meter stick, and you determine that the stream is 1.32 meters wide. However, because it is hard to measure the width of a stream with a meter stick, it turns out that you didn't do a very good job. The stream is actually 1.14 meters wide. Therefore, even though your estimate was less precise than your measurement, your estimate was actually more accurate.

Making Data Tables and Graphs

Data tables and graphs are useful tools for both recording and communicating scientific data.

Making Data Tables

You can use a **data table** to organize and record the measurements that you make. Some examples of information that might be recorded in data tables are frequencies, times, and amounts.

EXAMPLE

Suppose you are investigating photosynthesis in two elodea plants. One sits in direct sunlight, and the other sits in a dimly lit room. You measure the rate of photosynthesis by counting the number of bubbles in the jar every ten minutes.

1. Title and number your data table.

2. Decide how you will organize the table into columns and rows.

3. Any units, such as seconds or degrees, should be included in column headings, not in the individual cells.

Table 1. Number of Bubbles from Elodea

Time (min)	Sunlight	Dim Light
0	0	0
10	15	5
20	25	8
30	32	7
40	41	10
50	47	9
60	42	9

> Always number and title data tables.

The data in the table above could also be organized in a different way.

Table 1. Number of Bubbles from Elodea

Light Condition	Time (min)						
	0	10	20	30	40	50	60
Sunlight	0	15	25	32	41	47	42
Dim light	0	5	8	7	10	9	9

> Put units in column heading.

Making Line Graphs

You can use a **line graph** to show a relationship between variables. Line graphs are particularly useful for showing changes in variables over time.

EXAMPLE

Suppose you are interested in graphing temperature data that you collected over the course of a day.

Table 1. Outside Temperature During the Day on March 7

	Time of Day						
	7:00 A.M.	9:00 A.M.	11:00 A.M.	1:00 P.M.	3:00 P.M.	5:00 P.M.	7:00 P.M.
Temp (°C)	8	9	11	14	12	10	6

1. Use the vertical axis of your line graph for the variable that you are measuring—temperature.

2. Choose scales for both the horizontal axis and the vertical axis of the graph. You should have two points more than you need on the vertical axis, and the horizontal axis should be long enough for all of the data points to fit.

3. Draw and label each axis.

4. Graph each value. First find the appropriate point on the scale of the horizontal axis. Imagine a line that rises vertically from that place on the scale. Then find the corresponding value on the vertical axis, and imagine a line that moves horizontally from that value. The point where these two imaginary lines intersect is where the value should be plotted.

5. Connect the points with straight lines.

Be sure to add a number and a title to your graph.

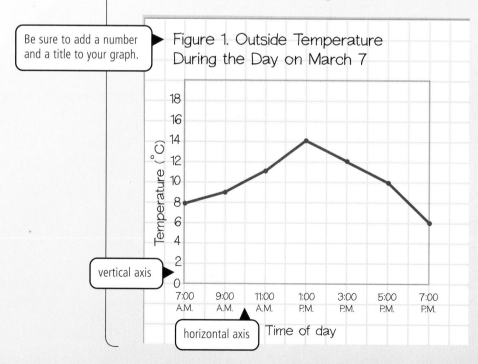

Figure 1. Outside Temperature During the Day on March 7

vertical axis

horizontal axis

Time of day

Making Circle Graphs

You can use a **circle graph,** sometimes called a pie chart, to represent data as parts of a circle. Circle graphs are used only when the data can be expressed as percentages of a whole. The entire circle shown in a circle graph is equal to 100 percent of the data.

EXAMPLE

Suppose you identified the species of each mature tree growing in a small wooded area. You organized your data in a table, but you also want to show the data in a circle graph.

1. To begin, find the total number of mature trees.

   $$56 + 34 + 22 + 10 + 28 = 150$$

2. To find the degree measure for each sector of the circle, write a fraction comparing the number of each tree species with the total number of trees. Then multiply the fraction by 360°.

   Oak: $\frac{56}{150} \times 360° = 134.4°$

3. Draw a circle. Use a protractor to draw the angle for each sector of the graph.

4. Color and label each sector of the graph.

5. Give the graph a number and title.

Table 1. Tree Species in Wooded Area

Species	Number of Specimens
Oak	56
Maple	34
Birch	22
Willow	10
Pine	28

Figure 1. Tree Species in Wooded Area

Willow 10
Birch 22
Pine 28
Oak 56
Maple 34

Instead of labeling each sector, you could make a color key.

Oak 56
Maple 34
Pine 28
Birch 22
Willow 10

Bar Graph

A **bar graph** is a type of graph in which the lengths of the bars are used to represent and compare data. A numerical scale is used to determine the lengths of the bars.

EXAMPLE

To determine the effect of water on seed sprouting, three cups were filled with sand, and ten seeds were planted in each. Different amounts of water were added to each cup over a three-day period.

Table 1. Effect of Water on Seed Sprouting

Daily Amount of Water (mL)	Number of Seeds That Sprouted After 3 Days in Sand
0	1
10	4
20	8

1. Choose a numerical scale. The greatest value is 8, so the end of the scale should have a value greater than 8, such as 10. Use equal increments along the scale, such as increments of 2.

2. Draw and label the axes. Mark intervals on the vertical axis according to the scale you chose.

3. Draw a bar for each data value. Use the scale to decide how long to make each bar.

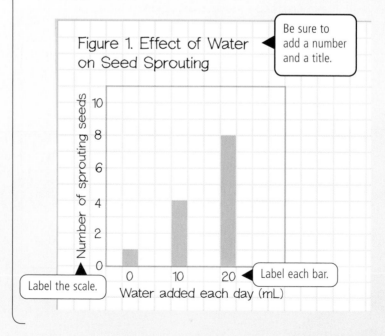

Figure 1. Effect of Water on Seed Sprouting

Be sure to add a number and a title.

Label the scale.

Label each bar.

Double Bar Graph

A **double bar graph** is a bar graph that shows two sets of data. The two bars for each measurement are drawn next to each other.

EXAMPLE

The same seed-sprouting experiment was repeated with potting soil. The data for sand and potting soil can be plotted on one graph.

1. Draw one set of bars, using the data for sand, as shown below.
2. Draw bars for the potting-soil data next to the bars for the sand data. Shade them a different color. Add a key.

Table 2. Effect of Water and Soil on Seed Sprouting

Daily Amount of Water (mL)	Number of Seeds That Sprouted After 3 Days in Sand	Number of Seeds That Sprouted After 3 Days in Potting Soil
0	1	2
10	4	5
20	8	9

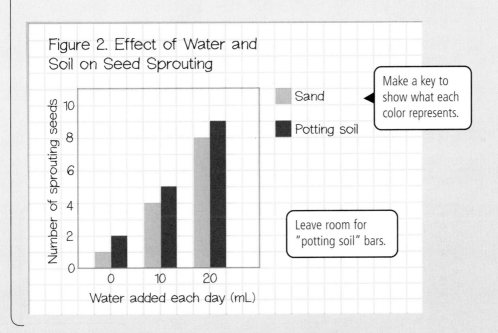

Figure 2. Effect of Water and Soil on Seed Sprouting

Make a key to show what each color represents.

Leave room for "potting soil" bars.

Designing an Experiment

Use this section when designing or conducting an experiment.

Determining a Purpose

You can find a purpose for an experiment by doing research, by examining the results of a previous experiment, or by observing the world around you. An **experiment** is an organized procedure to study something under controlled conditions.

Don't forget to learn as much as possible about your topic before you begin.

1. Write the purpose of your experiment as a question or problem that you want to investigate.

2. Write down research questions and begin searching for information that will help you design an experiment. Consult the library, the Internet, and other people as you conduct your research.

EXAMPLE

Middle school students observed an odor near the lake by their school. They also noticed that the water on the side of the lake near the school was greener than the water on the other side of the lake. The students did some research to learn more about their observations. They discovered that the odor and green color in the lake came from algae. They also discovered that a new fertilizer was being used on a field nearby. The students inferred that the use of the fertilizer might be related to the presence of the algae and designed a controlled experiment to find out whether they were right.

Problem
How does fertilizer affect the presence of algae in a lake?

Research Questions
- Have other experiments been done on this problem? If so, what did those experiments show?
- What kind of fertilizer is used on the field? How much?
- How do algae grow?
- How do people measure algae?
- Can fertilizer and algae be used safely in a lab? How?

Research
As you research, you may find a topic that is more interesting to you than your original topic, or learn that a procedure you wanted to use is not practical or safe. It is OK to change your purpose as you research.

LAB HANDBOOK

Writing a Hypothesis

A **hypothesis** is a tentative explanation for an observation or scientific problem that can be tested by further investigation. You can write your hypothesis in the form of an "If . . . , then . . . , because . . ." statement.

Hypothesis

If the amount of fertilizer in lake water is increased, then the amount of algae will also increase, because fertilizers provide nutrients that algae need to grow.

◀ **Hypotheses**
For help with hypotheses, refer to page R3.

Determining Materials

Make a list of all the materials you will need to do your experiment. Be specific, especially if someone else is helping you obtain the materials. Try to think of everything you will need.

Materials

- 1 large jar or container
- 4 identical smaller containers
- rubber gloves that also cover the arms
- sample of fertilizer-and-water solution
- eyedropper
- clear plastic wrap
- scissors
- masking tape
- marker
- ruler

Determining Variables and Constants

EXPERIMENTAL GROUP AND CONTROL GROUP

An experiment to determine how two factors are related always has two groups—a control group and an experimental group.

1. Design an experimental group. Include as many trials as possible in the experimental group in order to obtain reliable results.

2. Design a control group that is the same as the experimental group in every way possible, except for the factor you wish to test.

> **Experimental Group:** two containers of lake water with one drop of fertilizer solution added to each
>
> **Control Group:** two containers of lake water with no fertilizer solution added

> Go back to your materials list and make sure you have enough items listed to cover both your experimental group and your control group.

VARIABLES AND CONSTANTS

Identify the variables and constants in your experiment. In a controlled experiment, a **variable** is any factor that can change. **Constants** are all of the factors that are the same in both the experimental group and the control group.

1. Read your hypothesis. The **independent variable** is the factor that you wish to test and that is manipulated or changed so that it can be tested. The independent variable is expressed in your hypothesis after the word *if*. Identify the independent variable in your laboratory report.

> **Hypothesis**
> If the amount of fertilizer in lake water is increased, then the amount of algae will also increase, because fertilizers provide nutrients that algae need to grow.

2. The **dependent variable** is the factor that you measure to gather results. It is expressed in your hypothesis after the word *then*. Identify the dependent variable in your laboratory report.

Table 1. Variables and Constants in Algae Experiment

Independent Variable	Dependent Variable	Constants
Amount of fertilizer in lake water	Amount of algae that grow	• Where the lake water is obtained • Type of container used • Light and temperature conditions where water will be stored

> Set up your experiment so that you will test only one variable.

LAB HANDBOOK

MEASURING THE DEPENDENT VARIABLE

Before starting your experiment, you need to define how you will measure the dependent variable. An **operational definition** is a description of the one particular way in which you will measure the dependent variable.

Your operational definition is important for several reasons. First, in any experiment there are several ways in which a dependent variable can be measured. Second, the procedure of the experiment depends on how you decide to measure the dependent variable. Third, your operational definition makes it possible for other people to evaluate and build on your experiment.

EXAMPLE 1

An operational definition of a dependent variable can be qualitative. That is, your measurement of the dependent variable can simply be an observation of whether a change occurs as a result of a change in the independent variable. This type of operational definition can be thought of as a "yes or no" measurement.

Table 2. Qualitative Operational Definition of Algae Growth

Independent Variable	Dependent Variable	Operational Definition
Amount of fertilizer in lake water	Amount of algae that grow	Algae grow in lake water

A qualitative measurement of a dependent variable is often easy to make and record. However, this type of information does not provide a great deal of detail in your experimental results.

EXAMPLE 2

An operational definition of a dependent variable can be quantitative. That is, your measurement of the dependent variable can be a number that shows how much change occurs as a result of a change in the independent variable.

Table 3. Quantitative Operational Definition of Algae Growth

Independent Variable	Dependent Variable	Operational Definition
Amount of fertilizer in lake water	Amount of algae that grow	Diameter of largest algal growth (in mm)

A quantitative measurement of a dependent variable can be more difficult to make and analyze than a qualitative measurement. However, this type of data provides much more information about your experiment and is often more useful.

Writing a Procedure

Write each step of your procedure. Start each step with a verb, or action word, and keep the steps short. Your procedure should be clear enough for someone else to use as instructions for repeating your experiment.

> If necessary, go back to your materials list and add any materials that you left out.

> **Controlling Variables**
> The same amount of fertilizer solution must be added to two of the four containers.

> **Controlling Variables**
> All four containers must receive the same amount of light.

Procedure

1. Put on your gloves. Use the large container to obtain a sample of lake water.

2. Divide the sample of lake water equally among the four smaller containers.

3. Use the eyedropper to add one drop of fertilizer solution to two of the containers.

4. Use the masking tape and the marker to label the containers with your initials, the date, and the identifiers "Jar 1 with Fertilizer," "Jar 2 with Fertilizer," "Jar 1 without Fertilizer," and "Jar 2 without Fertilizer."

5. Cover the containers with clear plastic wrap. Use the scissors to punch ten holes in each of the covers.

6. Place all four containers on a window ledge. Make sure that they all receive the same amount of light.

7. Observe the containers every day for one week.

8. Use the ruler to measure the diameter of the largest clump of algae in each container, and record your measurements daily.

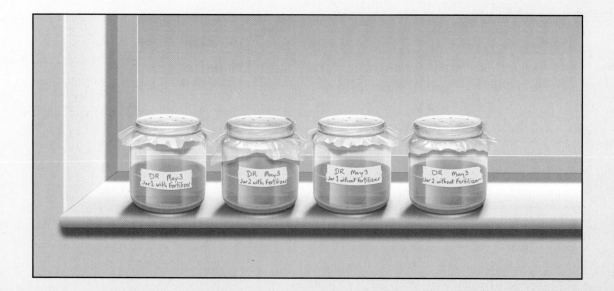

Recording Observations

Once you have obtained all of your materials and your procedure has been approved, you can begin making experimental observations. Gather both quantitative and qualitative data. If something goes wrong during your procedure, make sure you record that too.

Observations
For help with making qualitative and quantitative observations, refer to page R2.

For more examples of data tables, see page R23.

Table 4. Fertilizer and Algae Growth

| Date and Time | Experimental Group | | Control Group | | |
	Jar 1 with Fertilizer (diameter of algae in mm)	Jar 2 with Fertilizer (diameter of algae in mm)	Jar 1 without Fertilizer (diameter of algae in mm)	Jar 2 without Fertilizer (diameter of algae in mm)	Observations
5/3 4:00 P.M.	0	0	0	0	condensation in all containers
5/4 4:00 P.M.	0	3	0	0	tiny green blobs in jar 2 with fertilizer
5/5 4:15 P.M.	4	5	0	3	green blobs in jars 1 and 2 with fertilizer and jar 2 without fertilizer
5/6 4:00 P.M.	5	6	0	4	water light green in jar 2 with fertilizer
5/7 4:00 P.M.	8	10	0	6	water light green in jars 1 and 2 with fertilizer and in jar 2 without fertilizer
5/8 3:30 P.M.	10	18	0	6	cover off jar 2 with fertilizer
5/9 3:30 P.M.	14	23	0	8	drew sketches of each container

Notice that on the sixth day, the observer found that the cover was off one of the containers. It is important to record observations of unintended factors because they might affect the results of the experiment.

Use technology, such as a microscope, to help you make observations when possible.

Drawings of Samples Viewed Under Microscope on 5/9 at 100x

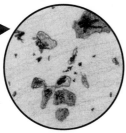

Jar 1 with Fertilizer

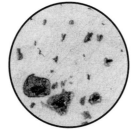

Jar 2 with Fertilizer

Jar 1 without Fertilizer

Jar 2 without Fertilizer

Summarizing Results

To summarize your data, look at all of your observations together. Look for meaningful ways to present your observations. For example, you might average your data or make a graph to look for patterns. When possible, use spreadsheet software to help you analyze and present your data. The two graphs below show the same data.

EXAMPLE 1

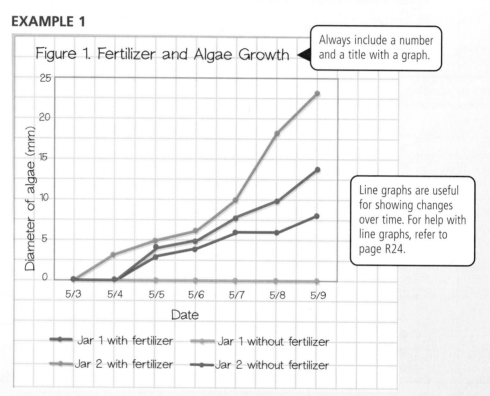

Always include a number and a title with a graph.

Line graphs are useful for showing changes over time. For help with line graphs, refer to page R24.

EXAMPLE 2

Bar graphs are useful for comparing different data sets. This bar graph has four bars for each day. Another way to present the data would be to calculate averages for the tests and the controls, and to show one test bar and one control bar for each day.

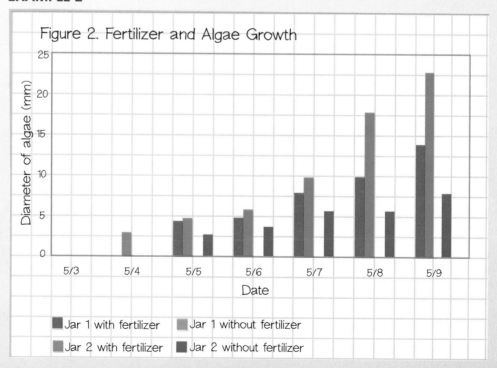

Drawing Conclusions

RESULTS AND INFERENCES

To draw conclusions from your experiment, first write your results. Then compare your results with your hypothesis. Do your results support your hypothesis? Be careful not to make inferences about factors that you did not test.

> For help with making inferences, see page R4.

Results and Inferences

The results of my experiment show that more algae grew in lake water to which fertilizer had been added than in lake water to which no fertilizer had been added. My hypothesis was supported. I infer that it is possible that the growth of algae in the lake was caused by the fertilizer used on the field.

> Notice that you cannot conclude from this experiment that the presence of algae in the lake was due only to the fertilizer.

QUESTIONS FOR FURTHER RESEARCH

Write a list of questions for further research and investigation. Your ideas may lead you to new experiments and discoveries.

Questions for Further Research

- What is the connection between the amount of fertilizer and algae growth?
- How do different brands of fertilizer affect algae growth?
- How would algae growth in the lake be affected if no fertilizer were used on the field?
- How do algae affect the lake and the other life in and around it?
- How does fertilizer affect the lake and the life in and around it?
- If fertilizer is getting into the lake, how is it getting there?

Math Handbook

Describing a Set of Data

Means, medians, modes, and ranges are important math tools for describing data sets such as the following widths of fossilized clamshells.

13 mm   25 mm   14 mm   21 mm   16 mm   23 mm   14 mm

Mean

The **mean** of a data set is the sum of the values divided by the number of values.

> **Example**
>
> To find the mean of the clamshell data, add the values and then divide the sum by the number of values.
>
> $$\frac{13\ mm + 25\ mm + 14\ mm + 21\ mm + 16\ mm + 23\ mm + 14\ mm}{7} = \frac{126\ mm}{7} = 18\ mm$$
>
> **ANSWER** The mean is 18 mm.

Median

The **median** of a data set is the middle value when the values are written in numerical order. If a data set has an even number of values, the median is the mean of the two middle values.

> **Example**
>
> To find the median of the clamshell data, arrange the values in order from least to greatest. The median is the middle value.
>
> 13 mm   14 mm   14 mm   16 mm   21 mm   23 mm   25 mm
>
> **ANSWER** The median is 16 mm.

Mode

The **mode** of a data set is the value that occurs most often.

Example

To find the mode of the clamshell data, arrange the values in order from least to greatest and determine the value that occurs most often.

13 mm 14 mm 14 mm 16 mm 21 mm 23 mm 25 mm

ANSWER The mode is 14 mm.

A data set can have more than one mode or no mode. For example, the following data set has modes of 2 mm and 4 mm:

2 mm 2 mm 3 mm 4 mm 4 mm

The data set below has no mode, because no value occurs more often than any other.

2 mm 3 mm 4 mm 5 mm

Range

The **range** of a data set is the difference between the greatest value and the least value.

Example

To find the range of the clamshell data, arrange the values in order from least to greatest.

13 mm 14 mm 14 mm 16 mm 21 mm 23 mm 25 mm

Subtract the least value from the greatest value.

13 mm is the least value.
25 mm is the greatest value.

25 mm − 13 mm = 12 mm

ANSWER The range is 12 mm.

Using Ratios, Rates, and Proportions

You can use ratios and rates to compare values in data sets. You can use proportions to find unknown values.

Ratios

A **ratio** uses division to compare two values. The ratio of a value a to a nonzero value b can be written as $\frac{a}{b}$.

> ### Example
>
> The height of one plant is 8 centimeters. The height of another plant is 6 centimeters. To find the ratio of the height of the first plant to the height of the second plant, write a fraction and simplify it.
>
> $$\frac{8 \text{ cm}}{6 \text{ cm}} = \frac{4 \times \overset{1}{\cancel{2}}}{3 \times \underset{1}{\cancel{2}}} = \frac{4}{3}$$
>
> **ANSWER** The ratio of the plant heights is $\frac{4}{3}$.

You can also write the ratio $\frac{a}{b}$ as "a to b" or as $a:b$. For example, you can write the ratio of the plant heights as "4 to 3" or as $4:3$.

Rates

A **rate** is a ratio of two values expressed in different units. A unit rate is a rate with a denominator of 1 unit.

> ### Example
>
> A plant grew 6 centimeters in 2 days. The plant's rate of growth was $\frac{6 \text{ cm}}{2 \text{ days}}$. To describe the plant's growth in centimeters per day, write a unit rate.
>
> *Divide numerator and denominator by 2:* $\quad \frac{6 \text{ cm}}{2 \text{ days}} = \frac{6 \text{ cm} \div 2}{2 \text{ days} \div 2}$
>
> You divide 2 days by 2 to get 1 day, so divide 6 cm by 2 also.
>
> *Simplify:* $\quad = \frac{3 \text{ cm}}{1 \text{ day}}$
>
> **ANSWER** The plant's rate of growth is 3 centimeters per day.

Proportions

A **proportion** is an equation stating that two ratios are equivalent. To solve for an unknown value in a proportion, you can use cross products.

Example

If a plant grew 6 centimeters in 2 days, how many centimeters would it grow in 3 days (if its rate of growth is constant)?

Write a proportion:	$\dfrac{6 \text{ cm}}{2 \text{ days}} = \dfrac{x \text{ cm}}{3 \text{ days}}$
Set cross products:	$6 \cdot 3 = 2x$
Multiply 6 and 3:	$18 = 2x$
Divide each side by 2:	$\dfrac{18}{2} = \dfrac{2x}{2}$
Simplify:	$9 = x$

ANSWER The plant would grow 9 centimeters in 3 days.

Using Decimals, Fractions, and Percents

Decimals, fractions, and percentages are all ways of recording and representing data.

Decimals

A **decimal** is a number that is written in the base-ten place value system, in which a decimal point separates the ones and tenths digits. The values of each place is ten times that of the place to its right.

Example

A caterpillar traveled from point *A* to point *C* along the path shown.

A   **36.9 cm**   **B**   **52.4 cm**   C

ADDING DECIMALS To find the total distance traveled by the caterpillar, add the distance from *A* to *B* and the distance from *B* to *C*. Begin by lining up the decimal points. Then add the figures as you would whole numbers and bring down the decimal point.

```
  36.9 cm
+ 52.4 cm
  89.3 cm
```

ANSWER The caterpillar traveled a total distance of 89.3 centimeters.

Example *continued*

SUBTRACTING DECIMALS To find how much farther the caterpillar traveled on the second leg of the journey, subtract the distance from *A* to *B* from the distance from *B* to *C*.

$$
\begin{array}{r}
52.4 \text{ cm} \\
- \ 36.9 \text{ cm} \\
\hline
15.5 \text{ cm}
\end{array}
$$

ANSWER The caterpillar traveled 15.5 centimeters farther on the second leg of the journey.

Example

A caterpillar is traveling from point *D* to point *F* along the path shown. The caterpillar travels at a speed of 9.6 centimeters per minute.

MULTIPLYING DECIMALS You can multiply decimals as you would whole numbers. The number of decimal places in the product is equal to the sum of the number of decimal places in the factors.

For instance, suppose it takes the caterpillar 1.5 minutes to go from *D* to *E*. To find the distance from *D* to *E*, multiply the caterpillar's speed by the time it took.

$$
\begin{array}{rl}
9.6 & \quad 1 \quad \text{decimal place} \\
\times \ 1.5 & \quad + \ 1 \quad \text{decimal place} \\
\hline
480 & \\
96 \quad\ \ & \\
\hline
14.40 & \quad 2 \quad \text{decimal places}
\end{array}
$$

> Align as shown.

ANSWER The distance from *D* to *E* is 14.4 centimeters.

DIVIDING DECIMALS When you divide by a decimal, move the decimal points the same number of places in the divisor and the dividend to make the divisor a whole number.

For instance, to find the time it will take the caterpillar to travel from *E* to *F*, divide the distance from *E* to *F* by the caterpillar's speed.

$$
9.6 \overline{)33.6}
$$

> Move each decimal point one place to the right.

$$
\begin{array}{r}
3.5 \\
96 \overline{)336.} \\
288 \\
\hline
480 \\
480 \\
\hline
0
\end{array}
$$

> Line up decimal points.

ANSWER The caterpillar will travel from *E* to *F* in 3.5 minutes.

Fractions

A **fraction** is a number in the form $\frac{a}{b}$, where b is not equal to 0. A fraction is in **simplest form** if its numerator and denominator have a greatest common factor (GCF) of 1. To simplify a fraction, divide its numerator and denominator by their GCF.

Example

A caterpillar is 40 millimeters long. The head of the caterpillar is 6 millimeters long. To compare the length of the caterpillar's head with the caterpillar's total length, you can write and simplify a fraction that expresses the ratio of the two lengths.

Write the ratio of the two lengths: $\quad \dfrac{\text{Length of head}}{\text{Total length}} = \dfrac{6 \text{ mm}}{40 \text{ mm}}$

Write numerator and denominator as products of numbers and the GCF: $\qquad = \dfrac{3 \times 2}{20 \times 2}$

Divide numerator and denominator by the GCF: $\qquad = \dfrac{3 \times \overset{1}{\cancel{2}}}{20 \times \underset{1}{\cancel{2}}}$

Simplify: $\qquad = \dfrac{3}{20}$

ANSWER In simplest form, the ratio of the lengths is $\frac{3}{20}$.

Percents

A **percent** is a ratio that compares a number to 100. The word *percent* means "per hundred" or "out of 100." The symbol for *percent* is %.

For instance, suppose 43 out of 100 caterpillars are female. You can represent this ratio as a percent, a decimal, or a fraction.

Percent	Decimal	Fraction
43%	0.43	$\dfrac{43}{100}$

Example

In the preceding example, the ratio of the length of the caterpillar's head to the caterpillar's total length is $\frac{3}{20}$. To write this ratio as a percent, write an equivalent fraction that has a denominator of 100.

Multiply numerator and denominator by 5: $\quad \dfrac{3}{20} = \dfrac{3 \times 5}{20 \times 5}$

$\qquad = \dfrac{15}{100}$

Write as a percent: $\qquad = 15\%$

ANSWER The caterpillar's head represents 15 percent of its total length.

Using Formulas

A mathematical **formula** is a statement of a fact, rule, or principle. It is usually expressed as an equation.

In science, a formula often has a word form and a symbolic form. The formula below expresses Ohm's law.

Word Form

$$\text{Current} = \frac{\text{voltage}}{\text{resistance}}$$

Symbolic Form

$$I = \frac{V}{R}$$

In this formula, I, V, and R are variables. A mathematical **variable** is a symbol or letter that is used to represent one or more numbers.

> The term *variable* is also used in science to refer to a factor that can change during an experiment.

Example

Suppose that you measure a voltage of 1.5 volts and a resistance of 15 ohms. You can use the formula for Ohm's law to find the current in amperes.

Write the formula for Ohm's law: $I = \dfrac{V}{R}$

Substitute 1.5 volts for V and 15 ohms for R: $I = \dfrac{1.5 \text{ volts}}{15 \text{ ohms}}$

Simplify: $I = 0.1$ amp

ANSWER The current is 0.1 ampere.

If you know the values of all variables but one in a formula, you can solve for the value of the unknown variable. For instance, Ohm's law can be used to find a voltage if you know the current and the resistance.

Example

Suppose that you know that a current is 0.2 amperes and the resistance is 18 ohms. Use the formula for Ohm's law to find the voltage in volts.

Write the formula for Ohm's law: $I = \dfrac{V}{R}$

Substitute 0.2 amp for I and 18 ohms for R: $0.2 \text{ amp} = \dfrac{V}{18 \text{ ohms}}$

Multiply both sides by 18 ohms: $0.2 \text{ amp} \cdot 18 \text{ ohms} = V$

Simplify: $3.6 \text{ volts} = V$

ANSWER The voltage is 3.6 volts.

Finding Areas

The area of a figure is the amount of surface the figure covers.

Area is measured in square units, such as square meters (m²) or square centimeters (cm²). Formulas for the areas of three common geometric figures are shown below.

Area = (side length)²
$A = s^2$

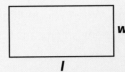

Area = length × width
$A = lw$

Area = $\frac{1}{2}$ × base × height

$A = \frac{1}{2}bh$

Example

Each face of a halite crystal is a square like the one shown. You can find the area of the square by using the steps below.

Write the formula for the area of a square:	$A = s^2$
Substitute 3 mm for s:	$= (3 \text{ mm})^2$
Simplify:	$= 9 \text{ mm}^2$

3 mm

3 mm

ANSWER The area of the square is 9 square millimeters.

Finding Volumes

The volume of a solid is the amount of space contained by the solid.

Volume is measured in cubic units, such as cubic meters (m³) or cubic centimeters (cm³). The volume of a rectangular prism is given by the formula shown below.

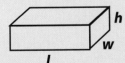

Volume = length × width × height
$V = lwh$

Example

A topaz crystal is a rectangular prism like the one shown. You can find the volume of the prism by using the steps below.

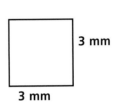

10 mm

12 mm

20 mm

Write the formula for the volume of a rectangular prism:	$V = lwh$
Substitute dimensions:	$= 20 \text{ mm} \times 12 \text{ mm} \times 10 \text{ mm}$
Simplify:	$= 2400 \text{ mm}^3$

ANSWER The volume of the rectangular prism is 2400 cubic millimeters.

Using Significant Figures

The **significant figures** in a decimal are the digits that are warranted by the accuracy of a measuring device.

When you perform a calculation with measurements, the number of significant figures to include in the result depends in part on the number of significant figures in the measurements. When you multiply or divide measurements, your answer should have only as many significant figures as the measurement with the fewest significant figures.

Example

Using a balance and a graduated cylinder filled with water, you determined that a marble has a mass of 8.0 grams and a volume of 3.5 cubic centimeters. To calculate the density of the marble, divide the mass by the volume.

$$\textit{Write the formula for density:} \quad \text{Density} = \frac{\text{mass}}{\text{Volume}}$$

$$\textit{Substitute measurements:} \quad = \frac{8.0 \text{ g}}{3.5 \text{ cm}^3}$$

$$\textit{Use a calculator to divide:} \quad \approx 2.285714286 \text{ g/cm}^3$$

ANSWER Because the mass and the volume have two significant figures each, give the density to two significant figures. The marble has a density of 2.3 grams per cubic centimeter.

Using Scientific Notation

Scientific notation is a shorthand way to write very large or very small numbers. For example, 73,500,000,000,000,000,000,000 kg is the mass of the Moon. In scientific notation, it is 7.35×10^{22} kg.

Example

You can convert from standard form to scientific notation.

Standard Form	Scientific Notation
720,000	7.2×10^5
5 decimal places left	Exponent is 5.
0.000291	2.91×10^{-4}
4 decimal places right	Exponent is −4.

You can convert from scientific notation to standard form.

Scientific Notation	Standard Form
4.63×10^7	46,300,000
Exponent is 7.	7 decimal places right
1.08×10^{-6}	0.00000108
Exponent is −6.	6 decimal places left

Note-Taking Handbook

Note-Taking Strategies

Taking notes as you read helps you understand the information. The notes you take can also be used as a study guide for later review. This handbook presents several ways to organize your notes.

Content Frame

1. Make a chart in which each column represents a category.
2. Give each column a heading.
3. Write details under the headings.

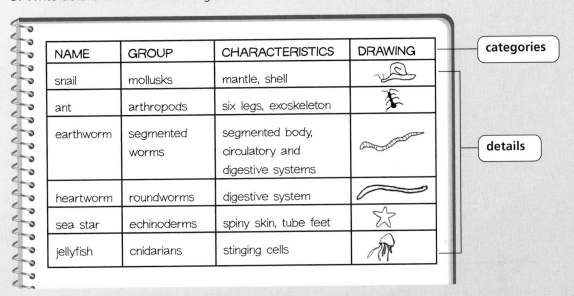

categories

details

NAME	GROUP	CHARACTERISTICS	DRAWING
snail	mollusks	mantle, shell	
ant	arthropods	six legs, exoskeleton	
earthworm	segmented worms	segmented body, circulatory and digestive systems	
heartworm	roundworms	digestive system	
sea star	echinoderms	spiny skin, tube feet	
jellyfish	cnidarians	stinging cells	

Combination Notes

1. For each new idea or concept, write an informal outline of the information.
2. Make a sketch to illustrate the concept, and label it.

NOTES

Types of forces
- contact force
- gravity
- friction

forces on a box being pushed

sketch with labels

contact force

gravity

friction

informal outline

Make flash cards to help you study for a test. Write a concept on one side of each card and draw the sketch that goes with it on the other side. Use the cards to review concepts with a friend.

Main Idea and Detail Notes

1. In the left-hand column of a two-column chart, list main ideas. The blue headings express main ideas throughout this textbook.

2. In the right-hand column, write details that expand on each main idea.

You can shorten the headings in your chart. Be sure to use the most important words.

When studying for tests, cover up the detail notes column with a sheet of paper. Then use each main idea to form a question—such as "How does latitude affect climate?" Answer the question, and then uncover the detail notes column to check your answer.

MAIN IDEAS	DETAIL NOTES
1. Latitude affects climate.	1. Places close to the equator are usually warmer than places close to the poles.
	1. Latitude has the same effect in both hemispheres.
2. Altitude affects climate.	2. Temperature decreases with altitude.
	2. Altitude can overcome the effect of latitude on temperature.

main idea 1

main idea 2

details about main idea 1

details about main idea 2

Main Idea Web

1. Write a main idea in a box.

2. Add boxes around it with related vocabulary terms and important details.

You can find definitions near highlighted terms.

definition of *work*

Work is the use of force to move an object.

formula

Work = force · distance

main idea

Force is necessary to do work.

The joule is the unit used to measure work.

definition of *joule*

Work depends on the size of a force.

important detail

Mind Map

1. Write a main idea in the center.
2. Add details that relate to one another and to the main idea.

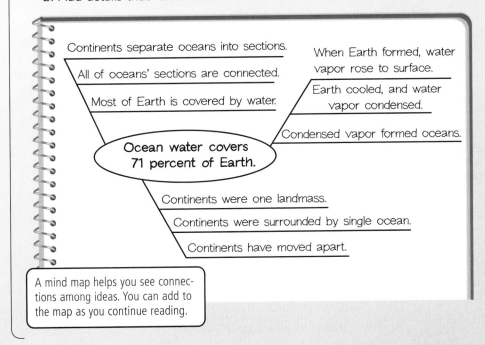

Continents separate oceans into sections.

All of oceans' sections are connected.

Most of Earth is covered by water.

When Earth formed, water vapor rose to surface.

Earth cooled, and water vapor condensed.

Condensed vapor formed oceans.

Ocean water covers 71 percent of Earth.

Continents were one landmass.

Continents were surrounded by single ocean.

Continents have moved apart.

A mind map helps you see connections among ideas. You can add to the map as you continue reading.

Supporting Main Ideas

1. Write a main idea in a box.
2. Add boxes underneath with information—such as reasons, explanations, and examples—that supports the main idea.

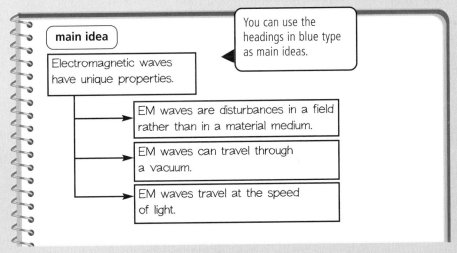

main idea

Electromagnetic waves have unique properties.

You can use the headings in blue type as main ideas.

EM waves are disturbances in a field rather than in a material medium.

EM waves can travel through a vacuum.

EM waves travel at the speed of light.

Outline

1. Copy the chapter title and headings from the book in the form of an outline.

2. Add notes that summarize in your own words what you read.

Cell Processes

1st key idea

I. Cells capture and release energy.

1st subpoint of I

  A. All cells need energy.

2nd subpoint of I

  B. Some cells capture light energy.

1st detail about B

    1. Process of photosynthesis

2nd detail about B

    2. Chloroplasts (site of photosynthesis)

    3. Carbon dioxide and water as raw materials

    4. Glucose and oxygen as products

  C. All cells release energy.

    1. Process of cellular respiration

    2. Fermentation of sugar to carbon dioxide

    3. Bacteria that carry out fermentation

II. Cells transport materials through membranes.

  A. Some materials move by diffusion.

    1. Particle movement from higher to lower concentrations

    2. Movement of water through membrane (osmosis)

  B. Some transport requires energy.

    1. Active transport

    2. Examples of active transport

Correct Outline Form

Include a title.

Arrange key ideas, subpoints, and details as shown.

Indent the divisions of the outline as shown.

Use the same grammatical form for items of the same rank. For example, if A is a sentence, B must also be a sentence.

You must have at least two main ideas or subpoints. That is, every A must be followed by a B, and every 1 must be followed by a 2.

Concept Map

1. Write an important concept in a large oval.
2. Add details related to the concept in smaller ovals.
3. Write linking words on arrows that connect the ovals.

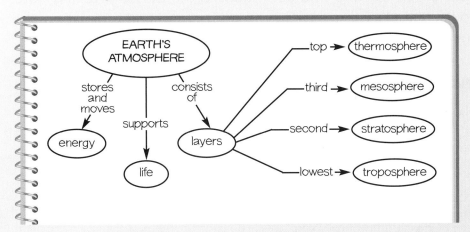

The main ideas or concepts can often be found in the blue headings. An example is "The atmosphere stores and moves energy." Use nouns from these concepts in the ovals, and use the verb or verbs on the lines.

Venn Diagram

1. Draw two overlapping circles, one for each item that you are comparing.
2. In the overlapping section, list the characteristics that are shared by both items.
3. In the outer sections, list the characteristics that are peculiar to each item.
4. Write a summary that describes the information in the Venn diagram.

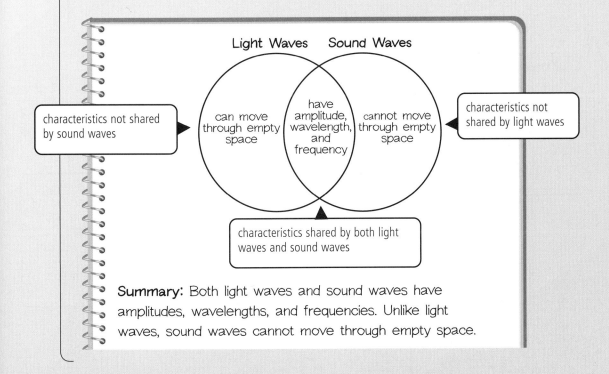

Summary: Both light waves and sound waves have amplitudes, wavelengths, and frequencies. Unlike light waves, sound waves cannot move through empty space.

Vocabulary Strategies

Important terms are highlighted in this book. A definition of each term can be found in the sentence or paragraph where the term appears. You can also find definitions in the Glossary. Taking notes about vocabulary terms helps you understand and remember what you read.

Description Wheel

1. Write a term inside a circle.
2. Write words that describe the term on "spokes" attached to the circle.

When studying for a test with a friend, read the phrases on the spokes one at a time until your friend identifies the correct term.

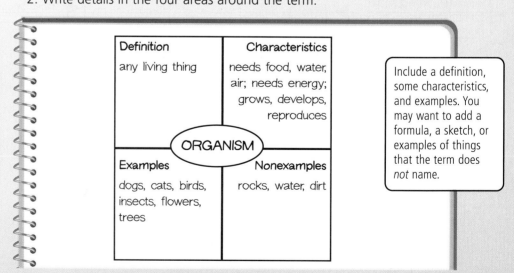

Four Square

1. Write a term in the center.
2. Write details in the four areas around the term.

Definition	Characteristics
any living thing	needs food, water, air; needs energy; grows, develops, reproduces

ORGANISM

Examples	Nonexamples
dogs, cats, birds, insects, flowers, trees	rocks, water, dirt

Include a definition, some characteristics, and examples. You may want to add a formula, a sketch, or examples of things that the term does *not* name.

Frame Game

1. Write a term in the center.
2. Frame the term with details.

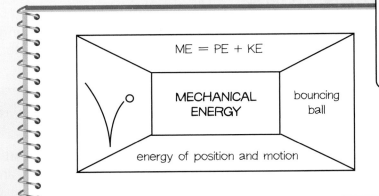

Include examples, descriptions, sketches, or sentences that use the term in context. Change the frame to fit each new term.

Magnet Word

1. Write a term on the magnet.
2. On the lines, add details related to the term.

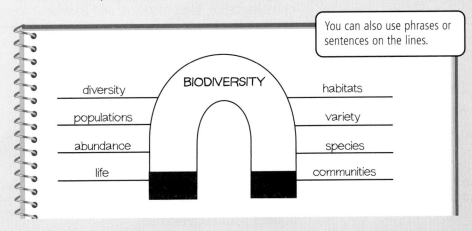

You can also use phrases or sentences on the lines.

Word Triangle

1. Write a term and its definition in the bottom section.
2. In the middle section, write a sentence in which the term is used correctly.
3. In the top section, draw a small picture to illustrate the term.

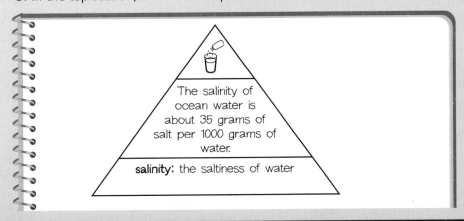

Classification of Living Things

Living things are classified into three domains. These domains are further divided into kingdoms, and then phyla. Major phyla are described in the table below, along with important features that are used to distinguish each group.

Classification of Living Things			
Domain	**Kingdom**	**Phylum**	**Common Name and Description**
Archaea	**Archaea**		Single-celled, with no nucleus. Live in some of Earth's most extreme environments, including salty, hot, and acid environments, and the deep ocean.
Bacteria	**Bacteria**		Single-celled, with no nucleus, but chemically different from Archaea. Live in all types of environments, including the human body; reproduce by dividing from one cell into two. Includes blue-green bacteria (cyanobacteria), *Streptococcus,* and *Bacillus.*
Eukarya			Cells are larger than archaea or bacteria and are eukaryotic (have a nucleus containing DNA). Single-celled or multicellular.
	Protista		Usually single-celled, but sometimes multicellular. DNA contained in a nucleus. Many phyla resemble plants, fungi, or animals but are usually smaller or simpler in structure.
	Animal-like protists	Ciliophora	Ciliates; have many short, hairlike extensions called cilia, which they use for feeding and movement. Includes paramecium.
		Zoomastigina	Zooflagellates; have usually one or two long, hairlike extensions called flagella.
		Sporozoa	Cause diseases in animals such as birds, fish, and humans. Includes *Plasmodium,* which causes malaria.
		Sarcodina	Use footlike extensions to move and feed. Includes foraminifers and amoebas. Sometimes called Rhizopoda.
	Plantlike protists	Euglenozoa	Single-celled, with one flagellum. Some have chloroplasts that carry out photosynthesis. Includes euglenas and *Trypanosoma,* which causes African sleeping sickness.
		Dinoflagellata	Dinoflagellates; usually single-celled; usually have chloroplasts and flagellum. In great numbers, some species can cause red tides along coastlines.

Classification of Living Things (cont.)

Domain	Kingdom	Phylum	Common Name and Description
		Chrysophyta	Yellow algae, golden-brown algae, and diatoms; single-celled; named for the yellow pigments in their chloroplasts (*chrysophyte*, in Greek, means "golden plant").
		Chlorophyceae	Green algae; have chloroplasts and are chemically similar to land plants. Unicellular or forms simple colonies of cells. Includes *Chlamydomonas, Ulva* (sea lettuce), and *Volvox*.
		Phaeophyta	Brown seaweed; contain a special brown pigment that gives these organisms their color. Multicellular, live mainly in salt water; includes kelp.
		Rhodophyta	Red algae; contain a red pigment that makes these organisms red, purple, or reddish-black. Multicellular, live in salt water.
	Funguslike protists	Acrasiomycota	Cellular slime molds; live partly as free-living single-celled organisms, then fuse together to form a many-celled mass. Live in damp, nutrient-rich environments; decomposers.
		Myxomycota	Acellular slime molds; form large, slimy masses made of many nuclei but technically a single cell.
		Oomycota	Water molds and downy mildews; produce thin, cottonlike extensions called hyphae. Feed off of dead or decaying material, often in water.
	Fungi		Usually multicellular; eukaryotic; cells have a thick cell wall. Obtain nutrients through absorption; often function as decomposers.
		Chytridiomycota	Oldest and simplest fungi; usually aquatic (fresh water or brackish water); single-celled or multicellular.
		Basidiomycota	Multicellular; reproduce with a club-shaped structure that is commonly seen on forest floors. Includes mushrooms, puffballs, rusts, and smuts.
		Zygomycota	Mostly disease-causing molds; often parasitic.
		Ascomycota	Includes single-celled yeasts and multicellular sac fungi. Includes *Penicillium*.

Classification of Living Things (cont.)

Domain	Kingdom	Phylum	Common Name and Description
	Plantae		Multicellular and eukaryotic; make sugars using energy from sunlight. Cells have a thick cell wall of cellulose.
		Bryophyta	Mosses; small, grasslike plants that live in moist, cool environments. Includes sphagnum (peat) moss. Seedless, nonvascular plants.
		Hepatophyta	Liverworts; named for the liver-shaped structure of one part of the plant's life cycle. Live in moist environments. Seedless, nonvascular plants.
		Anthoceratophyta	Hornworts; named for the visible hornlike structures with which they reproduce. Live on forest floors and other moist, cool environments. Seedless, nonvascular plants.
		Psilotophyta	Simple plant, just two types. Includes whisk ferns found in tropical areas, a common greenhouse weed. Seedless, vascular plants.
		Lycophyta	Club mosses and quillworts; look like miniature pine trees; live in moist, wooded environments. Includes *Lycopodium* (ground pine). Seedless vascular plants.
		Sphenophyta	Plants with simple leaves, stems, and roots. Grow about a meter tall, usually in moist areas. Includes *Equisetum* (scouring rush). Seedless, vascular plants.
		Pterophyta	Ferns; fringed-leaf plants that grow in cool, wooded environments. Includes many species. Seedless, vascular plants.
		Cycadophyta	Cycads; slow-growing palmlike plants that grow in tropical environments. Reproduce with seeds.
		Ginkgophyta	Includes only one species: *Ginkgo biloba*, a tree that is often planted in urban environments. Reproduce with seeds in cones.
		Gnetophyta	Small group includes desert-dwelling and tropical species. Includes *Ephedra* (Mormon tea) and *Welwitschia*, which grows in African deserts. Reproduce with seeds.
		Coniferophyta	Conifers, including pines, spruces, firs, sequoias. Usually evergreen trees; tend to grow in cold, dry environments; reproduce with seeds produced in cones.

Classification of Living Things (cont.)

Domain	Kingdom	Phylum	Common Name and Description
		Anthophyta	Flowering plants; includes grasses and flowering trees and shrubs. Reproduce with seeds produced in flowers, becoming fruit.
	Animalia		Multicellular and eukaryotic; obtain energy by consuming food. Usually able to move around.
		Porifera	Sponges; spend most of their lives fixed to the ocean floor. Feed by filtering water (containing nutrients and small organisms) through their body.
		Cnidaria	Aquatic animals with a radial (spokelike) body shape; named for their stinging cells (cnidocytes). Includes jellyfish, hydras, sea anemones, and corals.
		Ctenophora	Comb jellies; named for the comblike rows of cilia (hairlike extensions) that are used for movement.
		Platyhelminthes	Flatworms; thin, flattened worms with simple tissues and sensory organs. Includes planaria and tapeworms, which cause diseases in humans and other hosts.
		Nematoda	Roundworms; small, round worms; many species are parasites, causing diseases in humans, such as trichinosis and elephantiasis.
		Annelida	Segmented worms; body is made of many similar segments. Includes earthworms, leeches, and many marine worms.
		Mollusca	Soft-bodied, aquatic animals that usually have an outer shell. Includes snails, mussels, clams, octopus, and squid.
		Arthropoda	Animals with an outer skeleton (exoskeleton) and jointed appendages (for example, legs or wings). Very large group that includes insects, spiders and ticks, centipedes, millipedes, and crustaceans.
		Echinodermata	Marine animals with a radial (spokelike) body shape. Includes feather stars, sea stars (starfish), sea urchins, sand dollars, and sea cucumbers.
		Chordata	Mostly vertebrates (animals with backbones) that share important stages of early development. Includes tunicates (sea squirts), fish, sharks, amphibians, reptiles, birds, and mammals.

The Periodic Table of the Elements

1								
1 **H** Hydrogen 1.008	**2**							

Period

Each row of the periodic table is called a **period**. As read from left to right, one proton and one electron are added from one element to the next.

3 **Li** Lithium 6.941	**4** **Be** Beryllium 9.012
11 **Na** Sodium 22.990	**12** **Mg** Magnesium 24.305

		3	4	5	6	7	8	9
19 **K** Potassium 39.098	**20** **Ca** Calcium 40.078	**21** **Sc** Scandium 44.956	**22** **Ti** Titanium 47.87	**23** **V** Vanadium 50.942	**24** **Cr** Chromium 51.996	**25** **Mn** Manganese 54.938	**26** **Fe** Iron 55.845	**27** **Co** Cobalt 58.933
37 **Rb** Rubidium 85.468	**38** **Sr** Strontium 87.62	**39** **Y** Yttrium 88.906	**40** **Zr** Zirconium 91.224	**41** **Nb** Niobium 92.906	**42** **Mo** Molybdenum 95.94	**43** **Tc** Technetium (98)	**44** **Ru** Ruthenium 101.07	**45** **Rh** Rhodium 102.906
55 **Cs** Cesium 132.905	**56** **Ba** Barium 137.327	**57** **La** Lanthanum 138.906	**72** **Hf** Hafnium 178.49	**73** **Ta** Tantalum 180.95	**74** **W** Tungsten 183.84	**75** **Re** Rhenium 186.207	**76** **Os** Osmium 190.23	**77** **Ir** Iridium 192.217
87 **Fr** Francium (223)	**88** **Ra** Radium (226)	**89** **Ac** Actinium (227)	**104** **Rf** Rutherfordium (261)	**105** **Db** Dubnium (262)	**106** **Sg** Seaborgium (266)	**107** **Bh** Bohrium (264)	**108** **Hs** Hassium (269)	**109** **Mt** Meitnerium (268)

Group

Each column of the table is called a **group.** Elements in a group share similar properties. Groups are read from top to bottom.

58 **Ce** Cerium 140.116	**59** **Pr** Praseodymium 140.908	**60** **Nd** Neodymium 144.24	**61** **Pm** Promethium (145)	**62** **Sm** Samarium 150.36
90 **Th** Thorium 232.038	**91** **Pa** Protactinium 231.036	**92** **U** Uranium 238.029	**93** **Np** Neptunium (237)	**94** **Pu** Plutonium (244)

 Metal   Metalloid Nonmetal   Solid   Liquid   Gas

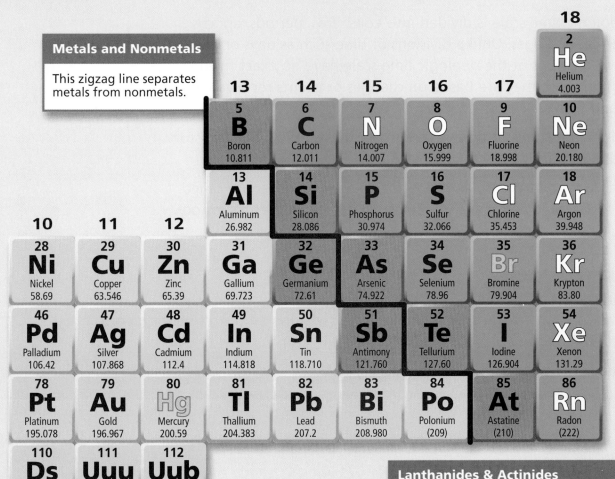

Metals and Nonmetals

This zigzag line separates metals from nonmetals.

Lanthanides & Actinides

The Lanthanide series (elements 58–71) and Actinide series (elements 90–103) are usually set apart from the rest of the periodic table.

18
2 **He** Helium 4.003

13	14	15	16	17
5 **B** Boron 10.811	6 **C** Carbon 12.011	7 **N** Nitrogen 14.007	8 **O** Oxygen 15.999	9 **F** Fluorine 18.998	10 **Ne** Neon 20.180

| | | | 13 **Al** Aluminum 26.982 | 14 **Si** Silicon 28.086 | 15 **P** Phosphorus 30.974 | 16 **S** Sulfur 32.066 | 17 **Cl** Chlorine 35.453 | 18 **Ar** Argon 39.948 |

10	11	12						
28 **Ni** Nickel 58.69	29 **Cu** Copper 63.546	30 **Zn** Zinc 65.39	31 **Ga** Gallium 69.723	32 **Ge** Germanium 72.61	33 **As** Arsenic 74.922	34 **Se** Selenium 78.96	35 **Br** Bromine 79.904	36 **Kr** Krypton 83.80
46 **Pd** Palladium 106.42	47 **Ag** Silver 107.868	48 **Cd** Cadmium 112.4	49 **In** Indium 114.818	50 **Sn** Tin 118.710	51 **Sb** Antimony 121.760	52 **Te** Tellurium 127.60	53 **I** Iodine 126.904	54 **Xe** Xenon 131.29
78 **Pt** Platinum 195.078	79 **Au** Gold 196.967	80 **Hg** Mercury 200.59	81 **Tl** Thallium 204.383	82 **Pb** Lead 207.2	83 **Bi** Bismuth 208.980	84 **Po** Polonium (209)	85 **At** Astatine (210)	86 **Rn** Radon (222)
110 **Ds** Darmstadtium (269)	111 **Uuu** Unununium (272)	112 **Uub** Ununbium (277)						

63 **Eu** Europium 151.964	64 **Gd** Gadolinium 157.25	65 **Tb** Terbium 158.925	66 **Dy** Dysprosium 162.50	67 **Ho** Holmium 164.930	68 **Er** Erbium 167.26	69 **Tm** Thulium 168.934	70 **Yb** Ytterbium 173.04	71 **Lu** Lutetium 174.967
95 **Am** Americium (243)	96 **Cm** Curium (247)	97 **Bk** Berkelium (247)	98 **Cf** Californium (251)	99 **Es** Einsteinium (252)	100 **Fm** Fermium (257)	101 **Md** Mendelevium (258)	102 **No** Nobelium (259)	103 **Lr** Lawrencium (262)

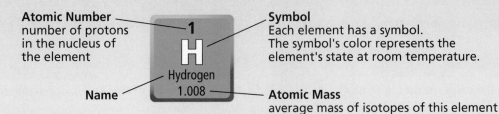

Atomic Number number of protons in the nucleus of the element

1 **H** Hydrogen 1.008

Symbol Each element has a symbol. The symbol's color represents the element's state at room temperature.

Name

Atomic Mass average mass of isotopes of this element

Divisions of Geologic Time

The geologic time scale is divided into eons, eras, periods, epochs (ehp-uhks), and ages. Unlike divisions of time such as days or minutes, the divisions of the geologic time scale have no exact fixed lengths. Instead, they are based on changes or events recorded in rocks and fossils.

Eon The largest unit of time is an eon. Earth's 4.6-billion-year history is divided into four eons.

The Hadean, Archean, and Proterozoic eons together are called Precambrian time and make up almost 90 percent of Earth's history.

Geologic Time Scale

This geologic time scale shows the longest divisions of Earth's history: eons, eras, and periods.

Hadean eon		Archean eon	
	Precambrian time – 4.6 bya to 544 mya		

4.6 bya* | 4 bya | 3.5 bya | 3 bya | Carboniferous period

*bya = billion years ago
†mya = million years ago

Phanerozoic eon				
Paleozoic era				
Cambrian period	Ordovician period	Silurian period	Devonian period	

544 mya | 490 mya | 443 mya | 417 mya | 354 mya

Precambrian Time at 3.6 Billion Years Ago

For nearly 4 billion years, during most of Precambrian time, no plants or animals existed.

Paleozoic Era at 544 Million Years Ago

At the beginning of the Paleozoic era, all life lived in the oceans.

The fossil record for Precambrian time consists mostly of tiny organisms that cannot be seen without a microscope. Other early forms of life had soft bodies that rarely formed into fossils.

The Phanerozoic eon stretches from the end of Precambrian time to the present. Because so many more changes are recorded in the fossil record of this eon, it is further divided into smaller units of time called eras, periods, epochs, and ages.

The Phanerozoic eon is divided into three eras: the Paleozoic, the Mesozoic, and the Cenozoic. Each era is subdivided into a number of periods. The periods of the Cenozoic, the most recent era, are further divided into epochs, which are in turn further divided into ages. The smaller time divisions relate to how long certain conditions and life forms on Earth lasted and how quickly they changed or became extinct.

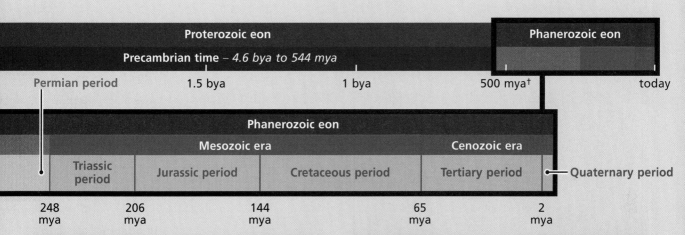

Proterozoic eon				Phanerozoic eon
Precambrian time – 4.6 bya to 544 mya				
Permian period	1.5 bya	1 bya	500 mya†	today

Phanerozoic eon				
	Mesozoic era		Cenozoic era	
Triassic period	Jurassic period	Cretaceous period	Tertiary period	Quaternary period
248 mya	206 mya	144 mya	65 mya	2 mya

During the Mesozoic era, dinosaurs lived along with the first mammals, birds, and flowering plants.

Cenozoic Era at Present Day

The first humans appeared in the later part of the Cenozoic era, which continues today.

Fossils in Rocks

If an organism is covered by or buried in sediment, it may become a fossil as the sediments become rock. Many rock fossils are actual body parts, such as bones or teeth, that were buried in sediment and then replaced by minerals and turned to stone. Fossils in rock include molds and casts, petrified wood, carbon films, and trace fossils.

1 Molds and Casts Some fossils that form in sedimentary rock are mold fossils. A mold is a visible shape that was left after an animal or plant was buried in sediment and then decayed away. In some cases, a hollow mold later becomes filled with minerals, producing a cast fossil. The cast fossil is a solid model in the shape of the organism. If you think of the mold as a shoeprint, the cast would be what would result if sand filled the print and hardened into stone.

Fossils in Rocks

Rock fossils show shapes and traces of past life.

1 Molds and Casts

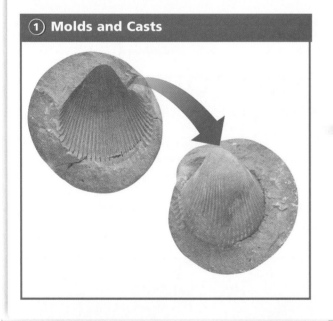

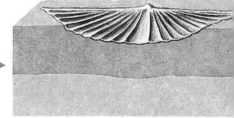

An organism dies and falls into soft sediment.

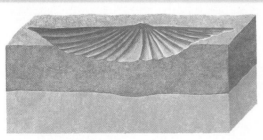

Over time, the sediment becomes rock and the organism decays, leaving a mold.

Minerals fill the mold and make a cast of the organism.

APPENDIX

② Petrified Wood The stone fossil of a tree is called petrified wood. In certain conditions, a fallen tree can become covered with sediments. Over time, water passes through the sediments and into the tree's cells. Minerals that are carried in the water take the place of the cells, producing a stone likeness of the tree.

In this close-up, you can see the minerals that replaced the wood, forming petrified wood.

③ Carbon Films Carbon is an element that is found in every living thing. Sometimes when a dead plant or animal decays, its carbon is left behind as a visible layer. This image is called a carbon film. Carbon films can show details of soft parts of animals and plants that are rarely seen in other fossils.

This carbon film of a moth is about 10 million years old. Carbon films are especially useful because they can show details of the soft parts of organisms.

④ Trace Fossils Do you want to know how fast a dinosaur could run? Trace fossils might be able to tell you. These are not parts of an animal or impressions of it, but rather evidence of an animal's presence in a given location. Trace fossils include preserved footprints, trails, animal holes, and even feces. By comparing these clues with what is known about modern animals, scientists can learn how prehistoric animals may have lived, what they ate, and how they behaved.

A trace fossil, such as this footprint of a dinosaur in rock, can provide important information about where an animal lived and how it walked and ran.

Half-Life

Over time, a radioactive element breaks down at a constant rate into another form.

The rate of change of a radioactive element is measured in half-lives. A half-life is the length of time it takes for half of the atoms in a sample of a radioactive element to change from an unstable form into another form. Different elements have different half-lives, ranging from fractions of a second to billions of years.

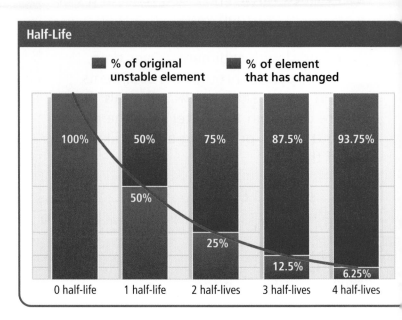

Half-Life

■ % of original unstable element ■ % of element that has changed

100%	50%	75%	87.5%	93.75%
	50%	25%	12.5%	6.25%
0 half-life	1 half-life	2 half-lives	3 half-lives	4 half-lives

Radiometric Dating

Radiometric dating works best with igneous rocks. Sedimentary rocks are formed from material that came from other rocks. For this reason, any measurements would show when the original rocks were formed, not when the sedimentary rock itself formed.

Elements with half-lives of millions to billions of years are used to date rocks.

Radioactive Breakdown and Dating Rock Layers

Igneous rocks contain radioactive elements that break down over time. This breakdown can be used to tell the ages of the rocks.

① **1408 Million Years Ago**

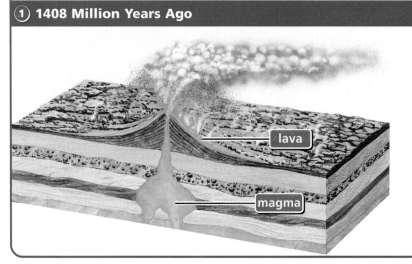

lava

magma

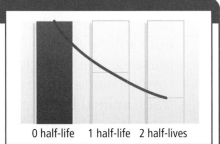

0 half-life	1 half-life	2 half-lives

When magma first hardens into rock, it contains some uranium 235 and no lead 207.

APPENDIX

Uranium 235, an unstable element found in some igneous rocks, has a half-life of 704 million years. Over time, uranium 235 breaks down into lead 207.

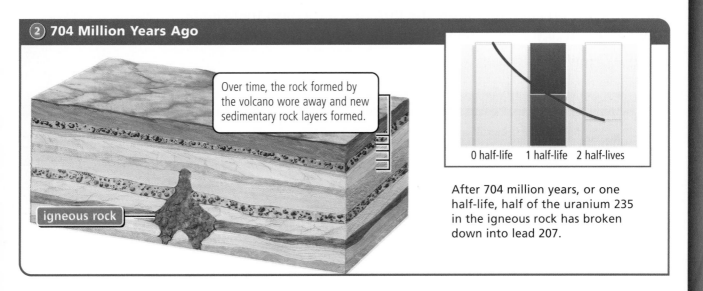

2 704 Million Years Ago

Over time, the rock formed by the volcano wore away and new sedimentary rock layers formed.

igneous rock

0 half-life   1 half-life   2 half-lives

After 704 million years, or one half-life, half of the uranium 235 in the igneous rock has broken down into lead 207.

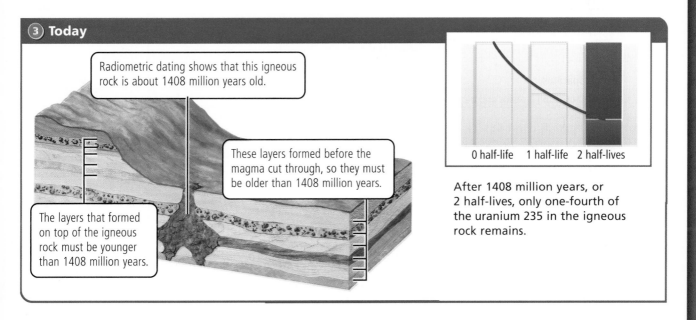

3 Today

Radiometric dating shows that this igneous rock is about 1408 million years old.

These layers formed before the magma cut through, so they must be older than 1408 million years.

The layers that formed on top of the igneous rock must be younger than 1408 million years.

0 half-life   1 half-life   2 half-lives

After 1408 million years, or 2 half-lives, only one-fourth of the uranium 235 in the igneous rock remains.

Just as uranium 235 can be used to date igneous rocks, carbon 14 can be used to find the ages of the remains of some things that were once alive. Carbon 14 is an unstable form of carbon, an element found in all living things. Carbon 14 has a half-life of 5730 years. It is useful for dating objects between about 100 and 70,000 years old, such as the wood from an ancient tool or the remains of an animal from the Ice Age.

Plant and Animal Cells

Plants and animals are eukaryotes, that is, their cells contain a nucleus and other membrane-bound structures called organelles. The diagrams on page R65 show the different structures that can be found in plant and animal cells. The table below lists the functions of the structures.

Cell Structures and Their Functions	Plant Cell	Animal Cell
Nucleus	✔	✔
stores genetic material that enables a cell to function and divide		
Cell Membrane	✔	✔
controls what comes into and goes out of a cell		
Cell wall	✔	
tough outer covering provides support		
Ribosome	✔	✔
uses genetic material to assemble materials needed to make proteins		
Endoplasmic reticulum	✔	✔
manufactures proteins and other materials a cell needs to function		
Golgi apparatus	✔	✔
finishes processing proteins and transports them		
Vesicle	✔	✔
stores and transports materials and wastes		
Mitochondrion	✔	✔
releases chemical energy stored in sugars		
Chloroplast	✔	
uses energy from sunlight to make sugars		
Lysosome		✔
breaks down food particles and wastes		

Plant Cell

Found in plant cells, not animal cells:

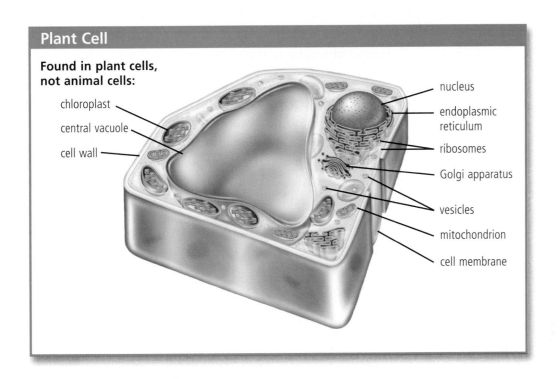

- chloroplast
- central vacuole
- cell wall

- nucleus
- endoplasmic reticulum
- ribosomes
- Golgi apparatus
- vesicles
- mitochondrion
- cell membrane

Animal Cell

Found in animal cells, not plant cells:

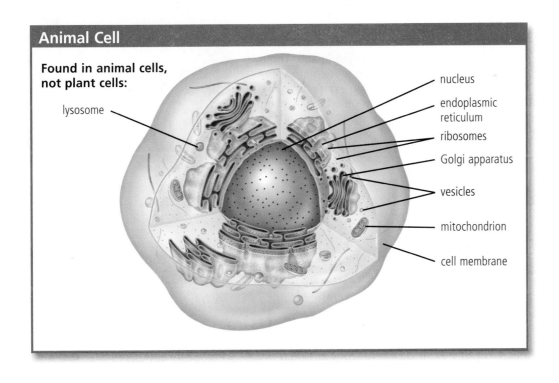

- lysosome

- nucleus
- endoplasmic reticulum
- ribosomes
- Golgi apparatus
- vesicles
- mitochondrion
- cell membrane

How a Light Microscope Works

Microscopes are used to see objects that are too small to see well with the naked eye. An ordinary light microscope works by combining convex lenses. A lens is a piece of glass or plastic shaped in such a way as to bend light. A convex lens has a bend similar to the curve of a sphere. It is thicker at its center than around the edges.

The object being viewed is mounted on a slide and placed on the stage of the microscope. The lens closer to the object is called the objective. This lens focuses an enlarged image of the object inside the microscope. The other microscope lens—the one you look through—is called the eyepiece. You use this lens to look at the image formed by the objective. Like a magnifying glass, the eyepiece lens forms an enlarged image of the first image.

Very small objects do not reflect much light. Most microscopes use a lamp or a mirror to shine more light on the object.

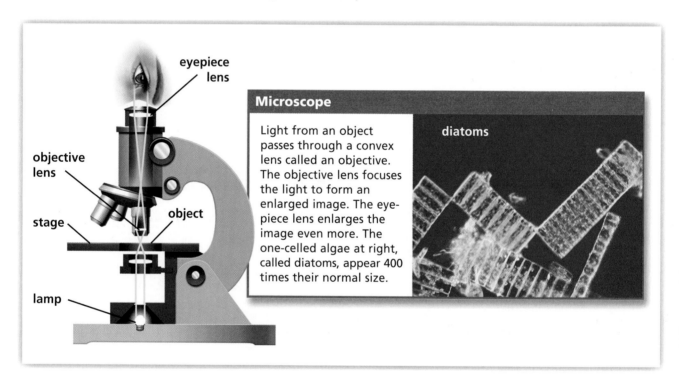

eyepiece lens

objective lens

stage

object

lamp

Microscope

Light from an object passes through a convex lens called an objective. The objective lens focuses the light to form an enlarged image. The eyepiece lens enlarges the image even more. The one-celled algae at right, called diatoms, appear 400 times their normal size.

diatoms

You will notice that many of the photographs of microscopic images included in this book have a magnification factor, for example 400×. This is the power of magnification of the microscope.

Glossary

A

abiotic factor (AY-by-AHT-ihk)
A nonliving physical or chemical part of an ecosystem. (p. D10)

   factor abiótico Una parte física o química sin vida de un ecosistema.

active transport
The process of using energy to move materials through a membrane. (p. A60)

   transporte activo El proceso de usar energía para mover sustancias a través de una membrana.

adaptation
A characteristic, a behavior, or any inherited trait that makes a species able to survive and reproduce in a particular environment. (p. xxxvii)

   adaptación Una característica, un comportamiento o cualquier rasgo heredado que permite a una especie sobrevivir o reproducirse en un medio ambiente determinado.

addiction
A physical or psychological need for a habit-forming substance, such as alcohol or drugs. (p. E145)

   adicción Una necesidad física o psicológica de una sustancia que forma hábito, como el alcohol o las drogas.

adolescence (AD-uhl-EHS-uhns)
The stage of life from the time a human body begins to mature sexually to adulthood. (p. E135)

   adolescencia La etapa de la vida que va desde que el cuerpo humano empieza a madurar sexualmente hasta la edad adulta.

adulthood
The stage of life that begins once a human body completes its growth and reaches sexual maturity. (p. E136)

   edad adulta La etapa de la vida que empieza una vez que el cuerpo humano completa su crecimiento y alcanza la madurez sexual.

algae
Protists that live mostly in water and use sunlight as a source of energy. *Algae* is a plural word; the singular is *alga.* (p. C31)

   algas Protistas que viven principalmente en el agua y que usan la luz solar como fuente de energía.

allele (uh-LEEL)
An alternate form of a gene for a specific trait or gene product. (p. A103)

   alelo Una forma alterna de un gen para un rasgo específico o un producto del gen.

amphibian
A cold-blooded vertebrate animal that lives in water and breathes with gills when it is young; as an adult, it moves onto land and breathes air with lungs. (p. C167)

   anfibio Un vertebrado de sangre fría que vive en el agua y respira con branquias cuando es juvenil; cuando es adulto, se mueve a la tierra y respire aire con pulmones.

ancestor
A distant or early form of an organism from which later forms descend. (p. B29)

   ancestro Una forma distante o temprana de un organismo a partir de la cual descienden formas posteriores.

angiosperm (AN-jee-uh-SPURM)
A plant that has flowers and produces seeds enclosed in fruit. (p. C107)

   Angiosperma Una planta que tiene flores y que produce semillas dentro de frutas.

Animalia (AN-uh-MAL-yuh)
Part of a classification system that divides all living things into six kingdoms. Kingdom Animalia includes multicellular organisms, from humans and lions to insects and microbes, that rely on food for energy. (p. B63)

   Animalia Parte de un sistema de clasificación que divide a todos los organismos vivos en seis reinos. El reino Animalia incluye a organismos multicelulares, desde humanos y leones hasta insectos y microbios, que dependen del alimento como fuente de energía.

antibiotic

A medicine that can block the growth and reproduction of bacteria. (p. E81)

antibiótico Una medicina que puede impedir el crecimiento y la reproducción de las bacterias.

antibody

A protein produced by some white blood cells to attack specific foreign materials. (p. E75)

anticuerpo Una proteína producida por algunos glóbulos blancos para atacar materiales extraños específicos.

antigen

A marker that a pathogen carries and that stimulates the production of antibodies. (p. E78)

antígeno Un marcador que lleva un patógeno y que estimula la producción de anticuerpos.

appendicular skeleton (AP-uhn-DIHK-yuh-luhr)

The bones of the skeleton that function to allow movement, such as arm and leg bones. (p. E16)

esqueleto apendicular Los huesos del esqueleto cuya función es permitir el movimiento, como los huesos del brazo y los huesos de la pierna.

Archaea (AHR-kee-uh)

Part of a classification system that divides all living things into six kingdoms. Kingdom Archaea includes microscopic single-celled organisms with a distinctive cell structure that allows them to live in extreme environments. (p. B63)

Archaea Parte de un sistema de clasificación que divide a todos los organismos vivos en seis reinos. El reino Archaea incluye a organismos microscópicos de una sola célula con una estructura celular distintiva que les permite vivir en medios ambientes extremosos.

artery

A blood vessel with strong walls that carries blood away from the heart. (p. E69)

arteria Un vaso sanguíneo con paredes fuertes que lleva la sangre del corazón hacia otras partes del cuerpo.

arthropod

An invertebrate animal with an exoskeleton, a segmented body, and jointed legs. (p. C142)

artrópodo Un animal invertebrado con un exoesqueleto, un cuerpo segmentado y patas articuladas.

asexual reproduction

The process by which a single organism produces offspring that have the same genetic material. (p. A88)

reproducción asexual El proceso mediante el cual un solo organismo produce crías que tienen el mismo material genético.

atom

The smallest particle of an element that has the chemical properties of that element.

átomo La partícula más pequeña de un elemento que tiene las propiedades químicas de ese elemento.

autotroph (AW-tuh-TRAHF)

An organism that captures energy from sunlight and uses it to produce energy-rich carbon compounds, usually through the process of photosynthesis. (p. C52)

autótrofo Un organismo que capta energía de la luz solar y la usa para producir compuestos de carbono ricos en energía, usualmente mediante el proceso de fotosíntesis.

axial skeleton

The central part of the skeleton, which includes the cranium, the spinal column, and the ribs. (p. E16)

esqueleto axial La parte central del esqueleto que incluye al cráneo, a la columna vertebral y a las costillas.

B

bacteria (bak-TEER-ee-uh)

A large group of one-celled organisms that sometimes cause disease. *Bacteria* is a plural word; the singular is *bacterium.* (pp. A14, E149)

bacterias Un grupo grande de organismos unicelulares que algunas veces causan enfermedades.

Bacteria (bak-TEER-ee-uh)

Part of a classification system that divides all living things into six kingdoms. Kingdom Bacteria includes microscopic single-celled organisms found in many environments. Bacteria can be associated with disease in other organisms. (p. B63)

Bacteria Parte de un sistema de clasificación que divide a todos los organismos vivos en seis reinos. El reino Bacteria incluye a organismos microscópicos de una sola célula que se encuentran en muchos medios ambientes. Las bacterias pueden estar asociadas a enfermedades en otros organismos.

behavior
An organism's action in response to a stimulus. (p. C62)

> **comportamiento** La acción de un organismo en respuesta a un estímulo.

binary fission
A form of asexual reproduction by which some single-celled organisms reproduce. The genetic material is copied, and one cell divides into two independent cells that are each a copy of the original cell. Prokaryotes such as bacteria reproduce by binary fission. (pp. A89, C12)

> **fisión binaria** Una forma asexual de reproducción mediante la cual algunos organismos unicelulares se reproducen. El material genético se copia y una célula se divide en dos células independientes las cuales son copias de la célula original. Los organismos procariotas, tales como las bacterias, se reproducen mediante fisión binaria.

binomial nomenclature
(by-NOH-mee-uhl NOH-muhn-KLAY-chuhr)
The two-part naming system used to identify species. The first part of the name is the genus, and the second part of the name is the species. (p. B52)

> **nomenclatura biológica** El sistema de denominación de dos partes que se usa para identificar a las especies. La primera parte del nombre es el género y la segunda parte del nombre es la especie.

biodiversity
The number and variety of living things found on Earth or within an ecosystem. (p. D91)

> **biodiversidad** La cantidad y variedad de organismos vivos que se encuentran en la Tierra o dentro de un ecosistema.

biology
The scientific study of life and all living things; ecology, zoology, and botany are examples of biological sciences. (p. D8)

> **biología** El estudio científico de la vida y de todos los organismos vivos; la ecología, la zoología y la botánica son ejemplos de ciencias biológicas.

biome (BY-ohm)
A region of Earth that has a particular climate and certain types of plants. Examples are tundra, taiga, desert, grassland, temperate and tropical forests.

> **bioma** Una región de la Tierra que tiene un clima particular y ciertos tipos de plantas. La tundra, la taiga, el desierto, la estepa, la selva tropical y el bosque templado son ejemplos de biomas.

biotic factor (by-AHT-ihk)
A living thing in an ecosystem.

> **factor biótico** Un organismo vivo en un ecosistema.

blood
A fluid in the body that delivers oxygen and other materials to cells and removes carbon dioxide and other wastes. (p. E65)

> **sangre** Un fluido en el cuerpo que reparte oxígeno y otras sustancias a las células y elimina dióxido de carbono y otros desechos.

blubber
A layer of fat in some sea mammals that lies beneath the skin. It insulates the animal from cold and stores reserve energy. (p. C184)

> **grasa de ballena** Una capa de tejido graso en algunos mamíferos marinos que yace bajo la piel. Aísla al animal del frío y almacena energía de reserva.

budding
A process of asexual reproduction in which an organism develops as an outgrowth of the parent. Each bud can grow into a new organism, breaking free and becoming separate and independent. (p. A93)

> **gemación** Un proceso de reproducción asexual en el cual un organismo se desarrolla a partir de una porción del progenitor. Cada yema puede convertirse en un nuevo organismo, separándose del progenitor y volviéndose independiente.

C

capillary
A narrow blood vessel that connects arteries with veins. (p. E69)

> **capilar** Un vaso sanguíneo angosto que conecta a las arterias con las venas.

carbohydrate (KAHR-boh-HY-drayt)
A type of molecule made up of subunits of sugars and used for energy and structure. (p. A42)

> **carbohidrato** Un tipo de molécula compuesta de unidades de azúcares y usada como fuente de energía y como material estructural.

carbon cycle
The continuous movement of carbon through Earth, its atmosphere, and the living things on Earth. (p. D18)

> **ciclo del carbono** El movimiento continuo del carbono en la Tierra, su atmósfera y todos los seres vivos en ella.

cardiac muscle
The muscle that makes up the heart. (p. E24)

> **músculo cardiaco** El músculo del cual está compuesto el corazón.

carrying capacity

The maximum size that a population can reach in an ecosystem. (pp. B82, D65)

capacidad de carga El tamaño máximo que una población puede alcanzar en un ecosistema.

cell

The smallest unit that is able to perform the basic functions of life. (p. xxxi)

célula La unidad más pequeña capaz de realizar las funciones básicas de la vida.

cell cycle

The normal sequence of growth, maintenance, and division in a cell. (p. A80)

ciclo celular La secuencia normal de crecimiento, mantenimiento y división en una célula.

cell membrane

The outer boundary of the cytoplasm, a layer that controls what enters or leaves the cell; a protective covering enclosing an entire cell. (p. A20)

membrana celular El límite exterior del citoplasma, una capa que controla lo que entra y sale de la célula, una cubierta protectora que encierra una célula entera.

cellular respiration

A process in which cells use oxygen to release energy stored in sugars. (pp. A50, C53, E38)

respiración celular Un proceso en el cual las células usan oxígeno para liberar energía almacenada en las azúcares.

cell wall

A protective outer covering that lies just outside the cell membrane of plant cells. (p. A21)

pared celular Una cubierta exterior protectora que se encuentra justo fuera de la membrana celular de las células vegetales.

central nervous system

The brain and spinal cord. The central nervous system communicates with the rest of the nervous system through electrical signals sent to and from neurons. (p. E104)

sistema nervioso central El cerebro y la médula espinal. El sistema nervioso central se comunica con el resto del sistema nervioso mediante señales eléctricas enviadas hacia y desde las neuronas.

chemical energy

Energy that is stored in the chemical composition of matter. The amount of chemical energy in a substance depends on the types and arrangement of its atoms. When wood or gasoline burns, chemical energy produces heat. The energy used by the cells in your body comes from chemical energy in the foods you eat. (p. A47)

energía química Energía almacenada en la composición química de la materia. La cantidad de energía química en una sustancia depende de los tipos y la disposición de sus átomos. Cuando se quema madera o gasolina, la energía química produce calor. La energía usada por las células en tu cuerpo proviene de la energía química en los alimentos que comes.

chemical reaction

The process by which chemical changes occur. In a chemical reaction, atoms are rearranged, and chemical bonds are broken and formed. (p. A42)

reacción química El proceso mediante el cual ocurren cambios químicos. En una reacción química, se reacomodan átomos y se rompen y se forman enlaces químicos.

childhood

The stage of life after infancy and before the beginning of sexual maturity. (p. E134)

niñez La etapa de la vida después de la infancia y antes del comienzo de la madurez sexual.

chlorophyll (KLAWR-uh-fihl)

A light-absorbing chemical, a pigment, that traps the energy in sunlight and converts it to chemical energy. Found in chloroplasts of plant cells and the cells of other photosynthetic organisms. (p. A48)

clorofila Una sustancia química que absorbe luz, un pigmento, que atrapa la energía de la luz solar y la convierte a energía química. Se encuentra en los cloroplastos de células vegetales y en las células de otros organismos fotosintéticos.

chloroplast (KLAWR-uh-PLAST)

An organelle in a plant cell that contains chlorophyll, a chemical that uses the energy from sunlight to make sugar. (p. A23)

cloroplasto Un organelo en una célula vegetal que contiene clorofila, una sustancia química que usa la energía de la luz solar para producir azúcar.

chromosome

A structure formed when the DNA in the nucleus of a eukaryotic cell condenses before the cell divides. (p. A75)

cromosoma Una estructura formada cuando el ADN en el núcleo de una célula eucariota se condensa antes de que la célula se divida.

circulatory system
The group of organs, consisting of the heart and blood vessels, that circulates blood through the body. (p. E65)

sistema circulatorio El grupo de órganos, que consiste del corazón y los vasos sanguíneos, que hace circular la sangre por el cuerpo.

classification
The systematic grouping of different types of organisms by their shared characteristics.

clasificación La agrupación sistemática de diferentes tipos de organismos en base a las características que comparten.

cloning
The process of using DNA technology to produce an offspring that is genetically identical to its one parent. (p. A154)

clonación El proceso de usar tecnología de ADN para producir una cría que es genéticamente idéntica a su único progenitor.

cnidarian (ny-DAIR-ee-uhn)
An invertebrate animal such as a jellyfish that has a body with radial symmetry, tentacles with stinging cells, and a central internal cavity. (p. C128)

cnidario Un animal invertebrado tal como una medusa que tiene un cuerpo con simetría radial, tentáculos con células urticantes y una cavidad central interna.

commensalism (kuh-MEHN-suh-LIHZ-uhm)
An interaction between two species in which one species benefits without harming the other; a type of symbiosis. (p. D59)

comensalismo Una interacción entre dos especies en la cual una especie se beneficia sin causar daño a la otra; un tipo de simbiosis.

community
All the populations that live and interact with each other in a particular place. The community can live in a place as small as a pond or a park, or it can live in a place as large as a rain forest or the ocean. (p. D48)

comunidad Todas las poblaciones que viven e interactúan entre sí en un lugar. La comunidad puede vivir en un lugar tan pequeño como una laguna o un parque o en un lugar tan grande como un bosque tropical o el océano.

compact bone
The tough, hard outer layer of a bone. (p. E15)

hueso compacto La capa exterior, resistente y dura de un hueso.

competition
The struggle between two or more living things that depend on the same limited resource. (p. D55)

competencia La lucha entre dos o más organismos vivos que dependen del mismo recurso limitado.

competitor
A species characterized by a relatively longer life span, with relatively few offspring, when compared with an opportunist species. (p. B96)

competidor Una especie caracterizada por una vida relativamente larga, con relativamente pocas crías, en comparación con una especie oportunista.

compound
A substance made up of two or more different types of atoms.

compuesto Una sustancia formada por dos o más diferentes tipos de átomos enlazados.

coniferous (koh-NIHF-uhr-uhs)
A term used to describe cone-bearing trees and shrubs that usually keep their leaves or needles during all the seasons of the year; examples are pine, fir, and spruce trees. (p. D32)

conífero Un término usado para describir a los árboles y los arbustos que producen conos o piñas y que generalmente conservan sus hojas o agujas durante todas las estaciones del año; el pino, el abeto y la picea son ejemplos de coníferas.

conservation
The process of saving or protecting a natural resource. (p. D99)

conservación El proceso de salvar o proteger un recurso natural.

consumer
A living thing that gets its energy by eating other living things in a food chain; consumers are also called heterotrophs. (pp. C58, D24)

consumidor Un organismo vivo que obtiene su energía alimentándose de otros organismos vivos en una cadena alimentaria; los consumidores también son llamados heterótrofos.

cooperation
A term used to describe an interaction between two or more living things in which they are said to work together. (p. D57)

cooperación Un término que describe la interacción entre dos o más organismos vivos en la cual se dice que trabajan juntos.

cycle

n. A series of events or actions that repeat themselves regularly; a physical and/or chemical process in which one material continually changes locations and/or forms. Examples include the water cycle, the carbon cycle, and the rock cycle.

v. To move through a repeating series of events or actions.

ciclo Una serie de eventos o acciones que se repiten regularmente; un proceso físico y/o químico en el cual un material cambia continuamente de lugar y/o forma. Ejemplos: el ciclo del agua, el ciclo del carbono y el ciclo de las rocas.

cytokinesis (SY-toh-kuh-NEE-sihs)

The division of a parent cell's cytoplasm following mitosis. (p. A81)

citocinesis La división del citoplasma de la célula madre después de la mitosis.

cytoplasm (SY-tuh-PLAZ-uhm)

A thick, gelatin-like material contained within the cell membrane. Most of the work of the cell is carried out in the cytoplasm. (p. A20)

citoplasma Un material espeso, parecido a la gelatina, contenido dentro de la membrana celular. La mayor parte del trabajo de la célula se realiza en el citoplasma.

D

data

Information gathered by observation or experimentation that can be used in calculating or reasoning. *Data* is a plural word; the singular is *datum.*

datos Información reunida mediante observación o experimentación y que se puede usar para calcular o para razonar.

deciduous (dih-SIHJ-oo-uhs)

A term used to describe trees and shrubs that drop their leaves when winter comes; examples are maple, oak, and birch trees. (p. D33)

caducifolio Un término usado para describir árboles y arbustos que dejan caer sus hojas cuando llega el invierno; el arce, el roble y el abedul son ejemplos de árboles caducifolios.

decomposer

An organism that feeds on and breaks down dead plant or animal matter. (pp. C19, D25)

descomponedor Un organismo que se alimenta de y degrada materia vegetal o animal.

density

A property of matter representing the mass per unit volume.

densidad Una propiedad de la materia que representa la masa por unidad de volumen.

dermis

The inner layer of the skin. (p. E84)

dermis La capa interior de la piel.

dichotomous key (dy-KAHT-uh-muhs)

A series of questions, each with only two answers, that can be used to help identify an organism's genus and species. (p. B56)

clave dicotómica Una serie de preguntas, cada una con solo dos respuestas, que puede usarse para ayudar a identificar el género y especie de un organismo.

diffusion (dih-FYOO-zhuhn)

The tendency of a substance to move from an area of higher concentration to an area of lower concentration. (p. A56)

difusión La tendencia de una sustancia a moverse de un área de mayor concentración a un área de menor concentración.

digestion

The process of breaking down food into usable materials. (p. E46)

digestión El proceso de descomponer el alimento en sustancias utilizables.

digestive system

The structures in the body that work together to transform the energy and materials in food into forms the body can use. (p. E46)

sistema digestivo Las estructuras en el cuerpo que trabajan juntas para transformar la energía y las sustancias en el alimento a formas que el cuerpo puede usar.

diversity

A term used to describe the quality of having many differences; *biodiversity* describes the great variety and many differences found among living things. (p. D80)

diversidad Un término usado para describir la cualidad de tener muchas diferencias; la biodiversidad describe la gran variedad y las muchas diferencias encontradas entre organismos vivos.

DNA

The genetic material found in all living cells that contains the information needed for an organism to grow, maintain itself, and reproduce. Deoxyribonucleic acid (dee-AHK-see-RY-boh-noo-KLEE-ihk). (p. A74)

ADN El material genético que se encuentra en todas las céulas vivas y que contiene la información necesaria para que un organismo crezca, se mantenga a sí mismo y se reproduzca. Ácido desoxiribunucleico.

domain

One of three divisions in a classification system based on different types of cells. The six kingdoms of living things are grouped into three domains: Archaea, Bacteria, and Eukarya. (p. B61)

dominio Una de las tres divisiones en un sistema de clasificación basado en los diferentes tipos de células. Los seis reinos de los organismos vivos esta agrupados en tres dominios: Archaea, Bacteria y Eukarya.

dominant

A term that describes the allele that determines the phenotype of an individual organism when two different copies are present in the genotype. (p. A107)

dominante Un término que describe al alelo que determina el fenotipo de un organismo cuando están presentes dos copias diferentes en el genotipo.

E

echinoderm

An invertebrate sea animal with a spiny skeleton, a water vascular system, and tube feet. (p. C139)

equinodermo Un animal invertebrado marino con esqueleto espinoso, sistema vascular acuífero y pies ambulacrales.

ecology

The scientific study of how living things interact with each other and their environment. (p. D9)

ecología El estudio científico de cómo interactúan los organismos vivos entre sí y con su medio ambiente.

ecosystem

All the living and nonliving things that interact in a particular environment. An ecosystem can be as small as a meadow or a swamp, or as large as a forest or a desert. (p. D9)

ecosistema Todos los organismos vivos y las cosas que interactúan en un medio ambiente específico. Un ecosistema puede ser tan pequeño como un prado o un pantano, o tan grande como un bosque o un desierto.

ectotherm

An animal whose body temperature changes with environmental conditions. (p. C170)

poiquilotermo o poiquilotérmico Un animal cuya temperatura corporal cambia con las condiciones del medio ambiente.

egg

A female reproductive cell (gamete) that forms in the reproductive organs of a female and has just a single copy of the genetic material of the parent. (p. A118)

óvulo Una célula reproductiva femenina (gameto) que se forma en los órganos reproductivos de una hembra y tiene una sola copia del material genético de la madre.

element

A substance that cannot be broken down into a simpler substance by ordinary chemical changes. An element consists of atoms of only one type.

elemento Una sustancia que no puede descomponerse en otra sustancia más simple por medio de cambios químicos normales. Un elemento consta de átomos de un solo tipo.

embryo (EHM-bree-OH)

A multicellular organism, plant or animal, in its earliest stages of development. (pp. C98, E121)

embrión Una planta o un animal en su estadio mas temprano de desarrollo.

emigration

In population studies, the movement of individuals out of an ecosystem. (p. B91)

emigración En estudios poblacionales, el movimiento de individuos fuera de un ecosistema.

endocrine system

A group of organs called glands and the hormones they produce that help regulate conditions inside the body. (p. E110)

sistema endocrino Un grupo de órganos llamados glándulas y las hormonas que producen que ayudan a regular las condiciones dentro del cuerpo.

endoskeleton

An internal support system; such a skeleton made of bone tissue is a distinguishing characteristic of vertebrate animals. (p. C157)

endoesqueleto Un sistema de soporte interno, como un esqueleto formado de tejido óseo es una característica distintiva de los animales vertebrados.

endotherm

An animal that maintains a constant body temperature. (p. C174)

homeotermo o endotermo Un animal que mantiene una temperatura corporal constante.

energy

The ability to do work or to cause a change. For example, the energy of a moving bowling ball knocks over pins; energy from food allows animals to move and to grow; and energy from the Sun heats Earth's surface and atmosphere, which causes air to move.

energía La capacidad para trabajar o causar un cambio. Por ejemplo, la energía de una bola de boliche en movimiento tumba los pinos; la energía proveniente de su alimento permite a los animales moverse y crecer; la energía del Sol calienta la superficie y la atmósfera de la Tierra, lo que ocasiona que el aire se mueva.

energy pyramid

A model used to show the amount of energy available to living things in an ecosystem. (p. D28)

pirámide de energía Un modelo usado para mostrar la cantidad de energía disponible para organismos vivos en un ecosistema.

environment

Everything that surrounds a living thing. An environment is made up of both living and nonliving factors. (p. xxxv)

medio ambiente Todo lo que rodea a un organismo vivo. Un medio ambiente está compuesto de factores vivos y factores sin vida.

epidermis

The outer layer of the skin. (p. E84)

epidermis La capa exterior de la piel.

estuary

The lower end of a river where it meets the ocean and fresh and salt waters mix. (p. D36)

estuario La parte baja de un río donde desemboca en el océano y donde el agua dulce del río se mezcla con el agua salada del mar.

eukaryotic cell (yoo-KAR-ee-AHT-ihk)

A cell in which the genetic material is enclosed within a nucleus, surrounded by its own membrane. (p. A20)

célula eucariota Una célula en la cual el material genético esta dentro de un núcleo, rodeado por su propia membrana.

evolution

The process through which species change over time; can refer to the changes in a particular population or to the formation and extinction of species over the course of Earth's history. (p. B17)

evolución El proceso mediante el cual las especies cambian con el tiempo; puede referirse a cambios en una población en particular o a la formación y extinción de especies en el curso de la historia de la Tierra.

exoskeleton

The strong, flexible outer covering of some invertebrate animals, such as arthropods. (p. C143)

exoesqueleto La cubierta exterior fuerte y flexible de algunos animales invertebrados, como los artrópodos.

experiment

An organized procedure to study something under controlled conditions. (p. xl)

experimento Un procedimiento organizado para estudiar algo bajo condiciones controladas.

extinction

The permanent disappearance of a species. (p. xxxvii)

extinción La desaparición permanente de una especie.

F

fermentation

A chemical process by which cells release energy from sugar when no oxygen is present. (p. A52)

fermentación Un proceso químico mediante el cual las células liberan energía del azúcar cuando no hay oxígeno presente.

fertilization

Part of the process of sexual reproduction in which a male reproductive cell and a female reproductive cell combine to make a new cell that can develop into a new organism. (pp. A118, C48, E121)

fertilización El proceso mediante el cual una célula reproductiva masculina y una célula reproductiva femenina se combinan para formar una nueva célula que puede convertirse en un organismo nuevo.

flower

The reproductive structure of an angiosperm, containing male and female parts. (p. C108)

flor La estructura reproductiva de una angiosperma, contiene las partes masculinas y femeninas.

food chain

A model used to show the feeding relationship between a single producer and a chain of consumers in an ecosystem. In a typical food chain, a plant is the producer that is eaten by a consumer, such as an insect; then the insect is eaten by a second consumer, such as a bird. (p. D26)

cadena alimentaria Un modelo usado para mostrar la relación de ingestión entre un solo productor y una cadena de consumidores en un ecosistema. En una cadena alimentaria típica, una planta es la productora que es ingerida por un consumidor como un insecto, y luego el insecto es ingerido por un segundo consumidor como un pájaro.

food web

A model used to show a feeding relationship in which many food chains overlap in an ecosystem. (p. D26)

red trófica Un modelo usado para mostrar una relación de consumo en la cual muchas cadenas alimentarias se empalman en un ecosistema.

fossil

The imprint or hardened remains of a plant or animal that lived long ago. (p. B9)

fósil La huella o los restos endurecidos de una planta o un animal que vivió hace mucho tiempo.

fruit

The ripened ovary of a flowering plant that contains the seeds. (p. C108)

fruta El ovario maduro de una planta floreciente que contiene las semillas.

Fungi (FUHN-jy)

Part of a classification system that divides all living things into six kingdoms. Kingdom Fungi includes multicellular mushrooms and molds and single-celled yeasts. (p. B63)

Fungi Parte de un sistema de clasificación que divide a todos los organismos vivos en seis reinos. El reino Fungi incluye a los hongos multicelulares, a los mohos y a las levaduras unicelulares.

G

gamete

A sperm or egg cell, containing half the usual number of chromosomes of an organism (one chromosome from each pair), which is found only in the reproductive organs of a plant or animal. (p. A118)

gameto Un óvulo o un espermatozoide, que contiene la mitad del número usual de cromosomas de un organismo (un cromosoma de cada par), que se encuentra sólo en los órganos reproductivos de una planta o de un animal.

gene

The basic unit of heredity that consists of a segment of DNA on a chromosome. (pp. A102, B33)

gen La unidad básica de herencia que consiste en un segmento de ADN en un cromosoma.

genetic engineering

The scientific process in which DNA is separated from an organism, changed, and then reinserted into the same or a different organism. (p. A151)

ingeniería genética El proceso científico en el cual se extrae el ADN de un organismo, se modifica y luego se reinserta en el mismo organismo o en uno diferente.

genetic material

The nucleic acid DNA that is present in all living cells and contains the information needed for a cell's growth, maintenance, and reproduction.

material genético El ácido nucleico ADN, ue esta presente en todas las células vivas y que contiene la información necesaria para el crecimiento, el mantenimiento y la reproducción celular.

genome (JEE-nohm)

All the DNA of an organism, including its genes; the genetic material of an organism. (p. A154)

genoma Todo el ADN de un organismo, incluyendo sus genes; el material genético de un organismo.

genotype (JEHN-uh-TYP)

The genetic makeup of an organism; all the genes that an organism has. (p. A106)

genotipo La estructura genética de un organismo; todos los genes que tiene un organismo.

genus

The first part of a binomial name that groups together closely related species. The genus *Felis* includes all species of small cats. (p. B52)

género La primera parte de un nombre biológico que agrupa a especies muy relacionadas entre sí. El género Felis incluye a todas las especies de gatos pequeños.

germination (JUR-muh-NAY-shuhn)

The beginning of growth of a new plant from a spore or a seed. (p. C99)

germinación El inicio del crecimiento de una nueva planta a partir de una espora o una semilla.

gestation

In mammals, the period of time spent by a developing offspring inside the mother's body. (p. C186)

gestación En los mamíferos, el periodo de tiempo que pasa una cría en desarrollo dentro del cuerpo de la madre.

gill
A respiratory organ that filters oxgen dissolved in water. (p. C137)

branquia Un órgano respiratorio que filtra oxígeno disuelto en el agua.

gland
An organ in the body that produces a specific substance, such as a hormone. (p. E112)

glándula Un órgano en el cuerpo que produce una sustancia específica, como una hormona.

glucose
A sugar molecule that is a major energy source for most cells, produced by the process of photosynthesis. (p. A47)

glucosa Una molécula de azúcar que es la principal fuente de energía para la mayoría de las células, producida mediante el proceso de fotosíntesis.

gymnosperm (JIHM-nuh-SPURM)
A plant that produces seeds that are not enclosed in flowers or fruit. (p. C102)

Gimnosperma Una planta que produce semillas que no están dentro de las flores o las frutas.

H

habitat
The natural environment in which a living thing gets all that it needs to live; examples include a desert, a coral reef, and a freshwater lake. (p. D46)

hábitat El medio ambiente natural en el cual un organismo vivo consigue todo lo que requiere para vivir; ejemplos incluyen un desierto, un arrecife coralino y un lago de agua dulce.

heredity
The passing of genes from parents to offspring; the genes are expressed in the traits of the offspring. (p. A102)

herencia La transferencia de genes de los progenitores a las crías; los genes se expresan en los rasgos de las crías.

heterotroph (HEHT-uhr-uh-TRAWF)
An organism that consumes other organisms to get energy. (p. C58)

heterótrofo Un organismo que consume a otros organismos para obtener energía.

hibernation
A sleeplike state in which certain animals spend the winter. Hibernation reduces an animal's need for food and helps protect it from cold. (p. C64)

hibernación Un estado parecido al de sueño en el cual ciertos animales pasan el invierno. La hibernación reduce la necesidad de alimento de un animal y le ayuda a protegerse del frío.

homeostasis (HOH-mee-oh-STAY-sihs)
The process by which an organism or cell maintains the internal conditions needed for health and functioning, regardless of outside conditions. (p. E12)

homeostasis El proceso mediante el cual un organismo o una célula mantienen las condiciones internas necesarias para la salud y el funcionamiento, independientemente de las condiciones externas.

hormone
A chemical that is made in one organ and travels through the blood to another organ. (p. E111)

hormona Una sustancia química que se produce en un órgano y viaja por la sangre a otro órgano.

host cell
A cell that a virus infects and uses to make copies of itself. (p. C26)

célula hospedera Una célula que un virus infecta y usa para hacer copias de sí mismo.

hyphae
Threadlike tubes that form the structural parts of the body of a fungus. *Hyphae* is a plural word; the singular is *hypha.* (p. C67)

hifas Los tubos, similares a hilos, que forman las partes estructurales del cuerpo de un hongo.

hypothesis
A tentative explanation for an observation or phenomenon. A hypothesis is used to make tentative predictions. (p. xl)

hipótesis Una explicación provisional de una observación o de un fenómeno. Una hipótesis se usa para hacer predicciones que se pueden probar.

I, J, K

immigration
In population studies, the movement of an organism into a range inhabited by individuals of the same species. (p. B91)

inmigración En estudios poblacionales, el movimiento de un organismo hacia un territorio habitado por individuos de la misma especie.

immune system
A group of organs that provides protection against disease-causing agents. (p. E75)

sistema immune o inmunológico Un grupo de órganos que provee protección contra agentes que causan enfermedades.

immunity
Resistance to a disease. Immunity can result from antibodies formed in the body during a previous attack of the same illness. (p. E80)

inmunidad La resistencia a una enfermedad. La inmunidad puede resultar de anticuerpos formados en el cuerpo durante un ataque previo de la misma enfermedad.

incubation
The process of keeping eggs warm by bodily heat until they hatch. (p. C179)

incubación El proceso de mantener huevos cálidos por medio de calor corporal hasta que eclosionen.

infancy
The stage of life that begins at birth and ends when a baby begins to walk. (p. E134)

infancia La etapa de la vida que inicia al nacer y termina cuando el bebe empieza a caminar.

insect
An arthropod with three body segments, six legs, two antennae, and compound eyes. (p. C145)

insecto Un artrópodo con tres segmentos corporales, seis patas, dos antenas y ojos compuestos.

integumentary system (ihn-TEHG-yu-MEHN-tuh-ree)
The body system that includes the skin and its associated structures. (p. E83)

sistema tegumentario El sistema corporal que incluye a la piel y a sus estructuras asociadas.

interaction
The condition of acting or having an influence upon something. Living things in an ecosystem interact with both the living and nonliving parts of their environment. (p. xxxv)

interacción La condición de actuar o influir sobre algo. Los organismos vivos en un ecosistema interactúan con las partes vivas y las partes sin vida de su medio ambiente.

interphase
The period in the cell cycle in which a cell grows, maintains itself, and prepares for division. (p. A81)

interfase El período en el ciclo celular en el cual una célula crece, se mantiene y se prepara para la división.

invertebrate
An animal that has no backbone. (p. C123)

invertebrado Un animal que no tiene columna vertebral.

involuntary muscle
A muscle that moves without conscious control. (p. E24)

músculo involuntario Un músculo que se mueve sin control consciente.

L

larva
A free-living early form of a developing organism that is very different from its adult form. (p. C126)

larva Una etapa temprana de vida libre de un organismo en desarrollo que es muy diferente a su etapa adulta.

law
In science, a rule or principle describing a physical relationship that always works in the same way under the same conditions. The law of conservation of energy is an example.

ley En las ciencias, una regla o un principio que describe una relación física que siempre funciona de la misma manera bajo las mismas condiciones. La ley de la conservación de la energía es un ejemplo.

lichen (LY-kuhn)
An organism that results from a close association between single-celled algae and fungi. (p. C70)

liquen Un organismo que resulta de una asociación cercana entre algas unicelulares y hongos.

limiting factor
A factor or condition that prevents the continuing growth of a population in an ecosystem. (pp. B92, D64)

factor limitante Un factor o una condición que impide el crecimiento continuo de una población en un ecosistema.

lipid
A type of molecule made up of subunits of fatty acids. Lipids are found in the fats, oils, and waxes used for structure and to store energy. (p. A43)

lípido Un tipo de molécula compuesta de unidades de ácidos grasos. Los lípidos se encuentran en las grasas, los aceites y las ceras usadas como materiales estructurales y para almacenar energía.

lung
A respiratory organ that absorbs oxygen from the air. (p. C137)

pulmón Un órgano respiratorio que absorbe oxígeno del aire.

M

mammal
A warm-blooded vertebrate animal whose young feed on milk produced by the mother's mammary glands. (p. C183)

mamífero Un animal vertebrado de sangre caliente cuyas crías se alimentan de leche producida por las glándulas mamarias de la madre.

mass
A measure of how much matter an object is made of.

masa Una medida de la cantidad de materia de la que está compuesto un objeto.

mass extinction
One of several periods in Earth's history when large numbers of species became extinct at nearly the same time. (p. B14)

extinción masiva Uno de varios períodos en la historia de la Tierra cuando grandes números de especies se extinguieron casi al mismo tiempo.

matter
Anything that has mass and volume. Matter exists ordinarily as a solid, a liquid, or a gas.

materia Todo lo que tiene masa y volumen. Generalmente la materia existe como sólido, líquido o gas.

meiosis (my-OH-sihs)
A part of sexual reproduction in which cells divide to form sperm cells in a male and egg cells in a female. Meiosis occurs only in reproductive cells. (pp. A119, C48)

meiosis Una parte de la reproducción sexual en la cual las células se dividen para formar espermatozoides en los machos y óvulos en las hembras. La meiosis sólo ocurre en las células reproductivas.

menstruation
A period of about five days during which blood and tissue exit the body through the vagina. (p. E119)

menstruación Un período de aproximadamente cinco días durante el cual salen del cuerpo sangre y tejido por la vagina.

metamorphosis
The transformation of an animal from its larval form into its adult form. (p. C146)

metamorfosis La transformación de un animal de su forma larvaria a su forma adulta.

microorganism
A very small organism that can be seen only with a microscope. Bacteria are examples of microorganisms. (pp. C10, E148)

microorganismo Un organismo muy pequeño que solamente puede verse con un microscopio. Las bacterias son ejemplos de microorganismos.

microscope
An instrument that uses glass lenses to magnify an object. (p. A12)

microscopio Un instrumento que usa lentes de vidrio para magnificar un objeto.

migration
The movement of animals from one region to another in response to changes in the seasons or the environment. (p. C64)

migración El movimiento de animales de una región a otra en respuesta a cambios en las estaciones o en el medio ambiente.

mitochondria (MY-tuh-KAWN-dree-uh)
Organelles that release energy by using oxygen to break down sugars. (p. A23)

mitocondrias Organelos que liberan energía usando oxígeno para romper los azúcares.

mitosis
The phase in the cell cycle during which the nucleus divides. (p. A81)

mitosis La fase en el ciclo celular durante la cual se divide el núcleo.

mobile
Able to move from place to place. (p. C130)

móvil Capaz de moverse de un lugar a otro.

molecule
A group of atoms that are held together by covalent bonds so that they move as a single unit.

molécula Un grupo de átomos que están unidos mediante enlaces covalentes de tal manera que se mueven como una sola unidad.

mollusk
An invertebrate animal with a soft body, a muscular foot, and a mantle. Many mollusks have a hard outer shell. (p. C136)

molusco Un animal invertebrado con cuerpo blando, un pie muscular y un manto. Muchos moluscos tienen una concha exterior dura.

molting
The process of an arthropod shedding its exoskeleton to allow for growth. (p. C143)

muda El proceso mediante el cual un artrópodo se despoja de su exoesqueleto para poder crecer.

multicellular
A term used to describe an organism that is made up of many cells. (p. A11)

multicelular Un término usado para describir a un organismo que esta formado por muchas células.

multicellular organism
An organism that is made up of many cells. (p. B13)

organismo multicelular Un organismo compuesto de muchas células.

muscular system
The muscles of the body that, together with the skeletal system, function to produce movement. (p. E23)

sistema muscular Los músculos del cuerpo que, junto con el sistema óseo, sirven para producir movimiento.

mutation
Any change made to DNA. (p. A145)

mutación Cualquier cambio hecho al ADN.

mutualism (MYOO-choo-uh-lihz-uhm)
An interaction between two species in which both benefit; a type of symbiosis. (p. D58)

mutualismo Una interacción entre dos especies en la cual ambas se benefician; un tipo de simbiosis.

N

natural resource
Any type of matter or energy from Earth's environment that humans use to meet their needs. (p. D84)

recurso natural Cualquier tipo de materia o energía del medio ambiente de la Tierra que usan los humanos para satisfacer sus necesidades.

natural selection
The process through which members of a species that are best suited to their environment survive and reproduce at a higher rate than other members of the species. (p. B21)

selección natural El proceso mediante el cual los miembros de una especie que están mejor adecuados a su medio ambiente sobreviven y se reproducen a una tasa más alta que otros miembros de la especie.

neuron
A nerve cell. (p. E105)

neurona Una célula nerviosa.

niche (nihch)
The role a living thing plays in its habitat. A plant is a food producer, whereas an insect both consumes food as well as provides food for other consumers. (p. D47)

nicho El papel que juega un organismo vivo en su hábitat. Una planta es un productor de alimento mientras que un insecto consume alimento y a la vez sirve de alimento a otros consumidores.

nitrogen cycle
The continuous movement of nitrogen through Earth, its atmosphere, and the living things on Earth. (p. D19)

ciclo del nitrógeno El movimiento continuo de nitrógeno por la Tierra, su atmósfera y los organismos vivos de la Tierra.

nucleic acid (noo-KLEE-ihk)
A type of molecule, made up of subunits of nucleotides, that is part of the genetic material of a cell and is needed to make proteins. DNA and RNA are nucleic acids. (p. A43)

ácido nucleico Un tipo de molécula, compuesto de unidades de nucleótidos, que es parte del material genético de una célula y se necesita para producir proteínas. El ADN y el ARN son ácidos nucleicos.

nucleus (NOO-klee-uhs)
The structure in a eukaryotic cell that contains the genetic material a cell needs to reproduce and function. (p. A20)

núcleo La estructura en una célula eucariota que contiene el material genético que la célula necesita para reproducirse y funcionar.

nutrient (NOO-tree-uhnt)
A substance that an organism needs to live. Examples include water, minerals, and materials that come from the breakdown of food particles. (pp. D8, E45)

nutriente Una sustancia que un organismo necesita para vivir. Ejemplos incluyen agua, minerales y sustancias que provienen de la descomposición de partículas de alimento.

nutrition
The study of the materials that nourish the body. (p. E140)

nutrición El estudio de las sustancias que dan sustento al cuerpo.

O

offspring
The new organisms produced by one or two parent organisms. (p. A93)

crías Los nuevos organismos producidos por uno o dos organismos progenitores.

opportunist
A species characterized by a relatively short life span, with relatively large quantities of offspring, as compared with a competitor species. (p. B95)

oportunista Una especie caracterizada por una vida relativamente corta, que produce relativamente grandes cantidades de crías, en comparación con una especie competidora.

organ
A structure in a plant or an animal that is made up of different tissues working together to perform a particular function. (pp. A30, C44, E11)

órgano Una estructura en una planta o en un animal compuesta de diferentes tejidos que trabajan juntos para realizar una función determinada.

organelle (AWR-guh-NEHL)
A structure in a cell that is enclosed by a membrane and that performs a particular function. (p. A20)

organelo Una estructura en una célula, envuelta en una membrana, que realiza una función determinada.

organism
An individual living thing, made up of one or many cells, that is capable of growing and reproducing. (p. A9)

organismo Un individuo vivo, compuesto de una o muchas células, que es capaz de crecer y reproducirse.

organ system
A group of organs that together perform a function that helps the body meet its needs for energy and materials. (p. E12)

sistema de órganos Un grupo de órganos que juntos realizan una función que ayuda al cuerpo a satisfacer sus necesidades energéticas y de materiales.

osmosis (ahz-MOH-sihs)
The movement of water through a membrane from an area of higher concentration to an area of lower concentration. (p. A59)

osmosis El movimiento de agua a través de una membrana desde un área de mayor concentración hacia un área de menor concentración.

P, Q

parasite
An organism that absorbs nutrients from the body of another organism, often harming it in the process. (p. C19)

parásito Un organismo que absorbe nutrientes del cuerpo de otro organismo, a menudo causándole daño en el proceso.

parasitism (PAR-uh-suh-TIHZ-uhm)
A relationship between two species in which one species is harmed while the other benefits; a type of symbiosis. (p. D59)

parasitismo Una relación entre dos especies en la cual una especie es perjudicada mientras que la otra se beneficia; un tipo de simbiosis.

parent
An organism that produces a new organism or organisms similar to or related to itself. (p. A93)

progenitor Un organismo que produce un nuevo organismo u organismos parecidos a o relacionados a él.

passive transport
The movement of materials through a membrane without any input of energy. (p. A58)

transporte pasivo El movimiento de sustancias a través de una membrana sin aporte de energía.

pathogen
An agent that causes disease. (p. E74)

patógeno Un agente que causa una enfermedad.

pedigree
A chart that shows family relationships, including two or more generations. (p. A147)

pedigrí Un diagrama de las relaciones de dos o más generaciones de una familia.

percentage
A ratio that states the number of times an outcome is likely to occur out of a possible 100 times. (p. A112)

porcentaje Una razón que establece el número de veces que es probable que ocurra un resultado en 100 veces.

peripheral nervous system
The part of the nervous system that lies outside the brain and spinal cord. (p. E106)

sistema nervioso periférico La parte del sistema nervioso que se encuentra fuera del cerebro y la médula espinal.

peristalsis (PEHR-ih-STAWL-sihs)
Wavelike contractions of smooth muscles in the organs of the digestive tract. The contractions move food through the digestive system. (p. E46)

peristalsis Contracciones ondulares de músculos lisos en los órganos del tracto digestivo. Las contracciones mueven el alimento por el sistema digestivo.

phenotype
The observable characteristics or traits of an organism. (p. A106)

fenotipo Las características o rasgos visibles de un organismo.

photosynthesis (FOH-toh-SIHN-thih-sihs)
The process by which green plants and other producers use simple compounds and energy from light to make sugar, an energy-rich compound. (pp. A48, C52, D23)

fotosíntesis El proceso mediante el cual las plantas verdes y otros productores usan compuestos simples y energía de la luz para producir azúcares, compuestos ricos en energía.

pioneer species
The first species to move into a lifeless environment. Plants like mosses are typical pioneer species on land. (p. D66)

especie pionera La primera especie que ocupa un medio ambiente sin vida. Las plantas como los musgos son típicas especies pioneras terrestres.

placenta
An organ that transports materials between a pregnant female mammal and the offspring developing inside her body. (p. C186)

placenta Un órgano que transporta sustancias entre un mamífero hembra preñado y la cría que se está desarrollando dentro de su cuerpo.

plankton
Mostly microscopic organisms that drift in great numbers through bodies of water. (p. C33)

plancton Organismos, en su mayoría microscópicos, que se mueven a la deriva en grandes números por cuerpos de agua.

Plantae (PLAN-tee)
Part of a classification system that divides all living things into six kingdoms. Kingdom Plantae includes multicellular organisms, such as trees, grass, and moss, that are capable of photosynthesis, capturing energy from the Sun. (p. B63)

Plantae Parte de un sistema de clasificación que divide a todos los organismos vivos en seis reinos. El reino Plantae incluye a organismos multicelulares, como árboles, pasto y musgo, que son capaces de fotosintetizar, capturando la energía del Sol.

pollen
Tiny multicellular grains that contain the undeveloped sperm cells of a plant. (p. C100)

polen Los diminutos granos multicelulares que contienen las células espermáticas sin desarrollar de una planta.

pollution
The release of harmful substances into the air, water, or land. (pp. B104, D91)

contaminación La descarga de sustancias nocivas al aire, alagua o a la tierra.

population
A group of organisms of the same species that live in the same area. For example, a desert will have populations of different species of lizards and cactus plants. (p. D46)

población Un grupo de organismos de la misma especie que viven en la misma área. Por ejemplo, un desierto tendrá poblaciones de distintas especies de lagartijas y de cactus.

population density

A measure of the number of organisms that live in a given area. The population density of a city may be given as the number of people living in a square kilometer. (pp. B85, D86)

densidad de población Una medida de la cantidad de organismos que viven un área dada. La densidad de población de una ciudad puede expresarse como el número de personas que viven en un kilómetro cuadrado.

population dynamics

The study of the changes in the number of individuals in a population and the factors that affect those changes. (p. B82)

dinámica de población El estudio de los cambios en el número de individuos en una población y los factores que afectan a estos cambios.

predator

An animal that hunts other animals and eats them. (pp. C63, D55)

predador Un animal que caza otros animales y se los come.

prey

An animal that other animals hunt and eat. (pp. C63, D55)

presa Un animal que otros animales cazan y se comen.

probability

The likelihood or chance that a specific outcome will occur out of a total number of outcomes. (p. A112)

probabilidad La posibilidad de que ocurra un resultado específico en un número total de resultados.

prokaryotic cell (proh-KAR-ee-AWT-ihk)

A cell that lacks a nucleus and other organelles, with DNA that is not organized into chromosomes. (p. A20)

célula procariota Una célula que carece de núcleo y otros organelos, con ADN que no esta organizado en cromosomas.

producer

An organism that captures energy from sunlight and transforms it into chemical energy that is stored in energy-rich carbon compounds. Producers are a source of food for other organisms. (pp. C19, D23)

productor Un organismo que capta energía de la luz solar y la transforma a energía química que se almacena en compuestos de carbono ricos en energía. Los productores son una fuente de alimento para otros organismos.

protein

One of many types of molecules made up of chains of amino acid subunits. Proteins control the chemical activity of a cell and support growth and repair. (p. A43)

proteína Uno de muchos tipos de moléculas formadas por cadenas de aminoácidos. Las proteínas controlan la actividad química de una célula y sustentan el crecimiento y la reparación.

Protista (proh-TIHS-tuh)

Part of a classification system that divides all living things into six kingdoms. Kingdom Protista includes mostly single-celled organisms with cells similar to those of the Plantae, Animalia, and Fungi kingdoms. (p. B63)

Protista Parte de un sistema de clasificación que divide a todos los organismos vivos en seis reinos. El reino Protista incluye principalmente a organismos unicelulares con células parecidas a las de los reinos Plantae, Animalia y Fungi.

protozoa

Animal-like protists that eat other organisms or decaying parts of other organisms. *Protozoa* is a plural word; the singular is *protozoan*. (p. C34)

protozoarios Protistas parecidos a los animales que comen otros organismos o partes en descomposición de otros organismos.

Punnett square

A chart used to show all the ways genes from two parents can combine and be passed to offspring; used to predict all genotypes that are possible. (p. A110)

cuadro de Punnett Una tabla que se usa para mostrar todas las formas en que los genes de dos progenitores pueden combinarse y pasarse a la crías; se usa para predecir todos los genotipos que son posibles.

R

ratio

A comparison between two quantities, often written with a colon, as 3 : 4. (p. A112)

razón Una comparación entre dos cantidades, a menudo se escribe con dos puntos, como 3 : 4.

recessive

A term that describes an allele that is not expressed when combined with a dominant form of the gene. (p. A107)

recesivo Un término que describe un alelo que no se expresa cuando se combina con una forma dominante del gen.

red blood cell

A type of blood cell that picks up oxygen in the lungs and delivers it to cells throughout the body. (p. E67)

glóbulos rojos Un tipo de célula sanguínea que toma oxígeno en los pulmones y lo transporta a células en todo el cuerpo.

regeneration

In some organisms, the process by which certain cells produce new tissue growth at the site of a wound or lost limb; also a form of asexual reproduction. (p. A90)

regeneración En algunos organismos, el proceso mediante el cual ciertas células producen crecimiento de tejido nuevo en el sitio de una herida o de una extremidad perdida; también un tipo de reproducción asexual.

replication

The process by which DNA is copied before it condenses into chromosomes. Replication takes place before a cell divides. (p. A137)

replicación El proceso mediante el cual el ADN se copia antes de condensarse en los cromosomas. La replicación se realiza antes de que una célula se divida.

reptile

A cold-blooded vertebrate that has skin covered with scales or horny plates and has lungs. (p. C168)

reptil Un vertebrado de sangre fría que tiene la piel cubierta de escamas o placas callosas y que tiene pulmones.

resistance

The ability of an organism to protect itself from a disease or the effects of a substance. (p. E153)

resistencia La habilidad de un organismo para protegerse de una enfermedad o de los efectos de una sustancia.

respiratory system

A system that interacts with the environment and with other body systems to bring oxygen to the body and remove carbon dioxide. (p. E37)

sistema respiratorio Un sistema que interactúa con el medio ambiente y con otros sistemas corporales para traer oxígeno al cuerpo y eliminar dióxido de carbono.

RNA

A molecule that carries genetic information from DNA to a ribosome, where the genetic information is used to bring together amino acids to form a protein. Ribonucleic acid (RY-boh-noo-KLEE-ihk). (p. A138)

ARN Una molécula que lleva información genética del ADN al ribosoma, donde la información genética se usa para unir aminoácidos para formar una proteína. Ácido ribonucleico.

S

scale

One of the thin, small, overlapping plates that cover most fish and reptiles and some other animals. (p. C161)

escama Una de las pequeñas y delgadas placas traslapadas que cubren a la mayoría de los peces y reptiles y algunos otros animales.

seed

A plant embryo that is enclosed in a protective coating and has its own source of nutrients. (p. C100)

semilla El embrión de una planta que esta dentro de una cubierta protectora y que tiene su propia fuente de nutrientes.

selective breeding

The process of breeding plants and animals with specific traits to produce offspring that have these traits. (p. A151)

reproducción selectiva El proceso de reproducir plantas y animales con rasgos específicos para producir crías que tengan estos rasgos.

sessile (SEHS-eel)

The quality of being attached to one spot; not free-moving. (p. C125)

sésil La cualidad de estar sujeto a un punto; sin libre movimiento.

sexual reproduction

A type of reproduction in which male and female reproductive cells combine to form offspring with genetic material from both cells. (pp. A102, C48)

reproducción sexual Un tipo de reproducción en el cual se combinan las células reproductivas femeninas y masculinas para formar una cría con material genético de ambas células.

skeletal muscle

A muscle that attaches to the skeleton. (p. E24)

músculo esquelético Un músculo que está sujeto al esqueleto.

skeletal system

The framework of bones that supports the body, protects internal organs, and anchors all the body's movement. (p. E14)

sistema óseo El armazón de huesos que sostiene al cuerpo, protege a los órganos internos y sirve de ancla para todo el movimiento del cuerpo.

smooth muscle
Muscle that performs involuntary movement and is found inside certain organs, such as the stomach. (p. E24)

músculo liso Músculos que realizan movimiento involuntario y se encuentran dentro de ciertos órganos, como el estómago.

specialization
The specific organization of a cell and its structure that allows it to perform a specific function. (p. A28)

especialización La organización específica de una célula y de su estructura que le permite realizar una función específica.

speciation
The evolution of a new species from an existing species. (p. B24)

especiación La evolución de una nueva especie a partir de una especie existente.

species
A group of living things that are so closely related that they can breed with one another and produce offspring that can breed as well. (p. xxxvii)

especie Un grupo de organismos que están tan estrechamente relacionados que pueden aparearse entre sí y producir crías que también pueden aparearse.

sperm
A male reproductive cell (gamete) that forms in the reproductive organs of a male and has just a single copy of the genetic material of the parent. (p. A118)

espermatozoide Una célula reproductiva masculina (gameto) que se forma en los órganos reproductivos de un macho y tiene una sola copia del material genético del progenitor.

sponge
A simple multicellular invertebrate animal that lives attached to one place and filters food from water. (p. C125)

esponja Un animal invertebrado multicelular simple que vive sujeto a un lugar y filtra su alimento del agua.

spongy bone
Strong, lightweight tissue inside a bone. (p. E15)

hueso esponjoso Tejido fuerte y de peso ligero dentro de un hueso.

spore
A single reproductive cell that can grow into a multicellular organism. (p. C67)

espora Una célula reproductiva individual que puede convertirse en un organismo multicelular.

stimulus
Something that causes a response in an organism or a part of the body. (pp. C55, E102)

estímulo Algo que causa una respuesta en un organismo o en una parte del cuerpo.

succession (suhk-SEHSH-uhn)
A natural process that involves a gradual change in the plant and animal communities that live in an area. (p. D66)

sucesión Un proceso natural que involucra un cambio gradual en las comunidades de plantas y animales que viven en un área.

sustainable
A term that describes the managing of certain natural resources so that they are not harmed or used up. Examples include maintaining clean groundwater and protecting top soil from erosion. (p. D102)

sostenible Un término que describe el manejo de ciertos recursos naturales para que no se deterioren o se terminen. Ejemplos incluyen mantener limpia el agua subterránea y proteger de la erosión a la capa superficial del suelo.

symbiosis (SIHM-bee-OH-sihs)
The interaction between individuals from two different species that live closely together. (p. D58)

simbiosis La interacción entre individuos de dos especies distintas que viven en proximidad.

system
A group of objects or phenomena that interact. A system can be as simple as a rope, a pulley, and a mass. It also can be as complex as the interaction of energy and matter in the four parts of the Earth system.

sistema Un grupo de objetos o fenómenos que interactúan. Un sistema puede ser algo tan sencillo como una cuerda, una polea y una masa. También puede ser algo tan complejo como la interacción de la energía y la materia en las cuatro partes del sistema de la Tierra.

T

taxonomy
The science of classifying and naming organisms.
(p. B44)

> **taxonomía** La ciencia de clasificar y ponerle nombre a los organismos.

technology
The use of scientific knowledge to solve problems or engineer new products, tools, or processes.

> **tecnología** El uso de conocimientos científicos para resolver problemas o para diseñar nuevos productos, herramientas o procesos.

tentacle
A long, slender, flexible extension of the body of certain animals, such as jellyfish. Tentacles are used to touch, move, or hold. (p. C128)

> **tentáculo** Una extensión larga, delgada y flexible del cuerpo de ciertos animales, como las medusas. Los tentáculos se usan para tocar, mover o sujetar.

theory
In science, a set of widely accepted explanations of observations and phenomena. A theory is a well-tested explanation that is consistent with all available evidence.

> **teoría** En las ciencias, un conjunto de explicaciones de observaciones y fenómenos que es ampliamente aceptado. Una teoría es una explicación bien probada que es consecuente con la evidencia disponible.

tissue
A group of similar cells that are organized to do a specific job. (pp. A29, C44, E10)

> **tejido** Un grupo de células parecidas que juntas realizan una función específica en un organismo.

trait
Any type of feature that can be used to tell two species apart, such as size or bone structure. (p. B46)

> **rasgo** Cualquier característica que puede usarse para diferenciar a dos especies, como el tamaño o la estructura ósea.

transpiration (TRAN-spuh-RAY-shuhn)
The movement of water vapor out of a plant and into the air. (p. C88)

> **transpiración** El movimiento de vapor de agua hacia fuera de una planta y hacia el aire.

U

unicellular
A term used to describe an organism that is made up of a single cell. (p. A11)

> **unicelular** Un término usado para describir a un organismo que está compuesto de una sola célula.

unicellular organism
An organism that is made up of a single cell. (p. B12)

> **organismo unicelular** Un organismo compuesto de una sola célula.

urban
A term that describes a city environment. (p. D80)

> **urbano** Un término que describe el medio ambiente de una ciudad.

urinary system
A group of organs that filter waste from an organism's blood and excrete it in a liquid called urine. (p. E53)

> **sistema urinario** Un grupo de órganos que filtran desechos de la sangre de un organismo y los excretan en un líquido llamado orina.

urine
Liquid waste that is secreted by the kidneys. (p. E53)

> **orina** El desecho líquido que secretan los riñones.

V

vaccine
A small amount of a weakened pathogen that is introduced into the body to stimulate the production of antibodies. (p. E78)

> **vacuna** Una pequeña cantidad de un patógeno debilitado que se introduce al cuerpo para estimular la producción de anticuerpos.

variable
Any factor that can change in a controlled experiment, observation, or model. (p. R30)

> **variable** Cualquier factor que puede cambiar en un experimento controlado, en una observación o en un modelo.

vascular system (VAS-kyuh-lur)
Long tubelike tissues in plants through which water and nutrients move from one part of the plant to another.
(p. C87)

> **sistema vascular** Tejidos largos en forma de tubo en las plantas a través de los cuales se mueven agua y nutrientes de una parte de la planta a otra.

vein

A blood vessel that carries blood back to the heart. (p. E69)

> **vena** Un vaso sanguíneo que lleva la sangre de regreso al corazón.

vertebrate

An animal with an internal backbone. (p. C157)

> **vertebrado** Un animal que tiene columna vertebral interna.

vestigial organ (veh-STIHJ-ee-uhl)

A physical structure that was fully developed and functional in an earlier group of organisms but is reduced and unused in later species. (p. B30)

> **órgano vestigial** Una estructura física que fue completamente desarrollada y funcional en un grupo anterior de organismos pero que está reducido y en desuso en especies posteriores.

virus

A nonliving disease-causing particle that uses the materials inside cells to make copies of itself. A virus consists of genetic material enclosed in a protein coat. (pp. C14, E149)

> **virus** Una particular sin vida, que causa enfermedad y que usa los materiales dentro de las células para reproducirse. Un virus consiste de material genético encerrado en una cubierta proteica.

volume

An amount of three-dimensional space, often used to describe the space that an object takes up.

> **volumen** Una cantidad de espacio tridimensional; a menudo se usa este término para describir el espacio que ocupa un objeto.

voluntary muscle

A muscle that can be moved at will. (p. E24)

> **músculo voluntario** Un músculo que puede moverse a voluntad.

W, X, Y, Z

water cycle

The continuous movement of water through Earth, its atmosphere, and the living things on Earth. (p. D17)

> **ciclo del agua** El movimiento continuo de agua por la Tierra, su atmósfera y los organismos vivos de la Tierra.

Index

Page numbers for definitions are printed in **boldface** type.
Page numbers for illustrations, maps, and charts are printed in *italics*.

brain, E104–105, E*105*, E106
　and senses, E3–5
bread, A53
breathing. *See* respiratory system.
breeding, B21, B*21*. *See also* reproduction.
　development of, A128–130
　and Mendel's research, A104–105, A129
　selective, A**151**
bristlecone pine trees, B64, C86, C*86*
bronchial tubes, E40, E*41*
brood parasitism, D61
budding, A89, A*89*, C49, C*49*, C91
Burgess Shale, B75
burns, E87
butterflies
　monarch, C64, C*64*
　symmetry of, C*131*

C

cactus, C90, C*90*
cancer, A148, A*148*
capillaries, E**69**
capsid, C25, C26
caracals, B45, B*45*
carbohydrates, A**42**, A*42*, E46, E140
carbon 14, R61
carbon cycle, D**18**, D*18*, D18–19, D38
carbon dioxide, D18, D*18*, E38, E40
　and cellular respiration, A50, A*51*, A*52*
　need for, C14
　and photosynthesis, A48, A*49*, A*52*, C52, C88–90,
　　C*89*
carbon films, R61
carbon monoxide, D92
carcinogens, A148
cardiac muscle, E**24**. *See also* heart.
carnivores, C59
carpooling, D104
carrying capacity, B**82**, D**65**
　for humans, B98
　Internet activity, D43
cars. *See* automobiles.
Carson, Rachel, D*76*
　Silent Spring, D76, D99
cartilage, C161, E18
cartilaginous fish, C*160*, C161
casts, R*60*
cats, B45, B*45*, B54, B*54*
cause-and-effect relationship, R**5**
cell cycle, A**80**, A80–82, A*81*
　cell division phase, A*81*, A81–82
　interphase, A**81**, A*81*
cell division, A70–97, C48, E121
　and asexual reproduction, A88–91
　and cell cycle, A**80**, A80–82, A*81*
　and cytokinesis, A**81**, A*81*, A81–82, A84, A*85*
　discovery of, A129
　and genetic material, A*74*, A74–75, A*75*
　and growth, development, and repair, A73, A76–78
　Internet Activity on, A71
　and mitosis, A**81**, A*81*, A81–82, A*83*
　and sexual reproduction, A92
　cell division phase, A**81**, A*81*

cell membranes, A**20**, A*20*, A*21*, A*22*
　in algae, C*33*
　in bacteria, C*17*
　and diffusion, A58, A*58*
　and lipids, A45, A*45*
　in organisms, C11
　in protozoa, C*34*
　and transport, A62–63
cell plate, A84, A*85*
cells, xxxi, A11–37, E9, E10. *See also* heredity;
　　organisms.
　animal and virus, C*14*
　of animals and plants, C58
　of bacteria and archaea, C18
　diploid and haploid, A118–119, A122
　discovery of, A12, A128–130
　elements of, A41–45
　and energy, A47–54
　eukaryotic, A**20**, A*20*, A20–24, A*21*, A*22*
　and genetic material, A*74*, A74–75, A*75*
　Internet Activity on, A7
　and microscope, A12, A18–19, A128–130
　modeling, A32
　and nucleus, C11
　and nutrients, E46
　of organisms, C11
　organization of, A29–31
　and oxygen, E38
　prokaryotic, A**20**, A*20*
　and respiratory system, E37
　size of, A62–63
　structure of, A20–24
　theory of, A*13*, A13–15
　and transport, A56–63
　types of, A26–28
　water and, xxxiii
cell theory, A13, A*13*
　proof of, A15
　use of, A14
cellular respiration, A**50**, A50–52, A*51*, A*52*, C53, C61,
　　E**39**. *See also* respiratory system.
cellulose, A42, C21, E46
cell walls, A**21**, A*21*, A*22*
　in algae, C*33*
　in bacteria, C*12*, C*17*
　in virus and bacteria, C17
Cenozoic era, R*59*
centipedes, C149, C*149*
central nervous system, E*104*, E104–105, E*106*
centromere, A75, A*75*, A82, A*83*
cephalopods, C138, C*138*. *See also* mollusks.
cerebellum, E107
cerebral cortex, E3
changes, population, B87–88, B*88*. *See also* growth,
　　population.
Chapter Investigations
　bacteria, C22–23
　bird beaks, C180–181
　cell cycles, A86–87
　diffusion, A64–65
　DNA, A142–143
　earthworms, C134–135
　field guides, B68–69
　heart rate and exercise, E73
　kidneys, E56–57

and photosynthesis, A48, A49, A52
glycerol, A**43**, A43
glyptodon, B18, B29
gnetophytes, C103
Golgi apparatus, A22, A24
Grand Canyon, D76
graphs
    bar, R26, R31
    circle, R25
    double bar, R27
    line, R24, R34
grasses, C53, D31, D33
    role in secondary succession, D67
grassland biome, D31, D32–33, D33
groundwater, D17, D83
growth, C11
    and cell division, A73, A76–77, A77
    living things and, xv
    of mammals, C186–187
    of organisms, A10
    of plants, C90, C91, C96
growth hormone, E111
growth plates, E18
growth, population, B81–83, B82, B83, B90–94
    Darwin's theory of, B83
    factors for, B101–102
    human, B99–103, B101, D83
    human limitations on, B101–102
    increase and decrease of, B91, D64, D69, E122
    limiting factors of, B92–94
    predicting, B87–88, B101–102
guanine (G), A136, A138–139
gymnosperms, C**102**, C102–103, C103
    compared to angiosperms, C108
    types of, C103

H

habitat, D**46**, D46–47, D47, D70
    for human populations, B99, B99
    loss of, D87, D94–96, D95, D96, D108
    and population growth, B87–88
    restoration of, D76
Hadeon eon, R58
hair, C183, E84, E86, E86
half-life, R62, R62–63
halophiles, C18, C18
hammer (ear), E103
haploid cells, A118–119, A122. See also meiosis.
harmful and helpful effects. See also disease.
    of bacteria, C20, C20–21, C21
    of fungi, C70–71
    and human use of plants, C113–114
    of plant adaptations, C54
    of viruses, C28
healing
    and cell replacement, A78, A78
    of nerve cells, A79
    skin, E87, E87
health, E140–147. See also disease; repair.
    and diet, E140–142
    and drug and alcohol abuse, E144–146
    and eating disorders, E146
    and exercise, E143–144

hearing, E103, E103, E105. See also nervous system.
heart, C44, C45, E66, E66–67, E68. See also circulatory system.
    and cardiac muscles, E24
    and hormones, E113
heat transfer, E117
herbivores, C59
heredity, A98–127, A**102**
    and alleles, A106–107
    discoveries in, A129–131
    and genes, A**102**, A102, A102–103
    Internet Activity on, A99
    and meiosis, A117–122
    Mendel's research on, A104–105, A105
    predicting patterns of, A110–115
heterotroph, C**58**
hibernation, C**64**, C184
hiccups, E43
hierarchy, B54, B54–56, B55. See also taxonomy.
high blood pressure, E70
hinge joints, E19
histamine, E76, E77
HIV, B102
hog farming, B104, B104
homeostasis, E**12**
hominid fossils, B76
homologs, A119–120, A121. See also meiosis.
Hooke, Robert, A12, A128
hormones, C**56**, E110–116, E**111**
    in adolescence, E135
    balance of, E116
    as chemical messengers, E110–111
    and glands, E111–113
    and reproductive system, E119
hornworts, C93
horsetails, C86, C86, C96
host cells, C**26**
Hox genes, A3, A3–5, A4, A5
human body, organization of, E9–12, E11
human development. See development, human.
human DNA, A118, A144, A145
Human Genome Project, A131, A154
human organism, A31
human populations, B98–105
    carrying capacity for, B98
    compared to mice, B34, B34
    density, D**86**, D86
    environmental impact of, B103, B103–105, B104, B105
    growth of, B99–103, B101, D81–87, D82, D108
    habitat for, B99, B99
    impact of technology on, B100, B100
    pressure on ecosystems from, D82–87
    projections of future growth, D81, D82
    proportion of urban dwellers, D86
humans, classification of, B56
humerus, E17
hydras, A89, A89, C128. See also cnidarians.
hydropower, D103
hydrothermal vents, xxxviii
hyphae, C67, C67, C68
    and other organisms, C70, C70–71
hypothalamus, E112, E113
    and feedback, E114, E115
hypothesis, xl, xli, **R3**, R29

INDEX

INDEX

compared to animal cells, C14
harmful and helpful, C28
multiplication of, C26, C27
vision, E4, E102, E*102*, E*105*
vitamins, E142, E*142*
vocabulary strategies, R50–51
description wheel, R50, *R50*
four square, D44, D*44*, R50, *R50*
frame game, D8, D*8*, R51, *R51*
magnet word, D80, D*80*, R51, *R51*
word triangle, R51, *R51*
vocal cords, E*42*
voice box, E42
volume, **R43**
voluntary motor nerves, E106
voluntary muscles, E24
voluntary nervous system, E107
volvox, C33

W

waste
disposal of, D*83*, D83–84
reducing, D*104*, D104–105
wastes. *See* urinary system.
water
as abiotic factor, D10, D11, D13
and animals, C61, C*61*
in cells, A*44*, A44–45
and cellular respiration, A50, A*51*, A*52*
and early organisms, B13–14
functions of, E142
and human technology, B100, B*100*
as limiting factor, B94
and mosses, C94–95
as natural resource, D84–85, D*85*, D*90*
need for, C13
as need of living things, xxxiii
and osmosis, A59
and photosynthesis, A48, A*49*, A52, C87–90, D13
physical form of, D17, D21
pollution, D93, D*93*, D94, D*94*
quality, D93
in soil, D*12*, D13
water balance, E55
water cycle, D**17**, D*17*, D*21*, D*38*
water ecosystems, D*23*, D35–37, D*36–37*, D38. *See also* aquatic biomes.
water molds, C35
water removal, E43
Watson, James, A32, A*32*, A130
weather, B93
West Nile virus, E153
wetlands, D36
food chain in, D26, D*27*
food web in, D26, D*27*
invasive species in, D95, D*96*
wetland ecosystems, D36. *See also* aquatic biomes.
wet mount, making, R15, *R15*
white blood cells, E67
and body defenses, E75–76
and feedback, E*115*
and T cells, E78
wildfire, B93, D33

renewal of ecosystems by, D3–5
wind farms, D103
wolves, D32, D33, D34
competition among, D56
population patterns, D64
womb. *See* uterus.
wood as natural resource, D84, D90
woody plants, C91
worms, C124, C*132*, C132–133, C*133*

X

X-chromosomes, A103, A*103*
and Punnett squares, A114, A*115*
x-rays, E94, E95
xylem, C87, C*89*, C9

Y

Y-chromosomes, A103, A*103*
and Punnett squares, A114, A*115*
yeasts, A89, B66, B*66*, C68, C69, C*69*
Yellowstone National Park, D*75*, D98
yogurt, A53

Z

zebrafish, A*4*, A4–5, A*5*
zebra mussels, B103

Acknowledgments

Photography

Cover Terry Whittaker/Photo Researchers, Inc.; **i** Terry Whittaker/Photo Researchers, Inc.; **iii** Photograph of James Trefil by Evan Cantwell; Photograph of Rita Ann Calvo by Joseph Calvo; Photograph of Kenneth Cutler by Kenneth A. Cutler; Photograph of Douglas Carnine by McDougal Littell; Photograph of Linda Carnine by Amilcar Cifuentes; Photograph of Donald Steely by Marni Stamm; Photograph of Sam Miller by Samuel Miller; Photograph of Vicky Vachon by Redfern Photographics; **vi** *bottom* © Kent Foster Photographs/Bruce Coleman, Inc.; **viii** *bottom* © Richard T. Nowitz/Corbis; **ix** © Burke/Triolo/Artville: Bugs and Insects; **x** © Orion Press/Corbis; **xii** © Jeff Schultz/Alaska Stock.com; **xiii** © Wolcott Henry/National Geographic Image Collection; **xiv** © Larry Dale Gordon/Getty Images; **xv** © Professors P.M. Motta & S. Correr/Photo Researchers, Inc.; **xx** Photograph by Ken O'Donoghue; **xxi** *bottom left* Photograph by Ken O'Donoghue *bottom right* Photograph by Frank Siteman, **xxx–xxxi** © Mark Hamblin/Age Fotostock; **xxxii–xxxiii** © Georgette Duowma/Taxi/Getty Images; **xxxiv–xxxv** © Ron Sanford/Corbis; **xxxvi–xxxvii** © Nick Vedros & Assoc./Stone/Getty Images; **xxxviii** *left* © Michael Gadomski/Animals Animals; *right* © Shin Yoshino/Minden Pictures; **xxxix**© Laif Elleringmann/Aurora Photos; **xl** © Pascal Goetgheluck/Science Photo Library/Photo Researchers, Inc.; **xli** *top left* © David Parker/Science Photo Library/Photo Researchers, Inc.; *top right* © James King-Holmes/Science Photo Library/Photo Researchers, Inc.; *bottom* Sinsheimer Labs/University of California, Santa Cruz; **xlii–xliii** *background* © Maximillian Stock/Photo Researchers, Inc.; **xlii** Courtesy, John Lair, Jewish Hospital, University of Louisville; **xliii** *top* © Brand X Pictures/Alamy; *center* Courtesy, AbioMed; **xlviii** © Chedd-Angier Production Company.

Cells and Heredity

Divider © Dr. Gopal Murti/Photo Researchers, Inc.; **A2, A3** © Mark Smith/Photo Researchers, Inc.; **A4** *top left to right* © Dr. Richard Kessel and Dr. Gene Shih/Visuals Unlimited; *bottom* © Chedd-Angier Production Company; **A5** *left* © Carolina Biological/Visuals Unlimited; *right* © Inga Spence/Visuals Unlimited; **A6, A7** © Biophoto Associates/Photo Researchers, Inc.; **A7** *top right* Photograph by Ken O'Donoghue; *center right* Photograph by Frank Siteman; **A9** Photograph by Ken O'Donoghue; **A10** © Heintges/Premium Stock/PictureQuest ; **A11** *bottom* © David Stone/Rainbow/ PictureQuest; *inset* © Science VU/Visuals Unlimited; **A12** *left* © American Registry of Photography; *right* Library of Congress, Prints and Photographs Division, #LC-USZ62-95187; **A13** *bottom* © Tom Walker/Visuals Unlimited; *inset* © Greg Theiman; **A14** © Will & Demi McIntyre/Corbis; **A16** *top* © Science VU/Visuals Unlimited; *center* Photograph by Frank Siteman; *bottom left, bottom right* Photographs by Ken O'Donoghue; **A18** *left* Photograph by Ken O'Donoghue; *right* © Dr. Gary Gaugler/Visuals Unlimited **A19** © Eye of Science/Photo Researchers, Inc.; **A20** *left* © Eric Grave/Photo Reseachers, Inc.; *right* © CNRI/Photo Reseachers, Inc.; **A21** *bottom left* © Biophoto Associates/Science Source/Photo Researchers, Inc.; *bottom right* © Dennis Kunkel/Phototake; **A22** *background* © John Edwards/Getty Images; *inset* © Gary Braasch/Getty Images; **A23** © Dr. Martha Powell/Visuals Unlimited; **A24** *top* © Dr. Henry Aldrich/Visuals Unlimited; *bottom* © Biophoto Associates/Photo Researchers, Inc.; **A25** *top* © Dr. Gary Gaugler/Visuals Unlimited; *bottom* © Dr. Tony Brain and David Parker/Photo Reseachers, Inc.; **A26** Photograph by Ken O'Donoghue; **A27** *center* © Ralph White/Corbis; *inset* © Alfred Pasieka/Photo Researchers, Inc.; **A28** © Stan Flegler/Visuals Unlimited; **A29** *left to right* © Ted Whittenkraus/Visuals Unlimited; © Gustav Verderber/Visuals Unlimited; © Dwight R. Kuhn; **A30** *left* © Eric and David Hosking/Corbis; *right* © Frans Lanting/Minden Pictures; **A31** Photograph by Ken O'Donoghue; **A32** *top* © Ken Eward/BioGrafx/Photo Researchers, Inc.; *inset* © A. Barrington Brown/Photo Researchers, Inc.; **A33** *left* © Photo Researchers, Inc.; *inset* © Dr. Linda Stannard, UCT/Photo Researchers, Inc.; **A34** *top left* David Stone/Rainbow/PictureQuest; *top right* © Science VU/Visuals Unlimited; *center left* © CNRI/Photo Reseachers, Inc.; © *bottom* Frans Lanting/Minden Pictures; **A35** © Dr. Martha Powell/Visuals Unlimited; **A36** *top* © Tom Walker/Visuals Unlimited; *inset* © Greg Theiman; **A38, A39** © Kent Foster Photographs/Bruce Coleman, Inc.; **A39** *top, center* Photographs by Ken O'Donoghue; **A41** Photograph by Ken O'Donoghue; **A42** © Corbis-Royalty Free; **A44** *top* © Alfred Pasieka/Photo Researhers, Inc.; *bottom* Photograph by Ken O'Donoghue; **A46** *background* © Andrew Syred/Photo Researchers, Inc.; *bottom left* © Anna Clopet/Corbis; *center right* Photograph by Tim Nihoff; *montage top to bottom* © Dr. Jeremy Burgess/Photo Researchers, Inc.; © Andrew Syred/Photo Researchers, Inc.; **A47** *top right* © David Young-Wolff/PhotoEdit; *top inset* John Durham/Photo Researchers, Inc.; *bottom inset* © Innerspace Imaging/Photo Researchers, Inc.; **A48** © Dr. Jeremy Burgess/Photo Researchers, Inc.; **A49** *top center* © Biophoto Associates/Science Source/Photo Researchers, Inc.; **A51** *top left* © Dr. Gopal Murti/Photo Researchers, Inc.; *top right* © Biophoto Associates/Science Source/Photo Researchers, Inc.; **A53** Photograph by Ken O'Donoghue; **A54** © Bob Daemmrich Photo, Inc.; **A55** © Roger Ressmeyer/Corbis; **A56** Photograph by Ken O'Donoghue; **A59** © Marilyn Schaller/Photo Researchers, Inc.; **A60** © Fred Bavendam/Peter Arnold, Inc.; **A62** Photograph by Frank Siteman; **A64** *top* Corbis/Royalty Free; *all others* Photograph by Frank Siteman; **A66** *bottom left* Photograph by Frank Siteman; *bottom right* © Fred Bavendam/Peter Arnold, Inc.; **A70, A71** © CNRI/Photo Researchers, Inc.; **A71** *top right* Photograph by Ken O'Donoghue; *center right* Photograph by Frank Siteman; **A73** Photograph by Ken O'Donoghue; **A74** © Will & Deni McIntyre/Photo Researchers, Inc.; **A76** Photograph by Frank Siteman; **A77** *background* © Rudiger Lehnen/Photo Researchers, Inc.; *left inset* © Alexis Rosenfeld/Photo Researchers, Inc.; *right inset* © David Hughes/Bruce Coleman, Inc.; **A79** *left* © Nancy Kedersha/UCLA/Photo Researchers, Inc.; *top right* Photograph of Elizabeth Gould by Denise Applewhite; **A80** © IFA/eStock Photo/PictureQuest; **A83** © Ed Reschke; **A84** Photograph by Ken O'Donoghue; **A85** *left* © Dr. Gopal Murti/Photo Researchers, Inc.; *right* © Carolina Biological/Visuals Unlimited; **A86** *top* © Michael Newman/PhotoEdit, Inc.; *top right, bottom left, bottom right* Photographs by Ken O'Donoghue; *center right* © Science VU/Visuals Unlimited; *center* © Custom Medical Stock Photo; **A88** © M.I. Walker/Photo Researchers, Inc.; **A89** *top* © CNRI/Photo Researchers, Inc.; *bottom* © Biophoto Associates/Photo Researchers, Inc.; **A90** © David B. Fleetham/Visuals Unlimited; **A91** *top* © Cytographics/Visuals

Unlimited; *bottom* Photograph by Ken O'Donoghue; **A93** © CNRI/Phototake; **A94** © Will & Deni McIntyre/Photo Researchers, Inc.; **A98, A99** © Norbert Rosing/National Geographic Image Collection; **A99** *top right* © Photodisc/Getty Images; *center right* Photograph by Ken O'Donoghue; **A101** © Florence Delva/Getty Images; **A103** *left* © CNRI/Photo Researchers, Inc.; *right* © Biophoto Associates/Photo Researchers, Inc.; **A106** © Mary Kate Denny/PhotoEdit; **A107** © Ken Weingart/Corbis; **A108** *top* © Johnny Johnson/Animals Animals; *bottom* Photograph by Ken O'Donoghue; **A09, A110** Photographs by Ken O'Donoghue; **A113** *background* © Ludovic Maisant/Corbis; *bottom right* © Jane Burton/Bruce Coleman, Inc.; **A114** Photograph by Frank Siteman; **A116** © Robert Dowling/Corbis; **A117** Photograph by Ken O'Donoghue; **A118** © Pascal Goetgheluck/Photo Researchers, Inc.; **A119** Photograph by Ken O'Donoghue; **A123** © David M. Phillips/Photo Researchers, Inc.; **A128** *center* Library of Congress, Prints and Photographs Division, #LC-USZ62-95187; *center right* Courtesy of The Royal Society of London; *bottom* Courtesy of Professor John Doebley, Genetics Department, University of Wisconsin; **A129** *top left* Library and Archives of the Royal Botanical Gardens, Kew; *center* Drawing by Edward Strasburger; *center left* © Margaret Stones; *center right* © Oliver Meckes/Photo Researchers, Inc.; *bottom* © Vic Small; **A130** *top left* Reproduced from *The Journal of Experimental Medicine*, 1944, vol. 79, 158-159, by copyright permission of the Rockefeller University Press; *top right* © Dr. Gopal Murti/Photo Researchers, Inc.; *center* © Omikron/Photo Researchers, Inc.; *bottom left* © Lennart Nilsson/Albert Bonniers Forlag AB; **A131** *top* © David Parker/Photo Researchers, Inc.; *center* Courtesy of The Whitehead Institute/MIT Center for Genome Research and reprinted by permission of Nature, 409:745-964 (2001), Macmillan Publishers Ltd.; *bottom* Courtesy of the USC-Keck School of Medicine and Ashanti DeSilva; **A132, A133** © Ted Horowitz/Corbis; **A133** *top right* Photograph by Ken O'Donoghue; *bottom right* © Corbis-Royalty Free; **A135** Photography by Ken O'Donoghue; **A139** Photograph by Ken O'Donoghue; **A142** *top* © Ken Eward/Photo Researchers, Inc.; *center* Photograph by Frank Siteman; *bottom* Photography by Ken O'Donoghue; **A143** Photograph by Frank Siteman; **A144** Photograph by Ken O'Donoghue; **A145** © David Pollack/Corbis; **A146** Photograph by Frank Siteman; **A147** © Meckes/Ottawa/Photo Researchers, Inc.; **A148** © Gladden Willis/Visuals Unlimited, Inc; **A149** © Dennis Kunkel Microscopy, Inc.; **A150** © Geoff Tompkinson/Photo Researchers, Inc.; **A151** © Doug Loneman/AP Wide World Photos; **A152** © Richard T. Nowitz/Corbis; **A153** © Mark C. Burnett/Stock Boston, Inc./PictureQuest ; **A154** © Getty Images; **A155** *left* © ImageState-Pictor/PictureQuest; *right* © PJ Green/Ardea London Limited; **A156** © Getty Images; **A160** Photograph by Ken O'Donoghue; **A168** *bottom right* Photograph by Ken O'Donoghue.

Life Over Time

Divider © Martin Siepman/Age Fotostock America Inc.; **B2, B3** *background* © Alfredo Maiquez/Lonely Planet Images; **B3** *top left* © Donald Windsor; *bottom right* Reprinted with permission from "Timing the Radiations of Leaf Beetles: Hispines on Gingers from Latest Cretaceous to Recent" Peter Wilf and Conrad C. Labandeira, SCIENCE V. 289:291-294 (2000). © 2000 AAAS.; **B4** *bottom* © The Chedd-Angier Production Company; *top* Courtesy, Earth Sciences and Image Analysis, NASA-Johnson Space Center; **B5** © The Natural History Museum, London; **B6, B7** © Richard T. Nowitz/Corbis; **B10** *top* © Mark A. Schneider/Photo Researchers, Inc.; *center* © Sinclair Stammers/Photo Researchers, Inc.; *bottom* © Novosti/Science Photo Library/Photo Researchers, Inc.; **B11** *bottom* © Field Museum/Photo Researchers, Inc.; **B13** *top* © Ken M. Johns/Photo Researchers, Inc.; **B14** *bottom* © Lynette Cook/Photo Researchers, Inc.; **B15** *top right* © D. Van Ravenswaay/Photo Researchers, Inc.; *bottom right* © David Parker/Photo Researchers, Inc.; *top left* © D. Van Ravenswaay/Photo Researchers, Inc.; **B16** *top* © Paddy Ryan/Animals Animals; *bottom* © Layne Kennedy/Corbis; **B17** *left* © Corbis-Royalty Free; **B18, B19** *background* © Ralph Lee Hopkins/Lonely Planet Images; *bottom* © The Natural History Museum, London; *top* © The Granger Collection, New York; **B19** *top right* © Volker Steger/Photo Researchers, Inc.; *right* © Zig Leszczynski/ Animals Animals; *left* © Theo Allots/Visuals Unlimited; **B20** *bottom right, top left, top right* © Tui De Roy/Minden Pictures; *bottom left* © Richard I'Anson/Lonely Planet Images; *background* © Ralph Lee Hopkins/Lonely Planet Images; **B21** *right* © Hans Reinhard/Bruce Coleman, Inc.; *center, left* © Larry Allan/Bruce Coleman, Inc.; **B23** *top left* © Bruce Coleman, Inc.; *background* © Paul Souders/Accent Alaska; **B24** *top* © Hans Reinhard/Bruce Coleman, Inc.; *bottom, center* © Jane Burton/Bruce Coleman, Inc.; **B25** © John Winnie, Jr./DRK Photo; **B26** *top* © Marian Bacon/Animals Animals; **B28** © Ed Degginger/Color-Pic, Inc.; **B29** © Mark A. Schneider/Photo Researchers, Inc.; **B31** *background* © Corbis-Royalty Free; **B32** *center, left* © Photodisc/Getty Images; *right* © Mark Smith/Photo Researchers, Inc.; **B34** © Photodisc/Getty Images; **B35** © Norbert Wu; **B36** *bottom* © Mark A. Schneider/Photo Researchers, Inc.; *top* © Tui de Roy/Bruce Coleman, Inc.; **B38** © Hans Reinhard/Bruce Coleman, Inc.; **B40, B41** © Burke/Triolo/Artville: Bugs and Insects; **B41** *top right* © Ed Block/Corbis; **B43** *top* © Robert Pickett/Corbis; *bottom* © U.S. Fish & Wildlife Service; **B44** *left* © David I. Roberts/Photo Researchers, Inc.; *right* © S.J. Krasemann/Photo Researchers, Inc.; **B45** *center* © Renee Lynn/Photo Researchers, Inc.; *bottom left* © Tom McHugh/Photo Researchers. Inc.; *top right* © Len Rue, Jr./Bruce Coleman, Inc.; *bottom right* © Frans Lanting/Minden Pictures; **B47** *right* © Bill Kamin/Visuals Unlimited; *bottom left* © Norbert Wu; *center, top left* © Dave Fleetham/Tom Stack & Associates; *background* © E.R. Degginger/Photo Researchers, Inc.; **B48** *top* © D. Ditchburn/Visuals Unlimited; *bottom* © M.H. Sharp/Photo Researchers, Inc.; **B49** *top right* © Tom Brakefield/Bruce Coleman, Inc.; *top left* © Fritz Polking/POLKI/Bruce Coleman, Inc.; *bottom left* © G.C. Kelley/Photo Researchers, Inc.; *bottom right* © Tom McHugh/Photo Researchers, Inc.; *background* © Corbis-Royalty Free; **B50** © Mary Evans Picture Library; **B51** *top* © Photodisc/Getty Images; **B53** *left, right* © Judy White/GardenPhotos.com; *center* © Tom J. Ulrich; **B54** *left* © Joe McDonald/Visuals Unlimited; *right* © Photodisc/Getty Images; **B55** *right* © John Mitchell/Photo Researchers, Inc.; *background* © Visuals Unlimited; **B57** *top right* © Robert Della-Piana/photolibrary/PictureQuest; *background* © Photodisc/Getty Images; **B58** From *A Field Guide To The Birds Of Eastern And Central North America*, Fifth Edition by Roger Tory Peterson. Text copyright © 2002 by Marital Trust B u/a Roger Tory Peterson and the Estate of Virginia Peterson. Reprinted by permission of Houghton Mifflin Company. All rights reserved.; **B59** *background* © Link/Visuals Unlimited; *bottom* © George Bryce/Animals Animals; **B60** © Ken Lucas/Visuals Unlimited; **B61** *left* © CNRI/Photo Researchers, Inc.; *center* © Wolfgang Baumeister/Photo Researchers, Inc.; *right* © Biophoto Associates/Photo Researchers, Inc.; **B62** *top to bottom* © Corbis-Royalty Free; © Sharna Balfour/Gallo Images/Corbis; © Eric Grave/Photo Researchers, Inc.; © Rico & Ruiz/Nature Picture Library; © Dr. Jeremy Burgess/Photo Researchers, Inc.; © Eye of Science/Photo Researchers, Inc.; *background* © Courtesy of NASA/Corbis; **B64** *center* © Jim Zuckerman/Corbis; *right* © Masa Ushioda/Bruce Coleman, Inc.; *left* © M. & C. Photography/Peter Arnold, Inc.; *top* © Ed Degginger/Earthscenes; **B65** © Jeff Foott/Bruce Coleman, Inc.; **B66** *right* © Mark Taylor, Warren Photographic/Bruce Coleman, Inc.; *bottom* © Dr. M. Rohde, GBF/Photo Researchers, Inc.; *left* © Cordelia Molloy/Photo Researchers, Inc.; **B67** ©

Gary Gaugler/Visuals Unlimited; **B68** © Corbis-Royalty Free; **B70** © John Mitchell/Photo Researchers, Inc.; **B72** © Tom McHugh/Photo Researchers, Inc. **B74** *bottom right* © Visuals Unlimited; *bottom left, top right* The Natural History Museum Picture Library, London; **B75** *top left* American Museum of Natural History Library; *bottom right* © O. Louis Mazzatenta/National Geographic Image Collection; *center* © Peter Scoones/Photo Researchers, Inc.; *top right* © Geoff Bryant/Photo Researchers, Inc.; **B76** *top left* © Science/Visuals Unlimited; *top right* © Kevin O. Mooney/Odyssey/Chicago; *center right* © Ira Block/National Geographic Image Collection; *bottom left* © James King-Holmes/Photo Researchers, Inc.; **B77** *top left* © John Reader/Science Photo Library; *bottom left* © David Parker/Photo Researchers, Inc.; **B78, B79** *background* NASA; **B81** © David M. Phillips/Photo Researchers, Inc.; **B83** *left* © Photo Researchers, Inc.; *right* © Wayne Lynch/DRK Photo; **B84** *right* © Darrell Gulin/DRK Photo; *left* © Thomas Wiewandt/Corbis; **B85** *left* © Stephen J. Krasemann/DRK Photo; *right* © D. Cavagnaro/DRK Photo; **B86** *center* © Visuals Unlimited; *right* © Judy White/GardenPhotos.com; *left* © Betty Press/Animals Animals; **B87** © Jim Sulley/The Image Works; **B88** © Anthony Mercieca/Photo Researchers, Inc.; **B89** *left* © Rod Planck/Photo Researchers, Inc.; *right* © Michael Abbey/Photo Researchers, Inc.; **B91** © OSF/N. Rosing/Animals Animals; **B92** © Tom Brakefield/Corbis; **B93** © Najlah Feanny/Corbis; **B95** *right* © Martha Cooper/Peter Arnold, Inc.; *bottom* © Dennis Flaherty/Photo Researchers, Inc.; **B96** © Stephen J. Krasemann/DRK Photo; **B97** *left* © Ted Spiegel/Corbis; *top right* © Wesmar; **B99** *bottom right* © Rob Crandall/The Image Works; *bottom left* © Grant Heilman/Grant Heilman Photography; *top right* © Ed Degginger/Color-Pic, Inc.; **B100** *left* © Bob Daemmrich/The Image Works; *right* © Geri Engberg/The Image Works; **B101** NASA; **B103** *top* © Ray Coleman/Photo Researchers, Inc.; *bottom* © John Serrao/Photo Researchers, Inc.; **B104** *top* © Donald Speckler/Animals Animals; *bottom* © Janis Burger/Bruce Coleman, Inc.; **B105** © Jeff Greenberg/The Image Works; **B106** © Gaetano/Corbis; **B108** *center* © Najlah Feanny/Corbis; *bottom* © Bob Daemmrich/The Image Works; **B110** © Photo Researchers, Inc.; **B111** © Wayne Lynch/DRK Photo.

Diversity of Living Things

Divider © Buddy Mays/Corbis; **C2, C3** © *background* Yva Momatiuk/John Eastcott/Minden Pictures; **C3** *top* © Pat O'Hara/Corbis; *bottom* © Darrell Gulin/Corbis; **C4** *top left* © Bruce Marlin/Cirrus Digital Imaging; *top right* © A.B. Sheldon; *bottom* © Chedd-Angier Production Company; **C6, C7** © Science VU/Visuals Unlimited; **C7** *top* Photograph by Frank Siteman; *center* Photograph by Ken O'Donoghue; *bottom* © Custom Medical Stock Photo; **C9** Photograph by Ken O'Donoghue; **C10** *background* © Lynda Richardson/Corbis; *inset* © Astrid & Hanns-Frieder Michler/Photo Researchers, Inc.; **C12** © A.B. Dowsett/Science Photo Library/Photo Researchers, Inc.; **C13** Photograph by Ken O'Donoghue; **C14** *right* © Dr. Gopal Murti/Photo Researchers, Inc.; *left* © K.G. Murti/Visuals Unlimited; **C15** © CNRI/Photo Researchers, Inc.; **C16** © Dennis Kunkel/Visuals Unlimited; **C17** *left* © Tina Carvalho/Visuals Unlimited; *center* © D.M. Phillips/Visuals Unlimited; *right* © CNRI/Photo Researchers, Inc.; **C18** *left* © Grant Heilman/Grant Heilman Photography; *left inset* © Dr. Kari Lounatmaa/Photo Researchers, Inc.; *center* © Roger Tidman/Corbis; *center inset* © Alfred Pasieka/Science Photo Library/Photo Researchers, Inc.; *right* © ML Sinbaldi/Corbis; *right inset* © Wolfgang Baumeister/Photo Researchers, Inc.; **C19** *left* © Jack Novak/Photri-Microstock; *left inset* © Dr. Kari Lounatmaa/Photo Researchers, Inc.; *center* © Dennis Flaherty/Photo Researchers, Inc.; *center inset* © Microfield Scientific LTD/Science Photo Library/Photo Researchers, Inc.; *right* © Dr. P. Marazzi/Science Photo Library/Photo Researchers, Inc.; *right inset* © Dr. Kari Lounatmaa/Photo Researchers, Inc.; **C20** © *background* Runk/Schoenberger/Grant Heilman Photography; *left inset* © Simko/Visuals Unlimited; *right inset* © Dwight R. Kuhn; **C21** © T.A. Zitter/Cornell University; **C22** *top* © Adam Hart-Davis, Leeds Public Health Laboraory/Photo Researchers, Inc. ; *bottom (both)* Photographs by Ken O'Donoghue; **C24, C25** Photographs by Frank Siteman; **C26** © Hans Gelderblom/Visuals Unlimited; **C27** *(both)* © Lee D. Simon/Photo Researchers, Inc.; **C28** © Bettmann/Corbis; **C29** *left* © Judy White/GardenPhotos.com; *right* © Dennis Kunkel Microscopy; **C30** © Corbis; **C31** Photograph by Ken O'Donoghue; **C32** *left* © R. Kessel-G. Shih/Visuals Unlimited; *center* © Jan Hinsch/Photo Researchers, Inc.; *right* © Runk/Schoenberger/Grant Heilman Photography; **C33** © R. Kessel-C.Y. Shih/Visuals Unlimited; **C34** © Andrew Syred/Photo Researchers, Inc.; **C35** © Ed Reschke/Peter Arnold, Inc.; **C36** *top* © CNRI/Photo Researchers, Inc.; *bottom left* © Runk/Schoenberger/Grant Heilman Photography; *bottom center* © Ed Reschke/Peter Arnold, Inc.; *bottom right* © Andrew Syred/Photo Researchers, Inc.; **C38** *left* © A.B. Dowsett/Science Photo Library/Photo Researchers, Inc.; *right* © Science VU/Visuals Unlimited; **C40, C41** © Orion Press/Corbis; **C41** *top, center* Photographs by Ken O'Donoghue; **C43** © David G. Massey/AP Wide World Photos; **C44** Photograph by Frank Siteman; **C45** © Joe McDonald/Bruce Coleman, Inc.; **C46** © Michael Doolittle/ PictureQuest; **C47** *background* © Photospin; *top* © A. Mercieca/Photo Researchers, Inc.; *center* © Jim Brandenburg/Minden Pictures; *center inset* © Yva Momatiuk/John Eastcott/Minden Pictures; *bottom* © Tim Fitzharris/Minden Pictures; **C48** © Matt Brown/Corbis; **C49** *left* © Joe McDonald/Corbis; *right* © David J. Wrobel/Visuals Unlimited; **C50** © Frans Lanting/Minden Pictures; **C51, C52** Photographs by Ken O'Donoghue; **C53** *top* © Peter Dean/Grant Heilman Photography; *inset* © Pascal Goetgheluck/Science Photo Library/Photo Researchers, Inc.; **C54** *(both)* © D. Suzio/Photo Researchers, Inc.; **C55** *left* © Joel Arrington/Visuals Unlimited; *right* © Gary W. Carter/Visuals Unlimited; **C57** © Josiah Davidson/Picturesque/PictureQuest; **C58** © Yva Momatiuk/John Eastcott/Minden Pictures; **C59** *left* © Brandon Cole; *right* © Rauschenbach/Premium Stock/PictureQuest ; **C60** Photograph by Frank Siteman; **C61** *left and left inset* © Dwight R.Kuhn; *center* © Steve Maslowski/Visuals Unlimited; *right* © Belinda Wright/DRK Photo; **C62** © J. Sneesby/B. Wilkins/Getty Images; **C63** *top* © Shin Yoshino/Minden Pictures; *bottom left* © Charles V. Angelo/Photo Researchers, Inc.; *bottom right* © Fred McConnaughey/Photo Researchers, Inc.; **C64** *left* © Ron Austing/Photo Researchers, Inc.; *right* © Kevin Schafer; **C65** *left, top right* © Steve Winter/National Geographic Image Collection; *bottom right* © Brian J. Skerry/National Geographic Image Collection; **C66** Photograph by Ken O'Donoghue; **C68** © IFA/eStock Photography/PictureQuest ; **C69** *top* © Andrew Syred/Science Photo Library/Photo Researchers; *bottom* © Simko/Visuals Unlimited; **C71** *(both)* © Lennart Nilsson/Albert Bonniers Forlag AB; **C72** *top* © Bob Daemmrich/Stock Boston, Inc./PictureQuest; *bottom* Photograph by Ken O'Donoghue; **C73** Photograph by Frank Siteman; **C74** *top* © Matt Brown/Corbis; *center* © Rauschenbach/Premium Stock/PictureQuest ; *bottom* © IFA/eStock Photography/PictureQuest; **C78** *top* © Academy of Natural Sciences of Philadelphia/Corbis; *bottom* © The Granger Collection, New York; **C79** *top left, top right* © The Natural History Museum, London; *bottom left* © Photo Researchers, Inc.; *bottom right* © The Granger Collection, New York; **C80** *top left* © B. Boonyaratanakornit & D.S. Clark, G. Vrdoljak/EM Lab, UC Berkeley/Visuals Unlimited, Inc.; *top right* © OAR/National Undersea Research Program; *center* © Terry Erwin/ Smithsonian Institution; *bottom* © Emory Kristoff/National Geographic Image

Collection; **C81** © Michael Bordelon/Smithsonian Institution; **C82, C83** © David J. Job/AlaskaStock.com; **C83** *(both)* Photographs by Ken O'Donoghue; **C85** Photograph by Ken O'Donoghue; **C86** *left* © Nick Garbutt/Nature Picture Library; *center* © D. Cavagnaro/Visuals Unlimited; *right* © Hal Horwitz/Corbis; **C87** © Andrew Syred/Photo Researchers, Inc.; **C88** *(both)* © Dr. Jeremy Burgess/Science Photo Library/Photo Researchers, Inc.; **C89** *background* © Donna Disario/Corbis; *top left* © Photodisc/Getty Images; **C90** © Craig K. Lorenz/Photo Researchers, Inc.; **C91** *top* © Delphoto/Premium Stock/ PictureQuest; *inset* © Unicorn Stock Photo; **C92** Photograph by Frank Siteman; **C93** *top* © Ray Simmons/Photo Researchers, Inc.; *bottom* The Field Museum of Natural History, #GEO85637c; **C94** Photograph by Frank Siteman; **C95** © Dwight R. Kuhn; **C96** *left* © Dr. Jeremy Burgess/Science Photo Library/Photo Researchers, Inc.; *inset* School Division, Houghton Mifflin Co.; *right* © Michael & Patricia Fogden/Corbis; **C97** *left* © Dwight R. Kuhn; *right* © Sylvester Allred/Fundamental Photographs; **C98** © Keren Su/Corbis; **C99** © Dwight R. Kuhn; **C100** © Martha Cooper/Peter Arnold, Inc.; **C101** *background* © Photospin; *top* © Scott Barrow/ImageState; *bottom* © Bryan Mullenix/Getty Images; **C102** Photograph by Ken O'Donoghue; **C103** © Robert Gustafson/Visuals Unlimited; **C104** *top* © Michael J. Doolittle/The Image Works; *bottom right* © James A. Sugar/Corbis; **C105** Photograph by Frank Siteman; **C106** *left* © Raymond Gehman/Corbis; *top right* © David Sieren/Visuals Unlimited, Inc.; *bottom right* © George Bernard/Science Photo Library; **C107** Photograph by Ken O'Donoghue; **C109** *background* © John Marshall; *left* © George D. Lepp/Corbis; *center* © Sergio Piumatti; *right* © Gary Braasch/Corbis; **C110** © Ed Reschke; **C111** *top* Photograph by Ken O'Donoghue; *bottom* © Custom Medical Stock Photo; **C112** *left* © Frank Lane Picture Agency/Corbis; *right* © Eastcott/Momatiuc/Animals Animals; **C113** *right* © Craig Aurness/Corbis; *inset* © Michael Newman/PhotoEdit; **C114** *background* © Lance Nelson/Corbis; *top, left* National Cotton Council of America; *right* © Mary Kate Denny/PhotoEdit; **C115** *left* © Patricia Agre/Photo Researchers, Inc.; *right* © Martin B. Withers, Frank Lane Picture Agency/Corbis; **C116** *top* © Hal Horwitz/Corbis; *center left* © Martha Cooper/Peter Arnold, Inc.; *center right* © Dwight R. Kuhn; *bottom left* © Gary Braasch/Corbis; *bottom right* © George D. Lepp/Corbis; **C117** *(both)* © Wolfgang Bayer/Bruce Coleman, Inc./PictureQuest ; **C120, C121** © Norbert Wu; **C121** *top* Photograph by Frank Siteman; *bottom* © Photospin; **C123** © Andrew J. Martinez/Visuals Unlimited; **C124** Photograph by Ken O'Donoghue; **C125** *background* © Viola's Photo Visions, Inc./Animals Animals; **C126** © Marty Snyderman/Visuals Unlimited; **C127** *left* © Dwight R. Kuhn; *inset* © Thomas Kitchin/Tom Stack & Associates; **C128** Photograph by Ken O'Donoghue; **C129** © Photodisc/Getty Images; **C130** *top left, bottom left* © John D. Cunningham/Visuals Unlimited; **C131** *left* © Bob Evans/Peter Arnold, Inc.; *right* © Visuals Unlimited; **C132** © Dwight R.Kuhn; **C133** *top* © Larry Lipsky/DRK Photo; *center* © A. Flowers & L. Newman/Photo Researchers, Inc.; *bottom* © Richard Kessel/Visuals Unlimited; **C134** *top* © Robert Pickett/Corbis; *bottom* Photograph by Ken O'Donoghue; **C135** *top* Photograph by Ken O'Donoghue; *bottom* Photograph by Frank Siteman; **C136** © Sinclair Stammers/Photo Researchers, Inc.; **C137** *top* © Andrew J. Martinez/Photo Researchers, Inc.; *bottom* © Konrad Wothe/Minden Pictures; **C138** *top* Photograph by Ken O'Donoghue; *bottom* © Fred Bavendam/Minden Pictures; **C139** *top* © Andrew J. Martinez; *bottom* © David Wrobel/Visuals Unlimited; **C140** *left* © Fred Winner/Jacana/Photo Researchers, Inc.; *right* © Gerald & Buff Corsi/Visuals Unlimited; **C141** © Kevin Schafer/Getty Images; **C142** Photograph by Frank Siteman; **C143** *top* © Kelvin Aitken/Peter Arnold, Inc.; *bottom* © Barry Runk/Grant Heilman Photography; **C144** *background* © Corbis-Royalty Free; *top* © Tim Davis/Corbis; *center* © Steve Wolper/DRK Photo; *bottom* © George Calef/DRK Photo; **C146** Photograph by Ken O'Donoghue; **C147** *top (all)* © Dwight R. Kuhn; *bottom* © Frans Lanting/Minden Pictures; **C148** *top* © David Scharf/Peter Arnold, Inc.; *bottom* © E.R. Degginger/Color-Pic, Inc.; **C149** *left* © Science Photo Library/Photo Researchers, Inc.; *right* © Claus Meyer/Minden Pictures; **C150** *top right* © Viola's Photo Visions, Inc./Animals Animals; *center left* © John D. Cunningham/Visuals Unlimited; *bottom left* © Konrad Wothe/Minden Pictures; *bottom right* © Gerald & Buff Corsi/Visuals Unlimited; **C154, C155** © Paul A. Souders/Corbis; **C155** *top* Photograph by Frank Siteman; *center left* © Steven Frame/Stock Boston Inc./PictureQuest; *center right* © Rod Planck/Photo Researchers, Inc.; **C157** Photograph by Frank Siteman; **C158** © Corbis-Royalty Free; **C159** *background* © SeaLifeStyles Signature Series/Imagin; **C160** *background* © Colla - V&W/Bruce Coleman, Inc.; *left* © Norbert Wu; *left inset* © Brandon Cole; *center* © Georgienne E. Bradley & Jay Ireland/Bradley Ireland Productions; *right* © Brandon Cole; **C162** © David Doubilet; **C163** *left* © Kennan Ward/Corbis; *right* © Frans Lanting/Minden Pictures; **C164** *left* © Bianca Lavies/National Geographic Image Collection; *right* Photograph by Frank Siteman; **C165** *left* © Dwight R. Kuhn; *right* © Joe McDonald/Bruce Coleman, Inc.; **C166** *all* © Dwight R. Kuhn; **C168** © Francois Gohier/Photo Researchers, Inc.; **C169** © Carmela Leszczynski/Animals Animals; **C170** *top* Photograph by Frank Siteman; *bottom* © Tui de Roy/Minden Pictures; **C171** © Michael Fogden/Animals Animals; **C172** *left* ©Frans Lanting/Minden Pictures; *center* © E.R. Degginger/Color-Pic, Inc.; *right* © Science Photo Library/Photo Researchers, Inc.; **C173** Photograph by Ken O'Donoghue; **C174** © Michael Quinton/Minden Pictures; **C175** *left* © Julie Habel/Corbis; *center* © Randy Faris/Corbis; *right* © David-Young Wolff/PhotoEdit; **C177** *background* © Tim Bird/Corbis; **C178** *left* © Jim Brandenburg/Minden Pictures; *right* © Fritz Polking/Visuals Unlimited; **C179** *top* © Ron Austing/Photo Researchers, Inc.; *bottom* © S. Nielsen/DRK Photo; **C180** *top* © DigitalVision/PictureQuest; *bottom* Photograph by Frank Siteman **C181** *top* Photograph by Frank Siteman; *bottom left* © Corbis-Royalty Free; *bottom center* © Frans Lemmens/Getty Images; *bottom right* © Arthur Morris/Corbis; **C182** © Carleton Ray/Photo Researchers, Inc.; **C183** *top* © Mitsuaki Iwago/Minden Pictures; *bottom* © Don Enger/Animals Animals; **C184** Photograph by Frank Siteman; **C185** *background* © Stephen Frink/Corbis; **C186** *left* © Photodisc/Getty Images; *right* © Frans Lanting/Minden Pictures; **C187** © Comstock; **C188** *top left* © Dwight R. Kuhn; *top right* © Michael Fogden/Animals Animals; *center right* © Fritz Polking/Visuals Unlimited; *bottom left* © Frans Lanting/Minden Pictures; *bottom right* © Photodisc/Getty Images.

Ecology

Divider © Richard du Toit/Nature Picture Library; **D2, D3** *background* © Mark Thiessen/National Geographic Image Collection; **D3** *top* © Frank Oberle/Getty Images; *bottom* © Hal Horwitz/Corbis; **D4** *top (both)* © Lawrence J. Godson; *bottom* Chedd-Angier Production Company; **D6, D7** © Jeff Schultz/Alaska Stock.com; **D7** *top* Photograph by Ken O'Donoghue; *center* Photograph by Frank Siteman; **D9** Photograph by Frank Siteman; **D10** © Mark Allen Stack/Tom Stack & Associates; **D11** *left* © Jim Brandenburg/Minden Pictures; *right* © Ted Kerasote/Photo Researchers, Inc.; **D12** *bottom left* © Grant Heilman Photography; **D13** © Frans Lemmens/Getty Images; **D14** *top* © Michael J. Doolittle/The Image Works, Inc.; *bottom* Photograph by Ken O'Donoghue; **D16** Photograph by Ken O'Donoghue; **D19** Photograph by Frank Siteman; **D21** © Randy Wells/Corbis; **D22** Photograph by Frank Siteman; **D23** *left* © Eric Crichton/Corbis; *top right* © E.R. Degginger/Color-Pic, Inc.; *bottom right* © T.E. Adams/Visuals Unlimited, Inc.; **D24** © Anthony Mercieca Photo/Photo Researchers, Inc.; **D25** *top* © Fred Bruemmer/DRK Photo; *bottom* Photograph by Ken O'Donoghue; **D27** *background* © Raymond Gehman/Corbis; **D29** *left* ©

Arthur Gurmankin & Mary Morina/Visuals Unlimited, Inc.; *top right* © Carmela Leszczynski/Animals Animals; **D30** © Charles Melton/Visuals Unlimited, Inc.; **D31** © Michio Hoshino/Minden Pictures; **D32** *top left* © Tom Bean; *top right* © E.R. Degginger/Color-Pic, Inc.; *bottom* © Joe McDonald/Visuals Unlimited, Inc.; **D33** *left* © David Wrobel/Visuals Unlimited, Inc.; *right* © Tom Bean; **D34** *left* © Owaki-Kulla/Corbis; *right* © Frans Lanting/Minden Pictures; **D35** *top* Photograph by Ken O'Donoghue; *bottom* © Stephen Dalton/Photo Researchers, Inc.; **D36** *left* © Aaron Horowitz/Corbis; *center* © Hans Pfletschinger/Peter Arnold, Inc.; *right* © Arthur Gurmankin & Mary Morina/Visuals Unlimited, Inc.; **D37** *left* © Paul Rezendes; *center* © Richard Herrmann/Visuals Unlimited, Inc.; *right* © Norbert Wu; **D42, D43** © Wolcott Henry/National Geographic Image Collection; **D43** *top* Photograph by Frank Siteman; *center* Photograph by Ken O'Donoghue; **D45** Photograph by Frank Siteman; **D46** *left and center* © Frans Lanting/Minden Pictures; *right* © Robin Karpan/Visuals Unlimited, Inc.; **D50** © Walt Anderson/Visuals Unlimited, Inc.; **D51** ©Alan & Linda Detrick/Photo Researchers, Inc.; **D52** *top* © Patrick J. Endres/Visuals Unlimited, Inc.; *bottom left* Photograph by Frank Siteman; *bottom right* Photograph by Ken O'Donoghue; **D53** Photograph by Ken O'Donoghue; **D54** © Spencer Grant/PhotoEdit, Inc.; **D55** © Gary Braasch; **D56** *top* © Joe McDonald/Visuals Unlimited, Inc.; *bottom* © Stephen J. Krasemann/Photo Researchers, Inc.; **D57** *top* Photograph by Ken O'Donoghue; *bottom* © Michael Fogden/Bruce Coleman Inc.; **D58** © Michael & Patricia Fogden/Minden Pictures; **D59** © Bradley Sheard; **D60** *clockwise from top* © S.J. Krasemann/Peter Arnold, Inc.; © Ray Coleman/Visuals Unlimited, Inc.; © Astrid & Hanns-Frieder Michler/Science Photo Library; © E.R. Degginger/Color-Pic, Inc.; © Dwight R. Kuhn; © Phil Degginger/Color-Pic, Inc.; **D61** © Arthur Morris/Visuals Unlimited, Inc.; **D62** *left* © Kevin Fleming/Corbis; *inset* © David M. Dennis/Animals Animals; **D63** Photograph by Ken O'Donoghue; **D64** *top* © Shin Yoshino/Minden Pictures; *bottom* © Tim Fitzharris/Minden Pictures; **D65** Photograph by Frank Siteman; **D66** *bottom (background)* © Leo Collier/Getty Images; **D67** *bottom (background)* © David R. Frazier/Getty Images; **D69** © A. & J. Visage/Peter Arnold, Inc.; **D70** *top left* © Frans Lanting/Minden Pictures; **D74** *bottom left* Denver Public Library, Western History Collection, call#F-4659; *top center* © James Randklev/Getty Images; *bottom right* Library of Congress, Prints and Photographs Division (LC-USZ62-16709 DLC) cph 3a18915; **D75** *top left* © H.H. French/Corbis; *top right* © Bill Ross/Corbis; *center left* The Bancroft Library, University of California, Berkeley; *center right* © Corbis; *bottom* © Michael Sewell/Peter Arnold, Inc.; **D76** *top left* © Alfred Eisenstaedt/Getty Images; *top right* © Tom Bean/DRK Photo; *center right* © David Muench/Corbis; *bottom left* © Kevin Schafer/Corbis; *bottom right* Habitat Quality for San Joaquin Kit Fox on Managed and Private Lands reprinted from ESRI Map Book, Vol. 16 and used herein with permission. Copyright © 2001 ESRI. All rights reserved.; **D77** *top* © Tom Soucek/Alaska Stock Images; *bottom* © Richard Galosy/Bruce Coleman, Inc.; **D78, D79** ©Alex Maclean/Photonica; **D79** *top and center* Photographs by Ken O'Donoghue; **D81** Photograph by Frank Siteman; **D83** © Ray Pfortner/Peter Arnold, Inc.; **D84** Photograph by Ken O'Donoghue; **D85** *top* © John Elk III; *bottom* © Ted Spiegel/Corbis; **D86** *background* © ChromoSohm/Sohm/Photo Researchers, Inc.; *insets* Courtesy, USGS: EROS Data Center; **D87** © Mark E. Gibson/Visuals Unlimited, Inc.; **D88** © David Zimmerman/Corbis; **D89** © David Young-Wolff/PhotoEdit, Inc.; **D90** *left* © Richard Stockton/Iguazu Falls/Index Stock Imagery, Inc.; *right* © Bill Ross/Corbis; **D91** Photograph by Ken O'Donoghue; **D92** *bottom* © Tom Bean/DRK Photo; *inset* © Jenny Hager/The Image Works, Inc.; **D93** *bottom* © Natalie Fobes/Corbis; *inset* © Natalie Fobes/Getty Images; **D95** © Kent Foster Photgraphs/Visuals Unlimited, Inc.; **D96** *top* © Andrew J. Martinez/Photo Researchers, Inc.; *inset* © D. Cavagnaro/Visuals Unlimited, Inc.; **D97** © Tom Edwards/Visuals Unlimited, Inc.; **D98** Photographs by Ken O'Donoghue and Frank Siteman; **D99** © Frank Pedrick/The Image Works, Inc.; **D100** © Joe McDonald/Visuals Unlimited, Inc.; **D101** *top (background)* © Jim Wark/Airphoto; *top (inset)* Photograph by Scott Williams/U.S. Fish and Wildlife Service; *bottom (background)* © Tom Bean/Corbis; *bottom (insets)* Courtesy, San Diego State University, Soil Ecology and Restoration Group; **D102** © Melissa Farlow/National Geographic Image Collection; **D103** © Klein/Hubert/Peter Arnold, Inc.; **D104** *top* © Janis Miglavs; *bottom* © David Young-Wolff/PhotoEdit, Inc.; **D105** © Kevin Schafer/Corbis; **D106** *top* Tom Myers/Photo Researchers, Inc.; *bottom* Photograph by Frank Siteman; **D108** *center left* © Natalie Fobes/Corbis; *center right* © Kent Foster Photographs/Visuals Unlimited, Inc.; *bottom left* © Joe McDonald/Visuals Unlimited, Inc.; *bottom right* © Klein/Hubert/Peter Arnold, Inc.

Human Biology

Divider RNHRD NHS Trust; **E2–E3** © Peter Byron/PhotoEdit; **E3** *top right* © ISM/Phototake; **E4** *top* © Wellcome Department of Cognitive Neurology/Photo Researchers, Inc., *bottom* Chedd-Angier Production Company; **E5** © Myrleen Ferguson Cate/PhotoEdit; **E6–E7** © Chris Hamilton/Corbis; **E7** *top* Frank Siteman, *bottom* Ken O'Donoghue; **E9** © SuperStock; **E10** Frank Siteman; **E11** *left* © Martin Rotker/Phototake; **E12** © SW Production/Index Stock Imagery/PictureQuest; **E13** *background* © Hulton-Deutsch Collection/Corbis, *center* © Underwood & Underwood/Corbis; **E14** Frank Siteman; **E15** © Prof. P. Motta/Dept. of Anatomy/University "La Sapienza," Rome/Photo Researchers, Inc.; **E16** © Photodisc/Getty Images; **E18** *bottom* © Science Photo Library/Photo Researchers, Inc., *bottom left* © Zephyr/Photo Researchers, Inc.; **E19** *top* © Zephyr/Photo Researchers, Inc., bottom Frank Siteman; **E20** *top left* © Stock Image/SuperStock, top right © Science Photo Library/Photo Researchers, Inc.; **E21** © Dennis Kunkel/Phototake; **E22** Frank Siteman; **E23** © Kevin R. Morris/Corbis; **E25** *background* © Mary Kate Denny/PhotoEdit, *top* © Martin Rotker/Phototake, *left* © Triarch/Visuals Unlimited, *bottom* © Eric Grave/Phototake; **E26** © Ron Frehm/AP Wide World Photos; **E27** © Jeff Greenberg/PhotoEdit; **E28** *top* © Gunter Marx Photography/Corbis, *bottom, all* Frank Siteman; **E30** © Martin Rotker/Phototake; **E31** *top* © Stock Image/SuperStock; **E34–E35** © Larry Dale Gordon/Getty Images; **E35** *top* Frank Siteman, *bottom* Ken O'Donoghue; **E37** Frank Siteman; **E38** © Amos Nachoum/Corbis; **E39** Ken O'Donoghue; **E41** *bottom left* © Michael Newman/PhotoEdit, *bottom right* © Science Photo Library/Photo Researchers, Inc.; **E43** © Kennan Harvey/Getty Images; **E44** *background* © Jim Cummins/Getty Images, *center* © Steve Casimiro/Getty Images; **E45** Ken O'Donoghue; **E47** Ken O'Donoghue; **E48** © Professors P. Motta & A. Familiari/University "La Sapienza," Rome/Photo Researchers, Inc.; **E49** © David Young-Wolff/PhotoEdit; **E50** © Dr. Gladden Willis/Visuals Unlimited; **E51** © David Gifford/SPL/Custom Medical Stock Photo; **E52** Frank Siteman; **E55** © LWA-Dann Tardif/Corbis; **E56** *top* © Myrleen Ferguson Cate/PhotoEdit, *bottom left* Ken O'Donoghue, *bottom right* Frank Siteman; **E57** Frank Siteman; **E59** © Professors P. Motta & A. Familiari/University "La Sapienza," Rome/Photo Researchers, Inc.; **E62–E63** © Professors P.M. Motta & S. Correr/Photo Researchers, Inc.; **E63** *both* Frank Siteman; **E65** Frank Siteman; **E67** © Science Photo Library/Photo Researchers, Inc.; **E68** © Myrleen Ferguson Cate/PhotoEdit; **E69** © Susumu